SO-EMD-995

DISCARD

BIBLIOGRAPHY OF MEDIEVAL DRAMA

BIBLIOGRAPHY
OF MEDIEVAL DRAMA

Carl J. Stratman, C. S. V.

Second Edition

Revised and Enlarged

VOLUME I

FREDERICK UNGAR PUBLISHING CO.

NEW YORK

Copyright © 1972 by Frederick Ungar Publishing Co., Inc.
Printed in the United States of America
Library of Congress Catalog Card No. 78-163141
ISBN 0-8044-3272-4

PREFACE

In this revised edition of *Bibliography of Medieval Drama* the format has been altered in some details, and more than 5,000 entries have been added to the 1954 edition. The arrangement of divisions has been changed, with greater prominence as well as treatment being accorded to the liturgical Latin drama. Within the various sections devoted to scholarly studies the entries now appear in chronological rather than in alphabetical order.

The continued listing of material relating to the French, German, Italian, and Spanish drama is not meant to be exhaustive, although each of these sections has been enlarged. Rather, sections devoted to the Continental medieval drama have been included on a selective basis, as the material is intended primarily as an aid for students of the English drama. Further, the material has been selected primarily for those students of the English drama who are searching for more information about Continental influences, parallel developments, and subsequent borrowings relative not only to the liturgical drama, but to the development of such types as the French "mystères," "miracles," "moralités," "farces," and "sotties"; the German "Osterspiels," "Passionsspiels," and "Weihnachtsspiels"; the Italian "sacre rappresentazioni"; and the Spanish "autos," "entremés," and "farsas." No effort has been made toward supplanting any bibliographies that may deal exclusively with the medieval drama in any of the countries represented.

Although there have been a number of changes from the first edition, many features remain more or less the same. Thus, each entry gives the full name of the author, the complete title of the work, together with the place of publication and the publisher, the date, and the major pagination. If the work is of sufficient importance, and contains a bibliography, the pages of the bibliography are noted.

Whenever possible an entry includes a symbol that indicates in what library a copy of the work may be found. Although it is still not feasible to annotate a bibliography of this size and complexity, the editor has continued the practice of placing an asterisk before the entry numbers to indicate the more important books and articles. Entries from the *Stationers' Register,* and the *Short Title Catalogue* numbers are still given when appropriate. The locations of manuscripts of medieval collections of plays, e.g., the Chester Cycle of Mystery Plays, as well as manuscripts of individual plays, remain a feature of this edition. Finally, the Festschriften continue to occupy a separate section.

Among the changes that appear in this edition are these:

1. The work has been divided into ten main categories rather than twelve.

2. A far greater emphasis is placed upon the liturgical Latin drama, mainly because it forms the basis for the development of English medieval drama, and a new interest in the form has begun to appear.

3. The section devoted to the English drama has been revised in some detail, as a comparison of the two editions will immediately show. For example, the division for the English drama now includes a bibliography devoted solely to the drama in English. In addition, the section entitled "Collections of Plays" has been incorporated into the English drama portion of the work, with the titles of the various plays given under the entry for the individual volumes. Further, for the category comprising the mystery and miracle plays a single alphabetical arrangement by place of dramatic activity or title of play has been adopted, to replace the former three-fold division "Cycle," "Non-Cycle," and "Drama in Other Cities."

4. "Morality Plays and Interludes" is the title of the section formerly listed simply as "Morality Plays." The new category has been adopted because of the confusion that always arises in attempting to make a strict distinction between individual morality plays and interludes, especially when the playwrights themselves compound the confusion by sometimes calling the one the other.

5. In the section devoted to "Morality Plays and Interludes" the arrangement remains alphabetical for the anonymous plays, but for plays written by a known author, the titles appear under his name in alphabetical sequence. Further, all the studies of an author's plays also

appear under his name, and are placed in chronological rather than in alphabetical order.

6. The play *Everyman* has been inserted within the section "Morality Plays and Interludes."

7. Instead of remaining a separate category, the greatly expanded material devoted to the tenth-century nun of Gandersheim, Hrotsvitha, now forms part of the section entitled "German Drama."

8. A new section appears in this edition entitled "Low Countries' Drama."

9. The very brief section of some forty-six entries entitled "Latin Drama" now becomes part of a new division, "Liturgical Latin Drama," which contains more than a thousand entries.

10. Within a specific section, such as "General Studies" or "Bibliography," the entries are now arranged in a chronological rather than an alphabetical order. For example, if one is interested in the development of scholarly interest in the Towneley or Wakefield Cycle, he will find that the chronological arrangement allows him to discover, with a minimum of effort, the particular trend of study in any decade or period.

11. Within any section devoted to secondary works, the former arrangement of one division for books, another for periodicals, and a third for theses and dissertations, has been abandoned. All such works are now entered in the same division and are placed in chronological sequence.

12. The use of entry numbers at the end of a section, for the purpose of cross reference to a particular topic or subject, is no longer followed. For example, at the conclusion of the entries devoted to Chester plays, the first edition listed some twenty-one entries that could also be consulted for material treating of these plays. In the present edition these cross references by number are deleted, and if the specific items are of any value for an understanding of Chester drama they are entered under their full titles in the Chester section. If the works are not of value, they do not belong in the bibliography even as a cross reference.

13. A more consistent attempt has been made in this edition to list those works that are of significance in more than one category under each pertinent category. For example, a book that covers the Chester, Ludus Coventriae, Wakefield, and York Cycles, will be listed under each cycle.

14. Two former sections, one devoted to "Pageants" and the other to "Guilds" in English drama, are now incorporated in the sections devoted to studies of English drama, or in the section "Mystery and Miracle Plays."

15. Wherever errors of date, pagination, authorship, spelling, etc., have been discovered, these errors have been corrected.

16. Book reviews are no longer indicated.

17. Appendix I, "Guide to Plays in Collections," has been omitted as the plays appear in the body of the text.

18. Appendix II, "Guide to Listed Serials in Libraries," has also been omitted as the locations for any serial or journal can be found very simply by consulting the *Union List of Serials* and *New Serial Titles*.

19. The entire title of a serial, journal, or periodical is given in this edition rather than the symbols used to represent them in the first edition. Because the title is used in each case the preliminary pages devoted to symbols for periodicals are now omitted.

20. The holdings of the British Museum are now included for secondary works as well as for primary texts.

Although, as stated earlier, an attempt has been made to correct the errors present in the first edition, it is possible not only that some of these errors have remained but entirely new ones have appeared. The compiler accepts all responsibility for such errors but begs the indulgence of those who use this work; he hopes that the advantages will outweigh any weaknesses.

In addition to the debt of gratitude owed to those who helped with advice and encouragement in preparing the first edition, the compiler acknowledges the considerable help of a leave of absence granted by Loyola University, and the encouragement and understanding of his chairman, John Gerrietts, in helping to arrange the leave as well as more compact teaching schedules. Two other people to whom thanks are due, in addition to my understanding and patient publisher, Frederick Ungar, are Mrs. Marion McCann of Loyola University Press, who among other tasks undertook the very arduous labor of typing the manuscript, and Mrs. Muriel Friedman of Loyola University, who not only proofread the entire manuscript but also prepared the index. Without their capable assistance this book would not now be in print.

CONTENTS

VOLUME I

SYMBOLS FOR LIBRARIES

BM   British Museum, London, England

C   Cambridge University, Cambridge, England

CLSU   University of Southern California, Los Angeles, Cal.
CSmH   Henry E. Huntington Library, San Marino, Cal.
CSt   Stanford University, Stanford, Cal.
CU   University of California, Berkeley, Cal.

CtY   Yale University, New Haven, Conn.

DFo   Folger Shakespeare Library, Washington, D.C.
DLC   Library of Congress, Washington, D.C.

Dyce   Dyce Collection, Victoria and Albert Museum, London, England

IC   Chicago Public Library, Chicago, Ill.
ICJ   John Crerar Library, Chicago, Ill.
ICLoy   Loyola University, Chicago, Ill.
ICN   Newberry Library, Chicago, Ill.
ICU   University of Chicago, Chicago, Ill.
IEN   Northwestern University, Evanston, Ill.
IU   University of Illinois, Urbana, Ill.

IaU   University of Iowa, Iowa City, Ia.

LNHT   Tulane University Library, New Orleans, La.
LU   Louisiana State University, Baton Rouge, La.

MB   Boston Public Library, Boston, Mass.
MBAt   Boston Athenaeum, Boston, Mass.
MH   Harvard University, Cambridge, Mass.
MWelC   Wellesley College, Wellesley, Mass.

MdBJ   Johns Hopkins University, Baltimore, Md.
MdBP   Peabody Institute, Baltimore, Md.
MdU   University of Maryland, College Park, Md.

MiD   Detroit Public Library, Detroit, Mich.
MiU   University of Michigan, Ann Arbor, Mich.

MiU-C   University of Michigan, William L. Clements Library,
         Ann Arbor, Mich.

MnU   University of Minnesota, Minneapolis, Minn.

MoSU   Saint Louis University, St. Louis, Mo.
MoU   University of Missouri, Columbia, Mo.

NB   Brooklyn Public Library, Brooklyn, N.Y.
NBC   Brooklyn College, Brooklyn, N.Y.
NBuG   Grosvenor Reference Division, Buffalo and Erie County Public
         Library, Buffalo, N.Y.
NIC   Cornell University, Ithaca, N.Y.
NN   New York Public Library, New York, N.Y.
NNC   Columbia University, New York, N.Y.
NNF   Fordham University, New York, N.Y.
NNU   New York Universities Library, New York, N.Y.
NNU-W   New York University, Washington Square Library, New York,
         N.Y.
NNUT   Union Theological Seminary, New York, N.Y.
NPV   Vassar College, Poughkeepsie, N.Y.
NRU   University of Rochester, Rochester, N.Y.

NcD   Duke University, Durham, N. C.
NcU   University of North Carolina, Chapel Hill, N.C.

NhD   Dartmouth College, Hanover, N.H.

NjP   Princeton University, Princeton, N.J.
NjR   Rutgers University, New Brunswick, N.J.

O   Bodleian Library, Oxford, England

OC   Public Library of Cincinnati and Hamilton County, Cincinnati, O.
OCU   University of Cincinnati, Cincinnati, O.
OCX   Xavier University, Cincinnati, O.
OCl   Cleveland Public Library, Cleveland, O.
OClCC   Cleveland College Library, Cleveland, O.
OClW   Western Reserve University, Cleveland, O.
ODW   Ohio Wesleyan University, Delaware, O.
OEac   East Cleveland Public Library, East Cleveland, O.
OO   Oberlin College, Oberlin, O.
OOxM   Miami University, Oxford, O.
OU   Ohio State University, Columbus, O.

PB　　　　Bethlehem Public Library, Bethlehem, Pa.
PBa　　　Academy of the New Church, Bryn Athyn, Pa.
PBm　　　Bryn Mawr College, Bryn Mawr, Pa.
PHC　　　Haverford College, Haverford, Pa.
PMA　　　Allegheny College, Meadville, Pa.
PP　　　　Free Library of Philadelphia, Philadelphia, Pa.
PPD　　　Drexel Institute of Technology, Philadelphia, Pa.
PPF　　　Franklin Institute, Philadelphia, Pa.
PPGi　　　Girard College, Philadelphia, Pa.
PPT　　　Temple University, Philadelphia, Pa.
PPPD　　　Divinity School of the Protestant Episcopal Church, Philadelphia, Pa.
PSC　　　Swarthmore College, Swarthmore, Pa.
PSt　　　Pennsylvania State University, University Park, Pa.
PU　　　　University of Pennsylvania, Philadelphia, Pa.
PU-F　　　University of Pennsylvania, H. H. Furness Memorial Library, Philadelphia, Pa.
PV　　　　Villanova College, Villanova, Pa.

RPV　　　Brown University, Providence, R.I.

ScU　　　University of South Carolina, Columbia, S.C.

TxU　　　University of Texas, Austin, Tex.

ViU　　　University of Virginia, Charlottesville, Va.

WU　　　　University of Wisconsin, Madison, Wis.

WaU　　　University of Washington, Seattle, Wash.

I GENERAL STUDIES

1   [Rabbotenu, Isaac.] The Bee-hive of the Romishe churche.
    Wherein the authour a zealous protestant, under the person of
    a superstitious papist, doth so driely repell the grose opinions
    of popery, and so divinely defend the articles of Christianitie,
    that (the sacred Scriptures excepted) there is not a booke to be
    founde, either more necessarie for thy profite, or sweeter for
    thy comforte. Translated out of the Dutch into English by Geo-
    rge Gilpin the Elder. London: Thomas Dawson for John Stell,
    1579. [28], 346 ff. [STC. 17445].
        BM.

2   Fabricius, Johann Albert. Codex apocryphus Novi Testamenti,
    collectus, castigatus testimoniisque censuris animadversion-
    ibus illustratus a Johanne Alberto Fabricio. 2 vol. Hamburg:
    Schiller, 1703.
        BM.

3   ----- Codex apocryphus Novi Testamenti, collectus, castigatus
    testimoniisque, censuris & animadversionibus illustratus a
    Johanne Alberto Fabricio. Editio secunda. 3 vol. Hamburg:
    Schiller and Kisner, 1719-1743.
        BM.

4   Hearne, Thomas, ed. Johannis de Fordun Scotichronicon genuinum,
    una cum ejusdem supplemento ac continuatione. 5 vol. Oxonii:
    e Theatro Sheldoniano, 1722. Index.
        BM.

5   Bonnet, Jacques. Histoire générale de la danse, sacrée et prophane;
    ses progrès & ses révolutions. Avec un supplément. A Paris:

chez d'Houry fils, 1724. xl, 269 pp.
BM. MB.

6   Chetwood, William Rufus. A General History of the Stage, from
Its Origin in Greece down to the Present Time. London: Printed
for W. Owen, 1749. 256 pp.
ICN. MB. WU.

7   Coupé, Jean Marie Louis, and others. Histoire universelle des
théâtres de toutes les nations, depuis Thespis jusqu' à nos
jours; par une société de gens de lettres [J. M. L. Coupé,
G. F. F. Des Hayes, Lefuel de Méricourt, et Testu]. 13 vol.
A Paris: chez les auteurs, 1779-1781.
MB.

8   Magnin, Charles. Les Origines du Théâtre moderne; ou, histoire
du génie dramatique depuis le Ier jusqu' au XVIe siecle, précédé
ed'une introduction contenant des études sur les origines du
théâtre antique. Tome I. Paris: L. Hachette, 1838. 522 pp.
ICU. IU. MB. NjP. NNF.

9   Alt, Heinrich. Theater und Kirche in ihrem gegenseitigen Ver-
hältniss historisch dargestellt. Berlin: Verlag der Plahnschen
Buchhandlung, 1846. vi, vii, 704 pp. Index.
BM.

10 Chassang, Alexis. Des Essais dramatiques imités de l'antiquité
au XIVe siècle. Paris: Auguste Durand, 1852. [6], 195, [2] pp.
BM. ICN. MH.

11 Wright, Thomas. "On the History of the Drama in the Middle
Ages." Bentley's Miscellany, XXXVIII (1855), 298-309.

12 [Anon.] "Mediaeval Theatricals." Knickerbocker's Magazine,
LXIII (1864), 237-247.

13 Klein, Julius Leopold. Geschichte des aussereuropäisen Dramas
und der lateinischen Schauspiele nach Christus bis ende des x.
Jahrhunderts. Leipzig: T. O. Weigel, 1866. 764 pp.
ICU. MnU.

14 Royer, Alphonse. Histoire universelle du théâtre. 6 vol. Paris:
A. Franck, 1869-1879.
BM.

15   Cutts, Rev. Edward L. Scenes and Characters of the Middle Ages.
       London: Virtue & Co., 1872. xiii, 546 pp. [Ministrels of the
       Middle Ages, pp. 267-310.]
          BM.

16   Fowler, James. "On Mediaeval Representations of the Months and
       Seasons." Archaeologia, XLIV (1873), 137-224.

17   Peiper, Rudolf, i.e., Leo Rudolf Samuel. Die profane Komoedie
       des Mittelalters. [Leipzig: B. G. Teubner, 187-?]. pp. [493]-542.
       (Archiv für litteraturgeschichte, V. BD.).
          ICU.

18   Gering, Hugo, ed. I slendzk Aeventyri: Isländische legenden
       Novellen und Märchen. 2 vol. Halle: Buchhandlung des Waisen-
       hauses, 1882-1883.
          BM.

19   Aymeric, Joseph, and Condamin, James, trans. Histoire générale
       de la littérature du moyen âge en Occident. 3 vol. Paris: E.
       Leroux, 1883-1889. [Translation of Ebert's work.]
          BM.

20   Holstein, Hugo. Die Reformation im Spiegelbilde der dramatischen
       Literatur des sechzehnten Jahrhunderts. Halle: Verein für Re-
       formationsgeschichte, 1886. viii, 287 pp. Index. (Verein für
       Reformations-Geschichte, Schrifte, 14/15).
          BM.

21   Weilen, Alexander. Der Ägyptische Joseph im Drama des XVI.
       Jahrhunderts. Vienna: Alfred Hölder, 1887. viii, 196 pp. Index.
          BM.

22   Cros-Mayresvieille, Gabriel. Le droit des pauvres sur les spectacles
       en Europe. Origine, législation, jurisprudence. Paris, Nancy:
       Berger-Levrault et Cie, 1889. xxi, 208 pp.
          BM. MB.

23   Sittard, Josef. Zur Geschichte der Musik und des Theaters am
       württembergischen Hofe. Nach Original-quellen. 2 vol. Stuttgart:
       Kohlhammer, 1890-1891.
          BM. MB.

24   Herford, I. "The Confraternities of Penitence, Their Dramas and
       Their Lamentations." English Historical Review, VI (1891), 646-
       673.

25 Soens, E. De rol van het booze beginsel op het middeleeuwsch
    Tooneel. Gent: A. Siffer, 1893. 146 pp.
        BM.

26 Dreves, G. M. "Zur Geschichte der Fête des fous." Stimmen aus
    Maria-Laach, XLVII (1894), 571-587.

27 Jeanroy, A. "Observations sur le théâtre méridional au XVe
    siècle." Romania, XXIII (1894), 523-560.

28 Jusserand, J. J. "Theatre of Our Ancestors. A Summary." Review
    of Reviews, IX (1894), 209.

29 Desrat, G. Dictionnaire de la danse, historique, théorique, prati-
    que et bibliographique, depuis l'origine de la danse jusqu'à
    nos jours. Avec préface de Ch. Nuitter [pseud. de C. L. E.
    Truinet]. Paris: Librairies-Imprimeries Réunies, 1895. [5],
    vi, 484 pp. Bibliography, pp. 385-459.
        BM.

30 Linder, Alfred, ed. Plainte de la Vierge, en vieux vénitien. Texte
    critique, précédé d'une introduction linguistique et littéraire.
    Upsala: Impr. Berling, 1898. 8, ccxliii, 98 pp. (Upsala Uni-
    versitets Arsskrift, 1898).
        BM.

31 Mantzius, Karl. Skuespilkunst i middelalder og renaissance.
    Kobenhaven: Gyldendal, 1899. 365 pp. "Literaturfortegnelse,"
    pp. [355]-258.
        BM. DLC. MnU.

32 Leendertz Jr., P. De Middelnederlandsche dramatische Poezie.
    Leiden: A. W. Sijrhoff, 1900-1907. 696, ccxvii pp. (Bibliotheek
    van Middelnederlandsche Letterkunde Afl. 63). [A completely
    new edition of the 1875 edition by Henri Ernest Moltzer.]

33 Broadbent, R. J. History of Pantomime. London: Simpkin, Marshall,
    Hamilton, Kent and Co., Ltd., [1901]. 226, [2] pp.
        ICN. ICU. MB. MiU. NN. OCl. PU.

34 Cook, A. S. "A Dramatic Tendency in the Fathers." Journal of
    English and Germanic Philology, V (1903), 62-64.

35 Glock, Anton. Uber den Zusammenhang des römischen Mimus
    und einer dramatischen Tätigkeit mittelalterlicher Spielleute

mit dem neueren homischen Drama. Berlin: Emil Felber, 1906.
　　　BM.

*36　Gofflot, L. V. Le Théâtre au Collège du moyen âge à nos jours. Avec bibliographie et appendices. Le Circle Francais de l'Université Harvard. Accompagné de nombreuses planches hors texte. Préface par Jules Claretie. Paris, 1907. xix, 336 pp.
　　　BM.

37　Haslinghuis, Edward Johannes. De duivel in het drama der middeleeuwen. Leiden: Van den Hoek, 1912. xvi, 208 pp. Bibliography, pp. [ii]-xvi.
　　　BM. MnU. NNC.

38　Hughes, Elizabeth Ann. "A Study of a Medieval Agency of Social Control." Ph.D. University of Chicago, 1915. 63, [4] pp.

39　Rondel, Auguste. Origines et Développement du théâtre en Europe du XVe au XVIIe siècle d' apres les textes les textes imprimés menade à travers une Bibliothèque Dramatique. Discours de Réception de M. Auguste Rondel. Réponse de M. José Silbert. Marseille: Typographie et Lithographie Barlatier, 1918. 44 pp. (Académie Des Sciences, Lettres et Beaux-Arts De Marseille).
　　　BM.

40　Walther, H. Das Streitgedicht in der lateinischen Literatur des Mittelalters. Munich: Oskar Beck, 1920. 254 pp. (Quellen und Untersuchungen zur lateinischen Philologie des Mittelalters V. Heft 2.)
　　　BM.

41　Worringer, W. Formprobleme der Gotik. Munich: R. Piper & Co., 1920. 127 pp. Index to Illustrations.
　　　BM.

42　Simons, L. Het drama en het tooneel in hun ontwikkeling I. Tot I. 1525. II. Tot I 1625; de zestiende eeuw. Amsterdam: Maatsch. voor goede en goedkoope Lecteur, 1921. x, 360, 247 pp.
　　　Royal Library, Brussels

43　Stammler, Wolfgang. Die Totentänze des Mittelalters. München: H. Stobbe, 1922. 64 pp. (Einzelschriften zur Bücher-und Hanschriftenkunde ... 4.bd.)

ICN. ICU.

44 Holzknecht, Karl Julius. "Literary Patronage in the Middle Ages."
Ph.D. University of Pennsylvania, 1923.

45 L., N. N. T. "The Stage in the Sixteenth and Seventeenth Centuries." Notes and Queries, XIII (1923), 130-131.

46 Braun, Joseph. Der christliche Altar in seiner geschichtlichen
Entwicklung. 2 vol. München: G. Koch & Co., 1924.
ICU.

47 Dvorak, Max. Kunstgeschichte als Geistesgeschichte. Munich:
R. Piper & Co., 1924. xv, 276 pp.
BM.

48 Faral, Edmond. Les Arts poetiques du XIIe et XIII e siècle;
recherches et documents sur la technique littéraire du moyen
âge. Paris: Champion, 1924. xvi, 384 pp. (Bibliothèque de l'
école du haute études fasc. 238).
BM.

49 Reynal, Albert. L'Église et le théâtre: essai historique. Paris:
Bloud & Gay, 1924. xi, 246 pp.
BM.

50 Albert, Heinrich. Der Stilcharakter des mittellateinischen
Dramas. Inaugural Dissertation. München, 1925. 89 pp.

51 Deslandres, P. "L'Eglise et le théâtre." Revue des Études
Historiques, XCI (1925), 131-136.

52 Mortier, Alfred. Le Démon dans ses incarnations dramatiques.
Paris: Peyronnet, 1925. 62 pp.   [BM.]

53 Künstle, Karl. Ikonographie der Heiligen. Freiburg i. B.:
Herder, 1926. xiv, 606 pp.
BM.

54 Haskins, Charles H. The Renaissance of the Twelfth Century.
Cambridge, Mass.: Harvard University Press, 1927. 437
pp. Bibliographical notes at end of chapters.
MB. MiU. NN. OC1. OCU. OO. PU. ViU. WaU.

55 Craig, Hardin. "Drama and the Stage, Including Selected Items

from the Fields of Mediaeval and Contemporary Drama."
Studies in Philology, XXV (1928), 195-210; XXVI (1929), 208-
222; XXVII (1930), 309-322; XXVIII (1931), 292-308.

56   Künstle, Karl. Ikonographie der Christlichen Kunst. Freiburg i.
B.: Herder, 1928. xvii, 670 pp. Index.
BM.

57   Macgrath, John Henry Vincent. "Religious Elements in the Classic
and Early Catholic Drama." Ph.D. Georgetown University,
1929.

58   McMahon, A.P. "Seven Questions on Aristotelian Definitions of
Tragedy and Comedy." Harvard Studies in Classical Philology,
XL (1929), 131-145.

59   Borcherdt, Hans Heinrich. "Theater und bildende Kunst im Wandel
der Zeiten." Euphorion, XXXII (1931), 179-187. (Reprinted,
1967).

60   Cottas, Vénétia. L'Influence du drame Christos paschon sur l'art
chrétien d'Orient. Paris: Librairie orientaliste Paul Geuthner,
1931. vi, 122 pp.
MnU. NN.

61   Dubech, Lucien. Histoire générale illustrée du théâtre. Par Lucien
Dubech avec la collaboration de Jacques de Montbrial et
Madeleine Horn-Monval. 5 vol. Paris: Librairie de France,
1931-1934.
BM. ICN.

62   Frank, Grace. "Popular Iconography of the Passion." Publications
of the Modern Language Association, XLVI (1931), 333-340.

63   Warren, Florence, ed. The Dance of Death, Edited from the MSS.
Ellesmere 26 / A. 13 and B. M. Landsdowne 699, Collated
with Other Extant MSS. With Introduction, Notes, etc. By
Beatrice White. London: Published for the Early English Text
Society by H. Milford, Oxford University Press, 1931. 118 pp.
BM. ICN. MB. MiU. OCU. OO. PHC. ViU.

64   Terry, Sir Richard Runciman. A Medieval Carol Book. London:
Burns, Oates, and Washbourne, Ltd., 1932. 66 pp.
BM.

65   Rushforth, Gordon MacNeil. Mediaevel Christian Imagery.
         Oxford: Clarendon Press, 1936. xx, 456 pp.
            BM. (Destroyed)

66   Nicoll, Allardyce. The Development of the Theatre. New York:
         Harcourt, 1937. 308 pp. Bibliography, pp. 289-300.
            BM. ICN. OC1. OU. PSC.

67   Schlee, Ernst. Die Ikonographie der Paradiesflüsse. Leipzig:
         Dieterisch'sche Verlagsbuchhandlung, 1937. ix, [1], 220 pp.
         (Studien über christliche Denkmaler. Neue Folge. H fr. 24).
            BM.

68   Coulton, George Gordon. Medieval Panorama. Cambridge: Uni-
         versity Press, 1938. xiv, 801 pp. Index.
            BM. ICN. NN.

69   Stoephasius, Renata von. Die Gestalt des Pilatus in den mittelal-
         terlichen Passionsspielen. Würzburg: K. Triltsch, 1938. 108
         pp.
            BM. NN. NNC.

70   Rost, Hans. Die Bibel im Mittelalter. Augsburg: Seitz, 1939.
         viii, 428 pp.
            BM.

71   Stegemeier, Henri. The Dance of Death in Folksong, with an
         Introduction on the History of the Dance of Death. [Chicago:
         Private Edition Distributed by the University of Chicago
         Libraries], 1939. 231 pp.
            DLC.

72   Boon, Jozef. De bouwmeester, mysterie in drei bedrijven. Brugge:
         Desclée, de Brouwer, 1941. 104 pp. "Van Denzelfden schrijver,"
         pp. [107]-110.
            DLC.

73   Nykl, Alois R. "Dice in an Old Czech Passion Play." Slavonic
         Year Book, I (1941), 200-205.

74   Reese, Gustave. Music in the Middle Ages with Introduction on
         Music of the Renaissance. London: J. M. Dent and Sons, 1941.
         xvii, 502 pp. Bibliography, pp. 425-463.
            BM. ICN.

75   Eastman, Fred, and Louis Wilson. Drama in the Church, a
       Manual of Religious Drama Production. New York, Los
       Angeles: S. French [1942]. xi, 187 pp. Selected List of Reli-
       gious Dramas, pp. 173-187.
                 BM.

76   Morey, Charles Rufus. Mediaeval Art. New York: W. W. Norton
       & Co., Inc., 1942. 412 pp. Index.
                 BM.

77   Salazar, Adolfo. La música en la sociedad europea. 4 vol.
       [Mexico]: El Colegio de México [1942-1946].
                 ICN.

78   Trapido, Joel. "An Encyclopaedic Glossary of the Classical and
       Medieval Theatres and of the Commedia Dell' Arte." Ph.D.
       Cornell University, 1942.

79   Atwood, E. Bagby, and Virgil K. Whitaker, eds. Excidium Troiae.
       Cambridge, Massachusetts: Mediaeval Academy, 1944. xci,
       81 pp.
                 BM. MH.

80   Murray, Sr. Elizabeth Marion. "The Place of the Lyric in the
       Drama before 1550." M.A. Fordham University, 1944.

81   Loomis, Roger S. "Were There Theatres in the Twelfth and
       Thirteenth Centuries?" Speculum, XX (1945), 92-95.

82   Bigongiari, Dino. "Were There Theatres in the Twelfth and
       Thirteenth Centuries?" Romanic Review, XXXVII (October,
       1946), 201-224.

83   Seydel, Irene. Zur Hegung des mittelalterlichen Theaters. In-
       augural Dissertation. Münster, 1946.

84   Tatlock, J. S. P. "Mediaeval Laughter." Speculum, XXI (1946),
       289-294.

85   Adolph, Helen. "On Mediaeval Laughter." Speculum, XXII (1947),
       251-253.

86   Geier, W. "O'Neill's Miracle Play." Religion in Life, XVI (1947),
       515-526.

87   Curtius, Ernst Robert. Europäische Literatur und Lateinisches
       Mittelalter. Bern: A. Francke A. G., 1948. 601 pp. Biblio-
       graphy, pp. 567-569. Index [2nd ed., 1954.]
       BM.

88   Philipps, Ronald. "The Church and Drama." <u>London</u> <u>Quarterly</u>
       <u>and</u> <u>Holborn</u> <u>Review</u>, CLXXII (1948), 213-217.

89   Stammler, Wolfgang. Der Totentanz: Enstehung und Deutung.
       Munich: Carl Hanser, 1948. 95 pp.
       BM.

90   Apel, Willi. The Notation of Polyphonic Music 900-1600. 4th ed. rev.
       Cambridge, Massachusetts: The Mediaeval Academy of America,
       1949. xxv, 462 pp.
       BM.

91   Arnold, Newton S. "A Swiss Resurrection Play of the Sixteenth
       Century." Ph.D. Columbia University, 1949.

92   Chailley, Jacques. "Un Document nouveau sur la danse ecclésiasti-
       que." <u>Acta</u> <u>Musicologica</u>, XXI (1949), 18-24.

93   Huizinga, Johan. Homo Ludens: a Study of the Play Element in
       Culture. (Translated by R. F. C. Hull from the German.)
       London: Routledge & Kegan Paul, 1949. 220 pp. Index. (Inter-
       national Library of Sociology and Reconstruction).
       BM.

94   Chailley, Jacques. Histoire musicale du moyen age. Paris: Presses
       Universitaires de France, 1950. 355 pp. "Notes et références,"
       pp. [313]-346.
       BM. ICN.

95   Clark, James M. "The Dance of Death in Medieval Literature:
       Some Recent Theories of its Origin." <u>Modern</u> <u>Language</u> <u>Review</u>,
       XLV (1950), 336-345.

96   ----- The Dance of Death in the Middle Ages and the Renaissance.
       Glasgow: Johnson, Son & Co., 1950. xi, 131 pp. (Glasgow Uni-
       versity Publications No. 86).
       BM.

97   Enklaar, D. Th. De Dodendans, een Cultur-Historische Studie.
       Amsterdam: L. J. Veens Uitgenersmaatschappij N.J., 1950,

162 pp.
BM.

98　Marshall, Mary H. "Boethius' Definition of 'Persona' and Mediaeval Understanding of the Roman Theater." Speculum, XXV (1950), 471-482.

99　----- "Theatre in the Middle Ages: Evidence from Dictionaries and Glosses." Symposium, IV (1950), 1-39, 366-389.

100　Steinbüchel, Theodor. Vom Menschenbild des christlichen Mittelalters, Donderausg. d. wiss. Buchgemeinschaft. Basel: B. Schwabe [Vorwert 1951]. 48 pp.
NN.

101　Ellis, Florence Hawley. "Passion Play in New Mexico." The New Mexico Quarterly, XXII (Summer, 1952), 200-212.

102　Nagler, A. M. Sources of Theatrical History. New York: Theatre Annual, Inc., 1952. xxiii, 611 pp. [Also, 1959, by Dover Publications.]
NN.

103　Strunk, Oliver. Source Readings in Music History. London: Faber & Faber, 1952. xxi, 919 pp.
BM.

104　Auerbach, Erich. Mimesis: The Representation of Reality in Western Literature. Translated from the German by Willard Trask. Princeton, New Jersey: Princeton University Press, 1953. 563 pp. [There is also a 1957 edition.]
BM. NN.

105　Hughes, Dom Anselm, ed. Early Medieval Music Up to 1300. London: Oxford University Press, 1953. xviii, 434 pp. (New Oxford History of Music. Vol. 2).
BM.

106　McDonnell, Sister M. Brideen. "Medieval Drama in Catholic Colleges." America, LXXXIX (June 20, 1953), 320-321.

107　Blom, Eric, ed. Grove's Dictionary of Music and Musicians. 9 vol. 5th ed. London: Macmillan & Co., Ltd., 1954. [Supplementary volume, 1961.]

108 Myrsky, A. "Aus Wissenschaft und Forschung; ein albanische Ostermysterium." Musica, VIII (November, 1954), 511-513.

109 Smits von Waesberghe, Joseph. Muziek en drama in de middele-euwen. 2. druk. Amsterdam: Bigot & Van Rossum [1954]. viii, 110 pp.
ICN.

110 Baltrusaitis, Jurgis. Le moyen âge fantastique: antiquités et exotismes dans l'art gothique. Paris: Colin, 1955. 299 pp. (Collection Henri Focillon, no. 3).
BM.

111 Herrick, Marvin T. "The New Drama of the Sixteenth Century." Journal of English and Germanic Philology, LIV (1955), 555-577.

112 ----- Tragicomedy: Its Origin and Development in Italy, France and England. Urbana: University of Illinois, 1955. vii, 331 pp. (Illinois Studies in Language and Literature, Vol. XXXIX).
BM. ICN. MH. NN. O. PU.

113 Hunningher, Benjamin. The Origin of the Theater: an Essay. The Hague: Nijhoff; Amsterdam; Querido, 1955. 139 pp. Bibliography, pp. 121-131. Index.
BM. ICN. NN.

114 Pearce, T. M. "Tracing a New Mexican Folk Play." Nueva Revista de Filologia Hispanica, IX (1955), 28.

115 Schuster, Sister M. F. "Twelfth Century Drama." Historical Bulletin, XXXIII (January, 1955), 85-91.

116 Kaff, Ludwig. Mittelalterliche Oster-und Passions-spiele aus Oberösterreich im Spiegel musikwissenschaftlicher Betrach-tung. [With the texts and airs of two of the plays.] Linz, 1956. 68 pp. [Schriftenreihe des Institutes für Landeskunde von Oberösterreich, No. 9.]
BM.

117 Lapkass, Nikolajs. "The Attitude of the Early Christians toward the Theatre from the Beginnings to the Middle of the Sixth Century." M.A. University of Indiana, 1956.

118 Réau, Louis. Histoire de la peinture au moyen âge: la miniature.

Melun: Librairie d'Argences, 1956. 256 pp.
    BM.

119   Bentley, Eric. What Is Theatre? A Query in Chronicle Form.
      London: Dennis Dobson, 1957. x, 273 pp.
        BM. NN.

120   Grube, Von Ernst. "Die abendländischchristliche Kunst des Mit-
      telalters und das geistliche Schauspiel der Kirche; eine
      kritische Untersuchung der theater-wissenschaftlichen Quel-
      lenforschung." Maske und Kothurn, III, Heft 1 (1957), 22-59.

121   Kindermann, Heinz. Das Theater der Antike und des Mittelalters.
      Salzburg: Otto Müller, 1957. 540 pp. Bibliography, pp. 453-501.
      Index.
        BM.

122   Thurston, Ethel. "Medieval Drama in New York." Catholic Art
      Quarterly, XXI (December, 1957), 25-26.

123   Cheyney, Sheldon. The Theatre. Three Thousand Years of Drama,
      Acting, and Stagecraft. Revised and edited by G. McKey. New
      York: Houghton, Mifflin and Co., 1958. 592 pp.
        BM.

124   Nicoll, Allardyce. The Development of the Theatre. 4th ed. rev.
      New York: Harcourt Brace [1958]. 318 pp.
        NN.

125   Parrish, Carl. The Notation of Medieval Music. London: Faber
      & Faber, 1958. xvii, 228 pp.
        BM.

126   Scarlett, Earle P. "The Dance of Death." Dalhousie Review,
      XXXVII (1958), 378-397.

127   Enck, John Jacob, Elizabeth T. Foster, and Alvin Whitley, eds.
      The Comic in Theory and Practice. New York: Appleton,
      Century-Crofts, 1960. 340 pp.
        CU. CSt. IaU. IU. LNHT. NjP. NNC. RPB.

128   Haulot, R. "Theatre in the Streets, Persistance des manifestations
      de tradition populaire." World Theatre, IX (Spring, 1960), 62-67.

129   Jackson, William Thomas Hobdell. The Literature of the Middle

Ages. New York: Columbia University Press, 1960. xiii, 432 pp. Index. "Bibliography," pp. 369-414.
BM.

130   White, Beatrice. "Medieval Mirth." Anglia, LXXVIII (1960), 284-301.

131   Wolff, Erwin. "Die Terminologie des Mittelalterlichen Dramas in Bedeutungsgeschichtlicher Sicht." Anglia, LXXVIII (1960), 1-27.

132   Richard, P. "Medieval Literature." Year's Work in Modern Language Studies, XXIII (1961), 45-55.

133   Salmon, P. B. "The 'Three Voices' of Poetry in Mediaeval Literary Theory." Medium Aevum, XXX (1961), 1-18.

134   Hatlen, Theodore W. Orientation to the Theatre. New York: Appleton-Century-Crofts, 1962. 286 pp.
BM. (London edition). NN.

135   Nicoll, Allardyce. The Theatre and Dramatic Theory. London: G. G. Harrap [1962]. 221 pp.
BM.

136   Ogden, Dunbar Hunt, III. "Costume and Character on the Medieval Religious Stage." Ph.D. Yale University, 1962.

137   Southern, Richard. The Seven Ages of the Theatre. London: Faber and Faber [1962]. 312 pp.
BM. NN.

138   Gardiner, Frank Cook. "The Medieval 'Pilgrim Plays' and the Pattern of Pilgrimage." Ph.D. University of Oregon, 1965.

139   Hurrell, John Dennis. "The Figural Approach to Medieval Drama." College English, XXVI (1965), 598-604.

140   Mancini, Valentino. "Public et espace scénique dans le théâtre du moyen âge." Revue d'Histoire du théâtre, XVII (1965), 387-403.

141   Sensebach, Alfred David. "Inter-Influence Between Drama and the Pictorial Arts During the Middle Ages." D.F.A. Yale University, 1965.

142   Mann, Nonnita. "Journal of the Direction of Christmas Revelles
      (A Selection from the Drama of the Middle Ages)." M.A.
      Humboldt State College, 1968.

143   Solá-Solé, J. M. "En torno a la 'Danca general de la muerte.'"
      Hispanic Review, XXXVI (1968), 303-327.

II FESTSCHRIFTEN

144 Joseph Quincy Adams Memorial Studies. Edited by James G.
     McManaway, Giles E. Dawson, and Edwin E. Willoughby.
     Washington, D.C.: Folger Shakespeare Library, 1948. x,
     808 pp.

     Farnham, Willard Edward. "The Medieval Comic Spirit in the
     English Renaissance," pp. 429-437.

145 Studies in Honor of T. W. Baldwin. Edited by Don Cameron Allen.
     Urbana: University of Illinois Press, 1958. [6], 276 pp.

     Herrick, Marvin T. "Susanna and the Elders in Sixteenth-
     Century Drama," pp. 125-135.

146 Homenaje a Bonilla y San Martin. Estudios eruditos in memoriam
     de Adolfo Bonilla y San Martin (1875-1926). Madrid: J. Ratés,
     1930. viii, 755 pp.

     Sorrento, Luigi. "I 'Trifoni' del Petrarca 'a lo divino' a
     l'allegoria religiosa negli 'Autos, '" pp. 397-435.

147 Niederdeutsche Studien. Festschrift für Konrad Borchling. New-
     munster: Karl Wachholz, 1932.

     Rosenhagen, Gustav. "Die Wolfenbütteler Spiele und das Spiel
     des Arnold von Immessen," pp. 78-90.

148 Essays and Studies in Honor of Carleton Brown. New York: Uni-
     versity Press; London: H. Milford, Oxford University Press,
     1940. xiii, 336 pp.

Frank, Grace. "Introduction to a Study of the Medieval French Drama," pp. 62-78.

Gillet, Joseph E. "The 'Memorias' of Felipe Fernández Vallejo and the History of the Early Spanish Drama," pp. 264-280.

Watt, Homer A. "The Dramatic Unity of the Secunda Pastorum," pp. 158-166.

148a In Memoria di Napoleone Caix e Ugo Angelo Cavello. Miscellanea di filologia e linguistica. Firenze: Successori le Monnier, 1886. xxxviii, 478 pp.

Miola, Alfonso. "Un testo drammatico spagnuolo del XV seculo," pp. 175-189.

149 Romanische Forschungen ... XIII. Mélanges Chabaneau. Volume offert à Camille Chabaneau à l'occasion du 75e anniversaire de sa naissance - 4 mars 1906 - par ses élèves, ses amis et ses admirateurs. Erlangen: Fr. Junge, 1907. xvi, 1117 pp.

Baist, Gottfried. "Das Osterspiel von Notre Dame aux Nonnains in Troyes," pp. 751-753.

150 Renaissance Studies in Honor of Hardin Craig. Stanford University, California: Stanford University Press; London: H. Milford, Oxford University Press, 1943. viii, 339 pp. [Reprinted from Philological Quarterly, Vol. XX, 1941.]

Coffman, George R. "The Miracle Play. Notes and Queries," pp. 13-19.

Frampton, Mendal G. "The York Play of Christ Led Up to Calvary. (Play XXXIV)," pp. 6-12.

150a Mélanges offerts à Rene Crozet Professeur à l'Université de Poitiers, Directeur du Centre d'Études Supérieures de Civilisation Médiévales à l'occasion de son soixante-dixieme anniversaire par ses amis, ses collègues, ses élèves et les membres du C. È. S. C. M. Edités par Pierre Gallais et Yves-Jean Riou. 2 vol. [paged continuously]. Poitiers: Société d'Études Médiévales, 1966. xxxi, [1], 1417 pp.

Guiette, Robert. "Réflexions sur le drame liturgique."

Chailley, Jacques. "Du drame liturgique aux prophètes de Notre-Dame-la-Grande."

151 Studies in Honor of A. H. R. Fairchild. Columbia: University of

Missouri Press, 1946. 191 pp. (University of Missouri Studies, XXI).

Craig, Hardin. "The Origin of the Passion Play: Matters of Theory As Well As Fact, " pp. 83-90.

152 Raccolta di Studi di storia e critica letteraria dedicata a Francesco Flamini da' suoi discepoli. Pisa: F. Mariotti, 1918. xxiv, 809 pp.

Ferri, Silvio. "Una imitazionè neogreca del Sacrificio d'Isaaco del Balcari, " pp. 429-438.

153 Mélanges de linguistique et de littérature romanes à la memoire d'István Frank. Offerts par ses anciens maîtres, ses amis et ses collègues de France et de l'étranger. [Saarbrucken]: Universität des Saarlandes, 1957. 695 pp. (Annales universitatis saraviensis philosophie-lettres, No. 6).

Henry, Albert. "Note sur le miracle de Berthe, " pp. 250-261.

154 An English Miscellany Presented to Dr. [F. J.] Furnivall in Honor of His Seventy-Fifth Birthday. Edited by W. P. Ker, A. S. Napier, and W. W. Skeat. Oxford: Clarendon Press, 1901. xiv, 500 pp.

Butler, Pierce. "A Note on the Origin of the Liturgical Drama, " pp. 46-51.
Craigie, W. A. "The Gospel of Nicodemus and the York Mystery Plays, " pp. 52-61.
Jusserand, J. J. "A Note on Pageants and 'Scaffolds Hye, '" pp. 183-195.
Leach, Arthur F., "Some English Plays and Players (1220-1548), " pp. 205-234.

155 Miscellanea di studi critici edita in onore di Arturo Graf. Bergamo: Instituto italiano d'arti grafiche, 1903. 850 pp.

Salza, Abd-el-Kader. "Una commedia pedantesca del cinquecento, " pp. 431-452.

156 Etudes de dialectologie romane dédiées à la mémoire de Charles Grandgagnage. Paris: E. Droz, 1932. 342 pp. (Société de littérature wallone, XVII).

Cohen, Gustave. "Le Plus ancien document du théâtre liégois. Mystères et moralités du manuscrit 217 de Chantilly," pp. 79-95.

Thomas-Bourgeois, C. A. "Le Drame religieux au Pays de Liege. Documents inédits," pp. 283-313.

157 Volume 47 of the Publications of the Modern Language Association is Dedicated to Professor Charles Hall Grandgent, on the Occasion of His 70th Anniversary. 1932. pp. 911-1534.

Gillet, Joseph E. "Tres Pasos de la Pasion y una Egloga de la Resurreccion (Burgos, 1520)," pp. 949-980.

158 Haverford Essays. Studies in Modern Literature Prepared by Some Former Pupils of Professor Francis B. Gummere. In Honor of the Completion of the Twentieth Year of His Teaching in Haverford College. Haverford, Pennsylvania, 1909. 303 pp.

Lester, John A. "Some Franco-Scottish Influences on the Early English Drama," pp. 131-152.

159 Studies in Language and Literature in Celebration of the Seventieth Birthday of James Morgan Hart. New York: Henry Holt and Co., 1910. vi, 520 pp.

Green, Antoinette. "An Index to the Non-Biblical Names in the English Mystery Plays," pp. 313-350.

160 Mélanges de philologie, d'histoire et de littérature offerts à Henri Hauvette. Paris: Presses francaises 1934. 845 pp.

Deanović, Mirko. "Le Théâtre francais et le théâtre italien à Zagreb du moyen âge au milieu du XIXe siècle," pp. 161-173.

161 Forschungen zur neueren Literaturgeschichte. Festgabe für Richard Heinzel. Weimar: E. Felber, 1898. 576 pp.

Luick, Karl. "Zur Geschichte des englischen Dramas im XVI. Jahrhundert," pp. 133-187.

162 Heller Memorial Volume. Washington University Studies. Humanistic Series, IX. 1922.

Mackenzie, William Roy. "The Debate Over the Soul in The Pride of Life," pp. 263-274.

162a Studies in Honor of John C. Hodges and Alwin Thaler. Edited by
      Richard Beale Davis, and John Leon Lievsay. Knoxville: Uni-
      versity of Tennessee, 1961. 209 pp. (Tennessee Studies in
      Literature. Special Number).

      Parker, Roscoe E. "Some Records of the 'Somyr Play,'" pp.
      19-26.

163   Mélanges de Philologie romane et de littérature médiévale offerts
      à E. Hoepffner. Paris: Les Belles Lettres, 1949. xii, 390 pp.

      Cohen, Gustave. "Un terme de scénologie médiévale et
      moderne: chape d'Hellequin; Manteau d'Arlequin," pp.
      113-115.

164   Monatshefte für deutschen Unterricht, XXX, No. 3, 4, 1938.
      A. R. Hohlfeld Number. [Madison]: University of Wisconsin
      Press, 1938. pp. 97-218.

      Evans, M. Blakemore. "A Medieval Pentecost. A Note on
      Foreign Languages in the Lucerne Passion Play," pp. 153-
      156.

165   Radcliffe College Monographs, XV. Studies in English and Com-
      parative Literature by Former and Present Students at Rad-
      cliffe College Presented to Agnes Irwin. Boston and London:
      Ginn, 1910. 170 pp.

      Harper, Carrie A. "A Comparison Between the Brome and
      Chester Plays of Abraham and Isaac," pp. 51-73.

166   Mélanges de linguistique et de lttérature offerts à M. Alfred
      Jeanroy par ses élèves et ses amis. Paris: E. Droz, 1928.
      xvi, 679 pp.

      Cohen, Gustave, "La comédie latine en France au XIIIe siècle,"
      pp. 255-263.
      Sneyders de Vogel, K. "Quelques annotations critiques à la
      Passion du Palatinus," pp. 597-602.

167   Anniversary Papers by Colleagues and Pupils of George Lyman
      Kittredge, Presented on the Completion of His Twenty-Fifth
      Year of Teaching in Harvard University. Boston and London:
      Ginn, 1913. vii, 462 pp.

Brown, Carleton. "Caiaphas As a Palm-Sunday Prophet," pp. 105-117.

168 Modern Language Notes, No. 57. Dedicated to Henry Carrington Lancaster, on the Occasion of His Sixtieth Birthday, November 10, 1942, pp. 489-613.

Cohen, Gustave. "Un Recueil de farces inédites du XVe siècle," pp. 520-526.

169 Mélanges offerts par ses amis et ses élèves à M. Gustave Lanson. Paris: Hachette, 1922. 534 pp.

Cohen, Gustave. "Le livre de scène du Mystere de la Passion, joué à Mons en 1501," pp. 63-76.

170 Mélanges de littérature, d'histoire et de philologie offerts à Paul Laumonier, Professeur à la Faculté des lettres de Bordeaux, par ses élèves et ses amis. Paris: E. Droz, 1935. xix, 682 pp.

Cohen, Gustave. "Emblèmes moraux inédits du XVe siècle," pp. 89-96.

170a Literature and Society: Nineteen Essays by Germain Brée and Others. Edited by Bernice Slote. Lincoln: University of Nebraska Press, 1964.

Taylor, Jerome. "The Dramatic Structure of the Middle English Corpus Christi, or Cycle Plays," pp. 175-186.

171 Mélanges d'histoire du moyen âge offerts à M. Ferdinand Lot par ses amis et ses élèves. Paris: E. Champion, 1925. xli, 740 pp.

Roques, Mario. "Pour le commentaire d'Aucassin et Nicolette esclairier le cuer," pp. 723-736.

171a Francipelegius: Medieval and Linguistic Studies in Honor of Francis Peabody Magoun, Jr. Edited by Jess B. Bessinger, Jr., and Robert P. Creed. New York: New York University Press; London: Allen & Unwin, 1965. 314 pp.

Brown, Arthur. "The Study of English Medieval Drama," pp. 265-273.

172   The Manly Anniversary Studies in Language and Literature ...
      To John Matthews Manly by His Students and Associates on
      the Completion of His Twenty-Fifth Year As Head of the
      Department of English in the University of Chicago. Chicago:
      University of Chicago Press, 1923. x, 432 pp.

        Coffman, George R. "A Note Concerning the Cult of St.
          Nicholas at Hildesheim," pp. 269-275.
        Smart, W. K. "The Castle of Perseverance: Place, Date,
          and a Source," pp. 42-53.
        Young, Karl. "Concerning the Origin of the Miracle Play,"
          pp. 254-268.

173   Hommage à Ernest Martineche. Etudes hispaniques et américaines.
      Paris: Artrey, 1939. 537 pp.

        Aubrun, Charles V. "Sur les debuts du théâtre en Espagne,"
          pp. 293-314.
        Le Gentil, G. "Les Thèmes de Gil Vicente dans les moralités,
          sotties et farces francaises," pp. 156-174.

174   Essays Contributed in Honor of President William Allan Neilson.
      Smith College Studies in Modern Languages, XXI. 1939. vii,
      269 pp.

        Withington, Robert. "Paranomasia in John Heywood's Plays,"
          pp. 221-239.

175   Etudes romanes dédiées à Gaston Paris, le 29 Décembre 1890
      (25e anniversaire de son doctorat des lettres), par ses élèves
      francais et ses élèves étrangers des pays de langue francaise.
      Paris: E. Bouillon, 1891. 552 pp.

        Sepet, Marius. "Observations sur le Jeu de la feuillée d'Adam
          de la Halle," pp. 69-81.

176   Homenaje ofrecido a Menendez Pedal. Miscelánea de estudios
      lingüisticos, literarios e históricos. Madrid: Hernando, 1925.
      Vol. I. 848 pp.

        Gillet, Joseph E. "Notes on the Language of the Rustics in the
          Drama of the Sixteenth Century," pp. 443-453.

177   Studi in onore di Carlo Pellegrini. Turin: Società Editrice Inter-
      nazionale, 1963. xxxix, 846 pp. (Biblioteca di Studi Francesi,
      No. 2).

    Lebègue, Raymond. "La survivance des personages des
        Mystères francais, " pp. 205-216.

178   Studies in French Language, Literature and History Presented to
      R. L. Graeme Ritchie. Cambridge: At the University Press,
      1949. xvi, 258 pp.

      Pope, Mildred K. "Variant Readings to Three Anglo-Norman
        Poems, " pp. 171-180. [Treats the Seinte Resureccion
        (Resureccion).]

179   [James Finch] Royster Memorial Studies. Chapel Hill: University
      of North Carolina Press, 1931. x, 329 pp. [Reprinted from
      Studies in Philology, Vol. XXVIII, 1931.]

      Brown, Carleton. "An Early Mention of a St. Nicholas Play in
        England, " pp. 62-69.

180   Mélanges de philologie offerts à Jean-Jacques Salverda de Grave
      ... à l'occasion de sa soixante-dixième année par ses amis et
      ses élèves. Groningue-La Haye-Batavia: J. B. Wolters, 1933.
      xii, 424 pp.

      Roques, Mario. "Sur deux lecons contestées du manuscrit
        d'Aucassin et Nicolette, " pp. 263-271.

181   Schelling Anniversary Papers. Dedicated to Felix E. Schelling by
      His Former Students on His Thirtieth Anniversary As John Welsh
      Centennial Professor of History and English Literature in the
      University of Pennsylvania. New York: The Century Co., 1923.
      x, 341 pp.

      Baugh, Albert C. "The Chester Plays and French Influence, "
        pp. 35-63.

182   Dai tempi antichi ai tempi moderni. Da Dante al Leopardi. Raccolta
      di scritti critici, di ricerche storiche, filologiche e litterarie
      ... Per le nozze di Michele Scherillo con Teresa Negri. Milano:
      U. Hoepli, 1904. xiv, 782 pp.

      Crescini, Vicenzo. "Postilla a Aucassin et Nicolette, " pp. 47-
        50.

182a Early English and Norse Studies: Presented to Hugh Smith in Honor
      of His Sixtieth Birthday. Edited by Arthur Brown, and Peter
      Foote. London: Methuen, 1963. 225 pp.

Brown, Arthur. "Some Notes on Medieval Drama in York,"
pp. 1-5.

183   Festschrift für Wolfgang Stammler zu seinem 65. Geburtstag
dargebracht von Freuden und Schülern. [Bielefeld]: E. Schmidt
[c. 1953]. 218 pp.

Hartl, E. "Untersuchungen zum St. Galler Passionsspiel."

184   Fribourg, Université. Philosophische Fakultät. Lebendiges Mittelalter. Festgabe für Wolfgang Stammler. Freiburg: Schweitz
[1958]. 316 pp.

Schneider, K. "Das Eisenacher Zehn-Jungfrauen-Spiel."

185   Mélanges de philologie, d'histoire et de littérature offerts à
Joseph Vianey. Paris: Presses francaises, 1934. xvi, 513 pp.

Catel, Jean. "Le Jeu de Robin et Marion. Pastourelle d'Adam
le Bossu, adaptee a la scene moderne," pp. 59-75.

186   Philologisch-philosophische Studien. Festschrift für Eduard
Wechssler zum 19 Oktober, 1929. Jena und Leipzig: W. Gronau,
1929. 404 pp. (Berliner Beiträge zur romanischen Philologie,
I).

Cohen, Gustave. "Fragment inédit d'un mystère de la passion,"
pp. 208-216.

187   Essays in Memory of Barrett Wendell, by His Assistants. Cambridge, Massachusetts: Harvard University Press, 1926. [12],
[3]-320 pp.

Withington, Robert. "The Development of the 'Vice,'" pp.
153-167.

188   Mélanges de philologie romane et d'histoire littéraire offerts à
M. Maurice Wilmotte . . . à l'occasion de son 25e anniversaire
d'enseignement ... Paris: H. Champion, 1910. Vol. I. xvii,
416 pp.

Cohen, Gustave. "La Scène des pelerins d'Emmäus. Contribution à l'étude des origines du théâtre comique," pp. 105-129.
----- "Le Thème de l'aveugle et du paralytique dans la littérature francaise," pp. 393-404.

III LITURGICAL LATIN DRAMA *

A Collections

*189 Adams, Joseph Quincy, ed. Chief Pre-Shakespearean Dramas.
        A Selection of Plays Illustrating the History of the English
        Drama from Its Origin Down to Shakespeare. Boston, New
        York: Houghton Mifflin Co., 1924. viii, [3], 712 pp.
                CtY. DLC. ICN. ICU. MH. MiU. NN. OU. PU. ViU. WU.

*190 Albrecht, Otto E. Four Latin Plays of St. Nicholas from the 12th
        Century Fleury Play-book. Text and Commentary, with a
        Study of the Music of the Plays and of the Sources and Icono-
        graphy of the Legends. Philadelphia: University of Pennsylvania
        Press; London: Humphrey Milford, Oxford University Press,
        1935. ix, 160 pp.

*191 Anz, Heinrich. Die lateinischen Magierspiele. Untersuchungen
        und Texte zur Vorgeschichte des deutschen Weihnachtsspiele.
        Leipzig: J. C. Hinrichs, 1905. viii, 163 pp. Bibliography, pp.
        5-11. Index.
                BM. CtY. MB. MH. MiU. NjP. NN. OC1W. OU. PU. WU.

———

    * Because of the absence of liturgical texts of plays written in England,
as well as the absence of any detailed historical accounts of liturgical
drama in that country, the texts of the liturgical plays, together with the
historical and critical studies, are placed separately in this section of
the bibliography.

192   Beeson, Charles Henry. A Primer of Medieval Latin. An Anthology
        of Prose and Poetry. Chicago: Scott, Foresman & Co., 1925.
        389 pp.
        BM.

*193   Brooks, Neil C. "Some New Texts of Liturgical Easter-Plays."
        Journal of English and Germanic Philology, VIII (1909), 463-
        488.

*194   Champollion-Figeac, J. J. Hilarii. Versus et Ludi. Lutetiae
        Parisiorum: Apud Techener Bibliopolam, 1838. xv, [1], 61,
        [2] pp.
        BM.

195   Chasles, Madeleine. "Le Drame liturgique." La Vie et les Arts
        liturgiques, III (1916-1917), 65-70, 121-134, 169-181, 258-
        266, 297-307, 403-412.

196   Chevalier, Ulysse. Ordinaires de l'Eglise Cathédrale de Laon
        (XIIe et XIIIe siècles) suivis de deux Mystères liturgiques
        publiés les manuscrits originaux. Avec deux planches en photo-
        typie. Paris: Alphonse Picard, Librairie, 1897. xliii, [1], 409
        pp.   DLC. ICU. NN. O.

*197   Cohen, Gustave. Anthologie du drame liturgique en France au
        moyen-âge. Textes originaux accompagnés de traductions.
        Préface du P. Roguet, o.p. Paris: Les Editions Du Cerf, 1955.
        290 pp.
        BM.

198   Cohen, Gustave, ed. La "Comédie" latine en France au XIIe
        siècle, textes publiés sous la direction et avec une introduction
        de Gustave Cohen. 2 vol. Paris: Belles Lettres, 1931.
        DFo. DLC. MiU. MnU. NN. OCU. PHC. PU. WaU.

*199   Coussemaker, Edmond de, ed. Drames Liturgiques du moyen age.
        (Texte et musique). Rennes: Imprimerie de H. Vatar, 1860. xix,
        350 pp. [The wrapper gives the imprint: Paris: Librairie Arch-
        éologique de Didron, 1861.]
        BM. CtY. DFo. DLC. IU. MH. PU.

200   ----- Drames liturgiques du moyen age (texte et musique). A
        Facsimile of the 1800 Rennes Edition. New York: Broude
        Brothers [1964]. [4], [iii]-xix, 350 pp.
        NN.

201 Du Cange, C. D. Glossarium Mediae et Infamiae Latinitatis.
7 vol. Parisiis, 1840-1846.

202 Du Méril, Edélstand. Origines Latines du théâtre moderne.
Publiées et annotées. Paris" Franck, 1849. [4], 418, [2] pp.
[A facsimile reproduction was published by Leipzig, by H.
Welter, in 1897.]
DLC. MiU. NjP. OC1. OO. PU. ViU. WU.

203 Froning, R. Das Drama des Mittelalters. Erster Teil. Die
lateinischen Osterfeiern und ihre Entwickelung in Deutschland.
Osterspiele. Passionsspiele. Zweiter Teil. Passionsspiele.
Dritter Teil. Passionsspiele. Weihnachts-und Dreikönigsspiele.
Fastnachtsspiele. 3 vol. Stuttgart: Union Deutsche Verlag-
sgesellschaft [1891-1892].

204 Fuller, John Bernard, ed. Hilarii Versus et Ludi. Edited from
the Paris Manuscript. New York: H. Holt and Company [c.
1929]. [10], 3-122 pp.
ICU. OCX.

*205 Gasté, Armand, ed. Les Drames liturgiques de la Cathédrale
de Rouen (Contribution à l'histoire des origines du théâtre en
France). Evreux: Imprimerie de l'Eure, 1893. [4], 81, [2] pp.
BM. ICU. MH. MnU. PU.

*206 Gautier, Léon. Histoire de la poésie liturgique au moyen age.
Les Tropes. Paris: Victor Palme, Alphonse Priard, 1886.
VIII, 280 pp. [Includes texts].
BM. CtY. DLC. ICN. IU. MdBP. MH. MnU. OU. PU. WaU.

207 Gofflot, L. V. Le Théâtre au College au moyen âge à nos jours.
Avec bibliographie et appendices. Le Circle Francais de
l'Université Harvard. Accompagné de nombreuses planches
hors texte. Préface par Jules Claretie. Paris, 1907. xix, 336
pp.
BM.

208 Harrington, Karl P. Medieval Latin. Chicago and London: University of Chicago Press, 1962. xxix, 698 pp.
BM.

209 Hartl, Eduard. Das Benediktbeurer Passionsspiel. Das St. Galler
Passionsspiel. Nach den Handschriften herausgegeben. Halle/
Saale: Max Niemeyer Verlag, 1952. 131 pp. (Nr. 41. Altdeutsche

Textbibliothek. Begründet von H. Paul. Herausgegeben Von G.
Baesecke).
BM.

210   Un dramma della passione del secolo XII (Seconda edizione).
D. M. Inguanez. Prefazione di Giulio Bertoni. Badia di
Montecassino, 1939. 55 pp. (Miscellanea Cassinese a cura
dei monaci di Montecassino).

*211   Jeanroy, Alfred, ed. and tr. Le Théâtre religieux en France du
XIe au XIIIe siècles. Paris. E. de Bocard, 1924. xxx, 159 pp.
DLC. ICN. ICU. MH. NjP. NN. OC1. OO. ViU. WU.

212   Lange, Carl. Die lateinischen Osterfeiern. In, Jahresbericht über
die Realschule erster Ordnung in Halberstadt. Programm No.
223. Halberstadt, 1881. pp. 3-35.

*213   ----- Die lateinischen Osterfeiern. Untersuchungen und die
Entwickelung der liturgischdramatischen Auferstehungsfeier
mit Zugrundelegung eines umfangreichen, neuaufgefunden
Quellenmaterials. München: Verlag von Ernst Stahl sen., 1887.
iv, 171 pp.
BM.

214   Langosch, Karl. Geistliche Spiele: lateinische Dramen des
Mittelalters mit deutschen Versen. Basel/Stuttgart: Benno
Schwabe & Co. [1957]. 284 pp. [Latin and German texts].
BM.

215   Manly, John Matthews, ed. Specimens of the Pre-Shakesperean
Drama. With an Introduction, Notes, and a Glossary. 2 vol.
Boston and New York: Ginn and Co., 1897-1898. [Also, 1903-
1904].
CtY. DLC. ICN. ICU. MH. MiU. NjP. NNC. OC.
PU. WaU.

216   Martène, E. De Antiquis Ecclesiae Ritibus. 4 vol. Antuerpiae,
1736-1738.

217   [Mélanges des Bibliophiles francais. Vol. VII. Paris, 1831-1832].
[The volume, which is in the British Museum, has no title-
page or date. The above title is taken from the cover. The
reputed editor is L. J. N. Monmerqué.]

*218   Milchsack, Gustav. Die Oster-und Passionsspiele. Literarhistorische

Untersuchungen ueber den Ursprung und die Entwickelung
derselben bis zum siebenzehnten Jahrhundert vornehmlich in
Deutschland. Nebst dem erstmaligen diplomatischen Abdruck
des Kuenzelsauer Fronleichnamsspieles. I. Die lateinischen
Osterfeiern. Wolfenbuettel: Julius Zwissler, 1880. vi, [2],
136 pp.

    BM. CtY. MiU. OCl. PU.

219   Mone, F. J. Schauspiele des Mittelalters. Aus Handschriften
herausgegeben und erklärt. 2 vol. Karlsruhe: Druck und Verlag
von C. Macklot, 1846.

    BM.

220   Monmerqué, L. J. N., et Francisque Michel, eds. Théâtre
Francais au moyen âge, publié d'après les manuscrits de la
Bibliothèque du Roi ... (XIe - XIVe siècles). Paris: Firmin
Didot Frères, 1842. xvi, 672 pp.

221   Pfeiffer, H. "Klosterneuburger Osterfeier und Osterspiel."
Jahrbuch des Stiftes Klosterneuburg, I (1908), 3-56.

222   Schmeller, J. A. Carmina Burana. Lateinische und deutsche
Lieder und Gedichte einer Handschrift des XIII. Jahrhunderts
aus Benedictbeuren auf der K. Bibliothek zu München. Zweite
unveränderte Auflage. Breslau: Wilhelm Koebner, 1883. x,
[2], 275 pp.

    O.

223   Thomas, L. P. "Les Strophes et la Composition du Sponsus
(Textes latin et roman)." Romania, LV (1929), 45-112.

224   Van Mierlo, J. "Een Utrechtsch Antiphonarium - Bijdrage tot de
Geschiedenis van het liturgisch Drama in de Nederlanden."
Leuvensche Bijdragen op het Gebied van de Germaansche
Philologie, VIII (1908-1909), 1-75.

225   Weinhold, Karl. Weihnacht-Spiele und Lieder aus Süddeutschland
und Schlesien. Mit Einleitung und Erläuterungen. Mit einer
Musikbeilage. Neue Ausgabe. Graz: Leuschner & Lubensky,
1870. vi, 456 pp.

    O.

226   Wright, Thomas, ed. Early Mysteries, and Other Latin Poems
of the Twelfth and Thirteenth Centuries: Edited from the
Original Manuscripts in the British Museum, and the Libraries

of Oxford, Cambridge, Paris, and Vienna. London: Nichols and
Son; Paris: Techener; Leipzig: F. A. Brockhaus, 1838. xxviii,
135 pp.
>BM. ICN. MB. MiU. MnU. NjP. NNUT. OC1.

227   Young, Karl. "A Contribution to the History of Liturgical Drama
at Rouen." Modern Philology, VI (1908-1909), 201-227.

*228   ----- The Drama of the Medieval Church. 2 vol. Oxford: At the
Clarendon Press, 1933. [Corrected reprint, 1951. Reprinted
from the corrected reprint of the first edition, 1962, 1967.]
>BM. CtY. DLC. ICN. ICU. MH. MiU. NN. O. OU. PU.

*229   ----- "The Harrowing of Hell in Liturgical Drama." Transactions
of the Wisconsin Academy of Sciences, Arts, and Letters, XVI,
Part 2 (1909), 889-947.

*230   ----- "Observations on the Origin of the Medieval Passion Play;
with Texts of Some Liturgical Dramas." Publications of the
Modern Language Association, XXV (1910), 309-354.

*231   ----- "Ordo Prophetarum." Transactions of the Wisconsin
Academy of Sciences, Arts, and Letters, XX (1922), 1-82.

*232   ----- Ordo Rachelis. Madison: University of Wisconsin Press,
1919. 65 pp. (University of Wisconsin Studies in Language and
Literature, No. 4).
>BM. ICN. IaU. WU.

*233   ----- "The Origin of the Easter Play." Publications of the Modern
Language Association, XXIX (1914), 1-58.

*234   ----- "Some Texts of Liturgical Plays." Publications of the
Modern Language Association, XXIV (1909), 294-331.

B INDIVIDUAL PLAYS

1 Easter Cycle *

a Quem Quaeritis (Trope)

APT
Manuscript
235 Apt, Bibl. Capit., MS. 4, Trop. Aptense, fol. 33v - 34r (10th
- 11th century)
Text
236 [Quem Queritis]. In, Young, Karl. The Drama of the Medieval
Church. Vol. I (Oxford, 1933), p. 212. [Incompletely edited
by Young, "Origin of the Easter Play," p. 23. Young simply
prints the text as a dramatic trope.]

BENEVENTO
Manuscript
237 Benevento, Bibl. Capit., MS. 27, Trop. Beneventanum, fol. 47v
(12th century).
Text
238 [Quem Queritis]. In, Young, Karl. The Drama of the Medieval
Church. Vol. I. (Oxford, 1933), p. 215. [Edited by Young,
"Origin of the Easter Play," pp. 37-38. Young simply prints
the text as a dramatic trope.]

BRESCIA
Manuscript
239 Brescia, Bibl. Civica Queriniana, MS. H. vi. 11, Ordin. Ecclesiae
Sanctae Juliae anni 1438, fol. 34r.
Text
240 [Quem Queritis]. In, Young, Karl. The Drama of the Medieval
Church. Vol. I. (Oxford, 1933), pp. 211-212. [Edited by
Young, "Origin of the Easter Play," pp. 47-48. Young simply
prints the text as a dramatic trope.]

IVREA
Manuscript
241 Ivrea, Bibl. Capit., MS. 60, Trop. Eporediense, fol. 69v (11th
century, 1001-1011).

---

* The entries are arranged in alphabetical order according to the
libraries which possess the various manuscripts. Where no manuscript
is located the arrangement is alphabetical according to the place of
representation.

Text
242 [Quem Queritis]. In, Young, Karl. The Drama of the Medieval
     Church. Vol. I. (Oxford, 1933), pp. 223-224. [Edited by
     Young, "Origin of the Easter Play," p. 28. Young simply
     prints the text as a dramatic trope.]

MODENA
                    Manuscript (Ravenna)
243 Modena, Bibl. Capit., MS. O. 1.7, Trop. Ravennatense, fol.
     102r - 102v (11th - 12th century).
                          Text
244 [Quem Queritis]. In, Young, Karl. The Drama of the Medieval
     Church. Vol. I. (Oxford, 1933), p. 206. [Edited by Young,
     "Origin of the Easter Play," p. 20. Young prints it simply as a
     dramatic trope.]

MONTE CASSINO
                       Manuscript
245 Monte Cassino, MS. 127, Miss. Monasticum, fol. 105v (11th
     century).
                          Text
246 [Quem Queritis]. In, Young, Karl. The Drama of the Medieval
     Church. Vol. I. (Oxford, 1933), p. 214. [Printed by Young,
     "Origin of the Easter Play," pp. 35-36; A. de la Fage, Essais
     de Diphthérographie musicale (Paris, 1862), p. 473. Young
     simply prints the text as a dramatic trope.]

247 [Quem Queritis]. In, Young, Karl. The Drama of the Medieval
     Church. Vol. I. (Oxford, 1933), p. 215. [Martene, Vol. IV,
     pp. 147-148, prints the text from an unidentified manuscript
     "older than the year 1105." Reprinted by Lange, No. 23, p. 23:
     Chambers, Vol. II, p. 12: Young, "Origin of the Easter Play,"
     p. 42; Bartholomaeis, p. 517. Young simply prints the text
     as a dramatic trope.]

MONZA
                       Manuscript
248 Monza, Bibl. Capit., MS. C. 13/76, Grad-Trop. Modoetinum,
     fol. 98v - 99r (11th century).
                          Text
249 [Quem Queritis]. In, Young, Karl. The Drama of the Medieval
     Church. Vol. I. (Oxford, 1933), p. 209. [Printed by Young,
     "Origin of the Easter Play," p. 29. Young prints the text
     simply as a dramatic trope.]
                       Manuscript
250 Monza, Bibl. Capit., MS. K. 11, Grad-Trop. Modoetinum, fol.

60r - 60v (12th century).
Text

251 [Quem Queritis]. In, Young, Karl. The Drama of the Medieval Church. Vol. I. (Oxford, 1933), p. 226. [Edited by Young, "Origin of the Easter Play," pp. 54-55.]

252 [Quem Queritis]. In, Young, Karl. The Drama of the Medieval Church. Vol. I. (Oxford, 1933), pp. 228-229. [Printed by A. F. Frisi, Memorie storiche di Monza e sua Corte, III (Milan, 1794), pp. 195-197.]

OXFORD
Manuscript (Heidenheim)

253 Oxford, Bodleian MS. Selden supra 27, Trop. Heidenhemense, fol. 69v - 70r (11th century).
Text

254 [Quem Queritis]. In, Young, Karl. The Drama of the Medieval Church. Vol. I. (Oxford, 1933), pp. 225-226. [Edited by Young, "Origin of the Easter Play," p. 50. Young simply prints the text as a dramatic trope.]
Manuscript (Novalesca)

255 Oxford, Bodleian, MS. Douce 222, Trop. Novaliciense, fol. 18r - 19r (11th century).
Text

256 [Quem Queritis]. In, Young, Karl. The Drama of the Medieval Church. Vol. I. (Oxford, 1933), pp. 215-216. [Edited by Young, "Origin of the Easter Play," p. 40; Brooks, New Texts, pp. 463-464: Young, Officium Pastorum, p. 309. Young simply prints the text as a dramatic trope.]

PARIS
Manuscript (Limoges)

257 Paris, Bibliothèque Nationale, MS. lat. 1118, Trop. Sancti Martialis Lemovicensis, fol. 40v (10th century, 988-996).
Text

258 [Quem Queritis]. In, Young, Karl. The Drama of the Medieval Church. Vol. I. (Oxford, 1933), pp. 211-212. [Edited by Young, "Origin of the Easter Play," p. 26. Young simply prints the text as a dramatic trope.]
Manuscript

259 Paris, Bibliothèque Nationale, MS. lat. 1119, Trop. Augustini Lemovicensis, fol. 21r - 21v (11th century).
Text

260 [Quem Queritis]. In, Young, Karl. The Drama of the Medieval Church. Vol. I. (Oxford, 1933), p. 209. [Edited by Young, "Origin of the Easter Play," p. 24. Young prints the text

simply as a dramatic trope.]

Manuscript

261   Paris, Bibliothèque Nationale, MS. lat. 1139, Trop. Sancti Martialis Lemovicensis, fol. 53r (11th - 12th century).

Text

262   [Quem Queritis]. In, Young, Karl. The Drama of the Medieval Church. Vol. I. (Oxford, 1933), p. 212. [Printed incompletely by Lange, p. 22; Young, "Origin of the Easter Play," pp. 33-34. Young simply prints the text as a dramatic trope.]

Manuscript

263   Paris, Bibliothèque Nationale, MS. lat. 1240, Trop. Sancti Martialis Lemovicensis, fol. 30v (10th century).

Text

264   [Quem Queritis.] In, Young, Karl. The Drama of the Medieval Church. Vol. I. (Oxford, 1933), p. 210. [Printed by Young, "Origin of the Easter Play," p. 22. Young prints the text simply as a dramatic trope.]

Manuscript

265   Paris, Bibliothèque Nationale, MS. lat. 887, Trop. S. Martini (?) Lemovicensis, fol. 19r (11th century).

Text

266   [Quem Queritis]. In, Young, Karl. The Drama of the Medieval Church. Vol. I. (Oxford, 1933), p. 569. [Edited by Young, "Origin of the Easter Play," p. 25.]

PIACENZA

Manuscript

267   Piacenza, Bibl. Capit., MS. 65, Grad.-Trop. Placentinum, fol. 235v (11th - 12th century).

Text

268   [Quem Queritis]. In, Young, Karl. The Drama of the Medieval Church. Vol. I. (Oxford, 1933), pp. 216-217. [Printed by Young, "Origin of the Easter Play," p. 41. Young simply prints the text as a dramatic trope.]

ROME

Manuscript (Monastery in the Abruzzi)

269   Rome, Bibl. Vatic., MS. lat. 4770, Miss. Benedictinum Sancti Petri in Aprutio, fol. 117r (10th - 11th century).

Text

270   [Quem Queritis]. In, Young, Karl. The Drama of the Medieval Church. Vol. I. (Oxford, 1933), pp. 207-208. [Printed by Young, "Origin of the Easter Play," p. 30; Bartholomaeis, pp. 517-518; Stapper, Münster, p. 21. Young prints the text simply as a dramatic trope.]

Manuscript
271 Rome, Bibl. Angelica, MS. 123 (B. III. 18), Trop. Bononiense
     (?), fol. 214r - 214v (11th century).
Text
272 [Quem Queritis]. In, Young, Karl. The Drama of the Medieval
     Church. Vol. I. (Oxford, 1933), p. 571. [Printed by Young,
     "Origin of the Easter Play," pp. 32-33; Bartholomaeis, p.
     518.]

ST. GALL

Manuscript
273 St. Gall, Stiftsbibliothek, MS. 376, Trop. Sangallense, pp. 196-
     197 (11th century).
Text
274 [Quem Queritis]. In, Young, Karl. The Drama of the Medieval
     Church. Vol. I. (Oxford, 1933), pp. 226-227. [Edited by
     Young, "Origin of the Easter Play," pp. 53-54.]
Manuscript
275 St. Gall, Stifsbibliothek, MS. 381, Trop. Sangallense, p. 247
     (11th century).
Text
276 [Quem Queritis]. In, Young, Karl. The Drama of the Medieval
     Church. Vol. I. (Oxford, 1933), p. 568.
Manuscript
277 St. Gall, Stiftsbibliothek, MS. 387, Brev. Sangallense, pp. 57-
     58 (11th century).
Text
278 [Quem Queritis]. In, Young, Karl. The Drama of the Medieval
     Church. Vol. I. (Oxford, 1933), pp. 227-228. [Young thinks
     that this is the first time that the entire text has been published.]
Manuscript
279 St. Gall, Stiftsbibliothek, MS. 484, Trop. Sangallense, p. 111
     (10th century).
Text
280 [Quem Queritis]. In, Young, Karl. The Drama of the Medieval
     Church. Vol. I. (Oxford, 1933), p. 201. [Printed by Gautier,
     Tropes, p. 220; Bartholomaeis, p. 128; Chambers, Vol. II,
     p. 9; Young, "Origin of the Easter Play," p. 2; Adams, p. 3.
     Young prints it simply as a dramatic trope.]

TURIN

Manuscript (Monastery of Bobbio)
281 Turin, Bibl. Reale, MS. G.V. 20, Grad.-Trop. Bobbiense, fol.
     97r (11th century).

Text

282   [Quem Queritis]. In, Young, Karl. The Drama of the Medieval
       Church. Vol. I. (Oxford, 1933), p. 207. [Edited by Young,
       "Origin of the Easter Play," p. 31. Young prints the text
       simply as a dramatic trope.]

TOURS

Text (Church of St. Martin, Tours)

283   [Quem Queritis]. In, Young, Karl. The Drama of the Medieval
       Church. Vol. I. (Oxford, 1933), pp. 224-225. [Printed by
       Martene, Vol. III, p. 173; Lange, No. 25, p. 24 (incomplete).
       Young simply prints the text as a dramatic trope.]

VERCELLI

Manuscript

284   Vercelli, Bibl. Capit., MS. 56, Miss. Vercellense (?), fol. 87v
       (11th - 12th century).

Text

285   [Quem Queritis]. In, Young, Karl. The Drama of the Medieval
       Church. Vol. I. (Oxford, 1933), p. 208. [Edited by Young,
       "Origin of the Easter Play," p. 27. Young prints the text
       simply as a dramatic trope.]

Manuscript

286   Vercelli, Bibl. Capit., MS. 161, Grad.-Trop. Vercellense,
       fol. 121r (12th century).

Text

287   [Quem Queritis]. In, Young, Karl. The Drama of the Medieval
       Church. Vol. I. (Oxford, 1933), p. 205. [Edited by Young,
       "Origin of the Easter Play," p. 14. Young prints it simply as a
       dramatic trope.]

VERONA

Manuscript (Mantua)

288   Verona, Bibl. Capit., MS. 107, Trop. Mantuanum, fol. 11
       (11th century).

Text

289   [Quem Queritis]. In, Young, Karl. The Drama of the Medieval
       Church. Vol. I. (Oxford, 1933), pp. 210-211. [Edited by
       Young, "Origin of the Easter Play," p. 19. Young simply
       prints the text as a dramatic trope.]

VICH

Manuscript (Ripoll, in Spain)

290   Vich, Museo, MS. 32, Trop. Ripollense, fol. 48v (12th - 13th
       century).

Text

291   [Quem Queritis]. In, Young, Karl. The Drama of the Medieval
        Church. Vol. I. (Oxford, 1933), p. 213. [Edited by Young,
        "Origin of the Easter Play," pp. 33-34. Young simply prints
        the text as a dramatic trope.]

VIENNA

Manuscript

292   Vienna, Nationalbibliothek, MS. lat. 1888, Miscellanea Moguntina
        (?), fol. 197r (10th century).

Text

293   [Quem Queritis]. In, Young, Karl. The Drama of the Medieval
        Church. Vol. I. (Oxford, 1933), p. 569. [Young thinks that
        this is the first time that the text has been printed.]

294   [Quem Queritis]. In, Young, Karl. The Drama of the Medieval
        Church. Vol. I. (Oxford, 1933), pp. 229-230. [From Martene,
        Vol. III, p. 180. Lange, No. 32, pp. 26-27, prints an excerpt.]

ZURICH

Manuscript

295   Zurich, Zentralbibliothek, Rheinau MS. 97, Trop. Rhenoviense
        (Sangallense?), pp. 16-17 (11th century).

Text

296   [Quem Queritis]. In, Young, Karl. The Drama of the Medieval
        Church. Vol. I. (Oxford, 1933), pp. 570-571. [Edited by
        Brooks, Easter Plays, pp. 191-192; Young, "Origin of the
        Easter Play," p. 15.]

   b Visitatio Sepulchri

ADMONT

Manuscript

297   Admont (Austria), Stiftsbibliothek of the Monastery, MS. 6
        (15th century).

Text

298   [Visitatio Sepulchri]. In, Brooks, Neil C. "Some New Texts of
        Liturgical Easter Plays." Journal of English and Germanic
        Philology, VIII (October, 1909), 467-468.

ANDENNE

Manuscript

299   Andenne (Belgium), Bibliothèque Capit., MS. II, Miss. Andennense,
        fol. 125r (13th - 14th century).

Text
300 [Visitatio Sepulchri]. In, Young, Karl. The Drama of the Medieval
Church. Vol. I. (Oxford, 1933), p. 589. [Young says that this
is the first time that the text has been printed.]

ANGERS
Text
301 [Visitatio Sepulchri]. In, Lange, Carl. Die lateinischen Osterfeiern. (Munich, 1887), p. 39.

302 Visitatio Sepulchri. In, Young, Karl. The Drama of the Medieval
Church. Vol. I. (Oxford, 1933), pp. 250-251. [From, J.
Eveillon, De Processionibus Ecclesiasticis Liber. (Paris,
1655), pp. 177-179].

AQUILEIA
Text
303 [Visitatio Sepulchri]. In Lange, Carl. Die lateinischen Osterfeiern. (Munich, 1887), No. 166, pp. 105-106.

304 [Visitatio Sepulchri]. In, Young, Karl. The Drama of the Medieval
Church. Vol. I. (Oxford, 1933), pp. 320-321. [From, Agenda
Dyocesis Aquilegiensis, Venice, 1495, fol. 126v - 128v (A).
Young also gives the variants from Agenda Diocesis Sanctae
Ecclesiae Aquilegiensis, Venice, 1575, pp. 115-117.]

AUGSBURG
Text
305 [Visitatio Sepulchri]. In, Young, Karl. The Drama of the Medieval
Church. Vol. I. (Oxford, 1933), pp. 311-312. [From, [Brevi-
arium Augustense], Augsburg, 1495, fol. 253r. Young reprints
the work from a copy in the British Museum (I.A. 6762).]

306 Ad visitandum Sepulcrum in Die Sancto Pasce. In, Young, Karl.
The Drama of the Medieval Church. Vol. I. (Oxford, 1933),
p. 645. [Found in Obsequiale siue Benedictionale secundum
ecclesiam Augustensem [Augusburg, 1499], fol. XXXIIv -
XXXIVv.]

307 [Visitatio Sepulchri]. In, Lange, Carl. Die lateinischen Osterfeiern. (Munich, 1887), pp. 85-86. [From, Munich, Staatsbibliothek, Liturg. 286, fol. 111r, Diurnale, 1508, Augsburg.]

308 [Visitatio Sepulchri]. In, Lange, Carl. Die lateinischen Oster-
feiern. (Munich, 1887), No. 170, pp. 108-110. [From, Munich,
Staatsbibliothek, Liturg. 4°. 15, fol. 47v, Agendae, 1547,
Augsburg.]

309 [Visitatio Sepulchri]. In, Young, Karl. The Drama of the
     Medieval Church. Vol. I. (Oxford, 1933), pp. 351-352.
     [From, Ritus Ecclesiastici Augustensis Episcopatus,
     Dillingen, 1580, pp. 593-598].

310 [Visitatio Sepulchri]. In, Milchsack, G. Die Oster- und Passions-
     spiele: I. Die lateinischen Osterfeiern. (Wolfenbüttel, 1880),
     pp. 131-132.

311 [Visitatio Sepulchri]. In, Froning, R. Das Drama des Mittelalters.
     Vol. I. (Stuttgart, 1891), pp. 16-17.

AVRANCHES
                            Manuscript (Mont-St.-Michel)
312 Avranches, Bibliothèque de la Ville, MS. 214, Ordin. Monasterii
     Sancti Michaëlis, pp. 236-238 (14th century).
                            Text
313 [Visitatio Sepulchri]. In, Young, Karl. The Drama of the Medieval
     Church. Vol. I. (Oxford, 1933), pp. 372-374. [Young says that
     this is the first time that the text has been printed.]

BAMBERG
                            Manuscript
314 Bamberg, Staatsbibliothek, MS. 22 (Ed. III. 2), Grad. Bamber-
     gense, fol. 128r (A), (12th - 13th century).
                            Text
315 [Visitatio Sepulchri]. In, Lange, Carl. Die lateinischen Oster-
     feiern. (Munich, 1887), No. 63, pp. 44-45.

316 [Visitatio Sepulchri]. In, Brooks, N. C. "Osterfeiern aus Bam-
     berger und Wolfenbüttler Handschriften." Zeitschrift für
     deutsche Altertum, LV (1914), 53-54.

317 Ad Sepulchrum. In, Young, Karl. The Drama of the Medieval
     Church. Vol. I. (Oxford, 1933), pp. 584-585. [Young attaches
     the variants found in Bamberg, Staatsbibliothek, MS. 27 (Ed.
     I. 13), Lib. resp. Bambergensis, fol. 170r (B), (15th century),
     and Bamberg, Staatsbibliothek, MS. 26 (Ed. IV. 2), Lib.
     resp. Bambergensis, fol. 50v (C), (13th century).]
                            Manuscript
318 Bamberg, Staatsbibliothek, MS. 101 (Ed. VII. 53), Ordin.
     Eystettense, fol. 103r - 103v (15th century).
                            Text
319 [Visitatio Sepulchri]. In, Brooks, N.C. "Osterfeiern aus Bam-
     berger und Wolfenbüttler Handschriften." Zeitschrift für

deutsche Altertum, LV (1914), 54-55.

320   [Visitatio Sepulchri]. In, Young, Karl. The Drama of the Medieval
       Church. Vol. I. (Oxford, 1933), pp. 612-613.

                             Manuscript

321   Bamberg, Staatsbibliothek, MS. 116 (Ed. IV. 1), Ordin, Bamber-
       gense, fol. 22v (13th century).

                             Text

322   [Visitatio Sepulchri]. In, Brooks, N.C. "Osterfeiern aus Bamberger
       und Wolfenbüttler Handschriften." Zeitschrift für deutsche
       Altertum, LV (1914), 54.

323   [Visitatio Sepulchri]. In, Young, Karl. The Drama of the Medieval
       Church. Vol. I. (Oxford, 1933), p. 585.

                             Manuscript

324   Bamberg, Staatsbibliothek, MS. Ed. IV, 2. 4°.

                             Text

325   [Visitatio Sepulchri]. In, Lange, Carl. Die lateinischen Oster-
       feiern. (Munich, 1887), pp. 44-45.

                           Manuscript (Reichenau)

326   Bamberg, Staatsbibliothek, MS. lit. 5 (Ed. V. 9), Trop.
       Augiense, fol. 45r - 45v (10th - 11th century).

                             Text

327   [Visitatio Sepulchri]. In, Lange, Carl. Die lateinischen Oster-
       feiern. (Munich, 1887), No. 39, p. 29.

328   [Visitatio Sepulchri]. In, Froning, R. Das Drama des Mittelalters.
       Vol. I. (Stuttgart, 1891), pp. 13-14.

329   [Visitatio Sepulchri]. In, Young, Karl. The Drama of the Medieval
       Church. Vol. I. (Oxford, 1933), pp. 259-260.

                             Manuscript

330   Bamberg, Staatsbibliothek, MS. lit. 118 (Ed. I. 19), Ordin.
       Bambergense, fol. 67v - 68r (16th century).

                             Text

331   [Visitatio Sepulchri]. In, Brooks, N.C. "Osterfeiern aus Bamberger
       und Wolfenbüttler Handschriften." Zeitschrift für deutsche
       Altertum, LV (1914), 55-56.

332   [Visitatio Sepulchri]. In, Young, Karl. The Drama of the Medieval
       Church. Vol. I. (Oxford, 1933), pp. 617-618.

                      Manuscript (Collegiate Church at Halle)

333   Bamberg, Staatsbibliothek, MS. lit. 19 (Ed. VI. 3), Brev. Hallense,
       fol. 98r - 98v (16th century).

Text

334   [Visitatio Sepulchri]. In, Brooks, N. C. "Osterfeiern aus
       Bamberger und Wolfenbüttler Handschriften." Zeitschrift
       für deutsche Altertum, LV (1914), 56-57.

335   [Visitatio Sepulchri]. In, Young, Karl. The Drama of the Medieval
       Church. Vol. I. (Oxford, 1933), pp. 340-342.

336   [Visitatio Sepulchri]. In, Lange, Carl. Die lateinischen Oster-
       feiern. (Munich, 1887), No. 141, pp. 93-95. [Lange indicates
       that the text is from Bamberg Agenda of 1597.]

337   [Visitatio Sepulchri]. In, Young, Karl. The Drama of the Medieval
       Church. Vol. I. (Oxford, 1933), pp. 323-324. [From, Agenda
       Bambergensis, Ingolstadt, 1587, pp. 597-604. Lange, in No.
       141, pp. 93-95, prints "virtually this identical text" as being
       from Bamberg Agenda of 1597.]

BARI
                               Manuscript
338   Bari, Bibl. Capit., MS. 7, Cantatorium Barense, p. 83 (13th
       century).
                               Text
339   Versus ad Sepulchrum. In, Young, Karl. The Drama of the
       Medieval Church. Vol. I. (Oxford, 1933), 609-610. [Young
       says that this text had not been published previously.]

BASEL
                               Text
340   [Visitatio Sepulchri]. In, Lange, Carl. Die lateinischen Oster-
       feiern. (Munich, 1887), p. 35. [Lange indicates that the text
       is from a Basel Brevier of 1515, in the Stadtbibliothek.]

BERLIN
                               Manuscript
341   Berlin, Staatsbibliothek, MS. theol. lat. 2°. 208, Brev. Berolin-
       ense (?), fol. 19v (16th century).
                               Text
342   [Visitatio Sepulchri]. In, Lange, Carl. Die lateinischen Oster-
       feiern. (Munich, 1887), No. 84, p. 57.
                               Manuscript
343   Berlin, Staatsbibliothek, MS. theol. lat. 2°. 208, Brev. Berolin-
       ense (?), fol. 19v (16th century).
                               Text
344   [Visitatio Sepulchri]. In, Young, Karl. The Drama of the Medieval

Church, Vol. I. (Oxford, 1933), p. 601.
Manuscript (Minden)
345 Berlin, Staatsbibliothek, MS. theol. lat. 4°. 15, Grad. Mindense, fol. 120r. (A) (11th century); MS. theol. lat. 4°, 11, Grad. Mindense, fol. 45v - 46r (B), a variant.
Text
346 Visitatio Sepulchri. In, Young, Karl. The Drama of the Medieval Church. Vol. I. (Oxford, 1933), pp. 243-244. [Young gives the variant.]
Manuscript (Cathedral of Magdeburg)
347 Berlin, Staatsbibliothek, MS. 4°. 113, Ordin. Cathedralis Magdeburgensis, fol. 89r (15th century).
Text
348 [Visitatio Sepulchri]. In, Brooks, N.C. The Sepulchre of Christ in Art and Liturgy. (Urbana, 1921), p. 103.

349 [Visitatio Sepulchri]. In, Young, Karl. The Drama of the Medieval Church. Vol. I. (Oxford, 1933), p. 630.

BESANCON
Manuscript
350 Besancon, Bibliothèque de la Ville, MS. 97, Ordin. Bisuntinum, pp. 59-60 (12th century; in the hand of the 18th century).
Text
351 [Visitatio Sepulchri]. In, Brooks, N.C. The Sepulchre of Christ in the Art and Liturgy. (Urbana, 1921), p. 94.

352 [Visitatio Sepulchri]. In, Young, Karl. The Drama of the Medieval Church. Vol. I. (Oxford, 1933), p. 577.
Manuscript
353 Besancon, Bibliothèque de la Ville, MS. 98, Ordin. ecclesiae Sancti Stephani Bisuntini, fol. 40r - 40v (13th century).
Text
354 [Visitatio Sepulchri]. In, Brooks, N.C. The Sepulchre of Christ in Art and Liturgy. (Urbana, 1921), pp. 94-95.

355 [Visitatio Sepulchri]. In, Young, Karl. The Drama of the Medieval Church. Vol. I. (Oxford, 1933), pp. 614-615.
Manuscript
356 Besancon, Bibliothèque de la Ville, MS. 99, Liber ceremoniarum ecclesiae Bisuntinae Sancti Johannis Evangelistae, fol. 29v - 30r (14th century).
Text
357 [Visitatio Sepulchri]. In, Brooks, N.C. The Sepulchre of Christ in Art and Liturgy. (Urbana, 1921), p. 95.

358   [Visitatio Sepulchri]. In, Young, Karl. The Drama of the Medieval
      Church. Vol. I. (Oxford, 1933), pp. 290-291.

BIGOT
Text
359   "Officium Sepulcri. (Ex ordinario offic. mss. bibliotecae Bigoti-
      anae)." In, Migne, J. P. Patrologiae Cursus Completus (1853),
      cols. 139-142. [Words and music. 11th century.]

BRESLAU
Manuscript
360   Breslau, Universitätsbibliothek, MS. I. Qu. 175, Ordin. ad usum
      Hierosolymitanum, fol. 45v - 46r (14th century).
Text
361   [Visitatio Sepulchri]. In, Young, Karl. "The Home of the Easter
      Play." Speculum, I (1926), 74.

362   [Visitatio Sepulchri]. In, Young, Karl. The Drama of the Medieval
      Church. Vol. I. (Oxford, 1933), p. 591. [Edited by A. Schön-
      felder, Historisches Jahrbuch, XXXII (1911), 588-589; J.
      Klapper, Zeitschrift für deutsche Philologie, I (1923), 52].

CAMBRAI
Manuscript (Arras)
363   Cambrai, Bibliotheque de la Ville, MS. 75, Grad.- Trop. Sancti
      Vedasti Atrebatensis, fol. 11v (11th century).
Text
364   Visitatio Sepulchri. In, Young, Karl. The Drama of the Medieval
      Church. Vol. I. (Oxford, 1933), p. 245. [Young believes that
      this is the first time that the text has been published.]

CAMBRIDGE (?)
Manuscript
365   Cambridge, Corpus Christi College, MS. 473, Trop. Wintoniense,
      fol. 26v (11th century).
Text
366   [Visitatio Sepulchri]. In, Frere, W. H., ed. The Winchester
      Troper. (London, 1894), p. 17.

367   Angelica de Christi Resurrectione. In, Young, Karl. The Drama
      of the Medieval Church. Vol. I. (Oxford, 1933), p. 587.

CASSEL
Manuscript (Fritzlar)
368   Cassel, Landesbibliothek, MS. Theol. 2⁰. 99, Directorium

Chori Fredeslariense, fol. 88v - 89r (15th century).
Text

369 [Visitatio Sepulchri]. In, Brooks, N. C. The Sepulchre of Christ in Art and Liturgy. (Urbana, 1921), p. 100.

370 [Visitatio Sepulchri]. In, Young, Karl. The Drama of the Medieval Church. Vol. I. (Oxford, 1933), p. 257.
Manuscript (Fritzlar)

371 Cassel, Landesbibliothek, MS. theol. 2⁰. 129, Lib. resp. Fredeslariensis, fol. 111r (14th century).
Text

372 [Visitatio Sepulchri]. In, Lange, Carl. Die lateinischen Oster-feiern. (Munich, 1887), No. 83, pp. 56-57.

373 [Visitatio Sepulchri]. In, Young, Karl. The Drama of the Medieval Church. Vol. I. (Oxford, 1933), pp. 588-589.
Manuscript (Fritzlar)

374 Cassel, Landesbibliothek, MS. theol. 4⁰. 25, Trop. Fredeslariense, fol. 114v (11th century).
Text

375 [Visitatio Sepulchri]. In, Lange, Carl. Die lateinischen Oster-feiern. (Munich, 1887), No. 22, p. 23.

376 [Visitatio Sepulchri]. In, Young, Karl. The Drama of the Medieval Church. Vol. I. (Oxford, 1933), p. 578.
Manuscript (Fritzlar)

377 Cassel, Landesbibliothek, MS. theol. 4⁰. 90, Brev. Fredeslariense, fol. 109v (14th century).
Text

378 [Visitatio Sepulchri]. In, Lange, Carl. Die lateinischen Oster-feiern. (Munich, 1887), No. 46, pp. 33-34.

379 [Visitatio Sepulchri]. In, Young, Karl. The Drama of the Medieval Church. Vol. I. (Oxford, 1933), p. 594.

CIVIDALE
Manuscript

380 Cividale, Reale Museo Archeologico, MS. CI, Process. Civi-dalense, fol. 77r - 79v (14th century).
Text

381 [Visitatio Sepulchri]. In, Coussemaker, E. de. Drames litur-giques du Moyen Age. (Rennes, 1860), pp. 298-306.

382 [Visitatio Sepulchri]. Reprinted from Coussemaker by, G. Milchsack. Die Oster- und Passionsspiele. I. Die latein-

ischen Osterfeiern. (Wolfenbüttel, 1880), pp. 66-81.

383 [Visitatio Sepulchri]. In, Lange, Carl. Die lateinischen Osterfeiern. In, Jahresbericht über die Realschule erster Ordnung
in Halberstadt, Programm No. 223. (Halberstadt, 1881), pp.
22-25.

384 [Visitatio Sepulchri]. In, Lange, Carl. Die lateinischen Osterfeiern. (Munich, 1887), No. 207, pp. 136-140.

385 [Visitatio Sepulchri]. In, Bartholomaeis, V. de. Le Origini della
Poesia drammatica italiana. (Bologna [1924]), pp. 523-524.

386 [Visitatio Sepulchri]. In, Young, Karl. The Drama of the Medieval
Church. Vol. I. (Oxford, 1933), pp. 378-380.

387 In Resvrrectione. In, Young, Karl. The Drama of the Medieval
Church. Vol. I. (Oxford, 1933), p. 598. [Cividale MS. T. VII.]

388 Le Jour de la Resurrection. In, Coussemaker, E. de. Drames
liturgiques du Moyen Age. (Rennes, 1860), pp. 307-310. [The
text is based on MS. T. VII (14th century), from the archives
of the cathedral of Cividale. The Manuscripts of the cathedral
are now in the Reale Museo Arechologico at Cividale, but
Young says that the MS. of this play is not among them.]

389 [Visitatio Sepulchri]. In, Milchsack, G. Die Osterund Passionsspiele. I. Die lateinischen Osterfeiern. (Wolfenbuttel, 1880),
p. 46.

390 [Visitatio Sepulchri]. In, Lange, Carl. Die lateinischen Osterfeiern. (Munich, 1887), pp. 58-59. [The text follows that of
Milchsack, p. 46.]

391 [Visitatio Sepulchri]. In, Young, Karl. The Drama of the Medieval
Church. Vol. I. (Oxford, 1933), p. 268. [This text was published by Coussemaker from MS. T. VII (14th century).]

CLERMONT-FERRAND
Manuscript
392 Clermont-Ferrand, Bibliothèque de la Ville, MS. 67, Brev.
Claromontense, fol. 120r - 120v (14th century).
Text
393 [Visitatio Sepulchri]. Printed by R. Twigge, in Dublin Review,
CXXI (1897), 362.

394   [Visitatio Sepulchri]. In, Young, Karl. The Drama of the Medieval
      Church. Vol. I. (Oxford, 1933), p. 580.

CLEVES
                              Manuscript
395   Cleves, Pfarrarchiv in der Oberstadt, Ordin. Clevense, fol. 10r
      (15th century).
                                Text
396   [Visitatio Sepulchri]. In, Stapper, R. "Mittelalterliche Osterge-
      bräuche der Stiftsherren zu Kleve." Romische Quartalschrift
      für christliche Altertumskunde und für Kirchengeschichte,
      XXXV (1927), 181-182.

397   [Visitatio Sepulchri]. In, Young, Karl. The Drama of the Medieval
      Church. Vol. I. (Oxford, 1933), pp. 592-593. [Young follows
      Stapper's text.]

COLOGNE
                                Text
398   [Visitatio Sepulchri]. In, Lange, Carl. Die lateinischen Oster-
      feiern. (Munich, 1887), p. 36.

399   [Elevatio Hostiae et Visitatio Sepulchri]. In, Young, Karl. "The
      Harrowing of Hell in Liturgical Drama." Transactions of the
      Wisconsin Academy of Sciences, Arts, and Letters, XVI,
      Part II, (1910), 912-914. [From, Munich, Staatsbibliothek,
      Liturg. 4°, 13*, pp. 251-255, Agenda, Coloniae, 1590.]

CONSTANCE
                                Text
400   [Visitatio Sepulchri]. In, Schubiger, A. Musikalische Spicelegien.
      (Berlin, 1876), pp. 75-76. [The text is from, Benedictionale
      Ecclesiae et Diocoesis Constantiensis (Constance, 1597), pp.
      183-187 (A).]

401   [Visitatio Sepulchri]. In, Lange, Carl. Die lateinischen Oster-
      feiern. (Munich, 1887), No. 71, p. 47. [Lange says that his
      text is based on Agenda of 1570, in Zurich, Stadbibliothek, Druck
      Ro 93, fol. 121v.]

402   [Visitatio Sepulchri]. In, Young, Karl. The Drama of the Medieval
      Church. Vol. I. (Oxford, 1933), pp. 301-302. [Young says that
      the text comes from, Benedictionale Ecclesiae et Diocoesis
      Constantiensis (Constance, 1597), pp. 183-187 (A).]

CRACOW

Manuscript

403   Cracow, Bibl. Capit., MS. 83, Lib. resp. Cracoviensis (12th century).

Text

404   [Visitatio Sepulchri]. In, Windakiewicza, S. "Dramat liturgiczny w Polsce sredniowiecznej." Rozpraw Wydzialu filologienznego Akademii Umiejetnosci w Krakowie, XXXIV (1903), 348-349. [With a photographic facsimile.]

405   [Visitatio Sepulchri]. In, Young, Karl. The Drama of the Medieval Church. Vol. I. (Oxford, 1933), p. 632.

Manuscript

406   Cracow, Bibl. Capit., MS. 85, Lib. resp. Cracoviensis anni 1471, fol. 116v - 117r.

Text

407   [Visitatio Sepulchri]. In, Windakiewicza, S. "Dramat liturgiczny w Polsce sredniowiecznej." Rozpraw Wydzialu filologieznego Akademii Umiejetnosci w Krakowie, XXXIV (1903), 352.

408   [Visitatio Sepulchri]. In, Young, Karl. The Drama of the Medieval Church. Vol. I. (Oxford, 1933), pp. 316-317.

DARMSTADT

Manuscript

409   Darmstadt, Landesbibliothek, MS. 545, Cantuale Bumagense, fol. 57v - 58r (14th century).

Text

410   [Visitatio Sepulchri]. In, Lange, Carl. Die lateinischen Oster-feiern. (Munich, 1887), No. 72, p. 48.

411   Versus Ante Sepulcrum. In, Young, Karl. The Drama of the Medieval Church. Vol. I. (Oxford, 1933), p. 588.

Manuscript

412   Darmstadt, Landesbibliothek, MS. 869, Brev. Darmstadiense, fol. 80r (15th century).

Text

413   [Visitatio Sepulchri]. In, Young, Karl. The Drama of the Medieval Church. Vol. I. (Oxford, 1933), p. 594. [Young thinks that this is the first time the play has been printed.]

Manuscript

414   Darmstadt, Landesbibliothek, MS. 977, Brevier (14th century).

Text

415   [Visitatio Sepulchri]. In, Lange, Carl. Die lateinischen Oster-feiern. (Munich, 1887), pp. 34-35.

Manuscript (Burgholz)
416   Darmstadt, Landesbibliothek, MS. 3183, Rituale Burgholtense,
      pp. 108-109 (13th century).
Text
417   [Visitatio Sepulchri]. In, Lange, Carl. Die lateinischen Oster-
      feiern. (Munich, 1887), No. 82, pp. 56-57.

418   [Visitatio Sepulchri]. In, Young, Karl. The Drama of the Medieval
      Church. Vol. I. (Oxford, 1933), p. 589.

DUBLIN

Manuscript
419   Dublin, Archbishop Marsh's Library, MS. Z. 4.2. 20 (olim V.
      3.2.10), Proces. ad usum ecclesiae Sancti Johannis Evangelistae
      Dublinensis, fol. 59r - 61r (B), (14th century).
Text
420   [Visitatio Sepulchri]. In, Manly, J. M. Specimens of the Pre-
      Shakespearean Drama. Vol. I. (Boston, 1900), pp. XXII-XXVI.

421   [Visitatio Sepulchri]. In, Chambers, E. K. The Mediaeval Stage.
      Vol. II. (Oxford, 1903), pp. 315-318.

EICHSTÄTT
Text
422   [Visitatio Sepulchri]. In, Lange, Carl. Die lateinischen Oster-
      feiern. (Munich, 1887), pp. 71-74. [From an Obsequiale of
      1539, at Eichstätt, Bibliothek, H. I. 79, fol. 159r.]

423   [Visitatio Sepulchri]. In, Lange, Carl. Die lateinischen Oster-
      feiern. (Munich, 1887), pp. 40-42. [From a Sacerdotale
      Romanum, 1560, at Eichstätt, Bibliothek, H. I. 86, fol. 257a.]

EINSIEDELN
Manuscript (Zurich)
424   Einsiedeln, Stiftsbibliothek, MS. 81, Brev. Turicense anni 1462,
      fol. 141v.
Text
425   [Visitatio Sepulchri]. In, Lange, Carl. Die lateinischen Oster-
      feiern. (Munich, 1887), No. 126, pp. 87-88.

426   [Visitatio Sepulchri]. In, Young, Karl. The Drama of the Medieval
      Church. Vol. I. (Oxford, 1933), pp. 308-309.
Manuscript
427   Einsiedeln, Stiftsbibliothek, MS. 300, Lib. resp. Einsidlensis,
      pp. 93-94 (12th - 13th century).

Text
428 [Visitatio Sepulchri]. In, Mone, F. J. Schauspiele des Mittelalters,
       Vol. I. (Karlsruhe, 1846), pp. 15-19.

429 [Visitatio Sepulchri]. In, Du Méril, Édelstand. Origines latines du
       théâtre moderne. (Paris, 1849), pp. 101-107.

430 [Visitatio Sepulchri]. In, Lange, Carl. Die lateinischen Oster-
       feiern. (Munich, 1887), No. 209, pp. 140-146.

431 [Visitatio Sepulchri]. In, Young, Karl. The Drama of the Medieval
       Church. Vol. I. (Oxford, 1933), pp. 390-392.
                                    Manuscript
432 Einsiedeln, Stiftsbibliothek, MS. 179 (12th century).
                                       Text
433 [Visitatio Sepulchri]. In, Mone, F. J. Schauspiele des Mittelalters.
       Vol. I. (Karlsruhe, 1846), p. 12.

434 [Visitatio Sepulchri]. In, Du Méril, Édelstand. Origines latines
       du théâtre moderne. (Paris, 1849), pp. 100-101.

435 [Visitatio Sepulchri]. In, Lange, Carl. Die lateinischen Oster-
       feiern. (Munich, 1887), p. 55. [The manuscript information is
       based on Lange.]
                              Manuscript (Frienbach)
436 Einsiedeln, Stiftsbibliothek, MS. 614, Lib. resp. Freienbacensis,
       fol. 17r - 17v (14th century).
                                       Text
437 [Visitatio Sepulchri]. In, Lange, Carl. Die lateinischen Oster-
       feiern. (Munich, 1887), pp. 90-91.

438 [Visitatio Sepulchri]. In, Young, Karl. The Drama of the Medieval
       Church. Vol. I. (Oxford, 1933), p. 635. [A shortened form].

ENGELBERG
                                    Manuscript
439 Engelberg, Stiftsbibliothek, MS. 314 (olim I. 4/25), Collectio
       cantilenarum, fol. 75v - 78v (14th century).
                                       Text
440 [Visitatio Sepulchri]. In, Mone, F. J. Schauspiele des Mittelalters.
       Vol. I. (Karlsruhe, 1846), pp. 23-27.

441 [Visitatio Sepulchri]. In, Lange, Carl. Die lateinischen Oster-
       feiern. (Munich, 1887), No. 206, pp. 136-140.

442 [Visitatio Sepulchri]. In, Young, Karl. The Drama of the Medieval
      Church. Vol. I. (Oxford, 1933), pp. 375-377.

443 [Visitatio Sepulchri]. In, Lange, Carl. Die lateinischen Oster-
      feiern. (Munich, 1887), pp. 34-35. [Lange indicates that the
      text is based on MS. I, 5/9, at Engelberg.]

ERLANGEN
                            Manuscript
444 Erlangen, Universitätsbibliothek, MS. 417, 4°, Lib. resp., fol.
      11r - 16v (16th century).
                              Text
445 [Visitatio Sepulchri]. In, Lange, Carl. Die lateinischen Oster-
      feiern. (Munich, 1887), No. 201, pp. 124-127.

446 [Visitatio Sepulchri]. In, Young, Karl. The Drama of the Medieval
      Church. Vol. I. (Oxford, 1933), p. 643.

ESSEN
                            Manuscript
447 Essen, Münsterarchiv, MS. sine sig. Ordin. Assindense, pp.
      80-83 (14th century).
                              Text
448 [Visitatio Sepulchri]. In, Arens, F. Der Liber Ordinarius der
      Essener Stiftskirche. (Paderborn, 1908), pp. 73-76.

449 [Visitatio Sepulchri]. In, Brooks, N. C. The Sepulchre of Christ
      in Art and Liturgy. (Urbana, 1921), pp. 98-99.

450 [Visitatio Sepulchri]. In, Young, Karl. The Drama of the Medieval
      Church. Vol. I. (Oxford, 1933), pp. 333-335.

FRAUENFELD
                            Manuscript
451 Frauenfeld, Kantonsbibliothek, MS. Y. 28, Brev. Crucelinense,
      fol. 152v (13th century).
                              Text
452 [Visitatio Sepulchri]. In, Young, Karl. The Drama of the Medieval
      Church. Vol. I. (Oxford, 1933), p. 579. [Young believes that
      this is the first time that the text has been printed.]

FREISING
                              Text
453 [Visitatio Sepulchri]. In, Lange, Carl. Die lateinischen Oster-
      feiern. (Munich, 1887), No. 160, pp. 102-103. [From, Brevarium

Frisingense, Venice, 1516, fol. 197v - 198r.]

454   [Visitatio Sepulchri]. In, Young, Karl. The Drama of the Medieval
       Church. Vol. I. (Oxford, 1933), pp. 322-323. [From, Breviarum
       Frisingense, Venice, 1516, fol. 197v - 198r.]

GOTHA

Manuscript
455   Gotha, Herzogliche Bibliothek, MS. II. 90, Brev. Gothanum (?),
       fol. 8v (13th century).

Text
456   [Visitatio Sepulchri]. In, Lange, Carl. Die lateinischen Oster-
       feiern. (Munich, 1887), No. 67, pp. 45-46.

457   [Visitatio Sepulchri]. In, Young, Karl. The Drama of the Medieval
       Church. Vol. I. (Oxford, 1933), pp. 595-596.

GRAN

Text
458   [Visitatio Sepulchri]. In, Lange, Carl. "Liturgischdramatische
       Auferstehungsfeiern aus Venedig, Gran, Meissen und Worms."
       Zeitschrift für deutsche Altertum, XLI (1897), 81-82.

459   [Visitatio Sepulchri]. In, Young, Karl. The Dramatic Associations
       of the Easter Sepulchre. (Madison, 1920), pp. 34-35.

460   [Visitatio Sepulchri]. In, Young, Karl. The Drama of the Medieval
       Church. Vol. I. (Oxford, 1933), p. 306. [From, Ordinarium
       Officii Divini secundum consuetudinem Metropolitanae Ecclesiae
       Strigoniensis (Tirnovo, 1580), sig. I 8r - K 1r.]

GRAZ

Manuscript (Monastery of St. Lambrecht)
461   Graz, Universitätsbibliothek, MS. I. 1459, Process. monasterii
       Sancti Lamberti anni 1571, fol. 54r - 56v (A).
Text
462   [Visitatio Sepulchri]. In, Wonisch, O. Osterfeiern und dramatische
       Zeremonien der Palmweihe. (Graz, [1927],) pp. 16-17.

463   [Visitatio Sepulchri]. In, Young, Karl. The Drama of the Medieval
       Church. Vol. I. (Oxford, 1933), pp. 360-361. [Young gives the
       variants in Graz, Universitätsbibliothek, MS. I. 1537, Process.
       Sancti Lamberti anni 1577, fol. 74r - 79r (B).]
Manuscript (Monastery of St. Lambrecht)
464   Graz, Universitätsbibliothek, MS. I. 1537, Process. Sancti Lamberti

anni 1577, fol. 74r - 79r (B).
> Text

465   [Visitatio Sepulchri]. In, Wonisch, O. Osterfeiern und dramatische
Zeremonien der Palmweihe. (Graz, [1927]), pp. 16-17.
> Manuscript (Monastery of St. Lambrecht)

466   Graz, Universitätsbibliothek, MS. I. 1549 (olim 40/6.8°), Brev.
Sancti Lamberti, fol. 135v - 136r (12th century).
> Text

467   [Visitatio Sepulchri]. In, A. Schönback, "Ueber einige Breviarien
von Sancti Lambrecht." Zeitschrift für deutsche Altertum, XX
(1876), 132-133.

468   [Visitatio Sepulchri]. In, Young, Karl. The Drama of the Medieval
Church. Vol. I. (Oxford, 1933), p. 634.
> Manuscript (Monastery of St. Lambrecht)

469   Graz, Universitätsbibliothek, MS. II. 208 (olim 42/13. 4°), Ordin.
Sancti Lamberti, fol. 29r (13th century).
> Text

470   [Visitatio Sepulchri]. In, A. Schönback, "Ueber einige Breviarien
von Sanct. Lambrecht." Zeitschrift für deutsche Altertum, XX
(1876), 131.

471   [Visitatio Sepulchri]. In, Young, Karl. The Drama of the Medieval
Church. Vol. I. (Oxford, 1933), p. 632.
> Manuscript (Monastery of St. Lambrecht)

472   Graz, Universitätsbibliothek, MS. II. 798, Brev. monasterii
Sancti Lamberti, fol. 52r - 53r (A), (12th century) with variants; also from Graz, MS. II, 193, Brev. Sancti Lamberti,
fol. 51v - 52r (B), (15th century); also from Graz, MS. III. 722,
Brev. Sancti Lamberti, fol. 37r - 37v (C), (14th century).
> Text

473   [Visitatio Sepulchri]. In, Young, Karl. The Drama of the Medieval
Church. Vol. I. (Oxford, 1933), pp. 363-365. [All the manuscript texts were edited by O. Wonisch. Osterfeiern und dramatische Zeremonien der Palmweihe. (Graz, [1927]), pp. 12-15.
> Manuscript (Monastery of St. Lambrecht)

474   Graz, Universitätsbibliothek, MS. III. 116, Lib. resp. Sancti
Lamberti, fol. 66r - 67r (B), (15th century).
> Text

475   [Visitatio Sepulchri]. In, Wonisch, O. Osterfeiern und dramatische
Zeremonien der Palmweihe. (Graz, [1927]), pp. 15-16.
> Manuscript (Monastery of St. Lambrecht)

476   Graz, Universitätsbibliothek, MS. III. 134, Brev. Sancti Lamberti,
fol. 247r (A), (13th century).

Text

477 [Visitatio Sepulchri]. In, Wonisch, O. Osterfeiern und dramatische Zeremonien der Palmweihe. (Graz, [1927], pp. 15-16.

478 [Visitatio Sepulchri. In, Young, Karl. The Drama of the Medieval
Church. Vol. I. (Oxford, 1933), pp. 656-657. [Young also gives
the variants from Graz, Universitätsbibliothek, MS. III. 116, Lib.
resp. Sancti Lamberti, fol. 66r - 67r (B), (15th century).]

HALBERSTADT
Manuscript
479 Halberstadt, Domschatz, MS. XVIII, Lib. resp. Halberstadensis
anni 1440, fol. 86r - 86v (A).
Text
480 [Visitatio Sepulchri]. In, Lange, Carl. Die lateinischen Osterfeiern. (Munich, 1887), No. 111, pp. 85-86.

481 Ad Uisitandum Sepulchrum. In, Young, Karl. The Drama of the
Medieval Church. Vol. I. (Oxford, 1933), p. 631. [Young attaches the variants from a printed Magdeburg Breviary of
1491, and from Wolfenbüttel.]

482 [Visitatio Sepulchri]. In, Milchsack, G. Die Osterund Passionsspiele; I. Die lateinischen Osterfeiern. (Wolfenbüttel,
1880), p. 47. [From a printed Magdeburg Breviary of 1491.]

483 [Visitatio Sepulchri]. In, Lange, Carl. "Die lateinischen Osterfeiern." Jahresbericht über die Realschule erster Ordnung in
Halberstadt, Programm No. 223. (Halberstadt, 1881), pp.
21-22. [A reprint of the Milchsack text.]
Manuscript
484 Halberstadt, Bibliothek des Domgymnasiums, MS. 92, Ordin.
Halberstadense, fol. 27r - 27v (15th century).
Text
485 [Visitatio Sepulchri]. In, Lange, Carl. Die lateinischen Osterfeiern. (Munich, 1887), No. 145, pp. 98-99.

486 [Visitatio Sepulchri]. In, Young, Karl. The Drama of the Medieval
Church. Vol. I. (Oxford, 1933), pp. 342-343.

487 [Visitatio Sepulchri]. In, Lange, Carl. Die lateinsichen Osterfeiern. (Munich, 1887), No. 139, pp. 91-92. [From, Breviar-
ium ... ecclesiae Halberstadensis, Nuremberg, 1515, fol.
39r.]

488   [Visitatio Sepulchri]. In, Young, Karl. The Drama of the Medieval
         Church. Vol. I. (Oxford, 1933), pp. 315-316. [From, Breviar-
         ium ... ecclesiae Halberstadensis, Nuremberg, 1515, fol.
         39r.]

HARLEM
                                  Manuscript
489   Harlem, Episcopal Museum, MS. 258, Brev. Harlemense, fol. 44v
         (13th century).
                                    Text
490   [Visitatio Sepulchri]. In, Lange, Carl. Die lateinischen Osterfeiern.
         (Munich, 1887), No. 142, pp. 93-95.

491   [Visitatio Sepulchri]. In, Van Mierlo, J. "Een Utrechtsch Anti-
         phonarium -- Bijdrage tot de Geschiedenis van het liturgisch
         Drama in de Nederlanden." Leuvensche Bijdragen op het Gebied
         van de Germaansche Philologie, VIII (1908), 51-52.

492   [Visitatio Sepulchri]. In, Young, Karl. The Drama of the Medieval
         Church. Vol. I. (Oxford, 1933), pp. 319-320.

HERZOGENBURG
                                  Manuscript
493   Herzogenburg, Stiftsbibliothek, MS. 67, Brev. Ducumburgense
         anni 1451, fol. 14 (old pagination).
                                    Text
494   [Visitatio Sepulchri]. In, Brooks, Neil C. "Some New Texts of
         Liturgical Easter Plays." Journal of English and Germanic
         Philology, VIII (October, 1909), 479-480.

495   [Visitatio Sepulchri]. In, Young, Karl. The Drama of the Medieval
         Church. Vol. I. (Oxford, 1933), pp. 636-637.
                                  Manuscript
496   Herzogenburg, Stiftsbibliothe, MS. 74, Liber ... Saltzburgensis
         ecclesie, A. 1475.
                                    Text
497   [Visitatio Sepulchri]. In, Brooke, Neil C. "Some New Texts of
         Liturgical Easter Plays." Journal of English and Germanic
         Philology, VIII (October, 1909), 483-484.
                           Manuscript (Klosterneuburg)
498   Herzogenburg, Stiftsbibliothek, MS. 180, Brev. Claustroneoburgense
         anni 1570, fol. 33v - 34r.
                                    Text
499   [Visitatio Sepulchri]. In, Brooks, Neil C. "Some New Texts of
         Liturgical Easter Plays." Journal of English and Germanic

Philology, VIII (October, 1909), 481-482.

500 [Visitatio Sepulchri]. In, Young, Karl. The Drama of the
Medieval Church. Vol. I. (Oxford, 1933), p. 639.
Manuscript (Passau)

501 Herzogenburg, Stiftsbibliothek, MS. 183, Brev. Pataviense,
fol. 122r - 122v (15th century).
Text

502 [Visitatio Sepulchri]. In, Brooke, Neil C. "Some New Texts of
Liturgical Easter Plays." Journal of English and Germanic
Philology, VIII (October, 1909), 487-488.

503 Visitatio Sepulchri. In, Young, Karl. The Drama of the Medieval
Church. Vol. I. (Oxford, 1933), pp. 354-355.

HILDESHEIM

Manuscript

504 Hildesheim, Dombibl. (Beverinische Bibl.), MS. 684, Brev.
Hildesiense, fol. 245v (A), (13th - 14th century).
Text

505 [Visitatio Sepulchri]. In, Brooke, Neil C. "Some New Texts of
Liturgical Easter Plays." Journal of English and Germanic
Philology, VIII (October, 1909), 468-469.

506 Visitatio Sepulchri. In, Young, Karl. The Drama of the Medieval
Church. Vol. I. (Oxford, 1933), p. 586. [Young attaches the
variants found in Hildesheim, Dombibl. (Beverinische Bibl.),
MS. 690, Brev. Hildesiense, fol. 7r (B), (15th century), and
also MS. 697, Lib. resp. Hildesiensis, fol. 182v (C), (16th
century).]

INNSBRUCK

Manuscript

507 Innsbruck, Universitätsbibliothek, MS. 610, Brev. Oenipontanum,
fol. 182v - 183v (15th century).
Text

508 Visitatio Sepulchri. In, Lange, Carl. Die lateinischen Osterfeiern.
(Munich, 1887), pp. 124-127.

509 Visitatio Sepulchri. In, Young, Karl. The Drama of the Medieval
Church. Vol. I. (Oxford, 1933), pp. 357-358.

KARLSRUHE

Manuscript (Villingen)

510 Karlsruhe, Hof- und Landesbibliothek, MS. Geo. 1. (Antiphonary

of the 15th century from the Monastery of St. George at
Villingen).

Text

511 [Visitatio Sepulchri]. In, "Some New Texts of Liturgical Easter
Plays." Journal of English and Germanic Philology, VIII
(October, 1909), 465-466.

KLOSTERNEUBURG

Manuscript

512 Klosterneuburg, Stiftsbibliothek, MS. 61, Brev. Claustroneoburgense, fol. 193r - 193v (A), (15th century).

Text

513 [Visitatio Sepulchri]. In, Pfeiffer, H. "Klosterneuburger Osterfeier und Osterspiel." Jahrbuch der Stiftes Klosterneuburg, I
(1908), 17-19.

514 [Visitatio Sepulchri]. In, Young, Karl. The Drama of the Medieval
Church. Vol. I. (Oxford, 1933), pp. 640-641. [Young appends
the variants from the text found in Klosterneuburg, Stiftsbibliothek,
MS. 590, Brev. Claustroneoburgense, fol. 300v - 301r (B), (15th
century).]

Manuscript

515 Klosterneuburg, Stiftsbibliothek, MS. 1021, Rituale Claustroneoburgense, fol. 60v - 61v (A), (14th century).

Text

516 [Visitatio Sepulchri]. In, Pfeiffer, H. "Klosterneuburger Osterfeier und Osterspiel." Jahrbuch der Stiftes Klosterneuburg, I
(1908), 17-19.

517 [Visitatio Sepulchri]. In, Young, Karl. The Drama of the Medieval
Church. Vol. I. (Oxford, 1933), pp. 317-318. [Young gives the
variants from MS. 629, Rituale Claustroneoburgense, fol. 103v
- 105r (B), (15th century(.]

Manuscript

518 Klosterneuburg, Stiftsbibliothek, MS. 1185, Brev. Claustroneoburgense, fol. 261v - 262r (13th century).

Text

519 [Visitatio Sepulchri]. In, Pfeiffer, H. "Klosterneuburger Oster-
feier und Osterspiel." Jahrbuch des Stiftes Klosterneuburg,
I (1908), 17-19 (C). [See, Young, Karl. The Drama of the
Medieval Church. Vol. I. (Oxford, 1933), p. 633.]

Manuscript

520 Klosterneuburg, Stiftsbibliothek, MS. 1193, Brev. Claustroneoburgense, fol. 240v - 241r (15th century).

Text

521 [Visitatio Sepulchri]. In, Pfeiffer, H. "Klosterneuburger Oster-

feier und Osterspiel." Jahrbuch des Stiftes Klosterneuburg,
I (1908), 17-19.

522   [Visitatio Sepulchri]. In, Young, Karl. The Drama of the Medieval
        Church. Vol. I. (Oxford, 1933), pp. 633-634.
                              Manuscript
523   Klosterneuburg, Stiftsbibliothek, MS. 1213, Ordin. Claustroneo-
        burgense anni 1325, fol. 83r - 83v (A).
                              Text
524   [Visitatio Sepulchri]. In, Pfeiffer, H. "Klosterneuburger Oster-
        feier und Osterspiel." Jahrbuch des Stiftes Klosterneuburg,
        I (1908), 17-19.

525   [Visitatio Sepulchri]. In, Young, Karl. The Drama of the Medieval
        Church. Vol. I. (Oxford, 1933), pp. 329-330. [Young gives
        the variants from, Klosterneuburg, Stiftsbibliothek, MS. 635,
        Ordin. Claustroneoburgense, fol. 57v - 58r (B), (15th century).]

526   [Visitatio Sepulchri]. In, Du Méril, Édelstand. Origines latines
        du théâtre moderne. (Paris, 1849), pp. 89-91. [MS. not indicated.]

527   [Visitatio Sepulchri]. In, Lange, Carl. Die lateinischen Oster-
        feiern. (Munich, 1887), pp. 95-98. [MS. not indicated.]

528   Ordo Paschalis. In, Langosch, Karl. Geistliche Spiele. Lateinische
        Dramen des Mittelalters mit deutschen Versen. (Basel, Stutt-
        gart, 1957), pp. 107-125. [MS. not indicated.]

KREMSMÜNSTER
                              Manuscript (Passau)
529   Kremsmünster, Stiftsbibliothek, MS. 100, Brev. Pataviense,
        fol. 168v - 169r (15th century).
                              Text
530   [Visitatio Sepulchri]. In, Young, Karl. The Drama of the Medieval
        Church. Vol. I. (Oxford, 1933), p. 655. [Young says that this
        is the first time that the text has been printed.]
                              Manuscript (Passau)
531   Kremsmünster, Stiftsbibliothek, MS. 274, Brev. Pataviense,
        fol. 306v (15th century).
                              Text
532   [Visitatio Sepulchri]. In, Brooks, Neil C. "Some New Texts of
        Liturgical Easter Plays." Journal of English and Germanic
        Philology, VIII (October, 1909), 484-485.

533   [Visitatio Sepulchri]. In, Young, Karl. The Drama of the Medieval

Church. Vol. I. (Oxford, 1933), pp. 337-338.

LAON

Manuscript

534 Laon, Bibliothèque de la Ville, MS. 216, Ordin. Laudunense,
fol. 129r - 129v (13th century).

Text

535 [Visitatio Sepulchri]. In, Chevalier, U. Ordinaires de l'Eglise
cathédrale de Laon. (Paris, 1897), pp. 118-119.

536 [Visitatio Sepulchri]. In, Young, Karl. The Drama of the Medieval
Church. Vol. I. (Oxford, 1933), pp. 302-303.

537 [Visitatio Sepulchri]. In, Lange, Carl. Die lateinischen Osterfeiern. (Munich, 1887), p. 30.

LE MANS

Manuscript

538 Le Mans, Bibliothèque de la Ville, MS. 165 (olim, 1175), Ordin.
Cenomanense, fol. 20v (15th century).

Text

539 [Visitatio Sepulchri]. In, Lange, Carl. Die lateinischen Osterfeiern. (Munich, 1887), pp. 66-67. [Incomplete]

540 [Visitatio Sepulchri]. In, Piolin, P. "Le Théâtre chrétien dans
le Maine au cours du Moyen Age." Revue historique et arch-
éologique du Maine, XXIX (1891), 210-211.

541 [Visitatio Sepulchri]. In, Piolin, P. Le Théâtre chrétien dans le
Maine au cours du Moyen Age. (Mamers, 1892), p. 19.

542 [Visitatio Sepulchri]. In, Young, Karl. The Drama of the Medieval
Church. Vol. I. (Oxford, 1933), pp. 288-289.

LICHTENTAL

Text

543 [Visitatio Sepulchri]. In, Mone, F. J. Schauspiele des Mittelalters.
Vol. II. (Karlsruhe, 1846), p. 19.

544 [Visitatio Sepulchri]. In, Du Méril, Édelstand. Origines latines du
théâtre moderne. (Paris, 1849), pp. 108-110.

LONDON

Manuscript

545 London, British Museum, Add. MS. 19415, Brev. Wormatense,

fol. 327r (15th century).
                        Text
546 [Visitatio Sepulchri]. In, Lange, Carl. "Liturgischdramatische
     Auferstehungsfeiern aus Venedig, Gran, Meissen und Worms."
     Zeitschrift für deutsche Altertum, XLI (1897), 82.

547 [Visitatio Sepulchri]. In, Young, Karl. The Drama of the Medieval
     Church. Vol. I. (Oxford, 1933), p. 591.
                        Manuscript (Strassburg)
548 London, British Museum, Add. MS. 23922, Lib. Resp. Argentora-
     tensis, fol. 41v - 42v (13th century).
                        Text
549 [Visitatio Sepulchri]. In, Lange, Carl. Die lateinischen Oster-
     feiern. (Munich, 1887), pp. 48-50.

550 [Visitatio Sepulchri]. In, Wilmart, A. L'ancien Cantatorium de
     l'Eglise de Strasbourg: Manuscrit additionnel 23922 du Musée
     Britannique ... avec un Mémoire de M. l'Abbé J. Walter.
     (Colmar, 1928), pp. 36-37.

551 Ad Celebrandam Resur[r]ectionem. In, Young, Karl. The Drama
     of the Medieval Church. Vol. I. (Oxford, 1933), pp. 587-588.
                        Manuscript (Silos, Spain)
552 London, British Museum, Add. MS. 30848, Brev. Silense, fol.
     125v (11th century).
                        Text
553 [Visitatio Sepulchri]. In, Lange, Carl. Die lateinischen Oster-
     feiern. (Munich, 1887), No. 27, pp. 24-25.

554 [Visitatio Sepulchri]. In, Young, Karl. The Drama of the Medieval
     Church. Vol. I. (Oxford, 1933), p. 577.
                        Manuscript (Silos, Spain)
555 London, British Museum, Add. MS 30850, Brev. Silense, fol.
     106v (11th century).
                        Text
556 [Visitatio Sepulchri]. In, Lange, Carl. Die lateinischen Oster-
     feiern. (Munich, 1887), No. 26, pp. 24-25.

557 [Visitatio Sepulchri]. In, Young, Karl. The Drama of the Medieval
     Church. Vol. I. (Oxford, 1933), p. 577.
                        Manuscript (Cologne)
558 London, British Museum, Add. MS. 31913, Brev. Coloniense,
     fol. 263v - 264 r (14th century).
                        Text
559 [Visitatio Sepulchri]. In, Lange, Carl. Die lateinischen Osterfeiern.

(Munich, 1887), No. 52, p. 35.

560   Ad Sepulchrum. In, Young, Karl. The Drama of the Medieval
      Church. Vol. I. (Oxford, 1933), pp. 593-594.
                         Manuscript (Paris)
561   London, British Museum, Add. MS. 37399, Brev. Parisiense,
      fol. 236v - 237r (13th - 14th century).
                              Text
562   Versus ad Sepulcrum. In, Young, Karl. The Drama of the Medieval
      Church. Vol. I. (Oxford, 1933), p. 610. [Young says that this
      is the first time that the text has been printed.]
                       Manuscript (Würzburg)
563   London, British Museum, MS. Arundel 156, Grad. Wirceburgense,
      fol. 35r (13th century).
                              Text
564   [Visitatio Sepulchri]. In, Lange, Carl. Die lateinischen Oster-
      feiern. (Munich, 1887), No. 144, pp. 95-98.

565   Ordo Sepulchri. In, Young, Karl. The Drama of the Medieval
      Church. Vol. I. (Oxford, 1933), pp. 629-630.
                 Manuscript (Regularis Concordia)
566   London, British Museum, MS. Cotton Faustina B. III, fol. 188v
      - 189v (new pagination).
                              Text
567   [Visitatio Sepulchri]. In, Young, Karl. The Drama of the Medieval
      Church. Vol. I. (Oxford, 1933), pp. 581-582.
                           Manuscript
568   London, British Museum, MS. Cotton Tiberius A. III, Regularis
      Concordia, fol. 21r - 21v (11th century).
                              Text
569   [Visitatio Sepulchri]. In, Lange, Carl. Die lateinischen Oster-
      feiern. (Munich, 1887), p. 38.

570   [Visitatio Sepulchri]. In, Manly, J. W. Specimens of the Pre-
      Shakespearean Drama. Vol. I. (Boston, 1900), pp. xix-xx.

571   [Visitatio Sepulchri]. In, Adams, Joseph Q. Chief Pre-Shakes-
      pearean Dramas. (Boston, New York, [1924]), pp. 9-10.

572   Visitatio Sepulchri. In, Young, Karl. The Drama of the Medieval
      Church. Vol. I. (Oxford, 1933), pp. 249-250. [Edited by S.
      Logeman, Anglia, XIII (1891), 426-428. Young says a less
      correct version is found in the Regularis Concordia in the
      British Museum, MS. Cotton Faustina B. III, fol. 188v -
      189v (11th century).]

Manuscript (Treves)
573 London, British Museum, MS. Harl. 2958, Ordin. Trevirense,
        fol. 37v (13th century).
Text
574 [Visitatio Sepulchri]. In, Lange, Carl. Die lateinischen Oster-
        feiern. (Munich, 1887), No. 105, pp. 71-74. [Edited, with
        omissions.]

575 [Visitatio Sepulchri]. In, Young, Karl. The Drama of the Medieval
        Church. Vol. I. (Oxford, 1933), pp. 280-281.

MADRID
Manuscript (Sicily)
576 Madrid, Bibl. Nac., MS. C. 132, Grad. ad usum ecclesiae
        Siculorum, fol. 102v - 103r (12th century).
Text
577 [Visitatio Sepulchri]. In, Young, Karl. The Drama of the Medieval
        Church. Vol. I. (Oxford, 1933), pp. 269-270. [Young says that
        this is the first time that the piece has been printed.]
Manuscript (Sicily)
578 Madrid, Bibl. Nac., MS. 289 (C. 153), Trop. ad usum ecclesiae
        Siculorum, fol. 115v - 116r (12th century).
Text
579 [Visitatio Sepulchri]. In, Young, Karl. "Some Texts of Liturgical
        Plays." Publications of the Modern Language Association, XXIV
        (June, 1909), 329.

580 [Visitatio Sepulchri]. In, Beeson, C. H. A Primer of Medieval
        Latin. (Chicago, [1925]), pp. 204-205. [Beeson reprints
        Young's text.]

581 [Visitatio Sepulchri]. In, Young, Karl. The Drama of the Medieval
        Church. Vol. I. (Oxford, 1933), p. 599.

MAINZ
Text
582 [Visitatio Sepulchri]. In, Würdtwein, S. A. Commentatio
        Historico-Liturgica de Stationibus Ecclesiae Moguntinae.
        (Mainz, 1782), pp. 179-181.

583 [Visitatio Sepulchri]. In, Young, Karl. The Drama of the Medieval
        Church. Vol. I. (Oxford, 1933), p. 612. [Young reprints the
        text from S. A. Würdtwein.]

MEISSEN

Text

584   [Visitatio Sepulchri]. In, Lange, C. "Liturgischdramatische
      Auferstehungsfeiern aus Venedig, Gran, Meissen und Worms."
      Zeitschrift für deutsche Altertum, XLI (1897), 82-83. [From,
      Breviarius ... insignis et ingenue Misnensis ecclesie, Meissen,
      1520, sig. F 4v - F 5r.]

585   [Visitatio Sepulchri]. In, Young, Karl. The Drama of the Medieval
      Church. Vol. I. (Oxford, 1933), pp. 330-331. [From, Breviarius
      ... insignis et ingenue Misnensis ecclesie, Meissen, 1520, sig.
      F 4v - F 5r.]

MELK

Manuscript (Passau)

586   Melk, Stiftsbibliothek, MS. 992, Brev. Pataviense (15th century).

Text

587   [Visitatio Sepulchri]. In, Young, Karl. The Drama of the Medieval
      Church. Vol. I. (Oxford, 1933), p. 648. [Young says that this
      is the first time that the text has been printed.]

Manuscript

588   Melk, Stiftsbibliothek, MS. 1056. (Ordinarium of the 11th or 12th
      century).

Text

589   [Visitatio Sepulchri]. In, Young, Karl. The Drama of the Medieval
      Church. Vol. I. (Oxford, 1933), pp. 241-242. [Young believes
      that this is the first printing of the text.]

Manuscript (Passau)

590   Melk, Stiftsbibliothek, MS. 1093, Ordin. Pataviense, fol. 37r
      (15th century).

Text

591   [Visitatio Sepulchri]. In, Young, Karl. The Drama of the Medieval
      Church. Vol. I. (Oxford, 1933), p. 646.

Manuscript

592   Melk, Stiftsbibliothek, MS. 1094, Process. monasticum, fol.
      35r - 38v (15th century).

Text

593   [Visitatio Sepulchri]. In, Brooks, Neil C. "Some New Texts of
      Liturgical Easter Plays." Journal of English and Germanic
      Philology, VIII (October, 1909), 476-478.

594   Ad Visitandum Sepulchrum. In, Young, Karl. The Drama of the
      Medieval Church. Vol. I. (Oxford, 1933), pp. 619-620.

Manuscript (Passau)

595   Melk, Stiftsbibliothek, MS. 1671, Brev. Pataviense, fol.

510v - 511v (15th century).
Text
596   [Visitatio Sepulchri]. In, Lange, Carl. Die lateinischen Oster-
      feiern. (Munich, 1887), No. 183, pp. 114-116.

597   [Visitatio Sepulchri]. In, Young, Karl. The Drama of the Medieval
      Church. Vol. I. (Oxford, 1933), pp. 352-353.

598   [Visitatio Sepulchri]. In, Lange, Carl. Die lateinischen Oster-
      feiern. (Munich, 1887), pp. 110-112. [Melk, Stiftsbibliothek,
      a. 3. 11, fol. 140v, Brevier, 1517.]

METZ

Manuscript
599   Metz, Bibliothèque Municipale, MS. 452, Trop. Sancti Arnulphi
      Metensis, fol. 25r (11th - 12th century).
Text
600   [Visitatio Sepulchri]. In, Young, Karl. The Drama of the Medieval
      Church. Vol. I. (Oxford, 1933), p. 578. [Young believes that
      this is the first time the text has been printed.]

MONT ST. MICHEL

Text
601   [Visitatio Sepulchri]. In, Du Méril, Édelstand. Origines latines
      du théâtre moderne. (Paris, 1849), pp. 94-96. [Bibliothèque
      d'Avranches, No. intér. 14, et extér. 2524. Early 14th cen-
      tury.]

MONTE CASSINO

Text
602   [Visitatio Sepulchri]. In, Lange, Carl. Die lateinischen Oster-
      feiern. (Munich, 1887), p. 23. [From, Martene, De Antiquis
      Ecclesiae Ritibus. Vol. 4. (Venice, 1788), p. 147.]

MUNICH

Manuscript (Augsburg)
603   Munich, Staatsbibliothek, MS. lat. 226, Ordin. Augustense,
      fol. 10v - 11r (12th century).
Text
604   [Visitatio Sepulchri]. In, Lange, Carl. Die lateinischen Oster-
      feiern. (Munich, 1887), No. 110, pp. 82-83.

605   [Visitatio Sepulchri]. In, Young, Karl. The Drama of the Medieval
      Church. Vol. I. (Oxford, 1933), pp. 310-311. [Edited by
      Lange, No. 110, pp. 82-83.]

Manuscript

606   Munich, Staatsbibliothek, MS. lat. 2725, Ordin. Alderspacense,
       fol. 71v - 72r (14th - 15th century).

Text

607   [Visitatio Sepulchri]. In, Young, Karl. The Drama of the Medieval
       Church. Vol. I. (Oxford, 1933), pp. 649-650.

Manuscript

608   Munich, Staatsbibliothek, MS. lat. 2988, Lib. resp. Ambergensus,
       fol. LIVv - LVr (15th century).

Text

609   [Visitatio Sepulchri]. In, Young, Karl. The Drama of the Medieval
       Church. Vol. I. (Oxford, 1933), p. 584. [Young says that this
       is the first time that the text has been printed.]

Manuscript (Aspach)

610   Munich, Staatsbibliothek, MS. lat. 3205, Brev. Aspacense, fol.
       1v (14th century).

Text

611   [Visitatio Sepulchri]. In, Lange, Carl. Die lateinischen Oster-
       feiern. (Munich, 1887), No. 64, pp. 44-45.

612   [Visitatio Sepulchri]. In, Young, Karl. The Drama of the Medieval
       Church. Vol. I. (Oxford, 1933), p. 583.

Manuscript (Eichstätt)

613   Munich, Staatsbibliothek, MS. lat. 3918, Ordin. Eystettense,
       fol. 75v - 76v (14th century).

Text

614   [Visitatio Sepulchri]. In, Young, Karl. The Drama of the Medieval
       Church. Vol. I. (Oxford, 1933), pp. 283-284. [Young says that
       this is the first time that the piece has been printed.]

Manuscript

615   Munich, Staatsbibliothek, MS. lat. 4117, Brev. Augustense, fol.
       131r (15th century).

Text

616   Ad Uisitandum Sepulchrum. In, Young, Karl. The Drama of the
       Medieval Church. Vol. I. (Oxford, 1933), pp. 626-627. [Young
       says that this is the first time that the text has been printed.]

Manuscript (Chiemsee)

617   Munich, Staatsbibliothek, MS. lat. 5349, Brev. Chiemense,
       fol. 199r - 199v (15th century).

Text

618   [Visitatio Sepulchri]. In, Lange, Carl. Die lateinischen Oster-
       feiern. (Munich, 1887), No. 162, pp. 102-103.

619   [Visitatio Sepulchri]. In, Young, Karl. The Drama of the Medieval
       Church. Vol. I. (Oxford, 1933), pp. 327-328.

Manuscript (Diessen)

620 Munich, Staatsbibliothek, MS. lat. 5545, Brev. Diessense, fol. 21r (15th century).

Text

621 [Visitatio Sepulchri]. In, Brooks, N. C. "Neue lateinischen Oster- feiern." Zeitschrift für deutsche Altertum, L (1908), 305-306.

622 [Visitatio Sepulchri]. In, Young, Karl. The Drama of the Medieval Church. Vol. I. (Oxford, 1933), pp. 358-359.

Manuscript (Diessen)

623 Munich, Staatsbibliothek, Cod. lat. 5546, fol. 152v - 153v (Diessen, Breviary, 15th century).

Text

624 [Visitatio Sepulchri]. In Lange, Carl. Die lateinischen Oster- feiern. (Munich, 1887), pp. 99-101.

625 [Visitatio Sepulchri]. In, Young, Karl. "The Harrowing of Hell in Liturgical Drama." Transactions of the Wisconsin Academy of Sciences, Arts and Letters, XVI, Part II (1910), 909-910.

Manuscript (Freising)

626 Munich, Staatsbibliothek, Cod. lat. 6423, Lib. resp. Frisingensis, fol. 1v (14th century). [A partially mutilated text.]

Text

627 [Visitatio Sepulchri]. In, Lange, Carl. Die lateinischen Oster- feiern. (Munich, 1887), No. 125, pp. 87-88.

Manuscript (Indersdorf)

628 Munich, Staatsbibliothek, MS. lat. 7691, Brev. Indersdorfense, pp. 120-121 (15th century).

Text

629 [Visitatio Sepulchri]. In, Lange, Carl. Die lateinischen Oster- feiern. (Munich, 1887), No. 168, pp. 107-108.

630 [Visitatio Sepulchri]. In, Young, Karl. "The Harrowing of Hell in Liturgical Drama." Transactions of the Wisconsin Academy of Sciences, Arts and Letters, XVI, Part II (1910), 905-906.

631 [Visitatio Sepulchri]. In, Young, Karl. The Drama of the Medieval Church. Vol. I. (Oxford, 1933), pp. 331-333.

Manuscript (Moosburg)

632 Munich, Staatsbibliothek, MS. lat. 9469, Brev. Mosburgense, fol. 59r - 59v (15th century).

Text

633 [Visitatio Sepulchri]. In, Brooks, N. C. "Neue lateinische Oster- feiern." Zeitschrift für deutsche Altertum, L (1908), 307- 308.

634 [Visitatio Sepulchri]. In, Young, Karl. The Drama of the Medieval
Church. Vol. I. (Oxford, 1933), pp. 361-363.
Manuscript (Pollingren)

635 Munich, Staatsbibliothek, MS. lat. 11735, Brev. Pollingense,
fol. 62v - 63r (15th - 16th century).
Text

636 [Visitatio Sepulchri]. In, Brooks, N. C. "Neue lateinische Osterfeiern." Zeitschrift für deutsche Altertum, L (1908), 304-305.

637 [Visitatio Sepulchri]. In, Young, Karl. The Drama of the Medieval
Church. Vol. I. (Oxford, 1933), p. 641.
Manuscript (Pollingren)

638 Munich, Staatsbibliothek, MS. lat. 11765, Brev. Pollingense,
fol. 147r (15th century).
Text

639 [Visitatio Sepulchri]. In, Young, Karl. The Drama of the Medieval
Church. Vol. I. (Oxford, 1933), p. 638.
Manuscript (Pollingren)

640 Munich, Staatsbibliothek, MS. lat. 11903a, Brev. Pollingense,
fol. 253v - 254r (15th century).
Text

641 [Visitatio Sepulchri]. In, Lange, Carl. Die lateinischen Osterfeiern. (Munich, 1887), No. 123, pp. 86-87.

642 Ad Uisitandum Sepulchrum. In, Young, Karl. The Drama of the
Medieval Church. Vol. I. (Oxford, 1933), p. 627.
Manuscript

643 Munich, Staatsbibliothek, MS. lat. 12301, Ordin, Raitenbuchense
anni 1431, fol. 90v.
Text

644 [Visitatio Sepulchri]. In, Young, Karl. The Drama of the Medieval
Church. Vol. I. (Oxford, 1933), p. 253. [Young believes this is
the first time the text has been printed.]
Manuscript

645 Munich, Staatsbibliothek, MS. lat. 12635, Ordin. Ranshofense,
pp. 59-60 (13th century).
Text

646 [Visitatio Sepulchri]. In, Young, Karl. The Drama of the Medieval
Church. Vol. I. (Oxford, 1933), p. 651. [Young says that this
is the first time that the play has been printed.]
Manuscript (St. Emmeran, Regensburg)

647 Munich, Staatsbibliothek, MS. lat. 14083, Trop. Emmeramense,
fol. 89r - 89v (11th - 12th century).
Text

648 [Visitatio Sepulchri]. In, Lange, Carl. Die lateinischen Oster-

feiern. (Munich, 1887), No. 40, p. 29.

649 Ad Sepvlchrvm. In, Young, Karl. The Drama of the Medieval
Church, Vol. I. (Oxford, 1933), p. 590.
Manuscript (St. Emmeram, Regensburg)
650 Munich, Staatsbibliothek, MS. lat. 14183, Ordin. Sancti Emmerammi Ratisponensis, fol. 50v - 51r (A), (15th century).
Text
651 [Visitatio Sepulchri]. In, Brooks, N. C. "Neue lateinische Osterfeiern." Zeitschrift für deutsche Altertum, L (1908), 300-
302.

652 [Visitatio Sepulchri]. In, Young, Karl. The Drama of thc Medieval
Church. Vol. I. (Oxford, 1933), pp. 295-297. [The variants in
MS. lat. 14428, Ordin. Sancti Emmerammi Ratisponensis, fol.
57r - 57v (B), are given in Young's text.]
Manuscript (St. Emmeram)
653 Munich, Staatsbibliothek, MS. lat. 14741, Brev. Sancti Emmerami,
fol. 207r (14th century).
Text
654 [Visitatio Sepulchri]. In Lange, Carl. Die lateinischen Osterfeiern. (Munich, 1887), No. 79, p. 53.

655 [Visitatio Sepulchri]. In, Young, Karl. The Drama of the Medieval
Church, Vol. I. (Oxford, 1933), p. 256.
Manuscript (Monastery in Germany)
656 Munich, Staatsbibliothek, MS. lat. 14765, Consuetudines Sigiberti Abbatis, fol. 93r - 94r (11th - 12th century).
Text
657 [Visitatio Sepulchri]. In, Albers, B. Consuetudines Monasticae.
Vol. II. (Monte Cassino, 1900-1912), pp. 104-106. [Albers
also published the text in Revue Bénédictine, XX (1903), 427-428.]

658 [Visitatio Sepulchri]. In, Young, Karl. The Drama of the Medieval
Church. Vol. I. (Oxford, 1933), p. 263.
Manuscript (St. Emmeram)
659 Munich, Staatsbibliothek, MS. lat. 14845, Hymnarium-Prosarium
Emmeramense, fol. 94r - 94v (12th century).
Text
660 Ad Sepulchrum Domini. In, Young, Karl. The Drama of the
Medieval Church. Vol. I. (Oxford, 1933), p. 590. [Young says
that this is the first time that the text has been printed.]
Manuscript (Passau)
661 Munich, Staatsbibliothek, MS. lat. 16141, Lib. resp. Pataviensis,
fol. 76v - 77r (14th century).

Text

662   Ad visitandum Sepulchrum. In, Young, Karl. The Drama of the
Medieval Church. Vol. I. (Oxford, 1933), pp. 634-635. [Young
calls it a "somewhat curtailed version."]

Manuscript (Tegernsee)

663   Munich, Staatsbibliothek, MS. Cod. lat. 19291, Brev. Tegernsee,
1432. fol. 119.

Text

664   [Visitatio Sepulchri]. In, Lange, Carl. Die lateinischen Osterfeiern. (Munich, 1887), pp. 86-87.

Manuscript (Prüfening)

665   Munich, Staatsbibliothek, MS. lat. 23037, Brev. Pruveningense,
fol. 176v (12th century).

Text

666   [Visitatio Sepulchri]. In, Young, Karl. "The Harrowing of Hell
in Liturgical Drama." Transactions of the Wisconsin Academy
of Sciences, Arts and Letters, XVI, Part II (1909), 943-944.

667   Ordo ad uisitandum Sepulchrum. In, Young, Karl. The Drama of
the Medieval Church. Vol. I. (Oxford, 1933), p. 597. [Young
gives the variants from Zurich, Zentralbibliothek, MS. Rheinau,
LIX, Ordin. Rhenoviense, pp. 112-113 (B), (13th century).]

Manuscript (Moosburg)

668   Munich, Staatsbibliothek, MS. lat. 23068, Brev. Mosburgense,
fol. 295v (14th century).

Text

669   [Visitatio Sepulchri]. In, Young, Karl. The Drama of the Medieval
Church. Vol. I. (Oxford, 1933), p. 346. [Young says that the
play is printed for the first time.]

Manuscript

670   Munich, Staatsbibliothek, MS. lat. 23181, Brev. fol. 265r - 265v
(15th century).

Text

671   [Visitatio Sepulchri]. In, Young, Carl. The Drama of the Medieval
Church. Vol. I. (Oxford, 1933), pp. 336-337. [Young says that
this is the first time that the play has been printed.]

Manuscript (Cathedral of Salzburg)

672   Munich, Staatsbibliothek, MS. lat. 24900, Brev. Salisburgense,
fol. 69r - 69v (15th century).

Text

673   [Visitatio Sepulchri]. In, Young, Karl. The Drama of the Medieval
Church. Vol. I. (Oxford, 1933), pp. 326-327. [Young thinks
that this is the first time that the play has been printed.]

Manuscript

674   Munich, Staatsbibliothek, MS. lat. 26947, Ordin. Ratisbonense,

fol. 121r - 121v (15th century).
                        Text
675   [Visitatio Sepulchri]. In, Brooks, N.C. "Neue lateinische Oster-
      feiern." Zeitschrift für deutsche Altertum, L (1908), 298-299.

676   [Visitatio Sepulchri]. In, Young, Karl. The Drama of the Medieval
      Church. Vol. I. (Oxford, 1933), p. 586.
                        Manuscript (Bamberg)
677   Munich, National-Museum, MS. 2494, Brev. Bambergense anni
      1448, fol. 154v.
                        Text
678   [Visitatio Sepulchri]. In, Young, Karl. The Drama of the Medieval
      Church. Vol. I. (Oxford, 1933), p. 585.

MÜNSTER
                        Manuscript
679   Münster, Chapter Library, MS. 4, Ordin. Monasteriense, fol.
      78v (13th century).
                        Text
680   [Visitatio Sepulchri]. In, Stapper, R. Die Feier des Kirchen-
      jahres an der Kathedrale von Münster im hohen Mittelalter.
      (Munster, 1916), p. 155. [Reprinted from Zeitschrift für
      vaterlandische Geschichte und Altertumskunde, LXXV
      (1917).]

681   [Visitatio Sepulchri]. In, Young, Karl. The Drama of the Medieval
      Church. Vol. I. (Oxford, 1933), p. 602.
                        Manuscript
682   Münster, Domarchiv, MS. circa 1489, fol. 39r - 39v.
                        Text
683   [Visitatio Sepulchri]. In, Stapper, R. Die Feier des Kirchen-
      jahres an der Kathedrale von Münster im hohen Mittelalter.
      (Munster, 1916), p. 45. [Reprinted from Zeitschrift für
      vaterlandische Geschichte und Altertumskunde, LXXV
      (1917).]

684   [Visitatio Sepulchri]. In, Young, Karl. The Drama of the Medieval
      Church. Vol. I. (Oxford, 1933), p. 602.
                        Manuscript
685   Münster, University Library, Cod. 354 (96); Münster Domarchiv,
      1696.
                        Text
686   [Visitatio Sepulchri]. In, Stapper, R. Die Feier des Kirchen-
      jahres an der Kathedrale von Münster im hohen Mittelalter.
      (Munster, 1916), pp. 48-49. Reprinted from Zeitschrift für

vaterlandische Geschichte und Altertumskunde, LXXV (1917).]

687   [Visitatio Sepulchri]. In, Young, Karl. The Drama of the Medieval Church. Vol. I. (Oxford, 1933), p. 603.

NARBONNE

Text

688   [Visitatio Sepulchri]. In, Martene, E. De Antiquis Ecclesiae Ritibus. Vol. III. (Venice, 1788), pp. 172-173. [Printed from a Narbonne Ordinary.]

689   [Visitatio Sepulchri]. In, Du Méril, Édélstand. Origines latines du théâtre moderne. (Paris, 1849), pp. 91-94.

690   [Visitatio Sepulchri]. In, Lange, Carl. Die lateinischen Oster-feiern. (Munich, 1887), No. 99, pp. 64-66. [The text follows that of Martene.]

691   [Visitatio Sepulchri]. In, Young, Karl. The Drama of the Medieval Church. Vol. I. (Oxford, 1933), pp. 284-286.

NUREMBERG

Manuscript

692   Nuremberg, Germanisches National-Museum, MS. 22923, Lib. resp. Noribergensis, fol. 105v - 107v (13th century).

Text

693   [Visitatio Sepulchri]. In, Lange, Carl. "Ungedruckte lateinische Osterfeiern." Zeitschrift für deutsche Altertum, XXVIII (1884), 125-128.

694   [Visitatio Sepulchri]. In, Lange, Carl. Die lateinischen Oster-feiern. (Munich, 1887), No. 208, pp. 140-146.

695   [Visitatio Sepulchri]. In, Froning, R. Das Drama des Mittelalters. Vol. I. (Stuttgart, 1891), pp. 17-20.

696   [Visitatio Sepulchri]. In, Young, Karl. The Drama of the Medieval Church. Vol. I. (Oxford, 1933), pp. 398-401.

697   [Visitatio Sepulchri]. In, Lange, Carl. Die lateinischen Oster-feiern. (Munich, 1887), pp. 90-91. [From, Nürnberg, Ger-manisches National-Museum, Liturg. 7823, fol. IIIv, Diurnale, 1522, Augsburg.]

ORLEANS
Manuscript (Fleury)
698   Orleans, Bibliothèque de la Ville, MS. 201 (olim 178), Miscellanea
      Floriacensia, pp. 220-225 (13th century).
Text
699   [Visitatio Sepulchri]. In, [Monmerque, L. J. N. (?), ed.] Mélanges
      des Bibliophiles francais. Vol. VII. (Paris, 1831-1832), pp.
      157-164.

700   [Visitatio Sepulchri]. In, Wright, T. Early Mysteries and Other
      Latin Poems of the Twelfth and Thirteenth Centuries. (London,
      1838), pp. 32-36.

701   [Visitatio Sepulchri]. In, Du Meril Édélstand. Origines latines
      du théâtre moderne. (Paris, 1849), pp. 110-116.

702   [Visitatio Sepulchri]. Barthelemy, C. Rational ou Manuel des
      divins Offices de Guillaume Durand. Vol. IV. (Paris, 1854),
      pp. 460-463. [Barthelemy reprints Monmerqué's text, with a
      French translation.]

703   [Visitatio Sepulchri]. In, Coussemaker, E. de. Drames liturgi-
      ques du Moyen Age. (Fennes, 1860), pp. 178-194.

704   [Visitatio Sepulchri]. In, Milchsak, G. Die Oster- Und Passions-
      spiele: I. Die lateinischen Osterfeiern. (Wolfenbüttel, 1880),
      pp. 67-81.

705   [Visitatio Sepulchri]. In, Lange, Carl. Die lateinischen Oster-
      feiern. (Munich, 1887), No. 223, pp. 160-165.

706   [Visitatio Sepulchri]. In, Davidson, C. Studies in the English
      Mystery Plays. (New Haven, 1892), pp. 33-39. [Davidson
      reprints Wright's text.]

707   [Visitatio Sepulchri]. In, Pollard, A. W. English Miracle Plays,
      Moralities and Interludes. (Oxford, 1904), pp. 157-161.
      [Pollard reprints Wright's text.]

708   [Visitatio Sepulchri]. In, Adams, Joseph Q. Chief Pre-Shakes-
      pearean Dramas. (Boston, New York, 1924), pp. 15-20.
      [Adams reprints Lange's text, with an English translation.]

709   [Visitatio Sepulchri]. In, Young, Karl. The Drama of the Medieval
      Church. Vol. I. (Oxford, 1933), pp. 393-397.

OXFORD

Manuscript

710   Oxford, Bodleian, MS. 775, Trop. Wintoniense saec. X (978-980), fol. 17r - 17v.

Text

711   [Visitatio Sepulchri]. In, Frere, W. H., ed. The Winchester Troper. (London, 1894), p. 17.

712   [Visitatio Sepulchri]. In, Manly, J. M. Specimens of the Pre-Shakespearean Drama. Vol. I. (Boston, 1900), p. XXI.

713   [Visitatio Sepulchri]. In, Chambers, E. K. The Mediaeval Stage. Vol. II. (Oxford, 1903), p. 13.

714   [Visitatio Sepulchri]. In, Beeson, C. H. A Primer of Medieval Latin. (Chicago, 1925), pp. 201-202. [Beeson reprints Manly's text.]

715   [Visitatio Sepulchri]. In, Young, Karl. The Drama of the Medieval Church. Vol. I. (Oxford, 1933), pp. 254-255.

716   [Visitatio Sepulchri]. In, Langosch, Karl. Geistliche Spiele. Lateinische Dramen des Mittelalters mit deutschen Versen. (Basel, Stuttgart, 1957), 99-105.

Manuscript (Novalesa)

717   Oxford, Bodleian, MS. Douce 222. [Benedictine Troper of the 12th century from Novalesa.]

Text

718   [Visitatio Sepulchri]. In, Brooks, Neil C. "Some New Texts of Liturgical Easter Plays." Journal of English and Germanic Philology, VIII (October, 1909), 463-464.

Manuscript (Sutri)

719   Oxford, Bodleian, MS. Misc. Liturg. 202, Brev. Dominicanum, fol. 72v - 73r (13th century).

Text

720   [Visitatio Sepulchri]. In, Lange, Carl. Die lateinischen Oster-feiern. (Munich, 1887), No. 108, pp. 81-82.

721   [Visitatio Sepulchri]. In, Young, Karl. "The Harrowing of Hell in Liturgical Drama." Transactions of the Wisconsin Academy of Sciences, Arts, and Letters, XVI, Part II (1910), 899-900.

722   [Visitatio Sepulchri]. In, Young, Karl. The Drama of the Medieval Church. Vol. I. (Oxford, 1933), pp. 309-310.

Manuscript (Würzburg)

723 Oxford, Bodleian, MS. Misc. lit. 297, Brev. Benedictum Ger-
     manicum, fol. 111r (12th century).

Text

724 [Visitatio Sepulchri]. In, Lange, Carl. Die lateinischen Oster-
     feiern. (Munich, 1887), No. 66, pp. 45-46.

725 Versvs Ad Sepvlcrvm. In, Young, Karl. The Drama of the
     Medieval Church. Vol. I. (Oxford, 1933), p. 595.

Manuscript (Germany)

726 Oxford, Bodleian, MS. Misc. Liturg. 325, Ordin. Benedictinum,
     fol. 82r - 82v (13th century).

Text

727 [Visitatio Sepulchri]. In, Young, Karl. "Some Texts of Liturgical
     Plays." Publications of the Modern Language Association,
     XXIV (1909), 312.

728 [Visitatio Sepulchri]. In, Young, Karl. The Drama of the Medieval
     Church. Vol. I. (Oxford, 1933), pp. 312-313.

Manuscript

729 Oxford, Bodleian, MS. Misc. Liturg. 346, Brev. Benedictinum,
     fol. 114v (13th century).

Text

730 [Visitatio Sepulchri]. In, Lange, Carl. Die lateinischen Oster-
     feiern. (Munich, 1887), pp. 91-92.

731 [Visitatio Sepulchri]. In, Brooks, Neil C. "Some New Texts of
     Liturgical Easter Plays." Journal of English and Germanic
     Philology, VIII (October, 1909), 478-479.

732 [Visitatio Sepulchri]. In, Young, Karl. The Drama of the Medieval
     Church. Vol. I. (Oxford, 1933), pp. 628-629.

Manuscript (Dublin)

733 Oxford, Bodleian, MS. Rawlinson Liturg. d. iv, Process. ad
     usum ecclesiae Sancti Johannis Evangelistae, Dubliensis,
     fol. 130r - 132r (A), (14th century).

Text

734 [Visitatio Sepulchri]. In, Chambers, E. K. The Mediaeval Stage.
     Vol. II. (Oxford, 1903), pp. 315-318.

735 [Visitatio Sepulchri]. In, Young, Karl. "The Harrowing of Hell
     in Liturgical Drama." Transactions of the Wisconsin Academy
     of Sciences, Arts, and Letters, XVI, Part II (1910), 918-924.

736 [Visitatio Sepulchri]. In, Adams, Joseph Q. Chief Pre-Shakespearean

Dramas. (Boston, New York, 1924). [Adams reprints
Chambers' text.]

737 [Visitatio Sepulchri]. In, Young, Karl. The Drama of the Medieval
Church. Vol. I. (Oxford, 1933), pp. 347-350. [Young gives the
variants from Dublin, Archbishop Marsh's Library, MS. Z.
4.2.20 (olim V.3.2.10) Proces ad usum ecclesiae Sancti
Johannis Evangelistae Dublinensis, fol. 59r - 61r (B), (14th
century).]

Manuscript (Barking, near London)

738 Oxford, University College, MS. 169, Ordin. Barkingense, pp.
121-124 (15th century).

Text

739 [Visitatio Sepulchri]. In, Young, Karl. "The Harrowing of Hell
in Liturgical Drama." Transactions of the Wisconsin Academy
of Sciences, Arts, and Letters, XVI, Part II (1909), 926-931.

740 [Visitatio Sepulchri]. In, Tolhurst, J. B. L. The Ordinale and
Customary of the Benedictine Nuns of Barking Abbey, II
(London, 1927-1928), pp. 378-379.

741 [Visitatio Sepulchri]. In, Young, Karl. The Drama of the Medieval
Church. Vol. I. (Oxford, 1933), pp. 381-384.

Manuscript

742 Oxford, Bodleian, Canonici Liturg. 325 (19414), Ordinarium
[Benedictine], (13th century - German).

Text

743 [Visitatio Sepulchri]. In, Young, Karl. "Some Texts of Liturgical
Plays." Publications of the Modern Language Association,
XXIV (June, 1909), 311-312.

PADUA

Manuscript

744 Padua, Bibl. Capit., MS. S, Ordin. Patavinense, fol. 98r - 99r
(13th century).

Text

745 [Visitatio Sepulchri]. In, Young, Karl. The Drama of the Medieval
Church. Vol. I. (Oxford, 1933), pp. 294-295.

PARIS

Manuscript

746 Paris, Bibliothèque de l'Arsenal, MS. 114, Ordo divini officii
secundum usum Sacrae Capellae, fol. 73v - 74r (15th century).

Text

747 [Visitatio Sepulchri]. In, Brooks, Neil C. "Some Texts of Liturgical
Easter Plays." Journal of English and Germanic Philology, VIII

(October, 1909), 471-473.

748   [Visitatio Sepulchri]. In, Young, Karl. The Drama of the Medieval
      Church. Vol. I. (Oxford, 1933), pp. 286-288.
                          Manuscript
749   Paris, Bibliothèque de l'Arsenal, MS. 133, Brev. Parisiense, fol.
      226r (15th century).
                          Text
750   [Visitatio Sepulchri]. In, Young, Karl. The Drama of the Medieval
      Church. Vol. I. (Oxford, 1933), pp. 275-276. [Young says that
      this is the first time that the piece has been printed.]
                          Manuscript
751   Paris, Bibliothèque de l'Arsenal, MS. 275, Brev. Cenomanense,
      fol. 129v (15th century).
                          Text
752   [Visitatio Sepulchri]. In, Young, Karl. The Drama of the Medieval
      Church. Vol. I. (Oxford, 1933), pp. 613-614. [Young says that
      this text was not published previously.]
                  Manuscript (Chalons-sur-Marne)
753   Paris, Bibliothèque de l'Arsenal, MS. 595, Brev.-Miss. Catalaun-
      ense. fol. 164v (14th century).
                          Text
754   [Visitatio Sepulchri]. In, Young, Karl. The Drama of the Medieval
      Church. Vol. I. (Oxford, 1933), p. 610. [Young says that this
      is the first time that this text has been printed.]
                          Manuscript
755   Paris, Bibliothèque Mazarine, MS. 342, Brev. Parisiense, fol.
      212r - 212v (14th century).
                          Text
756   [Visitatio Sepulchri]. In, Young, Karl. The Drama of the Medieval
      Church. Vol. I. (Oxford, 1933), p. 608.
                          Manuscript
757   Paris, Bibliothèque de l'Arsenal, MS. 660 (15th century).
                          Text
758   [Visitatio Sepulchri]. In, Brooks, Neil C. "Some New Texts of
      Liturgical Easter Plays." Journal of English and Germanic
      Philology, VIII (October, 1909), 474-475.
                  Manuscript (Bourges)
759   Paris, Bibliothèque Nationale, B. 453, fol. 69v (Bourges, Brevier,
      Druck, 1522).
                          Text
760   [Visitatio Sepulchri]. In, Lange, Carl. Die lateinischen Oster-
      feiern. (Munich, 1887), pp. 62-63.
                  Manuscript (Limoges)
761   Paris, Bibliothèque Nationale, fond. latin No. 119, fol. 42a

(Limoges, 11th century).
Text
762 [Visitatio Sepulchri]. In, Lange, Carl. Die lateinischen Osterfeiern. (Munich, 1887), p. 20.
Manuscript (Limoges)
763 Paris, Bibliothèque Nationale, MS. lat. 784, Lib. resp. Sancti
Martialis Lemovicensis (?), fol. 106v, (13th - 14th century).
Text
764 [Visitatio Sepulchri]. In, Young, Karl. The Drama of the Medieval
Church. Vol. I. (Oxford, 1933), p. 271. [Young says that this
is the first time that the piece has been printed.]
Manuscript (Rouen)
765 Paris, Bibliothèque Nationale, MS. lat. 904, Grad. Rothomagense,
fol. 101v - 102v (13th century).
Text
766 [Visitatio Sepulchri]. In, Coussemaker, E. de. Drames liturgiques du Moyen Age. (Rennes, 1860), pp. 250-255.

767 [Visitatio Sepulchri]. In, Milchsack, G. Die Osterund Passionsspiele: I. Die lateinischen Osterfeiern. (Wolfenbüttel, 1880),
p. 133.

768 [Visitatio Sepulchri]. In, Lange, Carl. Die lateinischen Osterfeiern. (Munich, 1887), No. 216, pp. 155-157.

769 [Visitatio Sepulchri]. In, Gasté, Armand. Les drames liturgiques de la Cathédral de Rouen. (Evreux, 1893), pp. 58-64.
[Combines both manuscripts.]

770 [Visitatio Sepulchri]. In, Lorique, H., J. Pothier, and A. Collette.
Le Graduel de l'Église cathédrale de Rouen au XIIIe Siècle.
Vol. II. (Rouen, 1907).] [Photographic facsimile].

771 [Visitatio Sepulchri]. In, Young, Karl. The Drama of the Medieval
Church. Vol. I. (Oxford, 1933), p. 660.

772 Office du Saint Sépulcre de Rouen. In, Cohen, Gustave. Anthologie
du drame liturgie en France au moyen-âge. (Paris, 1955), pp.
31-34.
Manuscript (Toul)
773 Paris, Bibliothèque Nationale, MS. lat. 975, Ordin. Tullense,
fol. 29v - 30r (13th century).
Text
774 [Visitatio Sepulchri]. In, Lange, Carl. Die lateinischen Osterfeiern. (Munich, 1887), No. 60, pp. 39-40. [A shortened form.]

775 [Visitatio Sepulchri]. In, Young, Karl. The Drama of the Medieval
       Church. Vol. I. (Oxford, 1933), pp. 265-266.
                              Manuscript
776 Paris, Bibliothèque Nationale, MS. lat. 978, Ordin. Parisiense,
       fol. 24r (A), (15th century).
                              Text
777 Officium Sepulchri. In, Young, Karl. "Some Texts of Liturgical
       Plays." Publications of the Modern Language Association,
       XXIV (June, 1909), 301.

778 Ad Sepulcrum. In, Young, Karl. The Drama of the Medieval
       Church. Vol. I. (Oxford, 1933), pp. 608-609. [Young gives
       the abbreviated form, with the variants from Paris, Biblio-
       thèque Nationale, MS. lat. 16317, Ordin. Parisiense, fol. 32r
       - 32v (B), (13th century).]
                              Manuscript (Metz)
779 Paris, Bibliothéque Nationale, MS. lat. 990 (Liber de Ordinatione
       et Officiis totius anni in ecclesia Metensi, fol. 52r (17th cen-
       tury copy of an original, whose date is not known).]
                              Text
780 [Visitatio Sepulchri]. In Brooks, Neil C. "Some New Texts of
       Liturgical Easter Plays." Journal of English and Germanic
       Philology, VIII (October, 1909), 464-465.

781 [Visitatio Sepulchri]. In, Young, Karl. The Drama of the Medieval
       Church. Vol. I. (Oxford, 1933), p. 261.
                              Manuscript (Limoges)
782 Paris, Bibliothèque Nationale, fonds lat. No. 1119, fol. 21a
       (Limoges, Troparium, 11th century).
                              Text
783 [Visitatio Sepulchri]. In, Lange, Carl. Die lateinischen Oster-
       feiern. (Munich, 1887), p. 20.
                              Manuscript (Navarre)
784 Paris, Bibliothèque Nationale, MS. 1123, Processionale
       Navarrense, fol. 25r (15th century).
                              Text
785 [Visitatio Sepulchri]. In, Lange, Carl. Die lateinischen Oster-
       feiern. (Munich, 1887), No. 17, p. 22. [Lange incorrectly
       numbers the manuscript 1223. Lange does not give the com-
       plete text.]

786 [Visitatio Sepulchri]. In, Young, Karl. The Drama of the Medieval
       Church. Vol. I. (Oxford, 1933), p. 576.
                              Manuscript (Limoges)
787 Paris, Bibliothèque Nationale, fonds Lat. No. 1139, fol. 53b

(Troparium, 11th century).
Text

788   [Visitatio Sepulchri]. In, Lange, Carl. Die lateinischen Oster-
      feiern. (Munich, 1887), p. 22.
Manuscript (Sens)

789   Paris, Bibliothèque Nationale, MS. lat. 1206, Ordin. Senonense,
      fol. 57v (13th century).
Text

790   [Visitatio Sepulchri]. In, Lange, Carl. Die lateinischen Oster-
      feiern. (Munich, 1887), p. 25.

791   [Visitatio Sepulchri]. In, Young, Karl. The Drama of the Medieval
      Church. Vol. I. (Oxford, 1933), pp. 580-581.
Manuscript (Rouen)

792   Paris, Bibliothèque Nationale, MS. 1213, Ordin. Rothomagense,
      p. 86 (A), (15th century).
Text

793   [Visitatio Sepulchri]. In, Lange, Carl. Die lateinischen Oster-
      feiern. (Munich, 1887), No. 218, pp. 155-157.

794   [Visitatio Sepulchri]. In, Young, Karl. "A Contribution to the
      History of Liturgical Drama at Rouen." Modern Philology, VI
      (1908-1909), 221-222.

795   [Visitatio Sepulchri]. In, Young, Karl. The Drama of the Medieval
      Church. Vol. I. (Oxford, 1933), p. 661. [Variants from Rouen,
      Bibliothèque de la Ville, MS. 382 (olim Y. 108), Ordin. Rotho-
      magense, fol. 70 bis^V - 71r (B), (15th century).]
Manuscript (Udine)

796   Paris, Bibliothèque Nationale, MS. lat. 1234, Ordin. Utinense,
      fol. 10v (14th century).
Text

797   [Visitatio Sepulchri]. In, Young, Karl. The Drama of the Medieval
      Church. Vol. I. (Oxford, 1933), pp. 298-299. [Young feels that
      this is the first time the play has been printed.]
Manuscript

798   Paris, Bibliothèque Nationale, Nouv. Acq., MS. Lat. 1235, Grad.-
      Trop. Nivernense, fol. 205r (12th century).
Text

799   [Visitatio Sepulchri]. In, Young, Karl. The Drama of the Medieval
      Church. Vol. I. (Oxford, 1933), p. 580. [Young says that this
      is the first time that the text has been printed.]
Manuscript (Beaunne)

800   Paris, Bibliothèque Nationale, fonds. lat. No. 1240, fol. 30v
      (Beaunne, Antiphonar, 11th century).

Text
801 [Visitatio Sepulchri]. In, Lange, Carl. Die lateinischen Oster-
     feiern. (Munich, 1887), pp. 22-23.
                              Manuscript
802 Paris, Bibliothèque Nationale, MS. lat. 1255, Brev. monasticum
     Gallicanum, fol. 151v - 152r (13th century).
                                 Text
803 [Visitatio Sepulchri]. In, Young, Karl. The Drama of the Medieval
     Church. Vol. I. (Oxford, 1933), p. 293. [Young thinks that this
     is the first time that the text has been printed.]
                              Manuscript
804 Paris, Bibliothèque Nationale, MS. lat. 1264, Brev. Parisiense,
     fol. 101v - 102r (14th century).
                                 Text
805 [Visitatio Sepulchri]. In, Lange, Carl. Die lateinischen Oster-
     feiern. (Munich, 1887), No. 88, pp. 60-62.

806 [Visitatio Sepulchri]. In, Young, Karl. The Drama of the Medieval
     Church. Vol. I. (Oxford, 1933), pp. 276-277.
                          Manuscript (Senlis)
807 Paris, Bibliothèque Nationale, MS. lat. 1268, Brev. Silvanectense,
     fol. 300r (A), (14th century).
                                 Text
808 [Visitatio Sepulchri]. In, Lange, Carl. Die lateinischen Oster-
     feiern. (Munich, 1887), pp. 27-28.

809 [Visitatio Sepulchri]. In, Young, Karl. The Drama of the Medieval
     Church. Vol. I. (Oxford, 1933), p. 245. [Young gives the
     variants found in the following: Bibliothèque Sainte-Geneviève,
     MS. 2636 (B. Bl. 4°. 22), Brev. Silvanectense, fol. 187r (B),
     (15th century).]
                         Manuscript (Chalons)
810 Paris, Bibliothèque Nationale, MS. lat. 1269, Brev. Catalaunense,
     fol. 279r - 279v (14th century).
                                 Text
811 [Visitatio Sepulchri]. In, Lange, Carl. Die lateinischen Oster-
     feiern. (Munich, 1887), No. 28, p. 25.

812 [Visitatio Sepulchri]. In, Young, Karl. The Drama of the Medieval
     Church. Vol. I. (Oxford, 1933), p. 579.
                     Manuscript (Clermont-Ferrand)
813 Paris, Bibliothèque Nationale, MS. lat. 1274, Brev. Claromontense,
     fol. 128v (14th century).
                                 Text
814 [Visitatio Sepulchri]. In, Lange, Carl. Die lateinischen Oster-

feiern. (Munich, 1887), No. 33, pp. 26-27. [Lange incorrectly numbers the manuscript 1272.]

815   [Visitatio Sepulchri]. In, Young, Karl. The Drama of the Medieval Church. Vol. I. (Oxford, 1933), p. 244.
Manuscript
816   Paris, Bibliothèque Nationale, MS. lat. 1293, fol. 113r.
Text
817   Officium Sepulchre. In, Young, Karl. "Some Texts of Liturgical Plays." Publications of the Modern Language Association, XXIV (June, 1909), 298-299.
Manuscript (Coutances)
818   Paris, Bibliothèque Nationale, MS. lat. 1301, Ordin. Constaniense, fol. 143v - 145v (15th century).
Text
819   [Visitatio Sepulchri]. In, Lange, Carl. Die lateinischen Osterfeiern. (Munich, 1887), No. 222, pp. 157-160.

820   [Visitatio Sepulchri]. In, Gasté, A. Les Drames liturgiques de la Cathédrale de Rouen. (Évreux, 1893), pp. 63-64.

821   [Visitatio Sepulchri]. In, Young, Karl. The Drama of the Medieval Church. Vol. I. (Oxford, 1933), pp. 408-410.
Manuscript (Xanten)
822   Paris, Bibliothèque Nationale, MS. lat. 1307, Brev. Xantense, fol. 92v (15th century). [Incomplete version of the text in, Bibliothèque Nationale, MS. lat. 1308, fol. 101r.]
Text
823   [Visitatio Sepulchri]. In, Lange, Carl. Die lateinischen Osterfeiern. (Munich, 1887), No. 42, pp. 29-30.

824   [Visitatio Sepulchri]. In, Young, Karl. The Drama of the Medieval Church. Vol. I. (Oxford, 1933), p. 269.
Manuscript (Xanten)
825   Paris, Bibliothèque Nationale, MS. lat. 1308, Brev. Xantense, fol. 101r (15th century).
Text
826   [Visitatio Sepulchri]. In, Lange, Carl. Die lateinischen Osterfeiern. (Munich, 1887), No. 41, pp. 29-30.

827   [Visitatio Sepulchri]. In, Young, Karl. The Drama of the Medieval Church. Vol. I. (Oxford, 1933), p. 599.
Manuscript (Worms)
828   Paris, Bibliothèque Nationale, MS. lat. 1310, Wormatiensis, fol. 198v - 199r (13th century).

Text
829 [Visitatio Sepulchri]. In, Young, Karl. "Some Texts of Liturgical
     Plays." Publications of the Modern Language Association,
     XXIV (June, 1909), 316-317.
                              Manuscript (Sainte-Chapelle)
830 Paris, Bibliothèque Nationale, MS. lat. 1435, Ordin. ad usum
     Capellae Regis, fol. 17v - 18r (14th century).
                              Text
831 [Visitatio Sepulchri]. In, Brooks, Neil C. "Some New Texts of
     Liturgical Easter Plays." Journal of English and Germanic
     Philology, VIII (October, 1909), 473-474.

832 [Visitatio Sepulchri]. In, Young, Karl. The Drama of the Medieval
     Church. Vol. I. (Oxford, 1933), pp. 277-278.
                              Manuscript
833 Paris, Bibliothèque Nationale, MS. lat. 9448, Trop. Prumiense,
     vol. 33v (10th - 11th century).
                              Text
834 [Visitatio Sepulchri]. In, Young, Karl. The Drama of the Medieval
     Church. Vol. I. (Oxford, 1933), p. 579. [Young believes that
     this is the first time the text has been printed.]
                              Manuscript
835 Paris, Bibliothèque Nationale, MS. lat. 9449, Trop. Nivernense,
     fol. 34r (11th century).
                              Text
836 [Visitatio Sepulchri]. In, A. Reiners, Unbekannte Tropen-
     Gesänge des feierlichen Messamtes im Mittelalter. (Luxem-
     burg, 1887), p. 36.

837 [Visitatio Sepulchri]. In, Young, Karl. The Drama of the Medieval
     Church. Vol. I. (Oxford, 1933), p. 579. [Young appends the
     single variant from Angels, Bibliothèque de la Ville, MS. 96,
     Grad. Andegavense, fol. 74v (12th century), not previously
     published.]
                              Manuscript (Remiremont)
838 Paris, Bibliothèque Nationale, MS. lat. 9486, Ordin. Romaricense,
     fol. 60r - 60v (12th century).
                              Text
839 [Visitatio Sepulchri]. In, Brooks, Neil C. "Some New Texts of
     Liturgical Easter Plays." Journal of English and Germanic
     Philology, VIII (October, 1909), 466.

840 [Visitatio Sepulchri]. In, Young, Karl. "Observations on the
     Origin of the Medieval Passion Play; with Texts of Some
     Liturgical Dramas." Publications of the Modern Language

Association, XXV (1910), 351.

841   Visitatio Sepulchri. In, Young, Karl. The Drama of the Medieval
       Church. Vol. I. (Oxford, 1933), p. 248.
                            Manuscript
842   Paris, Bibliothèque Nationale, MS. lat. 9508 (Supplément latin
       184), fol. 179 (17th century).
                            Text
843   [Visitatio Sepulchri]. In, Lange, Carl. Die lateinischen Oster-
       feiern. (Munich, 1887), p. 26.
                            Manuscript
844   Paris, Bibliothèque Nationale, MS. lat. 10510, Trop. Epternacense,
       fol. 11r (11th century).
                            Text
845   [Visitatio Sepulchri]. In, Young, Karl. The Drama of the Medieval
       Church. Vol. I. (Oxford, 1933), p. 578. [Young believes that
       this is the first time the text has been printed.]
                            Manuscript (Châlons-sur-Marne)
846   Paris, Bibliothèque Nationale, MS. lat. 10579, Ordin. Catalaun-
       ense, fol. LXXVIv - LXXVIIr (13th century).
                            Text
847   [Visitatio Sepulchri]. In, Lange, Carl. Die lateinischen Oster-
       feiern. (Munich, 1887), No. 97, pp. 62-63. [This edition
       has omissions.]

848   [Visitatio Sepulchri]. In, Young, Karl. The Drama of the Medieval
       Church. Vol. I. (Oxford, 1933), pp. 279-280.
                            Manuscript
849   Paris, Bibliothèque Nationale, MS. lat. 13233, Brev. Paris, fol.
       189r (14th century).
                            Text
850   [Visitatio Sepulchri]. In, Lange, Carl. Die lateinischen Osterfeiern.
       (Munich, 1887), pp. 60-62.
                            Manuscript
851   Paris, Bibliothèque Nationale, MS. lat. 16317, Ordin. (13th century).
                            Text
852   [Visitatio Sepulchri]. In, Brooks, Neil C. "Some New Texts of
       Liturgical Easter Plays." Journal of English and Germanic
       Philology, VIII (October, 1909), 476.
                            Manuscript (Bellovacensin)
853   Paris, Bibliothèque Sainte-Geneviève, MS. 117 (B. Bl. in fol. 26),
       Lib. resp. Bellovacensis, fol. 101r (13th century).
                            Text
854   [Visitatio Sepulchri]. In, Young, Karl. The Drama of the Medieval
       Church. Vol. I. (Oxford, 1933), p. 580. [Young says that this

is the first time that the text has been printed.]

PARMA
                                    Text
855   [Visitatio Sepulchri]. In, Barbieri, L. Ordinarium Ecclesiae
          Parmensis e vetustioribus excerptum reformatum A. 1417.
          (Parma, 1866), pp. 147-149. [From the Cathedral of Parma.]

856   [Visitatio Sepulchri]. In, Lange, Carl. Die lateinischen Oster-
          feiern. (Munich, 1887), No. 38, p. 28. [Follows Barbieri"s
          text.]

857   [Visitatio Sepulchri]. In, D'Ancona, A. Origini del Teatro italiano.
          Vol. I. (Turin, 1891), pp. 30-31. [Follows Barbieri's text.]

858   [Visitatio Sepulchri]. In, Young, Karl. The Dramatic Associations
          of the Easter Sepulchre. (Madison, 1920), pp. 44-45. [Follows
          Barbieri's text.]

859   [Visitatio Sepulchri]. In, Young, Karl. The Drama of the Medieval
          Church. Vol. I. (Oxford, 1933), p. 300.

PASSAU
                                    Text
860   [Visitatio Sepulchri]. In, Lange, Carl. Die lateinischen Oster-
          feiern. (Munich, 1887), No. 172, pp. 110-112. [Found in a
          Passau Agenda of 1490, fol. XCIIIIr - XCVIr.]

861   [Visitatio Sepulchri]. In, Young, Karl. The Drama of the Medieval
          Church. Vol. I. (Oxford, 1933), pp. 653-654. [Found in a Passau
          Agenda of 1490, fol. XCIIIIr - XCVIr.]

862   [Visitatio Sepulchri]. In, Lange, Carl. Die lateinischen Oster-
          feiern. (Munich, 1887), No. 171, pp. 110-112. [From, Breui-
          arium ... secundum chorum Patauiensis ecclesie, Venice, 1517,
          fol. 140v.]

863   [Visitatio Sepulchri]. In, Young, Karl. The Drama of the Medieval
          Church. Vol. I. (Oxford, 1933), pp. 652-653. [From Breui-
          arium ... secundum chorum Patauiensis ecclesie, Venice,
          1517, fol. 140v.]

POSTEL
                                    Text
864   [Visitatio Sepulchri]. In, Van Mierlo, J. "Een Utrechtsch Anti-

phonarium -- Bijdrage tot de Geschiedenis van het liturgisch
Drama in de Nederlanden." Leuvensche Bidragen op het
Gebied van de Germaansche Philologie, VIII (1908-1909), 48.
[From an antiphonary of the 14th century, from the monastery
of Postel.]

865   [Visitatio Sepulchri]. In, Young, Karl. The Drama of the Medieval
      Church. Vol. I. (Oxford, 1933), p. 589. [A reprint of Van
      Mierlo's text.]

PRAGUE
Manuscript

866   Prague, Verejná a Universitni Knihovna, MS. I. D. 20, Lib.
      resp. Pragensis (?), fol. 69v (15th century).
Text

867   [Visitatio Sepulchri]. In, Lange, Carl. Die lateinischen Oster-
      feiern. (Munich, 1887), No. 181, pp. 113-114.

868   [Visitatio Sepulchri]. In, Young, Karl. The Drama of the Medieval
      Church. Vol. I. (Oxford, 1933), p. 654.
Manuscript

869   Prague, Verejná a Universitni Knihovna, MS. VI. E. 4°. Brev.
      (14th century).
Text

870   [Visitatio Sepulchri]. In, Lange, Carl. Die lateinischen Oster-
      feiern. (Munich, 1887), pp. 122-124.
Manuscript

871   Prague, Verejná a Universitni Knihovna, MS. VI. E. 13. 4°.
      fol. 3, Brev. (12th century).
Text

872   [Visitatio Sepulchri]. In, Lange, Carl. Die lateinischen Oster-
      feiern. (Munich, 1887), pp. 146-148.
Manuscript

873   Prague, Verejná a Universitni Knihovna, MS. VI. G. 3b, Process.
      Sancti Georgii Pragensis, fol. 84r - 90r (14th century).
Text

874   [Visitatio Sepulchri]. In, Lange, Carl. Die lateinischen Oster-
      feiern. (Munich, 1887), No. 212, pp. 148-151.

875   [Visitatio Sepulchri]. In, Young, Karl. The Drama of the Medieval
      Church. Vol. I. (Oxford, 1933), pp. 402-404.
Manuscript

876   Prague, Verejná a Universitni Knihovna, MS. VI. G. 5. 4°.
      Antiph. (13th century).

Text

877   [Visitatio Sepulchri]. In, Lange, Carl. Die lateinischen Osterfeiern. (Munich, 1887), pp. 146-148.

Manuscript

878   Prague, Verejná a Universitni Knohovna, MS. VI. G. 10. 4°.
Process. (13th century).

Text

879   [Visitatio Sepulchri]. In, Lange, Carl. Die lateinischen Osterfeiern. (Munich, 1887), pp. 151-154.

Manuscript

880   Prague, Verejná a Universitni Knihovna, MS. XI. D. 21. 4°.
Rituale (14th century).

Text

881   [Visitatio Sepulchri]. In, Lange, Carl. Die lateinischen Osterfeiern. (Munich, 1887), pp. 130-131.

Manuscript

882   Prague, Verejná a Universitni Knihovna, MS. XII. E. 15a. 4°.
Antiph. (13th century).

Text

883   [Visitatio Sepulchri]. In, Lange, Carl. Die lateinischen Osterfeiern. (Munich, 1887), pp. 148-151.

Manuscript

884   Prague, Verejná a Universitni Knihovna, MS. XIII. C. 7. 4º,
Lib. resp. Pragensis, fol. 2v - 3v (14th century).

Text

885   [Visitatio Sepulchri]. In, Lange, Carl. Die lateinischen Osterfeiern. (Munich, 1887), No. 86, pp. 58-59.

886   [Visitatio Sepulchri]. In, Young, Karl. The Drama of the Medieval
Church. Vol. I. (Oxford, 1933), p. 600.

Manuscript

887   Prague, Verejná a Universitni Knihovna, MS. XIII. E. 14d, Ordin.
Sancti Georgii Pragensis, fol. 77r - 78r (14th century).

Text

888   [Visitatio Sepulchri]. In, Young, Karl. The Drama of the Medieval
Church. Vol. I. (Oxford, 1933), pp. 405-407. [Young says that
this is the first time that the play has been printed.]

Manuscript

889   Prague, Národni Museum, MS. XV. A. 10, Brev. Pragense, fol.
192r - 192v (14th century).

Text

890   [Visitatio Sepulchri]. In, Young, Karl. The Drama of the Medieval
Church. Vol. I. (Oxford, 1933), pp. 344-345. [Young says that
he believes that the play is printed for the first time.]

891   [Visitatio Sepulchri]. In, Lange, Carl. Die lateinischen Oster-
        feiern. (Munich, 1887), pp. 122-124. [Vienna, Hofbibliothek,
        Druck 22A. 13. 2°, fol. 171r, Brevier, 1572.]

RHEIMS

Manuscript

892   Rheims, Bibliothèque de la Ville, MS. 265 (C. 206), Grad. Sancti
        Dionysii Remensis, fol. 22v (12th - 13th century).

Text

893   [Visitatio Sepulchri]. In, Young, Karl. The Drama of the Medieval
        Church. Vol. I. (Oxford, 1933), p. 592. [Young says that this
        is the first time this text has been published.]

RHEINAU

Text

894   [Visitatio Sepulchri]. In, Brooks, Neil C. "Liturgical Easter
        Plays from Rheinau Manuscripts." Journal of English and Ger-
        manic Philology, X (April, 1911), 191-192. (Rheinau, MS.
        XCVII. Perhaps, 11th century.]

895   [Visitatio Sepulchri]. In, Brooks, Neil C. "Liturgical Easter Plays
        from Rheinau Manuscripts." Journal of English and Germanic
        Philology, X (April, 1911), 192. [Rheinau, MS. LXV, Anti-
        phonarium.]

896   [Visitatio Sepulchri]. In, Brooks, Neil C. "Liturgical Easter Plays
        from Rheinau Manuscripts." Journal of English and Germanic
        Philology, X (April, 1911), 192-196. [Rheinau, MS. XVIII,
        Lectionarium, 11th or 12th century. Belongs to the Einsiedeln
        group.]

897   [Visitatio Sepulchri]. In, Lange, Carl. Die lateinischen Oster-
        feiern. (Munich, 1887), pp. 51-52. [Rheinau, Directorium.]

898   [Visitatio Sepulchri]. In, Lange, Carl. Die lateinischen Oster-
        feiern. (Munich, 1887), pp. 68-69. [Einsiedeln, Cod. 757, fol.
        63a, Processionale, 1573.]

ROME

Manuscript (Fulda)

899   Rome, Bibl. Vatic., MS. Palatino 525, Brev. Fuldense, fol. 208v
        - 209r (15th century).

Text

900   [Visitatio Sepulchri]. In, Young, Karl. "Some Texts of Liturgical
        Plays." Publications of the Modern Language Association, XXIV
        (1909), 318.

901   [Visitatio Sepulchri]. In, Young, Karl. The Drama of the Medieval
         Church. Vol. I. (Oxford, 1933), p. 243.
                                    Manuscript
902   Rome, Bibl. Vaticana, MS. Palat. lat. 619, Miscellanea, fol. 25v
         (12th - 15th century).
                                      Text
903   [Visitatio Sepulchri]. In, Young, Karl. The Drama of the Medieval
         Church. Vol. I. (Oxford, 1933), p. 581. [Young says that this
         fragment has never been published previously.]
                                Manuscript (Jerusalem)
904   Rome, Bibl. Vatic., MS. Barberini lat. 659, Ordin. ad usum
         Hierosolymitanum anni 1160, fol. 75v - **76r**.
                                      Text
905   [Visitatio Sepulchri]. In, Young, Karl. "The Home of the Easter
         Play." Speculum, I (1926), 71-86.

906   [Visitatio Sepulchri]. In, Young, Karl. The Drama of the Medieval
         Church. Vol. I. (Oxford, 1933), p. 262.

ROUEN
                                    Manuscript
907   Rouen, Bibliothèque de la Ville, MS. 252, (A. 486), Lib. resp.
         S. Audoeni Rothomagensis, fol. 101v - 102r (14th century).
                                      Text
908   [Visitatio Sepulchri]. In, Lange, Carl. Die lateinischen Oster-
         feiern. (Munich, 1887), No. 56, pp. 36-37.

909   [Visitatio Sepulchri]. In, Young, Karl. The Drama of the Medieval
         Church. Vol. I. (Oxford, 1933), pp. 599-600.
                             Manuscript (Monastery of Fécamp)
910   Rouen, Bibliothèque de la Ville, MS. 253 (olim A. 538), Ordin.
         Fiscannense, fol. 54r - 55r (14th century).
                                      Text
911   [Visitatio Sepulchri]. In, Lange, Carl. Die lateinischen Oster-
         feiern. (Munich, 1887), No. 57, pp. 36-37.

912   [Visitatio Sepulchri]. In, Young, Karl. "The Harrowing of Hell
         in Liturgical Drama." Transactions of the Wisconsin Academy
         of Sciences, Arts, and Letters, XVI, Part II (1909), 903-904.

913   [Visitatio Sepulchri]. In, Young, Karl. The Drama of the Medieval
         Church. Vol. I. (Oxford, 1933), p. 254.
                             Manuscript (Cathedral of Rouen)
914   Rouen, Bibliothèque de la Ville, MS. 384 (olim Y 110), Ordin.
         Rothomagense, fol. 82v - 83r (14th century).

Text

915 [Visitatio Sepulchri]. In, Gasté, A. Les Drames liturgiques
de la Cathédrale de Rouen. (Evreux, 1893), pp. 58-62.

916 [Visitatio Sepulchri]. In, Young, Karl. The Drama of the Medieval
Church. Vol. I. (Oxford, 1933), pp. 370-371.

917 Officium Sepulchri. In, Joannis Abrincensis Episcopi deinde
Rotomangensis Archiepiscopi Liber De Officio Ecclesiasticis,
Notis D. Johannis Prevotii. (Rotomagi, 1679), pp. 211-215.

918 Office de Sepulcre. In, Du Méril, Édélstand. Origines latines du
théâtre moderne. (Paris, 1849), pp. 96-98.

919 Officium Sepulchri. In, Migne, J. P. Patriologiae Cursus Completus. (1856). Vol. 147, cols. 139-142.

SALZBURG

Text

920 [Visitatio Sepulchri]. In, Lange, Carl. Die lateinischen Osterfeiern. (Munich, 1887), pp. 99-101. [Vienna, Hofbibliothek,
Incun. 3993, fol. 116r, Salzburg, Brevier, 1497.]

921 [Visitatio Sepulchri]. In, Lange, Carl. Die lateinischen Osterfeiern. (Munich, 1887), No. 163, pp. 104-105. [From, Salzburg
Agenda of 1575, pp. 264-272 (B).]

922 [Visitatio Sepulchri]. In, Young, Karl. The Drama of the Medieval
Church. Vol. I. (Oxford, 1933), pp. 638-639. [From a Salzburg
Agenda of 1511, fol. 58v - 60v (A). Young appends the variants
from the text in a Salzburg Agenda of 1575, pp. 264-272 (B).]

SENS

Text

923 [Visitatio Sepulchri]. In, Mélanges de Bibliophiles francais.
Vol. VII. (Paris, 1831-1832), pp. 165-167.

924 [Visitatio Sepulchri]. In, Du Méril, Édélstand. Origines latines
du théâtre moderne. (Paris, 1849), pp. 98-100.

925 [Visitatio Sepulchri]. In, Milchsack, G. Die Oster- und Passionsspiele: I. Die lateinischen Osterfeiern. (Wolfenbüttel, 1880),
pp. 58-59.

926 [Visitatio Sepulchri]. In, Lange, Carl. Die lateinischen Oster-

feiern. (Munich, 1887), No. 100, pp. 64-66.

927   [Visitatio Sepulchri]. In, Young, Karl. The Drama of the Medieval Church. Vol. I. (Oxford, 1933), pp. 615-616. [Young uses the text from Mélanges.]

SOISSONS

Text

928   [Visitatio Sepulchri]. In, Lange, Carl. Die lateinischen Oster-feiern. (Munich, 1887), p. 26. [Soissons, from, Martene, p. 496.]

929   [Visitatio Sepulchri]. In, Young, Karl. The Dramatic Associations of the Easter Sepulchre. (Madison, 1920), pp. 47-48. [From, Rituale seu Mandatum insignis ecclesiae Suessionensis (Soissons, 1856), pp. 109-110.

930   [Visitatio Sepulchri]. In, Young, Karl. The Drama of the Medieval Church. Vol. I. (Oxford, 1933), pp. 304-305. [From, Rituale seu Mandatum insignis ecclesiae Suessionensis (Soissons, 1856), pp. 109-110.]

ST. BLAISE

Text

931   [Visitatio Sepulchri]. In, Gerbert, M. Monumenta Veteris Liturgiae Alemannicae. Vol. II. (St. Blaise, 1777-1779), p. 237.

932   [Visitatio Sepulchri]. In, Lange, Carl. Die lateinischen Oster-feiern. (Munich, 1887), No. 44, pp. 30-31.

933   [Visitatio Sepulchri]. In, Young, Karl. The Dramatic Associations of the Easter Sepulchre. (Madison, 1920), p. 7.

934   [Visitatio Sepulchri]. In, Young, Karl. The Drama of the Medieval Church. Vol. I. (Oxford, 1933), p. 260.

ST. FLORIAN

Manuscript

935   St. Florian, Stiftsbibliothek, MS. XI. 398, Ordin. Florianense anni 1512, fol. 76v - 77v.

Text

936   [Visitatio Sepulchri]. In, Lange, Carl. Die lateinischen Oster-feiern. (Munich, 1887), No. 204, pp. 127-129.

937   [Visitatio Sepulchri]. In, Mühlbacher, E. Die literarischen

Leistungen des Stiftes St. Florian bis zur Mitte des 19.
Jahrhunderts. (Innsbruck, 1905), pp. 387-390.

938   [Visitatio Sepulchri]. In, Young, Karl. The Drama of the Medieval
      Church. Vol. I. (Oxford, 1933), p. 657.
                              Manuscript
939   St. Florian, Stiftsbibliothek, MS. XI, 403. Brev. Florianense,
      fol. 235v - 236v (15th century).
                                 Text
940   [Visitatio Sepulchri]. In, Lange, Carl. Die lateinischen Oster-
      feiern. (Munich, 1887), No. 185, pp. 116-118.

941   [Visitatio Sepulchri]. In, Young, Karl. The Drama of the Medieval
      Church. Vol. I. (Oxford, 1933), p. 642.
                              Manuscript
942   St. Florian, Stiftsbibliothek, MS. XI, 420, Brev. Florianense anni
      1482, fol. 319r - 319v.
                                 Text
943   [Visitatio Sepulchri]. In, Lange, Carl. Die lateinischen Oster-
      feiern. (Munich, 1887), No. 193, pp. 119-122.

944   [Visitatio Sepulchri]. In, Young, Karl. The Drama of the Medieval
      Church. Vol. I. (Oxford, 1933), pp. 355-357.
                              Manuscript
945   St. Florian, Stiftsbibliothek, MS. XI. 434, Liber Benedictionum
      Florianensis, fol. 165r - 170r (15th century).
                                 Text
946   [Visitatio Sepulchri]. In, Lange, Carl. Die lateinischen Oster-
      feiern. (Munich, 1887), pp. 127-129.

947   [Visitatio Sepulchri]. In, Franz, A. Das Rituale von St. Florian
      aus zwölften Jahrhundert (Freiburg, 1904), pp. 195-196.

948   [Visitatio Sepulchri]. In, Mühlbacher, E. Die literarischen
      Leistungen des Stiftes St. Florian bis zur Mitte des 19.
      Jahrhunderts. (Innsbruck, 1905), pp. 387-390.

949   [Visitatio Sepulchri]. In, Schiffmann, K. Drama und Theater in
      Oesterreich ob der Enns bis zum Jahre 1803. (Linz, 1905),
      pp. 12-14.

950   [Visitatio Sepulchri]. In, Young, Karl. The Drama of the Medieval
      Church. Vol. I. (Oxford, 1933), pp. 366-367.
                              Manuscript
951   St. Florian, Stiftsbibliothek, MS. XI. 435. 2⁰, Brev. Florianense,

fol. 226v (A), (15th century).

Text

952   [Visitatio Sepulchri]. In, Lange, Carl. Die lateinischen Osterfeiern. (Munich, 1887), pp. 116-118.

953   [Visitatio Sepulchri]. In, Young, Karl. The Drama of the Medieval
Church. Vol. I. (Oxford, 1933), pp. 339-340. [Young gives the
variants from Vienna, Nationalbibliothek, MS. lat. 1843, Brev.
Pataviense, fol. 271v - 272r (B), (15th century).]

Manuscript

954   St. Florian, Stiftsbibliothek, MS. XI. 435. 2^O, Brev. Florianense,
fol. 235r (A), (15th century).

Text

955   [Visitatio Sepulchri]. In, Lange, Carl. Die lateinischen Osterfeiern. (Munich, 1887), pp. 116-118.

Manuscript

956   St. Florian, Stiftsbibliothek, MS. XI. 471. 4°, Brev. Florianense,
fol. 152r - 152v (15th century).

Text

957   [Visitatio Sepulchri]. In, Lange, Carl. Die lateinischen Osterfeiern. (Munich, 1887), No. 180, pp. 113-114.

958   Ad Visitationem Sepulchri. In, Young, Karl. The Drama of the
Medieval Church. Vol. I. (Oxford, 1933), pp. 650-651.

ST. GALL

Manuscript

959   St. Gall, Stiftsbibliothek, MS. 360, Versus Sangallenses, pp.
31-32 (12th century).

Text

960   [Visitatio Sepulchri]. In, Young, Karl. The Drama of the Medieval
Church. Vol. I. (Oxford, 1933), p. 246. [Young says that this
is the first time the work has been printed.]

Manuscript

961   St. Gall, Stiftsbibliothek, MS. 374, Antiphonar., fol. 101r
(11th century).

Text

962   [Visitatio Sepulchri]. In, Lange, Carl. Die lateinischen Osterfeiern. (Munich, 1887), p. 22.

963   [Visitatio Sepulchri]. In, Froning, R. Das Drama des Mittelalters.
Vol. I. (Stuttgart, 1891), p. 13.

Manuscript

964   St. Gall, Stiftsbibliothek, MS. 384, Brev. Sangallense (?), p.
240 (14th century).

Text
965 [Visitatio Sepulchri]. In, Young, Karl. The Drama of the Medieval
Church. Vol. I. (Oxford, 1933), p. 602. [Fragment].
Manuscript
966 St. Gall, Stiftsbibliothek, MS. 392, Lib. resp. Sangallensis (?),
pp. 109-110 (16th century).
Text
967 [Visitatio Sepulchri]. In, Brooks, N. C. "Neue lateinische Osterfeiern." Zeitschrift für deutsche Altertum, I (1908), 299.

968 [Visitatio Sepulchri]. In, Young, Karl. The Drama of the Medieval
Church. Vol. I. (Oxford, 1933), p. 581.
Manuscript
969 St. Gall, Stiftsbibliothek, MS. 1262, Ordin. Sangallense anni 1583,
pp. 142-143.
Text
970 [Visitatio Sepulchri]. In, Lange, Carl. Die lateinischen Osterfeiern. (Munich, 1887), No. 103, pp. 69-71. [Incomplete
text].

971 [Visitatio Sepulchri]. In, Young, Karl. The Drama of the Medieval
Church. Vol. I. (Oxford, 1933), pp. 621-622.
Manuscript
972 St. Gall, Stiftsbibliothek, MS. 1290, fol. 22r, Responsoriale,
1582.
Text
973 [Visitatio Sepulchri]. In, Lange, Carl. Die lateinischen Osterfeiern. (Munich, 1887), pp. 69-71.

STRASSBURG
Text
974 [Visitatio Sepulchri]. In, Lange, Carl. Die lateinischen Osterfeiern. (Munich, 1887), pp. 48-50. [From an Agende, 1513,
Strassburg.]

975 [Visitatio Sepulchri]. In, Froning, R. Das Drama des Mittelalters.
Vol. I. (Stuttgart, 1891), p. 14. [Strassburg, Antiphonary,
1200.]

976 [Visitatio Sepulchri]. In, Young, Karl. "The Harrowing of Hell
in Liturgical Drama." Transactions of the Wisconsin Academy
of Sciences, Arts, and Letters, XVI, Part II (1909), 913-914.

977 [Visitatio Sepulchri]. In, Young, Karl. The Drama of the Medieval
Church. Vol. I. (Oxford, 1933), pp. 255-256. [From a service

book, Agenda Ecclesiae Argentinensis, Cologne, 1590, pp.
252-255.]

STUTTGART
                    Manuscript (Monastery of Zwiefalten)
978   Stuttgart, Landesbibliothek, MS. 4°. 36, Lib. resp. Zwifaltensis,
       fol. 122v - 123v (12th century).
                                  Text
979   [Visitatio Sepulchri]. In, Young, Karl. The Drama of the Medieval
       Church. Vol. I. (Oxford, 1933), pp. 266-267. [Young thinks
       that this is the first time the play has been printed.]
                               Manuscript
980   Stuttgart, Landesbibliothek, MS. Ascet. 55, 4°, Lib. resp.
       Weingartensis, fol. 81r - 81v (13th century).
                                  Text
981   [Visitatio Sepulchri]. In, Lange, Carl. Die lateinischen Osterfeiern.
       (Munich, 1887), No. 132, pp. 89-90.

982   [Visitatio Sepulchri]. In, Young, Karl. The Drama of the Medieval
       Church. Vol. I. (Oxford, 1933), p. 628.
                           Manuscript (Hirsau)
983   Stuttgart, Landesbibliothek, MS. theol. et. phil. 249, 4°.,
       Ordin. Hirsaviense, fol. 79v - 80r (15th century).
                                  Text
984   [Visitatio Sepulchri]. In, Lange, Carl. Die lateinischen Oster-
       feiern. (Munich, 1887), No. 77, pp. 51-52.

985   [Visitatio Sepulchri]. In, Young, Karl. The Drama of the Medieval
       Church. Vol. I. (Oxford, 1933), p. 596.

TOURS
                                  Text
986   [Visitatio Sepulchri]. In, Lange, Carl. Die lateinischen Oster-
       feiern. (Munich, 1887), No. 24, p. 24. [Found in Martene,
       Leyden, 1706, pp. 481-482.]

987   [Visitatio Sepulchri]. In, Adams, Joseph Q. Chief Pre-Shakes-
       pearean Dramas. (Boston, New York, 1924), p. 6.

988   [Visitatio Sepulchri.] In, Young, Karl. The Drama of the Medieval
       Church. Vol. I. (Oxford, 1933), pp. 240-241. [Young notes
       that the text has been printed by Martene, III, pp. 179-180.]

989   Drame pascal de la Résurrection de Marmoutier. Tours. In,
       Cohen, Gustave. Anthologie du drame liturgie en France au

moyen-âge. (Paris, 1955), pp. 35-65.

TREVES

Manuscript
990   Treves, Stadtbibl., MS. 1238, Consuetudines Monasticae, fol.
       202v (15th century).

Text
991   [Visitatio Sepulchri]. In, Albers, B. Consuetudines Monasticae.
       Vol. V. (Monte Cassino, 1900-1912), pp. 39-41.

992   [Visitatio Sepulchri]. In, Young, Karl. The Drama of the Medieval
       Church. Vol. I. (Oxford, 1933), p. 299.

Manuscript
993   Treves, Stadtbibliothek, MS. 1635, Ordin. monasterii Sancti
       Maximini, fol. 79v (15th century).

Text
994   [Visitatio Sepulchri]. In, Brooks, Neil C. "Some Texts of Liturgical
       Easter Plays." Journal of English and Germanic Philology. VIII
       (October, 1909), 469-470.

Text
994   [Visitatio Sepulchri]. In, Young, Karl. The Drama of the Medieval
       Church. Vol. I. (Oxford, 1933), pp. 252-253.

Manuscript
996   Treves, Stadbibliothèque, MS. 1738, Ordin. Trevirense, fol.
       54v (15th century).

Text
997   [Visitatio Sepulchri]. In, Brooks, Neil C. "Some New Texts of
       Liturgical Easter Plays." Journal of English and Germanic
       Philology, VIII (October, 1909), 470-471.

998   [Visitatio Sepulchri]. In, Young, Karl. The Drama of the Medieval
       Church. Vol. I. (Oxford, 1933), p. 611.

999   [Visitatio Sepulchri]. In, Würdtwein, S. A. Commentatio Historico-
       Liturgica de Stationibus Ecclesiae Moguntinae. (Main, 1782),
       pp. 187-188.

1000   [Visitatio Sepulchri]. In, Young, Karl. The Drama of the Medieval
       Church. Vol. I. (Oxford, 1933), pp. 611-612. [Young reprints
       the text from S. A. Würdtwein.]

TRIER

Text
1001   [Visitatio Sepulchri]. In, Froning, R. Das Drama des Mittelalters.
       Vol. I. (Stuttgart, 1891), pp. 15-16.

TROYES

Manuscript

1002 Troyes, Bibliotheque de la Ville, MS. 792, fol. 301v - 302v
(13th century).

Text

1003 [Visitatio Sepulchri]. In, Young, Karl. The Drama of the Medieval
Church. Vol. I. (Oxford, 1933), pp. 603-604. [Edited by G.
Baist, Romanische Forschungen, ed. K. Vollmöller, XXIII (1907),
752-753. The text is basically in French.]

Manuscript

1004 Troyes, Bibliothèque, MS. 833, Ordin. Trecense, fol. 49r (14th
century).

Text

1005 [Visitatio Sepulchri]. In, Brooks, Neil C. The Sepulchre of Christ
in Art and Liturgy. (Urbana, 1921), pp. 108-109.

1006 [Visitatio Sepulchri]. In, Young, Karl. The Drama of the Medieval
Church. Vol. I. (Oxford, 1933), p. 615.

Manuscript

1007 Troyes, Bibliothèque de la Ville, MS. 1150, Ordin. Trecense, fol.
172r - 172v (14th century).

Text

1008 [Visitatio Sepulchri]. In, Brooks, Neil C. The Sepulchre of Christ
in Art and Liturgy. (Urbana, 1921), p. 108.

1009 [Visitatio Sepulchri]. In, Young, Karl. The Drama of the Medieval
Church. Vol. I. (Oxford, 1933), pp. 291-292.

UDINE

Manuscript

1010 Udine, Bibliothèque Arcivescovile, MS. F. 25, Lib. Resp.
Tarvisinus (?), fol. 94v - 95r (12th century).

Text

1011 [Visitatio Sepulchri]. In, Young, Karl. The Drama of the Medieval
Church. Vol. I. (Oxford, 1933), p. 590. [Young says that this
is the first time that the text has been printed.]

UTRECHT

Manuscript

1012 Utrecht, Bibliothek de Rijksuniversiteit, MS. 406 (olim Spript.
Eccles. 318), Lib. resp. Ultrajectensis, fol. 97v (B), (12th
century).

Text

1013 [Visitatio Sepulchri]. In, Milchsack, G. Die Oster- und Passionsspiele: I. Die lateinischen Osterfeiern. (Wolfenbüttel, 1880),
p. 65.

1014 [Visitatio Sepulchri]. In, Van Mierlo, J. "Een Utrechtsch Anti-
     phonarium -- Bijdrage tot de Geschiedenis van het liturgisch
     Drama in de Nederlanden." Leuvensche Bidragen op het Gebied
     van de Germaansche Philologie, VIII (1908-1909), 36.
                           Manuscript
1015 Utrecht, Bibliothek de Rijksuniversiteit, MS. 407 (olim, Scrip.
     Eccles. 316), Lib. resp. Ultrojectensis, fol. 116v (12th
     century).

                              Text
1016 [Visitatio Sepulchri]. In, Lange, Carl. Die lateinischen Oster-
     feiern. (Munich, 1887), No. 19, p. 23.

1017 [Visitatio Sepulchri]. In, Young, Karl. The Drama of the Medieval
     Church. Vol. I. (Oxford, 1933), pp. 242-243. [Young also gives
     the variant found in MS. 406 (olim Script. Eccles. 318), Lib.
     resp. Ultrajectensis, fol. 97v (B), (12th century).]

VERDUN
                              Text
1018 [Visitatio Sepulchri]. In, Martene, E. De Antiquis Ecclesiae
     Ritibus. Vol. IV. (Venice, 1788), p. 299. [From, Consuetudines
     insignis monasterii Sancti Vitoni Verdunensis, 10th century.]

1019 [Visitatio Sepulchri]. In, Albers, B. Consuetudines Monasticae.
     Vol. V. (Monte Cassino, 1900-1912), pp. 123-124. [A reprint
     of Martene.]

1020 [Visitatio Sepulchri]. In, Young, Karl. The Drama of the Medieval
     Church. Vol. I. (Oxford, 1933), p. 378. [Young reprints the
     text from Martene.]

SALZBURG
                           Manuscript
1021 Vienna, Nationalbibliothek, MS. lat. 1672, Brev. Salisburgense,
     fol. 266r - 266v (15th century).
                              Text
1022 [Visitatio Sepulchri]. In, Brooks, Neil C. "Some New Texts of
     Liturgical Easter Plays." Journal of English and Germanic
     Philology, VIII (October, 1909), 482-483.

1023 [Visitatio Sepulchri]. In, Young, Karl. The Drama of the Medieval
     Church. Vol. I. (Oxford, 1933), pp. 637-638.

VIENNA
                           Manuscript
1024 Vienna, Nationalbibliothek, MS. lat. 1768, Brev. Vindobonense

(?), fol. 190r (13th century).

Text

1025 [Visitatio Sepulchri]. In, Milchsack, G. Die Oster- und Passion-
　　　sspiele: I. Die lateinischen Osterfeiern. Wolfenbüttel, 1880.

1026 [Visitatio Sepulchri]. In, Lange, Carl. Die lateinischen Oster-
　　　feiern. (Munich, 1887), No. 165, pp. 104-105. [Lange says
　　　that the manuscript is from the 15th century.]

1027 [Visitatio Sepulchri]. In, Young, Karl. The Drama of the Medieval
　　　Church. Vol. I. (Oxford, 1933), pp. 325-326.

Manuscript (Speyer)

1028 Vienna, Nationalbibliothek, MS. lat. 1882, Directorium Spirense,
　　　vol. 41v (14th century).

Text

1029 [Visitatio Sepulchri]. In, Lange, Carl. Die lateinischen Oster-
　　　feiern. (Munich, 1887), No. 47, pp. 33-34.

1030 [Visitatio Sepulchri]. In, Young, Karl. The Drama of the Medieval
　　　Church. Vol. I. (Oxford, 1933), p. 247.

Manuscript

1031 Vienna, Nationalbibliothek, MS. lat. 1890, Brev. fol. 163r -
　　　163v (12th century).

Text

1032 [Visitatio Sepulchri]. In, Lange, Carl. Die lateinischen Oster-
　　　feiern. (Munich, 1887), No. 109, pp. 81-82.

1033 [Visitatio Sepulchri]. In, Young, Karl. The Drama of the Medieval
　　　Church. Vol. I. (Oxford, 1933), p. 629.

Manuscript (Monsee)

1034 Vienna, Nationalbibliothek, MS. lat. 1919, Brev. Monseense, fol.
　　　262v - 263r (15th century).

Text

1035 [Visitatio Sepulchri]. In, Lange, Carl. Die lateinischen Oster-
　　　feiern. (Munich, 1887), No. 182, pp. 114-116.

1036 [Visitatio Sepulchri]. In, Young, Karl. The Drama of the Medieval
　　　Church. Vol. I. (Oxford, 1933), pp. 646-647.

Manuscript

1037 Vienna, National-Bibliothek, MS. lat. 1928, Ordin. Ordinis
　　　Hospitalis Hiersolymitani, fol. 44r - 44v (14th century).

Text

1038 [Visitatio Sepulchri]. In, Brooks, Neil C. "Some New Texts of
　　　Liturgical Easter Plays." Journal of English and Germanic
　　　Philology, VIII (October, 1909), 467.

1039 [Visitatio Sepulchri]. In, Young, Karl. The Drama of the Medieval
Church. Vol. I. (Oxford, 1933), pp. 594-595.
Manuscript (Prague)

1040 Vienna, Nationalbibliothek, MS. lat. 1977, Brev. Pragense, fol.
264v and 309r (14th century).
Text

1041 [Visitatio Sepulchri]. In, Young, Karl. The Drama of the Medieval
Church. Vol. I. (Oxford, 1933), p. 644.
Manuscript (Monsee)

1042 Vienna, Nationalbibliothek, MS. lat. 3569, Brev. Monseense, fol.
276v - 277r (15th century).
Text

1043 [Visitatio Sepulchri]. In, Lange, Carl. Die lateinischen Osterfeiern. (Munich, 1887), No. 192, pp. 119-122.

1044 [Visitatio Sepulchri]. In, Young, Karl. The Drama of the Medieval
Church. Vol. I. (Oxford, 1933), pp. 655-656.
Manuscript (Monsee

1045 Vienna, Nationalbibliothek, MS. lat. 3824, Brev. Monseense, fol.
132r (A), (15th century).
Text

1046 [Visitatio Sepulchri]. In, Lange, Carl. Die lateinischen Osterfeiern. (Munich, 1887), No. 127, pp. 88-89.

1047 [Visitatio Sepulchri]. In, Young, Karl. The Drama of the Medieval
Church. Vol. I. (Oxford, 1933), p. 633. [Young attaches the
variants from Munich, Staatsbibliothek, MS. lat. 19932, Brev.
Tegirinsense, fol. 294r - 294v (B), (15th - 16th century), and
from Klosterneuburg, Stiftsbibliothek, MS. 1185.
Manuscript (Passau)

1048 Vienna, Nationalbibliothek, MS. lat. 4924, Brev. Pataviense,
fol. 394v - 395v (15th century).
Text

1049 [Visitatio Sepulchri]. In, Lange, Carl. Die lateinischen Osterfeiern. (Munich, 1887), No. 188, pp. 118-119.

1050 [Visitatio Sepulchri]. In, Young, Karl. The Drama of the Medieval
Church. Vol. I. (Oxford, 1933), p. 649. [Young says that
Lange's edition, No. 188, pp. 118-119, is defective.]
Manuscript (Prague)

1051 Vienna, Nationalbibliothek, MS. lat. 13427, Brev. Pragense,
fol. 129r - 129v (14th century).
Text

1052 [Visitatio Sepulchri]. In, Lange, Carl. Die lateinischen Osterfeiern. (Munich, 1887), No. 107, pp. 74-75.

1053 [Visitatio Sepulchri]. In, Young, Karl. The Drama of the Medieval
Church. Vol. I. (Oxford, 1933), p. 618. [Edited by Lange, No.
107, pp. 74-75.]

VORAU

Manuscript

1054 Vorau, Stiftsbibliothek, MS. 90, Brev. Pataviense, fol. 180v -
181v (13th century).

Text

1055 [Visitatio Sepulchri]. In, Young, Karl. The Drama of the Medieval
Church. Vol. I. (Oxford, 1933), p. 647.

WOLFENBÜTTEL

Manuscript

1056 Wolfenbüttel, Herzog-August-Bibliothek, MS. Helmst. 505, fol.
2r (14th century).

Text

1057 [Visitatio Sepulchri]. In, Brooks, N. C. "Osterfeiern aus Bamberger
und Wolfenbüttler Handschriften." Zeitschrift für deutsche
Altertum, LV (1914), 57-58.

1058 [Visitatio Sepulchri]. In, Young, Karl. The Drama of the Medieval
Church. Vol. I. (Oxford, 1933), p. 584.

Manuscript

1059 Wolfenbüttel, Herzogliche Bibliothek, MS. Helmst. 1156, Brev.
anni 1465, fol. 2v - 3r (A).

Text

1060 [Visitatio Sepulchri]. In, Young, Karl. The Drama of the Medieval
Church. Vol. I. (Oxford, 1933), pp. 635-636. [Young says that
this is the first time that it has been printed. He prints it with
variants found in Wolfenbüttel, Herzogliche Bibliothek, MS.
Helmst., 536 (583), Brev., fol. 76r - 76v (B), (14th century).]

WÜRZBURG

Manuscript

1061 Würzburg, Universitatsbibliothek, MS. Theol. 2^O. 127a, Brev.
Wirceburgense, fol. 68v - 69r (14th century).

Text

1062 [Visitatio Sepulchri]. In, Lange, Carl. Die lateinischen Osterfeiern. (Munich, 1887), No. 80, pp. 53-54.

1063 [Visitatio Sepulchri]. In, Young, Karl. The Drama of the Medieval
Church. Vol. I. (Oxford, 1933), pp. 257-258.

1064 [Visitatio Sepulchri]. In, Lange, Carl. Die lateinischen Oster-

feiern. (Munich, 1887), No. 101, p. 67. [Reprint of, Directorium Herbipolense, Speyer, 1477, fol. 39v.]

1065 [Visitatio Sepulchri]. In, Young, Karl. The Drama of the Medieval
Church. Vol. I. (Oxford, 1933), p. 282. [Reprint of, Directorium Herbipolense, Speyer, 1477, fol. 39v.]

ZURICH
Manuscript (Monastery of Rheinau)
1066 Zurich, Zentralbibliothek, Rheinau MS. XVIII, Lectionarium
Rhenoviense, pp. 282-283 (13th century).
Text
1067 [Visitatio Sepulchri]. In, Brooks, Neil C. "Some New Texts of
Liturgical Easter Plays." Journal of English and Germanic
Philology, VIII (October, 1909), 192-196.

1068 [Visitatio Sepulchri]. In, Young, Karl. The Drama of the Medieval
Church. Vol. I. (Oxford, 1933), pp. 385-389.
Manuscript (Rheinau)
1069 Zurich, Zentralbibliothek, MS. Rheinau, LIX, Ordin. Rhenoviense, pp. 112-113 (B), (13th century).
Text
1070 [Visitatio Sepulchri]. In, Lange, Carl. Die lateinischen Osterfeiern. (Munich, 1887), No. 78, pp. 51-52.
Manuscript
1071 Zurich, Zentralbibliothek, MS. C. 8b, Brev. Turicense anni
1260, fol. 55v - 56r.
Text
1072 [Visitatio Sepulchri]. In, Gerbert, M. Vetus Liturgia Alemannica.
(St. Blaise, 1776), p. 864. [Incomplete].

1073 [Visitatio Sepulchri]. In, Brooks, N. C. The Sepulchre of Christ
in Art and Liturgy. (Urbana, 1921), p. 110.

1074 [Visitatio Sepulchri]. In, Young, Karl. The Drama of the Medieval
Church. Vol. I. (Oxford, 1933), pp. 314-315.
Manuscript
1075 Zurich, Zentralbibliothek, MS. 65, Lib. resp. Augiensis, p.
103 (11th - 12th century).
Text
1076 [Visitatio Sepulchri]. In, Brooks, Neil C. "Some New Texts of
Liturgical Easter Plays." Journal of English and Germanic
Philology, VIII (October, 1909), 192.

1077 Ad Visitandvm Sepvlchrvm. In, Young, Karl. The Drama of the

Medieval Church. Vol. I. (Oxford, 1933), p. 583.

Other Texts

1078 [Visitatio Sepulchri]. In, Young, Karl. The Drama of the Medieval
Church. Vol. I. (Oxford, 1933), pp. 616-617. [From, Breuiarium
Sancte Patriarcalis et Metropolitane Bituricensis Ecclesie,
1522, fol. LXX^V. Reprinted, incompletely, by Lange, No. 98,
pp. 62-63.]

1079 [Visitatio Sepulchri]. In, Young, Karl. The Drama of the Medieval
Church. Vol. I. (Oxford, 1933), p. 652. [Young follows the text
by G. M. Dreves, in Stimmen aus Maria-Laach, XXXIII (1887),
423.] [15th century].

1080 [Visitatio Sepulchri]. In, Young, Karl. The Drama of the Medieval
Church. Vol. I. (Oxford, 1933), p. 614. [From an Ordinarius
...ecclesiae Moguntinae, of the year 1547, printed by Rueff,
p. 71, and now reprinted by Young.]

c Ludus Paschalis *

ST. QUENTIN

Manuscript (Origny-Sainte-Benoîte)

1081 St. Quentin, Bibliothèque de la Ville, MS. 86 (olim 75), Miscellanea
Oriniacensia, pp. 609-625, (14th century). [Incomplete at the
end.]

Text

1082 [Ludus Paschalis]. In, Coussemaker, E. de. Drames liturgiques
du moyen âge. (Rennes, 1860), pp. 256-279.

1083 [Ludus Paschalis]. In, Young, Karl. The Drama of the Medieval
Church. Vol. I. (Oxford, 1933), pp. 413-419.

1084 Ludus Paschalis (Jeu de Pâques). In, Cohen, Gustave. Anthologie
du drame liturgie en France au moyen-âge. (Paris, 1955),
pp. 275-287.

KLOSTERNEUBURG

Manuscript

1085 Klosterneuburg, Stiftsbibliothek, MS. 574, Miscellanea, fol.
142v - 144v (13th century).

Text

1086 Ordo Paschalis. In, Pfeiffer, H. "Klosterneuburger Osterfeier

---

* The four plays are listed here so as to follow Young's arrangement in The Drama of the Medieval Church.

und Osterspiel." Jahrbuch des Stiften Klosterneuburg, I
(1908), 27-40.

1087 Ordo Paschalis. In, Pfeiffer, H. "Das Klosterneuburger Osterspiel." Musica Divina: Sonderheft Klosterneuburg, I (1913),
161-167.

1088 Ordo Paschalis. In, Young, Karl. The Drama of the Medieval
Church. Vol. I. (Oxford, 1933), pp. 421-429.

MUNICH
Manuscript (Benedictbeuern)
1089 Munich, Staatsbibliothek, MS. lat. 4660a, Carmina Burana,
fol. v^r - vi^v (13th century).
Text
1090 [Ludus Paschalis]. In, Meyer, W. Fragmenta Burana. (Berlin,
1901), pp. 126-130.

1091 [Ludus Paschalis]. In, Young, Karl. The Drama of the Medieval
Church. Vol. I. (Oxford, 1933), pp. 432-437.

TOURS
Manuscript
1092 Tours, Bibliothèque de la Ville, MS. 927, Miscellanea Turon-
ensia fol. 1r - 8v (13th century).
Text
1093 Officium Sepulchri seu Resurrectionis. In, Luzarche, Victor.
Office de Paques ou de la Résurrection accompagné de la
notation musicale et suivi d'hymnes et séquences inédites.
Publié pour la première fois d'apres un manuscrit du XIIe
de la Bibliothèque de Tours. (Tours, 1856), pp. 1-26.

1094 La Résurrection. In, Coussemaker, E. de. Drames liturgiques
du moyen âge. (Rennes, 1860), pp. 21-48.

1095 [Ludus Paschalis]. In, Milchsack, G. Die Oster- und Passionsspiele: I. Die lateinischen Osterfeiern. (Wolfenbüttel, 1880),
pp. 97-102.

1096 [Ludus Paschalis]. In, Lange, Carl. Die lateinischen Osterfeiern.
Programm No. 223. (Halberstadt, 1881), pp. 29-34.

1097 [Ludus Paschalis]. In, Young, Karl. The Drama of the Medieval
Church. Vol. I. (Oxford, 1933), pp. 438-447.

d Peregrinus (Journey to Emmaus)

MADRID
Manuscript (Sicily)
1098 Madrid, Biblioteca Nacional, MS. C. 132, Grad. ad usum Ecclesiae
      Siculorum, fol. 105v - 108r (12th century).
Text
1099 [Peregrinus]. In, Young, Karl. "A New Version of the Peregrinus."
      Publications of the Modern Language Association, XXXIV (1919),
      120-124.

1100 Versus Ad Faciendum Peregrinum. In, Young, Karl. The Drama
      of the Medieval Church. Vol. I. (Oxford, 1933), pp. 477-480.
Manuscript (Sicily)
1101 Madrid, Biblioteca Nacional, MS. 289 (olim C. 153), Trop. ad
      usum Ecclesiae Siculorum, fol. 117r - 118v (12th century).
Text
1102 [Peregrinus]. In, Young, Karl. "Some Texts of Liturgical Plays."
      Publications of the Modern Language Association, XXIV (1909),
      329-331.

1103 [Peregrinus]. In, Bartholomaeis, V. De. Le Origini della Poesia
      drammatica italiana. (Bologna, [1924]), pp. 527-528. [Reprinted
      from Young's edition of 1909.]

1104 [Peregrinus]. In, Beeson, C. H. A Primer of Medieval Latin.
      (Chicago, [1925]), pp. 205-206. [Reprinted from the Young
      edition of 1909.]

1105 De Peregrino in Die Lune Pasche. In, Young, Karl. The Drama
      of the Medieval Church. Vol. I. (Oxford, 1933), pp. 459-460.

MUNICH
Manuscript (Carmina Burana)
1106 Munich, Staatsbibliothek, MS. lat. 4660a, Carmina Burana, fol.
      vii^r - vii^v (13th century).
Text
1107 [Discipuli duo et Christi]. In, Meyer, W. Fragmenta Burana.
      (Berlin, 1901), pp. 136-137, and Plates 12 and 13.

1108 [Peregrinus]. In, Young, Karl. The Drama of the Medieval Church.
      Vol. I. (Oxford, 1933), pp. 463-465.

ORLEANS
                              Manuscript (St. Benoît-sur-Loire)
1109 Orleans, Bibliothèque de la Ville, MS. 201 (olim 178), Miscel-
      lanea Floriacensia, pp. 225-230 (13th century).
                              Text
1110 [Peregrinus]. In, Mélanges des Bibliophiles francais. Vol. VII.
      (Paris, 1831-1832), pp. 175-183.

1111 [Peregrinus]. In, Wright, T. Early Mysteries and Other Latin
      Poems of the Twelfth and Thirteenth Centuries. (London,
      1838), pp. 37-41.

1112 Mystère de l'apparition à Emmaüs. In, Du Méril, Édelstand.
      Origines latines du théâtre moderne. (Paris, 1849), pp. 120-
      126.

1113 L'Apparition a Emmaus. In, Coussemaker, E. de. Drames
      liturgiques du moyen âge. (Rennes, 1860), pp. 195-209.

1114 [Peregrinus]. In, Young, Karl. The Drama of the Medieval Church.
      Vol. I. (Oxford, 1933), pp. 471-475.

PARIS
                              Manuscript (Rouen)
1115 Paris, Bibliothèque Nationale, MS. lat. 1213, Ordin. Rothoma-
      gense, p. 90 (C), (15th century).
                              Text
1116 [Peregrinus]. In, Young, Karl. "A Contribution to the History of
      Liturgical Drama at Rouen." Modern Philology, VI (October,
      1908), 222-223.
                              Manuscript (Beauvais)
1117 Paris, Bibliothèque Nationale, Nouvelles Acquisitions, MS. lat.
      1064, Miscellanea liturgica, fol. 8r - 11v (12th century).
                              Text
1118 [Peregrinus]. In, Desjardins, G. Histoire de la Cathédrale de
      Beauvais. (Beauvais, 1865), pp. 269-275.

1119 [Peregrinus]. In, Omont, Henri Auguste. "Le Mystère d'Emmaüs
      (Ordo ad Peregrinum), d'après un manuscrit du XIIe siecle de
      la cathédrale de Beauvais." Bibliothèque de l'Ecole des Chartes,
      LXXIV (1913), 263-266. [This supersedes the edition by Des-
      jardins.]

1120 Ordo ad Peregrinum. In, Young, Karl. The Drama of the Medieval
      Church. Vol. I. (Oxford, 1933), pp. 467-469.

Manuscript (Saintes)

1121 Paris, Bibliothèque Nationale, MS. lat. 16309, Brev. Santonense, fol. 604r - 605r (14th century).

Text

1122 "Discipuli duo et Christus." In, Bibliothèque de l'Ecole des Chartes, XXXIV (1873), 314-315. [Edited anonymously.]

1123 [Peregrinus]. In, Young, Karl. The Drama of the Medieval Church. Vol. I. (Oxford, 1933), pp. 453-454.

ROUEN

Manuscript

1124 Rouen, Bibliothèque de la Ville, MS. 222 (olim A. 551), Process. Rothomagense, fol. 43v - 45r (13th century).

Text

1125 Officium Peregrinorum. In, Young, Karl. "A Contribution to the History of Liturgical Drama at Rouen." Modern Philology, VI (October, 1908), 212-214.

1126 [Peregrinus]. In, Young, Karl. The Drama of the Medieval Church. Vol. I. (Oxford, 1933), pp. 461-462.

1127 Les Pelerins d'Emmaus, de Rouen. In, Cohen, Gustave. Anthologie du Drame liturgie en France au moyen-âge. (Paris, 1955), pp. 66-69.

Manuscript

1128 Rouen, Bibliothèque de la Ville, MS. 384 (Y. 110), Ordinarium Rothomangense, fol. 86r - 86v (14th century).

Text

1129 [Officium Peregrinorum]. In, Gaste, Armand. Les Drames liturgiques de la Cathédral de Rouen. (Evereux, 1893), pp. 65-68.

1130 [Peregrinus]. In, Adams, Joseph Q. Chief Pre-Shakespearean Dramas. (Boston, New York, 1924), pp. 21-24. [A reprint of Gaste's text.]

1131 [Peregrinus]. In, Young, Karl. The Drama of the Medieval Church. Vol. I. (Oxford, 1933), p. 693. [Young also gives the variants MS. 382, fol. 73r - 73v (15th century), and from Paris, Bibliothèque Nationale, MS. lat. 1213, Ordin. Rothomangense, p. 90 (C), (15th century).]

1132 Office des Voyageurs. In, Du Méril, Édelstand. Origines latines du théâtre moderne. (Paris, 1849), pp. 117-120.

e Passion Play

Planctus (Mariae)

MUNICH

Manuscript (Regensburg)

1133 Munich, Staatsbibliothek, MS. lat. 26947, Ordin. Ratisbonense, fol. 116r - 117v (15th century).

Text

1134 [Planctus]. In, Young, Karl. The Drama of the Medieval Church. Vol. I. (Oxford, 1933), pp. 504-506. [Young says that this is the first time that the full text has been printed.]

CIVIDALE

Manuscript (Cividale del Friuli)

1135 Cividale, Reale Museo Archeologico, MS. CI, Process. Cividalense, fol. 74r - 76v (14th century).

Text

1136 [Planctus]. In, Coussemaker, E. de. Drames liturgiques du Moyen Age. (Rennes, 1860), pp. 285-297.

1137 [Planctus]. In, Bartholomaeis, V. De. Il Teatro abruzzese del Medio Evo. (Bologna, [1924]), pp. 532-535. [Reprinted from Coussemaker.]

1138 Planctus Marie. In, Young, Karl. The Drama of the Medieval Church. Vol. I. (Oxford, 1933), pp. 507-512.

Passion - Planctus   Liturgical

Planctus Mariae (The Lament of Mary), An Acting Version of a 14th-Century Liturgical Music-drama. Transcribed and Translated by W. L. Smoldon, for Four Soloists (Two Sopranos, Contralto, and Tenor) and Mixed Chorus, with Suggested Acc. for Chamber Organ, and Chime Bells. London: Oxford University Press [c. 1965]. x p., Score (14) pp. [Words in Latin and English; also printed as text on pp. vii-x.]
ICN.

Ludus Breviter de Passione

MUNICH

Manuscript (Carmina Burana)

1139 Munich, Staatsbibliothek, MS. lat. 4660a, Carmina Burana, fol. IIIv - IVv (13th century).

Text

1140 [Ludus Breuiter de Passione.] In, Meyer, W. Fragmenta
      Burana. (Berlin, 1901), pp. 123-124. [With photographic
      facsimiles.]

1141 Ludus Breuiter de Passione. In, Young, Karl. The Drama of the
      Medieval Church. Vol. I. (Oxford, 1933), pp. 514-516.

                        Manuscript (Carmina Burana)

1142 Munich, Staatsbibliothek, MS. lat. 4660, Carmina Burana, fol.
      107r - 112v.

                                Text

1143 [Ludus de Passione]. In, Du Méril, Édelstand. Origines latines
      du théâtre moderne. (Paris, 1849), pp. 126-147 (D).

1144 [Ludus de Passione]. In, Froning, R. Das Drama des Mittelalters.
      Vol. I. (Stuttgart, 1891), pp. 284-299 (F).

1145 [Ludus de Passione]. In, Schmeller, J. A. Carmina Burana.
      (Breslau, 1894), pp. 95-107 (S).

1146 [Ludus de Passione]. In, Young, Karl. The Drama of the Medieval
      Church. Vol. I. (Oxford, 1933), pp. 518-532.

                        Manuscript (Sulmona)

1147 MS. Archivo capitolare di S. Panfilo, Fasc. 47, n. 9. (14th
      century). [Fragment].

                                Text

1148 Testo di Sulmona. In, Inguanez, D. M. Un dramma della pas-
      sione del secolo XII. (Montecassino, 1939), pp. 43-55.

1149 [Sulmona Fragment]. In, Young, Karl. The Drama of the Medieval
      Church. Vol. I. (Oxford, 1933), pp. 701-708.

      f Ascension

MOOSBURG

                              Manuscript

1150 Munich, Staatsbibliothek, MS. lat. 9469, Ordin. Mosburgense,
      fol. 72v - 73v (14th century).

                                Text

1151 [Ascension]. In, Brooks, N. C. "Eine liturgischdramatische
      Himmelfahrtsfeier." Zeitschrift für deutsche Altertum,
      LXII (1925), 91-96.

1152 [Ascension]. In, Young, Karl. The Drama of the Medieval
      Church. Vol. I. (Oxford, 1933), pp. 484-488.

2 The Christmas Cycle

a The Shepherds

CLERMONT-FERRAND
Manuscript

1153 Clermont-Ferrand, Bibliothèque de la Ville, MS. 67, Brev. Claromontense, fol. 28v (15th century).
Text

1154 [Officium Pastorum]. In, Twigge, R. Dublin Review CXXI (1897), 362. [Incomplete edition].

1155 [Officium Pastorum]. In, Young, Karl. "Officium Pastorum: A Study of the Dramatic Developments within the Liturgy of Christmas." Transactions of the Wisconsin Academy of Sciences, Arts, and Letters, XVII, Part I (1912), 321.

1156 [Officium Pastorum]. In, Young, Karl. The Drama of the Medieval Church. Vol. II. (Oxford, 1933), p. 11.
Manuscript

1157 Paris, Bibliothèque Nationale, MS. lat. 1274, Brev. Claromontense, fol. 40v (14th century).
Text

1158 [Officium Pastorum]. In, Young, Karl. "Officium Pastorum: A Study of the Dramatic Developments within the Liturgy of Christmas." Transactions of the Wisconsin Academy of Sciences, Arts, and Letters, XVII, Part I (1912), 322. [See pp. 369-378.]

1159 [Officium Pastorum]. In, Young, Karl. The Drama of the Medieval Church. Vol. II. (Oxford, 1933), p. 12.

MONTPELLIER
Manuscript (Rouen)

1160 Montpellier, Bibliothèque de la Faculté de Médecine, MS. H. 304, Miscellanea ecclesiastica, fol. 41r - 41v (12th century).
Text

1161 [Officium Pastorum]. In, Young, Karl. "A Contribution to the History of Liturgical Drama at Rouen." Modern Philology, VI (1908-1909), 207-208.

1162 [Officium Pastorum]. In, Young, Karl. "Officium Pastorum: A Study of the Dramatic Developments within the Liturgy of Christmas." Transactions of the Wisconsin Academy of Sciences, Arts, and Letters, XVII, Part I (1912), 323-324.

1163 [Officium Pastorum]. In, Young, Karl. The Drama of the
      Medieval Church. Vol. II. (Oxford, 1933), pp. 12-13.

1164 Office des Bergers. In, Cohen, Gustave. Anthologie du drame
      liturgie en France au moyen-âge. (Paris, 1955), pp. 117-
      119.

PADUA

Manuscript

1165 Padua, Bibl. Capit., MS. S, Ordin. Pataviense, fol. 40v - 41v
      (13th century).

Text

1166 [Officium Pastorum]. In, Dondi Orologio, F. S. Dissertazione
      sopra li Riti, Disciplinia, Costumanze della Chiesa di Padova
      sino al xiv Secolo. (Padua, 1816), p. 42. [Part of the text].

1167 [Officium Pastorum]. In, Bartholomaeis, V. De. Le Origini
      della Poesia drammatica italiana. (Bologna, [1924]), pp. 147-
      148, 525-526.

1168 [Officium Pastorum]. In, Young, Karl. The Drama of the
      Medieval Church. Vol. II. (Oxford, 1933), pp. 9-10.

1169 Officium Pastorum (Die Weihnachtsfeier von Padua). In, Langosch,
      Karl. Geistliche Spiele. Lateinische Dramen des Mittelalters
      mit deutschen Versen. (Bassel, Stuttgart, 1957), pp. 127-129.

PARIS

Manuscript (Limoges)

1170 Paris, Bibliothèque Nationale, MS. lat. 887, Trop. Lemovicense,
      fol. 9v (11th century).

Text

1171 [Officium Pastorum]. In, Young, Karl. "Officium Pastorum: A
      Study of the Dramatic Developments within the Liturgy of
      Christmas." Transactions of the Wisconsin Academy of
      Sciences, Arts, and Letters, XVII, Part I (1912), 300-301.

1172 [Quem Queritis]. In, Young, Karl. The Drama of the Medieval
      Church. Vol. II. (Oxford, 1933), p. 4.

1173 Les Berges à la crèche. In, Cohen, Gustave. Anthologie du
      drame liturgie en France au moyen-âge. (Paris, 1955), pp.
      109-110.

Manuscript (Rouen)

1174 Paris, Bibliothèque Nationale, MS. lat. 904, Grad. Rothomagense, fol. 11v - 14r (13th century).

Text

1175 [Officium Pastorum]. In, Coussemaker, E. de. Drames liturgiques du moyen âge. (Rennes, 1860), pp. 235-241. [Without
the liturgical sequel, but with the music.]

1176 [Officium Pastorum]. In, Young, Karl. "Officium Pastorum: A
Study of the Dramatic Developments within the Liturgy of
Christmas." Transactions of the Wisconsin Academy of
Sciences, Arts, and Letters, XVII, Part I (1912), 325-329.

1177 [Officium Pastorum]. In, Chasles, Madeleine. "Le Drame liturgique." La Vie et les Arts liturgiques, III (1916-1917), 177-179.
[With facsimiles, pp. 174-176].

1178 [Officium Pastorum]. In, Young, Karl. The Drama of the Medieval
Church. Vol. II. (Oxford, 1933), pp. 16-19.

1179 Office des Bergers de Rouen. In, Cohen, Gustave. Anthologie
du drame liturgie en France au moyen-âge. (Paris, 1955),
pp. 111-116.

Manuscript (Rouen)

1180 Paris, Bibliothèque Nationale, MS. lat. 1213, Ordin. Rothomagense, pp. 17-18 (15th century).

Text

1181 Officium Pastorum. In, Young, Karl. "A Contribution to the
History of Liturgical Drama at Rouen." Modern Philology, VI
(October, 1908), 214-216.

1182 [Officium Pastorum]. In, Young, Karl. "Officium Pastorum: A
Study of the Dramatic Developments within the Liturgy of
Christmas." Transactions of the Wisconsin Academy of
Sciences, Arts, and Letters, XVII, Part I (1914), 387-390.

ROUEN

Manuscript (Rouen)

1183 Rouen, Bibliothèque de la Ville, MS. 384 (olim Y. 110), Ordin.
ad usum cathedralis Rothomagensis, 22r - 23r (14th century).

Text

1184 [Officium Pastorum]. In, Gasté, A. Les Drames liturgiques de
la Cathédrale de Rouen. (Évreux, 1893), pp. 25-32.

1185 [Officium Pastorum]. In, Young, Karl. "Officium Pastorum: A
Study of the Dramatic Developments within the Liturgy of
Christmas." Transactions of the Wisconsin Academy of Sciences,

Arts, and Letters, XVII, Part I (1912), 330-333.

1186 [Officium Pastorum]. In, Adams, Joseph Q. Chief Pre-Shakespearean Dramas. (Boston, New York, 1924), pp. 25-27. [A
reprint of Gasté's text.]

1187 [Officium Pastorum]. In, Young, Karl. The Drama of the Medieval
Church. Vol. II. (Oxford, 1933), pp. 14-16.

1188 Office des Pasteurs. In, Du Méril, Edelstand. Origines latines
du théâtre moderne. (Paris, 1849), pp. 147-151. [From a MS.
at Rouen, No. 48 Y (14th century), and a MS. No. 50 Y (15th
century). Abridged in a MS. at Paris, Bibliothèque Nationale,
No. 1213, p. 17.]

b The Coming of the Magi

(Officium Stellae)

BESANCON
Text
1189 [Three Kings]. In, Crombach, H. Primitiae Gentium, seu Historia SS. Trium Regum Mägorum. (Cologne, 1654), pp. 732-
734. [The date of the manuscript used is uncertain.]

1190 [Three Kings]. In, Anz, H. Die lateinischen Magierspiele.
(Leipzig, 1905), pp. 142-145. [A reprint of Crombach's text.]

1191 [Three Kings]. In, Young, Karl. "La Procession des Trois Rois
at Besancon." The Romanic Review, IV (1913), 76-79. [A
reprint of Crombach's text.]

1192 [Three Kings]. In, Young, Karl. The Drama of the Medieval
Church. Vol. II. (Oxford, 1933), pp. 37-40.

BRUSSELS
Manuscript (Bilsen)
1193 Brussels, Bibliothèque des Bollandistes, MS. 299, Evangeliarium
Belisiense, fol. 179v - 180v (12th century).
Text
1194 [Officium Stellae]. In, Cahier, C., and A. Martin, Mélanges
d'Archéologie, d'Histoire et de Littérature, Vol. I. (Paris,
1847), pp. 258-260.

1195 [Officium Stellae]. In, Clément, F. Histoire générale de la Musiique religieuse. (Paris, 1861), pp. 115-118.

1196 [Officium Stellae]. In, Cohen, Gustave, and Karl Young. "The
Officium Stellae from Bilsen." Romania, XLIV (1916-1917),
359-368.

1197 [Officium Stellae]. In, Gessler, J. Le Drame liturgique de
Munsterbilsen. (Antwerp, 1928), pp. 19-30.

1198 Ordo [Stelle]. In, Young, Karl. The Drama of the Medieval
Church. Vol. II. (Oxford, 1933), pp. 75-80.

1199 L'Office de l'étoile. In, Cohen, Gustave. Anthologie du drame
liturgique en France au moyen-âge. (Paris, 1955), pp. 137-153.

EINSIEDELN
Manuscript
1200 Einsiedeln, Stiftsbibliothek, MS. 366 (olim 179), Fragmenta
liturgica, p. 53 (11th - 12th century). [A fragment].
Text
1201 [Officium Stellae]. In, Pilger, VIII (1849), 401-403.

1202 [Officium Stellae]. In, Schubiger, A. Musikalische Spicilegien.
(Berlin, 1876), pp. 45-46.

1203 [Officium Stellae]. In, Anz, H. Die lateinischen Magierspiele.
(Leipzig, 1905), pp. 152-153.

1204 [Officium Stellae]. In, Young, Karl. The Drama of the Medieval
Church. Vol. II. (Oxford, 1933), pp. 447-448.

LIMOGES
Text
1205 [Office des Mages]. In, Martene, E. De Antiquis Ecclesiae
Ritibus. Vol. III. (Venice, 1788), p. 44. [From an "ordinarium
ecclesie Lemovicensis," of uncertain date.]

1206 [Office des Mages]. In, Daniel, H. A. Codex Liturgicus Ecclesiae
Universae in epitomen redactus. Vol. I. (Leipzig, 1847), pp.
128-129. [A reprint of Martene's text.]

1207 Office des Mages. In, Du Méril, Édélstand. Origines latines du
théâtre moderne. (Paris, 1849), pp. 151-153. [A reprint of
Martene's text.]

1208 [Office des Mages]. In, Anz, H. Die lateinischen Magicrspiele.
      (Leipzig, 1905), pp. 140-141. [A reprint of Martene's text.]

1209 [Office des Mages]. In, Böhme, M. Das lateinische Weihnacht-
      spiel. (Leipzig, 1917), pp. 48-49. [A reprint of Martene's
      text.]

1210 [Office des Mages]. In, Young, Karl. The Drama of the Medieval
      Church. Vol. II. (Oxford, 1933), pp. 34-35.

LONDON

Manuscript (Strassburg)

1211 London, British Museum, Additional MS. 23922, Lib. resp.
      Argentoratensis, fol. 8v - 11r (13th century).

Text

1212 [Officium Stellae]. In, Birch, W. de G., Transactions of the
      Royal Society of Literature, 2d ser., X (1874), 413-416.

1213 [Officium Stellae]. In, Lange, Carl., Zeitschrift für deutsches
      Altertum, XXXII (1888), 413-415.

1214 [Officium Stellae]. In, Wilmart, A., ed. L'ancien Cantatorium
      de l'Église de Strasbourg: Manuscrit additionnel 23922 du
      Musée Britannique ... avec un Mémoire de M. l'Abbé J.
      Walter. (Colmar, 1928), pp. 8-10.

1215 [Officium Stellae]. In, Young, Karl. The Drama of the Medieval
      Church. Vol. II. (Oxford, 1933), pp. 64-66.

MADRID

Manuscript (Sicily)

1216 Madrid, Biblioteca Nacional, MS. 289 (olim C. 153), Trop. ad
      usum ecclesiae Siculorum, fol. 107v - 110r (12th century).

Text

1217 [Officium Stellae]. In, Young, Karl. "Some Texts of Liturgical
      Plays." Publications of the Modern Language Association,
      XXIV (June, 1909), 325-329.

1218 [Officium Stellae]. In, Bartholomaeis, V. De. Le Origini della
      Poesia drammatica italiana. (Bologna, [1924], pp. 528-530.
      [A reprint of Young's 1909 text.]

1219 [Officium Stellae]. In, Beeson, C. H. A Primer of Medieval
      Latin. (Chicago, [1925]), pp. 202-204. [A reprint of Young's
      1909 text.]

1220 [Officium Stellae]. In, Young, Karl. The Drama of the Medieval
Church. Vol. II. (Oxford, 1933), pp. 59-62.

MONTPELLIER

Manuscript (Rouen)

1221 Montpellier, Bibliothèque de la Faculté de Médecine, MS. H.
304, Miscellanea ecclesiastica, fol. 41v - 42v (12th century).

Text

1222 [Officium Stellae]. In, Gasté, A. Les Drames liturgiques de la
Cathédrale de Rouen. (Évreux, 1893), pp. 53-57. [Extracts from
the play].

1223 [Officium Stellae]. In, Young, Karl. "A Contribution to the History
of Liturgical Drama at Rouen." Modern Philology, VI (October, 1908), 208-211.

1224 [Officium Stellae]. In, Young, Karl. The Drama of the Medieval
Church. Vol. II. (Oxford, 1933), pp. 68-72.

1225 Adoration des Mages. In, Cohen, Gustave. Anthologie du drame
liturgie en France au moyen-âge. (Paris, 1955), pp. 171-184.

MUNICH

Manuscript (Freising)

1226 Munich, Staatsbibliothek, MS. lat. 6264a, Miscellanea Frisin-
gensia, fol. 1r (11th century).

Text

1227 Mystère de l'adoration des Mages. In, Du Méril, Édelstand.
Origines latines du théâtre moderne. (Paris, 1849), pp. 156-
162.

1228 Herodes sive Magorum adoratio. In, Weinhold, Karl. Weihnacht-
Spiele und Lieder aus Süddeutschland und Schlesien. (Graz,
1870), pp. 56-61.

1229 [Officium Stellae]. In, Wilken, E. Geschichte der geistlichen
Spiele in Deutschland. (Göttingen, 1872), pp. 6-9.

Manuscript (Freising)

1230 Munich, Staatsbibliothek, MS. lat. 6264a, Miscellanea Frisin-
gensia, fol. 1r (11th century).

Text

1231 [Officium Stellae]. In, Davidson, C. Studies in the English
Mystery Plays. (New Haven, 1892), pp. 50-64. [Based upon
the texts by Du Méril and Weinhold.]

1232 [Officium Stellae]. In, Anz, H. Die lateinischen Magierspiele.
       [Leipzig, 1905), pp. 154-158.

1233 [Officium Stellae]. In, Young, Karl. The Drama of the Medieval
       Church. Vol. II. (Oxford, 1933), pp. 93-97.
                                    Manuscript
1234 Munich, Staatsbibliothek, MS. lat. 14477, fol. 1r - 1v (12th
       century). [A mere fragment. The transcript was found among
       the papers of Wilhelm Meyer.]
                                      Text
1235 [Officium Stellae]. In, Young, Karl. The Drama of the Medieval
       Church. Vol. II. (Oxford, 1933), p. 445. [See the note by
       Young regarding a fourth fragment.]

ORLEANS
                         Manuscript (St. Benoît-sur-Loire)
1236 Orleans, Bibliothèque de la Ville, MS. 201 (olim 178), Miscellanea
       Floriacensia, pp. 205-214 (13th century).
                                      Text
1237 [Officium Stellae]. In, Mélanges des Bibliophiles francais. Vol.
       VII. (Paris, 1831-1832), pp. 133-144. [The MS. text has been
       translated into modern French by P. Piolin in, Le Théâtre
       chrétien dans le Maine au cours du Moyen Age. (Mammers,
       1892), pp. 21-32.]

1238 Herodes, sive Magorum adoratio. In, Wright, Thomas. Early
       Mysteries and Other Latin Poems of the Twelfth and Thirteenth
       Centuries. (London, Paris, Leipzig, 1838), pp. 23-28.

1239 Adoration des Mages. In, Du Méril, Édélstand. Origines latines
       du théâtre moderne. (Paris, 1849), pp. 162-171.

1240 [Officium Stellae]. In, Coussemaker, E. de. Drames liturgiques
       du moyen âge. (Rennes, 1860), pp. 143-165. [Coussemaker
       includes the music.]

1241 [Officium Stellae]. In, Davidson, C. Studies in the English Mys-
       tery Plays. (New Haven, 1892), pp. 51-65. [A reprint of
       Wright's text.]

1242 [Officium Stellae]. In, Adams, Joseph Q. Chief Pre-Shake-
       spearean Dramas. (Boston, New York, 1924), pp. 32-40.
       [A reprint of Coussemaker's text.]

1243 [Officium Stellae]. In, Young, Karl. The Drama of the Medieval
       Church. Vol. II. (Oxford, 1933), pp. 84-89.

1244 Adoration des Mages de l'Abbaye de Fleury-sur-Loire. In, Cohen, Gustave. Anthologie du drame liturgie en France au moyen-âge. (Paris, 1955), pp. 154-157.

PARIS

Manuscript (Rouen)

1245 Paris, Bibliothèque Nationale, MS. lat. 904, Grad. Rathomagense, fol. 28v - 30r (13th century).

Text

1246 [Officium Stellae]. In, Coussemaker, E. de. Drames liturgiques du moyen âge. (Rennes, 1860), pp. 242-249.

1247 [Officium Stellae]. In, Clément, F. Histoire générale de la Musique religieuse. (Paris, 1861), pp. 107-113.

1248 [Officium Stellae]. In, Lorique, H., J. Pothier, and A. Collette. Le Graduel de l'Église cathédrale de Rouen au XIIIe Siècle. Vol. II. (Rouen, 1907). [Facsimile].

1249 [Officium Stellae]. In, Chasles, Madeleine. "Le Drame liturgique." Le Vie et les Arts liturgiques, III (1916-1917), 302-307. [Facsimiles and text.]

1250 Officium Stellae. In, Young, Karl. The Drama of the Medieval Church. Vol. II. (Oxford, 1933), pp. 436-437.

Manuscript (France)

1251 Paris, Bibliothèque Nationale, MS. lat. 1152, (10th or 11th century). [On the upper half of a flyleaf at the end of the volume. A mere fragment.]

Text

1252 [Officium Stellae]. In, Bibliothèque de l'Ecole des Chartes, XXXIV (1873), 657-658. [Merely a fragment. Anonymous edition.]

1253 [Officium Stellae]. In, Young, Karl. The Drama of the Medieval Church. Vol. II. (Oxford, 1933), p. 443. [Merely a fragment].

Manuscript (Rouen)

1254 Paris, Bibliothèque Nationale, MS. lat. 1213, Ordin. Rothomagense, pp. 34-35 (15th century).

Text

1255 [Officium Stellae]. In, Young, Karl. "A Contribution to the History of Liturgical Drama at Rouen." Modern Philology, VI (1908-1909), 220-221.

1256 [Officium Stellae]. In, Young, Karl. The Drama of the Medieval Church. Vol. II. (Oxford, 1933), pp. 437-438. [With variants

from Rouen, MS. 382 (Y. 108), fol. 35v - 36r.]
Manuscript (Nevers)
1257 Paris, Bibliothèque Mazarine, MS. 1708, Lib. resp. Niver-
    nensis, fol. 81v (11th century).
Text
1258 [Officium Stellae]. In, Young, Karl. "Some Texts of Liturgical
    Plays." Publications of the Modern Language Association,
    XXIV (June, 1909), 296-297.

1259 [Officium Stellae]. In, Young, Karl. The Drama of the Medieval
    Church. Vol. II. (Oxford, 1933), pp. 50-51.
Manuscript (Nevers)
1260 Paris, Bibliothèque Nationale, MS. lat. 9449, Trop. Niver-
    nense, fol. 17v - 18r (11th century).
Text
1261 [Officium Stellae]. In, Delisle, L., Romania, IV (1875), 2-3.

1262 [Officium Stellae]. In, Chasles, Madeleine. "Le Drame liturgique."
    La Vie et les Arts liturgiques, III (1916-1917), 259-261.

1263 Versus Ad Stellam Faciendam. In, Young, Karl. The Drama of
    the Medieval Church. Vol. II. (Oxford, 1933), p. 439.
Manuscript (Compiègne)
1264 Paris, Bibliothèque Nationale, MS. lat. 16819, Lectionarium
    Compendiense, fol. 49r - 49v (11th century).
Text
1265 [Officium Stellae]. In, Hartmann, K. A. Martin. Ueber das
    altspanische Dreikönigsspiel. (Boutzen, 1879), pp. 43-46.

1266 [Officium Stellae]. In, Young, Karl. The Drama of the Medieval
    Church. Vol. II. (Oxford, 1933), pp. 54-56.
Manuscript (Nevers)
1267 Paris, Bibliothèque Nationale, Nouvelles Acquisitions, MS. lat.
    1235, Grad.-Trop. Nivernense, fol. 198r - 199v (12th
    century).
Text
1268 [Officium Stellae]. In, Delisle, L., Romania, IV (1875), 3-6.
Manuscript (Nevers)
1269 Paris, Bibliothèque Nationale, Nouvelles Acquisitions, MS. lat.
    1235, Grad.-Trop. Nivernense, fol. 198r - 199v (12th cen-
    tury).
Text
1270 [Officium Stellae]. In, Blume, C., ed. Analecta Hymnica Medii
    Aevi. Vol. 49. (Leipzig, 1886 -), pp. 12-13.

1271 [Officium Stellae]. In, Reiners, A. Unbekannte Tropen-Gesange des feierlichen Messamtes im Mittelalter. (Luxemburg, 1887), p. 33. [In part].

1272 [Officium Stellae]. In, Anz, H. Die lateinischen Magierspiele. (Leipzig, 1905), pp. 146-147. [Reprinted from Delisle's text.]

1273 [Officium Stellae]. In, Chasles, Madeleine. "Le Drame liturgique." La Vie et les Arts liturgiques, III (1916-1917), 259-261. [In part].

1274 [Officium Stellae]. In, Young, Karl. The Drama of the Medieval Church. Vol. II. (Oxford, 1933), pp. 440-441.

ROME

Manuscript (Malmédy, Belgium)

1275 Rome, Bibl. Vatic., MS. lat. 8552, fol. 1v (in a volume containing a version of Josepephus' Antiquitates Judaicae. A mere fragment.]

Text

1276 [Officium Stellae]. In, Young, Karl. "A New Text of the Officium Stellae." Modern Language Notes, XXVII (March, 1912), 70-71.

1277 [Officium Stellae]. In, Young, Karl. The Drama of the Medieval Church. Vol. II. (Oxford, 1933), pp. 443-445.

ROUEN

Manuscript

1278 Rouen, Bibliothèque de la Ville, MS. 222 (A. 551), Process. Rothomagense, fol. 4r - 4v (13th century).

Text

1279 [Officium Stellae]. In, Young, Karl. "A Contribution to the History of Liturgical Drama at Rouen." Modern Philology, VI (1908-1909), 212.

1280 [Officium Stellae]. In, Young, Karl. The Drama of the Medieval Church. Vol. II. (Oxford, 1933), p. 438. [Fragment]

Manuscript

1281 Rouen, Bibliothèque de la Ville, MS. 384 (olim Y. 110), Ordin. Rothomagense, fol. 38v - 39v (14th century).

Text

1282 Officium Stellae. In, Gasté, Armand. Les Drames liturgiques de la Cathédrale de Rouen. (Evreux, 1893), pp. 49-52.

1283 [Officium Stellae]. In, Böhme, M. Das lateinische Weihnachtspiel. (Leipzig, 1917), pp. 58-60. [A reprint of Gasté's
text.]

1284 [Officium Stellae]. In, Adams, Joseph Q. Chief Pre-Shakespearean
Dramas. (Boston, New York, 1924), pp. 28-31. [A reprint of
Gasté's text.]

1285 Officium Regum Trium Secundum Usum Rothomagensem. In,
Young, Karl. The Drama of the Medieval Church. Vol. II.
(Oxford, 1933), pp. 43-45. [Young says that he completes the
speeches and liturgical forms from the Officium Stellae in the
Rouen gradual of the thirteenth century (Paris, Bibl. Nat., MS.
lat. 904).

Other Texts

1286 Officium Stellae. In, Joannis Abrincensis Episcopi deinde Roto-
mangensis Archiepiscopi Liber Rotomangensis Archiepiscopi
Liber De Officiis Ecclesiasticis, Notis D. Johannis Prevotii.
(Rotomagi, 1679), pp. 206-210.

1287 Officium Stellae, Seu Trium Regum. In, Migne, J. P. Patrologiae
Cursus Completus (1856), Vol. 147, Cols. 135-140.

1288 Text des altspanischen Dreikönigsspiels. In, Hartmann, K. A.
Martin. Ueber das altspanishe Dreikönigsspiel. (Boutzen,
1879), pp. 46-51.

1289 Das Tegernseer Drama. In, Froning, R. Das Drama des Mittelalters. Vol. I. (Stuttgart, 1891), pp. 206-224.

    c The Slaughter of the Innocents

    (Ordo Rachelis, Interfectio Puerorum, Officium Infantum,
    Officium Stellae)

LAON

Manuscript

1290 Laon, Bibliothèque de la Ville, MS. 263, Troparium-Hymn-
arium Laudunense, fol. 149r - 151r (13th century).

Text

1291 Ordo Stelle. In, Chevalier, Ulysse. Ordinaires de L'Église
Cathédrale de Laon (XIIe et XIIIe siècles) suivis de deux
Mystères liturgiques publiées d'après les manuscrits
originaux. (Paris, 1897), pp. 389-394.

1292 [Ordo Stelle]. In, Young, Karl. Ordo Rachelis. (Madison, 1919), pp. 13-17.

1293 Ordo Stelle. In, Young, Karl. The Drama of the Medieval Church. Vol. II. (Oxford, 1933), pp. 103-106.

MUNICH

Manuscript (Freising)

1294 Munich, Staatsbibliothek, MS. lat. 6264, Lectionarium Frisingense, fol. 27v (11th - 12th century).

Text

1295 Rachel. In, Du Méril, Édélstand. Origines latines du théâtre moderne. (Paris, 1849), pp. 171-175.

1296 Ordo Rachelis. In, Weinhold, Karl. Weihnacht-Spiele und Lieder aus Süddeutschland und Schlesien. (Graz, 1870), pp. 62-65.

1297 Ordo Rachelis. In, Froning, R. Das Drama des Mittelalters. Vol. III. (Stuttgart, 1891), pp. 871-874. [Reprints Weinhold's text.]

1298 Ordo Rachelis. In, Young, Karl. Ordo Rachelis. (Madison, 1919), pp. 42-45.

1299 Ordo Rachelis. In, Young, Karl. The Drama of the Medieval Church. Vol. II. (Oxford, 1933), pp. 117-120.

ORLEANS

Manuscript (Fleury)

1300 Orleans, Bibliothèque de la Ville, MS. 201 (olim 178), Miscellanea Floriacensia, pp. 214-220 (13th century).

Text

1301 [Interfectio Puerorum]. In, Mélanges des Bibliophiles francais. Vol. VII. (Paris, 1831-1832), pp. 147-154. [Ordo Rachelis].

1302 Interfectio Puerorum. In, Wright, Thomas, ed. Early Mysteries and Other Latin Poems of the Twelfth and Thirteenth Centuries. (London, Paris, Leipzig, 1838), pp. 29-31. [Ordo Rachelis].

1303 Massacre des saints Innocents. In, Du Méril, Édélstand. Origines latines du théâtre moderne. (Paris, 1849), pp. 175-179. [Ordo Rachelis].

1304 Le Massacre des Innocents. In, Coussemaker, E. de. Drames liturgiques du moyen âge. (Rennes, 1860), pp. 166-167.

1305 [Ordo Stelle]. In, Young, Karl. Ordo Rachelis. (Madisoн, 1919),
      pp. 27-31.

1306 Ordo Rachelis. In, Young, Karl. The Drama of the Medieval
      Church. Vol. II. (Oxford, 1933), pp. 110-113.

1307 La Plainte de Rachel. Fête des Innocents. In, Cohen, Gustave.
      Anthologie du drame liturgie en France au moyen-âge. (Paris,
      1955), pp. 194-204.

PARIS
                           Manuscript (St. Martial, Limoges)
1308 Paris, Bibliothèque Nationale, MS. lat. 1139, Trop. Martialense,
      fol. 32v - 33r (11th - 12th century).
                                   Text
1309 [Officium Stellae]. In, Magnin, C., Journal des Savants (1846), 93.
      [In a review of L. J. N. Monmerqué and F. Michel's work,
      Théâtre francais au Moyen Âge (Paris, 1839).]

1310 [Officium Stellae]. In, Du Méril, Édélstand. Origines latines du
      théâtre moderne. (Paris, 1849), p. 46. [Fragmentary text].

1311 [Officium Stellae]. In, Coussemaker, E. de. Histoire de l'Har-
      monie au Moyen Âge. (Paris, 1852), p. 128.

1312 [Officium Stellae]. In, Gautier, L. Histoire de la Poèsie litur-
      gique au Moyen Âge. Les Tropes. (Paris, 1886), p. 168.

1313 [Officium Stellae]. In, Anz, H. Die lateinischen Magierspiele.
      (Leipzig, 1905), pp. 72-73. [A reprint of Gautier's text.]

1314 [Officium Stellae]. In, Chasles, Madeleine. "Le drame liturgi-
      que." La Vie et les Arts liturgiques, III (1916-1917), 407.

1315 [Officium Stellae]. In, Young, Karl. Ordo Rachelis. (Madison,
      1919), pp. 24-25.

1316 [Officium Stellae]. In, Young, Karl. The Drama of the Medieval
      Church. Vol. II. (Oxford, 1933), p. 109.
                             Manuscript (Rouen)
1317 Paris, Bibliothèque Nationale, MS. lat. 1213, Ordin. Rothom-
      agense, pp. 25-27 (15th century).
                                   Text
1318 Officium Infantum. In, Young, Karl. "A Contribution to the
      History of Liturgical Drama at Rouen." Modern Philology,

VI (October, 1908), 216-220.

ROUEN

Manuscript
1319 Rouen, Bibliothèque de la Ville, MS. 384 (olim Y 110), Ordin. Rothomagense, fol. 28.

Text
1320 Officium Infantum. In, Gasté, Armand. Les Drames liturgiques de la Cathédrale de Rouen. (Evreux, 1893), 35-48.

1321 Officium Infantum. In, Joannis Abrincensis Episcopi Abrincensis Episcopi deinde Rotomangensis Archiepiscopi Liber De Officiis Ecclesiasticis, Notis D. Johannis Prevotii. (Rotomagi, 1679), pp. 202-205.

1322 Officium Pastorum. In, Migne, J. P. Patriologiae Cursus Completus (1856), Vol. 147. Cols. 135-136.

d The Procession of the Prophets

(Ordo Prophetarum)

EINSIEDELN

Manuscript
1323 Einsiedeln, Stiftsbibliothek, MS. 366, Fragmenta liturgica, pp. 53-55 (11th - 12th century). [Fragment].

Text
1324 [Ordo Prophetarum]. In, Mone, F. J. Shauspiele des Mittelalters. Vol. I. (Karlsruhe, 1846), pp. 10-12.

1325 [Ordo Prophetarum]. In, Schubiger, A. Musikalische Spicilegien. (Berlin, 1876), pp. 46-47.

1326 [Ordo Prophetarum]. In, Young, Karl. "Ordo Prophetarum." Transactions of the Wisconsin Academy of Sciences, Arts, and Letters, XX (1922), 72-74.

LAON

Manuscript
1327 Laon, Bibliothèque de la Ville, MS. 263, Troparium-Hymn-arium Lauduense, fol. 147v - 149r (13th century).

Text
1328 Mystères de Prophètes du Christ (Ordo Prophetarum). In, Chevalier, Ulysse. Ordinaires de l'Eglise Cathédrale de Laon (XIIe et XIIIe siècles) suivis de deux Mystères

liturgiques publies les manuscrits originaux. (Paris, 1897), pp. 385-389.

1329 Ordo Prophetarum. In, Chasles, Madeleine. "Le Drame liturgique." La Vie et les Arts liturgiques, III (1916-1917), 129-134. [Reprints Chevalier's text.]

1330 Ordo Prophetarum. In, Young, Karl. "Ordo Prophetarum." Transactions of the Wisconsin Academy of Sciences, Arts, and Letters, XX (1921), 40-45.

1331 Ordo Prophetarum. In, Adams, Joseph Q. Chief Pre-Shakespearean Dramas. (Boston, New York, 1924), pp. 41-48. [Reprints Chevalier's text.]

1332 Ordo Prophetarum. In, Young, Karl. The Drama of the Medieval Church. Vol. II. (Oxford, 1933), pp. 145-150.

PARIS

Manuscript (St. Martial, Limoges)
1333 Paris, Bibliothèque Nationale, MS. lat. 1139, Trop. Martialense, fol. 55v - 58r (11th - 12th century).

Text
1334 [Ordo Prophetarum]. In, Wright, T. Early Mysteries and Other Latin Poems of the Twelfth and Thirteenth Centuries. (London, 1838), 60-62.

1335 [Ordo Prophetarum]. In, Magnin, C., Journal des Savants (1846), pp. 88-93. [A review of Théâtre francais au Moyen Âge, by L. J. N. Monmerqué, and F. Michel.]

1336 Mystère des Prophètes du Christ. In, Du Méril, Édélstand. Origines latines du théâtre moderne. (Paris, 1849), pp. 179-187.

1337 Les Prophètes du Christ. In, Coussemaker, E. de. Drames liturgiques du moyen âge. (Rennes, 1860), pp. 11-20.

1338 [Ordo Prophetarum]. In, Monmerqué, L. J. N., and F. Michel. Théâtre francais au Moyen Âge. (Paris, 1865), pp. 6-9.

1339 Ordo Prophetarum. In, Young, Karl. "Ordo Prophetarum." Transactions of the Wisconsin Academy of Sciences, Arts, and Letters, XX (1921), 25-31.

1340 [Ordo Prophetarum]. In, Young, Karl. The Drama of the Medieval
   Church. Vol. II. (Oxford, 1933), pp. 138-143.

ROUEN

Manuscript

1341 Rouen, Bibliothèque de la Ville, MS. 384 (olim Y. 110), Ordin.
   Rothomagense, fol. 33r - 35r (14th century).

Text

1342 [Ordo Processionis Asinorum]. In, Gasté, Armand, ed. Les
   Drames liturgiques de la Cathédrale de Rouen... (Evreux,
   1893), pp. 4-20. [Has some of the variants from Rouen,
   Bibliothèque de la Ville, MS. 382.]

1343 [Ordo Processionis Asinorum]. In, Young, Karl. "Ordo Prophetarum." Transactions of the Wisconsin Academy of Sciences,
   Arts, and Letters, XX (1922), 50-63. [Edited from MS. 384, MS.
   382, and from the text copied into MS. lat. 1232, of the Bibliothèque Nationale, Paris, fol. 26r - 27r (in a hand probably
   of the seventeenth century).]

1344 Ordo Processionis Asinorum Secundum Rothomagensem Vsum.
   In, Young, Karl. The Drama of the Medieval Church. Vol. II.
   (Oxford, 1933), pp. 154-165.

1345 Processione des Prophètes ou Fête de l'ane. In, Cohen, Gustave.
   Anthologie du drame liturgie en France au moyen-âge. (Paris,
   1955), pp. 120-136.

SALERNO

Text

1346 [Lectio Prophetarum]. In, Young, Karl. "Ordo Prophetarum."
   Transactions of the Wisconsin Academy of Sciences, Arts,
   and Letters, XX (1921), pp. 18-22. [From the British Museum
   copy of the 1594 Naples text.]

1347 [Lectio Prophetarum]. In, Officia propria Festorum Salernitanae
   Ecclesiae. (Naples, 1594), pp. 75-79.

1348 [Lectio Prophetarum]. In, Young, Karl. The Drama of the Medieval
   Church. Vol. II. (Oxford, 1933), pp. 133-137.

e Benedictbeuren Christmas Play

MUNICH

Manuscript

1349 Munich, Staatsbibliothek, MS. lat. 4660, Carmina Burana, fol.
99r - 104v (13th century).

Text

1350 [Benediktbeuern Christmas Play]. In, Du Méril, Edélstand. Les
Origines latines du théâtre moderne. (Paris, 1849), pp. 187-
206.

1351 [Benedicktbeuern Christmas Play]. In, Schmeller, J. A. Carmina
Burana. (Breslau, 1883), pp. 80-85.

1352 [Benediktbeuern Christmas Play]. In, Froning, Richard. Das
Drama des Mittelalters. (Stuttgart, 1891-1893), pp. 877-896.

1353 [Benedicktbeuern Christmas Play]. In, Young, Karl. The Drama
of the Medieval Church. Vol. II. (Oxford, 1933), pp. 172-190.

1354 Das Benediktbeuerer Weinachtsspiel (Aus den Carmina Burana).
In, Langosch, Karl. Geistliche Spiele. Lateinische Dramen
des Mittelalters mit deutschen Versen. (Basel, Stuttgart,
1957), pp. 131-177.

f Ludus de Rege Aegypti

Manuscript

1355 Munich, Staatsbibliothek, MS. lat. 4660, Carmina Burana, fol.
105r - 106v (13th century). [Fragment].

Text

1356 [Ludus de Rege Aegypti]. In, Du Méril, Edélstand. Les Origines
latines du théâtre moderne. (Paris, 1849), pp. 187-206.

1357 [Ludus de Rege Aegypti]. In, Schmeller, J. A. Carmina Burana.
(Breslau, 1883), pp. 91-95.

1358 [Ludus de Rege Aegypti]. In, Froning, Richard. Das Drama des
Mittelalters. (Stuttgart, 1891-1893), pp. 896-901.

1359 [Ludus de Rege Aegypti]. In, Young, Karl. The Drama of the
Medieval Church. Vol. II. (Oxford, 1933), pp. 463-468.

3 Plays Based on Old Testament Subjects

a Isaac and Rebecca

Manuscript

1360 Chorherrenstift at Vorau, Steiermark, Austria, MS. 223 (12th century). [Fragment].

Text

1361 Ordo de Ysaac et Rebecca et Filiis eorum Recitandus. Published by Otakar Kernstock, in Anzeiger für Kunde der deutschen Vorzeit, No. 6 (1877), col. 170-173.

1362 Ordo de Ysaac et Rebecca et Filiis eorum Recitandus. In, Young, Karl. The Drama of the Medieval Church. Vol. II. (Oxford, 1933), pp. 259-264.

b Joseph

Manuscript (Laon)

1363 Laon, Bibliothèque de la Ville, MS. 263, Troparium-Hymn-arium Laudunense, fol. 151r - 153v (13th century).

Text

1364 Ordo Joseph. In, Young, Karl. "A Liturgical Play of Joseph and His Brethren." Modern Language Notes, XXVI (February, 1911), 33-37.

1365 Ordo Ioseph. In, Young, Karl. The Drama of the Medieval Church. Vol. II. (Oxford, 1933), pp. 267-274.

c Daniel

BEAUVAIS

Manuscript

1366 London, British Museum, MS. Egerton 2615, Officium Cir-cumcisionis et Danielis Ludus, fol. 95r - 108r (12th century).

Text

1367 Daniel. In, Danjou, F. "Le Théâtre religieux et populaire au XIIIe Siècle: Le Mystère de Daniel." Revue de la Musique religieuse, populaire et classique, IV (1848), 65-78. [Following page 96 of the volume is the Daniel play, numbered separately from pages 1-32.]

1368 Daniel. In, Coussemaker, E. de. Drames liturgiques du moyen âge. (Rennes, 1860), pp. 49-82. [Words and music].

1369 Incipit Danielis Ludus. In, Young, Karl. The Drama of the

Medieval Church. Vol. II. (Oxford, 1933), pp. 290-301.

1370　Daniel. In, Cohen, Gustave. Anthologie du drame liturgie en France au moyen-âge. (Paris, 1955), pp. 205-235.

1371　The Play of Daniel. [New York, 1958?]. 16 leaves Typescript libretto. [Produced at the Chapel of the Intercession, New York, Jan. 5, 1959.] Text at the New York Public Library.

1372　The Play of Daniel, a Mediaeval Liturgical Drama, Transcribed and Edited by W. L. Smoldon. London: The Plaisong and Mediaeval Music Society, 1960. 41 pp.

HILARY
Manuscript
1373　Paris, Bibliothèque Nationale, MS. lat. 11331, Hilarii Versus et Ludi, fol. 12v - 16r (12th century).
Text
1374　Historia De Daniel Representanda. In, Champollion-Figeac, J. J. Hilarii. Versus et Ludi. (Lutetiae Parisiorum, 1838), pp. 43-60.

1375　Mystère de Daniel. In, Du Méril, Édélstand. Origines latines du théâtre moderne. (Paris, 1849), pp. 241-254.

1376　[Historia de Daniel Representanda]. In, Fuller, John Bernard, ed. Hilarii Versus et Ludi. (New York, [c. 1929]), pp. 98-117.

1377　[H]istoria de Daniel Representanda. In, Young, Karl. The Drama of the Medieval Church. Vol. II. (Oxford, 1933), pp. 276-286.

4　Plays Based on New Testament Subjects

a　The Annunciation
Manuscript
1378　Cividale, Reale Museo Archeologico, MS. CII, Process. Cividalense, fol. 69v - 71r (14th century).
Text
1379　L'Annonciation. In, Coussemaker, E. de. Drames liturgiques du moyen âge. (Rennes, 1860), pp. 280-284. [Latin words, and music].

1380　In Annunciatione beate Marie. In, Bartholomaeis, V. de. Il Teatro abruzzese del Medio Evo. (Bologna, [1924]), p. 531.

1381 In Annunciatione Beate Marie Virginis Representatio. In, Young,
      Karl. The Drama of the Medieval Church. Vol. II. (Oxford,
      1933), pp. 247-250.

      b The Wise and Foolish Virgins

         (Sponsus)

                          Manuscript (Limoges)
1382 Paris, Bibliothèque Nationale, MS. lat. 1139, Trop. Martialense,
      fol. 53r - 55v (11th - 12th century).
                                Text
1383 Mysterium Fatuarum Virginum. In, Wright, Thomas. ed. Early
      Mysteries and Other Latin Poems of the Twelfth and Thirteenth
      Centuries. (London, Paris, Leipzig, 1838), pp. 55-62.

1384 Mystère des Vierges sages et des Vierges folles. In, Du Méril,
      Édélstand. Origines latines du théâtre moderne. (Paris,
      1849), 233-237.

1385 Les Vierges Sages et Les Vierges Folles. In, Coussemaker, E. de.
      Drames liturgiques du moyen âge. (Rennes, 1860), pp. 1-10.
      [Words and music].

1386 Sponsus. In, Foerster, Wendelin, and Eduard Koschwitz. Alt-
      französisches Übungsbuch, zum Gegrauch bei Vorlesungen
      und Seminarübungen. (Heilbronn, 1884-1886), col. 93-100.

1387 [Sponsus]. In, Cloetta, W. "Le Mystère de l'Epoux." Romania,
      XXII (1893), 177-229.

1388 Sponsus. In, Foerster, Wendelin, and Eduard Koschwitz. Alt-
      französisches Übungsbuch zum Gebrauch bei Vorlesungen
      und seminarübungen. (Leipzig, 1902), col. 91-98.

1389 [Sponsus]. In, Monaci, E. Facsimili di Documenti per la Storia
      delle Lingue e delle Letterature romanze. (Rome, [1910]),
      plates 37-42. [Facsimile].

1390 [Sponsus]. In, Koschwitz, E. Les plus anciens Monuments de la
      Langue francaise: Textes diplomatiques. (Leipzig, 1913),
      pp. 48-53.

1391 Sponsus. In, Foerster, Wendelin, and Eduard Koschwitz. Alt-
      französisches Übungsbuch. 6th ed. by A. Hilka. (Leipzig,
      1921), cols. 91-98, 293-298.

1392 [Sponsus]. In, Thomas, L. P. "La Versification et les Lecons douteuses du Sponsus (Texte Roman)." <u>Romania,</u> LIII (1927), 43-81.

1393 [Sponsus]. In, Thomas, L. P. "Les Strophes et la Composition du Sponsus (Textes latin et roman)." <u>Romania,</u> LV (1929), 45-112.

1394 The Wise Virgins and the Foolish Virgins ... Written and Produced Probably About the Middle of the 12th Century. Translated Especially for This Work by Babette and Glen Hughes. In, Clark, B. H., ed. World Drama. Vol. I. (New York, 1933), pp. 322-324.

1395 Sponsus. In, Young, Karl. The Drama of the Medieval Church. Vol. II. (Oxford, 1933), pp. 362-364.

1396 Le Sponsus ou Drame de l'Epoux ou Drame des vierges sages et des vierges folles. In, Cohen, Gustave. Anthologie du drame liturgie en France au moyen-âge. (Paris, 1955), pp. 259-274.

   c The Raising of Lazarus

ORLEANS
                            Manuscript (Fleury)
1397 Orleans, Bibliothèque de la Ville, MS. 201 (olim 178), Miscellanea Floriacensia, pp. 233-243 (13th century).
                                 Text
1398 [Incipiun Uersus de Resuscitacione Lazari]. In, Mélanges des Bibliophiles francais. Vol. VII. (Paris, 1831-1832), pp. 197-213.

1399 Miraculum Resurrectionis B. Lazari. In, Wright, Thomas, ed. Early Mysteries, and Other Latin Poems of the Twelfth and Thirteenth Centuries. (London, 1838), pp. 45-53.

1400 Mystère De La Résurrection Du Lazare. In, Du Méril, Édélstand. Les Origines latines du théâtre moderne. (Paris, 1849), pp. 213-225.

1401 [La Resurrection De Lazare.] In, Coussemaker, Edmond de, ed. Drames liturgiques du moyen âge. (Rennes, 1860), pp. 220-234.

1402 Incipiunt Uersus de Resuscitacione Lazari. In, Young, Karl. The

Drama of the Medieval Church. Vol. II. (Oxford, 1933), pp. 199-208.

Manuscript (Fleury)

1403 Orleans, Bibliothèque de la Ville, MS. 201 (olim 178), Miscellanea Floriacensia, pp. 233-243 (13th century).

Text

1404 La Résurrection de Lazare, de Fleury-sur-Loire. In, Cohen, Gustave. Anthologie du drame liturgique en France au moyen-âge. (Paris, 1955), pp. 70-91.

PARIS

Manuscript

1405 Paris, Bibliothèque Nationale, MS. lat. 11331, Hilarii Versus et Ludi, fol. 9r - 10v (13th century).

Text

1406 Suscitatio Lazari. In, Champollion-Figeac, J. J. Hilarii. Versus et Ludi. Paris, 1838), pp. 24-33.

1407 Suscitacio Lazari. In, Du Méril, Édélstand. Les Origines latines du théâtre moderne. (Paris, 1849), pp. 225-232.

1408 Suscitacio Lazari. In, Gaselee, S., ed. The Oxford Book of Medieval Latin Verse. (Oxford, 1928), pp. 99-106. [Reprints the text of Champollion-Figeac, with modifications.]

1409 Suscitacio Lazari. In, Fuller, John Bernard, ed. Hilarii Versus et Ludi. (New York, [c. 1929]), pp. 75-86.

1410 Suscitacio Lazari. In, Young, Karl. The Drama of the Medieval Church. Vol. II. (Oxford, 1933), pp. 212-218.

1411 La Résurrection de Lazare, par Hilaire. In, Cohen, Gustave. Anthologie du drame liturgique en France au moyen-âge. (Paris, 1955), pp. 92-106.

d Conversion of St. Paul

Manuscript (Fleury)

1412 Orleans, Bibliothèque de la Ville, MS. 201 (olim 178), Miscellanea Floriacensia, pp. 230-233 (13th century).

Text

1413 [Conversio Beati Pauli]. In, Mélanges des Bibliophiles francais. Vol. VII. (Paris, 1831-1832), pp. 189-194.

1414 Mysterium Conversionis Beati Pauli Apostoli. In, Wright, Thomas,

ed. Early Mysteries and Other Latin Poems of the Twelfth
and Thirteenth Centuries. (London, Paris, Leipzig, 1838),
pp. 42-44.

1415 Conversion de saint Paul. In, Du Méril, Edélstand. Origines
latines du théâtre moderne. (Paris, 1849), pp. 237-241.

1416 La Conversion de Saint Paul. In, Coussemaker, E. de. Drames
liturgiques du moyen âge. (Rennes, 1860), pp. 210-219.
[Latin text, with words and music.]

1417 The Conversion of St. Paul. In, Young, Karl. The Drama of the
Medieval Church. Vol. II. (Oxford, 1933), pp. 219-222.

e Antichrist

Manuscript (Tegernsee)
1418 Munich, Staatsbibliothek, MS. lat. 19411, Miscellanea Tegirin-
sensia, pp. 6-15 [old pagination]. (12th - 13th century).
Text
1419 Ludus Paschalis, de Adventu et interitu Antichrist. In, Pez,
Bernardo. Thesaurus Anecdotorum Novissimus. Tomi II,
Pars III. (Augusburg, 1721), cols. 185-196 [i.e., 200].

1420 Antichrist. In, Wright, T. The Chester Plays. Vol. II. (London,
1847). [Reprints the text of B. Pez, 1721.]

1421 Ludus Paschalis De Adventu et Interitu Antichrist. In scena
saeculo XII exhibitus. In, Migne, J. P. Patrologiae Cursus
Completus. Vol. 213. (1855), cols. 949-960.

1422 Zezschwitz, G. von. Vom römischen Kaisertum deutscher
Nation: ein mittelalterliches Drama. (Leipzig, 1877), pp.
217-241.

1423 [Antichrist]. In, Froning, R. Das Drama des Mittelalters.
(Stuttgart, [1891]), pp. 206-224.

1424 [Antichrist]. In, Meyer, W. Gesammelte Abhandlungen zur
mittellateinischen Rythmik. Vol. I. (Berlin, 1905), pp. 150-
170. [This edition supersedes his earlier one in 1882.]

1425 [Antichrist]. In, Wilhelm, F. Der Ludus de Antichristo. (Munich,
1912). (Münchener Texte, F. Wilhelm, i).

1426 Antichrist. In, Barrow, Sarah F., and W. H. Hulme. Antichrist
      and Adam. (Cleveland, 1925), pp. 15-32. [Translation into
      English.]

1427 [Antichrist]. In, Young, Karl. The Drama of the Medieval Church.
      Vol. II. (Oxford, 1933), pp. 371-387.

1428 Steigleder, Paul. Das Spiel vom Antichrist. Eine Geistesgechicht-
      liche Untersuchung. Würzburg-Aumühle: Konrad Triltsch ver-
      lag, 1938. [4], 79, [1] pp. (Bonner Beiträge zur deutschen
      Philologie, Hft. 6).

1429 Ludus de Antichristo. (Das Spiel vom deutschen Kaiser und vom
      Antichrist). In, Langosch, Karl. Geistliche Spiele. Latinische
      Dramen des Mittelalters mit deutschen Versen. (Basel, Stutt-
      gart, 1957), pp. 179-239.

1430 Wright, John, tr. The Play of Antichrist. With an Introduction.
      Toronto: Pontifical Institute of Mediaeval Studies, 1967.

  5 St. Nicholas Plays

    a The Dowry

       Tres Filiae

LONDON
                              Manuscript (Hildesheim)
1431 London, British Museum, Add. MS. 22414, Miscellanea Hildesi-
      ensia, fol. 3v - 4v (11th - 12th century).
                                   Text
1432 [Tres Filiae]. In, Dümmler, E. Zeitschrift für deutsche Alter-
      tums, XXXV (1891), 402-405.

1433 [Tres Filiae]. In, Young, Karl. The Drama of the Medieval
      Church. Vol. II. (Oxford, 1933), pp. 311-314.

ORLEANS
                               Manuscript (Fleury)
1434 Orleans, Bibliothèque de la Ville, MS. 201 (olim 178), Miscellanea
      Floriacensia, pp. 176-182 (13th century).
                                   Text
1435 Tres Filiae. In, Lebeuf, J. "Lettres d'un solitaire à M. D. L. R.
      au sujet des nouveaux livres sur les anciennes Représentations
      Théâtrales." Mercure de France, April, 1735, pp. 698-708.

[Partial text of the play.]

1436 [Tres Filiae]. In, Mélanges des Bibliophiles francais, Vol. VII.
     (Paris, 1831-1832), pp. 91-92.

1437 Primum Miraculum. In, Wright, Thomas, ed. Early Mysteries,
     and Other Latin Poems of the Twelfth and Thirteenth Centuries.
     (London, Paris, Leipzig, 1838), pp. 3-7.

1438 Miracle de saint Nicolas [Tres Filiae]. In, Du Méril, Edélstand.
     Origines latines du théâtre moderne. (Paris, 1849), pp. 254-
     262.

1439 Les Filles Dotées. Miracle de Saint Nicolas. In, Coussemaker, E.
     de. Drames liturgiques du moyen äge. (Rennes, 1860), pp. 83-
     99. [Words and Music].

1440 [Tres Filiae]. In, Young, Karl. The Drama of the Medieval
     Church. Vol. II. (Oxford, 1933), pp. 316-321.

1441 [Tres Filiae]. In, Albrecht, Otto E. Four Latin Plays of St.
     Nicholas from the 12th Century Fleury Play-book. (Phila-
     delphia, London, 1935), pp. 118-125.

1442 Tres Filiae. In, Langosch, Karl. Geistliche Spiele. Lateinische
     Dramen des Mittelalters mit deutschen Versen. (Basel,
     Stuttgart, 1957), pp. 91-97.

   b Three Clerks

      Tres Clerici

LONDON
                              Manuscript (Hildesheim)
1443 London, British Museum, Add. MS. 22414, Miscellanea Hilde-
     siensia, fol. 4r (11th - 12th century).
                                    Text
1444 [Tres Clerici]. In, Dümmler, E., Zeitschrift für deutsche
     Altertums, XXXV (1891), 405-407.

1445 [Tres Clerici]. In, Young, Karl. The Drama of the Medieval
     Church. Vol. II. (Oxford, 1933), pp. 325-327.

ORLEANS

Manuscript (Fleury)

1446 Orleans, Bibliothèque de la Ville, MS. 201 (olim 178), Miscellanea Floriacensia, pp. 183-187 (13th century).

Text

1447 Tres Clerici. In, Leubeuf, J. "Remarques envoyées d'Auxerre, sur les spectacles que les ecclésiastiques ou religieux donnoient anciennement au public hors le temps de l'office." Mercure de France, December, 1729, pp. 2981-2995. [Article reprinted in A. G. Boucher d'Argis, Variétes historiques, physoques et litteraires. (Paris, 1752), III, pp. 184-188; in J. L. d'Ortique, Dictionnaire liturgique ... (Paris, 1853), cols. 1393-1399.]

1448 [Tres Clerici]. In, Mélanges des Bibliophiles francais. Vol. VII. (Paris, 1831-1832), pp. 103-107.

1449 Secundum Miraculum [Tres Clerici]. In, Wright, Thomas, ed. Early Mysteries, and Other Latin Poems of the Twelfth and Thirteenth Centuries. (London, Paris, Leipzig, 1838), pp. 8-10.

1450 Miracle de saint Nicolas [Tres Clerici]. In, Du Méril, Edélstand. Origines latines du théâtre moderne. (Paris, 1849), pp. 262-266.

1451 Les Trois Clercs. In, Coussemaker, E. de. Drames liturgiques du moyen âge. (Rennes, 1860), pp. 100-108. [Words and music.]

1452 Tres Clerici. In, Gofflot, L. V. Le Théâtre au Collège du moyen âge à nos jours. (Paris, 1907), pp. 16-20. [Translation].

1453 Tres Clerici. In, Adams, Joseph Q., ed. Chief Pre-Shakespearean Dramas. (Boston, New York, 1924), pp. 59-62. [Reprints Coussemaker's text.]

1454 [Tres Clerici]. In, Young, Karl. The Drama of the Medieval Church. Vol. II. (Oxford, 1933), pp. 330-332.

1455 [Tres Clerici]. In, Albrecht, Otto E. Four Latin Plays of St. Nicholas from the 12th Century Fleury Play-book. (Philadelphia, London, 1935), pp. 126-129.

1456 Saint Nicolas et les trois clergeons. In, Cohen, Gustave. Anthologie du drame liturgie en France au moyen-âge. (Paris, 1955), pp. 249-255.

1457 Tres Clerici. In, Harrington, Karl P. Medieval Latin. (Chicago
      and New York, 1962).

      c The Image of Saint Nicholas

         (Iconia Sancti Nicolai)

PARIS (HILARIUS)
                              Manuscript
1458 Paris, Bibliothèque Nationale, MS. lat. 11331, Hilarii Versus et
      Ludi, fol. 11r - 12r (12th century).
                                Text
1459 Iconia Sancti Nicolai. In, Champollion-Figeach, J. J. Hilarii.
      Versus et Ludi. (Lutetiae Parisiorum, 1838), pp. 34-39.

1460 [Iconia Sancti Nicolai]. In, Du Méril, Edélstand. Origines latines
      du théâtre moderne. (Paris, 1849), pp. 272-276.

1461 Ludus Super Iconia Sancti Nicolai. In, Pollard, Alfred W. English
      Miracle Plays, Moralities and Interludes. (Oxford, 1890), pp.
      162-165.

1462 Ludus Super Iconia Sancti Nicolai. In, Adams, Joseph Q., ed.
      Chief Pre-Shakespearean Dramas. (Boston, New York, 1924),
      pp. 55-58. [Reprints the text of Champollion-Figeac.]

1463 Iconia Sancti Nicholai. In, Albrecht, Otto E. Four Latin Plays of
      St. Nicolas from the 12th Century Fleury Play-book. (Philadelphia,
      London, 1935), pp. 129-134.

1464 Le Jeu de Saint Nicolas, par Hilaire. In, Cohen, Gustave. Antho-
      logie du drame liturgie en France au moyen-âge. (Paris,
      1955), pp. 239-248.

ORLEANS
                          Manuscript (Fleury)
1465 Orleans, Bibliothèque de la Ville, MS. 201 (olim 178), Miscellanea
      Floriacensia, pp. 188-196 (13th century).
                                Text
1466 [Iconia Sancti Nicolai]. In, Mélanges des Bibliophiles francais.
      Vol. VII. (Paris, 1831-1832), pp. 111-118.

1467 Tertium Miraculum [Iconia Sancti Nicolai]. In, Wright, Thomas,
      ed. Early Mysteries, and Other Latin Poems of the Twelfth
      and Thirteenth Centuries. (London, Paris, Leipzig, 1838), pp.
      11-14.

1468 [Iconia Sancti Nicolai]. In, Du Méril, Edélstand. Origines
      latines du théâtre moderne. (Paris, 1849), pp. 266-271.

1469 Le Juif Volé. In, Coussemaker, E. de. Drames liturgiques
      du moyen âge. (Rennes, 1860), pp. 109-122. [Words and
      music.]

1470 [Iconia Sancti Nicolai]. In, Young, Karl. The Drama of the
      Medieval Church. Vol. II. (Oxford, 1933), pp. 344-348.

      The Son of Getron

      (Filius Getronis)

ORLEANS
                         Manuscript (Fleury)
1471 Orleans, Bibliothèque de la Ville, MS. 201 (olim 178), Miscellanea
      Floriacensia, pp. 196-205 (13th century).
                              Text
1472 [Filius Getronis]. In, Melanges des Bibliophiles francais. Vol. VII.
      (Paris, 1831-1832), pp. 121-130.

1473 Quartum Miraculum [Filius Getronis]. In, Wright, Thomas, ed.
      Early Mysteries, and Other Latin Poems of the Twelfth and
      Thirteenth Centuries. (London, Paris, Leipzig, 1838), pp. 15-
      20.

1474 Miracle de saint Nicolas [Filius Getronis]. In, Du Méril, Edélstand.
      Origines latines du théâtre modernes. (Paris, 1849), pp. 276-284.

1475 Le Fils de Gédron. In, Coussemaker, E. de. Drames liturgiques
      du moyen âge. (Rennes, 1860), pp. 123-142. [Words and
      music.]

1476 Filius Getronis. In, Beeson, Charles Henry. A Primer of Medieval
      Latin. An Anthology of Prose and Poetry. (Chicago, 1925), pp.
      375-382.

1477 [Filius Getronis]. In, Young, Karl. The Drama of the Medieval
      Church. Vol. II. (Oxford, 1933), pp. 351-357.

1478 Filius Getronis. In, Albrecht, Otto E. Four Latin Plays of St.
      Nicolas from the 12th Century Fleury Play-book. (Philadelphia,
      London, 1935), pp. 134-142.

1479 The Son of Getron. A Medieval Music Drama, Transcribed and
Edited for Modern Performance, by C. C. Stemme. Pittsburgh:
University of Pittsburgh, 1962. 50 pp.

C STUDIES

1480 Moleon, Sieur de. Voyages liturgiques de France, ou recherches
faites en diverses ville du royaume. Contenant plusieurs parti-
cularitez touchant les Rits & les Usages des Eglises: Avec des
Découvertes sur l'Antiquité Ecclesiastique & Payenne. A Paris:
Chez Florentin Delaulne, 1718. XII, 580 [2] pp. Index.
BM.

*1481 Bianchini, Francesco. De sacris imaginibus musici operis à S.
Xysto, Papa III . . . in Basilica Liberiana constructis & de
Dominicae nativitatis praesepi, ac venerabilibus cunis infantiae
Christi Domini ibidem custoditis, dissertationes duae, etc.
Romae, 1727. VIII, 32 pp. [Christmas].
BM.

1482 Fant, Erik M[ichael]. Dissertation historica de origine ludorum
mimicorum proxime ante festum Passionis Dominicae, quam
... Praeside ... E.MF. ... proponit Jonas Zacharias Hjel-
merus, ... d. 24 April 1782. Upsaliae: J. Edman [1782].
12 pp.
NN.

1483 Docen, Bernard Joseph. Miscellaneen zur Geschichte der teut-
schen Literatur. 2 vol. München: Verlag der Schererschen
Kunst-und Buchhandlung, 1807.
BM.

1484 Magnin, Charles. "Les Origines du théâtre en Europe." Revue
des Deux Mondes, IV (1834), 578-597.

1485 "Les vierges sages et les vierges folles." Monmerque, L. J. N.,
and F. X. Michels, eds. Théâtre francais au moyen âge.
(Paris, 1839), pp. 1-9. [Sponsus].

1486 Wolf, Ferdinand Joseph. Über die Lais, Sequenzen und Leiche.
Ein Beitrag zur Geschichte der rhythmischen Formen und
Singweisen der Volkslieder und der volksmässigen Kirchen-
und Kunstlieder im Mittelalter. Heidelberg: C. F. Winter,
1841. xvi, 514 [2] pp.

1487 Delettre, Abbé. Histoire du Diocèse de Beauvais, depuis son
      établissement, au 3me siècle, jusqu' au 2 septembre 1792.
      3 vol. Beauvais: Impr. d' A. Desjardins, 1842-1843.
      ICU.

1488 Zacher, Julius, ed. Mittelnieder-ländisches Osterspiel."
      Zeitschrift für deutsches Altertum, II (1842), 302-350.

*1489 "Regularis Concordia." Migne, J. P. Patrologiae Cursus Com-
      pletus: Patrologia Latina (Paris, 1844-1864), Vol. 137,
      cols. 475-502.

*1490 Clément, Félix. "Liturgie, Musique et drame du moyen âge."
      Annales Archéologiques, VII (1847), 303-320; VIII (1848),
      36-48, 77-87.

1491 ----- "Le drame liturgique." Annales Archéologiques, VIII
      (1848), 304-311; IX (1849), 27-40, 162-174; X (1850), 154-
      159; XI (1851), 6-15.

*1492 Du Meril, Edélstand. Les Origines Latines du théâtre moderne,
      publiées et annotées. Paris: Frank, 1849. 418 pp. [Facsimile
      reprint, 1896.]
      DFo. ICN. ICU. MdBP. PHC.

1493 Didron, A. M. "Drame liturgique." Annales Archéologiques,
      XI (1851), 211-212.

1494 Bechstein, Ludwig. Das grosse thüringische Mysterium; oder,
      Das geistliche Spiel von den zehn Jungfrauen. Ausgeführt zu
      Eisenach am 24. April 1322. Nach der einzigen bis jetzt auf-
      gefundenen Handschrift. Halle: C. E. Pfeffer, 1855. xiv,
      75 pp. [Ten Maidens].
      NN.

1495 Office du sépulchre selon l'usage de l'Abbaye d'Origny--Sainte-
      Bénoit. Rapport à la section d'Archéologie du Comité de la
      langue de l'histoire et des arts de la France, le 20 avril 1857.
      Paris: Imprimerie impériale, 1858. 11 pp.
      DLC.

1496 Schubiger, Anselm. Die Sängerschule St. Gallens, vom achten
      bis zwölften Jahrhundert. Ein Beitrag zur gesanggeschichte
      des Mittelalters. Mit vielen facsimile und Beispielen.
      Einsiedeln und New York: K. und N. Benziger, 1858. vi, 96

pp.
       BM. DLC.

1497 Schubiger, Père Anseleme. La Séquence de Pâques "Victimae
       Pascali Laudes" et son auteur. Paris: Charles de Mourgues
       Frères, 1858. 24 pp. (Extrait du Journal La Maîtrise).
       BM.

*1498 Clément, Felix. Histoire générale de la musique religieuse.
       Paris: Adrien Le Clerc et Cie., 1860. xiii, 597 pp. Biblio-
       graphie musicale, pp. 561-594. Index.
       BM.

*1499 Coussemaker, Edmund de., ed. Ludus Paschalis from Origny-
       Sainte-Bénoite. Drames liturgiques du moyen âge. (Rennes,
       1860), pp. 271-279.

1500 Rieger, Max, ed. "Das Spiel von den Zehn Jungfrauen." Ger-
       mania, X, Heft 3 (1865), 311-337. [Ten Maidens].

1501 Bechstein Reinhold. "Zum Spiel von den zehn Jungfrauen." Ger-
       mania, XI, Heft 2 (1866), 129-166. [Also published separately
       at Jena, 1866. 38 pp. Located at BM.] [Ten Maidens].

1502 Drosihn, Fr. Über das Redentiner Osterspiel. Neustettin, 1866.
       36 pp.
       ICU.

1503 Klein, Julius Leopold. Geschichte des aussereuropäischen
       Dramas und der lateinischen Schauspiele nach Christus bis
       Ende des X. Jahrhunderts. Leipzig: T. O. Weigel, 1866.
       764 pp.
       ICU. MnU.

1504 Sepet, Marius. "Les Prophètes du Christ." Bibliothèque de l'
       École des Chartes, XXVIII (1867), 1-27, 211-264; XXIX
       (1868), 105-139, 261-293; XXXVIII (1877), 397-443.
       [Published also as a separate volume, Paris, 1878.]

1505 Walcott, Mackenzie, E. C. Sacred Archaeology. London: L.
       Reene & Co., 1868. xvi, 640 pp.

1506 Freybe, Albert. "Ein altes Weihnachtsspiel nach einer Hs.
       aus dem Nachlasse des Herrn Prof. A. F. C. Vilmar mit
       möglichster Schonung der sprachlichen Form des 14. Jhs.

ins Neuhochdeutsche übertragen." Zeitschrift für die historische Theologie, XXXIX, Heft 4 (1869), 575-604.

1507 Heales, Alfred. "Easter Sepulchres: Their Origin, Nature, and
History." Archaeologia, XLII (1869), 263-308.

1508 Kampers, Frans. Die deutsche Kaiseridee in Prophetie und Sage.
München: H. Lüneburg, 1869. 231 pp. (Zugleich als 2. bis zur
gegenwart und Kaisersagen im mittelalter.) [Antichrist].
BM. ICN.

1509 Schröder, Karl. "Zum Redentiner Spiel." Germania, Viertel-
jahrschrift für deutsche Altertumsskunde, XIV (1869), 181-
196.

1510 Czerny, Albin. Die Handschriften der Stiftsbibliothek St. Florian.
Linz: Franz Ebenhöch, 1871. viii, 333 pp. "Verzeichnis der
Autorem," pp. 319-333. Index.
BM.

1511 Delisle, Léopold Victor. Inventaire des Manuscrits latins de
Notre-Dame et d' autres fonds conservés à la Bibliothèque
Nationale sous les numeros 16719-18613. Paris, 1871.

1512 Delisle, L. "Note sur le manuscrit de Tours. Renfermant des
drames liturgiques et des légendes pieuses en vers francais."
Romania, II (1873), 91-95. [Le Manuscrit D'Adam.]

1513 Drosihn, Fr. "Bemerkungen zum Redentiner Osterspiel." Zeitschrift für deutsche Philologie, IV (1873), 400-406.

1514 Kehrein, J. Lateinische Sequenzen des Mittelalters, aus Handschriften und Drucken. Mainz: F. Kupferberg, 1873. 620 pp.
CtY. MdBJ. MH. MiU. NN. NNUT. OC1E. PU.

1515 Birch, Walter De Gray. On a Thirteenth Century Service Book of
Strasbourg, with Dramatic Representations. [London, 1874].
21 pp. (British Museum, Additional MS 23932, Liturgical.)
BM. ICU. PU.

1516 Freybe, Albert, ed. Das Mecklenburger Osterspiel vollendet im
jahre 1464 zu Redent, übertragen und behandett von dr. Albert
Freybe. Bremen: J. Kühtmann, 1874. xiv, [1], 427 [1] pp.
ICU.

1517 Haupt, Joseph. "Bruchstïk eines Osterspiels aus dem 13. Jahr-
      hundert." Archiv für die Geschichte deutscher Sprach und
      Dichtung, I (1874), 355-381.
                 BM.

1518 Foulques de Villaret, A. "L'Enseignement des Lettres et des
      Sciences dans l'Orléanais." Mémoires de la Société arché-
      ologique et historique de l'Orléanais, XIV (1875), 299-440.

1519 Scherer, Gustav. Verzeichniss der Handschriften der Stifts-
      bibliothek von St. Gallen, hrsg. auf Veranstaltung und mit
      Unterstützung des Kath. Administrationsrathes des Kantons
      St. Gallen. Halle: Buchhandlung des Waisenhauses, 1875. xii,
      [2], 650 pp.
                 ICU.

1520 Weinhold, Karl. Weihnachtspiele und Lieder aus Süddeutschland
      und Schlesien. Mit Einleitungen und Erläuterungen. Vienna:
      Wilhelm Braumüller, 1875. viii, 456 pp.
                 BM.

* 1521 Schubiger, Anselm. Musikalische Spicilegien über das liturgische
      Drama. Orgelbau und Orgelspiel, das ausserliturgische Lied
      und die Instrumentalmusik des Mittelalters. Berlin: L. Liep-
      mannssohn, 1876. 76 pp. [Das liturgische Drama des Mittel-
      alters und seine Musik.]
                 BM.

1522 Bohn, P. "Marienklage Handschrift der Trierischen Stadtbibliothek aus
      dem 15 Jahrhundert." Monatshefte für Musikgeschichte, IX, No. 1
      (1877), 1-4.

1523 Gausseron, Henri. "The Passion of Christ." Notes and Queries,
      5th Ser., VII (April 21, 1877), 309-310. [Reply to Ward's
      question.]

1524 Ward, C. A. "Passion of Christ." Notes and Queries, 5th Ser.,
      VII (March 24, 1877), 227. [Question.]

1525 Woeste, F. "Beitrage aus dem Niederdeutschen. Zum Redentiner
      Spiel." Zeitschrift für deutsche Philologie, VIII (1877), 106-
      108.

1526 Kressner, A. "St. Nicolaus in der Tradition und in der mittelalter-
      lichen Dichtung, eine literar-historische Skizze." Archiv für

das Studium der neueren Sprachen und Literaturen," LIX
(1878), 33-60.

*1527 Sepet, Marius Cyrille Alphonse. Les Prophètes du Christ. Paris:
Didier, 1878. 193 pp.
BM. MH. MnU. PU.

1528 Binns, William. "The Religious Drama." Modern Review, I
(1880), 792-819.

1529 Boutillier, Abbé F. Drames liturgiques et Rites figurés, ou
cérémonies symboliques dans l'église de Nevers. Nevers: G.
Vallière, 1880. 89 pp.
BM.

1530 Gross, Peter. Die Tropen und Figuren. Ein Hilfsbuch für den
deutschen, lateinischen und griechischen Unterricht an
höheren lehranstalten. Koeln: C. Roemke & Co., 1880. VIII,
282, [7] pp.
ICU.

*1531 Hase, Karl August von. Miracle Plays and Sacred Dramas. A
Historical Survey. Translated by A. W. Jackson, and Edited
by Rev. W. W. Jackson. London: Trübner and Co., 1880.
273 pp.
BM. ICN. MB.

1532 Rosieres, Raoul. Histoire de la société francaise au moyen âge,
(987-1483). 2 vol. Paris: Librairie A. Laisney, 1880.

1533 Lange, Carl. "Die lateinischen Osterfeiern." Jahresbericht über
die Realschule erster Ordnung in Halberstadt. Programn No.
223, Halberstadt, 1881. Pp. 1-35.

1534 Wycliff, John. The English Works of Wyclif Hitherto Unprinted.
Edited by F. D. Matthew. London: Trübner & Co., for
E. E. T. S., 1881. viii, li, 572 pp. [See, "De Officio Pastor-
ali," pp. 405-457.]
BM.

1535 Keppler, P."Zur Passionspredigt des Mittelalters." Historisches
Jahrbuch, III (1882), 285-315; IV (1883), 161-188.

*1536 Meyer, Wilhelm, ed. Der Ludus de Antichristo und Bemerkungen
über die lateinischen Rhythmen des 12. Jahrhunderts. München:

F. Straub, 1882. [1], 192 pp. [Based upon Adso's Libellus de
Antichristo.]
ICU.

1537 Guéranger, Prosper. The Liturgical Year. Translated from the
French by the Rev. Dom Laurence Shepherd [and others]. 2nd
edit. 15 vol. Dublin: Duffy, 1883-1903.
BM.

1538 Froning, Richard. Zur Geschichte und Beurteilung der geistlichen
Spiel des Mittelalters, insonderheit der Passionsspiele. [Frank-
furt a.M.: C. Jügel, 1884.] 29 pp.
NN.

*1539 Lange, Karl. "Ungedruckt lateinische Osterfeiern." Zeitschrift
für deutsche Altertum und deutsche Literatur, XXVIII (1884),
119-129; XXIX (1885), 246-259.

1540 Reiners, Adam. Die Tropen-, Prosen, und Präfationsgesänge
des feierlichen Hochamtes im Mittelalter; aus drei Handschriften
der Abteien Prüm und Echternach aufbewahrt in der Nationalbibliothek zu Paris. Luxemburg: I. Hary, 1884. [1], iii, 122,
ii pp.
BM. ICU.

*1541 Dreves, G. M., and C. Blume, eds. Analecta Hymnica Medii Aevi.
55 Parts in 19 vol. Leipzig: Altenburg, 1886-1922.
BM.

1542 Schöne, Alexander. Deutsche Altertümer im mecklenburger
Osterspiel. Ludwigslust: C. Kober, 1886. [3], 33 pp.
ICU.

1543 Gihr, Nikolaus. Die Sequenzen des romischen Messbuches dogmatisch
und ascetisch erklärt. Nebst einer Abhandlung über die Schmerzen
Mariä. Mit fünf Bildern. Freiburg im Breisgau: Herder's sche
Verlagshandlung, 1887. viii, 548 pp. Index. (Theologische Bib-
liothek. Zweite Serie).
BM.

*1544 Lange, Carl. Die lateinischen Osterfeiern. Untersuchungen über
den Ursprung und die Entwickelung der liturgisch-dramatischen
Auferstehungsfeier mit Zugrundelegung eines Umfangreichen,
neuaufgefundenen Quellenmaterials. München: E. Stahl, 1877.
iv, 171 pp. Bibliography, pp. 3-17.

CtY. ICN. ICU. MH. NjP. OC1W. OU.

1545 Holstein, Hugo. "Zur Litteratur des lateinischen Schauspiels
des 16. Jahrhunderts." Zeitschrift für Deutsche Philologie,
XX (1888), 97-108.

1546 Wirth, Ludwig. Die Oster- und Passionsspiele bis zum 15.
Jahrhundert. Beiträge zur Geschichte des deutschen Dramas.
Halle a.S.: Max Niemeyer, 1889. viii, 351 pp. Bibliography,
pp. 344-349.
BM.

*1547 Schmid, Max. Die Darstellung der Geburt Christi in der bildenden
Kunst. Entwicklungsgeschichtliche Studie. Stuttgart: J. Hoff-
mann, 1890. [1], iv, [2], 128 pp. [Christmas].
ICU.

1548 Walther, C. "Zum Redentiner Spiel." Jahrbuch des Vereins für
niederdeutsche Sprachforschung, XVI (1890), 44-53.

1549 Andrews, William. Old Church Lore. Hull: William Andrews &
Co., 1891. 255 pp.
BM.

1550 Dyer, T. F. Church-Lore Gleanings. London: A. D. Innes & Co.,
1891. vi, 352 pp. Index.
BM.

1551 Holstein, Hugo. "Zur Litteratur des lateinischen Schauspiels
des 16. Jahrhunderts." Zeitschrift für Deutsche Philologie,
XXIII (1891), 436-451.

1552 Holthausen, F. "Zu alt-und mittelenglischen Dichtungen."
Anglia, XIII (1891), 357-362. [Abraham and Isaac.]

*1553 Logeman, W., ed. "Regularis Concordia." Anglia, XIII (1891),
265-348; XV (1893), 20.

*1554 Logeman, W. S. "De consuetudine monarchorum." Anglia, XIII
(N.F.B and I), (1891), 365-454. [From British Museum, MS.
Cotton Tiberius A. III., "Regularis Concordia."]

1555 Rinn, H. "Deutsche Osterspiele im Mittelalter." Die Christliche Welt, V (1891), 284-289.

*1556 Chevalier, Cyr Ulysse. Repertorium Hymnologicum: Catalogue
        des chants, hymnes, proses, sequences, tropes en usage
        dans l'église latine depuis les origines jusqu' a nos jours.
        6 vol. Louvain et Brussels, 1892-1920. [Vols. 1-4 printed
        in Louvain; Vols. 5-6 printed in Brussels.]
              BM. ICU.

1557 Freybe, Albert, Ed. Die Handschrift des Redentiner Osterspiels
        im Lichtdruck mit einigen Beiträgen zu seiner Geschichte und
        Litteratur. Schwerin: Bärensprungschen Hofbuchdruckerei,
        1892. iv, [24], 47 pp.
              BM. ICU.

1558 Bahlmann, Paul. Die lateinischen Dramen von Wimpheling's
        Stylpho bis zur Mitte des sechzehnten Jahrhunderts: 1480-
        1550. Münster: Verlag der Regensberg'schen Buchhandlung,
        1893. 114 pp.
              BM. ICN. MB. MH. NjP. OU. PU.

1559 Bates, Katherine L. The English Religious Drama. New York
        and London: Macmillan and Co., 1893. 254 pp. Bibliography,
        pp. 240-254.
              BM. DLC. MB. MiU. NjP. OC1. PU. ViU. WaU.

1560 Batiffol, Pierre. L'Histoire du breviaire romain. Paris: Alphonse
        Picard et fils, 1893. xiv, 356 pp. Bibliography, pp. xiii-xiv.
              BM.

1561 Köppen, Wilhelm. Beiträge zur Geschichte des deutschen Weih-
        nachtsspiele. Paderborn: Druck und Verlag von Ferdinand
        Schöningh; Münster, i. W.: Osnabrück und Mainz, 1893. 132
        pp.
              BM.

1562 Schöne, Alexander. "Zum Redentiner Spiel." Zeitschrift für den
        deutschen Unterricht, VII (1893), 17-30.

1563 Sielmann, W. "R. Schroder: D. Red. Osterspiel." Deutsche
        Literaturzeitung, XIV (1893), 367-369.

1564 Bateson, Mary. "The Supposed Latin Penitential of Egbert and
        the Missing Work of Halitgar of Cambrai." English Historical
        Review, IX (April, 1894), 320-326.

1565 Chevalier, [Cyr] Ulysse. Poésie liturgique traditionnelle de l'

Église catholique en Occident. Tournai: Desclée, Lefebvre et
Cie, 1894. lxviii, 288 pp.
BM.

*1566 Frère, Walter Howard, ed. The Winchester Troper From MSS.
of the Xth and XIth Centuries. With Other Documents Illustrating
the History of Tropes in England and France. London: [Harrison
and Sons], 1894. xlvii, 248 pp. (Henry Bradshaw Society, Vol.
VIII).
BM. ICN. MH. NjP. NNUT. OClW. PBm. PU.

1567 Bousset, Wilhelm. Der Antichrist in der Überlieferung des
Judentums, des Neuen Testaments und der alten Kirche. Ein
Beitrag zur Auslegung der Apocalypse. Göttingen: Vanden-
hoeck und Ruprecht, 1895. [6], 186 pp.
ICU.

1568 Cabrol, Fernand. Les Eglises de Jérusalem: la discipline et la
liturgie en quatrième siècle. Paris, Poitiers: H. Oudin, 1895.
viii, 208 pp. Index.
BM.

1569 Freybe, Albert. "Das Redentiner Osterspiel." Österreichisches
Litteraturblatt, IV (1895), 109-110.

1570 Hautcoeur, Edouard, ed. Documents liturgiques et necrologiques
de l'Eglise collégiale de Saint Pierre de Lille. Lille: Quarré;
Paris: Picard, 1895. xix, 480 pp. Index.
BM.

1571 Montaiglon, A. de. Le Drame paschal de la Resurrection. Tours,
1895. 32 pp. [On the Latin text of MS. 927 de la Bibl. num. de
Tours.]
BM.

1572 Sprenger, R. "Zum Redentin Osterspiel." Zeitschrift für deutsche
Philologie, XXVII (1895), 301-308, 561-563.

*1573 Bahlmann, Paul. Jesuiten-dramen der niederrheinischen Orden-
sprovinz. Leipzig: O. Harrassowitz, 1896. 351 pp.
ICU.

1574 Bousset, Wilhelm. The Antichrist Legend; A Chapter in Christian
and Jewish Folklore, Englished from the German of W. Bousset,
with a prologue on the Babylonian Myth, by A. H. Keane.

London: Hutchinson and Co., 1896. xxxi, 307, [1] pp.
ICU.

1575 Ebner, Adalbert. Quellen und Forschungen zur Geschichte und
Kunstgeschichte des Missale Romanum im Mittelalter: Iter
Italicum. Freiburg im Breisgau: Herder'sche Verlagshand-
lung, 1896. x, 487 pp. Indices.
BM.

*1576 Chevalier, Cyr Ulysse Joseph, ed. Ordinaires de l'Église
cathédrale de Laon (XIIe et XIIIe siècles) suivis de deux
mystères liturgiques publiées d'après les manuscrits originaux. Paris: A. Picard, 1897. xliii, 409 pp. Index. (Bibliothèque liturgique, t. 6).
DLC. ICU. NN. O.

1577 Feasey, Henry J. Ancient English Holy Week Ceremonial.
London: T. Baker, 1897. 247 pp.
BM. MiU. OCl. PP. PU. PV.

1578 Morin, G. "Saint Lazare et Saint Maximin." Mémoires de la
Société Nationale des Antiquaires de France, LVI (1897),
27-51. [Lazarus].

1579 Venzmer, Berthold. Die Chöre im geistlichen Drama des
deutschen Mittelalters. Inaugural Dissertation. Rostock,
1897. 70 pp.

1580 Kuhl, G. "Die Bordesholmer Marienklage, herausgegeben und
eingeleitet." Jahrbuch des Vereins für niederdeutsche Sprachforschung, XXIV (1898), 1-75, I-XIV.

1581 Schwartz, Rudolf. Esther im deutschen und neulateinischen Drama
des Reformations-zeitalters. Eine litterärhistorische Untersuchung. Oldenburg und Leipzig: A. Schwartz, 1898.
BM. ICU.

1582 Teuber, Valentin. Die Entwicklung der Weihnachtsspiele seit
den ältesten Zeiten bis zum XVI. Jahrhundert. Komotau,
1898. 32 pp.
ICU.

1583 Vodoz, Jules. Le Théâtre latin de Ravisius Textor 1470-1524.
Winterhür: Impr. Geschwister Ziegler, 1898. 174 pp.
ICU.

1584 Wordsworth, Christopher. Notes on Mediaeval Services in Eng-
land, with an Index of Lincoln Ceremonies. London: Thomas
Baker, 1898. xiii, 313 pp. Index.
BM.

1585 Porter, Alice Downey. "The Religious Drama in France and
England from the Beginning of the Ninth to the Close of the
Thirteenth Century." Ph.D. Cornell University, 1899.

1586 Cesaresco, Evelyn M. "Puer Parvulus." Contemporary Review,
LXXVII (1900), 117-123. [Christmas].

1587 Bannister, H. M. "The Earliest French Troper and Its Date."
Journal of Theological Studies, II (April, 1901), 420-429.

1588 Butler, Pierce. "A Note on the Origin of the Liturgical Drama."
An English Miscellany Presented to Dr. Furnivall. (Oxford,
1901), pp. 46-52.

*1589 Daux, Camille, ed. Tropaire-Prosier de l'Abbaye Saint-Martin
de Montauriol publié d' après le manuscrit original
(XIe - XIIIe siècles). Paris: A. Picard et fils, 1901. liii,
210 pp. (Bibliothèque liturgique, pub. par U. Chevalier, t. 9.)
ICU.

1590 Lafond, P. "La Crèche de la Cathédrale Sainte-Marie d'Oloron."
Reunion des Sociétés des Beaux-Arts des Départements, XXI
(1901), 567-572.

1591 Robertson, John M. "The Gospel Mystery-Play." The Reformer,
III, New Ser., No. 35 (November 15, 1901), 657-666.

*1592 Sepet, Marius Cyrille Alphonse. Origines Catholiques du théâtre
moderne. Les Drames liturgiques et les jeux scolaires; les
mystères; les origines de la comédie au moyen âge; la renaissance. Paris: P. Lethielleux, 1901. viii, 576 pp.
BM. DLC. ICN. MB. MiU. MnU. NjP. PBm. PU. ViU.
WU.

1593 Stötzner, Paul, Ed. Osterfeiern. Hgg. nach einer Zwickauer
Handschrift aus dem Anfange des 16. Jahrhunderts. Zwickau,
1901. 28 pp.
ICU.

1594 Vermeylen, A. Le Théâtre dans l' église. Les origines du drame

moderne. Brussels: Impr. J. H. Moreau, 1901. 20 pp.
CtY. ICU.

1595 Werner, Jakob. Notkers Sequenzen. Beiträge zur Geschichte
der lateinischen Sequenzendichtung. Aus Handschriften
gesammelt. Aarau: H. R. Sauerländer & Co., 1901, iv,
130 pp.
NN.

1596 Wilmotte, Maurice. "Les origines du drame liturgique." Bul-
letin de la Classe des Lettres (Académie Royale, Brussels),
No. 7 (1901), 715-748.
BM. NN.

*1597 Chevalier, Cyr Ulysse Joseph, ed. Ordinaire et coutumier de
l'église cathédrale de Bayeux (XIIIe siècle). Publiées d'
après les manuscrits originaux. Paris: A. Picard et fils,
1902. 1, [1], 478, [1] pp. (Bibliothèque liturgique, t. 8).
ICU.

1598 Dawson, William Francis. Christmas: Its Origin and Associations,
Together with Its Historical Events and Festive Celebrations
during Nineteen Centuries: Depicting, by Pen and Pencil,
Memorable Celebrations, Stately Meetings of Early Kings,
Remarkable Events, Romantic Episodes, Brave Deeds, Pic-
turesque Customs, Time-Honoured Sports, Royal Christmases,
Coronations and Royal Marriages, Chivalric Feats, Court
Banquetings and Revellings, Christmas at the Colleges and
Inns of Court. Popular Festivities, and Christmas-Keeping in
Different Parts of the World, Derived from the Most Authentic
Sources, and Arranged Chronologically. London: E. Stock,
1902. 366 pp.
ICN.

*1599 Hager, George. Die Weihnachtskrippe. Ein Beitrag zur Volk-
skunde und Kunstgeschichte aus dem Bayerischen National-
museum. München: Kommissionsverlag der Gesellschaft
für Christliche Kunst, 1902. 144, [4] pp. [Christmas].
BM.

1600 Sprenger, R., und C. Walther. "Zum Redentiner Osterspiel."
Korrespondenblatt des Vereins für niederdeutsche Sprachforschung, XXIII (1902), 45-46.

1601 Albers, B. "Les 'Consuetudines Sigiberti Abbatis' dans CLM
14765." Revue bénédictione, XX (1903), 420-433. [On the

Visitatio Sepulchri from Munich MS lat. 14765.]

1602 Albers, B. "Les plus grand Coutumier de Cluny." Revue bénédictine, XX (1903), 174-184.

1603 Chambers, E. K. "Liturgical Plays." The Mediaeval Stage, Vol. II. (London, 1903), pp. 1-67.

1604 Gastoué, A. "Un petit drame liturgique parisien pour Pâques." La Tribune de Saint-Gervaise, 9e Année (1903), 155-156.

1605 Graham, R. "The Intellectual Influence of English Monasticism between the Tenth and the Twelfth Centuries." Transactions of the Royal Historical Society, New Ser., XVII (1903), 23-65. [Regularis Concordia].

1606 "Roman Catholic Church and the Sacred Play." American Monthly Review of Reviews, XXVIII (1903), 485-486.

1607 Walther, C. "Zum Redentiner Spiel 243 ff." Korrespondenblatt des Vereins für niederdeutsche Sprachforschung, XXIV (1903), 36-38.

1608 Arndt, Wilhelm. Die Personennamen der deutschen Schauspiele des Mittelalters. Marburg, 1904. 69 pp.

1609 Franz, Adolph. Das rituale von St. Florian aus dem Zwölften Jahrhundert. Freiburg im Breisgau: Herdersche, 1904. xii, 207 pp.
     BM.

1610 Kehrer, Hugo. Die "Heiligen drei Könige in der Legende und in der deutschen bildenden Kunst bis Albrecht Durer. Strassburg: J. H. Ed. Heitz, 1904. viii, 131 pp. "Literatur," pp. 122-124. (Studien zur deutschen Kunstgeschichte, Hft. 53).
     BM.

1611 Klein, David. "A Study of the Medieval Biblical Drama in English." M.A. Columbia University, 1904.

1612 Kock, E. A. "Zum Redentiner Osterspiel." Korrespondenblatt des Vereins für niederdeutsche Sprachforschung, XXV (1904), 94-95.

1613 Legband, Hans. Die Alsfelder Dirigierrolle. Dissertation.
      Göttingen, 1904. 62 pp.

1614 Meyer, Paul, ed. "Les Trois Maries: mystère liturgique de
      Reims." Romania, XXXIII (1904), 239-245.

1615 Pflaum, Hiram. "Der allegorische Streit Zwischen Synagoge und
      Kirche in der europäischen Dichtung des Mittelalters." Arch-
      ivum Romanicum, XVIII (1904), 243-340. [Antichrist].

1616 Pöllmann, Anasgar. "Das Kasseler Weihnachtsspiel in die Sprache
      unserer Zeit umgesetzt." Gottesminne Monatsschrift für reli-
      giöse Dichtkunst, II (1904), 556-557, 609-617, 671-672; III
      (1905), 49-53, 167-168, 221-224, 277-279, 386-389, 446-447,
      500-502, 565-567, 627-630, 694-695. [Nativity].

1617 Rand, E. K. "Sermo de Confusione Diaboli." Modern Philology,
      II (1904), 261-278. [Discusses the "Harrowing of Hell."]

1618 Schelling, Felix E. "Old English Sacred Drama." Lippincott's
      Magazine, LXXIV (1904), 441-453.

1619 Albers, B. Untersuchungen zu den ältesten Mönchsgewohnheiten;
      ein Beitrag zur Benediktinerordensgeschichte des X.-XII.
      Jahrhunderts. München: J. J. Lentner, 1905. xii, 132 pp.
      (Veröffentlichungen aus dem Kirchen-historischen seminar
      München . . . II. reihe, nr. 8).
           ICU.

1620 Feasey, Henry. "The Easter Sepulchre." Ecclesiastical Review,
      XXXII (1905), 337-355, 468-499.

1621 Mercati, G. "Antiche Omilie e sacre Rappresentazioni medievali."
      Rassegna gregoriana, IV (1905), 15-20.

1622 Plyer, M. T. "David in the English Drama." M.A. University
      of North Carolina, 1905.

1623 Batka, Richard. Die Musik in Böhmen. Berlin: Bard, Marquardt
      & Co. [1906]. iv, 100 pp. Bibliography, p. 100.
           BM.

1624 Berliere, V. "Les Coutumiers monastiques." Revue bénédictine,
      XXIII (1906), 260-267; XXV (1908), 95-107; XXIX (1912),
      357-367. [Regularis Concordia].

*1625 Cabrol, Fernand. Les origines liturgiques. Paris: Letowzey &
       Ané, 1906. viii, 372 pp. (Conférences données à L'Institut
       Catholique de Paris en 1906.)
       BM. ICU.

1626 Frere, Walter Howard. The Principles of Religious Ceremonial.
      London: Longmans, Green, 1906. xii, 324 pp. (Oxford Lib-
      rary of Practical Theology).
      BM.

1627 Lawson, Robb. "Religious Drama." Littell's Living Age,
      CCXLIX (1906), 611-616.

1628 Michael, Emil. Geschichte des deutschen Volkes vom 13 Jahr-
      hundert bis zum Ausgange des Mittelalters. Curturzustände
      des deutschen Volkes während des dreizehnten Jahrhunderts.
      Vol. 4. Freiburg im Breisgau: Herder, 1906. xxvii, 457 pp.
      Index. [See, "Die liturgischen Festspiele und die Anfänge
      des Dramas," pp. 400-448.]
      BM.

1629 Walton, Pauline. "The Supernatural in the English Drama." M.A.
      Northwestern University, 1906.

1630 Cabrol, F., and H. Leclercq. Dictionnaire d'Archéologie Chré-
      tienne et de Liturgie. Paris: Letouzey et Ané, 1907-1953.
      15 Vol. in 29.
      ICU.

1631 Cohen, Gustave. Geschichte der Inszenierung im geistlichen
      Schauspiele des Mittelalters in Frankreich. Vermehrte und
      verbesserte Ausgabe ins Deutsche übertragen von Dr.
      Constantin Bauer. Leipzig: Werner Klinkhardt, 1907. xiv,
      256 pp.
      NN.

1632 Gaaf, W. Van der. "The Easter Sepulchre." Englische Studien,
      XXXVII (1907), 461.

1633 Hörburger, Franz. Das Sonthofner Passionsspiel. Inaugural
      Dissertation. Innsbruck, 1907.

*1634 Male, Emile. "Les Influences du drame liturgique sur la
       sculpture romane." Revue de l'art ancien et moderne, XXII
       (August, 1907), 81-92.

1635 Moore, E. Hamilton. English Miracle Plays and Moralities.
      London and Manchester: Sherratt and Hughes, 1907. vi,
      199 pp.
           BM. DLC. MB. MiU. MnU. NjP. NN. OC1. OCU. WU.

*1636 Sepet, Marius Cyrille Alphonse. Le Drame religieux au moyen
      âge. Paris: Bloud & Cie, 1908. 63 pp. "Bibliographie," pp.
      [62]-63.
           BM. DLC. MiU. PBm. PSC. PU.

*1637 Young, Karl. "A Contribution to the History of Liturgical Drama
      at Rouen." Modern Philology, VI (1908), 201-227.

*1638 Brooks, Neil C. "Neue lateinische Osterfeiern." Zeitschrift
      (Anzeiger) für Deutsches Altertum und Deutsche Literatur,
      L (1909), 297-312.

1639 Cady, Frank W. "Liturgical Basis of the Towneley Mysteries."
      Publications of the Modern Language Association, XXIV
      (1909), 419-469.

1640 Genner, Arnold von. Les rites de passage: étude systématique
      des rites de la porte et du seuil, de l'hospitalité, de l'
      adoption, de la grossesse et de l'accouchement, de la nais-
      sance, de l' enfance, de la puberté, de l' initiation, de l'
      ordination, du couronnement, des financailles et du mariage,
      des funérailles, des saisons, etc. Paris: E. Nourry, 1909.
      ii, 288 pp. Index.
           BM.

1641 Robert, Gabriel. Les Écoles et l' Enseignement de la Théologie
      pendant la première Moitié du XIIe Siècle.
      Paris: J. Gabalda & Cie, 1909. xvi, 249 pp. (Etudes d' his-
      toire des dogmes et d' ancienne littérature ecclésiastique).
      "Index bibliographique": pp. [ix]-xvi.
           ICN.

*1642 Wilmotte, Maurice. "La naissance du drame liturgique." Etudes
      critiques sur la tradition littéraire en France. (Paris, 1909),
      pp. 1-47.

*1643 Young, Karl. "The Harrowing of Hell in Liturgical Drama."
      Transactions of the Wisconsin Academy of Science and
      Letters, XVI (1909), 889-947.

*1644 Young, Karl. "Some Texts of Liturgical Plays." Publications
       of the Modern Language Association, XXIV (1909), 294-331.

*1645 Chevalier, Ulysse. Institutions liturgiques de l'église de Mar-
       seille (XIIIe siècle) Copiées et annotées par le Chanoine J.
       H. Albanès. Publiées d'après le manuscrit original des
       Archives de la Préfecture de Marseille avec le Mortuologe
       de la même Église. Paris: Alphonse Picard et Fils, 1910.
       xxxii, 175 pp. Index.
            O.

*1646 Cohen, Gustave, ed. "La Scène des Pélerins d'Emmaus. Con-
       tribution à l'étude des origines du théâtre comique." Mélanges
       de philologie romane et d'histoire littéraire offert à M. Maurice
       Wilmotte. (Paris, 1910), pp. 105-129.

 1647 Male, Emile. "Les Trois Mages et le drame liturgique." Gazette
       des beaux-arts, 4e pér., IV (July-December, 1910), 261-270.

 1648 Royster, James F. "Richard III, IV, 4, and the Three Maries of
       the Medieval Drama." Modern Language Notes, XXV (1910),
       173-174.

 1649 Villetard, H. "I Giudei nella Liturgia." Rassegna Gregoriana,
       IX (1910), 429-444.

 1650 Weydig, Otto. Beiträge zur Geschichte des Mirakelspiels in
       Frankreich. Erfurt: Buchdrukerei von B. Hahne, 1910. 111
       pp.
            DLC. ICU. MH. NjP. WU.

 1651 Wordsworth, C., and H. Littlehales. The Old Service Books
       of the English Church. 2nd ed. London: Methuen & Co.,
       1910. xv, 319 pp. Index.
            BM.

 1652 Young, Karl. "Observations on the Origin of the Mediaeval
       Passion-Play." Publications of the Modern Language Asso-
       ciation, XXV (1910), 309-354.

 1653 Blume, C. "Vom Alleluja zur Sequenz." Kirchenmusikalisches
       Jahrbuch, XXIV (1911), 1-20.

 1654 Bohatta, Hanns. Liturgische Bibliographie des XV. Jahrhunderts
       mit Ausnahme der Missale und Linres d'Heures. Wien:

Gilhofer & Ranschburg, 1911. viii, 71, [1] pp.
ICU.

*1655 Brooks, Neil C. "Liturgical Easter-Plays from Rheinau MS."
Journal of English and Germanic Philology, X (1911), 191-
196.

1656 Kohler, Erwin. Entwicklung des biblischen Dramas des XVI.
Jahrhunderts in Frankreich unter dem Einfluss der literarischen
Renaissancebewegung. Leipzig: A. Deichert, 1911. xiv, 69 pp.
BM. WU.

1657 Krappe, Emil. Christi Leben von seiner Geburt bis zur Geschichte von der Samariterin Altfranzösische Version in ach-
tsilbingen Reimpaaren nach den Pariser Hss. Arsénal 5204,
Bibl. Nat. f. fr. 9588 und den entsprechenden Kapiteln der
Bible von Geufroi de Paris. Greifswald: E. Hartmann, 1911.
xiv, 63 pp. Bibliography, pp. v-vi.
NN.

1658 Luedtke, Helene. Les Croyances religieuses au moyen âge en
France, d'après les pièces du théâtre sérieux des XIIe,
XIIIe et XIVe siècles. Lausanne: Imprimeries Réunies
(S.A.) 1911. 164 pp.
NNC.

1659 Young, Karl. "A Liturgical Play of Joseph and His Brethren."
Modern Language Notes, XXVI (1911), 33-37.

*1660 ----- "Philippe de Mézièr's Dramatic Office for the Presenta-
tion of the Virgin." Publications of the Modern Language
Association, XXVI (1911), 181-234.

*1661 Chevalier, Ulysse. Poésie liturgique des églises de France aux
XVIIe et XVIIIe siècles ou recueil d'hymnes et de proses
usitées a cette époque et distribuées suivant l'orde du Brévi-
aire et du Missel. Paris: Alphonse Picard et Fils, Libraires,
1912. xcii, 255 pp. Index.
BM.

1662 Graves, T. S. "Some Allusions to Religious and Political Plays."
Modern Philology, IX (1912), 545-554.

1663 Norem, H. J. "Dramatic Elements in the English Sacred Drama."
M.A. University of Iowa, 1912.

*1664 Sondheimer, Isaac. Die Herodes-Partien im lateinischen
        liturgischen Drama und in den französischen Mysterien.
        Halle, a.S.: M. Niemeyer, 1912. 179 pp. "Benutze
        Werke," pp. [v]-viii.
            BM. IaU. IU. MiU. MnU. NN. OC1. PU. WU.

 1665 Young, Karl. "A New Text of the Officium Stellae." Modern
        Language Notes, XXVII (1912), 68-71.

 1666 ----- "Officium Pastorum: A Study of the Dramatic Develop-
        ments within the Liturgy of Christmas." Transactions of
        the Wisconsin Academy of Sciences, Arts, and Letters,
        XVII, Part 1 (1912), 299-396.

 1667 Coffman, George R. "New Theory Concerning the Origin of
        the Miracle Play." Ph.D. University of Chicago, 1913.

*1668 Craig, Hardin. "The Origin of the Old Testament Plays."
        Modern Philology, X (1913), 473-487.

 1669 Crosse, Gordon. Religious Drama. Edited by Percy Dearmer.
        London: A. R. Mowbray & Co., Ltd., 1913. xvi, 182 pp.
            BM. IaU. IU. MH. MiU. MnU. NN. OC1. PU. WU.

 1670 Faral, Edmond. Recherches sur les sources latines des contes
        et romane courtois du moyen âge. Paris: Champion, 1913.
        xi, 431 pp.
            BM.

 1671 Legris, A. "La Liturgie rouennaise en Italie." Revue des
        Questions historiques," Nouvelle Série, XLIX (1913), 450-
        460.

 1672 Michaelis, Eduard A. F. "Zum Ludus de Antichristo." Zeit-
        schrift (Anzeiger) für Deutsches Altertum und Deutsche
        Literatur, LIV (1913), 61-87.

 1673 Young, Karl. "La Procession des Trois Rois at Besancon."
        The Romanic Review, IV (1913), 76-83.

 1674 Rudwin, Josef M. "Relation of Religious Drama to Liturgies of
        the Church." Modern Language Notes, XXIX (1914), 108-109.

*1675 Young, Karl. "Officium Pastorum: A Study of the Dramatic
        Developments within the Liturgy of Christmas." Transactions

of the Wisconsin Academy of Science and Letters, XVII (1914),
229-230.

*1676 Young, Karl. "The Origin of the Easter Play." Publications of
the Modern Language Association, XXIX (1914), 1-58.

*1677 Dürre, Konrad. Die Mercatorscene in lateinisch-liturgischen,
altdeutschen und altfranzösischen religiösen Drama. Göttingen:
Druck von Heinrich, John Salle, 1915. 100 pp.
MH. MnU.

1678 Jenney, Adeline M. "A Further Word As to the Origin of the Old
Testament Plays." Modern Philology, XII (1915), 59-64.

1679 Whitmore, Charles Edward. Supernatural in Tragedy. Cambridge:
Harvard University Press, 1915. viii, 370 pp. Bibliography,
pp. [359]-362. [See pp. 113-127.]

*1680 Young, Karl, and Gustave Cohen. "The Officium Stellae from
Bilsen." Romania, XLIV (1915-1917), 357-372.

1681 Bonnell, J. K. "The Easter 'Sepulchrum' in Its Relation to the
Architecture of the High Altar." Publications of the Modern
Language Association, XXXI (1916), 664-712.

1682 Chasles, Madeleine. "Le Drame liturgique." La Vie et les arts
liturgiques, III (1916-1917), 65-70, 121-134, 169-181, 258-266,
297-307, 403-412.

*1683 Kretzmann, Paul Edward. The Liturgical Element in the Earliest
Forms of the Medieval Drama, with Special Reference to the
English and German Plays. Minneapolis: University of Minn-
esota, 1916. vii, 170 pp. Bibliography, pp. 165-170. (The
University of Minnesota Studies in Language and Literature,
No. 4).
BM. ICN. MiU. OC1. OCU. OU. PU. ViU.

1684 Omont, H. "Recherches sur la Bibliothèque de l'Église cathédrale
de Beauvais." Mémoires de l'Institut National de France:
Académie des Inscriptions et Belles-Lettres, XL (1916), 1-93.

*1685 Pierson, Merle. "The Relation of the Corpus Christi Procession
to the Corpus Christi Play in England." Transactions of the
Wisconsin Academy of Sciences, Arts, and Letters, XVIII
(1916), 110-165.

1686   Wanous, Hildegarde E. "The Bohemian Liturgical Drama."
       M.A. University of Minnesota, 1916.

1687   Anglès, H. "El Cant de la Sibila." Vida Cristiana, IV (1917),
       65-72.

1688   Böhme, Martin. Das lateinische Weihnachtsspiel, Grundzüge
       seiner (entwicklung). Leipzig: R. Voigtländer, 1917. 130 pp.

1689   Böhme, Martin. Das lateinische Weihnachtspiel. (Grundzüge seiner
       Entwichlung). Inaugural Dissertation. Leipzig, 1917. 132 pp.

1690   Nilson, Martin P. "Studien zur Vorgeschichte des Weihnachtsfestes."
       Archiv für Religionswissenschaft, XIX (December 14, 1917),
       50-150.

*1691 Young, Karl, and Gustave Cohen. "The Officum Stellae from
       Bilsen." Romania, XLIV (Janvier-Octobre, 1916-1917), 357-
       372.

1692   Gümbel-Seiling, Max. Das Niederdeutsche Osterspiel aus
       Redentin v. J. 1464 in der Übertragung. Leipzig: Breitkopf
       & Härtel, 1918. 95 pp.
              BM.

1693   Ursprung, Otto. "Die lateinische Osterfeiern und die Anfänge
       des neueren Dramas, sowie die Frühgeschichte des deutschen
       Kirchenliedes." Zeitschrift für Musikwissenschaft, II (1919-
       1920), 612-614.

1694   Weber, Toni. Die Präfigurationen im geistlichen Drama
       Deutschlands. Inaugural Dissertation. Marburg, 1919. 88 pp.

*1695 Young, Karl. "A New Version of the Peregrinus." Publications
       of the Modern Language Association, XXXIV (1919), 114-129.

*1696 ----- Ordo Rachelis. Madison: University of Wisconsin Press,
       1919. 65 pp. (University of Wisconsin Studies in Language and
       Liturature, No. 4).
              BM. ICN. IaU. WU.

1697   Heiberg, J. L. "Den hellige Nikolaos." Tilskueren (Copenhagen),
       XXXII, Part 2 (1920), 30-52.

*1698 Young, Karl. The Dramatic Associations of the Easter Sepulchre.

Madison: University of Wisconsin Press, 1920. 130 pp.
(University of Wisconsin Studies in Language and Literature,
No. 10).
   BM. IaU. ICN. MB. MiU. MnU. OC1. OCU. OO.
   ViU. WU.

*1699 Brooks, Neil Conwell. The Sepulchre of Christ in Art and Liturgy.
       Urbana: University of Illinois Press, 1921. 110 pp. Biblio-
       graphical footnotes. (University of Illinois Studies in Language
       and Literature, VII, No. 2.)
          BM. ICN. MB. MiU. MnU. OC1. OCU. PP. ViU.

1700 Fissen, Karl. Das Leben des heiligen Nikolaus in der altfran-
      zösischen Literatur und seine Quellen. Göttingen: Littmann,
      1921. 104 pp. Bibliography, pp. vi-viii.
         IaU. IU. NjP.

1701 Flood, W. H. Grattan. "Irish Origin of the Officium Pastorum."
      Month, CXXXVIII (1921), 545-549.

1702 Foerster, Wendelin and Edward Koschwitz. Altfranzösisches
      Uebungsbuch. Edited by A. Hilka. Leipzig, 1921.
         CU. IaU. LU. MdBJ. MnU. MoU. NhD. NNC.
         OO. TxU.

*1703 Male, Emile. "Le Drame liturgique et l'iconographie de la
       Resurrection." Revue de l'Art Ancien et Moderne, XXXIX
       (1921), 213-222.

1704 Stammler, Wolfgang. Mittelniederdeutsches Lesebuch. Hamburg:
      Hartung, 1921. 148 pp.
         ICU.

1705 Symons, T. "The Monastic Reforms of King Edgar." Downside
      Review, XXXIX (1921), 38-51.

1706 Williamson, Claude C. "Early Religious Drama." American
      Catholic Quarterly Review, XLVI (1921), 225-242.

*1707 Young, Karl. "Ordo Prophetarum." Transactions of the Wiscon-
       sin Academy of Science and Letters, XX (1921), 1-82.

1708 Benninghoff, Ludwig. Ludus de Antechristo oder das Spiel vom
      Kaiserreich und vom Antechrist. Hamburg: Hanseatische
      Verlagsanstalt, 1922. 113 pp. (Aus alten Bücherschranken).

[Original Latin and German translation.]
BM.

*1709 Cabrol, Fernand. Liturgical Prayer: Its History and Spirit.
London: Burns, Oates and Washbourne, Ltd., 1922. xiv,
382 pp. [Translated by a Benedictine of Stanbrook.]
BM. ICN.

1710 Farnham, Willard. "Scogan's 'Quem Quaeritis.'" Modern
Language Notes, XXXVII (1922), 289-292.

1711 Gougaud, L. "La Crèche de Noël avant Saint Francois d'Assise."
Revue des Sciences religieuses, II (1922), 26-34. [Christmas].

1712 Guardini, Romano. Vom Geist der Liturgie. Achte bis zwölfte
durchgesehene Auflage. Freiburg i.B.: Herder, 1922. xvii,
99 pp. (Ecclesia orans, 1).
BM.

1713 Heyne, Hildegard. Das Gleichnis von den klugen und torichten
Jungfrauen: eine literarischikonographische Studie zur alt-
christlichen Zeit. Leipzig: H. Haessel, 1922. 111 pp. "Die
Liturgie," pp. 21-30.
BM.

1714 Klein, Karl. Das geistliche Drama des Mittelalters. Versuch
einer Deutung als Gesamtphänomen. Inaugural Dissertation.
Köln, 1922. 184 leaves.

1715 Meyer, Emanuela. Die romanischen Elemente in den latenischen
Kirchendramen auf gallischem Boden. 2 vol. Inaugural Dissertation, Wien, 1922.

1716 Smith, Alison Moore. "The Iconography of the Sacrifice of
Isaac in Early Christian Art." American Journal of Archaeology, XXVI (1922), 159-173.

1717 Spener, Elisabeth. Die Entstehung des Redentiner Osterspiels.
Münster, 1922. 153 leaves.

1718 Sullivan, Blanche Gertrude. The Mystery Plays and Other Poems
of Hilary. M.A. Stanford University, 1922.

1719 Symons, T. "The Regularis Concordia." Downside Review, XL
(1922), 15-30.

1720 Tucker, Irwin St. John. "The Religious Origin of the Drama."
      Drama, XIII (1922), 47-51.

1721 Wilmart, A. "Le Samedi-Saint monastique." Revue bénédictine,
      XXXIV (1922), 159-163.

*1722 Young, Karl. "Ordo Prophetarum." Transactions of the Wiscon-
      sin Academy of Science and Letters, XX (1922), 1-82.

*1723 ----- "Concerning the Origin of the Miracle Play." The Manly
      Anniversary Studies in Language and Literature. (Chicago,
      1923), pp. 254-268.

1724 Blair, William Lawrence. "The Early Dramatic Activity of the
      Church in England." Ph.D. Yale University, 1923.

1725 Flood, W. H. Grattan. "The Irish Origin of the Easter Play."
      Month, CXLI (April, 1923), 349-352.

1726 Klapper, Joseph. "Der Ursprung der lateinischen Osterfeiern."
      Zeitschrift für deutsche Philologie, L (1923), 46-58.

1727 Molitor, R. "Passionspiel und Passionsliturgie." Benediktinische
      Monatschrift, V (1923), 105-116.

*1728 Young, Karl. "Concerning the Origin of the Miracle Play."
      The Manly Anniversary Studies in Language and Liter-
      ature. (Chicago, 1923), pp. 254-268.

1729 Grünes, Franz. Advent und Weihnachtsspiele im Erzgebirge.
      Inaugural Dissertation. Prag, 1924.

*1730 Muller, H. F. "Pre-History of the Medieval Drama. The Ante-
      cedents of the Tropes and the Conditions of Their Appearance."
      Zeitschrift für romanische Philologie, XLIV (1924), 544-575.

1731 Stapper, Richard. "Liturgische Ostergebräuche im Dom zu
      Münster." Zeitschrift für vaterländische Geschichte und
      Altertumskunde, LXXXII (1924), 19-51.

*1732 Coffman, George R. "A New Approach to Medieval Latin Drama."
      Modern Philology, XXI (February, 1925), 239-271.

1733 Faral, Edmond. La littérature latine du moyen âge; lecon d'
      ouverture prononcée au College de France le 24 Avril 1925.

Paris: Champion, 1925. 38 pp.
BM.

1734 Häne, Rafael. "Einsiedelns geistliche Spiele." Schweizerische
Rundschau, XXV (1925/6), 277-291.

1735 Rosenhagen, Gustav. "Das Redentiner Osterspiel im Zusammenhang mit den geistlichen Spielen seiner Zeit." Jahrbuch des
Vereins für niederdeutsche Sprachforschung, II (1925), 91-103.

1736 Samaran, C. "Miracle de saint Nicolas, Manuscrit du XVe
siècle." Romania, LI (April, 1925), 191-197.

1737 Tirabassi, Antonio. La parabole des Vierges sages et des Vierges
folles, d' après un Office noté du XIe siècle. Ixelles: M. Forton,
1925. 11 pp. [Conférence du 2 Juin, 1925].
BM.

1738 Clark, James Midgley. The Abbey of St. Gall As a Centre of
Literature and Art. Cambridge [England]: The University
Press, 1926. vi, [2], 322 pp. Bibliography, pp. [305]-313.

*1739 Young, Karl. "The Home of the Easter Play." Speculum, I (1926),
71-86.

1740 Bolte, Johannes, ed. Drei Schauspiele vom sterbenden Menschen.
1. Das Münchener Spiel von 1510. 2. Macropedius, Hecastus,
1539. 3. Neogeorgus, Mercator, 1540. Leipzig: K. W. Hiersemann, 1927. 319 pp. (Bibliothek des Literarischen vereins
in Stuttgart. Tübingen, CCLXIX/CCLXX.)
ICU.

1741 James, Stanley B. "A Study in Passion Plays." Month, CXLIX
(April, 1927), 309-315.

1742 Meyer, Kathi. Über die Melodiebildung in den geistlichen Spielen
des früheren Mittelalters. Internationaler musikhistorischer
Kongress (Beethoven-Zentenarfeier Wien 26. bis 31. März
1927). Vienna, 1927. 404 pp.
BM.

*1743 Raby, F. J. E. A History of Christian-Latin Poetry from the
Beginnings to the Close of the Middle Ages. Oxford: At the
Clarendon Press, 1927. xii, 491 pp. Bibliography, pp.
461-485. Index.

BM. DLC. IC Loy. ICN. ICU. IU. MH. NN. O.

1744 La Seinte resureccion. Anglonormanisches Osterspiel aus dem
      ende des XII. Jahrhunderts. Herausgegeben von Nikolaus
      Joseph Kiefer. Strassburg: Druck von J. H. Ed. Heitz, 1927.
      [4], 103, [1] pp. "Literatur, " pp. 98-100. [Text in French].
      BM.

1745 Samaran, C. "Mystère de saint Nicolas." [Fragment de Prologue;
      Texte avec améliorations à l'aide de rayons ultraviolets],
      Romania, LIII (July, 1927), 297-299.

1746 Stapper, Richard. "Mittelalterliche Ostergebräuche der Stift-
      sherren zu Klene." Römische Quartelschrift für christliche
      Altertumskunde und für Kirchengeschichte, XXXV (1927),
      171-182.

*1747 Thomas, Lucien-Paul. "La Versification et les lecons douteuses
       du Sponsus." Romania, LIII (1927), 43-81. (Texte Roman).

*1748 Brooks, Neil C. "The 'Sepulchrum Christi' and Its Ceremonies in
       Late Mediaeval and Modern Times." Journal of English and
       Germanic Philology, XXVII (April, 1928), 147-161.

*1749 Cohen, Gustave. "La Comédie latine en France au XIIe siècle."
       Mélanges de linguistique et de littérature offerts à M. Jeanroy
       par ses éleves et ses amis. (Paris, 1928), pp. 255-263.

1750 Coyle, Matthew Aloysius. "The Attitude of the Early Church
      Towards the Drama." M.A. Yale University, 1928.

1751 Haupt, Günther. Friedrich Hermann Flayders Moria Rediviva
      und die Bedeutendsten Vertreter des lateinischen Schuldramas
      im 16. und 17 Jahrhundert; zwei Beiträge zur Geschichte des
      lateinischen Schuldramas. Tübingen: Buchdruckerei der
      Tübinger Studenthilfe, 1928. 60 pp.
      ICU.

1752 Krogmann, Willy. "Die zweite weibliche Rolle im Redentiner
      Osterspiel." Zeitschrift für deutsche Philologie, LIII (1928),
      135-143.

1753 Marshall, Mary Hatch. "Antichrist in Mediaeval Drama and in
      the Drama of the Reformation in England." M.A. Yale Uni-
      versity, 1928.

1754 Muller, H. F. "Prehistory of the Medieval Drama. The Ante-
        cedent of the Tropes and the Conditions of Their Appearance."
        Zeitschrift für romanische Philologie, XLIV (1928), 544-575.

1755 Osgood, Phillips Endecott. Old-time Church Drama Adapted.
        New York, London: Harper, 1928. 291 pp.
        BM. DLC. IaU. MB. NN. OC1. OC1C. WU.

1756 Scholz, Felix. "Ein neues Osterleis von der 15. zum 16. Jahr."
        Zeitschrift für deutsche Philologie, LIII (1928), 49-54.

1757 Wilmart, André. L'ancien Cantatorium de l'église de Strasbourg.
        Colmar: Editions Alsatia, 1928. xxii, 116 pp.
        BM.

1758 Bäschlin, Hans Alfred. Die altdeutschen Salbenkrämerspiele.
        Inaugural Dissertation. Basel, 1929. [At the Bodleian.]

*1759 Brinkman, Alfons. Zum Ursprung des liturgischen Spieles.
        Bonn: Friedrich Cohen, 1929. 40 pp.
        MiU. MnU.

1760 Campbell, N. R. "Medieval Religious Drama." Truth, XXXIII
        (1929), 5-7.

1761 Eastman, Fred. "Religious Drama in England." Christian Cen-
        tury, XLVI (1929), 1212-1214.

1762 Hogan, A. J. "The Liturgical Origin and the Didactic Purposes
        of the Medieval Drama." Ph.D. Cambridge University, 1929.

1763 Lampen, Willibrord. Liturgie en drama. Leuven: Abdij Keizer-
        sberg; Brugge: Abdij Steenbrugge; 's Bosh, Federatie van Lit.
        Ver. in Nederland [1929]. 44 pp.
        Royal Library, Albert I, Brussels

*1764 Liuzzi, Fernando. "L'espressione musicale nel dramma liturgico."
        Studi Medievali, New Ser., II (April, 1929), 74-109.

*1765 Thomas, Lucien-Paul. "Les Strophes et la composition du Sponsus
        (Textes Latin et Roman)." Romania, LV (1929), 45-112. [The
        Bilingual Sponsus.]

1766 Walter, Joseph. "Le Mystère 'stella' des trois mages joué à la
        cathédrale de Strasbourg au XIIe siècle." Archives Alsaciennes
        d'histoire de l'art, VIII (1929), 39-50.

1767 Bloor, Robert Henry Underwood. Christianity and the Religious
        Drama. Boston: Beacon Press, 1930. 64 pp. (Essex Hall
        Lectures, 1928).
            BM. DLC. MH. WU.

1768 Cargill, Oscar. Drama and Liturgy. New York: Columbia Uni-
        versity Press, 1930. ix, 151 pp. Bibliography, pp. 145-148.
            BM. CSmH. CtY. DFo. DLC. IaU. ICN. ICU. MB.
            MH. MiU. OCl. OO. PU. ViU. WU.

1769 Eastman, Fred. Religion and Drama: Friends or Enemies?
        New York, London: Century, 1930. 19 pp.
            BM. DLC.

1770 Fleming, Willi. Das Ordensdrama. Leipzig: P. Reclam jun.,
        1930. 369 pp.
            ICU.

1771 Liuzzi, F. "Le Vergini savie e le Vergine folli." Studi Medievali,
        Nuova serie, III (1930), 82-109.

1772 Thulin, Oskar. Johannes der Täufer im geistlichen Schauspiel
        des Mittelalters und der Reformationszeit. Leipzig: Dieterich,
        1930. vii, 150 pp. (Studien über christliche Denkmäler. Heft.
        19). Bibliography, pp. 147-150.
            NN.

1773 Wellington, Sister St. Paul. "The Influence of the Medieval Hymn
        on Mediaeval Drama." Ph.D. University of Southern California,
        1930.

*1774 Young, Karl. "Dramatic Ceremonies of the Feast of the Purifica-
        tion." Speculum, V (1930), 97-102.

1775 Albrecht, Otto E. "The Nicholas Plays of the Fleury MS." Ph.D.
        University of Pennsylvania, 1931.

1776 Brown, Carleton. "An Early Mention of a St. Nicholas Play in
        England." Studies in Philology, XXVIII (October, 1931), 62-69.
        [Numbered 594-601 in continuous numbering in the volume.]

*1777 Duchesne, L. Christian Worship, Its Origin and Evolution. A
        Study of the Latin Liturgy up to the Time of Charlemagne.
        London: S.P.C.K., 1931. xx, 593 pp. Index.
            BM.

1778 Hayde, Sister Mary Loyola. "The Source of the Latin Trope."
      Ph.D. University of Illinois, 1931.

1779 Lipphardt, Walther. "Weihnachtsspiel und Liturgie." Die
      Singemeinde, VIII (1931-1932), 34-46.

1780 Siegl, Karl. "Das Egerer Fronleichnamsspiel." Unser Egerland,
      XXXV (1931), 33-39.

1781 Spanke, Hans. "Rhythmen - und Sequenzenstudien." Studi Medievali,
      New Ser., IV (1931), 286-320. [Trope-Sequence].

1782 Stender-Petersen, Adolf. Tragoediae sacrae; Materialien und
      Beiträge zur Geschichte der polnisch-lateinischen Jesuit-
      endramatik der Frühzeit. Tartu (Dorpat): [K. Mattiesens
      Buchdruckerei ant. ges]. 1931. 279 pp.
          BM. ICU.

1783 Wagner, Peter. "Ein vierstimmiger Agnustropus." Kirchen-
      musikalisches Jahrbuch, XXVI (1931), 7-12.

1784 Williamson, Claude C. "Early Religious Drama." Irish Ecclesi-
      astical Review, 5th Ser., XXXVIII (1931), 9-18, 157-169,
      267-284.

1785 App, Austin J. "Origin of Our Drama." Magnificat, XLIX (1932),
      236-240.

1786 Bischoff, B. "Regensburger Beiträge zur mittelalterlichen
      Dramatik und Ikonographie." Historische Vierteljahrs-
      chrift, XXVII (1932), 509-522.

1787 Breuer, Hans-Hermann. Das mittelniederdeutsche Osnabrücker
      Osterspiel. Der Ursprung des Osterspiels und die Prozession.
      Osnabrück: Ferdinand Schöningh, 1932. 118 pp. Bibliography,
      pp. 93-101. (Beiträge zur Geschichte und Kulturgeschichte
      des Bistums Osnabrück.]
          BM.

*1788 Brinkman, Alfons. Liturgische und volkstümliche Formen im
      geistlichen Spiel des deutschen Mittelalters. Münster: Aschen-
      dorff, 1932. 92 pp.
          CtY. ICN. MnU. OO. OU. WU.

1789 Burke, Mary Meda. "Realism in the Religious Drama of Mediaeval

England." M.A. University of Minnesota, 1932.

*1790 Cabrol, Fernand. The Books of the Latin Liturgy. Translated
by the Benedictines of Stanbrook. London: Sands & Co.; St.
Louis, Missouri: B. Herder Book Co., 1932. xii, 166 pp.
Bibliography, pp. 160-162, 165-166. (Vol. XXII of Catholic
Library of Religious Knowledge).
BM.

1791 Gérold, Théodore. La musique au moyen âge. Paris: Champion,
1932. xi, 441 pp. (Les classiques francais du moyen âge,
73).
BM.

1792 Lipphardt, Walther. "Marienklagen und Liturgie." Jahrbuch für
Liturgiewissenschaft, XII (1932), 198-205. [Mary plays].

1793 Marshall, Mary Hatch. "The Relation of the Vernacular Religious
Plays of the Middle Ages to the Liturgical Drama." Ph.D. Yale
University, 1932.

1794 McNeir, W. F. "Dramatic Values in the Passion Groups of the
Corpus Christi Cycles." M.A. University of North Carolina,
1932.

1795 Niedner, Helmut. Die deutschen und französischen Osterspiele bis
zum 15 Jahrhundert. Berlin: E. Ebering, 1932. 186 pp. (Ger-
manische Studien, Hft. 119.) "Literatur," pp. 181-186.
BM. DLC. ICN. MiU. MnU. WU.

1796 Pleister, Werner. "Die Aufführungsform des Ludus de Antichristo." Deutsches Volkstum, XIV (1932), 122-126.

1797 Schultze-Jahde, Karl. "Zum Tegernseer Antichristspiel."
Zeitschrift für Deutschkunde, XLVI (1932), 665-668.

1798 ----- "Zur Literatur über das Tegernseer Antichristspiel."
Zeitschrift für deutsche Philologie, LVII (1932), 180-183.

1799 Spanke, Hans. "Zur Geschichte der lateinischen nichtliturgischen
Sequenz." Speculum, VII (July, 1932), 367-382.

1800 Stallbaumer, O.S.V., Virgil R. "The Easter Trope. The Major
Source of the English Drama." Catholic World, CXXXIV
(1932), 652-659.

1801 Steinmann, Ulrich. "Der Weckruf des Michaels im Redentiner Osterspiel." Zeitschrift für deutsche Philologie, LVII (1932), 373-379.

1802 Bencker, Georg. Das deutsche Weihnachtsspiel. Inaugural Dissertation. Greifswald, 1933. ix, 68 pp.

1803 Dobbins, Dunstan J. "Drama of the Medieval Church." Catholic World, CXXXVIII (1933), 89-93.

1804 Dörrer, A. "Fronleichnamsspiel, Bozner." Stammler, Wolfgang, ed. Die deutsche Literatur des Mittelalters. Vol. I. (Berlin und Leipzig, 1933-1953), cols. 698-730.

1805 ----- "Fronleichnamsspiel, Freiburger." Stammler, Wolfgang, ed. Die deutsche Literatur des Mittelalters. Vol. I. (Berlin und Leipzig, 1933-1953), cols. 732-768.

1806 ----- "Fronleichnamsspiel, Künzelsauer." Stammler Wolfgang, ed. Die deutsche Literatur des Mittelalters. Vol. I. (Berlin und Leipzig, 1933-1953), cols. 768-773.

1807 ----- "'Ludus de Antichristo' (Antichrist-Dramen)." Langosch, Karl, ed. Die deutsche Literatur des Mittelalters. Vol. 3. (Berlin und Leipzig, 1933-1953), cols. 87-185.

1809 ----- "Passionsspiel, Egerer." Langosch, Karl, ed. Die deutsche Literatur des Mittelalters. Vol. 3. (Berlin und Leipzig, 1933-1953), cols. 738-741.

1810 ----- "Passionsspiel, Donaueschinger (Villinger)." Langosch, Karl, ed. Die deutsche Literatur des Mittelalters. Vol. 3. (Berlin und Leipzig, 1933-1953), cols. 726-738.

1811 ----- "Passionsspiel, Tiroler." Langosch, Karl, ed. Die deutsche Literatur des Mittelalters. Vol. 3. (Berlin und Leipzig, 1933-1953), cols. 741-835.

1812 ----- "Judenspiel, Endlingen, Rinner und Trienter." Stammler, Wolfgang, ed. Die deutsche Literatur des Mittelalters. Vol. 2. (Berlin und Leipzig, 1933-1953), cols. 667-717.

1813 ----- "Weihnachts- (Kindelwiegen-Spiel, Niederhessisches und Eisacktaler." Langosch, Karl. Die deutsche Literatur des Mittelalters. Vol. 4. (Berlin und Leipzig, 1933-1953), cols. 871-883.

1814 Dörrer, A. "Weihnachtsspiel, Unterinntaler." Langosch, Karl,
      ed. Die deutsche Literatur des Mittelalters. Vol. 4. (Berlin
      und Leipzig, 1933-1953), cols. 884-888.

1815 Gierach, Erich. "Fronleichnamsspiel, Egerer." Stammler,
      Wolfgang, ed. Die deutsche Literatur des Mittelalters. Vol.
      I. (Berlin und Leipzig, 1933-1953), cols. 730-732.

1816 Lipphardt, Walther. "Studien zu den Marienklagen." Die Singe-
      meinde, IX (1933), 65-79.

1817 McCabe, W. H. "The Drama in the Church." Times Literary
      Supplement, 1933, pp. 651-652.

1818 Fuller, Raymond Tifft. The World's Stage; Oberammergau,
      1934; a Book about the Passion Play; Its History, Its Mean-
      ing and Its People. New York: R. M. McBride and Co.;
      London: Cobden-Sanderson, Ltd., 1934. 58 pp.
          BM. DLC. IaU. MH. OCl.

1819 Kamlah, Wilhelm. "Der Ludus de Antichristo." Historische
      Vierteljahrschrift, XXVIII (1934), 53-87.

1820 Levi, E. "La Leggenda dell' Antichristo nel teatro medievale."
      Studi Medievali, New Ser., VII, fasc. 1 (1934), 52-63.

1821 Lipphardt, W. "Studien zu den Marienklagen. Marienklage und
      germanische Totenklage." Beiträge zur Geschichte der
      deutschen Sprache und Literatur, LVIII (Halle, 1934), 390-
      444. [Mary plays].

1822 Spanke, Hans. "Aus der Vorgeschichte und Frühgeschichte der
      Sequenz." Zeitschrift für deutsches alterum und deutsche
      Literatur, LXXI (1934), 1-3. [Trope].

1823 Petsch, Robert. "Die Vorspiele des Theophilus Dramas."
      Niederdeutsches Jahrbuch, LXV-LXVI (1935-1940, ersch.
      1941), 45-54.

1824 Rushton, Gerald Wayne. "Passion Plays and Their Origin."
      Catholic World, CXXXIX (1935), 40-46.

1825 Tabor, Lotte. Die Kultur des Klosters Tegernsee im frühen
      Mittelalter. Bottrop i.W.: Wilhelm Postberg, 1935. vi, 122 pp.
          BM.

1826 Dreimüller, Karl. Die Musik des Alsfelder Passionsspiels.
Ein Beitrag zur Geschichte der Musik in den geistlichen
Spielen des Mittelalters. Mit erstmaliger Veröffentlichung
der Melodien aus der Kasseller Handschrift des Alsfelder Spiels.
Inaugural Dissertation. Wien, 1936. 91 leaves.

1827 Meyer, Otto. "Ein Beitrag zur Geschichte des mittelalterlichen
Dramas." Neophilologus, XXII (1936), 63-69.

1828 Rauhut, Franz. "Der Sponsus." Romanische Forschungen, L
(1936), 21-50.

1829 Sievers, Heinrich. Die lateinischen liturgischen Osterspiele der
Stiftskirche von St. Blasien zu Braunschweig, Eine musik-
wissenschaftliche Untersuchung der liturgischen dramatischen
Osterfeiern in Niedersachsen mit besönderer beruck sichti-
gung des lateinischen liturgischen Osterspieles Braunschweig
IV. Berlin: Triltsch & Huther, 1936. 70, [2] pp.
DLC.

1830 Stumpfl, Robert. Kultspiele der Germanen als Ursprung des
mittelalterlichen Dramas. Berlin: Junker und Dünnhaupt,
1936. 448 pp.
BM. DLC. IaU. MH. MnU. NN. OCU. OO. OU. WU.

*1831 Wright, Edith Armstrong. The Dissemination of the Liturgical
Drama in France. Bryn Mawr: Bryn Mawr College, 1936.
201 pp. Bibliography, pp. 187-197.
DLC. IaU. MnU. OU. ViU. WU.

*1832 Hartl, Eduard. Das Drama des Mittelalters, sein wesen und
sein werden; Osterfeiern; mit einleitungen und anmerkungen
auf Grund der Handschriften. Leipzig: P. Reclam, un.,
1937. 266 pp. "Buchweiser," pp. [7]-12.
BM. DLC. IaU. IU. MB. OO. OU. PSC. PSt.

1833 Krogmann, Willy, ed. Das Redentiner Osterspiel. Leipzig:
Hirzel, 1937. 96 pp. (Altdeutsche Quellen. Heft. 3).
BM.

*1834 Shull, Virginia. "Clerical Drama in Lincoln Cathedral, 1318-
1561." Publications of the Modern Language Association, LII
(1937), 946-966.

1835 Zucker, A. E. "A Reconstruction of the Staging of the Redentin
Easter Play." Germanic Review, XII (1937), 1-13.

1836 Creamer, Sister John Elizabeth. "English Fifteenth Century Christmas Carols, Their Origin, Development and Relation to the Liturgy of the Christmas Cycle." M.A. Catholic University of America, 1938.

1837 Schröder, E. "Das Eisenacher Passionsspiel von 1227." Zeitschrift für deutsche Altertum und deutsche Literatur, LXXV (1938), 120.

1838 Spanke, Hans. "Sequenz und Lai." Studi Medievali, New Ser., XI (1938), 12-68.

1839 Ursprung, Otto. "Das Sponsusspiel." Archiv für Musikforschung, III (1938), 80-95.

1840 Breuer, Hans-Hermann. Das mittelnieder-deutsche Osnabrücker. Der Ursprung des Osterspiels und der Prozession, Untersuchungen, Einleitung und Ausgabe. Inaugural Dissertation. Munster, 1939. iv, 119 pp.

*1841 Creizenach, W. "Miracle-Plays and Moralities." The Cambridge History of English Literature. Vol. 5. (New York, Cambridge, 1939), pp. 40-67.

1842 Inguanez, Mauro, ed. Un dramma della passione del secolo XII. 2d ed. Pref. di Giulio Bertoni. Badia di Montecassino, 1939. 55 pp. (Miscellanea cassinese, 18).
BM. ICN.

1843 Rava, Arnaldo. Teatro medievale. L'Apparato scenico nella Visita delle Marie ae Sepolcro. Roma, 1939. 32 pp.
DLC. MnU. NN.

1844 Rushton, Gerald Wayne. "Passion Plays and Their Origin." Irish Ecclesiastical Review, 5th Ser., LIV (October, 1939), 375-384.

1845 Schlauch, Margaret. "The Allegory of Church and Synagogue." Speculum, XIV (1939), 448-464. [Antichrist].

*1846 Arnould, E. J. Le Manuel des Péchés. Etudes de littérature religieuse anglo-normande. Paris: E. Droz, 1940. ix, 451 pp. Bibliography, pp. 437-448.
BM.

1847 Ott, Hans. Personengestaltung im geistlichen Drama des Mittelalters. Inaugural Dissertation. Bonn, 1940. 159 pp.

1848 Rava, Arnaldo. Teatro medievale. L'apparato scenico negli
offici drammatici del tempo di natale. Roma: Libreria
Coletti, 1940. 53 pp.
ICU.

*1849 Toschi, Paolo. Dal Dramma Liturgico alla rappresentazione sacra.
Firenze: G. C. Sansoni, 1940. 169, [4] pp. (Biblioteca del
Leonardo, XVII).
BM. NN.

1850 Vijf Geestelijke Toneelspelen der Middeleeuwen. Amsterdam:
N. V. Uitgeners-mij. "Elsevier," 1940. [8], 379 pp. [Also
has the text of Elkerlijk.]
BM.

1851 Hartl, Eduard. "Das Regensburger Osterspiel und seine Beziehungen zum Freiburger Fronleichnamsspiel." Zeitschrift
für deutsche altertum und deutsche Literatur, LXXVIII
(1941), 121-132.

*1852 Marshall, Mary Hatch. "The Dramatic Tradition Established by
the Liturgical Plays. Publications of the Modern Language
Association, LVI (December, 1941), 962-991.

*1853 Pascal, R. "On the Origins of the Liturgical Drama of the Middle
Ages." Modern Language Review, XXXVI (1941), 369-387.

1854 Spanke, Hans. "Die Kompositionskunst der Sequenzen Adams von
St. Victor." Studi Medievali, New Ser., XIV (1941), 1-29.

1855 Symons, Thomas. "Sources of the 'Regularis Concordia.'" Downside Review, LIX (1941), 14-36, 143-170, 264-289.

*1856 Zucker, Adolf Edward, ed. and trans. The Redentin Easter Play.
Translated from the Low German of the Fifteenth Century,
with Introduction and Notes. New York: Columbia University
Press, 1941. x, 134 pp. (Records of Civilization, 32). [Prose
translation].
BM.

1857 Zucker, A. E., H. K. Russell, and Mary Margaret Russell.
"Redentin Easter Play." Poet Lore, XLVII (1941), 3-39.
["Condensed" version.]

1858 Coogan, Marjorie Dolores. "The Influence of the Liturgy on the
      English Cycle Plays." Ph.D. Yale University, 1942.

1859 Salazar, Adolfo. La musica en la sociedad Europea desde los
      primeros tiempos Cristianos. Vol. I. Mexico City: El Colegio
      de México, 1942.
          DLC.

1860 Yarham, E. R. "Medieval Easter Sepulchre." Atlantic Monthly,
      LV (1942), 432-434.

1861 Carlen, Albert. "Das Ordinarium Sedunense und die Anfänge der
      geistlichen Spiele im Wallis." Blätter aus der Walliser Ges-
      chichte, IX (1943), 349-373.

1862 Herzogenberg, Johanna Freiin von. Die Gestalten der deutschen
      geistlichen Spiele um 1500 als Ausdruck der seelischen Welt
      des späten Mittelalters. Inaugural Dissertation. Prag. 1943,
      101 leaves.

1863 Lynch, W. F. "Liturgy and the Theatre." Liturgical Arts, XII
      (1943), 3-4.

1864 Miller, E. S. "Medieval Biblical and Ritualistic Elements in
      the English Drama, 1497-1562." Ph.D. University of North
      Carolina, 1943.

1865 Ränke, Friedrich, ed. Das Osterspiel von Muris nach den alten
      und neueren Fragmenten. Aarau: H. R. Sauerländer, 1944.
      72 pp. [Text in German.]
          MH.

1866 Whittredge, Ruth, Ed. La Nativité et le Geu des Trois Roys.
      Two Plays from MS 1131 of the Bibliothèque Saint Geneviève,
      Paris. Bryn Mawr, Pennsylvania, 1944. 217 pp. Bibliography,
      pp. 89-93.
          DLC. ICN. MiU. NjP.

1867 Carlen, Albert. "Das Oberwalliser Theater im Mittelalter."
      Schweizerisches Archiv für Volkskunde, XLII (1945), 65-111.

1868 "Liturgical Nativity Play." Sower, CLVII (1945), 6-7.

1869 Pflueger, J. H. L. "On the English Translation of the 'Ludus de
      Antichristo' by W. H. Hulme." Journal of English and

Germanic Philology, XLIV (January, 1945), 24-27.

1870 Woerdeman, Jude, O.S.B. "The Transfer of the Easter Trope 'Quem quaeritis in Sepulchro' to its Position before the 'Te Deum' in Easter Matins." M.A. Catholic University of America, 1945.

*1871 Smoldon, W. L. "The Easter Sepulchre Music-Drama." Music and Letters, XXVII (1946), 1-17. [Visitatio Sepulchri].

1872 Woerdeman, Jude. "Source of the Easter Play; the Easter Quem quaeritis in Sepulchro." Orate Fratres, XX (1946), 262-272.

1873 Eastman, Fred. Christ in the Drama: A Study of the Influence of Christ on the Drama of England and America. New York: Macmillan Co., 1947. x, 174 pp. (The Shaffer Lectures of Northwestern University, 1946).
BM. DLC. IaU. MiU. MnU. WU.

1874 Harmon, Estelle B. K. "The Origin and Development of Early Liturgical Drama." M.A. University of Southern California, 1947.

1875 Liegey, Gabriel M. "Faith and the Origin of Liturgical Art." Thought, XXII (1947), 126-138.

1876 Stout, D. "Miracle Narrative and Play." Homiletic and Pastoral Review, XLVII (1947), 119-125, 191-195.

*1877 Wellesz, Egon. Eastern Elements in Western Chant: Studies in the Early History of Ecclesiastical Music. Oxford: University Press for the Byzantine Institute Inc., Boston, 1947. xv, 212 pp. Index. (Monumenta Musicae Byzantinae Subsidia, Vol. II).
BM. ICN.

1878 Abert, Anna Amalie. "Das Nachleben des Minnesangs im liturgischen Spiel." Die Musikforschung, I (1948), 95-105.

1879 Coucke, A. "Von liturgisch tot geestelijk drama. Bidrage tot de kennis van het middeleeuws toneel." In, Miscellanea J. Gessler (Deurne, 1948), pp. 317-324.

1880 Leitzmann, Albert. "Kleine Bemerkungen zum Redentiner Osterspiel." Niederdeutsche Mitteilungen, IV (1948), 48-49.

1881 Lipphardt, Walther. Die Weisen der lateinischen Osterspiele
      des 12. and 13. Jahrhunderts. Kassell: Bärenreiter, 1948.
      40 pp. (Gesellschaft für Musikforschung. Musikwissenschaft-
      liche Arbeiten, 2).
           BM.

1882 Philipps, Ronald. "The Church and Drama." London Quarterly
      and Holborn Review, CLXXIII (1948), 213-217.

1883 Schieb, Gabriele. "Zum Redentiner Osterspiel." Beiträge zur
      Geschichte der deutschen Sprache und Literatur, LXX (1948),
      295-303.

1884 Von den Steinen, Wolfram. Notker der Dichter und seine geist-
      liche Welt. 2 vol. Bern: A. Francke, 1948. "Literatur-
      Nachweise," Vol. 1, pp. 529-533. [Sequences, St. Gall].
           DLC. ICN.

1885 Appel, Willi. "From St. Martial to Notre Dame." Journal of the
      American Musicological Society, II (Fall, 1949), 145-158.

*1886 Hildburgh, Walter Leo. "English Alabaster Carvings As Records
      of the Medieval Religious Drama." Archaeologia, XCIII (1949),
      51-101.

1887 Reichert, George. "Strukturprobleme der älteren Sequenz."
      Deutsche Vierteljahrschrift für Literaturwissenschaft und
      Geistesgeschichte, XXIII (1949), 227-251.

1888 Boor, Helmut de. "Die lateinischen Grundlagen der deutschen
      Osterspiele." Hessische Blätter für Volkskunde, LXI (1950),
      45-66.

1889 Elsen, Vincent. "Translation of Five Medieval Liturgical Plays."
      M.A. Catholic University of America, 1950.

1890 Greuel, Herbert. Ein Beitrag zur Ursprungsfrage der mittelalter-
      lichen Fastnachtsspiele. Inaugural Dissertation. Koln, 1950.
      196 leaves.

1891 Lipphardt, Walther. "Studien zur Rhythmik der Antiphonen." Die
      Musikforschung, III (Kassel & Basel, 1950), 47-60.

1892 Love, Christopher C. "The Scriptural Latin Plays of the Renais-
      sance and Milton's Cambridge Manuscript." Ph.D. Toronto
      University, 1950.

1893 Marichal, Robert. "Les drames liturgiques du 'Livre de la Trésorerie d'Origny-Sainte-Benoite." Mélanges d'histoire du théâtre du moyen-âge et de la renaissance offerts à Gustave Cohen. (Paris, 1950), pp. 37-45.

*1894 Marshall, Mary H. "Aesthetic Values of the Liturgical Drama." English Institute Essays. 1950. Pp. 89-115.

1895 Mellot, Jean. "A Propos du théâtre liturgique de Bourges." Mélanges d'histoire du théâtre du Moyen-Age et de la Renaissance offerts à Gustave Cohen. (Paris, 1950), pp. 193-198.

1896 Thomas, Lucien-Paul. "Quatre systèmes de rubrication dramatique dans le MS. Paris Latin 1139." Scriptorium, IV (1950), 107-110.

1897 Hauck, Karl. "Zur Genealogie und Gestalt des Staufischen Ludus de Antichristo." Germanisch-romanische Monatsschrift, Neue Folge, II (1951-1952), 11-26.

1898 Jammers, Ewald. "Rhythmische und tonale Studien zur älterem Sequenz." Acta Musicologica, XXIII (1951), 1-40.

1899 Reinhardt, Heinz. "Uber den Ursprung des Dramas." Die Pforte, III (1951/52), 339-347.

*1900 Thomas, Lucien Paul, ed. Le "Sponsus" (mystère des vierges sages et des vierges folles) suivi des trois poèmes limousins et farcis du même manuscrit. Étude critique, textes, musique, notes et glossaire. Paris: Presses universitaires de France, 1951. 251 pp. (Brussels. Université libre. Philosophie et lettres. Faculté. Fravaux. [Tome 12]). BM. NN.

1901 Corbin, Solange. "Le 'Cantus Sibyllae': Origines et premiers textes." Revue de musicologie, XXXI (1952), 1-10. [Sibylline chant].

*1902 Hartl, Eduard, ed. Das Benediktbeurer Passionsspiel. Das St. Galler Passionsspiel. Nach den Handschriften. Halle/Saale: M. Niemeyer, 1952. 131 pp. (Altdeutsche Textbibliothek, Nr. 41). [The text of the Benediktbeurer Passionsspiel is from the Carmina Burana, Clm. 4660; of the St. Galler Passionsspiel from Stiftsbibliothek St. Gallen, Hs. Nr. 919.] BM. ICN. ICU.

1903 Hartl, Eduard. "Die Entwicklung des Benediktbeurer Passions-
      spiels." Euphorion, XLVI (1952), 113-137.

*1904 Henshaw, Millet. "The Attitude of the Church Toward the Stage
       to the End of the Middle Ages." Medievalia et Humanistica,
       VII (1952), 3-17.

1905 Hussman, Heinrich. "Zur Rhythmik des Trouveregesanges."
      Die Musikforschung, V (1952), 110-131.

1906 Rosenfeld, Hellmut. "Das Redentiner Osterspiel-ein Lübecker
      Osterspiel." Beiträge zur Geschichte der deutschen Sprache
      und Literatur, LXXIV (1952), 485-491.

1907 Schreyer, Brigitte. Das lateinisch-deutsche Osterspiel. Gestalt,
      Entwichlung, Urgestalt. Inaugural Dissertation. Halle, 1952.

*1908 Corbin, Solange. "Le Manuscrit 201 D'Orléans. Drame Liturgi-
       ques Dits de Fleury." Romania, LXXIV (1953), 1-43.

1909 Henry, Albert, ed. Chrestomathie de la littérature en ancien
      francais. Berne: A. Francke [1953]. 2 vol. in 1. (Biblio-
      theca romanica. Series altera. Scripta romanica selecta,
      3-4). [Has "Le Sponsus," words and music (in modern
      notation), Vol. 1, pp. 251-255.]
          NN.

1910 Husman, Heinrich. "Das Prinzip der Silbenzählung im Lied des
      zentralen Mittelalters." Die Musikforschung, VI (1953), 8-23.

*1911 Smoldon, W. L. "Mediaeval Music-Drama." Musical Times, XC
       (December, 1953), 557-560.

1912 Atkinson, B. "Church Classic; 'Quem Quaeritis,' Written in the
      Middle Ages Will Be Performed Today." New York Times,
      CIII (May 2, 1954), Section 2, p. 1.

1913 Frank, Grace. "The Beauvais Daniel." The Medieval French
      Drama. (Oxford, 1954), pp. 55-57.

*1914 ----- "Distribution, Dissemination, and Production of the
       Liturgical Drama." The Medieval French Drama. (Oxford,
       1954), pp. 66-73.

*1915 ----- "The Fleury Play-Book." The Medieval French Drama.

(Oxford, 1954), pp. 44-51.

*1916   Frank, Grace. "Hilarius." The Medieval French Drama. (Ox-
        ford, 1954), pp. 53-55.

*1917   ----- "Liturgical Christmas Plays. The Procession of Prophets.
        The Feast of Fools." The Medieval French Drama. (Oxford,
        1954), pp. 31-43.

*1918   ----- "Liturigical Easter Plays." The Medieval French Drama.
        (Oxford, 1954), pp. 18-30.

*1919   ----- "The Sponsus. The Presentation of the Virgin Mary in the
        Temple." The Medieval French Drama. (Oxford, 1954), pp.
        58-65.

*1920   Handschin, Jacques. "Trope, Sequence, and Conductus." Early
        Medieval Music Up to 1300. Edited by Dom Anselm Hughes.
        (London, New York, Toronto: Geoffrey Cumberlege, Ox-
        ford University Press, 1954), pp. 128-174. [The New Oxford
        History of Music].

 1921   Hunningher, Benjamin. De liturgische Oorsprong van het Theater.
        Amsterdam: N.V. Noord-Hollandsche, 1954. 20 pp. (Medede-
        lingen der koninklijke Nederlands Akademie van Wetenschappen,
        afd. Letterkunde, n. Reeks, Deel 17, No. 2).
        BM. ICU.

*1922   Smoldon, W. L. "Liturgical Drama." Early Medieval Music Up
        to 1300. Edited by Dom Anselm Hughes. (London, New York,
        1954), pp. 175-219.

*1923   ----- "Liturgical Music-Drama." Blom, Eric, ed. Grove's
        Dictionary of Music and Musicians. 5th ed., Vol. 5.
        (London, 1954), pp. 317-343. [See also, Supplementary
        Volume (London, 1961), pp. 271-272.]

 1924   Vecchi, Giuseppe. Uffici drammatici padovani. Firenze: L. S.
        Olschki, 1954. xii, 257 pp. (Biblioteca dell "Archivum
        Romanicum." Ser. 1: Storia, letteratura, paleografia, V.
        41).
        ICN.

 1925   Wolff, H. C. "Zur Wiedergeburt des religiösen Musiktheaters."
        Musica, VIII (December, 1954), 525-527.

*1926 Chailley, Jacques. "Le Drame liturgique médiéval a St. Martial
       de Limoges." Revue de l'Histoire du Théâtre, VII (1955),
       127-144.

1927   Eliot, Thomas Stearns. Religious Drama. Medieval and Modern.
       New York: House of Books, 1955. [25] pp.
       BM.

1928   Chailley, Jacques. Le Drame liturgique médiéval à Saint-Martial
       de Limoges. Paris: M. Brient, 1956. 20 pp.
       Bibliothèque National.

*1929 Cohen, Gustave. "Le drame liturgique en France." Etudes d'
       histoire du théâtre en France au moyen-âge et à la Renais-
       sance. 7th ed. (Paris, 1956), pp. 15-31.

1930   ----- "Le personnage de Marie-Madeleine dans le drame
       religieux francaise du Moyen Âge." Convivium, XXIV (1956),
       141-163.

1931   Crosland, Jessie. "Growth of the Drama in the Twelfth Century."
       Medieval French Literature. (Oxford, 1956), pp. 219-243.

*1932 Donovan, Richard Bertram. "The Medieval Liturgical Drama
       in the Hispanic Peninsula and Its Relation, with That of the
       Rest of Europe, Especially France." Ph.D. Yale University.
       1956.

1933   Hotze, Alphonse John. "Medieval Liturgical Drama, the Origin
       and Religiosity." Ph.D. University of Missouri, 1956.

1934   Jenks, Joseph B. "A Critical Edition of Meditations on the Pas-
       sion." Ph.D. Michigan State University, 1956.

1935   Kaff, Ludwig. Mittelalterliche Oster- und Passionsspiele aus
       Oberösterreich im Spiegel musikwissenschaftlicher Betrachtung.
       Linz: Oberösterreichischer Landesverlag in Kommission,
       1956. 68 pp. (Schriftenreihe des Instituts für Landeskunde von
       Oberösterreich, nr. 9). "Literaturverzeichnis," pp. 67-68.
       BM.

1936   Krieg, Edward. Das lateinische Osterspiel von Tours (aus der
       Handschrift 927 der Stadtbibliothek). Würzburg: K. Triltsch,
       1956. xvi, 130, 29 pp. [Literarhistorisch-musikwissen-
       schaftliche Abhandlungen. Bd. 13.] [With the text and a trans-

script of the music.]
BM.

1937 Noomen, W. "Remarques sur la versification du plus ancien
théâtre francais. L'enchaînement des répliques et la rime
mnémonique." Neophilologus, XL (1956), 179-193. [12th
- 15th century].

1938 ----- "Remarques sur la versification du plus ancien théâtre
francais: L'enchaînement des répliques et la rime mnémonique
(suite)." Neophilologus, XL (1956), 249-258.

1939 Somogyi-Schill Sarközi B., Stefan. L'Origine et le développement das "Osterspiele" (Jeux de Pâques) en Allemagne.
Thèse. Univ. Paris. Lettres. 1956, II, 296 leaves. Dactylographié.

*1940 Bradner, Leicester. "The Latin Drama of the Renaissance (1340
[sic for 1314] - 1640)." Studies in the Renaissance, IV (1957),
31-70. ["List of Original Neo-Latin Plays Published before
1650" appended, pp. 57-70.]

1941 Corbin, Solange. La Déposition liturgique du Christ, sa place
dans l'histoire des rites et du théâtre religieux. Thèse compl.
Lettres. Paris, 1957. vi, 369 leaves. Dactylographié.

1942 Larson, Orville K. "Bishop Abraham of Souzdal's Description of
'sacre rappresentazioni.'" Educational Theatre Journal, IX
(October, 1957), 208-213.

1943 ----- "Vasari's Description of Stage Machinery Used in 'sacre
rappresentazioni.'" Educational Theatre Journal, IX (December,
1957), 287-299.

1944 Rosenstock-Huessy, Eugen. "St. Tutilo of St. Gall and the Origin
of Drama." Catholic Art Quarterly, XX (Easter, 1957), 57-59.

*1945 Stevens, J. "Music in Mediaeval Drama." Proceedings of the Royal
Musical Association, LXXXIV (1957-1958), 81-95.

1946 Davis, F. H. "Three Liturgical Dramas at the Hunter College
Playhouse." Caecilia, LXXXV (February, 1958), 146-147.

*1947 Donovan, Richard B., C.S.B. The Liturgical Drama in Medieval
Spain. Toronto: Pontifical Institute of Mediaeval Studies, 1958.
[8], 229 pp.

*1948 Donovan, Richard B., C.S.B. "The Origin and Development of
       Liturgical Drama." The Liturgical Drama in Medieval Spain.
       (Toronto, 1958), pp. 6-19.

1949 "New York Pro Musica Antiqua." Musical Courier, CLVII (February, 1958), 20-21. [The play of Daniel].

1950 "A Twelfth-Century Musical Drama." The American Record
      Guide, XXV (December, 1958), 264-265. [Recording of the
      play Daniel.]

1951 Driver, Tom F. "Old Testament Christmas: Play of Daniel."
      Christian Century, LXXV (January, 1958), 135-136.

1952 Hildebrandt, William. "A Critical Edition of Richard Sherry's
      A Treatise of Schemes and Tropes." Ph.D. University of
      Wisconsin, 1958.

1953 Hussey, Maurice. "The Petitions of the Paternoster in Medieval
      English Literature." Medium Aevum, XXVII (1958), 8-16.

1954 Weakland, R. "The Beginnings of Troping." The Musical Quarterly, XLIV (October, 1958), 477-488.

1955 ----- "Daniel Revived." The Catholic Choirmaster, XLIV (Winter, 1958), 147-150. [The play of Daniel].

1956 Anderson, Mary Desirée. "The Twelfth Century Design Sources
      of the Worcester Cathedral Misericords." Archaeologica,
      XCVII (1959), 165.

*1957 Bowles, Edmund. "The Role of Musical Instruments in Medieval
       Sacred Drama." The Musical Quarterly, XLV (January, 1959),
       67-84.

1958 Campbell, Lily Bess. Divine Poetry and Drama in the Sixteenth
      Century England. Berkeley: University of California Press,
      1959. 267 pp.
           BM. NN (1961).

1959 Duprey, Richard. "Must Religious Plays Be Penance?" Catholic
      World, CXC (October, 1959), 36-41.

1960 Husman, H. "Sinn und Wesen der Tropen, veranschaulicht an den
      Introitustropen des Weihnachtsfestes." Archin für Musikwissenschaft, XVI (1959), 135-147.

1961 Labhardt, Frank. Das Sequentiar Cod. 546 der Stiftsbibliothek von St. Gallen und seine Quellen. 2 vol. [Stuttgart]: Paul Haupt Bern, 1959-1963. (Publikationen der Schweizerischen Musikforschenden Gesellschaft. Publications de la Société Suisse de Musicologie. Serie II. Vol. 8, I Textband).

*1961 Marshall, Mary. "Role of Musical Instruments in Medieval Sacred Drama." Musical Quarterly, XLV (January, 1959), 67-84.

1962 "Medieval Hit." Time, LXXIII (January 19, 1959), 72. [The play of Daniel].

1963 Stevens, D. "Medieval Music Drama." The Listener, LXI (June 18, 1959), 1084.

1964 Trimble, Lester. "New York Pro Musica antiqua Presentation of Play of Daniel." Nation, CLXXXVIII (January 31, 1959), 108.

*1965 Corbin, Solange. La déposition liturgique du Christ au Vendredi Saint, sa place dans l'histoire des rites et du théâtre religieux (analyse de documents portugais). Paris: Société d' éditions, "Les Belles Lettres," 1960. 346 pp. Bibliography, pp. [289]-310. (Collection portugais, 12).
   ICN. ICU.

1966 ----- "Le 'Jeu de Daniel' à l' abbaye de Royaumont." Cahiers de Civilisation médiévales, III (1960), 373-375.

1967 Gejou, F. "Fragment de drame liturgique (?) decouvert dans le manuscrit La Valliere de la Bibliothèque Nationale." Revue de Musicologie, XLV (1960), 76-83.

1968 Golea, A. "Streit um Das Spiel von Daniel." Neue Zeitschrift für Musik, CXXI (October 5, 1960), 354-355.

1969 Goodwin, N. "The Play of Daniel, Westminster Abbey." The Musical Times, CI (July, 1960), 438.

1970 Kirby, H. T. "The Jesse Tree Motif in Stained Glass." Journal of the British Society of Master Glass Painters, XIII (1960), 313-320; 434-441.
   BM.

1971 Murray, G. "Church and Stage: Song of Simeon." Christian
       Century, LXXVII (February 3, 1960), 137-138.

1972 Parmenter, A. "Daniel Comes Home." New York Times, CIX
       (April 23, 1960), Section 2, p. 9.

1973 Pocknee, C. E. "Christian Hymnody and the Drama." The Hymn
       Society of Great Britain and Ireland Bulletin, V, No. 2 (1960),
       30-32.

1974 Robinson, J. W. "The Play of Daniel Produced by the New York
       Pro Musica." Theatre Notebook, XV (1960), 33-34.

1975 Wagenaar-Nolthenius, Hélène. "Sur la construction musicale
       du drame liturgique." Cahiers de civilisation médiévales
       (Xe-XIIe siecles). III (1960), 449-456.

1976 Johnson, James Rosser. "The Tree of Jesse Window of Chartres:
       Laudes Regiae." Speculum, XXXVI (January, 1961), 1-22.

1977 McShane, Margaret Mary. "The Music of the Medieval Liturgical
       Drama." Ph.D. Catholic University of America, 1961. [Delete].

1978 Porebowiczowa, A. "Stredniowieczne misteria in Yorku." Ruch
       Muzyczny, V, No. 7 (1961), 10-11.

1979 Sticca, S. "The 'Planctus Mariae" and the Passion Plays." Symposium,
       XV (1961), 41-48.

1980 Weakland, R. "El drama liturgico en la Edad Media." Revista
       Musical Chilena, XV (1961), 52-60.

1981 Audiberti, J. "Mystères et miracles." Tableau de la littérature
       francaise, I (1962), 15-29.

1982 Craig, B. "Didactic Elements in Medieval French Serious Drama."
       L'Esprit créateur, II (1962), 142-148.

1983 Davidson, Nava Clark. "Potential Problems in Production of
       Liturgical Drama." M.A. University of Kansas, 1962.

1984 Duft, Johannes. "Wie Notker zu den Sequenzen kam." Zeitschrift
       für schweizerische Kirchengeschichte, LVI (1962), 201-214.
       [Notker Balbus].

1985 Ehrensperger, Harold Adam. Religious Drama: Ends and Means.
      New York: Abingdon Press [1962]. 287 pp.
          DLC.

1986 Falvy, Z. "Un 'Quem Queritis' en Hongrie au XIIe siècle."
      Studia Musicologica, III (1962), 101-107.

1987 Kreps, J. "L'apostolat de la musique orgue et chant." Musica
      sacra, LXIII (1962), 103-112.

1988 McShane, Margaret Mary. "The Music of the Medieval Liturgical
      Drama." Ph.D. Catholic University of America, 1962.

1989 Meyer-Baer, K. Liturgical Music Incunabula, A Descriptive
      Catalogue. London: Bibliographical Society, Oxford Univer-
      sity Press, 1962. 63 pp.
          BM.

1990 Nichols, Stephen G., Jr. "La tension dramatique du 'Sponsus.'"
      Romance Notes, III (Spring, 1962), 69-74.

1991 Pächt, Otto. The Rise of Pictorial Narrative in Twelfth-Century
      England. Oxford: Clarendon Press, 1962. xii, 63 pp. [See
      Part III, "Pictorial Representation and Liturgical Art.]
          BM.

*1992 Smoldon, William L. "Music of the Medieval Church Drama."
      Musical Quarterly, LXVIII (October, 1962), 476-497.

*1993 Anderson, M. Desirée. Drama and Imagery in English Medieval
      Churches. Cambridge: University Press; New York: Cam-
      bridge University Press, 1963 [i.e., 1964]. xi, 248 pp.
      Bibliography, pp. 219-238.
          BM.

1994 Gundry, I. "Medieval Church Drama: Some Practical Consider-
      ations." The Musical Times, CIV (March 4, 1963), 183-184.

1995 Riedel, J. "The Liturgical Play." Journal of Church Music, V
      (March, 1963), 2-5.

1996 Siegrist, Theodor. Herrscherbild und Weltscicht bei Notker
      Balbulus: Untersuchungen zu den Gesta Karoli. Zürich:
      Fretz & Wasmuth, 1963. 150 pp.
          BM.

1997 Werner, Wilfried. Studien zu den Passions-und Osterspielen des deutschen Mittelalters in ihrem Übergang vom Latein zur Volkssprache. Berlin: E. Schmidt, 1963. 151 pp. (Philologische Studien und Quellen, Heft. 18).
BM.

1998 Lüttuitz, H. von. "Polens glorreiches Osterspiel." Musica, XVIII (1964), 209-210.

1999 Modzelewski, Ks. Z. "Estetyka średniowiecznego dramatu liturgicznego." Roczniki humanistyczne, XII (1964), 5-68. [L'esthétique du drame liturgique médiéval.]

2000 Sticca, Sandro. "A Note on Latin Passion Plays." Italica, XLI (1964), 430-433.

2001 Ebel, Uda. Das altromanische Mirakel. Ursprung und Geschichte einer literarischen Gattung. Heidelberg: Winter, 1965. 144 pp. (Studia Romanica, Hft. 8).
BM.

2002 Grosse, Siegfried. "Ursprung und Entwicklung der österlichen Spiele des Mittelalters." Der Deutschunterricht, XVII (1965), 80-94.

2003 Grünberg, Alexander. Das religiöse Drama des Mittelalters; Österreich, Deutschland, Schweiz. 3 vol. in 1. Wien: Bergland Verlag [1965].
ICU.

*2004 Hardison, Jr., O. B. "The Early History of the Quem Quaeritis." Christian Rite and Christian Drama in the Middle Ages. (Baltimore, 1965), pp. 178-219.

*2005 ----- "From Quem Quaeritis to Resurrection Play." Christian Rite and Christian Drama in the Middle Ages. (Baltimore, 1965), pp. 220-252.

2006 Hess, Rainer. Das romanische geistliche Schauspiel als profane und religiöse Komödie. 15 und 16. Jahrhundert. München: W. Fink, 1965. 198 pp. (Freiburger Schriften zur romanischen Philologie, Bd. 4).
BM.

*2007 Jodogne, O. "Recherches sur les débuts du théâtre religieux en France." Cahiers de civilisation médiévale. VIII (1965), 1-24, 179-189.

2008 Sletsjoe, L. "Quelques réflexions sur la naissance du théâtre religieux." Actes du Xe Congrès internationale de linguistique et philologie romanes, X (Paris, 1965), 667-675.

*2009 Smoldon, William L. "Medieval Lyrical Melody and the Latin Church Dramas." Musical Quarterly, LI (July, 1965), 507-517.

2010 Chailley, Jacques. "Du drame liturgique aux prophètes de Notre-Dame-la-Grande." Gallais, Pierre, and Yves-Jean Riou, eds. Mélanges offerts à René Crozet a l'occasion de son soixante-dixième anniversaire. Vol. 2 (Poitiers, 1966), pp. 835-841.

2011 Gautier, Leon. Histoire de la poésie liturgique au moyen âge. Ridgewood, New Jersey: Gregg Press, 1966. viii, 280 pp. [A facsimile of the edition of 1886.]
BM.

2012 Guiette, Robert. "Reflexions sur le drame liturgique." Gallais, Pierre, and Yves-Jean Riou, eds. Mélanges offerts à René Crozet à l'occasion de son soixante-dixième anniversaire. Vol. 1. (Poitiers, 1966), pp. 197-202.

2013 Boor, Helmut Anton Wilhelm de. Die Textgeschichte der lateinischen Osterfeiern. Tübingen: M. Niemeyer, 1967. xi, 371 pp. (Hermaea. N. F. Bd. 22).
NN.

*2014 Shergold, N. D. "Dramatic Tropes of the Easter and Christmas Liturgies." A History of the Spanish Stage from Medieval Times Until the End of the Seventeenth Century. (Oxford, 1967), pp. 1-25.

2015 Kaltenbach, Carey W. "Evidence for a Quem Quaeritis Easter Matins Trope in the Divine Office at Poitiers, 'Annorum circiter 800.'" Emporia State Research Studies, XVIII, No. 4 (1968), 5-14.

2016 Kinghorn, A. M. "Liturgical Drama." Mediaeval Drama. (London, 1968), pp. 23-44.

2017 Michael, W. F. "Zum Innicher Osterspielfragment von 1340."

Zeitschrift für Deutschen Morgenländischen Gesellschaft, LXXXVII (1968), 387-390.

*2018 Smoldon, William L. "The Melodies of the Medieval Church-Drama and Their Significance."Comparative Drama, II (1968), 185-209.

IV ENGLISH DRAMA

A Bibliography

*2019 The Careless Shepherdess. A Tragi-comedy Acted before the
King & Queen, And at Salisbury-Court, with great Applause.
Written by Mr. T. G. Mr. of Arts. ... With an Alphabeticall
Catalogue of all such Plays that ever were Printed. London:
Printed for Richard Rogers and William Ley, 1656. 76 pp.
DFo.

2020 [Archer's Catalogue]. The Excellent Comedy, called The Old
Law: Or, A new way to please you. By Phil. Massinger. Tho.
Middleton. William Rowley. Acted before the King and Queene
at Salisbury House, and at severall other places, with great
Applause. Together with an exact and perfect Catalogue of all
the Playes, with the Authors Names, and what are Comedies,
Tragedies, Histories, Pastoralls, Masks, Interludes, more
exactly Printed than Ever before. London: Printed for Edward
Archer, 1656. 76 pp.
DFo.

*2021 [Kirkman, Francis]. A True, perfect, and exact Catalogue of
all the Comedies, Tragedies, Tragi-Comedies, Pastorals,
Masques and Interludes, that were ever yet printed and published, till this present year 1661. all which you may either
buy or sell at the several shops of Nath. Brook at the Angel
in Cornhil, Francis Kirkman at the John Fletchers Head, on
the Back-side of St. Clements, Tho. Johnson at the Golden
Key in St. Pauls Churchyard, and Henry Marsh at the Princes
Arms in Chancery-lane near Fleetstreet, 1661. 16 pp.
BM. DLC. ICN. OU.

2022 ----- A True, perfect and exact Catalogue of all the Comedies,
Tragedies, Tragi-Comedies, Pastorals, Masques and Inter-

ludes, that were ever yet Printed and Published, till this
present year 1671. all which you may either buy or sell, at
the Shop of Francis Kirkman, in Thames-street, over-
against the Custom House, London [1671]. 16 pp.
    CSmH. DFo. MB. MH. PU.

2023 Phillips, Edward. Theatrum Poetarum, Or A Compleat Collection
      of the Poets, Especially The most-Eminent of All Ages. The
      Antients distinguish't from the Moderns in their several Alpha-
      bets. With some Observations and Reflections upon many of
      them, particularly those of our own Nation. Together With a
      Prefatory Discourse of the Poets and Poetry in General....
      London: Printed for Charles Smith, M.DC. LXXV. [1675].
      [36], 192, 261, [3] pp.
          DFo.

2024 [Langbaine, Gerard]. An Exact Catalogue of All the Comedies,
      Tragedies, Tragi-Comedies, Operas, Masks, Pastorals, and
      Interludes That were ever yet Printed and Published, till this
      present year 1680. Oxon: Printed for L. Lichfield, Printer to
      the University, for Nicholas Cox, 1680. 16 pp.
          DFo.

2025 Winstanley, William. The Lives Of the most Famous English
      Poets, Or The Honour of Parnassus; In a Brief Essay Of above
      Two Hundred of them, from the Time of K. William the Con-
      queror, To the Reign of His Present Majesty King James II
      ... Written by William Winstanley, Author of the English
      Worthies. Licensed, June 16, 1686. Rob. Midgley. London:
      Printed by H. Clark, for Samuel Manship, 1687. [24], 221 pp.
          DFo.

*2026 Langbaine, Gerard. Momus Triumphans: Or, The Plagiaries Of
      The English Stage: Expos'd in a Catalogue Of All The Com-
      edies, Tragi-Comedies, Masques, Tragedies, Opera's,
      Pastorals, Interludes, &c. Both Ancient and Modern, that were
      ever yet Printed in English. The Names of their Known and
      Supposed Authors. Their several Volumes and Editions: With
      an Account of the various Originals, as well English, French,
      and Italian, as Greek and Latine, from whence most of them
      have Stole their Plots. By Gerard Langbaine, Esq.... London:
      Printed for Nicholas Cox, and are to be Sold by him in Oxford,
      MDCLXXXVIII [1688]. xvi, 32, [8] pp.
          BM. DFo. ICN. MiU.

2027   Langbaine, Gerard. A New Catalogue of English Plays, Containing
       All the Comedies, Tragedies, Tragi-Comedies, Opera's, Mas-
       ques, Pastorals, Interludes, Farces, &c. Both Ancient and
       Modern, that have ever yet been Printed, to this present year,
       1688. To which, are added, The Volumes, and best Editions;
       with divers Remarks, of the Originals of most Plays; and the
       Plagiaries of several Authors. By Gerard Langbaine, Gent...
       London: Printed for Nicholas Cox, and are to be Sold by him
       in Oxford MDCLXXXVIII [1688]. xvi, 32, [8] pp.

* 2028   ----- An Account of the English Dramatick Poets. Or, Some
       Observations and Remarks On the Lives and Writings, of all
       those that have Publish'd either Comedies, Tragedies, Tragi-
       Comedies, Pastorals, Masques, Interludes, Farces, or
       Opera's in the English Tongue. By Gerard Langbaine. Oxford:
       Printed by L. L. for George West, and Henry Clements,
       1691. [16], 556, [36] pp.
              BM. ICN.

2029   [Gildon, Charles]. The Lives and Characters Of The English
       Dramatick Poets. Also An exact Account of all the Plays that
       were ever yet Printed in the English Tongue; their Double
       Titles, the Places where Acted, the Dates when Printed, and
       the Persons to whom Dedicated; with Remarks and Observations
       on most of the said Plays. First begun by Mr. Langbaine, im-
       prov'd and continued down to this Time, by a Careful Hand.
       London: Printed for Nich. Cox, and William Turner, 1699.
       [16], 182, [13] pp.
              BM.

2030   [Mears, W.]. A True and Exact Catalogue Of All the Plays That
       were ever yet Printed in the English Tongue; with the Authors
       Names against each Play (Alphabetically Digested) and con-
       tinued down to October, 1713. London: Printed for W. Mears,
       1713. 48 pp.
              BM. ICN. MH.

2031   [Jacobs, Giles]. The Poetical Register: Or, The Lives and
       Characters of the English Dramatick Poets. With An Account
       of Their Writings. London: Printed for E. Curll, MDCCXIX.
       [1719]. [26], 433, [22] pp.
              BM.

2032   [Mears, W.]. A Compleat Catalogue Of all the Plays That were
       ever yet Printed in the English Language. Containing the Dates,

and the Number of Plays Written by every particular Author:
An Account of what Plays were Acted with Applause, and of those
which were never Acted; and also of the Authors now living. In
two separate Alphabets. London: Printed for W. Mears, 1719.
95 pp.
    CtY. DFo. DLC. ICN. MH.

*2033 [Mears, W.]. A Compleat Catalogue of All the Plays That were
ever yet Printed In the English Language. Containing The
Dates and Numbers of Plays Written by every particular Author:
An Account of what Plays were Acted with Applause, and of
those which were never Acted; and also the Authors now living.
In Two separate Alphabets. Continued to this present year, 1726.
The Second Edition. London: Printed for W. Mears, M.DCCXXVI
[1726]. 104 pp.
    CSmH. DLC. ICN. MH. NNC.

2034 [Feales, W.]. A True and Exact Catalogue Of all the Plays And
other Dramatic Pieces, That were ever yet Printed in the
English Tongue, In Alphabetical Order: Continu'd down to
April 1732. London: Printed for W. Feales, 1732. 35 pp.
    DFo. ICN. MH.

2035 Whincop, Thomas. Scanderbeg: Or, Love and Liberty. Written
by the late Thomas Whincop, Esq. To which are added A
List of all the Dramatic Authors, with some Account of their
Lives; and of all the Dramatic Pieces ever published in the
English Language, to the year 1747. London: Printed for W.
Reeve, MDCCXLVII [1747]. xix, [3], 320, [30] pp. [Attributed
to John Mottley.]
    BM. CSmH. DFo. DLC. ICN. ICU. MH. MiU. NN.
    O. TxU.

2036 [Chetwood, William Rufus]. The British Theatre. Containing The
Lives of the English Dramatic Poets; With An Account of all
their Plays. Together With The Lives of most of the Principal
Actors, as well as Poets. To which is prefixed, A short View
of the Rise and Progress of the English Stage. Dublin: Printed
for Peter Wilson, M.DCC, L. [1750]. [2], 16, [6], 200, [28] pp.
    CSmH. CtY. DFo. ICN. IU. MH. MiU. MnU. ODW.

2037 Cibber, [Theophilus]. The Lives of The Poets of Great Britain
and Ireland, To the Time of Dean Swift. Compiled from ample
Materials scattered in a Variety of Books, and especially from
MS. Notes of the late ingenious Mr. Coxeter and others, col-

lected for this Design. By Mr. Cibber. 5 vol. London:
Printed for R. Griffiths, 1753.

2038 Cibber, Colley. An Apology for the Life of Colley Cibber, Come-
dian. Written by Himself ... The Fourth Edition.... With
an Account of the Rise and Progress of the English Stage: a
Dialogue on Old Plays, and Old Players; and a List of Dramatic
Authors and Their Works. 2 vol. London: Printed for R. and
J. Dodsley, 1756.

2039 [Dodsley, Robert]. Theatrical Records: or, An Account of English Dramatic Authors, and Their Works. London: Printed
for R. and J. Dodsley, 1756. 135, [1], 32 pp.
     IaU. ICN. MH. MiU.

2040 [Baker, David Erskine]. The Companion To The Play-House: Or,
An Historical Account of all the Dramatic Writers (and their
Works) that have appeared in Great Britain and Ireland, From
The Commencement of our Theatrical Exhibitions, down to
the Present Year 1764. Composed in the Form of a Dictionary,
For the more readily turning to any particular Author, or Per-
formance. In Two Volumes. ... London: Printed for T. Becket
and P. A. Dehondt; C. Henderson, and T. Davies, 1764.
     BM. ICN. MB. MiU.

2041 [Capell, Edward]. Notitia Dramatica; or, Tables of Ancient Plays,
(from their Beginning, to the Restoration of Chares the second)
so many as have been printed, with their several Editions:
faithfully compiled, and digested in quite new Method, By E. C.
With a Preface. Notes and Various Readings to Shakespeare .
... 3 vol. London: Printed by Henry Hughs, for the Author
[1779].
     CtY. DLC. ICN. MB. MiU. NjP.

2042 The Playhouse Pocket-Companion, Or Theatrical Vade-Mecum:
Containing, I. A Catalogue of all the Dramatic Authors who
have written for the English Stage, with a List of their Works,
shewing the Dates of Representation or Publication. II. A
Catalogue of Anonymous Pieces. III. An Index of Plays and Authors. In a Method entirely new, Whereby the Author of any
Dramatic Performance, and the Time of its Appearance, may
be readily discovered on Inspection. To which is prefixed, a
Critical History of the English Stage from its Origin to the
present time; with an Enquiry into the Causes of the Decline
of Dramatic Poetry in England. London: Printed and sold by
Messrs. Richardson, and Urquhart; J. Wenman; and J.

Southern, 1779. [4], [13]-179 pp.
BM. DFo. ICN. MB.

*2043 [Reed, Isaac]. Biographia Dramatica, Or, A Companion To The
Playhouse: Containing Historical and Critical Memoirs, and
Original Anecdotes, of British and Irish Dramatic Writers,
from the Commencement of the most celebrated Actors. Also
An Alphabetical Account of their Works, the Dates when
printed, and occasional Observations on their Merits. Together With An Introductory View of the Rise and Progress of
the British Stage. By David Erskine Baker, Esq. A New Edition: Carefully Corrected; greatly enlarged; and continued
from 1764 to 1782. 2 vol. London: Printed for Messrs. Riving-
tons, T. Payne and Son, L. Davis, T. Longman, and G.
Robinson; J. Dodsley, J. Nichols, J. Debret, and T. Evans,
1782.
BM.

*2044 Egerton, Thomas. Egerton's Theatrical Remembrancer, Con-
taining A Complete List Of All The Dramatic Performances
In The English Language; Their Several Editions, Dates,
and Sizes, And The Theatre Where They Were Originally
Performed: Together With An Account Of Those Which Have
Been Acted And Are Unpublished, And A Catalogue Of Such
Latin Plays As Have Been Written By English Authors. From
The Earliest Production Of The English Drama To The End
Of The Year MDCCLXXXVIII. To Which Are Added Notitia
Dramatica, Being A Chronological Account Of Events Relative
To The English Stage. London: Printed for T. and J. Egerton,
MDCCLXXXVIII. [1788]. vi, [2], 354 pp.
DFo. ICN. MB. MH. MiU. MnU.

2045 A New Theatrical Dictionary. Containing An Account Of All The
Dramatic Pieces That Have Appeared From The Commence-
ment Of Theatrical Exhibitions To The Present Time. To-
gether With Their Dates When Written Or Printed, where
Acted, and Occasional Remarks on their Merits and Success.
To Which Is Added An Alphabetical Catalogue Of Dramatic
Writers, With The Titles of all the Pieces they have Written,
annexed to each Name. And Also A Short Sketch of the Rise
and Progress of the English Stage. London: Printed for S.
Bladon, 1792. [8], 400 pp.
BM. DFo. ICN. MB. MH.

2046 Oulton, Walley Chamberlain. Barker's Continuation of Egerton's

Theatrical Remembrancer, Baker's Biographia Dramatica,
&c. Containing, A complete List of all the Dramatic Performances their several Editions, Dates and Sizes, together
with those which are unpublished, and the Theatres where
they were originally performed; From MDCCLXXXVII to
MDCCCI. Including several Omissions, Additions and Corrections, Also a Continuation of the Notitia Dramatica, With
considerable Improvements. To Which Is Added A Complete
List of Plays, The Earliest Date, Size, and Author's Name,
(Where known). From the Commencement To 1801. The Whole
arranged, &c. by Walley Chamberlain Oulton. London: Printed
and Published by Barker & Son [1801?]. [4], 336 pp.
BM. MH.

2047 [Oulton, Walley Chamberlain]. Barker's Complete List Of Plays,
Exhibiting At One View, The Title, Size, Date, And Author,
From The Commencement Of Theatrical Performances, To
1803. To Which Is Added A Continuation To the Theatrical
Remembrancer, Designed To Shew Collectively Each Author's
Work. London: printed and published by [J.] Barker & Son
[1803]. [4], 350 pp.
BM. DFo. DLC. ICN. MB. MH. MiU. OCl.

2048 Jones, Stephen. Biographia Dramatica; Or, A Companion To The
Playhouse: Containing Historical and Critical Memoirs, and
original Anecdotes, Of British And Irish Dramatic Writers,
From The Commencement Of Our Theatrical Exhibitions;
Among Whom Are Some Of The Most Celebrated Actors: Also
An Alphabetical Account, And Chronological Lists, Of Their
Works, The Dates When Printed, And Observations On Their
Merits: Together With An Introductory View Of The Rise And
Progress Of The British Stage. Originally Compiled, To The
Year 1764, By David Erskine Baker. Continued Thence to
1782, By Isaac Reed, F.A.S. And brought down to the End
of November 1811, with very considerable Additions and Im-
provements throughout, by Stephens Jones. 3 vol. London:
Printed for T. Longman, Hurst, Rees, Orme, And Brown,
T. Payne, G. and W. Nicol, Nichols And Son, Scotcherd
and Letterman, J. Barker, W. Miller, R. H. Evans, J.
Harding, J. Faulder, And Gale And Curtis, 1812.
BM. CtY. ICN. MH. MiU. NjP. OU. PMA. ViU. WaU.

2049 Barker, J. The Drama Recorded; Or Barker's List of Plays,
Alphabetically Arranged, Exhibiting at One View, the Title,
Size, Date, and Author, With Their Various Alterations,

From the Earliest Period, to 1814; To Which Are Added,
Notitia Dramatica, Or, A Chronological Account of Events
Relative to the English Stage. London: Printed and Published
by J. Barker, (Dramatic Repository), Great Russell-Street,
Covent-Garden, 1814. [4], 212 pp.
DFo. DLC. ICN. MB. PPM.

2050 [Haslewood, Joseph]. The Prompter. [London? Lee Priory Press?
1814?] 308 pp. [Only copy printed?]
DFo.

2051 Delandine, Antoine Francois. Bibliographie dramatique, ou
tablettes alphabêtiques du thêâtre des diverses nations; avec
des observations littêraires et bibliographiques. Prêcêdêe
d'une notice sur l'origine du thêâtre francais. Paris: Renouard
[1818?]. [8], 588, [1] pp.
MB.

2052 Ebert, Friedrick Adolf. Allgemeines bibliographisches Lexicon.
2 vol. Leipzig: F. A. Brockhaus, 1821-1830.
BM.

2053 "Pageants on Particular Occasions." Sharp, Thomas. A Dissertation on the Pageants on Dramatic Mysteries Anciently
Performed at Coventry. (Coventry, 1825), pp. 145-158.

2054 Bellamy, B. P. General Catalogue of All the English Dramatic
Pieces I Have Been Able to Discover. 2 vol. Bath, 1834.

2055 Catalogue Of Early English Poetry, And Other Miscellaneous
Works Illustrating the British Drama, Collected by Edmund
Malone, esq., And Now Preserved In the Bodleian Library.
Oxford: University Press, 1836. viii, 52 pp.
BM. ICU. O.

2056 Chapman, John Kremble. A Complete History of Theatrical
Entertainments, Dramas, Masques, and Triumphs, at the
English Court, from the Time of King Henry the Eighth to
the Present Day, Including the Series of Plays Performed
before Her Majesty, at Windsor Castle, Christmas, 1848-
1849. Containing Many Curious Particulars of Our Early
Dramatic Literature and Art. London: Published by John
Mitchell, [1849]. 86 pp.
ICN. MB. MH. MiU. NB. PSC.

2057 Bibliotheca Dramatica. Catalogue of the Theatrical and Miscel-
        laneous Library of the Late William E. Burton. New York:
        J. Sabin and Co., 1860. 463 pp. (6, 154 entries, Classed).
        DLC. ICN. MiU. MnU.

2058 Halliwell, James O. A Dictionary of Old English Plays, Existing
        Either In Print Or In Manuscript, From the Earliest Times to
        The Close of The Seventeenth Century; Including Also Notices
        Of Latin Plays Written By English Authors During the Same
        Period. London: John Russell Smith, 1860. [8], 296 pp.
              BM. CtY. DFo. DLC. ICN. MH. MiU. NN. OC1.
              OCU. PU. TxU. WU.

2059 Kelly, William. Notices Illustrative of the Drama and Other
        Popular Amusements, Chiefly in the Sixteenth and Seventeenth
        Centuries, Incidentally Illustrating Shakespeare and His Con-
        temporaries: Extracted from the Chamberlain's Accounts
        and Other Manuscripts of the Borough of Leicester. With Intro-
        duction and Notes. London: J. Russell Smith, 1865. viii, 310 pp.
              BM. CtY. DFo. IaU. ICN. MH. MiU. NjP. OU. PHC.

2060 Hazlitt, W. Carew. Hand-Book To The Popular, Poetical, And
        Dramatic Literature of Great Britain, From the Invention of
        Printing to the Restoration. London: John Russell Smith, 1867.
        xii, 701, [3] pp.
              BM.

2061 Inglis, Ralston. The Dramatic Writers of Scotland. Glasgow:
        G. D. Mackellar, 1868. [2], 155, [1] pp.
              CtY. DLC. MB. MH. MiU. MnU.

*2062 Arber, Edward, ed. Transcript of the Registers of the Stationers'
        Company 1553-1640. 5 vol. London: Privately Printed, 1875-
        1894.
              BM. DLC. ICN. IaU. MH. MiU. MnU. NN. WU.

2063 Zeitschrift für romanische Philologie. Supplementhefte. 1-38,
        44-45. Halle: Niemeyer, 1878-1914, 1927-1938.

2064 "Mysteries, Miracle Plays, Moralities, and Religious Drama."
        Boston Public Library. Bulletin, IV (1879-1880), 131-135, 244.

*2065 Ticknor, George. Catalogue of the Spanish Library and of the
        Portuguese Books Bequeathed by George Ticknor to the Boston
        Pubic Library, Together with the Collection of Spanish and

Portuguese Literature in the General Library. By James
Lyman Whitney. Boston: by Order of the Trustees, 1879.
476 pp.
> DLC. IaU. ICN. MnU. WU.

2066   Brewer, E. Cobham. The Reader's Handbook of Allusions,
References, Plots and Stories. 4th ed. London: Chatto and
Windus, 1884. 1, 399 pp.

*2067   Stoddard, F. H. References for Students of Miracle Plays and
Mysteries. Sacramento, California: State Printing Office,
1887. 68 pp. (University of California. Library Bulletin,
No. 8.)
> BM. CU. DFo. ICN. ICU. MiU. NN. OU. ViU. WU.

2068   Lowe, Robert W. A Bibliographical Account of English Theatrical
Literature from the Earliest Times to the Present Day. London: John C. Nimmo, 1888. x, [2], 384 pp. [Reprint, 1966]
> BM. DFo. DLC. ICN. ICU. MH. MiU. NN. OC1.
> OU. PU. ViU. WU.

2069   Fleay, Frederick Gard. A Chronicle History of the London
Stage, 1559-1642. London: Reeves and Turner, 1890. x,
424 pp.
> BM.

2070   ----- A Biographical Chronicle of the English Drama, 1559-
1642. 2 vol. London: Reeves and Turner, 1891.
> DFo. DLC. ICN. MH. MiU. OC1. OU. PBm. ViU. WU.

2071   Cameron, James. A Bibliography of Scottish Theatrical Literature. Edinburgh, 1892. 8 pp. [Papers of the Edinburgh
Bibliographical Society, 1890-1895. Session 1891/92. no.
iv].
> MH.

2072   [Hazlitt, William Carew]. A Manual for the Collector of Old
English Plays. Edited from the Material Formed by Kirkman,
Langbaine, Downes, Oldys, and Halliwell-Phillips, with Ex-
tensive Additions and Corrections. London: Pickering &
Chatto, 1892. viii, 284 pp.
> BM. CSmH. DFo. DLC. IaU. ICN. MH. MiU. NjP.
> OU. PU. WU.

2073   Cameron, James. Supplement to a Bibliography. Edinburgh, 1896.

2 pp. [Papers of the Edinburgh Bibliographical Society. Session 1894/95, no. ii].

2074 Madan, Falconer. The Early Oxford Press. A Bibliography of Printing and Publishing at Oxford '1468-1640.' Oxford: Clarendon Press, 1895. 365 pp.
      BM. DLC. IaU. ICN. MiU. MnU. NjP. OU. PU. ViU.

2075 ----- A Summary Catalogue of Western MSS. in the Bodleian. 6 vol. Oxford, 1895-1937.
      BM. DLC. IaU. ICN. MiU. MnU.

2076 Bates, Katherine Lee. English Drama. A Working Basis. Department of Bibliography, Wellesley College. [Boston: Press of S. G. Robinson], 1896. 151 pp.
      DFo. IaU. ICN. MB. MH. NjP. NN. PSC. PU. WU.

2077 Mensch, Ella. Konversations-lexikon der Theater-litteratur. Praktisches Hand- und Nachschlagebuch zur schnellen und sicheren Orientierung über Die Dramen des in--und ausländer von den ältesten Zeiten bis zur Gegenwart. Stuttgart: Schwabacher, 1896. 348 pp.
      ICU.

2078 Tolman, A. H., and Ella A. Moore. Select Bibliography of the English Drama before Elizabeth. Chicago: University of Chicago Press, 1896. 16 pp.
      CtY.

*2079 Greg, Walter Wilson. A List of English Plays Written Before 1643 And Printed Before 1700. London: Printed for the Bibliographical Society, By Blades, East & Blades, March, 1900, for 1899. 158 pp.
      BM. DFo. DLC. ICN. ICU. MiU. NjP. OCU. PSC. TxU.

2080 James, Montague Rhodes. The Western Manuscripts in the Library of Trinity College, Cambridge. A Descriptive Catalogue. 4 vol. Cambridge: University Press, 1901.
      BM. CtY. DLC. ICN. ICU. IU. MH. MiU. MnU. NN.

*2081 Greg, Walter W. A List of Masques, Pageants, etc. Supplementary to a List of English Plays. London: Printed for the Bibliographical Society, 1902. 35, cxxxi pp.
      CtY. DLC. ICN. MH. MiU. NN. OC1. OU. PU. ViU. WU.

2082 Bates, Alfred, ed. The Drama, Its History, Literature and In-
fluence on Civilization. London: The Athenian Society, 1903.
[See Vol. 4: "Religious Drama," pp. 1-250].
CU. DLC. IaU. ICN. MB. MiU. MnU. OU. PU.

*2083 Chambers, Sir Edmund K. The Medieval Stage. 2 vol. Oxford:
Clarendon Press, 1903.
BM. CSmH. CtY. ICN. ICU. IU. MH. MiU. NjP. NN.
OCl. PU. ViU. WU.

2084 Adams, William Davenport, comp. Dictionary of the Drama. A
Guide to the Plays, Playwrights, Players, and Playhouses of
the United Kingdom and America, from the Earliest Times to
the Present. Philadelphia: Lippincott; London: Chatto and
Windus, 1904. viii, 627 pp. Vol. 1: A-G. [No more published].
BM. DLC. ICN. MH. MiU. MnU. NN. OCl. OU. PU.
TU. WU.

2085 Creizenach, Wilhelm Michael Anton. Register zur Geschichte
des Neueren Dramas. Band I-III bearb. von. dr. Paul Otto.
Halle a. s.: M. Niemeyer, 1904. 143 pp.
CtY. DLC. ICN. IU. MiU. NN. OCl. PU. ViU. WaU.

2086 Scott, Edward J. L. Index to the Sloane Manuscripts in the British
Museum. London: Printed by the Order of the Trustees, 1904.
583 pp.
ICN. MChB. MnU. NN. PPL.

2087 Courtney, William Pridaux. Register of National Bibliography.
3 vol. London: Constable, 1905-1912.
DLC. IaU. ICN. MiU. MnU. WU.

2088 Klein, David. "A Contribution to a Bibliography of Medieval
Drama: A Supplement to Chambers." Modern Language Notes,
XX (November, 1905), 202-205.
ICN.

2089 Readers Guide to Periodical Literature: a Consolidation of the
Cumulative Index to a Selected List of Periodicals and the
Readers' Guide to Periodical Literature. H. W. Wilson Co.,
Minneapolis. 1905--.

2090 Drama Index. Boston: F. W. Faxon Co., 1910-1952. 40 vol.
[Part II of the Annual Magazine Subject Index, 1907-1952].

2091 Schelling, Felix E. Elizabethan Drama, 1558-1642. A History
      of the Drama in England from the Accession of Queen Eliz-
      abeth to the Closing of the Theaters, to which is prefixed a
      Résumé of the Earlier Drama from its Beginning. 2 vol.
      London: Archibald Constable and Co., 1908.

2092 ["Clarence, Reginald," pseud. for H. J. Eldrege]. "The Stage"
      Cyclopaedia. A Bibliography of Plays. An Alphabetical List
      of Plays and other Stage Pieces of which any record can be
      found since the commencement of the English Stage, together
      with Descriptions, Author's Names, Dates and Places of
      Production, and other Useful Information, comprising in all
      nearly 50,000 Plays, and Extending Over a Period of Upwards
      of 500 Years. London: "The Stage," 1909. 503 pp.
           DLC. ICN. MH. MnU. WU.

2093 The Dramatic Index: Covering Articles and Illustrations Con-
      cerning the Stage and Its Players in the Periodicals of America
      and England; With a Record of Books on the Drama and of
      Texts of Plays. Issued yearly 1909--.
           ICN.

2094 Green, Antoinette. "An Index to the Non-Biblical Names in the
      English Mystery Plays." Studies in Honor of J. M. Hart.
      (New York: Henry Holt and Co., 1910), pp. 313-350.
           MB. OCU. OO. OU.

2095 Annual Magazine Subject Index. The Dramatic Index. Edited by
      Fredrick Winthrop Faxon. Boston: The Boston Book Co.,
      1911--.

*2096 Brooke, C. F. Tucker. The Tudor Drama. A History of English
      National Drama To The Retirement of Shakespeare. Boston,
      New York, Chicago, Dallas, San Francisco: Houghton Mifflin
      Company [1911]. xii, [2], 461 pp.

2097 Duval, L. "Curiosités bibliographiques relatives au Drame
      chrétien." Revue catholique de Normandie, XXI (1911),
      57-72.

2098 Farmer, John Stephen. A Rough Hand List to the Tudor Fac-
      simile Texts: Old English Plays, Printed & MSS. Rarities,
      Exact Collotype Reproductions in Folio and Quarto, Under
      the General Editorship and Supervision of John S. Farmer,
      Assisted by Craftsmen of Repute and Standing. Christmas,

1911. Amersham, Bucks: Issued for Subscribers by J. S.
Farmer, 1911. 24 pp. 1914. 48 pp.
   CtY. DLC. IaU. ICN. MiU. NjP. OU. ViU. WU.

*2099 Kretzmann, P. E. From Liturgy to Miracle Play: A Bibliography
in the Earliest Forms of the Medieval Drama. University of
Minnesota, [1912?] 77 pp. Typewritten MS.
   MnU.

2100 Materials for the Study of the English Drama (Excluding Shakespeare). Chicago: University of Chicago Press, 1912. 89 pp.
   DLC. IaU. MiU. OC1. OCU.

*2101 Greg, W. W. Bibliographical and Textual Problems of the English
Miracle Cycles. Lectures Delivered As Sanders Reader in
Bibliography in the University of Cambridge, 1913. Reprinted
from The Library, 1914. London: Alexander Morning Limited,
1914. 113 pp.
   BM.

*2102 Kirkman, Francis. A True, Perfect, and Exact Catalogue of
All the Comedies, Tragedies, Tragi-Comedies, etc. Edited
by John S. Farmer for Subscribers. Amersham, England,
1913. 15 pp. [Reprint].
   BM. ICN. MnU. PU.

2103 Gross, Charles. A Bibliography of British Municipal History,
Including Gilds and Parliamentary Representation. Cambridge,
Massachusetts: Harvard University Press, 1915. xxxiv, 461
pp. (Harvard Historical Studies, Vol. 5).
   BM. ICN. NN.

2104 Davis, Caroline Hill. Pageants in Great Britain and the United
States; a List of References. New York: New York Public
Library, 1916. 43 pp.
   DLC. ICN. ICJ. ICU. MB. MiU. OC1. OU. WU.

2105 Leach, Howard Seavoy. A Union List of Collections of English
Drama in American Libraries. Princeton, New York: The
University Library, 1916. 12 pp. (Reprinted from the Pro-
ceedings of the American Library Institute, 1916).
   DLC. IaU. MH. MiU. MnU. NjP. OU.

*2106 Wells, John Edwin. Manual of the Writings in Middle English,
1050-1400. New Haven, Connecticut: Connecticut Academy

of Arts and Sciences. Yale University Press, 1916. 941 pp.
Nine Supplements issued separately.
> BM. CtY. DLC. ICN. ICU. IU. MH. MiU. NN. OU.
> ViU. WU.

2107 Humphreys, Arthur Lee. A Handbook to County Bibliography.
Being a Bibliography of Bibliographies Relating to Counties
and Towns of Great Britain and Ireland. London: Strangeways
and Sons, 1917. x, 501 pp.
> BM. ICN.

2108 Mostyn, Llewelyn Nevill Vaughan Lloyd. Catalogue of a Collection
of Early English Plays, the Property of the Lord . . . Which
Will Be Sold By Auction By Messrs. Sotheby, Wilkinson and
Hodge . . . on . . . the 20th of March, 1919, and Following
Day . . . London: Dryden Press, J. Davy and Sons, 1919.
39 pp. (364 entries).
> CtY. DLC. ICN. MnU.

2109 Bibliography of English Language and Literature. Compiled by
Members of the Modern Humanities Research Association.
1920-- Date. Annual.

2110 Studies in Philology. A Quarterly Journal Published by the University of North Carolina. Beginning with Vol. XIX. 1922,
a Bibliography Published, entitled "Recent Literature of the
English Renaissance." Under Direction of Thornton S. Graves.
1922--.

*2111 Chambers, E. K. The Elizabethan Stage. 4 vol. Oxford: At the
Clarendon Press, 1923.

2112 Progress of Medieval and Renaissance Studies in the United States
of America. Boulder, Colorado: American Council of Learned
Societies, Committee on Medieval Latin, Mediaeval Academy
of America, 1923--date.

2113 International Index to Periodicals (Formerly Readers' Guide
Supplement): Devoted Chiefly to the Humanities and Science.
Vol. IV. 1924--. New York: H. W. Wilson Co.

2114 Northup, Clark Sutherland. A Register of Bibliographies of the
English Language and Literature. New Haven: Yale University
Press, 1925. [8], 507 pp. [Reprinted, 1962, by Hafner Pub-
lishing Company.]

*2115 Pollard, A. W., and G. R. Redgrave. A Short-Title Catalogue of
       Books Printed in England, Scotland, and Ireland and of English
       Books Printed Abroad, 1475-1640. London: Bibliographical
       Society, 1926. xviii, 609 pp.
           BM. ICN.

*2116 Albright, Evelyn May. Dramatic Publication in England, 1580-
       1640. A Study of Conditions Affecting Content and Form of
       Drama. New York: Heath and Co.; London: Oxford Univer-
       sity Press, 1927. 422 pp. Bibliography, pp. 385-419.
           BM. ICN. IU. MB. MH. MiU. OCl. OU. PU. ViU.

2117   Benham, Allen Rogers, and Lena Lucile Tucker. A Bibliography
       of Fifteenth Century Literature, With Special Reference to
       the History of English Culture. Seattle, Washington: Uni-
       versity of Washington Press, 1928. 274 pp. (University of
       Washington Publications in Language and Literature, Vol.
       2. No. 3, pp. 113-274.)
           BM. DFo. DLC. ICN. ICU. MiU. OCl. OO. ViU. WU.

2118   Gamble, William Burt, comp. The Development of Scenic Art
       and Stage Machinery. A List of References in the New York
       Public Library. New York: The New York Public Library,
       1928. 231 pp. Bibliography, pp. 149-198.
           DLC. IaU. ICN. MiU. MnU.

2119   Kress, Leona L. "Bibliography of Medieval English Religious
       Drama." Emerson Quarterly, VIII (May, 1928), 12.

2120   Tucker, Lena Lucile, and Allen Rogers Benham. A Bibliography
       of Fifteenth Century Literature. With Special Reference to
       the History of English Culture. Seattle, Washington: Uni-
       versity of Washington Press, 1928. 274 pp. (University of
       Washington Publications in Language and Literature, Vol. 2,
       No. 3, pp. 113-274.) [Delete 2117].
           BM. DFo. DLC. IaU. ICN. ICU. MiU. OCl. OO. ViU.
       ·   WU.

2121   Nungezer, Edwin. A Dictionary of Actors and of Other Persons
       Associated with the Public Representations of Plays in Eng-
       land before 1642. New Haven: Yale University Press; London:
       H. Milford, 1929. vi, 438 pp. Bibliography, pp. 405-438.
           BM. DLC. IaU. ICN. MnU. OCl. OO. OU. PHC. PU.
       ViU.

2122 The Catholic Periodical Index: A Cumulative Author and Subject
      Index to a Selected List of Catholic Periodicals. Published for
      the Catholic Library Association, by the H. W. Wilson Co.,
      New York. 1939. 1930--.
          ICN.

2123 Cole, George Watson. A Survey of Bibliography of English Liter-
      ature, 1475-1640. With Especial Reference to the Works of
      the Bibliographical Society of London. Chicago: Chicago Uni-
      versity Press, 1930. 95 pp.
          DLC. ICN. MB. MiU. MnU. NNC. PU.

2124 Kent, Violet, comp. The Player's Library and Bibliography of the
      Theatre. With Introductions by Geoffrey Whitworth and F. S.
      Boas. London: Gollancz, 1930. 401 pp.
          BM. DLC. MiU. WU.

2125 Lawrence, William W. Selected Bibliography of Medieval Liter-
      ature in England. Rev. ed. New York: Columbia University
      Press, 1930. 23 pp.
          BM. DLC. IaU. ICN. MiU. MnU. OC1W. ODW.

*2126 Coleman, Edward D. The Bible in English Drama. An Annotated
      List of Plays Dealing with Biblical Themes, Including Trans-
      lations from Other Languages. New York: New York Public
      Library, 1931. xiii, 212 pp. Indices. [Reprint, 1968].
          DFo. ICN. ICU. IU. MB. MH. NN. OC1. OU.

2127 Paetow, Louis John. A Guide to the Study of Medieval History.
      Rev. ed. New York: F. S. Crofts and Co., 1931. xix, 643
      pp.
          ICN.

2128 Niessen, Carl. Collection of Works on the History of the Theatre,
      Principally in Germany. Washington, D.C.: Library of Con-
      gress, 1932. [Typewritten. About 570 items.]

2129 Baker, Blanche Merritt. Dramatic Bibliography. New York: H.
      W. Wilson and Co., 1933. xvi, 320 pp.
          BM. DFo. IaU. ICN. MiU. NcD. NN. OU. PU. TU.
          ViU.

2130 Cole, George Watson. An Index to Bibliographical Papers Pub-
      lished by the Bibliographical Society and the Library Asso-
      ciation. London, 1877-1932. Chicago, Illinois: Published for

the Bibliographical Society of America at the University of
Chicago Press, 1933. ix, [1], 262 pp.
    BM. ICU.

*2131 Sibley, G. M. The Lost Plays and Masques, 1500-1642. Ithaca,
New York: Cornell University Press, 1933. 205 pp.
    IaU. ICN. MnU. PU.

*2132 Young, Karl. "List of Books." The Drama of the Medieval Church.
Vol. 2. (Oxford, 1933), pp. 544-562.

2133 Barrett, Wilfred Phillips. Chart of Plays 1584 to 1623. Published
under the Auspices of the Shakespeare Association. Cambridge:
University Press, 1934. 39 pp.
    DLC. ICN. MH. MnU. NcD. NN. OC1. OU. PU-F. WU.

2134 Doctoral Dissertations Accepted by American Universities. New
York: H. W. Wilson Co., 1934 -- date. Annual.

2135 Essay and General Literature Index, 1900-1933; An Index to About
40,000 Essays and Articles in 2,144 volumes of Collections of
Essays and Miscellaneous Works. Edited by Minnie Earl Sears
and Marian Shaw. New York: H. W. Wilson Co., 1934--.
    ICN.

2136 de Ricci, Seymour. Census of Medieval and Renaissance Manuscripts in the United States and Canada. 3 vol. New York: H.
W. Wilson, 1935-1940.
    DLC. IaU. ICN. ICU. IU. MH. MnU. OCU. PU. WU.

2137 Worthington, Mabel P., comp. English Miracle, Morality and
Mystery Plays. A List. New York: Federal Theatre Project,
1936. 22 pp. [Mimeographed.]
    CSmH. OC1W.

2138 Bibliographic Index: A Cumulative Bibliography of Bibliographies.
Edited by Dorothy Charles and Bea Joseph. New York: H. W.
Wilson Co., 1937--date.

2139 Coleman, Edward D. "The Jew in English Drama: An Annotated
Bibliography." Bulletin of the New York Public Library, XLII
(1938), 827-850, 919-932; XLIII (1939), 45-52, 374-378;
XLIV (1940), 361-372, 429-444, 495-504, 543-558, 620-634,
675-698, 777-788, 843-866.

2140 Dissertation Abstracts. A Guide to Dissertations and Monographs
      Available in Microfilm. Ann Arbor, Michigan: University
      Microfilms, 1938--date. Monthly. [Title, 1938-1951, Micro-
      film Abstracts].

2141 Poole's Index to Periodical Literature. By William Frederick
      Poole. Rev. ed. 6 vol. New York: Peter Smith, 1938.

*2142 Greg, W. W. A Bibliography Of The English Printed Drama To
      The Restoration. 4 vol. London: Printed For The Bibliographical
      Society At the University Press, Oxford, 1939-1959.
            BM. CSmH. CtY. DFo. DLC. ICN. ICU. MH. MiU.
            NNC. O. OO. PU. ViU.

*2143 Hiler, Hilaire and Meyer, comp. Edited by Helen Grant Cushing.
      Bibliography of Costume. A Dictionary Catalogue of about
      Eight Thousand Books and Periodicals. New York: H. W.
      Wilson Co., 1939. xxxix, 911 pp.
            BM. CSmH. DFo. DLC. ICN. MH. MiU. NjP. OU.
            PU. WU.

2144 The Carl H. Pforzheimer Library. Interludes 1553-1576. New
      York: Privately Printed, 1940. Pp. 525-536. [Reprint from the
      Catalogue of English Books and Manuscripts, 1475-1700, in
      the Carl H. Pforzheimer Library.]
            BN. DFo. ICN.

2145 Palfrey, Thos. R., and Coleman, Henry E., Jr. Guide to Biblio-
      graphies of Theses, United States and Canada. 2nd ed. Chicago,
      Illinois: American Library Association, 1940. 48 pp.
            DLC. ICN. ICU. MB. MH. NN. NNC. OCl. PU. WU.

*2146 The Cambridge Bibliography Of English Literature. Edited by
      F. W. Bateson. 4 vol. Cambridge, England: At the University
      Press; New York: The Macmillan Company, 1941. Supplement,
      1957.

*2147 "Renaissance to Restoration. 3. The Drama." The Cambridge
      Bibliography of English Literature. Vol. 1. (New York,
      Cambridge, 1941), pp. 487-522; Vol. 5. (Cambridge, 1957),
      pp. 241-249.

*2148 "The Middle English Period. 5. The Medieval Drama." The
      Cambridge Bibliography of English Literature. Vol. 1.
      (Cambridge, New York, 1941), pp. 274-279; Vol. 5. (Cam-
      bridge, 1957), pp. 156-158.

2149 Nineteenth Century Readers' Guide to Periodical Literature.
1890-1899. With Supplementary Indexing, 1900-1922. Edited
by Helen Grant Cushing and Adah V. Morris. New York:
H. W. Wilson Co., 1944. 2 vol.

2150 Farrar, Clarissa P., and Austin P. Evans. Bibliography of English Translation from Medieval Sources. New York: Columbia
University Press, 1946. 534 pp.
    CSmH. CtY. DFo. DLC. ICN. ICU. MiU. OCl. PU.
    ViU. WU.

2151 Pierpont Morgan Library. English Drama from the Mid-Sixteenth
to the Later Eighteenth Century. Catalogue of an Exhibition.
Oct. 22, 1945--March 2, 1946. New York: Printed by the
Gallery Press, 1946. 95 pp.
    ICN. MH.

2152 Rosenberg, Robert P. "Bibliographies of Theses in America."
Bulletin of Bibliography, XVIII (September/December, 1945),
181-182; (January/April, 1946), 201-203.

2153 Baldensperger, Fernand, and Werner P. Friedrich, eds. Bibliography of Comparative Literature. Chapel Hill: University
of North Carolina, 1950. 701 pp.
    DFo. DLC. ICN. ICU. MB. MH. MiU. OCl. PU. WU.

2154 Carter, M. J. "A Bibliography of the English Miracle and Popular
Morality Plays Printed to 1945." M.A. University of London,
1950.

*2155 Loewenberg, Alfred. The Theatre of the British Isles Excluding
London. A Bibliography. London: Printed for the Society for
Theatre Research, 1950 (for 1949). Distributed Only to
Members of the Society. xi, 75 pp.
    BM. ICN. MH. MiU. MnU.

*2156 Henshaw, Millett. A Survey of Studies in Medieval Drama, 1933-
1950. Reprinted for Private Circulation from: Progress of
Medieval and Renaissance Studies in the United States and
Canada, Bulletin No. 21, August, 1951. 35 pp.

2157 Williams, Harry F. An Index of Medieval Studies Published in
Festschriften 1865-1946, with Special Reference to Romanic
Materials. Berkeley and Los Angeles: University of California
Press, 1951. 165 pp.

CU. DLC. IaU. MnU.

2158 Baker, Blanche Merritt. Theatre and Allied Arts. A Guide to
      Books Dealing with the History, Criticism, and Technic of
      the Drama and Theatre and Related Arts and Crafts. Rev.
      ed. New York: H. W. Wilson Co., 1952. xiv, 536 pp.
            BM. CSmH. CtY. DFo. DLC. ICN. ICU. MH. MiU.
            OCU. PU. ViU.

2159 Index to Theses Accepted for Higher Degrees in the Universities
      of Great Britain and Ireland. London: Aslib, 1953--date.
      Annual.

2160 Stratman, Carl J., C.S.V. Bibliography of Medieval Drama.
      Berkeley and Los Angeles: University of California Press,
      1954. x, 423 pp. Index.
            BM. CSmH. CtY. DFo. DLC. ICN. ICU. MH. MiU.
            NN. O. OU. PU. TxU.

2161 Pantin, William Abel. The English Church in the Fourteenth
      Century. Cambridge: At the University Press, 1955. xi,
      291 pp.
            BM.

2162 Schwanbeck, Gisela. Bibliographie der deutschsprachigen Hoch-
      schulschriften zur Theaterwissenschaft von 1885 bis 1952.
      Berlin: Selbstverlag der Gesellschaft für Theatergeschichte,
      1956. xiv, 563 pp. Index. (Schriften der Gesellschaft für
      Theatergeschichte, Bd. 58).
            BM. ICU.

2163 Rea, John A. "Recent Books in the Field of Medieval Literature."
      Kentucky Foreign Language Quarterly, VI (1959), 98-99.

2164 Read, Conyers, ed. Bibliography of British History. Tudor Per-
      iod 1485-1603. Introduction by Edward P. Cheyney. 2nd ed.
      Oxford: Clarendon Press, 1959. xxiv, 624 pp. [Original edition,
      1933].
            IC Loy. ICN.

2165 Rojek, Hans Jürgen. Bibliographie der deutschsprachigen Hoch-
      schulschriften zur Theaterwissenschaft von 1953 bis 1960.
      Berlin: Selbstverlag der Gesellschaft für Theatergeschichte,
      1962. xvi, 170 pp. (Schriften der Gesellschaft für Theater-
      geschichte, Bd. 61).
            ICU.

*2166 Bergquist, G. William, ed. Three Centuries of English And American Plays: A Checklist. England: 1500-1800. United States: 1714-1830. New York and London: Hafner Publishing Company, 1963. xii, 281 pp.

*2167 Harbage, Alfred. Annals of English Drama 975-1700. Revised by S. Schoenbaum. London: Methuen & Co., Ltd., 1964. xvii, [1], 321, [2] pp.
BM. CtY. DFo. DLC. ICN. ICU. MH. NN. NNC. O. PU.

*2168 Besterman, Theodore. A World Bibliography of Bibliographies and of Bibliographical Catalogues, Calendars, Abstracts, Digests, Indexes, and the Like. 4th ed. 5 vol. Lausanne: Societas Bibliographica, 1965-1966.

2169 Cumulated Dramatic Index, 1909-1949. A Cumulation of The F. W. Faxon Company's Dramatic Index. Cumulated by G. K. Hall & Co. 2 vol. Boston, Massachusetts: G. K. Hall & Co., 1965.

2170 Ackerman, Robert W. "Middle English Literature to 1400." The Medieval Literature of Western Europe. A Review of Research, Mainly 1930-1960. (New York, 1966), pp. [73]-123.

2171 Bland, D. S. "A Checklist of Drama at the Inns of Court." Research Opportunities in Renaissance Drama, IX (1966), 47-61.

*2172 Fisher, John H., ed. The Medieval Literature of Western Europe. A Review of Research, Mainly 1930-1960. New York: Published for The Modern Language Association of America by the New York University Press; London: University of London Press Limited, 1966. xvi, 432 pp. Index.

2173 Friend, Albert C. "Medieval Latin Liturature." The Medieval Literature of Western Europe. A Review of Research, Mainly 1930-1960. (New York, 1966), pp. [1]-33.

2174 Kolve, V. A. "Bibliography." The Play Called Corpus Christi. (London, 1966), pp. 317-327.

2175 Coleman, Edward Davidson. The Bible in English Drama; an Annotated List of Plays Including Translations from Other Languages from the Beginnings to 1931. New York: New York Public Library [1968]. xiii, 212 pp. [Reprint of the 1931 edition, with A Survey of Recent Major Plays, 1968, by I. Sheffer.]

*2176 McNamee, Lawrence F. Dissertations in English and American
      Literature. Theses Accepted by American, British and Ger-
      man Universities, 1865-1964. New York, London: R. R.
      Bowker Company, 1968. xi, [1], 1124 pp. Indices.

2177 Palmer, Helen H., and Dyson, Anne Jane. European Drama
     Criticism. Hamden, Connecticut: The Shoe String Press, Inc.,
     1968. [8], 460 pp. ["Miracle, Morality, and Mystery Plays,"
     pp. 274-281.]

*2178 "Bibliography." Wilson, F. P. The English Drama 1485-1585.
      Edited with a Bibliography by G. K. Hunter. (Oxford, 1969),
      pp. 202-237. [For Moralities and Interludes.]

*2179 Litto, Frederic M. American Dissertations on the Drama and
      the Theatre; a Bibliography. [Kent, Ohio]: Kent State Univer-
      sity Press [1969]. ix, 519 pp.

B Collections of Plays

2180 Adams, Joseph Quincy, ed. Chief Pre-Shakespearean Dramas.
     A Selection of Plays Illustrating the History of the English
     Drama from Its Origin Down to Shakespeare. Boston, New
     York: Houghton Mifflin Co., 1924. viii, [3], 712 pp.

              CtY. DLC. ICN. ICU. MH. MiU. NN. OU. PU.
              ViU. WU.

         I Sources of the Liturgical Drama
               The Wordless "Alleluia" Sequence
               The "Quem Quaeritis" Trope
               The Easter Sepulchre ("Despositio Crucis,
                 Elevatio Crucis")
               Semi-Dramatic Trope (Easter)

        II Liturgical Plays Dealing with the Story of Christ
               Sepulchrum (The Visit of the Marys)
               Sepulchrum (The Visit of the Marys, and the Race
                 of Peter and John)
               Sepulchrum (The Visit of the Marys, The Race of
                 Peter and John, and The Appearance to Mary
                 Magdalene)
             Peregrini
             Pastores
             Magi

Herodes
Prophetae

III Liturgical Plays Dealing with Miscellaneous Biblical
       Stories and with the Legends of the Saints
     Conversio Beati Paul Apostoli
     Ludus Super Iconia Sancti Nicolai
     Tres Clerici
     Adeodatus

IV The Introduction of the Vernacular
     The Sepulchre
     The Wayfarers
     The Shepherds

  V The Craft Cycles
     Banns (N. Towne)
     The Fall of Lucifer (N. Towne)
     The Creation of Eve, with the Expelling of Adam and
         Eve out of Paradise (Norwich)
     The Killing of Abel (Wakefield)
     Noah (Wakefield)
     The Deluge (Chester)
     The Sacrifice of Isaac (Brome)
     Pharaoh (Wakefield)
     The Prophets (Chester)
     The Salutation and Conception (N. Towne)
     The Birth of Jesus (York)
     The Shepherds (Wakefield)
     The Magi, Herod, and the Slaughter of the Innocents
         (Coventry)
     Christ's Ministry (Chester)
     The Betraying of Christ (N. Towne)
     The Trial of Christ (N. Towne)
     The Harrowing of Hell (Chester)
     The Resurrection of Christ (Wakefield)
     The Judgment Day (York)

VI Non-Cycle Plays
     Dux Moraud
     The Conversion of St. Paul
     Mary Magdalene
     The Play of the Sacrament

VII Moralities
The Castle of Perseverance
Everyman
Mankind
Wyt and Science

VIII Folk Plays
Robin Hood and the Sheriff of Nottingham
Robin Hood and the Friar
Shetland Sword Dance
Oxfordshire St. George Play
Leicestershire St. George Play
The Revesby Sword Play

IX Farces
The Plays Called the Foure PP
The Mery Play betwene Johan Johan the Husbande, Tyb
His Wyfe, and Syr Johan the Preest
The Play of the Wether

X The Court Drama
Damon and Pithias

XI Plays of the Professional Troupes
Cambises

2181 Allen, John, ed. Three Medieval Plays: The Coventry Nativity
Play; Everyman; The Farce of Master Pierre Pathelin.
London: William Heinemann, Ltd., 1953. 43 pp.; 40 pp.;
54 pp.

BM.

2182 Amyot, Thomas, Jr. Payne Collier, etc., ed. A Supplement to
Dodsley's Old Plays. 4 vol. Printed for the Shakespeare
Society, and to be had of W. Skeffington, 1853.

CtY. DFo. DLC. MB. MH. MiU. NN. OU. PU. ViU.

Vol. 1 Chester
Vol. 2 Coventry
Marriage of Wit and Wisdom
Wit and Science

2183 The Ancient British Drama. 3 vol. London: Printed for William
Miller, 1810.

BM. CtY. CU. DLC. ICN. IU. MB. MH. MWelC.
NjP. OC.

Vol. 1 The Four P's
Damon and Pithias

2184 Armstrong, William A., ed. Elizabethan History Plays. With
an Introduction and Glossary. (World's Classics, 606). London: Oxford University Press, 1965. xv, 428 pp.

BM.

King John (John Bale)

2185 Ashton, John William, ed. Types of English Drama. New York:
Macmillan Co., 1940. 750 pp.

DLC. IaU. MnU. OCU. WU.

Plays of Abraham and Melchizedek and Lot
Sacrifice of Isaac
Everyman

2186 Bang, Willy, ed. Materialien zur Kunde des älteren des englischen
Dramas. 44 vol. Louvain and London: A. Uystpruyst, 1902-1914.
(Continued as: Materials for the Study of the Old English Drama,
by H. de Vocht, 1927--.)

BM. CtY. CU. DLC. ICN. ICU. MH. MiU. NIC.
OU. PP.

Vol. 4 Everyman
Vol. 5 Godly Queene Hester
Vol. 12 Enterlude of Youth
Vol. 24 Everyman
Vol. 25 King John (John Bale)
Vol. 26 Everyman
Vol. 33 Impatient Poverty

2187 Bates, Alfred, ed. The Drama. Its History, Literature, and
Influence on Civilization. 20 vol. London: The Athenian
Society, 1908.

Vol. 4 Everyman

2188 Bentley, Gerald Eades, ed. The Development of English Drama.
      An Anthology. New York: Appleton-Century-Crofts, Inc.,
      1950. vii, [1], 823 pp.

      Brome: Abraham and Isaac
      Chester: Deluge or Noah's Flood
      Towneley: Second Shepherds' Play
      The Summoning of Everyman

2189 Block, K. S., ed. Ludus Coventriae; Or, The Plaie Called Corpus
      Christi. Cotton MS. Vespasian D. VIII. London: Published for
      the Early English Text Society by H. Milford, Oxford Univer-
      sity Press, 1922. lx, [2], 402, [2] pp. [Extra Series, No. CXX,
      1922 (for 1917).) [Reprinted 1960].

          BM. CtY. DLC. ICN. ICU. MH. MiU. NjP. NN. O. OCU.
          PU.

      The Creation of Heaven and the Angels; Fall of Lucifer
      The Creation of the World and Man; Fall of Man
      Cain and Abel
      Noah
      Abraham and Isaac
      Moses
      The Prophets
      Mary in the Temple
      The Betrothal of Mary
      The Salutation and Conception
      Joseph's Return
      The Visit to Elizabeth
      The Trial of Joseph and Mary
      The Birth of Jesus
      The Adoration of the Shepherds
      The Adoration of the Magi
      The Purification
      The Massacre of the Innocents; The Death of Herod
      Christ and the Doctors
      The Baptism
      The Temptation
      The Woman Taken in Adultery
      The Raising of Lazarus
      The Passion Play. I.
      The Last Supper
      The Betrayal
      The Passion Play. II. (King Herod; Trial before Annas and
        Caiaphas)

The Death of Judas; The Trial before Pilate; The Trial be-
    fore Herod
Pilate's Wife's Dream; The Trial of Christ and the Thieves
    before Pilate
The Procession to Calvary; The Crucifixion
The Descent into Hell
The Burial; The Guarding of the Sepulchre
The Harrowing of Hell; The Resurrection
The Announcement to the Three Maries
The Appearance to Mary Magdalen
The Appearance to Cleophas and Luke; The Appearance to
    Thomas
The Ascension
The Day of Pentecost
The Assumption of the Virgin
Doomsday

2190 Boas, Frederick S., ed. Five-Pre-Shakespearean Comedies.
       London: Oxford University Press, H. Milford [1934]. 343 pp.

       BM. CtY. DFo. DLC. MH. MiU. MnU. OC1. WU.

       The Four PP.
       Fulgens and Lucrece

2191 Bond, Richard Warwick. Early Plays from the Italian. Oxford:
       University Press, 1911. 332 pp.

       DFo. PU.

       Misogonus

2192 Brandl, A., and O. Zippel, eds. Mittelenglische Sprach-und
       Literaturproben. Ersätz für Mätzners Altenglische Sprach-
       proben. Mit etymologischen Wörterbuch zugleich für Chaucer.
       Berlin: Weidmannsche Buchhandlung, 1917. vii, [1], 423 pp.

       BM.

       Interludium de Clerico et Puella
       York: The Journey to Bethlehem
               The Angels and the Shepherds
       Towneley: Secunda Pastorum

2193 ----- Mittelenglische Sprach-und Literaturproben. Neuausgabe

von Mätzners Altenglischen Wörterbuch zugleich für Chaucer.
Zweite Auflage. Berlin: Weidmannsche Buchhandlung, 1927.
vii, [1], 423 pp. [Reprint in 1947].

Interludium de Clerico et Puella
York: The Journey to Bethlehem
        The Angels & the Shepherds
Towneley: Second Shepherds

2194 Brandl, A., and O. Zippel, eds. Middle English Literature.
      (Mittelenglische Sprach-und Literaturproben.) 2nd ed. New
      York: Chelsea Publishing Company, 1947. vii, [1], 423 pp.

Interludium de Clerico et Puella
York: The Journey to Bethlehem
        The Angels and the Shepherds
Towneley: Second Shepherds

2195 Brandl, Alois. Quellen des weltlichen Dramas in England vor
      Shakespeare. Ein Ergänzungsband zu Dodsley's Old English
      Plays. Strassburg: Karl J. Trübner, 1898. cxxvi, 666, [1] pp.

    BM. CtY. DFo. DLC. ICN. ICU. IEN. MH. MiU. NN.
    OU. PU.

The Pride of Life
Mankind
Nature (Henry Medwall)
The Play of Love (John Heywood)
The Play of the Wether (John Heywood)
A Mery Play betwene Johan Johan the husbande / Tyb his wyfe /
    and syr johan the preest (John Heywood)
Respublica
Kyng Daryus
Misogonus
Horestes (John Pikeryng)
Gismond of Salern in Loue
Common Conditions

2196 Bridge, Joseph C., ed. Three Chester Whitsun Plays. With an
      Introduction and Notes. Chester: Phillipson and Golder, 1906.
      xiv, 49 pp.

    BM. CtY. ICN. MH. MiU. MnU. MWelC. NN.

The Banes or Proclamation of the Plays
The Salutation and Nativity
The Plays of the Shepherds
The Adoration of the Magi

2197 Brown, Carleton Fairchild, ed. The Stonyhurst Pageants. Göttingen: Vandenhoeck & Ruprecht; Baltimore: The Johns Hopkins
Press, 1920. 30, 302 pp. (Hesperia Ergänzungsreihe:
Schriften zur englischen Philologie...Heft 7). [MS. is in-
complete].

BM. IaU. MB. MiU. MnU. OCU. OU. PBm. PU. ViU. WU.

[The 6 Pagean] of Iacob
The 7 Pagean of Ioseph
The eight pagean of Moyses
The 9 pagean of Iosue
The 10 pagean of Gedeon
The 11 pagean of Iephte
The 12 pagean of Samson
[The 14 pagean of Saul]
The 15 pagean of Dauid
The 16 pageant of Salomon
The 17 pageant [of Elias]
[The 18 pageant of Naaman]

2198 Browne, E. Martin, ed. Mystery and Morality Plays. Selected
and Introduced. New York: Published by Meridian Books, Inc.,
1960. 317 pp. (Religious Drama 2. Living Age Books).

BM.

Brome: The Sacrifice of Isaac
Chester: Noah's Flood
Cornish: 1 David Takes the Shoots to Jerusalem
        2 David and Bathsheba
        The Three Maries
Coventry: Herod and the Kings
Ludus Coventriae: The Parliament of Heaven: The Annunci-
                ation and Conception
                The Woman Taken in Adultery
Towneley: The Play of the Shepherds
York: The Creation of the Heavenly Beings: The Fall of
        Lucifer
        The Creation of Man
        The Garden of Eden

The Fall of Man
The Birth of Christ
The Temptation of Christ
The Second Trial Before Pilate: The Scourging and Con-
    demnation
The Crucifixion
The Harrowing of Hell
The Ascension
The Last Judgment
Everyman

2199 Browne, E. Martin, ed. Religious Plays for Use in Churches.
    London: Philip Allan, 1932. 93 pp. Bibliography and Informa-
    tion, pp. 83-93.

Brome: Sacrifice of Isaac
Ludus Coventriae: Play of the Maid Mary
                   Mary the Mother
Towneley: Second Shepherds' Play
York: Nativity Play

2200 Cawley, A. C., ed. Everyman and Medieval Miracle Plays.
    Edited with an Introduction. New York: E. P. Dutton & Co.,
    Inc., 1959. xxi, [1], 266 pp.

    BM.

Brome: Abraham and Isaac
Chester: Noah's Flood
          The Harrowing of Hell
Cornwall: The Death of Pilate
Coventry: The Annunciation
Ludus Coventriae: Cain and Abel
                   The Woman Taken in Adultery
Wakefield: The Second Shepherds' Pageant
            Herod the Great
York: The Creation, and the Fall of Lucifer
       The Creation of Adam and Eve
       The Fall of Man
       The Crucifixion
       The Resurrection
       The Judgment
Everyman

2201 ----- The Wakefield Pageants in the Towneley Cycle. Man-
    chester: Manchester University Press [1958]. xxxix, 187 pp.

(Old and Middle English Texts Edited by G. L. Brook). [Re-printed 1963, 1968.]

Mactacio Abel
Processus Noe Cum Filiis
Prima Pastorum
Secunda Pastorum
Magnus Herodes
Coliphizacio

2202 Child, Clarence Griffin. The Second Shepherds Play, Everyman, And Other Early Plays. Translated with Introduction and Notes. Boston, New York, and Chicago: Houghton Mifflin Company, 1910. xlviii, 138 pp. [Reprinted 1957.]

DLC. MH. MiU. NjP. OCl. OCU. OU. PBm. PU. WU.

Quem Quaeritis
Brome: Abraham and Isaac
Towneley: The Second Shepherds' Play
Everyman
Robin Hood Plays
  Robin Hood and the Knight
  Robin Hood and potter
Saint George Play (Oxfordshire)

2203 Child, Francis James, ed. Four Old Plays. Three Interludes: Thersytes, Jack Jugler and Heywoods Pardoner and Frere: and Jocasta, a Tragedy by Gascoigne and Kinwelmarsh, with an Introduction and Notes. Cambridge: G. Nichols, 1848. 288 pp.

CtY. DLC. ICN. MA. MH. MiU. NIC. NN. PU. RPB.

2204 Clark, Barrett H., ed. World Drama. 2 vol. New York and London: D. Appleton & Co., 1933. [Reprint, 1955].

Adam
The Wise Virgin and the Foolish Virgins (From the French)
Towneley: The Second Shepherds' Play
Everyman

2205 Clark, David Lee, William Brian Gates, and Ernest Edwin Leisy, eds. The Voices of England and America. 2 vol. New York: Nelson, 1937.

Vol. 1 Second Shepherds' Play
        Everyman

2206 Cohen, Helen Louise, ed. Milestones of the Drama. New York,
      Chicago: Harcourt, Brace and Co., [c. 1940]. 580 pp.

      Everyman

2207 Collier, John Payne. Five Miracle Plays, or Scriptural Dramas.
      London: Privately Printed, 1836. 5 parts. iv, 19, 16, 44, 24,
      39, 4 pp. [25 copies printed.]

         BM. MnU.

      Chester: The Advent of Antichrist
      Dublin: The Sacrifice of Abraham
      Ludus Coventriae: The Marriage of the Virgin
      Towneley: Adoration of the Shepherds
      (From MS. Harl. 2253): Harrowing of Hell

2208 Collier, John Payne, ed. Five Old Plays, Illustrating the Early
      Progress of the English Drama. Edited from Copies, Either
      Unique, or of Great Rarity. London: W. Nicol, 1851. xx,
      426 pp. (Printed for the Roxburghe Club).

         BM. CtY. DLC. ICN. ICU. MH. NNC.

      Conflict of Conscience
      A Knack to Know a Knave
      The Rare Triumphs of Love and Fortune
      The Three Ladies of London
      The Three Lords and Three Ladies of London

2209 ----- Illustrations of Early English Popular Literature. 2 vol.
      London: Privately Printed, 1863-1864.

         BM. CSmH. DFo. ICN. ICU. MH. OCl. PP. PU.

      The Comedy of Tyde Taryeth No Man
      Enterlude of Godly Queene Hester

2210 ----- Illustrations of Old English Literature. 3 vol. London:
      Privately Printed, 1866.

         BM. ICN. MBAt. NN. PP.

Vol. 1 Respublica
Vol. 2 Horestes

2211 Craig, Hardin, ed. Two Coventry Corpus Christi Plays. 2nd
ed. London: Oxford University Press, 1957. xlii, 133 pp.
(E.E.T.S. Extra Series LXXXVII).

Pageant of the Shearmen and Taylors
Pageant of the Weavers

2212 Deimling, Hermann. The Chester Plays. Part I. Re-edited from
the MSS. by the Late Dr. Hermann Deimling. Part II. Re-
edited from the MSS. by Dr. Matthews. 2 vol. London: Published for the Early English Text Society by K. Paul, Trench
Trübner &Co. 1892-1916. (Early English Text Society.
Extra Series, No. LXII-CXV.) [Reprinted, 1935, 1959.]

BM. CtY. DLC. ICN. ICU. MH. MiU. NjP. NN. O.
OC1. PU.

The Fall of Lucifer
The Creation
The Deluge
The Sacrifice of Isaac
Balaam and Balak
The Nativity
Adoration of the Shepherds
Adoration of the Magi
The Magi's Oblation
Slaying of the Innocents
Purification
The Temptation
Christ. The Adulteress. Chelidonius
Christ's Visit to Simon the Leper
Christ's Betrayal
Christ's Passion
Christ's Descent into Hell
Christ's Resurrection
Christ Appears to Two Disciples
Christ's Ascension
The Sending of the Holy Ghost
The Prophets and Antichrist
The Coming of Antichrist
The Last Judgment

2213 The Digby Plays. With an Incomplete Morality of Wisdom, Who
      Is Christ. Re-issued from the Plates of the Text Edited by
      F. J. Furnivall for the New Shakespeare Society in 1882.
      London: Published for the Early English Text Society by Hum-
      phrey Milford, Oxford University Press, 1930. xxxii, 239 pp.

          BM.

2214 Dodsley, Robert, ed. A Select Collection of Old Plays. 12 vol.
      London: Printed for R. Dodsley in Pall-Mall, 1744.

          CtY. ICN. MH. MiU. MoU. NIC. NjP. PU. TxU. WU.

          Vol. 1 Chief Promises of God (God's Promises)
                 Damon and Pithias
                 The Four P's
                 New Custom

2215 ----- A Select Collection of Old Plays. The Second Edition.
      Corrected and Collated with the Old Copies. With Notes Critical
      and Explanatory. Edited by Isaac Reed. 12 vol. London: Printed
      by J. Nichols for J. Dodsley, 1780.

          BM. CtY. DFo. ICN. MH. MiU. NjP. NN. OU.

          Vol. 1 Damon and Pithias
                 God's Promises
                 The Four P's
                 New Custom
          Vol. 2 The World and the Chylde

2216 [Dodsley, Robert, ed.]. A Select Collection of Old Plays. A New
      Edition. With Additional Notes and Corrections. By the Late
      Isaac Reed, Octavius Gilchrist, and the Editor. 12 vol. Lon-
      don: Septimus Prowett, 1825.

          BM.

          Vol. 1 The Four P's (John Heywood)
                 God's Promises (John Bale)
                 New Custome
          Vol. 2 Tancred and Gismunda (Robert Wilmot)

2217 Dodsley, Robert, ed. A Select Collection of Old English Plays.
      Originally Published by Robert Dodsley in the Year 1744. 4th

ed. Now First Chronologically Arranged. Revised and En-
larged. With the Notes of All the Commentators, and New
Notes by W. Carew Hazlitt. 15 vol. London: Reeves and
Turner, 1874-1876.

BM. CtY. DLC. ICN. ICU. MH. MiU. NNC. OC1. PU.

Vol. 1 The Tragi-Comedy of Calisto and Melibaea
Everyman: a Moral Play
Interlude of the Four Elements
The Four P.P
God's Promises
Hickscorner
The Pardoner and the Friar
A New Interlude, Called Thersites
The World and the Child

Vol. 2 Disobedient Child
History of Jacob and Esau
Jack Juggler
Lusty Juventus
Marriage of Wit and Science
Nice Wanton
Interlude of Youth

Vol. 3 New Custom
The Trial of Treasure
Like Will to Like

Vol. 4 Cambises
Contention Between Liberality and Prodigality
Rare Triumphs of Love and Fortune

Vol. 6 A Knack to Know a Knave
Conflict of Conscience
The Three Ladies of London
The Three Lords and Three Ladies

Vol. 7 Tancred and Gismunda

2218 Dugdale, Sir William. Monasticon Anglicanum. New ed. Vol. 6,
Part 3. (London, 1830), pp. 1537-1543. [A reprint of the
1722 Stevens edition.]

2219 England, George, ed. The Towneley Plays. Re-edited from the

Unique MS. With Side-notes and Introduction by Alfred W.
Pollard. London: Published for the Early English Text Society
by K. Paul, Trench, Trubner & Co., 1897. xxxiv, [2], 416,
[2] pp. (Early English Text Society. Extra Series, No. LXXI.)
[Reprinted, 1907, 1925, 1952, 1966.]

BM. CtY. DLC. ICN. ICU. MH. MiU. NjP. NN. O. PU.

The Creation
Killing of Abel
Noah and the Ark
Abraham
Isaac
Sequitur Iacob
The Prophets
Pharaoh
Caesar Augustus
The Annunciation
The Salutation of Elizabeth
Shepherds' Play, I
Shepherds' Play, II
Offering of the Magi
The Flight into Egypt
Herod the Great
The Purification of Mary
The Play of the Doctors
Iohn the Baptist
The Conspiracy
The Buffeting
The Scourging
The Crucifixion
The Talents
The Deliverance of Souls
The Resurrection of the Lord
The Pilgrims
Thomas of India
The Lord's Ascension
The Judgment
Lazarus
The Hanging of Judas

2220 Everyman and Other Plays. Decorated by John Austen. [London]:
      Chapman and Hall, 1925. 201 pp.

         BM.

              Towneley: The Nativity
                        Second Shepherds Play
          Everyman

2221 Everyman, with Other Interludes, Including Eight Miracle Plays.
      London: J. M. Dent & Sons; New York: E. P. Dutton & Co.
      [1909]. xxi, 198 pp. (Everyman's Library). [Reprinted 1910,
      1912, 1914, 1915, 1917, 1920, 1924, 1926, 1930, 1935, etc.].

              Chester: The Deluge
                        Abraham, Melchisedec, and Isaac
              Cornish: The Three Maries
                        Mary Magdalene and the Apostles
              Coventry: The Nativity Play
              Towneley: The Crucifixion
                        The Harrowing of Hell
                        Second Shepherds' Play
          Everyman
          Bale, John: God's Promises

2222 Farmer, John Stephen, ed. Anonymous Plays. 3rd Series. Com-
      prising Jack Juggler; King Darius; Gammer Gurton's Needle;
      New Custom; Trial of Treasure; Note-book and Word-list.
      London: Privately Printed for Subscribers, 1906. 302 pp.
      (Early English Dramatists, Vol. 10.)

          BM. CtY. DLC. ICN. ICU. MB. MH. NjP. NN. OU. PU.
          ViU.

2223 ----- Five Anonymous Plays. 4th Series. Comprising Apius
      and Virginia; The Marriage of Wit and Science; Grim the
      Collier of Croydon; Common Conditions; The Marriage of
      Wit and Wisdom; Note-book and Word-list. London: Privately
      Printed for Subscribers, 1908. 328 pp. (Early English Dra-
      matists, Vol. 12).

          BM. CtY. DLC. ICN. ICU. MH. MiU. NjP. NNC. OU. PU.

2224 ----- Recently Recovered "Lost" Tudor Plays, with Some Others,
      Comprising Mankind--Nature - Wit and Science - Respublica -
      Wealth and Health - Impatient Poverty - John the Evangelist.
      Note-book and Word-list. London: Privately Printed for Sub-
      scribers, 1907. viii, 472 pp. (Early English Dramatists,
      Vol. 13).

BM. CtY. DLC. ICN. ICU. MH. MiU. NN. OU. PU. ViU.

2225 Farmer, John Stephen, ed. Six Anonymous Plays. 1st Series.
c. 1510-1537, Comprsing Four Elements. The Beauty and
Good Properties of Women (Usually Known As Calisto and
Melibaea): Everyman; Hickscorner; The World and the
Child; Thersites; Note-book and Word-list. London: Private-
ly Printed for Subscribers, 1905. 286 pp. (Early English
Dramatists, Vol. 4).

BM. CtY. DLC. ICN. ICU. MiU. NjP. NN. OU. PU. ViU.

2226 ----- Six Anonymous Plays. 2nd Series. Comprising Jacob and
Esau; Youth; Albion, Knight; Misogonous; Godly Queen Hester;
Tom Tyler and His Wife; Note-book and Word-list. London:
Privately Printed for Subscribers, 1906. 478 pp. (Early Eng-
lish Dramatists, Vol. 7).

BM. CtY. DLC. ICN. MH. MiU. NjP. NNC. OO.

2227 Franklin, Alexander, ed. Seven Miracle Plays: Cain and Abel,
Noah's Flood, Abraham and Isaac, The Shepherds, The Three
Kings, King Herod, and Adam and Eve. London and New York:
Oxford University Press, 1963. 158 pp.

BM.

Brome: Abraham and Isaac
Chester: King Herod
         Noah's Flood
         The Shepherds
Towneley: Cain and Abel
York: The Three Kings
Non-Cycle: Adam and Eve

2228 Feasey, Lynette. Old English At Play. Old Plays Adapted for
Young Players. London: G. G. Harrap and Co., Ltd., 1944.
144 pp.

Coventry: Nativity Play
York: Play of the Shepherds
Everyman
Play of Noah's Ark
St. George and the Dragon

2229 Fifteenth Century Prose and Verse, With an Introduction by
      Alfred W. Pollard. Westminster: A Constable & Co., Ltd.,
      1903. 324 pp.

      Coventry: Nativity Play
      Everyman

2230 Franklin, Alexander, ed. Seven Miracle Plays: Cain and Abel,
      Noah's Flood, Abraham and Isaac, The Shepherds, The Three
      Kings, King Herod, and Adam and Eve. London and New York:
      Oxford University Press, 1965. 158 pp. (Reprint).

      BM.

2231 Furnivall, F. J., ed. The Digby Mysteries... Edited from the
      MSS. London: Published for the New Shakespere Society, by
      N. Trübner & Co., 1882. xxxii, 239, [1] pp.

      NN.

      Herod's Killing of the Children
      The Conversion of St. Paul
      Mary Magdalene
      Christ's Burial and Resurrection

2232 ----- The Digby Plays, with An Incomplete 'Morality' of Wis-
      dom, Who Is Christ (Part of One of the Macro Moralities).
      Re-issued from the Plates of the Text Edited by F. J. Furnivall
      for the New Shakespere Society in 1882. London: Published for
      the Early English Text Society by K. Paul, Trench, Trübner
      & Co., 1896. [8], v-xxxii, 239 pp. (Early English Text Society.
      Extra Series [No.] 70.)

      BM. CtY. DLC. ICN. MH. MiU. NjP. NN. O. OC1. PU.
      ViU.

2233 Furnivall, F. J., and Alfred W. Pollard, eds. The Macro Plays.
      1. Mankind (ca. 1475). 2. Wisdom (ca. 1460). 3. The Cas-
      tle of Perseverance (ca. 1425). With Introduction and Glos-
      sarial Index. London: Published for the Early English Text
      Society by Humphrey Milford, Oxford University Press, 1904.
      xlii, 210 pp.

      BM.

2234 Gassner, John, ed. A Treasury of the Theatre [From Aeschylus
      to Turgenev]. Revised Edition. New York: Simon and Schuster,
      1951. xvii, [1], 718 pp. [The modernized versions are all by
      John Gassner.]

      Abraham and Isaac [Brome]
      The Second Shepherds' Play [Towneley]
      Everyman

2235 ----- Medieval and Tudor Drama. Edited, with Introductions
      and Modernizations by John Gassner. Toronto, New York,
      London: Bantam Books, 1963. xviii, 457 pp.

      Mystery and Miracle Plays
      Brome: Abraham and Isaac
      Chester: The Death of Herod
                The Betrayal of Christ
                The Resurrection, Harrowing of Hell, and the Last
                    Judgment
      Cornwall: Death of Pilate
      Coventry: The Pageant of the Shearmen and Tailors
      Wakefield: The Murder of Abel
                  The Deluge: Noah and His Sons
                  The Second Shepherds Play
                  The Crucifixion
      York: The Creation and Fall of Lucifer
            Man's Disobedience and the Fall of Man
      Moralities and Interludes
                  Everyman
                  The Play Called the Four PP (John Heywood)
      Folk
          A Christmas Mumming: The Play of Saint George

2236 Gayley, Charles Mills, ed. Representative English Comedies.
      With Introductory Essays and Notes. An Historical View of
      Our Earlier Comedy and Other Monographs by Various Writers.
      4 vol. New York: The Macmillan Co., 1903.

          BM. CtY. DLC. ICN. ICU. MH. MiU. NjP. NNC. OC. PU.

      Vol. 1 Play of the Weather
             Mery Play Betweene Johan Johan, Tyb, etc.

2237 Goodman, Randolph. Drama on Stage. New York: Holt, Rine-
      hart and Winston [c. 1961]. 475 pp.

Everyman

2238 Gordon, J., and Hunter, J. The Towneley Mysteries. London:
J. B. Nichols for the Surtees Society, 1836. xx, [2], 352 pp.

BM. CtY. ICN. ICU. MnU. MH. NN. NNUT. PPPD.

2239 Grosart, Alexander Balloch, ed. Miscellanies of the Fuller
Worthies Library. Edited with Memorial Introduction and
Notes. 4 vol. London: Privately Printed, 1871-1876.

BM. CtY. DLC. MH. MiU. NjP. O. OU. PU. WU.

Vol. 1 The Temptation by John Bale
Vol. 2 Jack Juggler
Godly Queen Hester

2240 Halliwell, James Orchard, ed. The Literature of the Sixteenth
and Seventeenth Centuries. Illustrated by Reprints of Very
Rare Tracts. London: for Private Circulation Only, 1851.
236 pp.

BM. DFo. ICN. NN.

2241 ----- Ludus Coventriae. A Collection of Mysteries, Formerly
Represented at Coventry on the Feast of Corpus Christi. London: Printed for the Shakespeare Society, 1841. xvi, 434 pp.

BM. ICN. NN.

The Creation of Heaven and the Angels; Fall of Lucifer
The Creation of the World and Man; Fall of Man
Cain and Abel
Noah and the Death of Lamech
Abraham and Isaac
Moses
The Prophets
The Conception of Mary
Mary in the Temple
The Betrothal of Mary
The Parliament of Heaven; The Salutation and Conception
Joseph's Return
The Visit to Elizabeth
The Trial of Joseph and Mary
The Birth of Christ

The Adoration of the Shepherds
The Adoration of the Magi
The Purification
The Massacre of the Innocents; The Death of Herod
Christ and the Doctors
The Baptism
The Temptation
The Woman Taken in Adultery
The Raising of Lazarus
Prologues of Demon and of John the Baptist; The Council of
    the Jews
The Entry into Jerusalem
The Last Supper, and The Conspiracy of the Jews and Judas
The Betrayal
The Trial of Christ before Annas and Caiaphas; Peter's
    Denial; The Death of Judas; The Trial of Christ before
    Pilate; The Trial of Christ before Herod
Pilate's Wife's Dream
The Trial of Christ and the Thieves before Pilate; The Con-
    demnation and the Scourging; The Procession to Calvary;
    The Crucifixion
The Descent into Hell of Anima Christi
The Embassy to Pilate of Joseph of Arimathea; The Episode
    of Longeus; The Descent from the Cross and the Burial
The Guarding of the Sepulchre; The Harrowing of Hell; The
    Resurrection and Appearance to the Virgin; The Compact
    of the Soldiers and Pilate
The Announcement to the Three Maries
The Appearance to Mary Magdalen
The Appearance on the Way to Emmaeus; The Appearance
    to Thomas
The Ascension and The Choice of Matthias
The Day of Pentecost
The Assumption of the Virgin
Doomsday

2242 Halliwell, James Orchard, ed. Ludus Coventriae. A Collection
      of Mysteries Formerly Represented at Coventry on the Feast
      of Corpus Christi. London: Printed for the Shakespeare
      Society, 1843. xvi, 434 pp. (In: Thomas Amyot, ed., A Sup-
      plement to Dodsley's Old Plays. [London], 1853. Vol. 2, No. 1).

2243 Hampden, John, ed. Everyman; The Interlude of Youth; The
      World and the Child. London and Edinburgh: Thomas Nelson
      and Sons, Ltd. [1931]. vii, [1], 9-96 pp.

BM.

2244 Hawkins, Thomas, ed. The Origin of the English Drama, Illustrated in Its Various Species, viz., Mystery, Morality,
Tragedy, and Comedy, by Specimens from Our Earliest
Writers. With Explanatory Notes. 3 vol. Oxford: Printed at
the Clarendon Press, for S. Leacroft, 1773.

BM. CtY. DLC. ICN. ICU. MH. NjP. NN. OU. PU. ViU.

Vol. 1 Cambises
Digby: Candlemas Day
Everyman
Hycke-scorner
Lusty Juventus

2245 Heilman, Robert B., ed. An Anthology of English Drama Before
Shakespeare. Edited with an Introduction. New York, Toronto:
Rinehart & Company, Inc., 1952. xxi, [3], 405 pp.

Ludus Coventriae: The N. Towne Betrayal
Wakefield: Noah
The Second Shepherds' Play
York: Crucifixion
Everyman

2246 Hemingway, Samuel Burdett, ed. English Nativity Plays. Edited
with Introduction, Notes, and Glossary. New York: Henry
Holt and Company, 1909. xlviii, 319 pp. (Yale Studies in
English, XXXVIII). [Reprinted 1964.]

BM. CtY. CU. DLC. ICN. ICU. MH. NN. OU. PU.

Chester: Nativity
Shepherds's Play
Ludus Coventriae: Incarnation
Joseph
Visitation
Nativity
Shepherds
Towneley: Annunciation
Salutacio Elizabeth
First Shepherds' Play
Second Shepherds' Play
York: Prophets, Annunciation, Visitation

Joseph
Nativity
Shepherds

2247 Hemingway, Samuel B., ed. English Nativity Plays. Edited with
      Introduction, Notes, and Glossary. New York: Russell &
      Russell, Inc., 1964. [8], xlviii, 319 pp. [Reprint of the 1909
      edition. See the 1909 edition for the plays.]

2248 Hinkson, Katharine Tynan. Miracle Plays: Our Lord's Coming
      and Childhood. London: John Lane, the Bodley Head; Chicago:
      Stone and Kimball, 1895. 97 pp.

      BM.

      The Annunciation
      The Finding in the Temple
      The Flight into Egypt
      The Nativity
      The Presentation in the Temple
      The Visitation

2249 Hopper, Vincent F., and Gerald B. Lahey, eds. Medieval Mys-
      tery Plays. Abraham and Isaac. Noah's Flood. The Second
      Shepherds' Play. Morality Plays. The Castle of Perseverance.
      Everyman. And Interludes. Johan, The Husband. The Four
      PP. Great Neck, New York: Barron's Educational Series, Inc.,
      1962. [8], 297, [2] pp.

      Brome: Abraham and Isaac
      Chester: Noah's Flood
      Towneley: The Second Shepherds' Play
      The Castle of Perseverance
      Everyman
      Johan, the Husband (John Heywood)
      The Four PP. (John Heywood)

2250 Hubbell, Jay Broadus, and John O. Beaty. An Introduction to
      Drama. New York: Macmillan Co., 1927. xi, 838 pp.

      Brome: Abraham and Isaac
      Towneley: Second Shepherds' Play
      Everyman

2251 Hussey, Maurice. The Chester Mystery Plays. Sixteen Pageant

Plays from the Chester Craft Cycle. Adapted into Modern English. Melbourne, London, Toronto: Heinemann, 1960. xxi, [1], 160 pp. [First Published in the Drama Library, 1957.]

BM.

The Fall of Lucifer
The Creation of Man: Adam and Eve
Noah's Deluge
Abraham and Isaac
The Nativity
The Adoration of the Shepherds
The Adoration of the Magi
The Magi's Oblation
The Slaying of the Innocents
Simon the Leper
The Betrayal of Christ
Christ's Passion
Christ's Resurrection
Christ's Ascension
Antichrist
The Last Judgment

2252 Kreymborg, Alfred, ed. Poetic Drama: an Anthology of Plays in Verse from the Ancient Greek to the Modern American. New York: Modern Age Books [1941]. 855 pp.

BM.

Towneley: The Second Shepherds' Play
Everyman

2253 Leverton, Garrett H., ed. Plays for the College Theatre. New York: Samuel French, 1939. 629 pp.

BM.

York: Nativity Play
Everyman

2254 Lieder, Paul R., ed. British Drama. New York: Houghton Mifflin Co., 1929. iv, 374 pp.

BM. DLC. IaU. MH. MiU. MnU. NN.

Brome: Abraham and Isaac
Towneley: Second Shepherds' Play
Everyman

2255 Loomis, Roger Sherman, & Wells, Henry W., eds. Representa-
      tive Medieval and Tudor Plays Translated and Modernized.
      New York: Sheed & Ward, 1942. [4], 301 pp. Bibliography,
      pp. 299-301.

      Ludus Coventriae
          The Mystery of the Redemption (Abridged)
              The Creation and Fall of Man
              The Procession of the Prophets
              The Parliament of Heaven and the Annunciation
              The Cherry Tree
              The Adoration of the Shepherds
              The Adoration of the Magi and Death of Herod
              The Raising of Lazarus
          The Passion Play, the Resurrection, and the Last Judgment
              The Prologue of Satan
              The Passion Play
              The Appearance to Magdalene
              The Last Judgment
      Wakefield: Annunciation
                  The Second Shepherds' Play
      Everyman
      John, Tyb, and Sir John (John Heywood)
      The Pardoner and the Friar (John Heywood)

2256 Malcolmson, Anne. Miracle Plays. Seven Medieval Plays for
      Modern Players. Adapted by Anne Malcolmson. Illustrated
      by Pauline Baynes. London: Constable and Co., 1960. [18],
      142 pp.

          BM.

      Brome: Abraham and Isaac
      Chester: Noah's Flood
      Wakefield: The Shepherds' Play [2nd Shepherds]
      York: Nativity
      Coventry: Herod and the Magi, Slaughter of the Innocents
          [Shearmen and Taylors]

2257 Malone Society Reprints. Oxford [London]: Oxford University
      Press, 1906 --. [The imprint information varies widely from
      volume to volume.]

Albion Knight
Calisto and Melebea (John Rastell)
The Cobler's Prophecy (Robert Wilson)
The Contention Between Liberality and Prodigality
The Cruel Debtor
The Four Cardinal Virtues
Gentleness and Nobility
The Most Virtuous and Godly Susanna (Thomas Garter)
Good Order
The Interlude of Vice [Horestes]. (John Pikeryng)
Jack Juggler (2)
Jacob and Esau
John the Evangelist
King John (John Bale)
A Knack to Know a Knave
Love Feigned and Unfeigned
The Play of Lucrece
The Marriage of Wit and Science
Pater Filius (Prodigal Son)
The Play of Patient Grissell (John Phillip)
The Pedlar's Prophecy
Processus Satanae
Rare Triumphs of Love and Fortune
Resurrection of Our Lord
A Play of Robin Hood for May-Games
Somebody and Others
Temperance and Humility
Tom Tyler and His Wife
Trial and Flagellation
The Interlude of Wealth and Health
Wit and Science (John Redford)

2258 Manly, John Matthews, ed. Specimens of the Pre-Shaksperean
      Drama. With an Introduction, Notes, and a Glossary. 2 vol.
      Boston and New York: Ginn and Co., 1897-1898. [Also, 1903-
      1904].

          CtY. DLC. ICN. ICU. MH. MiU. NjP. NNC. OC. PU.
          WaU.

      Vol. 1 Mystery and Miracle Plays
                  Brome: Abraham and Isaac
                  Chester: Antichrist
                          De Mose et Rege Balaak et Balaam
                          Propheta (Processus Prophetarum)

Coventry: The Pageant of the Shearmen and Tay-
                   lors (The Nativity and the Slaughter
                   of the Innocents)
Digby: The Conversion of St. Paul
Ludus Coventriae: Noah and Lamech
                              Salutation & Conception
Norwich: Creation and Fall, I, II
Play of the Sacrament
Shrewsbury Fragments: [Officium Pastorum,
                                    Resurrectionis,
                                    Peregrinorum]
Towneley: Processus Noe
                  Isaac
                  Iacob
                  Second Shepherds' Play
York: The Resurrection
          The Judgment Day

Folk Plays
       Revesby Sword Play
       Robin Hood Plays (1) Robin Hood and the Knight;
          (2) Robin Hood and the Friar; (3) Robin Hood
          and the Potter
       St. George Plays (Oxfordshire St. George Play;
          Christmas Lutterworth Play)

Moralities and Interludes
       Mankind
       Mundus et Infans
       Hycke-scorner
       Wyt and Science (John Redford)
       Nice Wanton
       The Foure PP (John Heywood)
       Kynge Johan (John Bale)

Vol. 2 Cambises (Thomas Preston)

2259 Manning, Rosemary, ed. The Shepherds' Play, and Noah and
        the Flood: Two Miracle Plays Arranged for Young People
        Glasgow, London: Grant [1955]. 43 pp.

        BM.

2260 Markland, James Heywood, ed. Chester Mysteries. De Deluvio
        Noe. De Occisione Innocentium. London: Printed by Bensley

and Sons, 1818. [10], xxii, [2], 70, [1] pp. (Roxburghe Club).

BM. DLC. MdBP. MH. NN.

2261 Marriott, William. A Collection of English Miracle-Plays Or
Mysteries; Containing Ten Dramas from the Chester, Coventry,
and Towneley Series, with Two of Latter [sic!] Date. To Which
Is Prefixed, An Historical View of This Description of Plays.
Basel: Schweighauser & Co.; Paris: Brockhaus & Avenarius,
1838. lxiii, [1], 271 pp.

DLC. IC Loy. IaU. MdBP. MiU. MnU. NN. OC1. ODW.

Chester: The Deluge
              Antichrist
Coventry: The Nativity (Shearmen and Tailors)
Digby: Candlemas Day, or the Killing of the Children of
              Israel
Ludus Coventriae: Joseph's Jealousy
                          The Trial of Mary and Joseph
Towneley: Pharao
              Pastores
              Crucifixio
              Extractio Animarum ab Inferno
              Juditium
Bale, John: God's Promises

2262 Matthews, Brander, and Paul Robert Lieder, eds. The Chief
British Dramatists, Excluding Shakespeare. London: George
G. Harrap and Co.; New York: Houghton, 1924. 1084 pp.

Brome: Abraham and Isaac
Towneley: Second Shepherds' Play

2263 McCallum, James Dow, ed. English Literature. The Beginnings
to 1500. New York, Chicago, Boston: Charles Scribner's Sons,
1929. xxvii, [1], 440 pp.

The Shepherds (Towneley)

2264 Mooney, Margaret S. A Rosary of Mystery Plays. Fifteen Plays
Selected from the York Cycle of Mysteries Performed by the
Crafts on the Day of Corpus Christi in the 14th, 15th, and 16th
Centuries, Translated from the Middle English of the Originals
into Our Mother Tongue. Albany, New York: F. H. Evory and
Co., 1915. 150 pp.

CtY. DLC. ICN. ICU. MH. NN.

The Annunciation
The Visit of Mary to Elizabeth
The Nativity
The Presentation of the Child Jesus
Christ with the Doctors in the Temple
The Agony in the Garden of Gethsemane
The Scourging of Jesus by Pilate's Orders
The Crowning of Jesus with Thorns
Christ Led Up to Calvary Bearing His Cross
The Crucifixion of Christ
The Resurrection
The Ascension
The Descent of the Holy Spirit
The Assumption of the Virgin
The Coronation of the Virgin

2265 Morley, Henry, ed. English Plays. Selected, Edited and Arranged. London, Paris and New York: Cassell, Petter, Galpin and Co. [c. 1880]. 440 pp. (Cassell's Library of English Literature, Vol. 3.)

Towneley: Second Shepherds' Play
The Four P's (John Heywood)
Hycke-Scorner

2266 Norris, Edwin, ed. The Ancient Cornish Drama. Edited and Translated. 2 vol. Oxford: At the University Press, 1859. [Text in old Celtic and modern English on facing pages.]

CtY. DLC. ICN. ICU. IU. MH. MiU. O. OC1. PU

Vol. 1 Origo Mundi
        Passio Domini Nostri
Vol. 2 Resurrexio Domini Nostri

2267 Osgood, Rev. Phillips Endecott. Old-Time Church Drama Adapted. Mystery Plays and Moralities of Earlier Days for Sundry Churchly Uses To-Day. New York and London: Harper & Brothers Publishers, 1928. [8], 291 pp.

BM. DLC. ICU. MH. NN. OC1.

Chester: The Miracle Play of Melchizedek, Abraham and Isaac

York: Annunciation
      Nativity
      Shepherds'
      Meeting of the Three Kings
      The Herod Play
      The Adoration of the Three Kings
        [Nativity Cycle, with Towneley Prologue]
Everyman

2268 Parks, Edd Winfield, and Richard Croom Beatty, eds. The English Drama. An Anthology 900-1642. New York: W. W. Norton and Co., Inc., 1935. viii, 1495 pp.

Brome: Abraham and Isaac
Towneley: The Second Shepherds' Play
Oxfordshire St. George Play
Robin Hood and the Friar
Shetland Sword Dance
Everyman
John, John (John Heywood)

2269 Parry, W. Dyfed, ed. Old Plays for Modern Players, Selected and Modernized. London: E. Arnold and Co., 1930. 150 pp.

NN. NNC.

Brome: Abraham and Isaac
Chester: Noah's Flood
Towneley: Second Shepherds' Play (Episodes)
Four PP's (John Heywood)
Play of the Weather (John Heywood)

2270 Pollard, Alfred William, ed. An English Garner. Westminster: Archibald Constable & Co., 1903. 324 pp. [Another edition, 1909.]

BM.

Towneley: Second Shepherds' Play
Everyman

2271 ----- English Miracle Plays, Moralities and Interludes. Oxford: Clarendon Press, 1927. lxxii, 250 pp. [Original edition, 1890. 8th edition, 1927.]

BM. DLC. ICN. ICU. MH. MiU. NN. OU. PU. ViU.

Mystery and Miracle Plays
 Harrowing of Hell (Harley MS.)
 Ludus Super Iconia Sancti Nicolai
 Mysterium Resurrectionis Domini Nostri Jesu Christi
 Brome: Abraham and Isaac
 Chester: Noah's Flood
     Sacrifice of Isaac
 Digby: Mary Magdalen (Abridged)
 Ludus Coventriae: Salutation and Conception
 Towneley: Secunda Pastorum
 York: Fall of Lucifer

Moralities and Interludes
 Castle of Perseverance
 Everyman
 Four Elements (John Rastell)
 King John (John Bale)
 Magnyfycence (John Skelton)
 Mary Magdalen (Lewis Wager)
 Pardoner and the Frere (John Heywood)
 Thersytes

2272 Purvis, J. S., ed. The York Cycle of Mystery Plays. A Shorter
   Version of the Ancient Cycle. With a Note on the Production
   Staged at the York Festival of 1951 by E. Martin Browne.
   London: S.P.C.K., 1951. [4], 200 pp.

  The Creation, Fall of Lucifer
  God Creates Adam and Eve
  Adam and Eve in the Garden of Eden
  Man's Disobedience and Fall
  Annunciation, and Visit of Elizabeth to Mary
  Joseph's Trouble About Mary
  Journey to Bethlehem: Birth of Jesus
  The Angels and the Shepherds
  Coming of the Three Kings, the Adoration
  Flight into Egypt
  Baptism of Jesus
  Temptation of Jesus
  Woman Taken in Adultery. Raising of Lazarus
  Entry into Jerusalem
  Conspiracy to Take Jesus
  The Agony and Betrayal
  Peter Denies Jesus: Jesus Examined by Caiaphas
  Death of Pilate's Wife: Jesus before Pilate

Second Accusation before Pilate: Remorse of Judas; Purchase
    of the Field of Blood
Second Trial Continued. Judgment of Jesus
Christ Led Up to Calvary
Crucifixio Christi
Mortificacio Christi
Harrowing of Hell
Resurrection; Fright of the Jews
Jesus Appears to Mary Magdalen after the Resurrection
Incredulity of Thomas
The Ascension
Coronation of Our Lady

2273 Purvis, J. S. The York Cycle of Mystery Plays. A Complete
      Version. London: S.P.C.K., 1962. 384 pp.

      BM. CtY. ICU. MH. NN. O. OC1. PU.

The Creation, and the Fall of Lucifer
The Creation, to the fifth day
God Creates Adam and Eve
God puts Adam and Eve in the Garden of Eden
Man's disobedience and fall from Eden
Adam and Eve driven from Eden
Sacrificium Cayme and Abell
The Building of the Ark
Noah and his wife, the Flood and its waning
Abraham's sacrifice of Isaac
The departure of the Israelites from Egypt, the ten plagues,
    and the passage of the Red Sea
The Annunciation, and visit of Elizabeth to Mary
Joseph's trouble about Mary
The Journey to Bethlehem; the birth of Jesus
The Angels and the Shepherds
The coming of the three Kings to Herod
The coming of the three Kings to Herod; the Adoration
The Flight into Egypt
The Purification of Mary; Simeon and Anna Prophesy
The Massacre of the Innocents
Christ with the Doctors in the Temple
The Baptism of Jesus
The Temptation of Jesus
The Transfiguration
The Woman taken in Adultery
The entry into Jerusalem upon the Ass

The conspiracy to take Jesus
The Last Supper
The Agony and the Betrayal
Peter denies Jesus; Jesus examined by Caiaphas
The Dream of Pilate's Wife: Jesus before Pilate
Trial before Herod
Second accusation before Pilate; remorse of Judas, and pur-
    chase of Field of Blood
The Second Trial before Pilate continued; the Judgment of
    Jesus
Christ led up to Calvary
Crucifixio Cristi
Mortificacio Cristi [and burial of Jesus]
The Harrowing of Hell
The Resurrection; fright of the Jews
Jesus appears to Mary Magdalene after the Resurrection
The Travellers to Emmaus meet Jesus
The Incredulity of Thomas
The Ascension
The Descent of the Holy Spirit
The Death of Mary
The Appearance of our Lady to Thomas
The Assumption and Coronation of the Virgin
The Judgment Day
A fragment? of a Coronation

2274 Robinson, Donald Fay, ed. The Harvard Dramatic Club Miracle
    Plays. Ten Plays Translated and Adapted by Various Hands.
    Edited with Notes on Production and Music. Preface by George
    Pierce Baker. New York: S. French; London: S. French, Ltd.,
    1928. xiii, 247 pp.

        DLC. ICU. MB. MnU. NN. OCl. OO. PP. WU.

    Coventry: The Pageant of the Shearmen and the Tailors
        (Adapted by J. M. Brown)
    The Towneley Play (Adapted by R. C. Burrell)
    The Nativity, the Chantilly Play (Translated and adapted by
        E. Sanchez, and D. F. Robinson)
    The Benediktbeuren Play (Translated and adapted by D. F.
        Robinson)
    The Wiseman, the Spanish Play (Translated and adapted by
        D. F. Robinson)
    The Provencal Play (Translated and adapted by D. F. Robin-
        son)

The Hessian Christmas Play (Translated and adapted by D. F. Robinson)

The Maastrict Play (Translated and adapted by D. F. Robinson)

The Star, the Bilsen Play (Translated and adapted by D. F. Robinson)

The Umbrian Play (Translated and adapted by D. F. Robinson)

2275 Rose, Martial, ed. The Wakefield Mystery Plays. London: Evans Brothers Limited, 1961. 464 pp.

Part 1 The Creation
The Killing of Abel
Noah
Abraham
Isaac
Jacob
Pharaoh
The Procession of the Prophets
Caesar Augustus

Part 2 The Annunciation
The Salutation of Elizabeth
The First Shepherds' Plays
The Second Shepherds' Play
The Offering of the Magi
The Flight Into Egypt
Herod the Great
The Purification of Mary
The Play of the Doctors

Part 3 John the Baptist
Lazarus
The Conspiracy
The Buffeting
The Scourging
The Hanging of Judas
The Crucifixion

Part 4 The Talents
The Deliverance of Souls
The Resurrection
The Pilgrims
Thomas of India
The Ascension of the Lord
The Judgment

2276   Rubinstein, H. F. Great English Plays. New York and London: Harper and Brothers, 1928. 1136 pp.

     DLC. IaU. MB. MnU. OC1. OCU. ViU. WU.

     Towneley: Nativity
     Everyman
     Johan, Tyb and the Curate (John Heywood)

2277   Sanders, Thomas E. The Discovery of Drama. [Glenview, Illinois]: Scott, Foresman and Company, 1968. [6], 632 pp.

     Everyman

2278   Schenkkan, Robert Frederick, and Kai Jurgensen, eds. Fourteen Plays for the Church. New Brunswick, New Jersey: Rutgers University Press, 1948. xii, 268, [7] pp.

     DLC. IaU. MB. MnU. NN. PP. WU.

     The Birth of Christ
     Herod and the Kings
     The Annunciation, the Birth and the Shepherds
     The Innocents
     The Second Shepherds' Play
     St. Nicholas and the Scholars
     The Fleury Sepulchre Play
     The Journey to Emmaus
     The King of Glory
     The Resurrection of Christ
     The Redentin Easter Play
     The Raising of Lazarus
     The Sacrifice of Isaac
     The Tragedy of Job

2279   Schweikert, Harry Christian, ed. Early Plays. New York: Harcourt, Brace & Co., 1928. vi, 845 pp.

     DLC. IaU. MnU. NN. PSC. ViU. WU.

     Brome: Abraham and Isaac
     Ludus Coventriae: The Fall of Lucifer
     Towneley: Noah
             The Second Shepherds' Play
     York: Judgment Day

Robinhood and the Friar
Everyman

2280 Shafer, Robert, ed. From Beowulf to Thomas Hardy. 2 vol. New
York: Doubleday and Page [1924]. [The 1939 edition also has
the Towneley Second Shepherds' Play.]

Everyman

2281 Sharp, Thomas, ed. Ancient Mysteries from the Digby Manuscripts.
Preserved in the Bodleian Library, Oxford. Edinburgh: Printed
for the Abbotsford Club, 1835. xlvii, [1], 200, viii pp.

CSmH. ICN. MiD.

Candlemas Day
Conversion of Saul
Mary Magdalene
A Morality [Wisdom].

2282 Smith, Lucy Toulmin, ed. York Plays. The Plays Performed by
the Crafts or Mysteries of York on the Day of Corpus Christi
in the 14th, 15th, and 16th Centuries. Now First Printed
From the Unique Manuscript in the Library of Lord Ashburnham. Edited with Introduction and Glossary. Oxford: Clarendon
Press, 1885. lxxviii, 557 pp. [Reissued, 1963.]

BM. CtY. DLC. ICN. ICU. MH. MiU. NjP. NN. O. OU.
PU. WU.

The Creation, and the Fall of Lucifer
The Creation, to the fifth day
God creates Adam and Eve
God puts Adam and Eve in the Garden of Eden
Man's disobedience and fall from Eden
Adam and Eve driven from Eden
Sacrificium Cayme and Abell
The building of the Ark
Noah and his wife, the Flood and its waning
Abraham's sacrifice of Isaac
The departure of the Israelites from Egypt, the ten plagues,
     and the passage of the Red Sea
The Annunciation, and visit of Elisabeth to Mary
Joseph's trouble about Mary
The Journey to Bethlehem; the birth of Jesus

The Angels and the Shepherds
The coming of the three Kings to Herod
The coming of the three Kings to Herod; the Adoration
The Flight into Egypt
The Massacre of the Innocents
Christ with the Doctors in the Temple
The Baptism of Jesus
The Temptation of Jesus
The Transfiguration
The Woman taken in Adultery. The raising of Lazarus
The entry into Jerusalem upon the Ass
The conspiracy to take Jesus
The Last Supper
The Agony and the Betrayal
Peter denies Jesus. Jesus examined by Caiaphas
The Dream of Pilate's Wife: Jesus before Pilate
Trial before Herod
Second accusation before Pilate: remorse of Judas, and
    purchase of Field of Blood
The second Trial before Pilate continued; the Judgment of Jesus
Christ led up to Calvary
Crucifixio Cristi
Mortificacio Cristi [and burial of Jesus]
The Harrowing of Hell
The Resurrection; fright of the Jews
Jesus appears to Mary Magdalene after the Resurrection
The Travellers to Emmaus meet Jesus
The Purification of Mary: Simeon and Anna prophesy
The Incredulity of Thomas
The Ascension
The Descent of the Holy Spirit
The Death of Mary
The Appearance of our Lady to Thomas
The Assumption and Coronation of the Virgin
The Judgment Day

2283 Stauffer, Ruth Matilda, comp. The Progress of the Drama
        through the Centuries. New York: Macmillan, 1927. 696 pp.

        Towneley: The Second Shepherds' Play
        Everyman

2284 Stevens, John. History of the Ancient Abbeys, Monasteries,
        Hospitals, Cathedrals and Collegiate Churches. Vol. 1
        (London, 1722), pp. 139-157. [Prints the first five plays of
        the Ludus Coventriae cycle.]

2285 Switz, Theodore Mac Lean, and Robert A. Johnston, eds. Great
       Christian Plays. A Collection of Classical Religious Plays
       in Acting Versions of Selected Choral Readings Suitable for
       a Worship Service. Greenwich, Connecticut: Seabury Press,
       1956. xii, 306 pp.

       MB. MH. NN. OrU. PPPD.

2286 Tatlock, J. S. P., and R. G. Martin, eds. Representative Eng-
       lish Plays from the Miracle Plays to Pinero. Edited with an
       Introduction and Notes. 2nd ed. revised and enlarged. New
       York: Appleton-Century-Crofts, Inc., 1938. x, 914 pp.
       [First edition, 1916].

       BM.

       Towneley: Noah's Flood
                      The Second Shepherd's Play
       Brome: Abraham and Isaac
       Everyman

2287 Thomas, R. George. Ten Miracle Plays. London: Edward Arnold
       (Publishers) Ltd., 1966. [8], 166 pp. Bibliography, pp. 15-16.

       Chester: Balaam and Balak
                     Christ's Passion
       Coventry: Herod & the Slaying of the Innocents
       Ludus Coventriae: Proclamation
                              Noah
                              Woman Taken in Adultery
                              Doomsday
       Towneley: Murder of Abel
                      The Conspiracy (and Capture of Christ)
       York: Annunciation
              Harrowing of Hell

2288 Tickner, Frederick James, ed. Earlier English Drama from
       Robin Hood to Everyman. Edited and Arranged for Acting.
       American Edition Revised by Thomas Whitfield Baldwin...
       New York: Thomas Nelson & Sons [cop. 1929]. xx, [1], 18-
       304 pp. (Nelson's English Series).

       BM. DLC. IaU. NjP. NN. OCl. MnU. WU.

       Brome: Abraham and Isaac

Chester: Christ Betrayed
              Harrowing of Hell
              Massacre of the Innocents
              Resurrection
              The Shepherds' Play
Cornish: Noah's Flood
Coventry: Pageant of Shearmen and Taylors
Digby: Conversion of St. Paul
Ludus Coventriae: Creation
                    Crucifixion
                    Doomesday
                    Prophets
                    Raising of Lazarus
                    Salutation
                    Trial of Christ
Towneley: The Flood
               The Second Shepherds' Play
York: The Sacrifice of Isaac

2289 The Tudor Facsimile Texts. Under the Supervision and Editor-
ship of John S. Farmer. London and Edinburgh: Issued for
Subscribers by T. C. & E. C. Jack, 1909--.

All for Money (Thomas Lupton)
Calisto and Melibaea (John Rastell)
Cambises (Thomas Preston)
Castle of Perseverance
Cobler's Prophecy (Robert Wilson)
Conflict of Conscience (Nathaniel Woodes)
Contention Between Liberality and Prodigality (2)
Damon and Pithias (Richard Edwards)
Disobedient Child (Thomas Ingelend)
Four PP (John Heywood)
Gentleness and Nobility
Gismond of Salern
God's Promises (John Bale)
Hickscorner
Horestes (John Pikeryng)
Impatient Poverty
Jack Juggler
Jacob and Esau
John John the Husband, Tyb His Wife (John Heywood)
John the Evangelist
A Knack to Know a Knave
Like Will to Like (Ulpian Fulwell)

Longer Thou Livest the More Fool (William Wager)
Lusty Juventus (Richard Wever)
Magnyfycence (John Skelton)
Mankind
Marriage of Wit and Science
Marriage of Wit and Wisdom (Francis Merbury)
Mary Magdalene (Lewis Wager)
Mind, Will and Understanding
Nature (Henry Medwall)
Nature of the Four Elements (John Rastell)
New Custom
Nice Wanton
Pardoner and the Friar (John Heywood)
Pedlar's Prophecy (Robert Wilson)
Play of Love (John Heywood)
Play of the Weather (John Heywood)
Respublica
Temptation of Our Lord (John Bale)
Thersytes
Three Ladies of London (Robert Wilson)
Three Laws (John Bale)
Three Lords and Three Ladies of London (Robert Wilson)
Tide Tarrieth No Man (George Wapull)
Tom Tyler and His Wife
Trial of Treasure
Wealth and Health
Wit and Science (John Redford)
Witty and Witless (John Heywood)
World and the Child
Youth

2290 Waterhouse, Osborn, ed. The Non-Cycle Mystery Plays. Together with the Croxton Play of the Sacrament and the Pride
of Life. Introduction and Glossary. London: Published for
the Early English Text Society, by Kegan, Paul, Trench,
Trubner and Co., Ltd., 1909. lxxiv, 112 pp.

BM. CtY. DLC. ICN. MH. MiU. NjP. NNC. OC. PP. WU.

Brome: Abraham's Sacrifice
Croxton Play of the Sacrament
Dublin: Abraham's Sacrifice
Newcastle: Noah's Ship
Norwich (A & B): Creation of Eve and the Fall
The Pride of Life

Shrewsbury Fragments: Officium Pastorum
                        Officium Resurrectionis
                        Officium Peregrinorum

2291 Woods, George Benjamin, Homer A. Watt, and George K.
      Anderson. The Literature of England. An Anthology and
      History. 2 vol. Chicago: Scott, Foresman and Company
      [1936].

         BM.

      Towneley: Second Shepherds' Play
      Everyman [In the revised edition of 1941]

2292 Wright, Thomas, ed. The Chester Plays: a Collection of Mys-
      teries Founded upon Scriptural Subjects, and Formerly Re-
      presented by the Trades of Chester at Whitsuntide. 2 vol.
      London: Printed for the Shakespeare Society, 1843-1847.

         BM. CtY. DLC. ICN. MB. MiU. MH. NN. O. OC1W.
         OU. PU. ViU.

      The Fall of Lucifer
      The Creation and Fall, and Death of Abel
      Noah's Flood
      The Histories of Lot and Abraham
      Balaam and His Ass
      The Salutation and Nativity
      The Play of the Shepherds
      The Three Kings
      The Offering and Return of the Three Kings
      The Slaughter of the Innocents
      The Purification
      The Temptation and the Woman Taken in Adultery
      Lazarus
      Christ's Entry into Jerusalem
      Christ Betrayed
      The Passion
      The Crucifixion
      The Harrowing of Hell
      The Resurrection
      The Pilgrims of Emaus
      The Ascension
      The Emission of the Holy Ghost
      Ezechiel

Antichrist
Doomsday

2293 Wright, Thomas, ed. Early Mysteries and Other Latin Poems of
        the Twelfth and Thirteenth Centuries. Edited from the Original
        Manuscripts in the British Museum, and the Libraries of Ox-
        ford, Cambridge, Paris, and Vienna. London: Nichols and
        Son, 1838. 135 pp. [This collection actually belongs with the
        liturgical and Latin plays.]

        BM. ICN. MB. MiU. MnU. NjP. NNUT. OC1. OC1W.

    1 Miracula IV. Sancti Nicolai
    2 Mysteria et Miraculum e libris Novi Testamenti Desumpta
        Herodes, sive Magorum adoratio
        Interfectio Puerorum
        Mysterium Resurrectionis D. N. Jhesu Christi
        Mysterium Apparitionis D. N. Jhesu Christi
        Mysterium duobus Discipulis in Emmaus vico
        Mysterium Conversionis beati Pauli Apostoli
        Miraculum Resurrectionis B. Lazari
    3 Mysterium Fatuarum Virginum

2294 Wright, Thomas, and James Orchard Halliwell, eds. Reliquiae
        Antiquae. Scraps from Ancient Manuscripts, Illustrating
        Chiefly Early English Literature and the English Language.
        2 vol. London: W. Pickering; Berlin: A. Asher, 1841-1843.
        [Another edition, 1845.]

        ICN. O.

        Vol. 2 A Mystery of the Burial of Christ
                A Mystery of the Resurrection

2295 Young, Karl. The Drama of the Medieval Church. 2 vol. Oxford:
        At the Clarendon Press, 1933. [Corrected reprint, 1951.
        Reprinted from the corrected reprint of the first edition, 1962,
        1967.]

        BM. CtY. DLC. ICN. ICU. MH. MiU. NN. O. OU. PU.

C General Studies

2296 Cotgrave, John. The English Treasury of Wit and Language:
       Collected Out of the Most and Best of Our English Drammatick
       Poems. Methodically Digested into Common Places for Gen-
       erall Use. London: Printed for H. Moseley, 1655. 311 pp.
           BM. CSmH. CtY. DLC. ICN. MB. PU-F.

2297 Thesaurus Dramaticus. Containing All the Celebrated Passages,
       Soliloquies, Similes, Descriptions, and Other Poetical
       Beauties in the Body of English Plays, Ancient and Modern.
       Digested under Proper Topics; with the Names of the Plays,
       and Their Authors, Referr'd to in the Margin. 2 vol. London:
       Printed by S. Aris for T. Butler, 1724.
           BM. DLC. IaU. ICN. ICU. MiU.

2298 Chetwood, William Rufus. A General History of the Stage, from
       its Origin in Greece down to the Present Time. London:
       Printed for W. Owen, 1749. 256 pp.
           ICN. MB. WU.

2299 The Beauties of the English Stage: Consisting of the Most Affecting
       and Sentimental Passages, Soliloquies, Similies, Descriptions,
       etc., in the English Plays, Ancient and Modern. Digested
       under Proper Heads in Alphabetical Order, with the Names
       and Dates of the Plays and Several Authors Referred to. 3rd
       ed. 3 vol. London: Printed for E. Withers, 1756.
           CtY. DFo. DLC. ICN. MBAt.

2300 Censor Dramaticus (pseud). A Complete History of the Drama,
       from the Earliest Periods to the Present Time. London:
       Printed and sold by T. Wilkins, 1793. 140 pp.
           BM. DFo. MB.

*2301 Jackson, John. The History of the Scottish Stage, from Its First
       Establishment to the Present Time; with a Distinct Narrative
       of Some Recent Theatrical Transactions. With Memoirs of
       His Own Life. Edinburgh: Printed for Peter Hill, 1793. xvi,
       [1], 424, 41 pp.
           BM. CtY. DLC. IaU. ICN. MiU. MnU. OCU. PPM.

2302 Roach, John. Roach's New and Complete History of the Stage,
       from Its Origin to Its Present State. London: Printed for &
       by J. Roach, 1796. 144 pp.
           BM. MB.

2303 Campbell, Alexander. An Introduction to the History of Poetry
in Scotland from the Beginning of the Thirteenth Century
Down to the Present Time. Edinburgh, 1798. viii, 374, [8],
222 pp.
NN.

2304 Dibdin, Charles. A Compendious History of the English Stage.
Containing a candid analysis of all dramatic writings, a
liberal and impartial criticism on the merits of theatrical
performers, and a sketch of the lives of such as have been
eminent in their profession. By Waldron, Dibdin, &c. London: Printed for J. S. Jordan by J. S. Barr, 1800. [4], 174 pp.
BM. MB.

2305 Irving, David. The Lives of the Scottish Poets; with Preliminary
Dissertations, on the Literary History of Scotland, and the
Early Scottish Drama. 2 vol. Edinburgh, 1804.
DLC. IaU. ICN. MB. OC1. OCU. OOxM. PP.

2306 Gilliland, Thomas. The Dramatic Mirror: Containing the History
of the Stage, from the Earliest Period to the Present Time;
Including a Biographical and Critical Account of All the
Dramatic Writers from 1660; and Also of the Most Distinguished
Performers, from the Days of Shakespeare to 1807; and a His-
tory of the Country Theatres in England, Ireland and Scotland.
2 vol. London: C. Chapple, 1808.
BM. CSmH. CtY. ICN. MB. MiU. NB. NjP. OU. PU-F.

*2307 Harleian Miscellany: A Collection of Scarce, Curious, and En-
tertaining Pamphlets and Tracts, As Well in Manuscripts As
in Print. Selected from the Library of Edward Harley, Second
Earl of Oxford. Interspersed with Historical, Political, and
Critical Annotations, by William Oldys ... and Some Additional Notes by Thomas Park. 10 vol. London: J. White, 1808-
1813. [Editions in 1744-1746; 1808-1811.]
BM. ICN.

2308 Wewitzer, Ralph. A Theatrical Pocket Book, Or Brief Dramatic
Chronology, from the Earliest Periods of History: with a
List of British Dramatists, and of Actors, &c. on the London
Stage, from the Introduction of Theatrical Entertainments
into England. London: The Editor, 1814. iv, [4], 127, [2] pp.
BM. MB.

2309 ----- A Brief Dramatic Chronology of Actors, &c. on the London

Stage, from the Introduction of Theatrical Entertainments into England, to the Present Time. New edition. Added, a miscellaneous appendix. London: Miller, 1817. 8, 115, [1] pp.
BM. MB.

2310 Hazlitt, William. A View of the English Stage; Or, a Series of Dramatic Criticisms. London: R. Stodart, 1818. 461 pp. [Other editions in 1821, and 1906.]
BM. IaU. ICN. MiU. OU.

*2311 Malone, E. Historical Account of the English Stage. In, Variorum Shakespeare. Vol. 3. (London, 1821), pp. 5-409.
BM.

*2312 Nichols, John. The Progresses and Public Processions of Queen Elizabeth. 2 vol. London: Printed by and for John Nichols and Son, 1823.
BM. DLC. ICN. MB. MH. NN. OC1. PU. WU.

2313 Dodsley, Robert. The Rise and Progress of the English Theatre, from Its Earliest Beginning, to the Death of King Charles the First. [London: Prowett, 1825.] pp. 109-138. [Extracted from the Preface to Dodsley's Select Collection of Old Plays.]
BM. MB.

2314 [Laneham's Letter]. Kenilworth Festivities: Comprising Lane-ham's Description of the Pageantry, and Gascoigne's Masques, Represented before Queen Elizabeth at Kenilworth Castle anno 1575; with Introductory Prefaces, Glossarial and Explanatory Notes. Warwick and Leamington: J. Merridew, 1825. 114 pp.
BM. DLC. MB. MnU. OO.

2315 Dibdin, Charles, Jr. History and Illustrations of the London Theatres: Comprising an Account of the Origin and Progress of the Drama in England; with Historical and Descriptive Ac-counts of the Theatres Royal, Covent Garden, Drury Lane, Haymarket, English Opera House, and Royal Amphitheatre. London: The Proprietors of the "Illustrations of London Buildings," 1826. [2], 94 pp.
BM. MB.

2316 Literary and Graphical Illustrations of Shakespeare, and the British Drama: Comprising an Historical View of the Origin and Improvement of the English Stage, and a Series of Critical and Descriptive Notices of Celebrated Tragedies,

Comedies, Operas, and Farces. London: Hurst, Chance & Co., 1831. xvi, 204 pp.
BM. MB.

2317 Aspin, Jehoshaphat. Ancient Customs, Sports, and Pastimes of the English; Explained from Authentic Sources, & in a Familiar Manner. London: Harris, 1832. viii, 256 pp.
BM. MB.

2318 Magnin, Charles. "Les Origines du théâtre en Europe." Revue des Deux Mondes, IV (1834), 578-597.

*2319 Herbert, William. The History of the Twelve Great Livery Companies of London; Principally Compiled from Their Grants and Records. With an Historical Essay, and Account of Each Company . . . Including Notices and Illustrations of Metropolitan Trade and Commerce, as Originally Concentrated in Those Societies . . . With Attested Copies and Translations of the Companies' Charters. 2 vol. London: Published by the author, 1837.
DFo. DLC. ICN. MH. MiU. NjP. OU. PBm. ViU.

2320 Cardwell, Edward. Documentary Annals of the Reformed Church of England. 2 vol. Oxford: University Press, 1839. Index.
BM.

2321 Tomlins, Frederick Guest. A Brief View of the English Drama, from the Earliest Period to the Present Time: with Suggestions for Elevating the Present Condition of the Art, and Its Professors. London: C. Mitchell, 1840. 152 pp.
BM. CSmH. DLC. ICN. MiU. OCl.

2322 Fairholt, Frederick. Lord Mayor's Pageants. London: T. R. Richards, for the Percy Society, 1843-1844. 2 Parts in 1.
MiU. OCl. OClW. OCU. OU. PBm. PU.

*2323 Northbrook, John. A Treatise against Dicing, Dancing, Plays, and Interludes. With Other Idle Pastimes. From the Earliest Edition, about A.D. 1577. With an Introduction and Notes. Reprinted from the Shakespeare Society, 1843. 188 pp.
BM. DLC. MB. MiU. NN. OCU. OU. PU-F.
TxU. ViU.

2324 Halliwell, James Orchard, ed. Letters of the Kings of England, Now First Collected from the Originals in Royal Archives

and from Other Authentic Sources. 2 vol. London: Colburn,
1846.
    BM.

2325 Mone, Franz Joseph. Schauspiele des Mittelalters. Aus Handschriften herausgegeben und erklärt. 2 vol. Karlsruhe: C.
Macklot. 1846.
    CtY. DFo. DLC. ICN. MnU. NjP. OCU. OU. PU. WU.

2326 Jupp, Edward Basil. An Historical Account of the Worshipful
Company of Carpenters of the City of London, Compiled Chiefly From Records In Their Possession. London: W. Pickering,
1848. xix, 338 pp. Index.
    BM.

2327 Stuart, John. Extracts from the Council Register of the Burgh
of the Aberdeen. Vol. 1. 1398-1570. Aberdeen: Printed for
the Spalding Club, 1848. lxxiii, 478 pp. Index.
    BM.

2328 [Anon.]. "Dramatic Poetry in the Age of Elizabeth." British
Quarterly Review, XIV (1851), 39-66.

2329 Harrod, H. "A Few Particulars Concerning Early Pageants."
Norfolk Archaeology, III (1852), 3-18.

2330 Nichols, John Gough, ed. Chronicle of the Gray Friars of London.
London: For the Camden Society, 1852. xxxv, 108 pp.
    BM.

2331 [Anon.]. "The Drama in the Middle Ages." National Magázine,
II (1853), 221-224; 367-369.

2332 Wright, Thomas. "On the History of the Drama in the Middle
Ages." Bentley's Miscellany, XXXVIII (1855), 298-309.

2333 ----- On the History of the Drama in the Middle Ages. A Sketch.
[London? 185-?]. 12 pp. [Reprinted in his, Essays on Arche-
ological Subjects.]
    BM. MB.

2334 Kelly, William. Notices Illustrative of the Drama and Other Popular Amusements, Chiefly in the Sixteenth and Seventeenth Centuries. London: J. R. Smith, 1865. viii, 310 pp.
    BM. CtY. ICN. MB. MH. MiU. NjP. OC1. OU. PHC.

2335 Maetzner, E. A. F. Altenglische Sprachproben. 2 vol. Berlin:
Weidmann, 1867-1900. [A - M only.]
BM.

2336 Riley, Henry Thomas, ed. Gesta Abbatum Monasterii Sancti
Albani a Thoma Walsingham ... compilata. 3 vol. London:
Longmans, Green, Reader, and Dyer, 1867-1869. Index
in Vol. 3.
BM.

2337 Inglis, Ralston. The Dramatic Writers of Scotland. Glasgow: G.
D. Mackellar, 1868. 155, [1] pp.
CtY. DLC. MB. MH. MiU. MnU.

2338 [Hazlitt, William Carew]. The English Drama and Stage under
the Tudor and Stuart Princes, 1543-1664, Illustrated by a
Series of Documents, Treatises, and Poems. With a Preface
and Index. London: Printed for the Roxburghe Library [by
Whittingham and Wilkins], 1869. xvi, 289 pp.
BM. CSmH. DFo. MB. MiU. NjP. NN. OU. PU. ViU.

*2339 Smith, Toulmin, ed. English Gilds. The Original Ordinances of
More Than One Hundred Early English Gilds: Together with
ye olde Vsages of ye Cite of Wynchester; The Ordinances of
Worcester; The Office of the Mayor of Bristol; and The Costom-
ary of the Manor of Tettenhall-Regis. From Original MSS.
of the Fourteenth and Fifteenth Centuries. Edited, with Notes.
With an Introduction and Glossary, &c. by His Daughter,
Lucy Toulmin Smith. And a Preliminary Essay in Five Parts,
On the History and Development of Gilds, by Lujo Brentano.
London: Published for the Early English Text Society by N.
Trübner & Co., 1870. cxcix, 483 pp.
BM. MdBP. MiU. OClW. ViU. WU.

2340 Warton, Thomas. History of English Poetry from the Twelfth to
the Close of the Sixteenth Century. Edited by W. C. Hazlitt.
4 vol. London: Reeves and Turner, 1871.
BM. IaU. ICN. MiU. MnU. NjP. OCl. OCU. ViU.

2341 Meyer, Heinrich. The Infancy of the English Drama. Hagen:
Butz, 1873. 19 pp.
NjP. NNC.

2342 Ebert, George Karl Wilhelm Adolf. Allgemeine Geschichte der
Literatur des Mittelalters im Abenlande. 3 vol. Leipzig:

F. C. W. Vogel, 1874-1878.
BM.

2343 Morris, Richard, ed. Cursor Mundi. 3 vol. London: Kegan Paul,
      Trench, Trübner & Co., 1874-1877. (Early English Text
      Society. Series I).
      BM.

2344 Lacroix, Paul. The Arts in the Middle Ages, and at the Period of
      the Renaissance. London: Chapman and Hall, 1875. xix, 520
      pp.
      BM.

2345 Robertson, James Craigie. Materials for the History of Thomas
      Becket. 7 vol. London: Longman & Co., 1875-1885.
      BM.

2346 Boedeker, Karl, ed. Altenglische Dichtungen des ms. Harl.
      2253. Mit Grammatik und Glossar. Berlin: Weidmann, 1878.
      463 pp.
           CtY. DLC. ICN. ICU. MH. MiU. NcU. OU. PU. WaU.

2347 Collier, John Payne. The History of English Dramatic Poetry to
      the Time of Shakespeare: and Annals of the Stage to the Resto-
      ration. New ed. 3 vol. London: G. Bell and Sons, 1879.
      BM. ICN. MB. MH. MiU. OC1. OU. PBm. PU-F.

2348 Herrtage, Sidney John Hervon, ed. The Early English Versions
      of the Gesta Romanorum. London: N. Trübner, 1879. xxxi,
      563 pp. (Early English Text Society, extra series, 33).
      BM.

*2349 Jusserand, Jean -J. Le Théâtre en Angleterre depuis la conquête
      jusqu' aux prédécesseurs immediats de Shakespeare. 2d ed.
      Paris: E. Leroux, 1881. 350 pp.
           BM. DFo. DLC. ICN. MB. OC1W. OCU.

2350 Lennox, Lord William Pit. Plays, Players and Playhouses at
      Home and Abroad, with Anecdotes of the Drama and the Stage.
      2 vol. London: Hurst & Blackett, 1881.
      BM. NN.

2351 Mézieres, Alfred Jean Francois. Prédecesseurs et contemporains
      de Shakespeare. 3d ed. Paris: Hachette, 1881. xiv, 367 pp.
           BM. CtY. ICN. MB. MH. MiU. NN. OC1.

2352 Prölss, Karl Robert. Geschichte des neuren Dramas. 3 vol. Leipzig:
      B. Schlicke, 1881-1883.
          ICN. MdPB. MnU. PBm. PHC.

2353 Ten Brink, Bernhard. Geschichte der englischen Litteratur.
      Revised by A. Brandl, and Translated by H. M. Kennedy. 2
      vol. in 3. New York: Henry Holt and Co., 1883-1896.
          BM. ICN. MB. OCU. OO. PBm. PPD. PV. ViU.

2354 Symonds, John A. Shakespeare's Predecessors in the English
      Drama. London: Smith, Elder and Co., 1884. xix, 668 pp.
          BM. CSmH. DFo. ICN. MdBP. MH. MiU. NjP. OU.
          ViU.

2355 Hodgetts, J. Frederick. The English in the Middle Ages; from the
      Norman Usurpation to the Days of the Stuarts. Their Mode of
      Life, Dress, Arms, Occupations, and Amusements. London:
      Whiting and Co., 1885. xv, 210 pp.
          BM. DLC. ICN. MnU. NcD. OC1. OU. PV.

2356 Ireson, Frank, Brother. A Sketch of the Pre-Shakespearian
      Drama. London: Imprynted by Brother C. H. Wyman, 1885.
      33 pp.
          BM. DLC. ICN. MB. MH. MnU. NN. PU.

2357 Herford, Charles. Studies in the Literary Relations of England and
      Germany in the Sixteenth Century. Cambridge: University Press,
      1886. 426 pp.
          CtY. DFo. IaU. MH. MiU. NjP. OU. PU. ViU.

2358 Hudson, Henry Norman. Shakespeare; His Life, Art, and
      Character. With an Historical Sketch of the Origin and
      Growth of the Drama in England. 2 vol. Boston: Ginn Brothers,
      1886.
          BM. DFo. ICN.

2359 Seligman, Edwin Robert Anderson. Two Chapters on the Mediaeval
      Guilds of England. Baltimore: American Economic Association.
      1887. 113 pp. "List of Authorities," pp. [107]-113. (American
      Economic Association Monographs, II, No. 5.)
          BM. DLC. ICN. MH. OO. OU. PU. WU.

2360 Clode, Charles Matthew. Early History of the Guild of Merchant
      Taylors of the Fraternity of St. John the Baptist. 2 vol. Lon-
      don: Harrison and Sons, 1888. [Also 1889].

ICN. MB. MH. MnU. NjP.

2361 Dibdin, James C. The Annals of the Edinburgh Stage. With an
     account of the rise and progress of dramatic writing in Scot-
     land. Edinburgh: Cameron, 1888. viii, 511 pp.
        BM. MB.

2362 Jusserand, J. J. English Wayfaring Life in the Middle Ages
     (Fourteenth Century). Translated by Lucy Toulmin Smith.
     London: T. F. Unwin, 1889 [1888]. 451 pp.
        BM.

2363 Metcalfe, William M. Legends of the Saints in the Scottish
     Dialect of the XIV Century. 3 vol. Edinburgh: Scottish
     Text Society, 1888-1896.
        BM.

2364 Böhck, A. Über die Anfänge des englischen Dramas. Breslau,
     1890.
        CtY. MH.

*2365 Cloetta, Wilhelm. Beiträge zur Litteraturgeschichte des Mittelal-
      ters und der Renaissance. 2 vol. Halle: M. Niemeyer, 1890.
      [See vol. 1: Komödie und Tragödie im Mittelalter.]
        BM. CtY. MdBP. MH. MiU. NjP. OC1. PU. ViU.

2366 Fleay, Frederick Gard. A Chronicle History of the London
     Stage, 1559-1642. London: Reeves and Turner, 1890. x, 424
     pp.
        BM. DFo. ICN. MB. MH. MiU. MnU. NjP. OC1. PU.

2367 Golden, William Echard. A Brief History of the English Drama
     from the Earliest to the Latest Times. New York: Welch,
     Fracker Co., 1890. 227 pp.
        BM. MB. NN.

*2368 Gross, Charles. The Gild Merchant: a Contribution to British
      Municipal History. 2 vol. Oxford: Clarendon Press, 1890.
        DLC. ICN. MH. MiU. NjP. NN. OCU. OO. PU.
        ViU. WU.

2369 Fleay, Frederick Gard. A Biographical Chronicle of the English
     Drama, 1559-1642. 2 vol. London: Reeves and Turner,
     1891.
        BM. DFo. IaU. ICN. MnU.

2370 Graf, Herman. Der Miles Gloriosus im englischen Drama bis
      zur Zeit des Bürgerkrieges. Schwerin, i.m.: E. Herberger's
      Buchdruckerei, [1891], 58 pp. Bibliographical footnotes.
      BM. CSmH. CtY. ICU. IU. MB. PU-F.

2371 Hibbert, Francis Aidan. The Influence and Development of Eng-
      lish Gilds; as Illustrated by the History of the Craft Gilds of
      Shrewsbury. Cambridge: University Press, 1891. xii, 168 pp.
      (Cambridge Historical Essays, No. 5.)
      BM. ICN. ICU.

*2372 Lambert, Joseph Malet. Two Thousand Years of Gild Life; Or,
      an Outline of the History and Development of the Gild System
      from Early Times, with Special Reference to Its Application
      to Trade and Industry; Together with a Full Account of the
      Gilds and Trading Companies of Kingston-upon-Hull: A. Brown
      and Sons, 1891. xi, 414 pp. Bibliography, pp. [399]-402.
      BM. ICN. ICU.

2373 Bates, Katherine L., and Lydia B. Godfrey. Outline Studies in
      the Early Drama. [Wellesley: Privately Printed, c. 1892].
      30 pp.
      ICU.

2374 Hazlitt, William Carew. A Manual for the Collector and Amateur
      of Old English Plays. London: Pickering and Chatto, 1892.
      viii, 284 pp.
      BM. CSmH. ICN. MH. MiU. NjP. OCl. OU. PU.

2375 Christie, James, Comp. Some Account of Parish Clerks. Lon-
      don: Privately Printed for The Worshipful Company of Parish
      Clerks by James Vincent, 1893. xxii, 219 pp. Index.
      BM.

2376 Cunliffe, John William. Influence of Seneca on Elizabethan
      Tragedy: An Essay. London and New York: Macmillan, 1893.
      155 pp.
      CtY. DLC. ICN. NjP. NN. NNC. OO. PU.

*2377 Creizenach, Wilhelm. Geschichte des neueren Dramas. 5 vol.
      Halle: M. Niemeyer, 1893-1916.
      CtY. DFo. ICN. ICU. IU. MiU. MnU. PU. ViU. WaU.

2378 Doren, Alfred Jacob. Untersuchungen zur Geschichte der Kauf-
      mannsgilden im Mittelalter. Leipzig: Duncker & Humblot,

1893. xii, 220 pp.
  DLC. IaU. MiU. MnU. OCl. PU. WU.

2379 Napier, Arthur Sampson. History of the Holy Rood-Tree. London: Kegan Paul, Trench, Trübner & Co., Ltd., 1894. lix, 86 pp. (Early English Text Society, Original Series, 103).
  BM.

2380 Collins, John Churton. Essays and Studies. London and New York: Macmillan and Co., 1895. ix, 369 pp.
  BM. DFo. ICN.

*2381 Courthope, W. J. History of English Poetry. 6 vol. New York and London: MacMillan and Co., 1895-1910. [See Vols. II-IV.]
  BM. ICN. MH. OClCC. OO. PBa. PP. PU. TxU. ViU.

*2382 Jusserand, Jean-J. A Literary History of the English People. 3 vol. New York: G. Putnam and Sons, 1895-1909.
  BM. ICN. OCl. OCU. OO.

2383 Winslow, Mrs. Catherine Mary (Reignolds). Readings from the Old English Dramatists. With notes. 2 vol. Boston: Lee and Shepard, 1895.
  BM. IaU. ICU. MB. NjP. OCl. ViU.

2384 Bates, Katherine L., and Lydia B. Godfrey. English Drama: A Working Basis. Boston: S. G. Robinson, 1896. 151 pp.
  BM. ICN. MB. NjP. NN. OCl. PPD. PSC. PU.

2385 Boas, Frederick Samuel. Shakespeare and His Predecessors. New York: C. Scribner's Sons, 1896. viii, 555 pp. (The University Series.)
  BM. DFo. ICN. MH. MiU. OCl. OCU. ViU. WaU.

2386 Ditchfield, Peter Hampson. Old English Customs Extant at the Present Time. London: Redway, 1896. 343 pp.
  IaU. PBm. PHC. PPL. PSt.

2387 Gee, Henry and Hardy, William John, compilers. Documents Illustrative of English Church History, Compiled from Original Sources. London: Macmillan, 1896. xii, 670 pp.
  BM.

2388 Sanborn, Katherine Abbott. My Favorite Lectures of Long Ago, For Friends Who Remember. Boston: [The Case; Lockwood and Brainard Co., Hartford, Conn., printers], 1898. 338 pp.

[See, "The Old Miracle Plays."]
ICU. MnU.

2389 Schelling, Felix E. "Studies in the Evolution of Dramatic Species
      from the Beginnings of the English Drama to the Year 1660."
      University of Pennsylvania Bulletin (1898).

2390 Hope, Robert Charles. Medieval Music: an Historical Sketch.
      2nd ed. London: Elliot Stock, 1899. 169 pp. Bibliography.
      Index.
      BM.

*2391 Ward, Sir Adolphus William. A History of English Dramatic
       Literature to the Death of Queen Anne. New, rev. ed. 3 vol.
       London: Macmillan and Co., Ltd.; New York, The Macmillan
       Co., 1899.
       BM. ICN. MH. MnU. NjP. OCU. OU. ViU. WaU.

2392 Cushman, Lysander William. The Devil and the Vice in the Eng-
      lish Dramatic Literature before Shakespeare. Halle a. S.:
      Max Niemeyer, 1900. xiv, 148 pp. Bibliography, pp. [146]-
      148. (Studien zur englischen Philologie, No. 6).
      BM. DLC. ICN. MB. MiU. NN. OC1. OO. PBm. PU.

2393 Eberstadt, Rudolph. Der Ursprung des Zunftwesens und die
      älteren Handerverbände des Mittelalters. Leipzig: Duncker
      & Humblot, 1900. 201 pp. Bibliography, pp. [194]-195.
      BM. CtY. DLC. ICN. MH. MiU. MnU. NN.

2394 Gairdner, James, ed. The Paston Letters, 1422-1509 A.D.; A
      Reprint of the Edition of 1872-5 ... to Which Are Now Added
      Others. 4 vol. Westminster: Constable, 1900-1901. Index.
      BM.

2395 Nettleton, George H. "The Evolution of the Shakespearean Clown."
      Ph.D. Yale University, 1900.

2396 Smith, G. Gregory. The Transition Period. Edinburgh: W.
      Blackwood and Sons, 1900. 422 pp.
      BM. IaU. ICN. MnU. NN. OC1. ViU.

2397 Cushman, Lysander W. Die Figuren des Teufels und des Vice
      in dem ernsten englischen Drama bis auf Shakespeare. In-
      augural Dissertation. Goettingen, 1901.

2398 Jusserand, J. J. "A Note on Pageants and 'Scaffolds Hye.'"

An English Miscellany Presented to Dr. Furnivall. (Oxford, 1901), pp. 183-195.

2399 Schücking, Levin Ludwig. Studien über die stofflichen Beziehungen der englischen Komödie zur italienischen bis Lilly. Halle a.S.: M. Niemeyer, 1901. [6], 109 pp. (Studien zur englischen Philologie, hrsg. von L. Morsbach...hft. IX).
ICN.

2400 Traill, Henry D., and J. S. Mann, eds. Social England. A Record of the Progress of the People in Religion, Laws, Learning, Arts, Industry, Commerce, Science, Literature, and Manners from the Earliest Times to the Present Day. New Illustrated Edition. 6 vol. London: Cassell and Co., 1901-1904. [Original edition, 1894-1898.]
ICN.

2401 Wilson, Louise Suzanne. "The Annals of the Pageants under the Early Tudors." M.A. Stanford University, 1901.

2402 Brotanek, Rudolf. Die englischen Maskenspiele. Wien und Leipzig: Wilhelm Braumüller, 1902. xiv, 371 pp.
BM. ICN. MH. NjP. NN. OCU. PHC. PSC. PU. ViU.

*2403 Greg, Walter Wilson. List of Masques and Pageants. London: Printed for the Bibliographical Society by Blades, East, and Blades, 1902. 35 pp.
CtY. DLC. MH. MiU. NN. OU. PU. ViU. WU.

2404 Hastings, Charles. The Theatre; Its Development in France and England, and a History of Its Greek and Latin Origins. Authorized translation by Frances A. Welby. London: Duckworth and Co.; Philadelphia: J. B. Lippincott and Co., 1902. xvi, 368 pp. Bibliography, pp. 342-346. [The French edition was published in 1900.]
BM. IaU. ICN. MB (1901). OCl (1901). PU (1901).

2405 Schelling, Felix E. The English Chronicle Play; A Study in the Popular Historical Literature Environing Shakespeare. New York: Macmillan Co.; London: Macmillan and Co., Ltd., 1902. xi, 310 pp. List of plays on historical subjects, pp. 278-286.
BM. ICN. MB. NjP. NN. OCl. ViU. WaU.

2406 Bates, Alfred, ed. Drama, Its History, Literature, and Influence on Civilization. 20 vol. London: Athenian Society, 1903.

*2407 Chambers, E. K. "Minstrel Guilds." The Mediaeval Stage.
        Vol. II. (London, 1903), pp. 258-262.

2408 "Hell As Staged 300 Years Ago; an Introductory Mediaeval
        Comparison with the Modern Inferno at Drury Lane." Sphere,
        XIII (June 27, 1903), 280.

2409 Mantzius, Karl. A History of Theatrical Art in Ancient and
        Modern Times. With an Introduction by William Archer.
        Authorized translation by Louise von Cossel. 6 vol. London:
        Duckworth and Co., 1903-1921. Bibliographies.
        CtY. MiU. OC1. OCX. PPT. PU. ViU.

2410 Matthews, Brander. "Medieval Drama." Modern Philology, I
        (June, 1903), 71-94.

2411 Peele, David Derrick. "Drama at the English Court in the 16th
        Century." M.A. University of Chicago, 1903.

2412 Strutt, Joseph. The Sports and Pastimes of the People of England:
        Including the Rural and Domestic Recreations, May Games,
        Mummeries, Shows, Processions, Pageants, and Pompous
        Spectacles from the Earliest Period to the Present Time.
        Edited by W. Hone. London: T. Tegg, 1831. 420 pp. New ed.,
        London: Methuen and Co., [1903]. 322 pp.

2413 Symmes, Harold S. Les Débuts de la critique dramatique en
        Angleterre jusqu' à la mort de Shakespeare. Paris: E. Leroux,
        1903. xiv, 276 pp. Bibliography, pp. [235]-267.
        BM. DLC. IaU. ICN. MB. MiU. NjP. NN. OCU.

2414 Adams, John Chester. "The Predecessors of the Seventeenth
        Century Court Masque in England." Ph.D. Yale University,
        1904.

2415 Bateson, Mary. "The Mediaeval Stage." Scottish Historical Re-
        view, I (July, 1904), 399-406.

2416 Driesen, Otto. Der Ursprung des Harlekin. Ein kulturgeschicht-
        liches Problem. Berlin: Alexander Duncker-Verlag, 1904. xii,
        286 pp. Index. (Forschungen zur neueren Literaturgeschichte,
        Heft. 25).
        BM.

2417 Tunison, J. S. Dramatic Traditions of the Middle Ages. Chicago:

University of Chicago Press, 1904. 350 pp.
BM. IaU. ICN. MB. MiU. MnU. NjP. OC1. OU. ViU.

*2418   Brand, John, and Henry Ellis. Observations on the Popular Anti-
         quities of Great Britain. 3 vol. London: Printed for F. C. and
         J. Rivington, 1902. [Rearranged as Faiths and Folklore, by
         William C. Hazlitt, 1905. 2 vol.]
         BM. DLC. ICN. ICU. MB. MdBP. MH. NN. OCU. PU.

2419   Brand's Popular Antiquities of Great Britain. Edited by William
         Carew Hazlitt. 2 vol. London: Reeves and Turner, 1905.

2420   Mönkemeyer, Paul. Prolegomena zu einer Darstellung der englischen
         Volksbühne zur Elisabeth--und Stuart zeit nach den alten Büchnen-
         anweisungen. Hannover: Eberlein, 1905. viii, 94 pp.
         BM. ICN.

2421   Moorman, F. W. "The Pre-Shakespearian Ghost." Modern Lan-
         guage Review, I (1905-1906), 85-95.

2422   [Anon.]. "Pageants of the Middle Ages." Spectator, CII (1905),
         887-888.

2423   Riblet, Mary Varian. "The Vice on the English Stage." M.A.
         Columbia University, 1905.

2424   Taylor, George Coffin. "Relation of Lyric and Drama in Mediaeval
         England." Ph. D. University of Chicago, 1905.

2425   Tierney, R. H. "Religious Element in the Mediaeval Guilds."
         American Catholic Quarterly Review, XXX (1905), 647-657.

2426   Ankenbrand, Hans. Die Figur des Geistes im Drama der eng-
         lischen Renaissance. Leipzig: A. Deichert, 1906. xi, 100 pp.
         Bibliography, pp. vii-ix.
         BM.

2427   Calthorp, Dion Clayton. English Costume from William I to
         George IV 1066-1830. 4 vol. London: A. and C. Black, 1906.
         [Frequently reprinted in one volume.]
         NN.

2428   Chambers, E. K. Notes on the History of the Revels Office
         under the Tudors. London: A. H. Bullen, 1906. 80 pp.
         BM. CtY. ICN. MB. MiU. NjP. NN. OU. PU.

*2429 Crowley, Timothy J. Character Treatment in the Medieval Drama.
        Notre Dame, Indiana, 1907. 181 pp. Bibliography, pp. 171-
        181.
            DLC. MH.

2430 Gayley, Charles Mills. Plays of Our Forefathers and Some of
        the Traditions upon Which They Were Founded. New York:
        Duffield and Co., 1907. 349 pp. [Also a London 1908 edition.]
            BM. ICN. MB. NjP. NN. OC1. OU. PU. WU.

*2431 Gofflot, L. V. Le Théâtre au college du moyen âge à nos jours,
        avec bibliographie et appendices. Paris: Champion, 1907.
        336 pp.

2432 Green, Alice S. Town Life in the Fifteenth Century. 2 vol. New
        York: Macmillan Co.; London: Macmillan & Co., Ltd., 1907.
            BM (1894).

2433 Manly, John Matthews. The Influence of the Tragedies of Seneca
        upon Early English Drama. Reprinted from the Tragedies of
        Seneca, by Professor F. J. Miller. [Chicago, Illinois, 1907].
        10 pp.
            BM. CtY. OC1W.

2434 Ristine, Frank Humphrey. "The Beginnings of Tragi-Comedy in
        English Dramatic Literature." M.A. Columbia University,
        1907.

*2435 Taylor, George C. "The Relation of the English Corpus Christi
        Play to the Middle English Lyric." Modern Philology, V
        (July, 1907), 1-38.

*2436 Chambers, E. K., and W. W. Greg, eds. "Dramatic Records
        from the Lansdowne Manuscripts." Malone Society. Col-
        lections. I. Part II (1908), pp. 143-215.

2437 Schelling, Felix E. Elizabethan Drama, 1558-1642. With a Re-
        sume of the Earlier Drama. 2 vol. Boston and New York:
        Houghton, Mifflin and Co., 1908. Bibliographical essay. Vol.
        2, pp. 443-537.
            BM. DFo. ICN. MB. MnU. NjP. NN. OC1. OCU. PBm.

2438 Forestier, A. "Origins of the English Stage." Illustrated London
        News, CXXXV (1909), 934; CXXXVI (1909), 57, 167, 225, 344,
        423.

2439 Lester, John A. "Some Franco-Scottish Influences on the Early
        English Drama." Haverford Essays. Studies in Modern Liter-
        ature Prepared by Some Former Pupils of Professor Francis
        B. Gummere. (Haverford, 1909), pp. 131-152.

2440 Lott, Bernhard [George]. Der Monolog im englischen Drama
        vor Shakespeare. Greifswald: J. Abel, 1909. 114, [2] pp.
        Bibliography, pp. 7-8.
              NN.

2441 Mangan, R. L. "Nativity in Early Pageants." Catholic World, XC
        (1909), 294-304.

2442 Allen, Philip Schuyler. "The Mediaeval Mimus. I." Modern
        Philology, VII (January, 1910), 329-344.

2443 ----- "The Mediaeval Mimus. II." Modern Philology,
        VIII (July, 1910), 1-44.

*2444 Bond, Francis. Wood Carvings in English Churches. I. Miseri-
        cords. London: Oxford University Press, 1910. xix, 237 pp.
        Index.
              BM.

2445 "Early Beginnings of the English Stage." Theatre, XI (April,
        1910), 125.

2446 Lee, Sir Sidney. The French Renaissance in England. An Ac-
        count of the Literary Relations of England and France in the
        Sixteenth Century. Oxford: Clarendon Press, 1910. xxiv, 494
        pp.
              BM. CtY. DLC. ICN. MiU. NN. OCl. OCU. OU.

*2447 Murray, John Tucker. English Dramatic Companies, 1558-1642.
        2 vol. London: Constable and Co., 1910.
              BM. IaU. ICN. MH. MnU. OCl. OCU.

2448 Schipper, J. M. History of English Versification. Oxford:
        Clarendon Press, 1910. xix, 390 pp. [Translation from the
        German.]
              BM.

*2449 Ward, Sir Adolphus William, and A. R. Waller, eds. Cambridge
        History of English Literature. 15 vol. Cambridge: University
        Press, 1910.

BM. DFo. DLC. ICN. ICU. IU. MB. MH.

*2450 Brooke, Charles Frederick Tucker. Tudor Drama. A History of
       English National Drama to the Retirement of Shakespeare.
       Boston: Houghton, 1911. xii, 461 pp.
            BM. DFo. ICN. MH. MiU. MnU. NjP. NN. OC1. OU.
            PPL. PU.

2451 Eckhardt, Eduard. Die Dialeckt-und äuslandertypen des älteren
       englische Dramas. 2 vol. Louvain: A. Uystpruyst, 1910-1911.
            BM. DFo. DLC. ICN. MiU. NjP. OC1. OCU. OU.
            PU. ViU.

2452 Flenley, Ralph, ed. Six Town Chronicles of England. Edited from
       the Manuscripts in the Bodleian Library, the Library of St.
       John's College, Oxford, the Library of Trinity College, Dublin,
       and the Library of the Marquis of Bath at Longleat; Now Printed
       for the First Time with an Introduction and Notes. Oxford:
       Clarendon Press, 1911. 208 pp.
            BM. DLC. ICN. MB. MnU. NjP. NN. PHC. PU.

2453 Fox, Harriet Ruth. "School Drama in England before 1580." M.A.
       Columbia University, 1911.

2454 Oelrich, Wilhelm. Die Personennamen in mittelalterlichen Drama
       Englands. Inaugural Dissertation. Kiel, 1911. 108 pp.

*2455 Spencer, Matthew Lyle. Corpus Christi Pageants in England. New
       York: Baker and Taylor Co., 1911. 276 pp. Bibliography, pp.
       263-269.
            DLC. ICN. MB. MnU. NjP. OC1W. OCU. OO. WU.

2456 Bates, Esther Willard. Pageants and Pageantry. New York: Ginn,
       1912. 294 pp.
            DLC. MiU. NN. OC1. OO. PU. ViU. WU.

2457 Henderson, T. F. "Scottish Popular Poetry before Burns."
       Cambridge History of English Literature, IX. (Cambridge,
       1912), pp. 359-380.

2458 Howells, W. D. "Pair of Pageants." North American Review,
       CXCV (1912), 607-614.

2459 Jack, Alexander Fingland. An Introduction to the History of Life
       Insurance. London and New York: S. King & Son, 1912. xii,

263 pp. Bibliography, pp. 246-256.
BM. DLC. MiU. MnU. OC1. PBm. PU. ViU. WU.

2460 McCaully, Martha Gause. "Function and Content of the Prologue,
Chorus and Other Non-Organic Elements in English Drama,
from the Beginnings to 1642." Ph.D. University of Pennsylvania,
1912.

2461 Oliver, D. E. The English Stage, Its Origin and Modern Develop-
ments; a Critical and Historical Study. London: John Ouseley,
Ltd., 1912. xv, 151 pp. Bibliography, pp. 151-[152].
BM. DLC. IaU. ICN. MB. MiU. PU. TxU. WU.

2462 Scott, J. F. "Apprenticeship Under the English Gild System."
Elementary School Teacher, XIII (1912), 180-188.

2463 Scotten, Hallie Gretchen. "Rogue and Vagabond Types in the
English Drama of the 16th Century." M.A. University of
Chicago, 1912.

2464 Wallace, Charles Williams. The Evolution of the English Drama
up to Shakespeare with a History of the First Blackfriars
Theatre; A Survey Based upon Original Records Now for the
First Time Collected and Published. Berlin: G. Reimer, 1912.
xxi, 246 pp.
BM. DFo. DLC. ICN. IU. MB. MiU. NjP. OC1. OO.

2465 Cox, John Charles. Churchwardens' Accounts from the Fourteenth
Century to the Close of the Seventeenth Century. London:
Methuen & Co., 1913. xvii, 365 pp. (The Antiquary Books).
BM.

2466 Hughes, Anselm, ed. Early English Harmony from the 11th to
the 15th Century. Vol. 1. Edited by H. E. Wooldridge. London: Quaritch, 1897. Vol. 2. Transcriptions and Notes. Edited
by Rev. H. V. Hughes. London: Plainsong and Medieval Music
Society, 1913.
BM.

2467 Jones, Bertrand Luscombe. "Introduction to the History of the
After-Piece and the Curtain-Raiser of the English Stage from
their Beginnings to 1740." M.A. University of Chicago, 1913.

2468 Semar, John. "The Pre-Shakespearean Stage. Some Facts About
It, with Comments and Notes." Mask, VI (1913), 135-158.

*2469 Stuart, Donald Clive. "The Stage Setting of Hell and the Icono-
        graphy of the Middle Ages." Romanic Review, IV (1913),
        330-342.

2470 Wieland, Karl Günther. Lustspielemente im mittelenglischen
        Drama (bis 1500). Buhl (Baden): Buchdruckerei Unitas [1913].
        159 pp.
            DLC.

2471 Campbell, Eva M. Satire in the Early English Drama. Columbus,
        Ohio: F. J. Heer, 1914. 136 pp.
            MiU. NjP. OO. PU.

*2472 Feuillerat, Albert. Great Britain. Office of the Revels. Docu-
        ments Relating to the Revels at Court in the Time of King
        Edward VI and Queen Mary (the Loseley Manuscripts). Edited
        with Notes and Indexes. Louvain: A. Uystpruyst, 1914. 339
        pp. (Materialien zur Kunde des älteren englischen Dramas.
        Hrsg. von W. Bang. 44 bd.)
            BM. DFo. ICN.

*2473 Johnson, Arthur Henry. The History of the Worshipful Company
        of the Drapers of London; Preceded by an Introduction on Lon-
        don and Her Guilds up to the Close of the XVth Century. 5
        vol. Oxford: Clarendon Press, 1914-1922.
            BM. IaU. ICN. OCU.

2474 Nelson, Lelia Stacy. "Portrayal of Witchcraft in the English
        Drama from 1558 to 1642." M.A. University of Chicago,
        1914.

2475 Parrott, Sir James Edward. The Pageant of English Literature.
        London: Thomas Nelson and Sons, 1914. viii, 480 pp.
            BM. MB. NN. OC1. PU.

2476 Schelling, Felix E. English Drama. London: Dent and Sons;
        New York: E. P. Dutton and Co., 1914. 341 pp.
            BM. DFo. ICN. IU. MiU. NjP. OCU. PU.

2477 Skeat, Walter William. Glossary of Tudor and Stuart Words,
        Especially from the Dramatists. London: Mayhew, 1914.
        461 pp.
            ICN.

2478 Wynne, Arnold. The Growth of English Drama. Oxford: The

Clarendon Press, 1914. 281. [1] pp.
BM. IaU. MB. MiU. NBuG. NjP. NN. OC1. OU.

2479 Gross, Charles. A Bibliography of British Municipal History,
Including Gilds and Parliamentary Representation. Cambridge: Harvard University Press, 1915. xxxiv, 461 pp. (Harvard Studies, Vol. 5.)
BM. ICN. NN.

2480 Moore, Hazelle S. "Comic Country and Village Scene in Sixteenth
Century Drama." M.A. University of Chicago, 1915.

2481 Whiteford, Margaret Bartlett. "The Children of the Chapel before
1597." M.A. Columbia University, 1915.

2482 Whitmore, Charles Edward. Supernatural in Tragedy. Cambridge: Harvard University Press, 1915. viii, 370 pp. Bibliography, pp. [359]-363.
BM. MiU. OC1. OCU. OCX. OU. ViU.

2483 Baskervill, C. R. "On Two Old Plays." Modern Philology, XIV
(1916-1917), 16.

2484 ----- "Some Evidence of Early Romantic Plays in England."
Modern Philology, XIV (August, 1916), 229-251; XIV (December, 1916), 467-512.

*2485 Creizenach, Wilhelm Michael Anton. The English Drama in the
Age of Shakespeare. Philadelphia: J. B. Lippincott Co.; Lon-
don, Sidgwick and Jackson, Ltd., [1916]. xv, 454 pp.
BM. CSmH. CtY. DFo. ICN. MiU. NN. OC1. ODW.
OO. PU. ViU. WaU.

2486 Davis, Caroline Hill. "Pageants in Great Britain and the United
States. A List of References." Bulletin of the New York Public
Library, XX (1916), 753-791.

2487 Fryar, John R. "Catholic Benefit Clubs of the Middle Ages."
Ecclesiastical Review, LIV (1916), 176-192.

2488 Herrington, Hunley Whateley. "Magic and Witchcraft in the
Elizabethan Drama from the Beginning to 1597." Ph.D. Harvard University, 1916.

2489 McMahon, Amos Philip. "The Mediaeval Conception of Tragedy and Comedy." Ph.D. Harvard University, 1916.

2490 Smallwood, Samuel. Some Ancient Mystery Towers Remaining
      in England. Kidsgrove, Staffordshire; Mow-Cop, Cheshire;
      Bradgate, Leicestershire; Plessey, Northumberland; Rottley,
      do; Perranzabuloe, Cornwall. [Hitchin: W. Carling and Co.,
      1916]. 74 pp.
          BM. NN.

2491 Adams, Elizabeth D. "A Fragment of a Lord Mayor's Pageant."
      Modern Language Notes, XXXII (May, 1917), 285-289.

2492 Adams, Joseph Quincy. Shakespearean Playhouses; A History
      of English Theatres from the Beginnings to the Restoration.
      Boston, New York: Houghton Mifflin Co., [c. 1917]. xiv,
      473 pp. Bibliography, pp. [433]-456.
          BM. CtY. DFo. DLC. ICN. ICU. IU. OC1. PU. WU.

*2493 Lawson, Robb. Story of the Scots Stage. Paisley, England: A.
      Gardiner, 1917. 303 pp. Bibliography, pp. [287]-292.
          BM. DLC. MB. MiU. MnU. NB. NN. OC1. WU.

2494 Wills, Helen Holton. "The Evolution of Women in the English
      Drama from its Beginnings to 1595." M.A. Columbia Uni-
      versity, 1917.

2495 Armitage, Frederick. The Old Guilds of England. London: Weare
      and Co., 1918. 226 pp.
          BM. DLC. IaU. ICN. MiU. NcD. PU. WU.

2496 Barnicle, Mary E. "The Exemplum of the Penitent Usurer."
      Publications of the Modern Language Association, XXXIII
      (1918), 409-428.

2497 Lau, Marie King. "Predecessors in English Drama of Shakespeare's
      Comic Monologs." M.A. University of Chicago, 1918.

2498 Renard, Georges Francois. Guilds in the Middle Ages. Translated,
      with an introduction by G. H. D. Cole. London: G. Bell & Sons,
      Ltd., 1918. xxv, 139 pp. Bibliography, pp. 137-[140].
          BM. DLC. ICN. MiU. NjP. NN. OC1. PU. WaU.

*2499 Withington, Robert. English Pageantry; an Historical Outline.
      2 vol. Cambridge: Harvard University Press, 1918-1920.
          DLC. MB. MiU. MnU. NN. OC1. OCU. ViU. WaU.

2500 Dilley, Maude Evelyn. "The Parasite; a Study in Dramatic
         Development." M.A. Columbia University, 1919.

2501 Rosé, Grace N. "Old English Plays Adapted for the House."
         House and Garden, XXXVI (Decmeber, 1919), 19-21, 62.

2502 Westlake, Herbert Francis. The Parish Gilds of Mediaeval Eng-
         land. London, Society for Promoting Christian Knowledge.
         New York: Macmillan Co., 1919. viii, 242 pp.
              BM. DLC. IaU. MB. MiU. MnU. NN. OC1. OU.

2503 Withington, Robert. "A Note on 'A Fragment of a Lord Mayor's
         Pageant.'" Modern Language Notes, XXXIV (Decmember,
         1919), 501-503.

2504 Brawley, Benjamin. Short History of the English Drama. New
         York: Harcourt, 1921. ix, 260 pp. Bibliography, pp. 239-249.
              BM (1922 ed.). ICN.

2505 Davey, Henry. History of English Music. 2nd ed. revised and
         rewritten. London: J. Curran and Sons, 1921. xix, 505 pp.
         Index.
              BM.

*2506 Reed, Arthur William. The Beginnings of the English Secular
         and Romantic Drama. London: Published for the Shakespeare
         Association by Humphrey Milford, Oxford University Press,
         1922. 31 pp. (Shakespeare Association Papers, No. 7).
              BM. DFo. DLC. IU. MB. NN. OCU. PBm. PU. ViU.
         WaU.

2507 Busby, Olive Mary. Studies in the Development of the Fool in
         the Elizabethan Drama. London: Humphrey Milford, Oxford
         University Press, 1923. 87 pp.
              BM. ICN.

*2508 Campbell, Lily B. Scenes and Machines on the English Stage
         during the Renaissance. A Classical Revival. Cambridge:
         University Press, 1923. x, 302 pp.
              BM. CtY. DLC. ICN. IU. MH. MiU. NN. NNC. OU. PU.

*2509 Chambers, E. K. The Elizabethan Stage. 4 vol. London: Oxford
         University Press, 1923. [Reprinted].

2510 Chambers, R. W. "The Lost Literature of Mediaeval England."

Library, V (1923), 326-330.

*2511 Creizenach, Wilhelm Michael Anton. Geschichte des neueren
         Dramas. Dirttes Band. Renaissance und Reformation. Zweiter
         Teil. Zweite, vermehrte und verbesserte Auflage bearbeitet
         und mit einem vollständigen Register zum zweiten und dritten
         Band versehen von Adalbert Hämel. Halle: Niemeyer, 1923.
         143 pp.
                BM. CtY. DLC. ICN. IU. MiU. NN. OCl. OO. PU.
                ViU. WU.

2512 Crum, Mason. Guide to Religious Pageantry. New York: Mac-
         millan, 1923. 134 pp.
                DLC. IaU. OCl. OO.

2513 Lemon, W. P. "Biblical Pageantry and Dramatics." Homiletic
         and Pastoral Review, LXXXV (1923), 395-404.

2514 Moore, John Robert. "The Tradition of Angelic Singing in Eng-
         lish Drama." Journal of English and Germanic Philology,
         XXII (January, 1923), 89-99.

2515 Barrow, Sarah Field. The Medieval Society Romances. New York:
         Columbia University Press, 1924. 141 pp. Bibliographical
         footnotes.
                ICN. OCl. OCU. OO. OOxM. OU. PBm. PU. ViU.

*2516 Brown, Carleton. Religious Lyrics of the Fourteenth Century.
         London: Clarendon Press, 1924. xxii, 358 pp.
                BM.

2517 Camp, Charles Wellner. The Artisan in Elizabethan Literature.
         New York: Columbia University Press, 1924. 170 pp. Biblio-
         graphy, pp. 151-163.
                BM. DLC. ICN. NN.

2518 Bradner, Leicester. "Stages and Stage Scenery in Court Drama
         before 1558." Review of English Studies, I (1925), 447-448.

2519 Flood, William Henry Grattan. Early Tudor Composers. Bio-
         graphical Sketches. London: Humphrey Milford, 1925.
         121 pp. (Oxford Musical Essays).
                BM.

2520 Jones, Warren. "Medieval Influences in Eighteenth Century

Tragedy after 1850." M.A. University of Chicago, 1925.

2521 Moore, John Brooks. The Comic and the Realistic in English
     Drama. Chicago: University of Chicago Press, [c. 1925].
     viii, 231 pp. Bibliography, pp. 216-223.
     ICN.

2522 Parrott, Alice Anne. "Scenery on the Tudor Stage." M.A. Col-
     umbia University, 1925.

2523 Reed, Edward Bliss, ed. Songs from the British Drama. New
     Haven: Yale University Press, 1925. xi, 386 pp.
         BM. DFo. DLC. ICN. MB. MiU. OC1. OU. PU.
         ViU. WU.

2524 Schelling, Felix E. Elizabethan Playwrights: A Short History of
     the English Drama from Medieval Times to the Closing of the
     Theatres in 1642. New York: Harper and Brothers, 1925. xiv,
     335 pp. Bibliography, pp. 287-302.
         BM. DFo. DLC. ICN. MiU. MnU. OC1. OU. PSC. ViU.

*2525 Taylor, Henry Osborn. The Mediaeval Mind. A History of the
     Development of Thought and Emotion in the Middle Ages. 4th
     ed. 2 vol. Cambridge, Massachusetts: Harvard University
     Press, 1925. [Original edition, 1911.]
         ICN.

*2526 Unwin, G. The Gilds and Companies of London. 2d ed. London:
     Methuen & Co., [1925], 397 pp. xvi, 397 pp.
         BM. DLC. ICN. MB. MnU. OU. WaU. WU.

2527 Child, Harold. "Revivals of English Dramatic Works, 1919-1925."
     Review of English Studies, II (April, 1926), 177-188.

2528 Dorman, Isabel Wait. "The Development of the Witch Figure in
     English Literature." M.A. Columbia University, 1926.

*2529 Hillebrand, Harold N. The Child Actors. 2 vol. Urbana: Uni-
     versity of Illinois, 1926. Bibliography, Vol. 2, pp. 339-347.
         BM. IaU. ICN. IU. MH. MiU. OC1. PU. ViU.

*2530 Owst, Gerald R. Preaching in Medieval England. Cambridge: At
     the University Press, 1926. xviii, 381 pp. Index. (Cambridge
     Studies in Medieval Life and Thought).
         BM.

2531 Potter, R. R. "Some Aspects of the Supernatural in English
Comedy from the Origins to the Closing of the Theatres in
1642." Ph.D. University of North Carolina, 1926.

2532 Wills, Mary Marguerite. "The History of the Development of
the Technique of Acting from the Earliest Greek Times to
the Nineteenth Century in England." M.A. Northwestern
University, 1926.

*2533 Winslow, Ola Elizabeth. Low Comedy as a Structural Element
in English Drama from the Beginnings to 1642. Private Edition. Distributed by the University of Chicago Libraries.
Chicago, Illinois, 1926. xi, 186 pp. Bibliography, pp. 172-
186.
BM. DLC. MB. MnU. ODW. OU.

2534 Wright, Louis B. "Vaudeville Elements in English Drama from
the Origins until the Closing of the Theatres in 1642." Ph.D.
University of North Carolina, 1926.

2535 Albright, Evelyn May. Dramatic Publication in England, 1580-
1640; A Study of Conditions Affecting Content and Form of
Drama. New York: D. C. Heath and Co.; London: Oxford
University Press, 1927. 442 pp. Bibliography, pp. 385-419.
BM. DFo. ICN. ICU. MH. MiU. OCl. OU. PU. ViU.
WU.

2536 Child, Harold. "Revivals of English Dramatic Works, 1901-1918,
1926." Review of English Studies, III (1927), 169-185.

2537 Flood, W. H. Grattan. "Early Tudor Drama." Review of English
Studies, III (1927), 445-446.

2538 Hogrefe, Pearl. "The Influence of Early English Humanists on
Pre-Elizabethan Drama." Ph.D. University of Chicago, 1927.

2539 Mackenzie, Agnes Mure. The Playgoers Handbook to the English
Renaissance Drama. London: Cape, 1927. 191 pp.
BM. CtY. DLC. IaU. ICN. MiU. OCl. WU.

*2540 Mill, Anna Jean. Mediaeval Plays in Scotland. University of St.
Andrews: Oxford University Press, 1927. 356 pp. (St. Andrews
University Publications, No. XXIV.)
ICN. ICU. MB. MiU. OCl. ODW. OU. PU. TxU.

2541 Nicoll, Allardyce. British Drama. London: G. G. Harrap and
       Co., Ltd., 1927. 497 pp. Bibliography, pp. 463-480. [4th
       ed., 1947.]
             BM (1925). IaU. ICN. MB. NN. OC1. OO. PPTU.

2542 Schelling, Felix E. English Literature during the Lifetime of
       Shakespeare. Rev. ed. New York: Henry Holt and Co., 1927.
       492 pp.
             BM. ICN. MH. MnU. MiU. OC1. OCU. PPD. PV. ViU.

2543 Wright, Louis B. "Animal Actors on the English Stage before
       1642." Publications of the Modern Language Association,
       XLII (1927), 656-669.

2544 ----- "Juggling Tricks and Conjury on the English Stage before
       1642." Modern Philology, XXIV (1927), 269-284.

2545 Albright, E. M. "Dramatic Publication in England, 1580-1640:
       A Reply." Review of English Studies, IV (1928), 193-202.

2546 Eckhardt, Eduard. Das englische Drama im Zeitalter der Re-
       formation und der Hochrenaissance. Vorstufen: Shakespeare
       und seine Zeit. Berlin: de Gruyter, 1928. xii, 293 pp. Biblio-
       graphy, pp. 9-12.
             BM. CSmH. CtY. IaU. IU. MH. MiU. NN. PU. WU.

2547 Gamble, William Burt. Development of Scenic Art and Stage
       Machinery. New York: New York Public Library, 1928. 231
       pp.
             DLC. IaU. MiU. MnU.

2548 Hirte, Helmuth. Entwicklung des Prologs und Epilogs im früh-
       neuenglischen Drama. Inaugural Dissertation. Giessen, 1928.

2549 Hughes, Dom Anselm, ed. Worcester Medieval Harmony of the
       Thirteenth and Fourteenth Centuries. London: The Plainsong
       and Medieval Music Society, 1928. 149 pp.
             BM.

2550 Kramer, Stella. The English Craft Gilds: Studies in Their Pro-
       gress and Decline. Oxford: University Press, 1928. xi, 228
       pp.
             DLC. ICN. MiU. NN. OC1. PU.

2551 Lucius, Eberhard. Gerichtsszenen im älteren englischen Drama.

Inaugural Dissertation. Giessen, 1928.

2552 Meyer, E. F. "Remarks on the English Medieval Gild: Borough
Relations with the Gilds." American Federationist, XXXV
(1928), 960-965, 1095-1100.

2553 Nicoll, Allardyce. The English Stage. London: E. Benn, Ltd.,
1928. 80 pp. Bibliography, pp. [79]-80. (Benn's Sixpenny
Library.)
BM. MnU. OCl. OO.

2554 Rossbach, Jakob. Das erste Auftreten der Personen im älteren
englischen Drama. Inaugural Dissertation. Giessen, 1928.

2555 Thorp, Willard. The Triumph of Realism in Elizabeth Drama,
1558-1612. Princeton: Princeton University Press, 1928. ix,
142 pp. Bibliography, pp. 139-142.
BM. DFo. DLC. IaU. ICN. MnU. OCl. OClW.

2556 Aronstein, Philipp. Das englische Renaissance-drama. Leipzig,
Berlin: Teubner, 1929. x, 336 pp. "Literatur," pp. 321-323.
BM. CtY. DLC. IaU. ICN. MnU. NN. OCl.

2557 Eckhardt, Eduard. Das englische Drama der Spätrenaissance.
Berlin: de Gruyter, 1929. viii, 202 pp.
BM. CtY. DFo. ICN. ICU. MnU. NcD. NN. OCl.

2558 Gregor, Josef. Das Theater des Mittelalters. Seine Wirkungen
in der Grafik, Miniatur und im Taffelbilde. München: Piper,
1929. 15 pp., 47 illus.

2559 Meyer, Erwin F. "The English Craft Gilds and the Borough Govern-
ment during the Later Middle Ages." Ph.D. University of Colorado, 1929.

*2560 ----- "English Craft Gilds and Borough Governments of the
Later Middle Ages I." University of Colorado Studies, XVI
XVI (1929), 323-378.

*2561 Motter, T. H. Vail. The School Drama in England. London, New
York, Toronto: Longmans, Green &Co., 1929. xiii, 325 pp.
Bibliography, pp. 299-310. Index.
BM. CtY. DFo. DLC. ICN. ICU. IU. MH. NN. OCl. PU.

2562 Schutt, J. H. "A Guide to English Studies: The Study of the Medieval

Drama." English Studies, XI (February, 1929), 11-17.

2563 Seymour, St. John Drelincourt. Anglo-Irish Literature, 1200-1582. Cambridge: The University Press, 1929. [10], 169, [1] pp. Index.
ICN. ICU.

*2564 Thorndike, Ashley Horace. English Comedy. New York: The Macmillan Co., 1929. vi, 635 pp.
BM. DFo. DLC. IaU. ICN.MB. MnU. NN. OCl. ViU.

*2565 Meyer, Erwin F. "English Craft Gilds and Borough Governments of the Later Middle Ages II." University of Colorado Studies, XVII (1930), 350-426.

2566 Scudder, Robert Earl. "Conventions of Satire by Early Tudor Dramatists." M.A. Northwestern University, 1930.

2567 Speck, Cornelius van der. The Church and the Churchman in English Dramatic Literature before 1642. Amsterdam: J. J. Paris, 1930. 188 pp. "List of Plays," pp. 177-184.
DFo. DLC. ICN.

2568 Bald, R. C. "The Development of Greek and Mediaeval English Drama. A Comparison." Englische Studien, LXVI (1931), 6-15.

2569 Collins, Fletcher. "The Relation of Tudor Halls to Elizabethan Public Theatres." Philological Quarterly, X (1931), 313-316.

2570 Fitzgibbon, H. Macaulay. "Instruments and Their Music in the Elizabethan Drama." Musical Quarterly, XVII (1931), 319-329.

*2571 Green, Adwin Wigfall. The Inns of Court and Early English Drama. With a Preface by Roscoe Pound. New Haven: Yale University Press; London: H. Milford, Oxford University Press, 1931. xii, 199 pp. Bibliography, pp. 183-187.
BM. DFo. DLC. IaU. ICN. MH. MnU. OCU. OU. PU.

2572 McGachen, F. "The History and Development of Scenery on the English Stage from Medieval Times to the Year 1700." M.A. McGill University, 1931.

2573 Mehrens, Harold E. "Los Pastores--a Survival of Medieval

Drama." M.A. New Mexico Normal University, 1931.

2574 Mountford, Winifred M. "The Devil in English Literature from the Middle Ages to 1700." Ph.D. London University (External), 1931.

*2575 Nicoll, Allardyce. Masks, Mimes and Miracles: Studies in the Popular Theatre. With Two Hundred and Twenty-Six Illustrations. New York: Harcourt, Brace and Co., 1931. 407 pp.
BM. IaU. ICN. IU. MH. MnU. OC1. OO. WaU.

2576 Poling, V. "Medieval Guild Scene." School Arts Magazine, XXXI (1931), 222-224.

2577 Rudwin, Maximilian. The Devil in Legend and Literature. Chicago and London: The Open Court, 1931. xi, 354 pp.
BM. DLC. ICN. MnU. OC1. OC1W. PBm. ViU.

2578 Sayle, Robert Theophilus Dalton. Lord Mayors Pageants of the Merchant Taylors' Company in the 15th, 16th, and 17th Centuries. [London: The Eastern Press, Ltd.], 1931. Printed for Private Circulation. 160 pp.
CSmH.

2579 Thompson, Francis J. "The Devils in Middle English Literature." M.A. Columbia University, 1931.

2580 Altpeter, Peter. "The History of Dramatic Censorship in England to the Year 1642." M.A. University of Southern California, 1932.

2581 Hobson, Martha Barbour. "The Development of Off-Stage Action in the English Drama." Ph.D. Northwestern University, 1932.

2582 McG., T. J. "Medieval Drama." Truth, XXXVI (1932), 23.

2583 Harris, M. Dormer. "Shakespeare and the Religious Drama." Notes and Queries, CLXV (1933), 254-255.

2584 Macdonald, J. F. "The Use of Prose in English Drama before Shakespeare." University of Toronto Quarterly, II (1933), 465-481.

*2585 Owst, Gerald Robert. Literature and Pulpit in Medieval England. Cambridge: University Press, 1933. xxiv, 616 pp.

BM. CtY. DLC. ICN. MiU. NN. NNC. OU. PU. ViU.

2586 Sibley, Gertrude M. The Lost Plays and Masques: 1500-1642.
Ithaca: Cornell University Press; London: Humphrey Milford,
1933. 205 pp. (Cornell Studies in English, Vol. XIX.)
BM. DFo. DLC. IaU. ICN. MB. MiU. OCl. OU. ViU.

2587 Tergau, Diedrich. Die sozialen Typen im Drama des englischen
Mittelalters. Inaugural Dissertation. Göttingen, 1933. 78 pp.
CtY. CSmH. DLC. ICN. MiU.

2588 Tiegs, Alexander. Zur Zusammenarbeit englische berufsdramaticker
Unmittelbar vor, neben und nach Shakespeare. Breslau: Trewendt
and Grainier, 1933. vii, 144 pp. "Bibliographie," pp. 129-137.
BM. DLC. ICN. MnU. NNU-W.

2589 Friedlaender, Ernst. Kontrast und Gleichfoermigkeit im alteren
englischen Drama. Inaugural Dissertation. Breslau, 1934.

2590 Meyer, E. F. "English Medieval Industrial Codes." American
Federationist, XLI (1934), 609-614.

2591 Risikoff, Seymour. "The Shrew in English Drama from the
Beginnings to 1642." M.A. Columbia University, 1934.

*2592 Tomlinson, Warren Everett. Der Herodescharakter im englischen
Drama. Leipzig: Mayer and Muller, 1934. x, 182 pp. "Literatur-
verzeichnis," pp. [viii]-x. (Palaestra, 195).
BM. CtY. DLC. IaU. ICN. MiU. MnU.

*2593 Withington, Robert. "'Vice' and 'Parasite.'" A Note on the Evolu-
tion of the Elizabethan Villain." Publications of the Modern
Language Association, XLIX (September, 1934), 743-751.

2594 Baesecke, Anna. Das Schauspiel der englischen Komödianten in
Deutschland. Halle: M. Niemeyer, 1935. xiii, 154 pp.
"Literatur," pp. ix-xii.
BM. DLC. ICN. MiU. NcD. NcU. NN. OCU. ViU.

2595 Bradbrook, M. C. Themes and Conventions of Elizabethan Tragedy.
Cambridge: University Press, 1935. viii, 275 pp.
BM. CtY. DLC. ICN. MB. MiU. OU. PHC. PV. WaU.

2596 Fischel, O. "A Study of the Middle Ages. Theatrical History
Through Pictorial Art of the Period." Burlington Magazine,

LXVI (1935), 4, 7-8, 13-14.

*2597 Harris, Mary Dormer, ed. The Register of the Guild of the Holy
Trinity, St. Mary, St. John the Baptist and St. Katherine of
Coventry. 2 vol. London: Published for the Dugdale Society
by H. Milford, Oxford University Press, 1935-1944.
BM. CtY. ICN.

2598 Hinks, Roger. Carolingian Art. London: Sidgwick & Jackson,
1935. x, 224 pp. Index. Bibliography.
BM.

2599 Rule, Margaret Brady. "Details and Accessories of Historical
Costume from the 14th through the 18th Centuries; A Reference
Book for the Designers of Theatrical Costumes." M.A. Uni-
versity of Iowa, 1935.

*2600 Welsford, Enid. The Fool. His Social and Literary History.
London: Faber and Faber, 1935. xv, 374 pp. Bibliography,
pp. 349-356. Index.
BM.

2601 Zühlsdorf, Harald. Die Technik des komischen Zwischenspiels
der frühen Tudorzeit. Berlin: Triltsch & Huther, 1935. 77 pp.
BM. PU. WU.

*2602 Farnham, Willard. The Medieval Heritage of Elizabethan Tragedy.
Berkeley: University of California Press, 1936. xiv, 487 pp.
BM. DFo. ICN. ICU. IU. MiU. NN. OCl. PU. ViU. WU.

2603 Gwatkin, H[enry] M., J. P. Whitney, et al., eds. The Cambridge
Medieval History. Planned by J. B. Bury. 8 vol. Cambridge:
University Press, 1911-1936. Bibliographies at the end of each
volume.
ICN.

2604 Nicoll, Allardyce. The English Theatre. London and New York:
T. Nelson and Sons, Ltd., 1936. xi, 252 pp.
BM. MB. NN. OCl. OU. PPTU.

2605 Rapp, Albert. Studien über den Zusammenhang des geistlichen
Theaters mit der bildenden Kunst im ausgehenden Mittelalter.
Kallmünz: Michael Lassleben, 1936. 99 pp. "Literatur (aus-
wohl)," pp. [96]-99.
BM. MiU.

2606 Spencer, Theodore. Death and Elizabethan Tragedy. Cambridge:
      Harvard University Press; London: Humphrey Milford, 1936.
      xii, 288 pp.
          BM. DLC. IaU. ICN. MnU. NN. OCU. OO. WaU. WU.

2607 Greer, Clayton A. "Relationships in the Plays of the York-Lancaster
      Tetralogy." Ph.D. University of Texas, 1937.

*2608 Hartl, Eduard. Das Dräma des Mittelalters, Sein Wesen und sein
      Werden; Osterfeiern; mit einleitungen und anmerkungen auf
      Grund der Handschriften. Leipzig: P. Reclam, 1937. 266 pp.
      "Buchweiser," pp. 7-12.
          BM. DLC. IaU. IU. MB. OO. OU. PSC. PSt.

2609 Mills, Laurens Joseph. One Soul in Bodies Twain; Friendship in
      Tudor Literature and Stuart Drama. Bloomington, Indiana:
      The Principia Press, Inc., 1937. vii, 470 pp. Bibliographical
      references in notes, pp. [379]-458.
          BM. DFo. DLC. ICN. MiU. OC1. OU. PSC. ViU.

2610 Koldewy, Eva. Über die Willensfreiheit im älteren englischen
      Drama. Inaugural Dissertation. Berlin, 1937.

2611 Taylor, George C. "The Medieval Element in Shakespeare."
      Shakespeare Association Bulletin, XII (1937), 208-216.

*2612 Withington, Robert. Excursions in English Drama. New York,
      London: D. Appleton-Century Co., Inc. [c. 1937]. xix, 264
      pp. Bibliographical note, pp. 247-251.
          BM. DFo. DLC. ICN. MnU. NN. ViU.

2613 Armbrister, Victor S. "The Origins and Functions of Subplots
      in Elizabethan Drama." Ph.D. Vanderbilt University, 1938.

2614 Coffman, George R. "Some Trends in English Literary Scholar-
      ship, with Special Reference to Mediaeval Backgrounds." Studies
      in Philology, XXXV (1938), 500-514.

2615 Coulton, G[eorge] G. Medieval Panorama. The English Scene from
      Conquest to Reformation. Cambridge: Cambridge University
      Press, 1938. xiv, 801 pp.
          ICN. NN.

2616 Hall, Adelia M. "Plays Written or Presented in England between
      1498 and 1576, with Certain Facts." M.A. University of Colorado,
      1938.

2617 Shirley, John W. "The Parasite, the Glutton, and the Hungry Knave in English Drama to 1625." Ph.D. University of Iowa, 1938.

2618 Stallmann, Heinz. Malapropism im englischen Drama von den Anfängen bis 1800. Berlin, 1938. 113 pp.
    BM.

2619 Thomas, Sidney. "The Social and Dramatic Origins of the Elizabethan Realistic Comedy." M.A. Columbia University, 1938.

*2620 Whiting, Bartlett Jere. Proverbs in the Earlier English Drama. Cambridge, Mass.: Harvard University Press; London: H. Milford, 1938. xx, 505 pp. (Harvard Studies in Comparative Literature, Vol. XIV.)
    BM. DFo. DLC. IaU. ICN. MnU. OCU. OO. ViU. WU.

2621 Griffin, William J. "Tudor Control of Press and Stage." Ph.D. University of Iowa, 1939.

2622 Lewis, Alice B. "Descriptions of the Devil and His Works in Early English Literature and the Development of These Ideas in Relation to Doctrine." Ph.D. London University, 1939.

2623 Martin, Marilynn--Natalie. "The Role of Kingship in English Drama to 1642." M.A. Yale University, 1939.

2624 Ward, A. W. "The Origins of English Drama." The Cambridge History of English Literature. Vol. 5. (New York, 1939), pp. 1-25.

2625 Bowers, Fredson Thayer. Elizabethan Revenge Tragedy, 1587-1642. Princeton: Princeton University Press, 1940. viii, 288 pp.
    BM. CtY. DLC. ICN. ICU. IU. MB. MH. NN. NNC. OU. WU.

2626 Fox, L. "Administration of Gild Property in Coventry in the Fifteenth Century." English Historical Review, LV (1940), 634-647.

2627 Fulford, G. L. "The History and Development of Scenery and Lighting of the English Stage from Medieval Times to the Year 1700." M.A. McGill University, 1940.

2628 Taylor, Joseph Richard. Story of the Drama: Beginning to the Commonwealth. Boston: Expression, 1940. xxvi, 555 pp.

BM. MB. MH. MnU. OC1. OC1W.

2629 Robbins, Edwin W. "The Drama in England during the Reign of Edward VI." M.A. University of Illinois, 1941.

2630 Shull, Virginia Moore. "Stagecraft in Mediaeval English Drama." Ph.D. Yale University, 1941.

*2631 Adams, Henry Hitch. English Domestic or Homiletic Tragedy 1575 to 1642. Being an Account of the Development of the Tragedy of the Common Man Showing Its Great Dependence on Religious Morality. New York: Columbia University Press, 1942. x, 228 pp. Bibliography, pp. 207-220. (Columbia University Studies in English and Comparative Literature, No. CLIX.)
BM. DFo. DLC. ICN. OC1. PV. RPV. ViU.

2632 Bukofzer, Manfred F. "Speculative Thinking in Mediaeval Music." Speculum, XVII (1942), 165-180.

2633 Jones, Juanita. "The Theory of Comic Drama in England before 1625." Ph.D. University of Iowa, 1942.

2634 Kelleher, Mother Margaret Mary. "The Friar in the English Drama from 1550 to 1616." M.A. Catholic University of America, 1942.

2635 Kernodle, George R., and Portia. "Dramatic Aspects of the Medieval Tournament." Speech Monographs, IX (1942), 161-172.

*2636 Clune, The Rev. George. The Medieval Gild System. Dublin: Browne and Nolan, Ltd. [1943]. 300 pp. Bibliography, pp. 281-285.
CtY. DLC. MnU.

2637 Detmold, George Ernst. "The Origins of Drama." Ph.D. Cornell University, 1943.

2638 Griffin, William J. "Notes on Early Tudor Control of the Stage." Modern Language Notes, LVIII (1943), 50-54.

2639 Kernodle, George R. "The Medieval Pageant Wagons of Louvain." Theatre Annual, (1943), 58-62.

2640 Lever, Katherine. "Early Tudor Drama and Old Greek Comedy: A Study of Didactic and Satiric Plays." M.A. Bryn Mawr University, 1943.

2641 Miller, Edwin Shephard. "Medieval Biblical and Ritualistic Ele-
      ments in English Drama, 1497-1562." Ph.D. University of
      North Carolina, 1943.

2642 Atkins, J. W. H. English Literary Criticism: The Medieval Phase.
      Cambridge: Cambridge University Press, 1944. ix, 211 pp.
      BM.

2643 Bouvier, Arthur Paul. "Studies in the Development of Dramatic
      Conventions in 16th Century England." Ph.D. University of
      Minnesota, 1944.

2644 Dunham, Richard Roy. "The Birth of the Modern Theatre." Ph.D.
      Cornell University, 1944.

2645 Frey, J. P. "Medieval Craft Guilds." American Federationist, LI
      (1944), 20-23, 23-26.

2646 Kernodle, George Riley. From Art to Theatre; Form and Conven-
      tion in the Renaissance. Chicago: University of Chicago Press,
      [1944]. 255 pp. Bibliography, pp. 220-243.
      MH.

2647 Murray, Sr. Elizabeth Marion. "The Place of the Lyric in the
      Drama before 1550." M.A. Fordham University, 1944.

2648 Ryan, S. J., Rev. Harold. "Heroic Play Elements in Earlier Eng-
      lish Drama." Ph.D. St. Louis University, 1944.

2649 Trachtenberg, Joshua. The Devil and the Jew. The Medieval Con-
      ception of the Jew and Its Relation to Modern Anti-Semitism.
      New Haven: Yale University Press, 1944. xiv, 279 pp.
      BM.

2650 Tristram, Ernest William. English Medieval Wall Painting, The
      Twelfth and Thirteenth Centuries. 3 vol. London: Oxford Uni-
      versity Press for Pilgrim Trust, 1944-1950.
      BM.

2651 Abegglen, Homer N. [Dissertation in five parts.] "1. The Methods
      of Staging in London Theaters in the Last Half of the 19th Century.
      2. Theatrical Satire on the American Business Man, 1900-1940.
      3. The Staging of Medieval and Elizabethan Plays. 4. A Com-
      parison between Plautine Farce and Romantic Comedy. 5. The
      Premiere of Wycherley's The Plain-Dealer." Ph.D. Western

Reserve University, 1945.

2652 Chambers, E. K. English Literature at the Close of the Middle Ages. Oxford: Clarendon Press, 1945. 248 pp. Bibliography, pp. 206-231. (Vol. 2, Part 2 of Oxford History of English Literature.)
BM. DLC. IaU. ICN. MnU. M3. TxU. ViU.

2653 Fermor, Una Ellis. The Frontiers of Drama. London: Methuen, 1945. vi, 154 pp.
BM. DFo. DLC. ICN. ICU. IU. MiU. OO. PU. TxU. ViU. WU.

2654 Gassner, John Waldhorn. Masters of the Drama. New York: Dover, 1945. 804 pp. Bibliography, pp. 739-764.
ICN.

2655 Bigongiari, Dino. "Were There Theatres in the Twelfth and Thirteenth Centuries?" Romanic Review, XXXVII (October, 1946), 201-224.

*2656 Greg, W. W. "Authorship Attributions in the Early Play-Lists." Edinburgh, Bibliographical Society Transactions. II (1946), 305-329.

*2657 Baldwin, Thomas Whitfield. Shakespeare's Five-Act Structure. Shakespeare's Early Plays on the Background of Renaissance Theories of Five-Act Structure from 1470. Urbana: University of Illinois Press, 1947. xiii, 848 pp.
BM. CtY. DFo. DLC. ICN. ICU. MH. NN. NjP. O. PU.

*2658 Gwynn, A. "End of Medieval Drama in England." Studies. (Dublin), XXXVI (1947), 283-295.

2659 Holzknecht, K. J. Outlines of Tudor and Stuart Plays, 1497-1642. New York: Barnes and Noble, 1947. ix, 442 pp.
BM.

2660 Karchmer, Estelle B. "Types of Early Medieval Drama." M.A. University of Southern California, 1947.

2661 Sabol, Andrew Joseph. "Music for the English Drama from the Beginning to 1642." Ph.D. Brown University, 1947. [Reproduces approximately 100 pieces of music.]

2662 Thorson, Une E. "Medieval Theatre in the Modern Day." M.A. University of Wisconsin, 1947.

2663 Butler, James Harmon. "A Study of Ancient Greek, Roman, and Medieval Theater Conventions and Devices." M.A. University of California, 1948.

*2664 Cave, C. J. P. Roof Bosses in Medieval Churches. Cambridge: University Press, 1948. viii, 235 pp. 367 plates. Index. BM.

2665 Evans, B. Ifor. A Short History of English Drama. Harmondsworth: Penguin Books, 1948. 172 pp.

2666 Jayne, Sears R. "Platonism in English Drama of the Renaissance, 1442-1642." Ph.D. Yale University, 1948.

2667 Jones, Donald Eric. "The Ghost in the Drama." M.A. Columbia University, 1948.

2668 McDowell, J. H. "Conventions of Medieval Art in Shakespearean Staging." Journal of English and Germanic Philology, XLVII (1948), 215-229.

2669 Meade, Anna McClymonds. "The Actor in the Middle Ages." M.A. Columbia University, 1948.

2670 Sabol, Andrew J. "Music for the English Drama from the Beginnings to 1642." Ph.D. Brown University, 1948. [Delete 2661].

2671 Buitenhuis, J. M. "The Beginning of English Drama." Theatre World, XLV (August, 1949), 34, 36.

2672 McCutchan, John W. "Personified Abstractions as Characters in Elizabethan Drama." Ph.D. University of Virginia, 1949.

2673 McDowell, J. H. "Medieval Influences in Shakespearian Staging." Players Magazine, XXVI (1949), 52-53.

2674 Powell, Arnold F. The Melting Mood, A Study of the Function of Pathos in English Tragedy through Shakespeare. Vanderbilt University Dissertation. Nashville, 1949. (Reprinted from the Bulletin of Birmingham-Southern Collection, XLII. No. 4) 26 pp.
    MiD. MiU.

2675 Trevelyan, George M. Illustrated English Social History. Il-
      lustrations Chosen by Ruth C. Wright. 4 vol. London, New
      York: Longmans, Green and Co., 1949-1952.
      ICU.

2676 Troller, George Stephen. "Expressionism and the Medieval Play."
      M.A. Columbia University, 1949.

2677 Carpenter, N. C. "Musicians in Early University Drama." Notes
      and Queries, CXCV (1950), 470-472.

2678 Coghill, Nevill. "The Basis of Shakespearian Comedy: A Study in
      Medieval Affinities." Essays and Studies, III (1950), 1-21.

2679 Craddock, Lawrence G., O.F.M. "Franciscan Influences on
      Early English Drama." M.A. Catholic University of America,
      1950.

2680 Elrod, James F. "The Influence of the Roman Mime on the Theatre
      and the Drama in France, England, and Italy Between 1000 and
      1500." M.A. University of Indiana, 1950.

2681 Feldman, Abraham. "Dutch Influence in the Tudor Theatre."
      Ph.D. University of Pennsylvania, 1950.

2682 Krzyzanowski, Julius. "Conjectural Remarks on Elizabethan
      Dramatists." Notes and Queries, CXCV (1950), 400-402.

2683 Lee, Nancy. "Analysis and Models of Wagon and Simultaneous
      Stages of the Medieval Theatre." M.F.A. Carnegie Institute
      of Technology, 1950.

2684 Oakeshott, Walter. The Sequence of English Medieval Art. Lon-
      don: Faber & Faber, Ltd., 1950. xi, 55 pp. 56 Plates. Index.
      BM.

*2685 Rossiter, Arthur Percival. English Drama from Early Times to
      the Elizabethans: Its Background, Origins, and Development.
      London, New York: Hutchinson's University Library, 1950.
      176 pp. Bibliographical references, pp. 164-169.
      BM. DFo. ICN. MnU. PU.

2686 Sayles, George O. The Medieval Foundations of England. 2nd
      ed. rev. London: Methuen, 1950. xxv, 482 pp.
      BM.

2687 Aldus, Paul John. "The Use of Physical Comic Means in English
        Drama from 1420-1603." Ph.D. University of Chicago, 1951.

2688 Cormican, L. A. "Medieval Idiom in Shakespeare. I: Shakespeare
        and the Liturgy. II. Shakespeare and the Medieval Ethic."
        Scrutiny, XVII (1951), 186-202, 298-317.

2689 Laver, James. Drama, Its Costume and Decor. London: Studio,
        1951. 276 pp. Bibliography, pp. 267-272. Index.
              BM.

2690 Lord, John Bigelow. "Certain Dramatic Devices Studied in the
        Comedies of Shakespeare and in Some of the Works of His Con-
        temporaries and Predecessors." Ph.D. University of Illinois,
        1951. 296 pp.

2691 Stamm, Rudolf. Geschichte des englischen Theaters. Bern: Francke,
        1951. 483 pp. Bibliographical references in "Anmerkungen," pp.
        417-453. "Ausgewählte Bibliographie," pp. [452]-458.
              BM. DFo. ICN. MiU.

2692 Bowen, Hoyt E. "The Stage with an Apron; Its History, Develop-
        ment and Significance for the Modern Theatre." M.A. Columbia
        University, 1952.

2693 Cazamian, Louis. The Development of English Humor. Part I: From
        the Early Times to the Renaissance; Part II: The Renaissance.
        Durham, North Carolina: Duke University Press, 1952. viii,
        421 pp. Index.
              BM. NN.

2694 Dreuth, Shirley Mae. "Theatrical Elements in the Staging of the
        Medieval Drama." B.A. University of Illinois, 1952.

2695 James, D. J., ed. Universities and the Theatre. With an Intro-
        duction by Tyrone Guthrie. London: George Allen, 1952.
        vii, 115 pp.
              BM. NN.

2696 Radford, Cecily. "Medieval Actresses." Theatre Notebook, VII
        (1952-1953), 48.

*2697 Southern, Richard. Changeable Scenery, Its Origin and Develop-
        ment in the British Theatre. London: Faber and Faber [1952].
        411 pp.
              BM. NN.

2698 Boughner, Daniel C. "Retribution in English Medieval Drama."
      Notes and Queries, CXCVIII (December, 1953), 506-508.

*2699 Curtius, Ernest Robert. European Literature and the Latin Mid-
      dle Ages. Translated by Willard R. Trask. London: Routledge
      & Kegan Paul, 1953. xv, 662 pp. Index.
              BM.

2700 Hayden, A. R. P. "The Development of the Technique of Comedy
      in Early English Drama." M.A. University of Wales, 1953-
      1954.

2701 Krempel, Daniel Sparlatus. "The Theatre in Relation to Art and
      to the Social Order from the Middle Ages to the Present."
      Ph.D. University of Illinois, 1953.

2702 McDonnell, Sister Mary. "Medieval Drama in Catholic Colleges."
      America, LXXXIX (June 20, 1953), 320-321.

2703 Sutherland, Raymond C., Jr. "Conceptions of Hell in Medieval
      Literature As Developed from Biblical, Patriotic, and Native
      Germanic Sources." Ph.D. University of Kentucky, 1953.

2704 Wickham, G. W. G. "Medieval Pageantry and the Court and Public
      Stages of the Sixteenth and Seventeenth Centuries." D. Phil.
      Oxford University (New College), 1953.

*2705 Boughner, Daniel C. The Braggart in Renaissance Comedy: A
      Study in Comparative Drama from Aristophanes to Shakespeare.
      Minneapolis: University of Minnesota Press, 1954. ix, 328 pp.
              BM. NN.

2706 Cunnington, C[ecil] Willett, and Phillis. Handbook of English Costume
      in the Sixteenth Century. With Illustrations by Barbara Phillipson.
      London: Faber and Faber, Ltd., 1954. 224 pp. "Sources," pp.
      206-209.
              BM. DLC.

*2707 Doran, Madeleine. Endeavors of Art: A Study of Form in Elizabethan
      Drama. Madison: University of Wisconsin Press, 1954. xv, 482
      pp.
              BM. ICN. NN.

2708 Enright-Clark, Doris. "Liber Apologeticus de Omni Statu Humanae
      Naturae by Thomas Chandler. Edited with an Introduction and

Notes." Ph.D. Bryn Mawr University, 1954.

2709 Hieatt, A. Kent. "Medieval Symbolism and the Dramatic Imagery of the English Renaissance." Ph.D. Columbia University, 1954.

2710 Kesler, Charlotte R. "The Importance of the Comic Tradition of English Drama in the Interpretation of Marlowe's Doctor Faustus." Ph.D. University of Missouri, 1954.

2711 Krempel, Daniel S. "The Theatre in Relation to Art and to the Social Order from the Middle Ages to the Present." Speech Monographs, XXI (1954), 195-196.

2712 McKinney, Treysa Dorene Seely. "A Study of the Background and History of the Medieval Drama in France and England." M.A. Baylor University, 1954.

2713 Radford, Cecily. "Medieval Actresses." Devon and Cornwall Notes and Queries, XXVI (1954), 26.

*2714 Anderson, Lady Mary Désirée Cox. The Imagery of British Churches. London: John Murray, 1955. xvi, 224 pp. Bibliography & Notes, pp. 195-216. Index.
BM.

2715 Carter, Joel Jackson. "English Dramatic Music to the Seventeenth Century and Its Availability for Modern Productions." Ph.D. Stanford University, 1955.

2716 Clark, William Smith. The Early Irish Stage. Oxford: Clarendon Press, 1955. x, 227 pp.
BM.

*2717 Craig, Hardin. English Religious Drama of the Middle Ages. Oxford: At the Clarendon Press, 1955. vi, 421 pp. Bibliography, pp. [390]-401. Index.
BM. CtY. DFo. DLC. ICN. ICU. MH. MiU. NN. OC1. PU.

2718 Freedley, George, and John A. Reeves. A History of the Theatre. Rev. ed. New York: Crown Publisher, Inc., [1955]. xvi, 784 pp.
BM. NN.

2719 Gordon, Max. "Medieval Tales." Contemporary Review,
      CLXXXVIII (1955), 106-109.

2720 Herrick, Marvin Theodore. Tragicomedy. Its Origin and Develop-
      ment in Italy, France, and England. Urbana: University of
      Illinois Press, 1955. vii, 331 pp. (Illinois Studies in Language
      and Literature. Vol. 39). [Reissued in 1962.]
      BM.

2721 Macgowan, Kenneth, and William Melnitz. The Living Stage: A
      History of the World Theatre. Englewood Cliffs, New Jersey:
      Prentice-Hall, Inc., 1955. xx, 543 pp.
      BM. NN.

2722 Tristram, Ernest William. English Wall Painting of the Fourteen-
      the Century. Edited by Eileen Tristram, with a Catalogue by
      E. W. Tristram. Compiled in Collaboration with Monica
      Bardswell. London: Routledge & Paul [1955]. xi, 311 pp.
      ICU.

2723 Wimsatt, Jr., W. K., ed. English Stage Comedy. New York:
      Columbia University Press, 1955. x, 182 pp. (English Institute
      Essays. 1954).
      NN.

2724 Arnold, Hugh. Stained Glass in the Middle Ages in England and
      France. New York: Macmillan Co., 1956. xiv, 269 pp. [Re-
      print of the 1939 edition.]
      BM. NN.

2725 Carter, Joel Jackson. "English Dramatic Music to the Seventeenth
      Century, and Its Availability for Modern Productions." Ph.D.
      Stanford University, 1956. [Delete 2715].

2726 Coggin, Philip A. Drama and Education: An Historical Survey from
      Greece to the Present Day. London: Thames and Hudson, 1956.
      vi, 327 pp.
      BM. NN.

*2727 Cohen, Gustave. "Le vocabulaire de la scénologie medievale."
      Zeitschrift für französische Sprache und Literatur, LXVI
      (1956), 15-21.

2728 Kleinstuck, Johannes. "Die mittelalterliche Tragödie in England."
      Euphorion, L (1956), 177-195.

2729 MacCarthy, S. "Shakespeare the Medievalist." Irish Ecclesiastical
     Review, LXXXIV (September, 1956), 193-200.

2730 Bridges-Adams, W. The Irresistible Theatre. Volume I. From
     the Conquest to the Commonwealth. London: Secker & Warburg,
     1957. xiv, 446 pp. Index.
     BM.

*2731 Farnham, Willard [Edward]. The Medieval Heritage of Elizabethan
     Tragedy. 1st Edition Reprinted with Corrections. Oxford:
     Blackwell, 1956. [i.e., January, 1957]. xiv, 487 pp. Index.
     [Original edition, 1936.]
     BM. NN.

2732 Lombardo, Agostino. Il Dramma Pre-Shakespeariano: Studi sul
     Teatro Inglese del Medioevo al Rinascimento. Venice: Neri
     Pozza Editora, 1957. viii, 224 pp.
     BM.

2733 Spivac, Bernard. "Falstaff and the Psychomachia." Shakespeare
     Quarterly, VIII (Fall, 1957), 449-459.

2734 Stamm, Rudolf. Englische Literatur. Bern: A. Francke, 1957.
     422 pp. Index. (Wissenschaftliche Forschungsberichte
     Geisteswissenschaftliche Reihe. Herausgegeben von Professor
     Dr. Karl Hönn. Band II). [See, "Theater und Drama bis 1642,"
     pp. 70-140.]
     O.

2735 Taylor, William Edwards. "The Villainess in Elizabethan Drama."
     Ph.D. Vanderbilt University, 1957.

2736 Braun, Margaret. "Das Drama vor Shakespeare und seine Bezie-
     hungen zum Publikum." Shakespeare Jahrbuch, XCIV (1958),
     191-199.

2737 Cuddon, J. A. B. "The Transition from the Late Medieval to the
     Renaissance Conceptions of Satan in English Literature with
     Especial Reference to the Drama." B. Litt. University of Ox-
     ford (Brasenose), 1958-1959.

2738 Gardiner, H. C. "First Stage: Recording by BBC." Discussion,
     C (October, 1958), 1.

*2739 Harrison, Frank L. Music in Medieval Britain. London: Routledge

and Kegan Paul, 1958. xix, [1], 491 pp. Bibliography, pp. 440-453. Index.
    O.

2740 Jewkes, Wilfred T. Act Division in Elizabethan and Jacobean Plays 1583-1616. Hamden, Connecticut: Shoe String Press, 1958. x, 374 pp. Bibliography, pp. 353-372.

2741 Poole, Austin Lane, ed. Medieval England. 2 vol. Oxford: Clarendon Press, 1958.
    BM.

*2742 Stevens, John. "Music in Medieval English Drama." Proceedings of the Royal Musical Association, LXXXIV (1958), 81-95.

2743 Auerbach, Erich. Scenes from the Drama of European Literature. Six Essays. New York: Meridian Books, 1959. 249 pp. (Meridian Books, M 63). [See, "Figura."]
    NN.

2744 Gibbs, Lloyd Graham. "A History of the Development of the Dumb Show As a Dramatic Convention." Ph.D. University of South Carolina, 1959.

2745 Jenkins, D. R. "The Antagonist: the Nature and Function of Oppositive Characters in Medieval Religious Drama. The Consideration of a Specific Problem of Characterization in an Attempt to Establish Certain Criteria upon Which a Critical Evaluation of the Texts May Be Found." M.A. University of Wales (Cardiff), 1959-1960.

2746 Klenke, Sister M. Amelia. "The 'Christus Domini' Concept of Medieval Art and Literature." Studies in Philology, LVI (January, 1959), 14-25.

2747 Martin, Charles Basil. "The Survivals of Medieval Religious Drama in New Mexico." Ph.D. University of Missouri, 1959.

2748 McKisack, May. The Fourteenth Century 1307-1399. Oxford: Clarendon Press, 1959. xix, 598 pp. Bibliography, pp. 533-566. Index. (Oxford History of England. Vol. 5).
    BM.

2749 Moe, Christian Hollis. "From History to Drama: A Study of the Influence of the Pageant, the Outdoor Epic Drama, and the

Historical Stage Play upon the Dramatization of Three American Historical Figures." Ph.D. Cornell University, 1959.

2750 Niva, Weldon N. "Significant Character Names in English Drama to 1603." Ph.D. University of Pennsylvania, 1959.

2751 Richmond, Vilma E. Bourgeois. "The Development of the Rhetorical Death Lament from the Late Middle Ages to Marlowe." Ph.D. University of North Carolina, 1959.

2752 Robinson, James Edward. "The Dramatic Unities in the Renaissance: A Study of the Principles, with Application to the Development of English Drama." Ph.D. University of Illinois, 1959.

*2753 Robinson, J. W. "Medieval English Acting." Theatre Notebook, XIII (Spring, 1959), 83-88.

2754 Tucker, Susie I. "Laughter in Old English Literature." Neophilologus, XLIII (1959), 222-226.

*2755 Wickham, Glynne. Early English Stages: 1300 to 1600. Vol. I. 1300 to 1576. 2 vol. London: Routledge and Kegan Paul; New York: Columbia University Press, 1959-1963.
BM. CtY. DFo. DLC. ICN. ICU. IU. MB. MH. NN. O. OCl. PU.

2756 Burton, Ernest James. The British Theatre; Its Repertory and Practice, 100-1900 A.D. Illustrated by Anne Brighton. London: H. Jenkins [1960]. 271 pp. Bibliography, pp. 259-262.
BM. NN.

2757 Gibbs, Lloyd Graham. "A History of the Development of the Dumb Show As a Dramatic Convention." Ph.D. University of South Carolina, 1960. [Delete 2744].

2758 Kernodle, George R. "Seven Medieval Theatres in One Social Structure." Theatre Review, II (1960), 26-36.

2759 Orr, David. "The Influence of Learned Italian Drama of the Sixteenth Century on English Drama before 1623." Ph.D. University of North Carolina, 1960.

2760 Putzel, Rosamond. "Structural Patterns in the Repertory of the Child Actors Through 1591." Ph.D. University of North Carolina, 1960.

2761 Stambusky, Alan A., Jr. "Toward Modern Perspective: Political and Ecclesiastical Origins of Dramatic Censorship." Ph.D. University of Wisconsin, 1960.

2762 Young, William Donald. "Devices and 'Feintes' of the Medieval Religious Theatre in England and France." Ph.D. Stanford University, 1960.

2763 Campos, Helen Kershner. "An Historical Study of English Pageant Wagon Dramaturgy with Suggestions for Effective Modern Presentation." M.A. University of Southern California, 1961.

2764 Clemen, Wolfgang. English Tragedy before Shakespeare. Translated from the German by T. S. Dorsch. London: Methuen and Company, 1961. 301 pp. Bibliography, pp. 293-294.
BM.

2765 Cook, David, ed., with Assistance from F. P. Wilson. Dramatic Records in the Declared Accounts of the Chamber 1558-1642. Malone Society. Collections. VI. 1961 (1962). xxviii, [2], 192 pp.

2766 Edwards, Ralph Williams. "Shakespearean Laughter: A Study of Shakespeare's Basis of Laughter and Their Implications." Ph.D. Boston University, 1961.

2767 Peet, Alice Lida. "The History and Development of Simultaneous Scenery in the West from the Middle Ages to Modern United States." Ph.D. University of Wisconsin, 1961.

2768 Stevens, John Edgard. Music and Poetry in the Early Tudor Court. London: Methuen & Co., 1961. xi, 483 pp.
BM.

*2769 Williams, Arnold. The Drama of Medieval England. East Lansing, Michigan: Michigan State University Press, 1961. 186 pp.
BM. CtY. DFo. DLC. ICN. ICU. IU. MH. NN. NNC. OCl. PU.

2770 Williamson, Ward. "Notes on the Decline of Provincial Drama in England, 1530-1642." Educational Theatre Journal, XIII (December, 1961), 280-288.

2771 Zesmer, David M. Guide to English Literature from Beowulf Through Chaucer and Medieval Drama. New York: Barnes and Noble, Inc., 1961. xi, 397 pp.

BM. DLC. ICU. MH.

*2772 Bradbrook, Muriel C. The Rise of the Common Player. A Study
of Actor and Society in Shakespeare's England. London:
Chatto & Windus, 1962. 320 pp.
BM.

2773 Roberts, Vera Mowry. On Stage: A History of Theatre. New York:
Harper & Row, 1962. 534 pp.
NN.

2774 Gousseff, James William. "The Staging of Prologues in Tudor
and Stuart Plays." Ph.D. Northwestern University, 1962.

2775 Ives, E. W. "In Aid of the Restoration Fund: A Medieval Example."
Notes and Queries, New Ser., IX (May, 1962), 162-163.

2776 Robinson, John W. "Medieval English Dramaturgy." Ph.D. University of Glasgow, 1962.

2777 Testar, Gerald. "An Experimental Theatre Series Presentation
of Selected Medieval Dramas with Wagon-Staging." M.F.A.
University of Portland, 1962.

2778 Britain, Kilbee Cormack. "The Sin of Despair in English Renaissance Literature." Ph.D. University of California (Los Angeles),
1963.

2779 Burton, Ernest James. The Student's Guide to the British Theatre
and Drama. Illustrated by Diana Quin. London: H. Jenkins,
1963. 191 pp. Bibliography, pp. 177-186.
BM. NN.

2780 Clunes, Alec Sheriff de Moro. The British Theatre. London: Cassell, 1963. 187 pp.
BM. NN.(1964)

2781 Joseph, Stephen. The Story of the Playhouse in England. London:
Barrie and Rockliff [1963]. xiv, 156 pp.
BM. NN.

2782 Lehmann, Paul Joachim Georg. Die Parodie im Mittelalter. Mit
24 ausgewählten parodistischen Texten. 2nd ed. Stuttgart:
A. Hiersemann, 1963. 267 pp.
ICN.

2783 Lev, Don David. "The Production of a Medieval Drama for the
Modern Audience." M.A. University of Oregon, 1963.

2784 Martin, Jo Ann. "The Secularization of the English Play." Ph.D.
Stanford University, 1963.

*2785 Ogilvy, J. D. "Mimi, Scurrae, Histriones: Entertainers of the
Early Middle Ages." Speculum, XXXVIII (October, 1963), 603-
619.

2786 Ross, Lawrence J. "Art and Study of Early English Drama."
Renaissance Drama, VI (1963), 35-46.

2787 Armstrong, William A. "Shakespeare and the Medieval Stage."
English, XV (Summer, 1964), 46-49.

2788 Bergeron, David Moore. "Allegory in English Pageantry 1558-
1625." Ph.D. Vanderbilt University, 1964.

*2789 Bowles, E. A. "Musical Instruments in the Medieval Corpus
Christi Procession." Journal of the American Musicological
Society, XVII (1964), 251-260.

2790 Galambos, Peter. "Classical and Secular Influences on Medieval
Drama." M.A. Syracuse University, 1964.

*2791 Harbage, Alfred. Annals of English Drama 975-1700. An Analytical
Record of All Plays, Extant Or Lost, Chronologically Arranged
and Indexed By Authors, Titles, Dramatic Companies, &c.
Revised by S. Schoenbaum. London: Methuen & Co., Ltd.,
1964. xvii, [1], 321, [2] pp. Index. [First edition, 1940.]
BM. CSmH. DFo. DLC. ICN. ICU. MH. NN. O. PU.

2792 Marsh, Joel Brace. "A Plan for the Design and Construction of
Stage Armor and Weapons for the Thirteenth Through the
Fifteenth Century." M.A. University of Indiana, 1964.

2793 McCollom, William G. "From Dissonance to Harmony: The Evolution
of Early English Comedy." Theatre Annual, XXI (1964), 69-96.

2794 Roston, Murray. "Shakespeare and the Biblical Drama." Iowa
English Yearbook, No. 9 (1964), 36-43.

2795 Siebert, Paul Earl. "A Study of English Costume, 1277 to 1668,
As Illustrated by a Progressive Compilation of Plates on Monu-

mental Brasses." M.A. University of Southern California,
1964.

2796 Bentley, Eric Russell. The Life of the Drama. New York: Athen-
eum Press, 1965. ix, 371 pp. Bibliography, pp. 355-359.
BM.

2797 Bradbrook, Muriel Clara. English Dramatic Form: A History
of Its Development. London: Chatto and Windus, 1965. xii,
13-205 pp.
BM. DLC. ICU. MH. NNC. PU.

2798 Kigata, Yosuki. English Drama before Shakespeare. Kyoto:
Apollon-sha, 1965. 637 pp.

2799 Knight, George Wilson. The Golden Labyrinth: A Study of British
Drama. London: Methuen, 1965. xiv, 402 pp.
BM. ICU. MH.

2800 Littlefield, Robert Lee. "Knowledge, Opinion, and Tragedy.
A Survey from Mythic Origins to Elizabethan Tragedy." Ph.D.
Texas Technological College, 1965.

2801 McAlindon, T. "Comedy and Terror in Middle English Literature:
The Diabolical Game." Modern Language Review, LX (1965),
323-332.

2802 Rosenfeld, Hellmut. "Der Totentanz als europäisches Phänomen."
Archiv für Kulturgeschichte, XLVIII (1966), 54-83.

2803 Axton, Richard. "Early Medieval Drama." Ph.D. Cambridge
University, 1967.

2804 Johnston, Alexandra F. "Medieval Drama in England--1966."
Queen's Quarterly, LXXIV (1967), 78-91.

*2805 Margesons, John Malcolm Russell. The Origins of English Tragedy.
Oxford: Clarendon Press, 1967. xiii, 195 pp.
BM.

2806 Staniforth, Gwendolyn E. "The Description of Character in English Drama, 1475-1575." Ph.D. University of California (Los
Angeles), 1967.

2807 Thornly, Eva M. "The Middle English Penitential Lyric and Hoc-

cleve's Autobiographical Poetry." Neuphilologische Mitteilungen, LXVIII (1967), 295-321.

2808 Tobin, Terence. "The Beginnings of Drama in Scotland." Theatre
Survey, VIII (May, 1967), 1-16.

2809 Weimann, Robert. "Die furchtbare Komik des Herodes: Drama-
turgie und Figurenaufbau des vorshakespeareschen Schurken."
Archiv, CCIV (1967), 113-123.

2810 Whitney, Dixie D. "A Slide Set with Accompanying Script on
Medieval Theatre on Statistical Results Proving the Educational Validity." M.A. Syracuse University, 1967.

2811 Wickham, Glynne. "Emblème et image: Quelques remarques sur
la manière de figurer et de représenter le lieu sur la scène
anglaise au XVIe siècle." In, Jacquot, Jean, avec la collab.
d'Elie Konigson et Marcel Oddon. Le lieu théâtral à la Renaissance. (Paris, 1964), pp. 317-322.

*2812 Young, Percy M. A History of British Music. London: Ernest Benn
Limited, 1967. xi, [1], 641 pp. Index.
          O.

2813 Berger, Harry, Jr. "Theater, Drama, and the Second World: a
Prologue to Shakespeare." Comparative Drama, II (1968), 3-20.

2814 Greenhoe, Joe A. "The Alien Hero: A Study of the Rhetoric of
Mutilation in Cult, Ritual and Early Drama." Ph.D. Tulane
University, 1968.

*2815 Hosley, Richard. "The Origins of the So-Called Elizabethan Mul-
tiple Stage." The Drama Review, XII, No. 2 (1968), 28-50.

2816 Huganir, Kathryn. "Medieval Theatres." Theatre Annual, XXIII
(1968), 34-35.

2817 Kaplan, Joel H., and George Shand. "The 'Poculi Ludique Societas': Medieval Drama at the University of Toronto." Research
Opportunities in Renaissance Drama, XI (1968), 141-161.

2818 Kinghorn, A. M. Mediaeval Drama. London: Evans Brothers, Ltd.,
1968. 160 pp. Bibliography, pp. 153-157. Index. (Literature
in Perspective).
          BM.

2819   Long, John H. Music in English Renaissance Drama. Lexington:
       University of Kentucky Press, 1968. xvi, 184 pp. [See the es-
       say by Nan C. Carpenter, "Music in the English Mystery
       Plays."]

2820   Meagher, John C. "The First Progress of Henry VII." Renais-
       sance Drama, New Ser., I (1968), 45-73.

2821   Nicholson, Jack L. "The Medieval Mystery, Miracle, and
       Morality Plays and Their Twentieth-Century Counterparts."
       M.A. University of Tulsa, 1968.

2822   Prater, Neal B. "The Origin of English Tragicomedy and Its
       Development before Shakespeare." Ph.D. Vanderbilt Uni-
       versity, 1968.

*2823 Smoldon, William. "The Melodies of the Medieval Church Dramas
       and Their Significance." Comparative Drama, II (Fall, 1968),
       185-209.

2824   Solá-Sole, J. M. "En torno a 'La danca general de la muerte.'"
       Hispanic Review, XXXVI (October, 1968), 303-327.

2825   Wickham, Glynne. Shakespeare's Dramatic Heritage: Collected
       Studies in Mediaeval, Tudor and Shakespearean Drama. New
       York: Barnes and Noble, 1969. xviii, 271 pp.

2826   Wilson, F. P. "The Vice." The English Drama 1485-1585. (Ox-
       ford, 1969), pp. 59-66.

   D   Mystery and Miracle Plays (Vernacular Drama)

       1 General Studies

2827   Prynne, William. Histrio-Mastix. London: Printed by E. A. and
       W. I. for Michael Sparke, 1633. 1006 pp.
           BM. CSmH. DFo. ICN. MH. NjP. OClW. PU. TxU.

2828   Stevens, John. Appendix to Dugdale's Monasticon (1722). Vol. I,
       538 pp. London: [For various booksellers].
           BM.

2829   "Mysteries, Moralities and Other Early Dramas." Retrospective
       Review, I (1820), 332-357.

*2830 Hone, William. Ancient Mysteries Described, Especially the
        English Miracle Plays, Founded on the Apocryphal New
        Testament Story, Extant Among the Unpublished Manuscripts
        in the British Museum. Including Notices of Ecclesiastical
        Shows. London: Printed for W. Hone, 1823. [2], x, [2], [13]-298
        pp.
                BM. CSmH. CtY. ICN. MnU. NN. OU. PU. ViU. WU.

2831   Sharp, Thomas. "Processions on Corpus Christi Day, Midsummer
        and St. Peter's Eves." A Dissertation on the Pageants or Dra-
        matic Mysteries Anciently Performed at Coventry. (Coventry,
        1825), pp. 159-206.

2832   "Sharp's Dissertation on the Pageants or Dramatic Mysteries."
        Retrospective Review, XIII (1826), 297-316.

2833   Collier, John Payne. The History of English Dramatic Poetry to
        the Time of Shakespeare; and Annals of the Stage to the Resto-
        ration. 3 vol. London: J. Murray, 1831.
                BM. CtY. ICN. MB. MiU. NjP. NN. OC1W. PU. ViU.

2834   Marriott, William. "An Historical View of English Miracle-
        Plays or Mysteries." A Collection of English Miracle-Plays
        Or Mysteries ... (Basel, 1838), pp. vii-lxiii.

*2835 Wright, Thomas, ed. Early Mysteries and Latin Poems of the
        Twelfth and Thirteenth Centuries. London: Nichols and Son,
        1838. 135 pp.
                BM. MB. MdBP. MiU. NjP. NNUT. OC1. OC1W.

2836   "A Poem Against the Friars and Their Miracle-Plays." In,
        Wright, Thomas, and James Orchard Halliwell, eds. Reli-
        quiae Antiquae. Vol. I. (London, 1841), pp. 322-323. [From
        M. S. Cotton. Cleop. B. ii. of the 15th century.]

2837   "A Sermon Against Miracle-Plays." In, Wright, Thomas, and
        James Orchard Halliwell, eds. Reliquiae Antiquae. Vol. II.
        (London, 1841), pp. 42-57. ["From a MS volume of English
        Sermons written at the latter end of the fourteenth Century."
        --Library of St. Martin's-in-the-Fields, London.]

*2838 Wright, Thomas and J. O. Halliwell, ed. Reliquiae Antiquae;
        Scraps from Ancient Manuscripts, Illustrating Chiefly Early
        English Literature and English Language. 2 vol. London: W.
        Pickering, 1841-1843.

BM. CSmH. ICN. MiU. NjP. NN. NNC. ODW. PPL.

2839 Weber, Paul. Geistliches Schauspiel und kirchliche Kunst in
ihrem Verhältnis erläutert an einer Ikonographie der Kirche
und Synagoge. Stuttgart, [1844]. 152 pp.
ICN. WU.

2840 Collier, John Payne. "The Performance of Dramas by Parish
Clerks and Players in Churches." Shakespeare Society
Papers, III (1847), 40-47.

*2841 Coussemaker, Charles Edmond Henrii de. Histoire de l'har-
monie au moyen âge. Paris: V. Didron, 1852. 374 pp. Bibliography, pp. 211-222.
BM. CtY. ICN. MdBP. MiU. NN. OC1. PB. PU.

2842 Bell, Robert. Ancient Poems, Ballads, and Songs of the Peasantry
of England. London: J. W. Parker and Son, 1857. 252 pp.
BM. ICN. MB. MdBP. NjP. NB. NN. OC1. PBm.

*2843 Hase, Karl. Das geistliche Schauspiel. Geschichtliche Ueber-
sicht. Leipzig: Druch und Verlag von Breitkopf und Hartel,
1858. xii [4], 320 pp. [Translated by A. W. Jackson and published in London in 1880.]
BM. NN. OC1. OO. PHC. PU.

2844 Ebert. Adolf. "Die englischen Mysterien." Jahrbuch für romanische und englische Sprache und Literatur, I (1859), 44-82;
130-170.

2845 "Mediaeval Theatricals." Knickerbocker, LXIII (1864), 237-
247.

2846 P. "The Dance of Death as a Mystery." Temple Bar, XII (1864),
292-302.

2847 Le grand mystère de Jésus, passion et resurrection; drame
breton du moyen âge avec une étude sur le théâtre Chez les
nations celtiques, par le vecomte Hersart de la Villemarqué
...2. éd. Paris: Didier et Cie, 1866. [2], cxxxv, 263 pp.
ICU.

2848 Cahour, A. "Dramatic Mysteries of the Fifteenth and Sixteenth
Centuries." Catholic World, I (1867), 577-598.

2849 [Smeken, Jan], supposed author. Dit is Tspel vanden heiligen
　　　sacramente vaneler nyeuwervaert. Uitg. en met aanteeken-
　　　ingen voorzien door Dr. Eelco Verwijs. Leeuwarden: H.
　　　Suringar, 1867. [4], viii, 107 pp.
　　　　　ICU.

2850 Froude, James Anthony. "The Mystery Plays." History of Eng-
　　　land, from the Fall of Wolsey to the Death of Elizabeth. Vol.
　　　I. (New York, 1868), pp. 73-78.
　　　　　NN.

2851 Reville, Albert. "Le drame religieux du moyen âge jusqu à
　　　nos jours." Revue des Deux Mondes, LXXVI (1868), 84-119.

2852 "Mystery or Passion Plays." Blackwood's Edinburgh Magazine,
　　　CVI (1869), 671-693.

2853 MacColl, Malcolm. The Ammergau Passion Play. With Some
　　　Introductory Remarks on the Origin and Development of
　　　Miracle Plays, and Some Practical Hints for the Use of In-
　　　tending Visitors. London: Rivington, 1870. 84 pp.
　　　　　BM. MB (also 1871 edition).

2854 [Anon.]. "Mysteries and Plays of the Middle Ages." Colburn's
　　　New Monthly Magazine, CLXVIII (1871), 667-668.

2855 P., J. "Mysteries, or Miracle Plays." Dublin University Mag-
　　　azine, LXXXVIII (1871), 361-373.

2856 Hudson, Henry Norman. "Miracle Plays." Shakespeare. Vol. 1.
　　　(Boston, 1872), pp. 55-71.

2857 Wülcker, Richard P. Das Evangelium Nicodemi in der abend-
　　　ländischen Literatur. Nebst drei Excursen über Joseph von
　　　Arimathia als Apostel Englands, das Drama Harrowing of
　　　Hell und Jehan Michels Passion Christ. Paderborn: F. Schön-
　　　ingh, 1872. vi, [2], 101 pp.
　　　　　BM. ICU.

2858 Klein, Julius Leopold. Geschichte des Dramas. 13 vol. Leipzig:
　　　T. O. Weigel, 1875-1876.
　　　　　BM. DLC. IaU. ICN. MiU. MnU. NN. PSC. WU.

2859 Verney, Lady F. P. "Mysteries, Moralities, and the Drama."
　　　Contemporary Review, XXV (1875), 595-609.

2860 Genée, Rudolf. Die englischen Mirakelspiele und Moralitäten
      als Vorläufer des englischen Dramas. Berlin: Carl Habel,
      1878. 32 pp.
           BM. ICN. MB. ICU. NcD. NN. OCl.

*2861 Sepet, Marius Cyrille Alphonse. Le Drame Chrétien au moyen
      âge. Paris: Didier et Cie., 1878. xii, 296 pp.
           BM. IaU. MB. MnU. NjP. NN. OCl. PSC. PU. WaU.

2862 Sheppard, J. P. "The Canterbury Marching Watch with Its
      Pageant of St. Thomas." Archaeologia Cantiana, XII (1878),
      27-46.

2863 Rovenhagen, Ludwig. Alt-englische Dramen. Die geistlichen
      Schauspiele. [Aachen, Palm, 1879]. 39 pp.
           MB. MH.

*2864 Hase, Karl. Miracle Plays and Sacred Dramas. A Historical
      Survey. Translated from the German by A. W. Jackson. Lon-
      don: Trübner & Co., 1880. x, [2], 273 pp.
           BM. DLC. ICN. MH. MiU. NjP. OCl. PHC. WU.

2865 [Anon.]. "Passion Plays." Colburn's New Monthly Magazine,
      CLXVII (1880), 1-12.

2866 Jusserand, Jean Adrien Antoine Jules. "Les mystères." Le
      Théâtre en Angleterre depuis la conquête. 2nd ed. (Paris,
      1881), pp. 39-106.

2867 Marin, William. At the Ober-Ammergau Passion Play. With an
      Introduction on the Ancient Mysteries. A lecture delivered
      on July 8, 1881. Buenos Ayres: Lowe, Anderson & Ca. [1881?].
      22 pp.
           MB.

2868 Prölss, Karl Robert. Geschichte des neueren Dramas. 5 vol.
      in 6. Leipzig: B. Schlicke, 1881-1883.
           BM. DLC. ICN. MH. MiU. OCl. OCU. OO.

2869 Howlett, Richard, ed. Monumenta Franciscana. Vol. 2. Being
      a Further Collection of Original Documents Respecting the
      Franciscan Order in England. London: Longmans, 1882.
      lxii, 331 pp. (Rerum Britannicarum medii aevi scriptores,
      or, Chronicles and Memorials of Great Britain and Ireland
      During the Middle Ages). [For miracle plays acted by the

Franciscans, see pp. xxviii-xxx.]
BM.

2870 "The Ancient, Mediaeval and Modern Stage." Edinburgh Review,
      CLVIII (1883), 57-89.

2871 Capes, F. J. "Poetry of the English Mysteries." Nineteenth
      Century, XIV (1883), 654-672.

2872 Gierth, F. "Ueber die älteste mittelenglische Version der
      Assumptio Mariae." Englische Studien, VII (1884), 1-33.

2873 A New Study of Shakespeare. An Inquiry into the Connection of
      the Plays and Poems with the Origins of the Drama and with
      Platonic Philosophy through the Mysteries. London: Trübner
      & Co., 1884. 372 pp.
      BM.

2874 Coit, Davida. "The Poetic Element in the Medieval Drama."
      Annales du Midi, LVI (1885), 407-415.

2875 Meyer, Karl. "Geistliches Schauspiel und kirchliche Kunst."
      Vierteljahrsschrift für Kultur und Literatur der Renaissance,
      I (1886), 162-186, 409-439.

*2876 Smith, Lucy Toulmin. A Common-place Book of the Fifteenth
      Century, Containing a Religious Play and Poetry, Legal Forms,
      and Local Accounts Printed from the Original Manuscript at
      Brome Hall, Suffolk, by Lady Caroline Kerrison. London:
      Trübner and Co., 1886. 176 pp.
      BM. ICN. NN.

2877 Hohlfeld, Alexander R. Die altenglischen Killektivmisterien.
      Leipzig: Halle, 1888. 69 pp.
      WU.

*2878 Holthausen, Ferdinand, ed. Vices and Virtues. Being a Soul's
      Confession of Its Sins, with Reason's Description of the
      Virtues. A Middle-English Dialogue of about 1200 A.D.
      Edited with an Introduction. Translation, Notes, and Glossary,
      from the Stowe MS. 240 in the British Museum. 2 vol. London:
      Published for the Early English Text Society by N. Trübner
      and Co., 1888-1921. Paged continuously.
      BM. DLC. IaU. ICN. MnU.

*2879 Creizenach, Wilhelm. Die Schauspiele der englischen Komö-
         dianten. Berlin und Stuttgart: W. Spemann, 1889. cxviii, 352 pp.
         BM. DFo. ICN. MiU. NjP. OCl. OO. PSC. PU.

*2880 Hohlfeld, Alexander R. "Die englischen Kollektiv-Mysterien."
         Anglia, XI (1889), 219-310.

2881   Pollard, Alfred William. "Easter Plays." Guardian, XLIV (1889),
         799-800.

2882   ----- "Old Christmas Plays." Universal Review, V (1889), 517-
         534.

2883   Clodd, Edward. "Miracle Plays." Longman's Magazine, XV (1890),
         621-629. [Reprinted in Eclectic Magazine, LI (1890), 742-746;
         and in Living Age, CLXXXV (1890), 431-436.]

2884   Hohlfeld, Alexander R. "Two Old English Mystery Plays on the
         Subject of Abraham's Sacrifice." Modern Language Notes, V
         (April, 1890), 111-119.

*2885 Bapst, Germain. "Etude sur les mystères au moyen âge. La
         mise en scène. (Suite)." Revue Archéologique, XVIII (1891),
         300-320; XIX (1892?), 193-213.

*2886 Froning, Richard. Das Drama des Mittelalters. Stuttgart: Union
         deutsche Verlagsgesellschaft [1891-1892]. 3 parts. viii, 1008
         pp.
         BM. DLC. ICN. MiU. OCl. OCU. ODW. OO. PSC.

2887   Zeidler, Jacob. Studien und Beiträge zur Geschichte der Jesuiten-
         Komödie und des Klosterdramas. Hamburg und Leipzig: L.
         Voss, 1891. 121 pp.
         CtY.

2888   Davidson, C. "Concerning English Mystery Plays." Modern
         Language Notes, VII (1892), 339-343.

2889   Davidson, Charles. "English Mystery Plays." Ph.D. Yale Uni-
         versity, 1892.

2890   ----- Studies in the English Mystery Plays. New Haven: Yale
         University Press, 1893. 173 pp. Bibliography, pp. [3]-5.
         BM. CSmH. CtY. DLC. ICN. MH. MiU. OU. ViU.
         WU.

2891 Zupitza, Julius. "Iak and His Step Dame." Archiv für Das
      Studium Der Neueren Sprachen und Literaturen, XC (1893),
      57-82.

2892 Green, Alice Stopford. Town Life in the Fifteenth Century. 2
      vol. New York: Macmillan and Co., 1894.
            BM. DFo. ICN. MH. NN. OO. OU. PU. TxU. ViU.

2893 Solymosy, Sandor. "Bethlehem in den Volksmysterien und in der
      Geschichte des Dramas." Egyetemes philologiai közlony,
      XVIII (1894), Hefte 2-4.

2894 Courthope, William John. "The Rise of the Drama in England."
      A History of English Poetry. Vol. 1. (London, 1895), pp.
      393-425.

2895 Harris, Herbert. "Was Paradise Lost Suggested by the Mystery
      Plays?" Modern Language Notes, X (November, 1895), 223.

2896 Kölbing, Eugen. "Kleine Beiträge zur Erklärung und Textkritik
      vor-Shakespeare'scher Dramen." Englische Studien, XXI
      (1895), 162-167.

2897 Bourne, Edward G. "Miracle Plays." Modern Language Notes, XI
      (1896), 124-125.

2898 Hughes, T. Cann. "Miracle Plays." Notes and Queries, Series
      8, X (1896), 364-365.

2899 Clarke, Sidney W. The Miracle Play in England. An Account of
      the Early Religious Drama. London: William Andrews Co.,
      1897. ix, 94 pp.
            BM. CtY. DLC. ICN. MB. MiU. NcU. OCl. PBm. ViU.

2900 Brandl, Alois Leonhard, ed. Quellen des weltlichen Dramas in
      England. Strassburg: K. J. Trübner, 1898. cxxvi, 666 pp.
            BM. CtY. ICN. PU.

2901 Sanborn, Katherine Abbott. "The Old Miracle Plays." My Favorite
      Lectures of Long Ago, for Friends Who Remember. (Boston,
      1898), pp. 174-216.

*2902 Hohlfeld, Alexander R. "Die altenglischen Kollektivmisterien,
      Unter besonderer Berüksichtigung des Verhältnisses der
      York- und Towneley - Spiele." Anglia, XI (1899), 219-310.

2903 Ward, Adolphus William. "Religious Drama in England." A
         History of English Dramatic Literature. Vol. 1. New ed.
         (London, 1899), pp. 40-98.

2904 Wesley, Edmund Alfred. "The English Miracle Play." Literary and
         Philosophical Society of Liverpool. Proceedings, LIII (1899),
         133-152.

*2905 Cushman, Lysander W. The Devil and the Vice in the English
         Dramatic Literature before Shakespeare. Halle, A. S.:
         Max Niemeyer, 1900. xiv, 148 pp.
            BM. ICN. ICU. MB. MiU. NN. OC1. OU. PU. ViU.

2906 Gauss, E. F. L. "The So-Called Mystery Plays." Open Court,
         XIV (1900), 415-421.

2907 Greg, Walter Wilson. "Herod the Great on the English Stage."
         Spectator, LXXXV (1900), 657-658.

2908 Mabie, Hamilton Wright. "The Forerunners of Shakespeare."
         Outlook, LXIV (January 6, 1900), 33-42.

2909 Symonds, John Addington. Shakespeare's Predecessors in the
         English Drama. New edition. London: Smith, Elder and Co.,
         1900. xix, 551 pp.
            BM. DLC. MB. MH. MiU. NjP. NN. OC1W. OO.

2910 Tisdel, Frederick M. "Comedy in the Mystery Plays of England,
         France and Germany." Ph.D. Harvard University, 1900.

2911 Carstensen, Cathrine. Kvindetyper i Middelalderens religiøse
         Skuespil, saerlig de engelske, af Cathrine Carstensen.
         København: Klein, 1901. 105 pp. (Det Filolgiskhistoriske
         Samfund. Studier fra Sprog-og Oldtidsforskning, Nr. 50.)
            BM. ICU. NN. PU.

2912 Davis, R.H. "English Passion Plays." Century Magazine, LXI
         (1901), 622-625.

2913 Jusserand, J. J. "A Note on Pageants and 'Scaffolds Hye,'"
         An English Miscellany Presented to Dr. Furnivall. (Oxford,
         1901).

*2914 Leach, Arthur F. "Some English Plays and Players (1220-1548)."
         In, An English Miscellany Presented to Dr. [F. J.] Furnivall
         in Honor of His Seventy-Fifth Birthday. (Oxford, 1901), pp.
         205-234.

2915 Mannying, Robert of Brunne. Handlyng Synne, A.D. 1303, with
Those Parts of the Anglo-French Treatise on Which It Was
Based, William of Wadington's 'Manuel des pechiez,' re-
edited by F. J. Furnivall. London: K. Paul, Trench, Trübner
and Co., for the Early English Text Society, 1901-1903.
396 pp.
BM. DLC. ICN. MnU. OC1. OCU. OO. PHC. PSC. PU.

2916 Carson, W. R. "Miracle Plays." American Ecclesiastical
Review, XXVII (1902), 141-160.

2917 Cook, Albert A. "A Remote Analogue to the Miracle Plays."
Journal of English and Germanic Philology, IV (1902), 421-
451.
2918 Eckhardt, Eduard. Die lustige Person im älteren englischen
Drama. Berlin: Mayer and Muller, 1902. xxxii, 478 pp.
Bibliography, pp. xii-xviii.
BM. ICN. MH. MiU. NjP. OCU. ODW. PU. ViU.

2919 Bateson, Mary. Medieval England: English Feudal Society from
the Norman Conquest to the Middle of the Fourteenth Century. New York: G. P. Putnam's Sons; London: T. F. Unwin,
1903. xxvii, 448 pp.
BM. ICN. MB. MiU. NjP. OC1. OU. PU. ViU.

2920 Becker, Maria Louise. "Maria Magdalena in der Kunst." Bühne
und Welt. Zeitschreft für Theaterwesen, Literatur und Musik,
5 Jg. (1903), 975-990, 1019-1030. Berlin.

*2921 Chambers, E. K. "Guild Plays and Parish Plays." The Mediaeval
Stage. Vol. II. (London, 1903), pp. 106-148.

*2922 ----- The Medieval Stage. 2 vol. Oxford: Clarendon Press,
1903.
BM. CSmH. CtY. ICN. ICU. MH. MiU. NjP. NN. OU.
PU.

2923 Mathews, Brander. "The Medieval Drama." Modern Philology,
I (1903), 71-94.

2924 ----- "The Medieval Drama." The Development of the Drama.
(New York, 1903), 107-146.

2925 Morgan, Stella Webster. Study of the Noah and Isaac Miracle
Plays, with Reference to Their Sources and Anachronisms.

B.A. University of Illinois, 1903.

2926 Schwab, Moise. "Mots hebreux dans les mystères du moyen âge." Revue des Études Juives, XLVI (1903), 148-151.

2927 Strutt, Joseph. The Sports and Pastimes of the People of England: Including the Rural and Domestic Recreations, May Games, Mummeries, Shows, Processions, Pageants, and Pompous Spectacles from the Earliest Period to the Present Time. Edited by W. Hone. London: T. Tegg, 1831. 420 pp. New ed., London: Methuen and Co., [1903], 322 pp. BM. ICN. MB. NjP. OOxM. OU.

2928 Symmes, Harold S. Les Débuts de la critique dramatique en Angleterre. Paris: E. Leroux, 1903. xiv, 276 pp. BM. ICN. MB. MiU. NjP. NN. OCU.

2929 Tisdel, Frederick Monroe. "The Influence of Popular Customs on the Mystery Plays." Journal of English and Germanic Philology, V (1903-1904), 323-340. [Delete 2933].

2930 Gagley, C. M. "The Earlier Miracle Play of England." Independent Quarterly, X (October, 1904), 108-129.

2931 Gothein, Marie. "Die Frau im englischen Drama vor Shakespeare." Shakespeare Jahrbuch, XL (1904), 1-49.

2932 Hooper, E. S. "Processus Torturum; a Suggested Emendation." Athenaeum, August 27, 1904, p. 284.

2933 Tisdel, Frederick M. "Influence of Popular Custom on Mystery Plays." Journal of English and Germanic Philology, V (1904), 323-340.

2934 The Educational Alliance. -- The Dramatic Club of the Thomas Davidson School. [Program and Explanation of the Miracle Plays.] [New York: F. V. Strauss & Co.,], 1905. 2 leaves. NN

2935 Leendertz, Pieter, Jr. "Die Quellen der ältesten mittelenglischen Version der Assumptio Mariae." Englische Studien, V (1905), 350-358.

2936 Emerson, Oliver F. "Legends of Cain." Publications of the Modern Language Association, XXI (1906), 831-838.

2937 Gayley, C. M. "The Later Miracle Plays of England." Independent
      Quarterly, XII (1906), 67-88.

2938 Grabo, Carl Henry. "The Stage for Which Shakespeare Wrote."
      Chautauquan, XLIV (1906), 98-106, 211-219, 354-366; XLV
      (1906), 79-89, 206-218, 331-343.

*2939 Crowley, Timothy. Character Treatment in the Medieval Drama.
      Notre Dame, Indiana, 1907. 181 pp. Bibliography, pp. 177-
      181.   DLC. MH.

2940 Medley, D. J. "The Setting of the Miracle Plays." Transactions
      of the Glasgow Archaeological Society, V (1906), 59-67.

2941 Moorman, F. W. "The Pre-Shakespearian Ghost." Modern
      Language Review, I (Janaury, 1906), 85-95.

2942 Parks, Allie V. "Stage Properties, Costumes, Scenery and
      Music of the English Miracle Plays." M.A. University of
      Illinois, 1906.

2943 Thien, Hermann. Über die englischen Marienklagen. Kiel: H.
      Fiencke, 1906. xii, 91 pp.
              BM. CtY. DLC. ICN. MB. MH. MnU. NjP.

2944 Creizenach, Wilhelm Michael Anton. "The Early Religious
      Drama." Cambridge History of English Literature. Vol. 5.
      (Cambridge, 1907-1927), pp. 36-51.

*2945 Manly, John M. "Literary Forms and the New Theory of the
      Origin of Species." Modern Philology, IV (April, 1907), 577-
      595.

2946 Markley, Mary Elizabeth. "A Study of the Lyric in the Drama
      from the Miracle Plays through the Plays of Lyly." M.A.
      Columbia University, 1907.

2947 Moore, E. Hamilton. "The Apocryphal Elements in Mediaeval
      Drama." International Journal of Apocrypha, No. 11 (1907),
      15-16.

2948 Moore, E. Hamilton. English Miracle Plays and Moralities.
      London: Sherrat and Hughes, 1907. vi, 199 pp.
              BM. DLC. MB. MiU. MnU. NjP. NN. OCl. WU.

2949 Schaff, David Schley. "The Religious Drama." In, Schaff, Philip. History of the Christian Church. Vol. 5. (New York, 1907), pp. 869-875.

2950 Solomon, Benvenuta. "Some Aspects of the Devil in English Dramatic Literature." Gentleman's Magazine, CCCII (1907), 583-601.

*2951 Taylor, G. C. "The English Planctus Mariae." Modern Philology, IV (1907), 605-637.

2952 Taylor, George Coffin. The Relation of Lyric and Drama in Medieval England. Chicago: University of Chicago Press, 1907. 38 pp.
 ICN. MB. NjP. NN. OCU.

2953 Taylor, G. C. "The Relation of the English Corpus Christi Play and the Middle English Lyric." Modern Philology, V (1907), 1-38.

2954 Beatty, Arthur. "Notes on the Supposed Dramatic Character of the 'Ludi' in the Great Wardrobe Accounts of Edward III." Modern Language Review, IV (1908-1909), 474-477.

*2955 Gayley, Charles M. Plays of Our Forefathers and Some of the Traditions upon Which They Were Founded. London: Chatto, 1908. xi, 349 pp.
 BM. IaU. ICN. MnU.

2956 Hemingway, Samuel Burdett. "A Critical Edition of the English Nativity Plays." Ph.D. Yale University, 1908.

*2957 Sepet, Marius Cyrille Alphonse. Le Drame religieux au moyen âge. Paris: Bloud et Cie, 1908. 63 pp.
 BM. IaU. MiU. PSC. PU.

2958 Tucker, Samuel M. Verse Satire in England before the Renaissance. New York: Columbia University Press, 1908. xi, 246 pp. Bibliography, pp. 228-234.
 BM. ICN. MiU. NjP. NN. OC1. OO. OU.

2959 Gayley, Charles M. "An Historical View of the Beginnings of English Comedy." Gayley, Charles M. Representative English Comedies. Vol. 1. (New York, 1909), pp. xiii-lxiv.

*2960 Greg, W. W. "Notes on Some Early Plays." Library, New Ser.,
      XI (1909), 44-56; 162-172.

2961 Harris, M. Dormer. "St. Christian Miracle Play." Notes and
     Queries, 10th Series, XI (1909), 230.

2962 Herrlich, Joseph. Das englische Bibeldrama zur Zeit der Renais-
     sance und Reformation mit besonderer Berücksichtigung von
     Udall's Komödie Jacob und-Esau. Bad Aibling: F. Haack, 1909.
     70 pp.
          CtY. MH.

2963 Lawrence, W. J. "Early French Players in England." Anglia,
     XXXII (1909), 61-89.

2964 Mangan, R. L. "The Nativity of Early Pageants." Catholic World,
     XC (1909), 294-304.

2965 O'Neill, Francis. "The English Miracle Play." Catholic Uni-
     versity. Bulletin, XV (1909), 464-473.

2966 Röhmer, Richard Andreas. Priestergestalten im englischen
     Drama bis zu Shakespeare. Inaugural Dissertation. Berlin,
     1909. 50 pp.
          ICU.

*2967 Allen, Philip Schuyler. "The Medieval Mimus II." Modern Philo-
      logy, VIII (1910), 1-44.

2968 Roosval, J. "The Altar Screens, or Reredoses of the 15th Cen-
     tury." Mask, III (1910), 1-5.

2969 Bertrin, George, and Arthur F. J. Remy. "Miracle Plays and
     Mysteries." Catholic Encyclopedia. Vol. 10. (New York,
     1911), pp. 348-350.

2970 Oelrich, Wilhelm. Die Personennamen im mittelalterlichen
     Drama Englands. Kiel: A. F. Jensen, 1911. 108 pp.
     Literaturverzeichnis, pp. 7-9.
          NN.

2971 O'Neill, Francis. "Ballad Influence on Miracle Plays." Amer-
     ican Catholic Quarterly Review, XXXVI (1911), 23-38.

2972 O'Neill, Francis, O.P. "Some Aspects of the Mediaeval Miracle

Play." Ph.D. Catholic University of America, 1911.

2973 Snell, Frederick John. "Miracle Plays." The Customs of Old England. (London, [1911]), pp. 49-60.
NN.

*2974 Spencer, Matthew Lyle. Corpus Christi Pageants in England. New York: Baker and Taylor Co., 1911. xi, 276 pp. Bibliography, pp. 263-269.
BM. DLC. MB. MnU. NjP. OC1W. OCU. OO.

2975 Syrett, Netta. The Old Miracle Plays of England. London & Oxford: A. R. Mowbray and Co., Ltd.; Milwaukee: The Young Churchman Co., [1911]. vii, 118 pp. [Texts.]
BM. DLC. MnU.

*2976 Haslinghuis, Edward Johannes. De Duivel in het Drama der Middeleuwen. Leiden: Van den Hoek, 1912. xvi, 208 pp. Bibliography, pp. [ii]-xvi.
BM. MnU. NNC.

2977 Lyle, Marie. "The Relation of the Lucifer Tradition in the Literary Composition of the Middle Ages to the Story of the Fall of the Angels in the Mystery Plays." M.A. University of Minnesota, 1912.

2978 McMurray, Wallace. "Elements in the Composition of the Medieval Play of the Nativity in Relation to their Final Form." M.A. University of Minnesota, 1912.

2979 "The Modern Church and Miracle Plays." Literary Digest, XLIV (1912), 336.

2980 Brown, Carleton. "Caiphas as a Palm-Sunday Prophet." Kittredge Anniversary Papers. (Boston, 1913), pp. 105-117.

2981 Christianson, Addie Olive. "The Comic Element in English Medieval Drama." M.A. Columbia University, 1913.

*2982 Craig, Hardin. "The Origin of the Old Testament Plays." Modern Philology, X (1913), 473-487.

2983 Crawford, M. "English Interjections in the 15th Century." University of Nebraska Studies, XIII (1913), 361-405.

*2984 Cron, Berthold. Zur entwicklungsgeschichte der englischen
        Misterien des alten Testaments. Marburg: A. L.; Noske:
        Borna-Leipzig, 1913. ix, 121 pp.
            CtY. DLC. IU. MH. MiU. PBm. PU. WaU. WU.

2985 Crosse, Gordon. The Religious Drama. London: A. R. Mow-
        bray, 1913. xvi, 182 pp.
            BM. IaU. IU. MH. OCl. ODW. PU. WU.

*2986 Foster, Frances Allen. The Northern Passion. 2 vol. London:
        K. Paul, Trench, Trubner and Co., Ltd., for the Early
        English Text Society, 1913-1916.
            BM. ICN.

2987 Moore, Edward R. "Mediaeval Religious Drama." Fordham
        Monthly, XXXI (1913), 328-333.

2988 Spaar, Otto. Prolog und Epilog im mittelalterlichen englischen
        Drama. Inaugural Dissertation. Kiel, 1913. 81 pp.

2989 Tisdel, Frederick Monroe. Studies in Literature. New York:
        Macmillan and Co., 1913. ix, 333 pp. Illus. Bibliography,
        pp. 319-325. Index, pp. 327-333. [Religious Plays of Mid-
        dle English Period, pp. 209-216.]
            BM. NN.

*2990 Coffman, George R. A New Theory Concerning the Origin of
        the Miracle Play. Menasha, Wisconsin: George Banta Pub-
        lishing Co., 1914. vi, 84 pp.
            BM. DLC. ICN. MiU. MnU. NjP. OU. PU. WU.

*2991 Craig, Hardin. "The Corpus Christi Procession and the Corpus
        Christi Play." Journal of English and Germanic Philology,
        XIII (1914), 589-602.

*2992 Dodds, M. H. "The Northern Stage." Archaeologia Aeliana,
        XI, 3rd Ser., (1914), 31-64.

*2993 Foster, Frances A. A Study of the Middle English Poem Known
        as the Northern Passion and Its Relation to the Cycle Plays.
        London and Bungay: R. Clay and Sons, Ltd., 1914. 101 pp.
            ICN. MiU. NjP. OCU. ODW. OO. OU. PHC. PU.

2994 Greg, W. W. "Christ and the Doctors. Inter-relation of the
        Cycles." The Library, 3rd Ser., V (July, 1914), 280-319.

[Part III of his article, "Bibliographical and Textual Problems of the English Miracle Cycles."]

2995 Hitzig, Walther. Zur Geschichte der Wechselwirkung zwischen der geistlichen Bühne und der bildenden Kunst des Mittel- alters ... I. Teil: Das Problem und die Grundlagen. Mannheim, 1914. 32 pp.
ICU.

2996 Ploch, W. W. "Staging and Costuming in the Pageant of the Early English Mystery Play." M.A. Ohio State University, 1914.

2997 Hughes, Elizabeth A. "The Use of the Drama by the Church As an Instrument of Social Control. The Ideals and Standards Which She Tried to Have Work Down to the People." A Study of a Mediaeval Agency of Social Control. (Chicago, 1915), pp. 14- 53.

2998 Jenney, Adeline M. "A Further Word As to the Origin of the Old Testament Plays." Modern Philology, XIII (May, 1915), 59-64.

2999 Kretzmann, P. E. "A Few Notes on the Harrowing of Hell." Modern Philology, XIII (1915), 49-51.

*3000 Pierson, Merle. "The Relation of the Corpus Christi Procession to the Corpus Christi Play in England." Transactions of the Wisconsin Academy of Science and Letters, XVIII (1915), 110-165. Bibliography, pp. 161-165.

3001 Whitmore, Charles Edward. "The Mediaeval Sacred Drama. Origin and Growth of the Liturgical Drama." The Supernatural in Tragedy. (Cambridge, 1915), 113-176.

3002 Bragdon, Elizabeth. "A Study of Extant Miracle Plays and Records of Lost Miracle Plays." M.A. University of Minnesota, 1916.

*3003 Coffman, George R. "The Miracle Play in England. Nomenclature." Publications of the Modern Language Association, XXXI (1916), 448-465.

3004 Coleman, A. I. DuP., and A. D. Compton. "Miracle Plays, Mysteries, Moralities." Encyclopedia of Religion and Ethics. Edited by James Hastings. Vol. 8. (New York, 1916), pp. 690-695.

3005 Gerould, Gordon Hall. "Saints' Lives in Drama." Saints' Legends.

(Boston and New York, 1916), pp. 300-308.
NN.

*3006 Haller, Julius. Die Technik des Dialogs im mittelalterlichen
  Drama Englands. Worms a Rh.: Wormser Verlags-und
  Druckereigesellschaft m.b.H., 1916. xv, [1], 157 pp.
  BM. IU. MH.

3007 Hulme, N. H. "A Valuable Middle English Manuscript." Modern
  Philology, XIV (1916), 67-73.

3008 Rudwin, Maximilian Josef. "Modern Passion Plays." Open Court,
  XXX (1916), 278-300.

3009 Weiner, K. Die Verwendung des Parallelismus als Kunstmittel
  im englischen Drama vor Shakespeare. Hamburg: Berngruber
  und Henning, 1916. 72 pp.
  DLC. MH. MiU. NNU-W. PU-F.

3010 Bonnell, J. K. "Serpent with a Human Head in Art and in Mystery
  Plays." American Journal of Archaeology, XXI (1917), 255-
  291.

3011 Gregg, M. T. "Christmas Miracle Plays." Educational Review,
  XXXVIII (1917), 86-101.

3012 Jones, Gwen Ann. "A Play of Judith." Modern Language Notes,
  XXXII (1917), 1-6.

3013 Painter, Anna Mercy. "Ecclesiastical Music in Early English
  Drama." M.A. Columbia University, 1917.

3014 Phillips, C. "Drama of the Nativity." Catholic World, CVI
  (1917), 289-301.

3015 Withington, Robert. "The Early 'Royal Entry.'" Publications
  of the Modern Language Association, XXXII (1917), 616-
  623.

*3016 Frank, Grace. "Revisions in the English Mystery Plays."
  Modern Philology, XV (1918), 565-572.

3017 Lanius, T. The Miracle Play. Medieval and Modern. M.A. University of Missouri, 1918.

*3018 Coffman, George R. "The Miracle Play in England--Some Re-
       cords of Presentation and Notes on Preserved Plays." Studies
       in Philology, XVI (1919), 56-66.

 3019 Dürrschmidt, Hans. Die Sage von Kain in der mittelalterlichen
       Literatur Englands. Bayrenth: Elwanger, 1919. viii, 131 pp.
       BM. MnU.

 3020 Lowden, Bertha E. "The Development of Dramatic Dialogue in
       English Mystery Plays." Ph.D. University of California,
       1919.

*3021 Miller, Frances H. "The Northern Passion and the Mysteries."
       Modern Language Notes, XXXIV (1919), 88-92.

 3022 Benedikt, Margarete. Die Darstellung der alttestamentarischen
       Stoffe im Mittelenglischen Drama. Inaugural Dissertation.
       Wien, 1920. 138 pp.

*3023 Frank, Grace. "The Palatine Passion and the Development of
       the Passion Play." Publications of the Modern Language Asso-
       ciation, XXXV (1920), 464-483.

 3024 Gilbert, Allan H. "Milton and the Mysteries." Studies in Philology,
       XVII (1920), 149-169.

 3025 Kirtlan, E. J. B. "Mystery and Miracle Plays." London Quarter-
       ly Review, CXXXIV (1920), 117-119.

 3026 Frank, Grace. "Critical Notes on the 'Palatine Passion.'"
       Modern Language Notes, XXXVI (April, 1921), 193-204.

 3027 Meier, Hermann. Die Strophenformen in den englischen Mys-
       terienspielen. Freiburg i. B.: Rebholz, 1921. 70 pp.
       NcU.

*3028 Phillips, William J. Carols, Their Origin, Music, and Con-
       nection with Mystery Plays. London: G. Routledge and Sons,
       Ltd.; New York: E. P. Dutton and Co., [1921], xv, 134 pp.
       Includes Texts.
           BM. ICN. MB. MiU. NN. OC1. OU. PHC. PPTU.

 3029 Sutton, V. R. "Mantle of the Virgin." Drama, XII (1921), 71-79.

 3030 Candler, Martha. Drama in Religious Service... . Illustrated

with Photographs. New York and London: Century Co., 1922.
xv, 259 pp. Bibliography, pp. 239-259.
NN.

3031 Fletcher, Jefferson B. "Herod in the Drama." Studies in Philology,
XIX (July, 1922), 292-307.

3032 Reed, Arthur William. The Beginnings of the English Secular
and Romantic Drama. Shakespeare Association, 1922. 31 pp.
BM. MB. MiU. NN. OC1. ODW. PU. ViU.

*3033 Smith, Alison Moore. "The Iconography of the Sacrifice of Isaac
in Early Christian Art." American Journal of Archaeology,
XXVI (1922), 159-173.

3034 Butterworth, Walter. "The Dance of Death." Manchester Quarterly, CLXV (January, 1923), 32-47.

3035 Crum, Mason. "Descriptive List of Plays and Pageants Suitable
for Use in Churches, Sunday Schools and Other Religious
Organizations." A Guide to Religious Pageantry. (New York,
1923), pp. 79-134.

3036 Lamont, John Wood. "The Origin of the Miracle Play." M.A.
Columbia University, 1923.

*3037 Moore, John Robert. "The Tradition of Angelic Singing in the
English Drama." Journal of English and Germanic Philology,
XXII (January, 1923), 89-99.

3038 Peele, D. D. "The History of Religious Pageantry." In Crum,
Mason. A Guide to Religious Pageantry. (New York, 1923),
pp. 16-31.

*3039 Young, Karl. "Concerning the Origin of the Miracle Play." The
Manly Anniversary Studies in Language and Literature.
(Chicago, 1923), pp. 254-268.

3040 Bonnell, J. K. "Cain's Jaw-Bone." Publications of the Modern
Language Association, XXXIX (1924), 140-146.

3041 Dearmer, Geoffrey. "Miracle Plays." Saturday Review of Literature, CXXXVII (January 5, 1924), 8-9.

3042 Dustoor, P. E. "The Origin of the Play of 'Moses and the Tables of the Law.'" Modern Language Review, XIX (October, 1924), 459-462.

3043 Pennington, Jo. "Mystery and Miracle Plays; Primarily Religious They Were the Foundations, Laid and Abandoned by the Church, of Modern Drama." International Studio, LXXX (1924), 207-213.

3044 Collingwood, Ava Farwell. "A Study of the Soliloquy in Pre-Shakespearean Drama." M.A. Columbia University, 1925.

3045 Harris, M. Dormer. "The 'World' in the Doomsday Mystery Play." Notes and Queries, CXLIV (1925), 243.

3046 Hyde, E. F. The Mystery Play: Medieval and Modern. M.A. University of Missouri, 1925.

3047 Mackay, Constance D'Arcy. "The Miracle Play Comes Back. Many Churches Are Now Reviving This Beautiful Old Custom." Delineator, CVII (December, 1925), 5, 80.

3048 Nicoll, Allardyce. "The Growth of Native Drama: Tropes and Liturgical Plays." British Drama. (London, [1925]), pp. 20-40.

*3049 Traver, Hope. "The Four Daughters of God: a Mirror of Changing Doctrine." Publications of the Modern Langauge Association, XL (March, 1925), 44-92.

3050 Albright, Victor E. The Shakespearian Stage. New York: Columbia University Press, 1926. xii, 194 pp.
          BM. DLC. IaU. ICN. MnU. NcD.

3051 Mentzer, Ethyl Grace. "The Devil of the English Mystery Play." M.A. Columbia University, 1926.

3052 Potter, R. R. "Some Aspects of the Supernatural in English Comedy from the Origins to the Closing of the Theatres in 1642." Ph.D. University of North Carolina, 1926.

3053 Winslow, Ola Elizabeth. "Low Comedy in the Scripture Cycles." Low Comedy As a Structural Element in English Drama. (Chicago, 1926), pp. 1-43.

3054 Wright, Louis B. "Vaudeville Elements in English Drama from the Origins until the Closing of the Theatres in 1642." Ph.D. University of North Carolina, 1926.

3055 Allison, Tempe E. "On the Body and Soul Legend." Modern Language Notes, XLII (1927), 102-106.

3056 Jagendorf, M. "Student Theatres in the Middle Ages." Theatre Arts Monthly, XI (September, 1927), 699-704.

3057 James, Stanley B. "A Study in Passion Plays." Month, CXLIX (1927), 309-315.

3058 Kroll, Joseph. "Zur Geschichte des Spieles von Christi Höllenfahrt." Kulturwissenschaftliche Bibliothek Warburg. Hamburg. Vorträge (1927-1928), 257-301.

*3059 Manly, John M. "The Miracle Play in Medieval England." Royal Society of Literature of the United Kingdom, Ser. III, n.s., VII (1927), 133-153.

*3060 Mill, Anna J. Medieval Plays in Scotland. London: W. Blackwood and Sons, Ltd., 1927. 356 pp.
        BM. ICN. ICU. MB. OC1. OU. PU. TxU.

3061 Wright, Louis Booker. "Juggling Tricks and Conjury on the English Stage before 1642." Modern Philology, XXIV (1927), 269-284.

3062 Bloor, Robert Henry Underwood. Christianity and the Religious Drama. London: The Lindsey Press, 1928. 61 pp. (The Essex Hall Lecture.)
        BM.

3063 Brunner, Thomas. Jacob und seine zwölf Sohne. Hrsg. v. Robert Stumpfl. Halle: M. Niemeyer, 1928. xxxvi, 111 pp.
        BM. DLC. ICN. MiU. OCU. OU. PHC. PU. ViU. WU.

3064 Chreitzberg, Margaret. "Prevailing Types of Women in English Drama from the Beginnings to 1640." M.A. University of North Carolina, 1928.

3065 Eckhardt, Eduard. Das englische Drama im Zeitalter der Reformation und der Hochrenaissance. Vorstufen, Shakespeare und seine Zeit. Berlin und Leipzig: Walter de Gruyter and Co., 1928. 293 pp. "Allgemeine Bibliographie," pp. ix-xii.

CSmH. CtY. IaU. ICN. MH. MnU. NN. PU.

3066 Kress, Leona L. (Sister M. Clarissa). "Religious Motive in
English Medieval Drama." The Emerson Quarterly, VIII
(January, 1928), 11-12, 28; (March, 1928), 11-12, 28.
(May, 1928), 11-12.

3067 Marshall, Mary Hatch. "Antichrist in Mediaeval Drama and in
the Drama of the Reformation in England." M.A. Yale University, 1928.

3068 Mellen, Frederic Davis. "The Antichrist Legend in Middle English." M.A. University of Chicago, 1928.

3069 Parker, Roscoe E., ed. The Middle English Stanzaic Versions
of the Life of Saint Anne. London: Humphrey Milford,
Oxford University Press for E.E.T.S., 1928. liv, 139 pp.
Bibliography, pp. 138-139. (Original Series, 174).
BM.

*3070 Vriend, Joannes, S. J. The Blessed Virgin Mary in the Medieval
Drama of England. Purmerend: J. Musses, 1928. xv, 160 pp.
Select Bibliography, pp. [xiii]-xv.
BM. DLC. ICN. ICU. IU. MH. MiU. MnU. NN. OCU.

3071 Wright, Louis Booker. "Variety-Show Clownery on the Pre-
Restoration Stage." Anglia, LII (1928), 51-68.

3072 Agius, Ambrose. "Mystery Plays in an English Village." Downside Review, XLVII (1929), 246-250.

3073 Carroll, K. M. "The Miracle Plays as Guides to Mediaeval Life
and Thoughts." Contemporary Review, CXXXV (January,
1929), 81-89.

*3074 Coffman, George R. "A Plea for the Study of the Corpus Christi
Plays as Drama." Studies in Philology, XXVII (October, 1929),
411-424.

3075 Beuscher, Elisabeth. Die Gesangseinlagen in den englischen
Mysterien. Münster i Westph.: Helios-Verlag, G.M.B.H.,
1930. ix, 106 pp. (Universitäts-Archiv; eine Sammlung
wissenschaftlicher Untersuchungen und Abhandlungen [Nr.
38]). Bibliography, pp. vii-ix.
CtY. ICN. MH. MnU. NN. OU.

3076 Cazamian, Louis Francois. Development of English Humour.
New York: The Macmillan Co., 1930. 162 pp. [Part II, 1952.]
ICN. MiU. OCl. OCU. OO. OU. PPD. PU.

3077 Coffman, George R. "Author's Corrections--'Corpus Christi
Plays As Drama.'" Studies in Philology, XXVII (October,
1930), 688.

3078 Glaymen, Rose Ebey. Recent Judith Drama and Its Analogues.
Philadelphia: University of Pennsylvania Press, 1930. 134 pp.
DLC. MB. MiU. OCl. OCU. OU. PSC. PU. WU.

3079 Rollenhagen, Georg. Spiel von Tobias, 1576. Halle: Niemeyer,
1930. xix, 152 pp.
BM. DLC. IaU. ICN. MiU. WU.

3080 Sachs, Hans. Seven Shrovetide Plays. Translated by E. U.
Ouless. London: H. F. W. Deane & Sons, [c. 1930]. 78 pp.
BM. DLC. ICN. MiU. MnU. NN. OCl. WU.

3081 Withington, Robert. "The Corpus Christi Plays as Drama."
Studies in Philology, XXVII (October, 1930), 573-582.

3082 Adrian, Gertrud. Die Bühnenanweisungen in den englischen
Mysterien. Bochum-Langendreer: H. Pöppinghaus, 1931.
vi, 70 pp. Bibliography, pp. iv-vi.
BM. CtY. CU. IU. McU. MH. MiU. MnU.

3083 Bald, R. C. "The Development of Greek and Medieval English
Drama: A Comparison." Englische Studien, LXVI (1931),
6-15.

3084 Coffman, George R. "A Note on Saints' Legends." Studies in
Philology, XXVIII (1931), 580-586.

3085 Colonius, Dorothy Elizabeth. "Costume on the English Stage
until 1590." M.A. University of Chicago, 1931.

*3086 Greg, Walter W. "Notes on Some Early Plays." Library, 4th
Ser., XI (1931), 44-56.

*3087 Nicoll, Allardyce. Masks, Mimes, and Miracles. London:
George C. Harrap and Co., 1931. 407 pp.
BM. IaU. IU. MH. MiU. MnU. OCl. OO. PU. WaU.

3088 Townsend, Walter and Leonard. Mystery and Miracle Plays in
England. London: Henry Hartley, [1931], 90 pp.
DLC. MiU. NN. OC1.

3089 Collins, Fletcher. "Music in Guild Plays." Ph.D. Yale University,
1932.

*3090 ----- "Music in the Craft Cycles." Publications of the Modern
Language Association, XLVII (September, 1932), 613-621.

3091 Pascoe, Margaret E. Les Drames religieux au milieu du XVIIe
siècle. Paris: Boivin, 1932. 216 pp. Bibliography, pp. [199]-209.
BM. IaU. ICN. MnU. OU.

*3092 Withington, Robert. "Ancestry of the Vice." Speculum, VII (1932),
522-529.

3093 Bardner, Jean. "Dramatic Problems in the Nativity Plays." M.A.
University of Wisconsin, 1933.

*3094 Cornelius, Brother Luke, The Role of the Virgin Mary in the
Coventry, York, Chester, and Towneley Cycles. Baltimore:
Catholic University of America Press, 1933. 121 pp.
DLC.

3095 Gaster, T. H. "The Earliest Known Miracle Play. Cuneiform
Tablets Unearthed at Ras-Shamura, Syria, a Poem Describing
the Combat Between the Gods of Rain and Verdure and the
God "Mot" (Death)." Folk-lore, XLIV (1933), 379-390.

3096 McKeehan, Irene Pettit. "The Book of the Nativity of St. Cuthbert." Publications of the Modern Language Association,
XLVIII (1933), 981-999.

3097 Moore, John Robert. "Miracle Plays, Minstrels, and Jigs."
Publications of the Modern Language Association, XLVIII
(September, 1933), 942-945.

3098 Parker, Roscoe E. "The Reputation of Herod in Early English
Literature." Speculum, VIII (1933), 59-67.

3099 Stephens, L. Louise. "The Christian Mystery Play." Theatre
and School, XII (1933), 14-15.

3100 Tergau, Diedrich. Die sozialen Typen im Drama des englischen
Mittelalters. Inaugural Dissertation. Göttingen, 1933. 78 pp.

CtY. CSmH. DLC. MiU.

3101 Young, Karl. "An 'Interludium' for a Gild of Corpus Christi." Modern Language Notes, XLVIII (February, 1933), 84-86.

3102 Young, S. "Production of Six Miracle Plays by the Stage Alliance." New Republic, LXXIV (1933), 71-73.

3103 Bamberger, Bernhard. Die Figur des Propheten in der englischen Literatur, von den ältesten Zeiten bis zum Ausgang des 18 Jahrhunderts. Eine typologische Untersuchung. Inaugural Dissertation. Würtzburg University, 1934.

3104 Brown, Carleton. "Sermons and Miracle Plays: Merton College MS 248." Modern Language Notes, XLIV (June, 1934), 394-396.

3105 Emrich, Wilhelm. Paulus im drama. Berlin und Leipzig: Walter de Gruyter, 1934. 145 pp. "Quellen," pp. 131-145. IaU. ICN. OC1W. PPTU.

3106 Garvin, K. "A Note on Noah's Wife." Modern Language Notes, XLIX (February, 1934), 88-90.

*3107 Knoll, Friedrich Otto. Die Rolle der Maria Magdalena im geistlichen Spiel des Mittelalters. Berlin: Walter de Gruyter, 1934. 122 pp. Bibliography, pp. 12-16. BM. CtY. IaU. ICN. MnU. OU.

3108 Owst, G. R. "Sermons and Miracle Plays." Modern Language Notes, XLIX (1934), 394-396.

3109 Pfander, H. G. "Dives et Pauper." The Library, Fourth Series, XIV (1934), 299-312.

3110 Rushton, Gerald Wynne. "Passion Plays and their Origin." Catholic World, CXXXIX (1934), 40-46.

*3111 Tomlinson, Warren Everett. Der Herodes Charakter im englischen Drama. Leipzig: Mayer and Muller, g.m.b.h., 1934. x, 182 pp. (Palaestra, 195.) BM. DLC. IaU. ICN. MiU. MnU. OU. ViU. WU.

3112 Withington, Robert. "Notes on the Corpus Christi Plays and 'The Green Pastures.'" Shakespeare Association Bulletin,

IX (October, 1934), 193-197.

*3113 Withington, Robert. "Vice and Parasite; a Note on the Evolution
       of the Elizabethan Villain." Publications of the Modern Lan-
       guage Association, XLIX (1934), 743-751.

 3114 Koho, Yosuke. "Medieval Drama and Gilds." Studies in English
       Literature (Imperial University, Tokyo), XV (1935), 183-193.

 3115 Richardson, H. G. "Dives et Pauper." The Library, Fourth
       Series, XV (1935), 31-37.

*3116 Brooks, Neil C. "An Ingolstadt Corpus Christi Procession and
       the Biblia Pauperum." Journal of English and Germanic
       Philology, XXXV (January, 1936), 1-16.

*3117 Farnham, Willard. The Medieval Heritage of Elizabeth Tragedy.
       Berkeley: University of California Press, 1936. 487 pp.
               BM (1957). ICN. MiU. MnU. NcD. NN. OC1. PU. ViU.

 3118 O'Brien, Rosemary Agnes. "Angels in Sixteenth Century Drama."
       M.A. Columbia University, 1936.

 3119 Pearson, Lu Emily. "Isolable Lyrics in the Mystery Plays."
       English Literary History, III (September, 1936), 228-252.

 3120 Ross, Hugh. "Medieval Drama Redivivus." American Scholar,
       V (1936), 49-63.

*3121 Withington, Robert. "Braggart, Devil, and Vice." Speculum, XI
       (January, 1936), 124-129.

 3122 Brunner, Rev. Francis A. "A Discussion of the Problems of the
       Dialog between Mary and Joseph in Christ I." M.A. Catholic
       University of America, 1937.

*3123 Deasy, Philip Cormac. St. Joseph in the English Mystery Plays.
       Washington, D.C.: Catholic University Press, 1937. ix, 112
       pp. Bibliography, pp. 107-112.
               BM. IaU. ICN. MH. OC1. WU.

*3124 Härtl, Eduard. Das Drama des Mittelalters. Leipzig: P. Reclam,
       1937. 266 pp.
               IaU. MnU.

3125 Hicks, Mother Mary Agatha, O.S.U. "The Apocryphal Gospels and the Craft Plays of the Nativity Cycle." M.A. (Missing). Catholic University of America, 1937.

3126 Withington, Robert. "The Biblical Drama in England." The Bible and Its Literary Associations. (New York, 1937), pp. 341-362.

3127 ----- Excursions in English Drama. New York: D. Appleton Century Co., 1937. xvii, 264 pp. Bibliographical note, pp. 247-251.
       BM. DFo. DLC. ICN. MnU. NN. ViU.

3128 Carver, James E. "The Northern Homily Cycle." Ph.D. New York University, 1938.

3129 Eliason, Mary H. "A Study of Some Relations between Literature and History in the Third Estate of the 14th Century: Chaucer, 'Piers the Plowman' and the English Mystery Cycles." Ph.D. University of North Carolina, 1938.

3130 Melchers, Paul. Kulturgeschichtliche Studien zu den mittelenglischen Misterienspielen. Würzburg: Konrad Triltsch, 1938. iii, 56 pp. Bibliography, pp. 54-56.
       BM. ICN. NNC.

3131 Whiting, Bartlett Jere. Proverbs in Earlier English Drama. Cambridge: Harvard University Press, 1938. xx, 505 pp.
       BM. DFo. DLC. IaU. MnU. OC1. OCU. OO. ViU.

3132 Blatherwick, D. P. "Religion and Drama." London Quarterly Review, CLXIV (1939), 513-520.

3133 Doyle, Sister M. Berenice. "The Characterization of Adam and Eve in the English Mystery Play." M.A. Catholic University of America, 1939.

3134 Weary, Erica H. "The Staging of the English Mystery Plays." Ph.D. University of Southern California, 1939.

*3135 Wells, Henry W. "Style in the English Mystery Plays." Journal of English and Germanic Philology, XXXVIII (1939), 496-524.

3136 Wells, Minnie E. "The Age of Isaac at the Time of the Sacrifice." Modern Language Notes, LIV (December, 1939), 579-582.

3137 Wood, Frederick T. "The Comic Elements in the English Mys-
      tery Plays." Neophilologus, XXV (October, 1939), 39-48.

*3138 Blair, Lawrence. "A Note on the Relation of the Corpus Christi
      Procession to the Corpus Christi Play in England." Modern
      Language Notes, LV (February, 1940), 83-95.

3139 Kernodle, George R. "England's Religious Drama Movement."
      College English, I (February, 1940), 414-426.

3140 Lusher, Patricia G. "Studies in the Guild Drama in London,
      from 1515 to 1550, in the Records of the Drapers Company."
      Ph.D. University of London, 1940.

3141 Valency, Maurice J. The Tragedies of Herod and Mariamne.
      Columbia University Studies in English and Comparative
      Literature, No. 145. 1940. ix, 304 pp.
            BM. ICN.

3142 Vijf geestelijke toneelspelen der middeleeuwen [Verzorgd door
      Dr. Hubert J. E. Endepols]. Amsterdam: "Elsevier," 1940.
      379 pp.
            BM. ICN. NNC.

3143 Wilson, Winifred Graham. "Skinners' Pageants." Life and Let-
      ters Today, XXVII (1940), 10-16.

3144 Wood, Frederick T. "The Comic Elements in the English Mys-
      tery Plays." Neophilologus, XXV (1940), 194-206.

*3145 Coffman, George R. "The Miracle Play: Notes and Queries."
      Philological Quarterly, XX (July, 1941), 204-211.

3146 Gardiner, Harold C. "Easter Drama's Six-hundred-year Run."
      America, LXV (1941), 19-20.

3147 Kearney, James J. "The Suppression of the Mystery Plays: Cul-
      mination of Social, Literary, and Religious Forces in the
      Sixteenth Century." Ph.D. Fordham University, 1941.

3148 Kispaugh, Sr. Mary Jerome. "The Feast of the Presentation of
      the Virgin Mary in the Temple: An Historial and Literary
      Study." Ph.D. Catholic University of America, 1941.

3149 Mill, Anna J. "Noah's Wife Again." Publications of the Modern

Language Association, LVI (September, 1941), 613-626.

3150 Thorsen, John Kehl. "A Project for the Staging of Four Nativity Plays from the English Miracle Cycles." M.A. Northwestern University, 1941.

3151 Cahill, Helen Catherine. "The Production of the Medieval Miracle Play." M.A. Louisiana State University. 1942.

3152 Coffman, George R. "Correction: The Miracle Play: Notes and Queries." Philological Quarterly, XXI (April, 1942), 249-250.

3153 Howell, James. "The Rogue in English Comedy to 1642." Ph.D. University of North Carolina, 1942.

3154 Mahr, August Carl. Relations of Passion Plays to St. Ephrem the Syrian. Columbus, Ohio: State University Press, 1942. vii, 34 pp. (Contributions in Language and Literature.)
        BM. DLC. MH. MiU. NN. OCU. OU. PU. ViU. WU.

3155 Schapiro, M. "Cain's Jaw-bone That Did the First Murder." Art Bulletin, XXIV (1942), 205.

3156 Weir, Evangeline G. "The Vernacular Sources of the Middle English Plays of the Blessed Virgin Mary; a Study of the Marian Elements in the Homilies and Other Works of Religious Instruction from 1200 to 1500 in Relation to the Mary Play." Ph.D. Stanford University, 1942.

3157 Miller, Edwin S. "Medieval Biblical and Ritualistic Elements in the English Drama, 1497-1562." Ph.D. University of North Carolina, 1943.

3158 Schlenk, Leon J. "Production of Medieval Guild Plays in England." M.A. Marquette University, 1943.

3159 Sullivan, S. S.J., Sr. John. "A Study of the Themes of the Passion in the Medieval Cyclic Drama." Ph.D. Catholic University of America, 1943.

3160 Cohen, Gustave. "Influence of Mysteries on Medieval Art." American Journal of Archaeology, XLVIII (1944), 385.

3161 Gaffney, H. "Early Drama and Corpus Christi." Irish Ecclesiastical Record, 5th ser., LXIII (1944), 155-166.

3162 Loomis, R. S. "Evidence for the Existence of the Secular
      Theatres in the 12th Century." Pubications of the Modern
      Language Association, LIX (1944), 1339.

*3163 Loomis, R. S. "Some Evidence for Secular Theatres in the 12th
      and 13th Centuries." Theatre Annual, III (1945), 33-43.

3164 Robertson, D. W. "A Study of Certain Aspects of the Cultural
      Tradition of Handlying Synne." M.A. University of North
      Carolina, 1945.

*3165 Craig, Hardin. "The Origin of the Passion Play: Matters of
      Theory as Well as Fact." Studies in Honor of A. H. R. Fair-
      child. (University of Missouri Studies, XXI, 1946), pp. 83-90.

*3166 Gardiner, S.J., Harold C. Mysteries' End. An Investigation of
      the Last Days of the Medieval Religious Stage. New Haven:
      Yale University Press; London: Geoffrey Cumberlege, 1946.
      xiv, 142 pp. Index. (Yale Studies in English, Vol. 103).
          BM. CtY. DFo. DLC. ICN. ICU. MH. NN. OC1. PU.

3167 Eastman, F. "Christ in the Drama." Review Christendom, XII
      (1947), 546-547.

3168 Eastman, Fred. Christ in the Drama. New York: Macmillan
      and Co., 1947. x, 174 pp.
          BM. DLC. ICU. IaU. MB. MH. MnU. TxU.

3169 Kenneth, Richard William. "Miracle, Mystery and Shakespeare."
      Poetry and the People. (London, 1947), pp. 53-81.

3170 Stout, D. "Miracle Narrative and Play." Homiletic and Pastoral
      Review, XLVIII (1947), 119-125.

3171 Allen, Don Cameron. The Legend of Noah. Renaissance Rational-
      ism in Art, Science and Letters. Urbana: University of Illinois
      Press, 1949. vii, 221 pp. (Illinois Studies in Language and
      Literature, Vol. 33, No. 3, 4.)
          BM. IU.

3172 Robbins, Rossell Hope. "A Sixteenth Century English Mystery
      Fragments." English Studies, XXX (August, 1949), 134-136.

3173 Southern, Richard. "The 'Houses' of the Westminster Play."
      Theatre Notebook, III (1949), 46-52.

*3174 Craddock, Lawrence G. "Franciscan Influences on Early Eng-
       lish Drama." Franciscan Studies, X (1950), 383-417.

3175   "Drama." Encyclopaedia Britannica. Vol. 7. (London, 1950),
       pp. 586-590.

3176   Garth, Hebn. M. Saint Mary Magdalene in Mediaeval Literature.
       Johns Hopkins University Studies, 67, No. 3. 1950. 114 pp.
       (History and Political Science, Series 67, No. 3).
            BM.

3177   Parker, Roscoe E. "Pilates Voys." Speculum, XXV (1950),
       237-244.

3178   Robbins, Rossell Hope. "An English Mystery Play Fragment
       Ante 1300." Modern Language Notes, LXV (January, 1950),
       30-35. [Two parts, French and English, each of 22 lines.]

3179   Chauvin, Sister Mary John, of Carmel. "The Role of Mary
       Magdalene in Medieval Drama." Ph.D. Catholic University
       of America, 1951.

3180   McNeir, Waldo F. "The Corpus Christi Passion Plays As Dra-
       matic Art." Studies in Philology, XLVIII (July, 1951), 601-
       628.

3181   ----- The Passion Plays in the Corpus Christi Cycles as Art:
       A Defense of Dramatic Values to be Found in Them. Baton
       Rouge: Louisiana State University, 1951.

*3182 Bloomfield, Morton Wilfred. The Seven Deadly Sins: An Intro-
       duction to the History of a Religious Concept, with Special
       Reference to Medieval English Literature. East Lansing
       Michigan State College Press, 1952. xiv, 482 pp. Bibliography,
       pp. 257-306.
            BM. ICN.

3183   Fenner, James L. "Humanization of the Gospel Narratives in the
       Medieval Nativity-Plays." M.A. Columbia University, 1952.

3184   Ulman, Seth P. "The Dramatic Art of the English Medieval Magi
       Plays." Ph.D. University of California, 1953.

*3185 Boughner, Daniel C. "The English Miracle Plays." The Brag-
       gart in Renaissance Comedy: A Study in Comparative Drama

from Aristophanes to Shakespeare. (Minneapolis, 1954), pp. 119-144.

3186 Broadbent, J. "An Edition of the Noah Pageant in the English Corpus Christi Cycles." M.A. University of Leeds, 1954-1955.

3187 Gassner, John Waldhorn. Masters of the drama. Third revised and enlarged edition. New York: Dover, 1954. xxi, 890 pp.
BM.

3188 Gruber, Christine. Das religiöse Theater Englands der Gegenwart in seinen zusammenhängen mit der Entwicklung im Mittelalter und in der Renaissance. Dissertation. Universität Wien, 1954. 187 leaves.

3189 Loomis, Roger Sherman. "Was There a Play on the Martyrdom of Hugh of Lincoln?" Modern Language Notes, LXIX (January, 1954), 31-34.

3190 Robbins, Rossell Hope. "A Dramatic Fragment from a Caesar Augustus Play." Anglia, LXXII (1954), 30-34. [M. S. Ashmole 750 contains a speech apparently from a lost play on the Slaughter of the Innocents.]

3191 Spitzer, Leo. "Reply to 'Was There a Play about Hugh of Lincoln?'" Modern Language Notes, LXIX (May, 1954), 383-384.

*3192 Craig, Hardin. English Religious Drama of the Middle Ages. Oxford: Clarendon Press; New York: Oxford University Press, 1955. vi, 421 pp. Bibliography, pp. 390-401.
BM. CtY. DLC. ICN. ICU. IU. MB. MH. NN. O. OU.

3193 ----- "The Miracle Play." English Religious Drama of the Middle Ages. (Oxford, 1955), pp. 81-87.

3194 ----- "Miracle Plays." English Religious Drama of the Middle Ages. (Oxford, 1955), pp. 320-334.

3195 ----- "Mystery and Miracle Plays." English Religious Drama of the Middle Ages. (Oxford, 1955), pp. 354-377.

3196 Halliday, Frank Ernest. The Legend of the Rood, with the Three Maries and the Death of Pilate, Done into English Verse with an Introduction. London: G. Duckworth, 1955. 142 pp.
BM. NN.

3197 Healer, Alphaleta. "The Mystery Play in England." M.A. Texas
      Technological College. 1955.

*3198 Browne, E. M. "The English Mystery Plays." Drama, XLIII
      (Winter, 1956), 34-36.

*3199 Dunn, Catherine E. "The Miracle Play As an Art Form."
      Catholic Art Quarterly, XIX (Easter, 1956), 48-56.

3200 Harder, Kelsie B. "Chaucer's Use of the Mystery Plays in the
      Miller's Tale." Modern Language Quarterly, XVII (September,
      1956), 193-198. Bibliographical footnotes.

3201 Pearce, T. M. "The New Mexican Shepherds' Play." Western
      Folklore, XV (April, 1956), 77-78.

3202 Bonventre, Brother Baldwin Peter. "A Classification of Comic
      Techniques in the English Cycle Plays." M.A. Fordham Uni-
      versity, 1957.

3203 Bridijes-Adams, W. "The Great Cycles." The Irresistible
      Theatre. Volume I From the Conquest to the Commonwealth.
      (London, 1957), pp. 41-45. See also pp. 22-40, 46-60.

3204 Fischer, E. "Some Mystery Plays are Refreshing." Ave Maria,
      LXXXVI (December 21, 1957), 15.

3205 Ingram, R. W. "The Use of Music in English Miracle Plays."
      Anglia, LXXV (1957), 64-65.

3206 Maltman, Sister Nicholas. "A Study of the Evil Characters in
      the English Corpus Christi Cycles." Ph.D. University of
      California, 1957.

3207 Maynard, T. "Green Plot Be Our Stage." Magnificat, CVIII
      (February, 1957), 51.

3208 Means, Michael Hugh. "A Comparison and Evaluation of the
      Moses Plays in the Medieval English Mystery Cycles."
      M.A. Ohio State University, 1957.

3209 Swart, J. "The Insubstantial Pageant." Neophilologus, XLI
      (1957), 127-141.

*3210 Woolf, Rosemary. "The Effect of Typology on the English

Medieval Plays of Abraham and Isaac." <u>Speculum</u>, XXXII (October, 1957), 805-825.

3211 Young, Wilfred. "Noah and His Wife: A Note on Three English Miracle Plays." <u>Hermathena</u>, XC (November, 1957), 17-32.

3212 Browne, E. Martin. "Medieval Plays in Modern Production." Religious Drama 2, Mystery and Morality Plays. (New York, 1958), pp. 305-315.

3213 Campbell, Parris. "A Historical Study on the Development of Religious Drama from the Medieval Period to the Present." M.A. Tennessee Agricultural and Industrial State University. 1958.

3214 Jones, P. R. "The Treatment of Old Testament Characters and Incidents in Old and Middle English Poetry and Drama." M.A. University of Wales, 1958-1959.

3215 Parker, John W. "Touches of Comedy and Realism in Early Religious Plays." <u>College Language Association Journal</u>, II (1958), 51-54.

3216 Scherer, Philip. "Aspects in the Old English of the Corpus Christi Manuscript." <u>Language</u>, II (April-June, 1958), 245-251.

3217 Weiner, Albert Bacon. "Acting on the Medieval Religious Stage." Ph.D. Yale University, 1958.

3218 Cooling, June, ed. "Unpublished Middle English Prologue." <u>Review of English Studies</u>, X (May, 1959), 172-173.

3219 McElroy, Sister Mary Immaculate. "The Assumption Theme in Medieval Drama." M.A. Fordham University, 1959.

*3220 Robbins, Rossell H. Historical Poems of the XIVth and XVth Centuries. New York: Columbia University Press, 1959.

3221 "Cardiff's First Corpus Christi Procession for over Twenty Years." Photograph. <u>Illustrated London News</u>, XXXVII (July 2, 1960), 33.

3222 Prosser, Eleanor. "Try What Repentance Can: A Re-evaluation of the English Mysteries As Religious Drama." Ph.D. Stanford University, 1960.

3223 Young, William Donald. "Devices and Feintes of the Medieval
      Religious Theater in England and France." Ph.D. Stanford
      University, 1960.

3224 Kennison, Louise. "Topical References in the Fourteenth Cen-
      tury Miracle Plays." M.A. Smith College, 1961.

3225 Maltman, Sister Nicholas. "Pilate--Os Malleatoris." Speculum,
      XXXVI (1961), 308-311.

*3226 Prosser, Eleanor. Drama and Religion in the English Mystery Plays:
      A Re-evaluation. Stanford, California: Stanford University
      Press, 1961. vi, 229 pp.
          BM. CtY. DLC. ICU. IU. MH. NNC. OU. PU.

3227 ----- "Joseph." Drama and Religion in the English Mystery
      Plays. (Standord, California, 1961), pp. 89-102.

3228 Roston, M. "The Use in English Drama of Themes from the
      Old Testament and Its Apocrypha." Ph.D. London University
      (External), 1961.

3229 Stevens, Richard. "The Wagon Stage." M.F.A. Carnegie In-
      stitute of Technology, 1961.

*3230 Williams, Arnold. The Drama of Medieval England. [Lansing]:
      Michigan State University Press, 1961. vi, 186 pp.
          CtY. DLC. ICN. ICU. MH. MiU. NN. OU. PU. ViU.
          WU.

3231 Janicka, Irena. The Comic Elements in the English Mystery Plays
      Against the Cultural Background, Particularly Art. Poznán:
      Praca Wydava z Zasilku Polskiej Adademii Nauk, 1962. 119
      pp. Bibliography, pp. [111]-115. (Poznanskie Towarzystwo
      Przyjaciol Nauk. Wydzial filologiczno-filozoficzny. Prace
      Komisji filologiczney. Tom. XVI, 6).
          ICU. Royal Library, Albert I, Brussels.

3232 Browne, E. Martin. "Producing the Mystery Plays for Modern
      Audiences." Drama Survey, III (May, 1963), 5-15.

3233 Campbell, A. P. "The Mediaeval Mystery Cycle, Liturgical in
      Impulse." Revue de l'Université d'Ottawa, XXXIII (March,
      1963), 23-37.

3234 "Carillons and Veills: New York Pro Musica Presentation of
      the Play of Herod." Newsweek, LXII (December 23, 1963),
      51.

3235 Gundry, Inglis. Medieval Church Drama. Musical Times, CIV
      (March, 1963), 183-184.

3236 Lewis, Leon Eugene. "The Play of Mary Magdalene." Ph.D.
      University of Wisconsin, 1963.

3237 McNaspy, C. J. "Presentation of the Play of Herod at the Clois-
      ters in New York City." America, CIX (December 21, 1963),
      808-809.

3238 Pace, George B. "Adam's Hell." Publications of the Modern
      Language Association, LXXVIII (June, 1963), 25-35.

3239 Cowling, George Herbert. Music on the Shakespearean Stage.
      New York: Russell & Russell, 1964. vi, 116 pp. [First
      published in 1913.]
          NN.

3240 Hussey, S. S. "How Many Herods in the Middle English Drama?"
      Neophilologus, XLVIII (1964), 252-259.

3241 McDermott, John James. "Mary Magdalene in English Liter-
      ature from 1500 to 1650." Ph.D. University of California
      (Los Angeles), 1964.

3242 Morgan, Margery M. "High Fraud: Paradox and Double-Plot
      in the English Shepherds' Plays." Speculum, XXXIX (1964),
      680-681.

*3243 Dawson, Giles, ed. Records of Plays and Players in Kent,
      1450-1642. The Malone Society. Collections. Vol. VII.
      Oxford: At the University Press, 1965. xxxi, [1], 211 pp.

3244 Gamer, Helena M. "Mimes, Musicians and the Origin of the
      Mediaeval Religious Play." Deutsche Beiträge zur Geistigen
      Überlieferung, V (1965), 9-28.

*3245 Hardison, Osborne Bennett, Jr. Christian Rite and Christian
      Drama: Essays in the Origin and Early History of Modern
      Drama. Baltimore: Johns Hopkins Press, 1965. xi, [5], 1-
      328 pp. Bibliographical footnotes.
          BM.

*3246 Hess, Rainer. Das romische geistliche Schauspiel als profane
       und religiöse Komödie, 15 und 16. Jahrhundert. München: W.
       Fink [1965]. 198 pp. (Freiburger Schriften zur romanischen
       Philologie, v. 4).
              ICN.

3247 Lazier, Gilbert N. "The Comedy of the English Medieval Mys-
      tery Cycle. A Descriptive Study." Ph.D. Southern Illinois Uni-
      versity, 1965.

3248 Macaulay, P. S. "The Treatment of Theology in the Mediaeval
      English Drama, with Particular Reference to the Mystery
      Cycles." B. Litt. University of Glasgow, 1965-1966.

3249 McClure, Hazel Dean. "Eschatological Themes in English Medi-
      eval Drama." Emporia State Research Studies, XIV (1965),
      14-28.

3250 "Mystery and Miracle Plays." Encyclopedia of Poetry and Poetics.
      Alex Preminger, editor. (Princeton, New Jersey, 1965), 536-
      538.

3251 Robinson, J. W. "The Late Medieval Cult of Jesus and the Mys-
      tery Plays." Publications of the Modern Langauge Association,
      LXXX (December, 1965), 508-515.

3252 Storwell, Donald Charles, Jr. "A Study of the Treatment of the
      Devil Figure in Medieval English Religious Drama." M.A.
      University of Miami, 1965.

*3253 Kolve, V. A. The Play Called Corpus Christi. London: Edward
       Arnold (Publishers) Ltd., 1966. viii, [4], 337 pp. Bibliography,
       pp. 317-327. Index.

*3254 Weimann, Robert. "'Platea' and 'locus' im Misterienspiel: zu
       einem Grundprinzip vorshakespearescher Dramaturgie."
       Anglia, LXXXIV (1966), 330-352.

3255 Cawte, E. C., A. Helm, & N. Peacock. English Ritural Drama.
      A Geographical Index. Folk-Lore Society [Vol. 127], 1967.
      132 pp. [Has a full bibliography of known performances of
      the Mummer plays.]

3256 Fry, Timothy. "The Antiquity of the Tradition of the Triads in
      the English Cycle Plays." American Benedictine Review,

XVIII (1967), 465-480.

3257 Gold, Edith Z. "Comedy and Theology in the Medieval Mystery
       Plays." Ph.D. University of Michigan, 1967.

3258 Nelson, Alan H. "The Contest of Guile in the English Corpus
       Christi Plays." Ph.D. University of California (Berkeley), 1967.

3259 Levine, Lee F. "The Concept of the Jew as a Character in the
       English Medieval Mystery Cycles." M.A. The American Uni-
       versity, 1967.

3260 Kinghorn, A. M. "Miracle Plays." Mediaeval Drama. (London,
       1968), pp. 61-87.

3261 ----- "Realism in the Miracle Plays." Mediaeval Drama.
       (London, 1968), pp. 88-111.

3262 Malina, Marilyn J. "The Middle English Cycle: A Preface."
       Ph.D. University of Virginia, 1968.

3263 Williams, Arnold. "Typology and the Cycle Plays: Some
       Criteria." Speculum, XLIII (October, 1968), 677-684.

3264 Steiner, Rudolf. The Easter Festival Considered in Relation to
       the Mysteries: Four Lectures Given in Dornach, Switzerland
       19th to 22nd April 1924. 3d ed. (New Translation). [Translated
       from the German by George Adams.] London: Rudolf Steiner,
       1968. 78 pp. [Translation of Das Osterfest als ein Stück
       Mysteriengeschichte der Menschheit.]

*3265 Elliott, Jr., John R. "The Sacrifice of Isaac As Comedy and
       Tragedy." Studies in Philology, LXVI (January, 1969), 36-59.

3266 Hone, William. Ancient Mysteries Described, Especially the
       English Miracle Plays, Founded in the Apocryphal New Testament
       Story Extant Among the Unpublished Manuscripts in the British
       Museum; Including Notices of Ecclesiastical Shows ... London:
       Printed for W. Hone, 1823. Detroit: Singing Tree Press, 1969.
       300 pp. [Reprint].
          DLC.

2 Texts of Plays and Places of Dramatic Activity
(Cycle, Non-Cycle, Miscellaneous Plays)

Aberdeen

3267 Stuart, John, ed. Extracts from the Council Register Of the
       Burgh Of Aberdeen. 2 vol. Aberdeen: Printed for the Spalding
       Club, 1844-1848.
              ICU.

3268 Bain, Ebenezer. "The Aberdeen Craftsmen and the Miracle
       Plays." Merchant and Craft Guilds; a History of the Aber-
       deen Incorporated Trades. (Aberdeen, 1887), pp. 47-61.

3269 Chambers, E. K. "Aberdeen, Scotland." The Mediaeval Stage.
       Vol. II. (London, 1903), pp. 330-337.

3270 Pierson, Merle. "Aberdeen." In, "The Relation of the Corpus
       Christi Procession to the Corpus Christi Play in England."
       Transactions of the Wisconsin Academy of Sciences, Arts,
       and Letters, XVIII (1916), 111-113.

Abingdon

3271 Chambers, E. K. "Abingdon, Berkshire." The Medieval Stage.
       Vol. II. (London, 1903), p. 337.

Adam
Texts
3272 Luzarche, Victor, ed. Adam: drame Anglo-normand du XIIe
       siècle, publié pour la première fois d'après un manuscrit de
       la Bibliothèque de Tours. Tours: J. Bouserez, 1854. [3], lxxiv,
       [1], 101 pp. [Incorrect transcript of the Ms. (MS. 927 de la Biblio-
       thèque deTours.)] Delisle, L. "Note sur le manuscrit de Tours
       [Nr. 927] renfermant des drames liturgique et des legendes
       pieuses en vers francais." Romania, II (1873), 91-95.
              BM. ICU.

3273 ----- Adam: representation de la chute du premier homme;
       imitation libre de la première partie du drame Anglo-normand
       du XIIe siècle. Paris: Wittersheim, 1855. 78 pp.
              BM.

3274 Palustre, Leon, tr. Adam, mystère du XIIe siècle. Texte
       critique accompagné d'une traduction. Paris: Dumoulin,

1877. [4], xii, 187, [1] pp.
BM. CtY. MnU.

3275 Grass, Karl, ed. Das Adamsspiel: Anglonormannisches Gedicht
des XII. Jahrhunderts, mit einem Anhang die fünfzehn Zeichen
des jüngsten Gerichts. Halle a.S.: Max Niemeyer, 1891.
viii, 173, [1] pp. (Romanische Bibliothek, 6).
BM. NN.

3276 ----- Das Adamsspiel, etc. Zweite verbesserte Auflage. Halle
a.S.: Max Niemeyer, 1907. lxix, 94 pp. (Romanische Bibliothek, 6).

3277 Studer, Paul, ed. Le Mystère d'Adam: an Anglo-Norman Drama
of the Twelfth Century. Manchester: University Press; London:
Longmans, Green, 1918. lviii, 80 pp. Bibliography, pp. 59-63.
(Modern language texts, French Series: Medieval Section).
BM. NN.

*3278 Chamard, Henri, ed. and tr. Le Mystère d'Adam, drame reli-
gieux du XIIe siècle. Texte du ms. de Tours et traduction
noubelle. Paris: A. Colin, 1925. xi, 101 pp.
DLC. IaU. MiU. MnU. NN. WU.

3279 Barrow, Sarah F., and W. H. Hulme. The Medieval Religious
Plays "Antichrist" and "Adam." Translated with an intro-
duction. Cleveland, Western Reserve University Bulletin,
XXVIII, No. 8 (1925).

*3280 Stone, Edward Noble. Adam; A Religious Play of the Twelfth
Century, Also Known as the Repraesentatio Adae and Le
Mystère d'Adam and Containing Three Parts, Adam and Eve,
Cain and Abel, and the Processus Prophetarum. Translated
from the Norman French and Latin into English Verse.
Seattle, Washington: University of Washington Press, 1926. 193
pp. (University of Washington Publications in Language and
Literature, IV, No. 2; 2d printing, 1928).
BM. DLC. MnU. NN.

3281 Grass, Karl, ed. Das Adamspiel. Anglonormannisches Mysterium des XII Jahrhunderts; mit einem Anhang die fünfzehn
Zeichen des jüngsten Gerichts. Halle: Niemeyer, 1928. 111
pp.
BM.

3282 Cohen, Gustave. Le Jeu d'Adam et Eve. Mystère du XIIe
      siècle. Adaptations musicales de Jacques Chailley. Paris:
      Delagrave, 1936. 90 pp. [10th edition, 1948].
          BM.

3283 Doyle, John W., trans. Adam, a Play. Translated from the
      Anglo-Norman. Sydney: Shakespeare Head Press, [1948].
      77 pp.
          NN.

3284 Le mystère d'Adam. Ordo representacionis Ade. Texte com-
      plet du manuscrit de Tours publié avec une introduction et
      un glossaire par Paul Aebischer. Genève: Droz; Paris:
      Minard, 1963. 119 pp. (Textes litteraires francais, 99).
          BM. ICN. ICU.

3285 Le Jeu d'Adam. In, Harden, A. Robert, comp. Trois pieces
      medievales. (New York, 1967).

3286 Sletsjöe, Leif, ed. Le Mystère d'Adam. Édition dipolmatique
      accompagnee d'une reproduction photographique du manuscrit
      de Tours et des lecons des éditions critiques. Paris: C.
      Klincksieck, 1968. xii, 89 pp. (Bibliothèque Francaise et
      Romane, Série D: Initiation, Textes et Documents, 2.)
          ICU.

                              Studies
3287 Grass, Karl Julius. Über Versmass und Reim des Anglonor-
      mannischen Adamsspieles und des Gedichtes von den Fünfzehn
      Zeichen des jüngsten Gerichts. Inaugural Dissertation. Bonn,
      1891. 26 pp.

3288 Roomsdonk, J. N. "'Ras' in 'Le mystère d'Adam.' v. 482."
      Modern Language Review, XVI (1921), 325 ff.

3289 Monteverdi, A. "Sul testo del Mistero d'Adamo." Archivum
      Romanicum, IX (1925), 446-453. [Corrections to the edition of
      the text by P. Studer.]

3290 Breuer, Hermann. "Untersuchungen zum lateinischen altfranz-
      ösischen Adamsspiel." Zeitschrift für Romanische Philologie,
      LI (1931), 625-664; LIII (1932), 1-66.

3291 Cherau, G. "Théâtre liturgique: le jeu d'Adam et Eve; adapté
      par G. Cohen, représente à Chartres." Illustration, CXCI
      (1935), 262-263.

3292 Cohen, Gustave. "Genesis and Staging of the Jeu d'Adam."
      Annales politiques et littéraires, CV (1935), 576-578.

3293 Urwin, Kenneth. "The Mystère d'Adam." Modern Language
      Review, XXXIV (1939), 70-72.

3294 Frank, Grace. "Genesis and Staging of the Jeu d'Adam." Pub-
      lications of the Modern Language Association, LIX (1944),
      7-17.

3295 ----- "Le Mystère d'Adam." The Medieval French Drama.
      (Oxford, 1954), pp. 74-84.

3296 Steadman, John M. "Adam's Tunica Rubea: Vestiary Symbolism
      of the Anglo-Norman Adam." Modern Language Notes, LXXII
      (November, 1957), 497-499.

3297 Calin, William C. "Cain and Abel in the Mystère d'Adam."
      Modern Language Review, LVIII (April, 1963), 172-176.

3298 Gregory, J. B. E. "A Note on Lines 113-122: Le mystère d'Adam."
      Modern Language Notes, LXXVIII (December, 1963), 536-537.

3299 Woolf, R. "The Fall of Man in 'Genesis B' and the Mystère
      d'Adam." In Studies in Old English Literature in Honor of
      A. G. Brodeur. (Eugene: University of Oregon, 1963), pp.
      187-199.

3300 Kaske, R. E. "The Character 'figura' in Le Mystère d'Adam."
      In, Medieval Studies in Honor of Urban I. Holmes. (Chapel
      Hill, 1965), pp. 103-110.

3301 Noomen, W. "Note sur l'élément liturgique du Jeu d'Adam."
      In, Omagiu lui Alexandru Rosetti la 70 de ani. (Bucharest,
      1965), 635-638.

3302 Sletsjøe, Leif. "Histoire d'un texte: Les vicissitudes qu' a con-
      nues de 'Mystère d'Adam' (1854-1963)." Studia Neophilo-
      logica, XXXVII (1965), 11-39.

3303 Mathieu, Michel. "La mise en scène du Mystère d'Adam."
      Marche Romane, XVI (1966), 47-56.

Appledore

3304 Chambers, E. K. "Appledore, Kent." The Mediaeval Stage.
      Vol. II. (London, 1903), p. 337.

Ashburton

3305 Blair, Lawrence. "Ashburton." In, "A Note on the Relation of
      the Corpus Christi Procession to the Corpus Christi Play in
      England." Modern Language Notes, LV (February, 1940),
      85.

Baddow

3306 Chambers, E. K. "Baddow, Essex." The Mediaeval Stage. Vol.
      II. (London, 1903), p. 338.

Barnstable

3307 Harper, Sidney. "The History of Drama in Barnstable." Devon-
      shire Association, Reports and Transactions. XLIX (Series 3,
      Vol. 9), (1917).

Bassingbourne

3308 Wortham, Rev. B. Hale. "Churchwardens' Accounts of Bassing-
      bourne." Antiquary, VII (1883), 24-26.

3309 Chambers, E. K. "Bassingbourne, Cambridgshire." The
      Mediaeval Stage. Vol. II. (London, 1903), p. 338.

Bath

3310 ----- "Bath, Somersetshire." The Mediaeval Stage. Vol. II.
      (London, 1903), p. 338.

3311 Pierson, Merle. "Bath." In, "The Relation of the Corpus Christi
      Procession to the Corpus Christi Play in England." Transactions
      of the Wisconsin Academy of Sciences, Arts and Letters, XVIII
      (1916), 155.

3312 Blair, Lawrence. "Bath." In, "A Note on the Relation of the
      Corpus Christi Procession to the Corpus Christi Play in Eng-
      land." Modern Language Notes, LV (February, 1940), 92.

Bethersden

3313 Chambers, E. K. "Bethersden, Kent." The Mediaeval Stage.
        Vol. II. (London, 1903), p. 338.

Beverley

3314 Oliver, George. The History and Antiquities of the Town and
        Minster of Beverley, in the County of York, from the Most
        Early Period; with Historical and Descriptive Sketches of the
        Abbeys of Watton and Meaux, the Convent of Haltemprise,
        the Villages of Cottingham, Leckonfield, Bishop and Cherry
        Burton, Walkington, Risby, Scarburgh, and the Hamlets
        Comprised within the Liberties of Beverley. Compiled from
        Public and Private Reocrds, and Manuscripts of Undoubted
        Authority; and Illustrated by Numerous Engravings on Copper,
        Wood, and Stone; and Other Valuable Embellishments. Bever-
        ley: Printed and Sold by M. Turner, 1829. xxiii, [1], 575 pp.
        BM.

3315 Leach, Arthur Francis. The Beverley Town Documents. Edited
        for the Selden Society. Vol. 14. London: B. Quaritch, 1900.
        253 pp.
            BM. NN.

3316 ----- "Some English Plays and Players, 1220-1548." In, An
        English Miscellany Presented to Dr. Furnivall. (Oxford, 1901),
        pp. 205-234.

3317 Chambers, E. K. "Beverley, Yorkshire." The Mediaeval Stage.
        Vol. II. (London, 1903), pp. 338-341.

3318 Pierson, Merle. "Beverley." In, "The Relation of the Corpus
        Christi Procession to the Corpus Christi Play in England."
        Transactions of the Wisconsin Academy of Sciences, Arts, and
        Letters, XVIII (1916), 114-121.

3319 Witty, J. R. "The Beverley Plays." Transactions of the Yorkshire
        Dialect Society, IV (1922), 18-42.

Billericay

3320 Chambers, E. K. "Billericay, Essex." The Mediaeval Stage.
        Vol. II. (London, 1903), p. 341.

Bishop Auckland

3321 Chambers, E. K. "Bishop Auckland, Durham." The Mediaeval
        Stage, Vol. II. (London, 1903), p. 342.

Boreham

3322 ----- "Boreham, Essex." The Mediaeval Stage. Vol. II.
        (London, 1903), p. 342.

Boxford

3323 ----- "Boxford, Suffolk." The Mediaeval Stage. Vol. II. (Lon-
        don, 1903), p. 342.

Braintree

3324 ----- "Braintree, Essex." The Mediaeval Stage. Vol. II. (Lon-
        don, 1903), p. 342.

Brentwood

3325 ----- "Brentwood, Essex." The Mediaeval Stage. Vol. II. (Lon-
        don, 1903), p. 342.

Bristol

3326 ----- "Bristol, Gloustershire." The Mediaeval Stage. Vol. II.
        (London, 1903), p. 342.

3327 Blair, Lawrence. "Bristol." In, "A Note on the Relation of the
        Corpus Christi Procession to the Corpus Christi Play in
        England." Modern Language Notes, LV (February, 1940), 86.

BROME ABRAHAM AND ISAAC

Manuscript
3328   "The Book of Brome." FF. 15^r-22^r. Yale University MS.

Texts
3329 Smith, Lucy T., ed. "Abraham and Isaac, A Mystery Play; from
        a Private Manuscript of the 15th Century." Anglia, VII (1884),
        316-337.

3330 Abraham and Isaac. In, Smith, Lucy T., ed. Commonplace Book of the Fifteenth Century. (London, 1886), pp. 46-69. [Reprint of the 1884 edition.]

3331 Smith, Lucy Toulmin. "Notes on A Common-place Book of the Fifteenth Century, with a Religious Play of Abraham and Isaac." The Norfolk Antiquarian Miscellany, III (1887), 115-167. [The text of the play is found on pp. 127-146].

3332 Abraham and Isaac. In, Pollard, A. W. English Miracle Plays. (Oxford, 1890), pp. 173-176. [An extract].

3333 Abraham and Isaac. In, Manly, John Matthews, ed. Specimens of the Pre-Shakespearean Drama. Vol. 1. (Boston, 1897), pp. 41-57.

3334 Abraham and Isaac. In, Manly, John Matthews. Specimens of the Pre-Shaksperean Drama. (Boston and New York, 1903-1904).

3335 The Old English Miracle Play of Abraham and Isaac. London: At the De La More Press, 1905. 33, [2] pp. [The De La More Booklets.] [Modernized version based on Lucy T. Smith's edition.]
       BM.

3336 Smith, Lucy Toulmin, ed. The Book of Brome. Edited from the MS. at Brome Hall. In, Smith, Lucy Toulmin. Commonplace Book of the Fifteenth Century. Norfolk Antiquarian Miscellany. Edited by Walter Rye. 6 vol. Norwich: Gibbs and Waller, 1907-1908. See Vol. III, 117-167.
       BM. CtY.

3337 Abraham and Isaac. In, Waterhouse, Osborn, ed. The Non-Cycle Mystery Plays. (London, 1909), pp. 36-53.

3338 The Brome Abraham and Isaac. In, Child, Griffin, ed. The Second Shepherd's Play. Everyman, and Other Plays. (New York, 1910), pp. 7-26.

3339 Abraham and Isaac. In, Tatlock, J. S.P., and R. G. Martin, eds. Representative English Plays. (New York, 1916), pp. 13-19.

3340 Abraham and Isaac. A Miracle Play Adapted from the Pageant of the Barbers and Wax Chandlers in the Chester Cycle of Miracles and from the Book of Brome Found at Brome Hall,

Suffolk. In, Eliot, Samuel A., ed. Little Theatre Classics.
Vol. 2. (Boston, 1918-1922), pp. 71-112.

3341 The Sacrifice of Isaac. In, Adams, Joseph Q., ed. Chief Pre-
Shakespearean Dramas. (Boston, 1924), pp. 117-124.

3342 The Brome Abraham and Isaac. In, Matthews, Brander, and P. R.
Lieder, eds. Chief British Dramatists. (Boston, 1924), pp.
1-9.

3343 Abraham and Isaac, Brome Play. In, Hubbell, J.B., and J. O.
Beaty, compilers. An Introduction to Drama. (New York,
1927), pp. 99-106.

3344 Abraham and Isaac. In, Pollard, Alfred W., ed. English Miracle
Plays, Moralities and Interludes. (Oxford, 1927).

3345 Abraham and Isaac. In, Schweikert, Harry Christian, ed. Early
English Plays. (New York, [1928]), pp. 90-123.

3346 Abraham and Isaac. In, Lieder, P. R., ed. British Drama.
(New York, 1929).

3347 Abraham and Isaac. In, Tickner, Frederick James, ed. Earlier
English Drama from Robin Hood to Everyman. (New York,
[1929]), pp. 82-99.

3348 Abraham and Isaac. In, Parry, W. D., compiler. Old Plays for
Modern Players. (London, 1930), pp. 26-36.

3349 Browne, E. Martin, ed. The Sacrifice of Isaac; Adapted from
the Brome MS. (XIV Century.) London: P. Allan [1932]. 24
pp. (Religious Plays, Series No. 2.).
NN.

3350 Sacrifice of Isaac. In, Browne, E. Martin, ed. Religious Plays
for Use in Churches. (London, 1932).

3351 Abraham and Isaac. In, Parks, Edd Winfield, and Richmond
Croom Beatty, eds. The English Drama. An Anthology 900-
1642. (New York, 1935), pp. 10-22.

3352 Abraham and Isaac. In, Tatlock, J. S. P., and R. G. Martin, eds.
Representative English Plays from the Miracle Plays to Pinero.
2nd ed. (New York, 1938), pp. 13-19.

3353 Abraham and Isaac. In, A Book of Short Plays. XV-XX Centuries. (London, 1940).

3354 Abraham and Isaac. In, Bentley, Gerald Eades, ed. The Development of English Drama. An Anthology. (New York, 1950), pp. 12-20.

3355 Abraham and Isaac. In, Gassner, John, ed. A Treasury of the Theatre. Rev. ed. (New York, 1951), pp. 189-193.

3356 Abraham and Isaac. In, Cawley, A. C., ed. Everyman and Medieval Miracle Plays. (New York, 1959), pp. 51-68.

3357 The Sacrifice of Isaac. In, Browne, E. Martin, ed. Mystery and Morality Plays. (New York, 1960), pp. 58-69.

3358 Abraham and Isaac. In Malcolmson, Anne. Seven Miracle Plays for Modern Players. (London, 1960).

3359 Abraham and Isaac. In, Hopper, Vincent F., and Gerald B. Lahey, eds. Medieval Mystery Plays. (New York, 1962), pp. 70-89.

3360 Abraham and Isaac. In, Franklin, Alexander, ed. Seven Miracle Plays: Cain and Abel, Noah's Flood, Abraham and Isaac, The Shepherds, The Three Kings, and Adam and Eve. (London and New York, 1963), pp. 52-71.

3361 Abraham and Isaac. In, Franklin, Alexander, ed. Seven Miracle Plays: Cain and Abel, Noah's Flood, Abraham and Isaac, The Shepherds, The Three Kings, and Adam and Eve. (London and New York, 1965), pp. 52-71.

Studies

3362 "Abraham and Isaac. A Mystery Play; from a Private Manuscript of the 15th Century." Anglia, VII (1884), 316-337.

3363 Hohlfeld, Alexander R. "Two Old English Mystery Plays on the Subject of Abraham's Sacrifice." Modern Language Notes, V (April, 1890), 111-119. [Columns 222-237]. [Gives a long section of each play, for basis of comparison.]

*3364 Holthausen, F. "Play of Abraham and Isaac (Brome)." Anglia, XIII (1891), 361-362. [Textual emendations.]

3365 Davidson, C. "Concerning English Mystery Plays." Modern

Language Notes, VII (1892), 339-341.

3366 Varnhagen, Hermannus. De fabula scenica immolationem Isaac
      tractante quae sermone medio-anglico conscripta in codice
      Bromensi asservats est. Erlangae: Typis Friderici uinge
      typographi aulae Reg. Bavar et univers. Erlangensis, 1899.
      [2], 20 pp.
           BM. ICU.

3367 Chambers, E. K. "Abraham and Isaac" (Brome MS). The
      Mediaeval Stage. Vol. II. (London, 1903), p. 426.

3368 Harper, Carrie A. "A Comparison between the Brome and Chester
      Plays of Abraham and Isaac." Studies in English and Compara-
      tive Literature. (Boston, 1910), pp. 51-75. (Radcliffe College
      Monographs, No. 15).
           NN.

3369 Wells, John Edwin. "The Brome Abraham." A Manual of the
      Writings in Middle English, 1050-1400. (New Haven, 1916-
      1951), pp. 568-569, 862, 1228, 1283, 1319, 1370, 1417,
      1468, 1637, 1729.

3370 Fort, Margaret Dancy. "The Metres of the Brome and Chester
      Abraham and Isaac Plays." Publications of the Modern Lan-
      guage Association, XLI (December, 1926), 832-839.

3371 Dustoor, P. E. "Textual Notes on Three Non-Cycle Mystery
      Plays." Modern Language Review, XXIII (April, 1928), 208-
      212.

3372 Greene, Richard L. "The Brome Manuscript." Times Literary
      Supplement, (March 31, 1932), p. 229.

3373 Brady, Sister Mary Patrick. "A Study of the Characterizations
      of Abraham, Sarah, and Isaac in the English Abraham and
      Isaac Plays with Special Reference to Scripture and to Apocryphal
      Writings." M.A. Catholic University of America, 1938.

3374 Wells, Minnie E. "The Age of Isaac at the Time of the Sacrifice."
      Modern Language Notes, XIV (1939), 579-582.

3375 Severs, J. Burke. "The Relationship between the Brome and
      Chester Play of Abraham and Isaac." Modern Philology, XLII
      (February, 1945), 137-151.

3376 Lombardo, Agostino. "'The Sacrifice of Isaac' e il Miracle
       Play." English Miscellany, IV (1953), 1-43.

3377 Craig, Hardin. "Abraham and Isaac - Manuscripts from Brome
       Hall and from Dublin." English Religious Drama of the Mid-
       dle Ages. (Oxford, 1955), pp. 305-310.

3378 Kahrl, Stanley J. "The Brome Hall Commonplace Book." Theatre
       Notebook, XXII (Summer, 1968), 157-161.

Brookland

3379 Chambers, E. K. "Brookland, Kent." The Mediaeval Stage.
       Vol. II. (London, 1903), p. 343.

Bungay

3380 ----- "Bungay, Suffolk." The Mediaeval Stage. Vol. II. (Lon-
       don, 1903), p. 343.

3381 Pierson, Merle. "Bungay." In, "The Relation of the Corpus
       Procession to the Corpus Christi Play in England." Trans-
       actions of the Wisconsin Academy of Sciences, Arts, and Let-
       ters, XVIII (1916), 123.

3382 Blair, Lawrence. "Bungay." In, "A Note on the Relation of the
       Corpus Christi Procession to the Corpus Christi Play in Eng-
       land." Modern Language Notes, LV (February, 1940), 93.

Burial and Resurrection

Manuscript
3383 Burial and Resurrection of Christ. Bodleian MS. E. Museo 160.

Texts
3384 A Mystery of the Burial of Christ. Wright, Thomas, and James
       Orchard Halliwell, eds. Reliquiae Antiquae. Vol. 2. (Lon-
       don, Berlin, 1843), pp. 124-143.

3385 A Mystery of the Resurrection. Wright, Thomas, and James
       Orchard Halliwell, eds. Reliquiae Antiquae. Vol. 2. (Lon-
       don, Berlin, 1843), pp. 144-161.

3386 Christ's Burial and Resurrection. A Mystery. In Two Parts, in
       the Northern Dialect. From the Bodleian MS. E Museo 160.

In, Furnivall, F. J., ed. The Digby Plays. (London, 1882),
pp. 169-228.

3387 Christ's Burial and Resurrection. In, Furnivall, Frederick J.,
ed. The Digby Plays. With an Incomplete Morality of Wisdom,
Who Is Christ. (London, 1896), pp. 169-228.

3388 Christ's Burial and Resurrection. In, Furnivall, Frederick J.,
ed. The Digby Plays. With an Incomplete Morality of Wisdom,
Who Is Christ. (London, 1930), pp. 169-228.

Studies

3389 Schmidt, K. "The Burial and Resurrection of Christ." In, "Die
Digby-Spiele." Anglia. Zeitschrift für Englische Philologie,
VIII. 3. Heft (1885), 393-404.

3390 Chambers, E. K. "Burial and Resurrection." The Mediaeval
Stage. Vol. II. (London, 1903), pp. 431-432.

3391 Wells, John Edwin. "The Bodley 'Burial and Resurrection.'"
A Manual of the Writings in Middle English, 1050-1400. (New
Haven, 1916-1951), pp. 569-570, 862, 993.

3392 Craig, Hardin. "Burial and Resurrection." English Religious
Drama of the Middle Ages. (Oxford, 1955), pp. 317-319.

3393 Baker, D. C., and J. L. Murphy. "The Bodleian MS. E. Mus.
160 Burial and Resurrection and the Digby Plays." Review
of English Studies, XIX (1968), 290-293.

Burnham

3394 Chambers, E. K. "Burnham, Essex." The Mediaeval Stage.
Vol. II. (London, 1903), p. 343.

Bury St. Edmunds

3395 ----- "Bury St. Edmund's Suffolk." The Mediaeval Stage. Vol.
II. (London, 1903), pp. 343-344.

3396 Pierson, Merle. "Bury St. Edmunds." "The Relation of the Corpus
Christi Procession to the Corpus Christi Play in England."
Transactions of the Wisconsin Academy of Sciences, Arts,
and Letters, XVIII (1916), 123.

3397 Wells, John Edwin. "The Bury St. Edmunds Fragment." A
         Manual of Writings in Middle English, 1050-1400. (New Haven,
         1916-1951), pp. 1079-1080, 1136, 1228, 1586, 1636.

Cambridge

3398 Masters, Robert. History of Corpus Christi College. Cambridge:
         Printed for the Author by J. Bentham Printer to the University,
         1753. iv, 428, 115, 54 pp. [In 2 parts.]
         BM.

3399 Chambers, E. K. "Cambridge, Cambridgeshire." The Mediaeval
         Stage. Vol. II. (London, 1903), p. 344.

3400 Pierson, Merle. "Cambridge." In, "The Relation of the Corpus
         Christi Procession to the Corpus Christi Play in England."
         Transactions of the Wisconsin Academy of Sciences, Arts,
         and Letters, XVIII (1916), 155-156.

3401 Sayle, C. "Drama in Cambridge." Times Literary Supplement,
         June 9, 1921, p. 372.

3402 Smith, G. C. Moore, ed. "The Academic Drama at Cambridge:
         Extracts from College Records." Malone Society. Collections.
         II, Part II (1923), pp. 150-230.

Canterbury

3403 Sheppard, J. F. "The Canterbury Marching Watch with Its Pageant
         of St. Thomas." Archaeologia Cantiana, XII (1878), 27-46.

3404 Chambers, E. K. "Canterbury, Kent." The Mediaeval Stage.
         Vol. II. (London, 1903), pp. 344-345.

3405 Pierson, Merle. "Canterbury." In, "The Relation of the Corpus
         Christi Procession to the Corpus Christi Play in England."
         Transactions of the Wisconsin Academy of Sciences, Arts,
         and Letters, XVIII (1916), 124.

3406 Plomer, Henry R. "Plays at Canterbury in 1570." Library, Third
         Series, IX (1918), 251-254.

3407 Blair, Lawrence. "Canterbury." In, "A Note on the Relation of
         the Corpus Christi Procession to the Corpus Christ Play in
         England." Modern Language Notes, LV (February, 1940), 87.

3408 Rackham, Bernard. The Ancient Glass of Canterbury Cathedral.
        London: Published for the Friends of Canterbury Cathedral
        by Lund Humphries & Co., 1949. xv, 194 pp.

3409 Dawson, Giles, ed. "Canterbury." Records of Plays and Players
        in Kent 1450-1642. Malone Society. (Oxford, 1965), pp. 1-
        21.

Chelmsford

3410 Chambers, E. K. "Chelmsford, Essex." The Mediaeval Stage.
        Vol. II. (London, 1903), pp. 345-348.

3411 Mepham, William Alfred. "The Chelmsford Plays of the Sixteenth
        Century." Essex Review, LVI (1947), 171-178.

CHESTER PLAYS

Manuscripts

3412 [c. 1500] National Library of Wales, Aberystwyth. MS. Peniarth
        399 [Formerly Hengwrt 229]. MS. of the Antichrist play. 10
        leaves.

3413 [c. 1575-1600] Manchester Free Library. Opening of the play
        of the Resurrection. Fragment of 41 lines.

3414 1591. San Marino, California. Huntington Library. HM. 2.
        Imperfect at the beginning. The first pageant supplied in a
        modern transcript. Signed, "By me Edward Gregorie scholler
        at Bunbury the yeare of our lord god 1591."

3415 1592. British Museum. MS. Additional 10,305. 168 folios. Muti-
        lated at the beginning and the end. 96 lines of text missing at
        the end. At the end of each play signed, "By me Georgi Bellin
        1592." [Wright used this manuscript for his edition.]

3416 1597-1756. Chester. Cooper's Guild. Cooper's Enrolment Book
        1597-1756. Cooper's play of the Trial and Flagellation, in
        the hand of George Bellin.

3417 1600. British Museum. MS. Harley 2013. 205 folios. Perfect.
        Several plays are signed at the end, "per me George Bellin
        1600."

3418 1604. Oxford. MS. Bodley 175. 176 folios. Perfect. The MS. is signed at the end, "1604, per me gulielmum Bedford."

3419 1607. British Museum. MS. Harley 2124. 142 folios. Written in two hands. MS. signed at the end in the second hand, "1607 Augusti quarto, per Jacobum Miller."

Collections

3420 [Markland, James Heywood, ed.]. Chester Mysteries. De Deluvio Noe. De Occisione Innocentium. London: Printed by Bensley and Sons, 1818. xxii, [2], 70 pp. [From MS. Harl. 2124. Has the Prologue also. Fifty copies printed.]
   BM. DLC. MdBP. MH. NN.

3421 Wright, Thomas, ed. The Chester Plays: A Collection of Mysteries Founded upon Scriptural Subjects, and Formerly Represented by the Trades of Chester at Whitsuntide. 2 vol. London: Printed for the Shakespeare Society, 1843-1847.
   BM. CtY. DLC. ICN. MH. MiU. NN. OU. PU. ViU.

3422 The Chester Plays. Re-edited from the MSS. by the Late Dr. Hermann Deimling. [Vol. 2 is Re-edited from the MSS. by Dr. Matthews.] Part I. London: Published for the Early English Text Society by Kegan Paul, Trench, Trubner & Co., 1893. Part II. London: Published for the Early English Text Society by Kegan Paul, Trench, Trubner & Co., Ltd., and by Humphrey Milford, Oxford University Press, 1916. xxxv, [1], 240, [6], xxv-lx, 241-458. [Vol. I reprinted 1926, 1959. Vol. II reprinted 1935, 1959. First printing of Vol. I was 1892.]
   CtY. IaU. MH. MiU. NN. OCl. OO. PHC. ViU.

3423 Bridge, Joseph C., ed. Three Chester Whitsun Plays. With an Introduction and Notes. Chester: Phillipson and Golder, 1906. xiv, 49 pp.
   BM. CtY. ICN. MH. MiU. MnU. NN. MWelC.

3424 Conroy, Frank M., and Roy Mitchell, eds. The Nativity and Adoration Cycle of the Chester Mysteries, As Performed in New York on Christmas Eve at the Greenwich Village Theatre, with a Prefatory Note on the Sources and Method of Playing, Including the Sheaphardes' Play. The Offering of the Sheaphardes, The Adoration of the Magi. New York: E. H. Arens, 1917. 23 pp.
   CtY. DLC. IaU. MB. MH. NN. OCl. ODW.

3425 Matthews, Godfrey W. The Chester Mystery Plays. Liverpool:
       E. Howell, Ltd., 1925. [4], 85, [4] pp. (Reprinted from the
       Transactions of the Historic Society of Lancashire and Che-
       shire, Vol. LXXVI.) [Plays 1-3 from British Museum, MS.
       Harl. 2124.]
             BM. MH. MnU. NN. WU.

3426 King, I., and O. Bolton, eds. The Chester Miracle Plays. Done
       into Modern English and Arranged for Acting; with an Intro-
       duction by Sir Barry V. Jackson. London: Society for Promoting
       Christian Knowledge; New York: The Macmillan Co., 1930.
       xvii, 177 pp.
             BM. CtY. DLC. ICN. MH. MiU. MnU. NN.

3427 Beaudoin, Kenneth. The Chester Trilogy; Rendered into Some-
       what More Contemporary English. 1950. 14 pp.
             NN.

3428 Hussey, Maurice. The Chester Mystery Plays. Sixteen Pageant
       Plays From the Chester Craft Cycle. Adapted into Modern
       English. Melbourne, London, Toronto: Heinemann, 1957.
       xxi, [1], 160 pp. [Reprinted, 1960].

Individual Plays
Texts

Fall of Lucifer

3429 The Fall of Lucifer. In, Wright, Thomas, ed. The Chester Plays.
       Vol. 1. (London, 1843), pp. 8-19.

3430 The Fall of Lucifer. In, Deimling, Hermann, ed. The Chester
       Plays. Vol. 1. (London, 1892), pp. 9-20.

3431 The Fall of Lucifer. In, Matthews, Godfrey W. The Chester
       Mystery Plays. (Liverpool, 1925).

3432 The Fall of Lucifer. In, Hussey, Maurice. The Chester Mystery
       Plays ... Adapted into Modern English. (Melbourne, London,
       Toronto, 1960), pp. 3-10.

The Creation

3433 The Childhood of Man. [In ten scenes]. In, King, I. and O. Bolton.
       The Chester Mystery Plays. Done into Modern English...
       (London, 1930), pp. 1-57. [Plays 1-4 adapted.]

3434 The Creation and Fall, and Death of Abel. In, Wright, Thomas, ed. The Chester Plays. Vol. 1. (London, 1843), pp. 20-44.

3435 The Creation. In, Deimling, Hermann, ed. The Chester Plays. Vol. 1. (London, 1892), pp. 20-47.

3436 The Creation. In, Matthews, Godfrey W. The Chester Mystery Plays. (Liverpool, 1925).

3437 The Creation of Man: Adam and Eve. In, Hussey, Maurice. The Chester Mystery Plays ... Adapted into Modern English. (Melbourne, London, Toronto, 1960), pp. 11-22.

De Deluvio Noe

3438 De Deluvio, Noe. In, Markland, J. H., ed. Chester Mysteries. (London, 1818), pp. 13-37.

3439 De Deluvio Noe. In, Marriott, William. A Collection of English Miracle-Plays. (Basel, 1838), pp. 3-15.

3440 De Deluvio Noe. In, Wright, Thomas, ed. The Chester Plays. Vol. 1. (London, 1843), pp. 45-56.

3441 De Deluvio Noe. In, Keltie, John S. The Works of the British Dramatists. (Edinburgh, 1870), pp. xl-xlii. [A selection only.]

3442 De Deluvio Noe. In, Pollard, A. W., ed. English Miracle Plays. (Oxford, 1890), pp. 8-20, 180-184.

3443 The Deluge. In, Deimling, Hermann, ed. The Chester Plays. Vol. 1. (London, 1892), pp. 48-63.

3444 De Deluvio Noe. In, Hawthorne, Julian, ed. The Masterpieces and the History of Literature. Vol. 4. (New York, 1906), pp. 332-335.

3445 De Deluvio Noe. In, Everyman, with Other Interludes, Including Eight Miracle Plays. (London, 1909), pp. 26-36.

3446 De Deluvio Noe. In, Smallwood, Samuel. Some Ancient Mystery Towers Remaining in England. [Hitchin, England, 1916], pp. 57-72.

3447 Noah's Flood. In, Eliot, Jr., Samuel A., ed. Little Theatre

Classics. Vol. 2. (Boston, 1918-1922).

3448   De Deluvio Noe. In, Adams, Joseph Quincy, ed. Chief Pre-
       Shakespearean Dramas. (Boston, 1924), pp. 111-116.

3449   The Deluge. In, Matthews, Godfrey W. The Chester Mystery
       Plays. (Liverpool, 1925).

3450   The Chester Play of the Deluge. Edited by J. Isaacs, with En-
       gravings on Wood by David Jones. Waltham Saint-Lawrence,
       Berkshire: Printed and Published at the Golden Cockerel Press,
       1927. iv, 16, [1] pp. [Text is based on that by A. W. Pollard,
       with variants from the manuscripts edited by Deimling.]
           BM. CSmH. CtY. MnU. NcD. NN. PBm.

3451   Noah's Flood. In, Pollard, Alfred W., ed. English Miracle
       Plays, Moralities and Interludes. (Oxford, 1927).

3452   Noah's Flood. In, Parry, W. D., ed. Old Plays for Modern
       Players, Selected and Modernized. (London, 1930), pp. 13-
       25.

3453   Noah's Deluge. In, Everyman And Other Interludes. (London,
       New York, [1935]).

3454   The Deluge or Noah's Flood. In, Bentley, Gerald Eades, ed. The
       Development of English Drama. An Anthology. (New York,
       1950), pp. 4-11.

3455   Britten, Benjamin. [Noy's fludde. English and German]. Noye's
       fludde; the Chester miracle play, set to music. Op. 59. Full
       score. London: Hawkes & Son [1958]. (score) 193 pp. [Text
       from "English Miracle Plays, Moralities and Interludes,"
       edited by Alfred W. Pollard.]
           ICN.

3456   Britten, Benjamin, and Colin Graham. Noye's Fludde. The Chester
       Miracle Play Set to Music by Benjamin Britten. Notes on the
       Production. [London]: Boosey & Haekes, [1958]. 8 pp.
           BM.

3457   Britten, Edward Benjamin. Noye's Fludde. The Chester Miracle
       Play set to music. Notes On The Production. [London] Boosey
       & Hawkes [1958]. [7] pp.
           BM.

3458 Britten, Benjamin. Noye's fludde; the Chester Miracle Play, Set
to Music. Op. 59. Vocal score by Imogen Holst. London, New
York: Hawkes; sole selling agents: Boosey & Hawkes [c. 1958].
76 pp.
ICN.

3459 Noye's Fludde. The Chester Miracle Play. Set to Music by Benjamin Britten. London, Paris, etc: Boosey and Hawkes, Ltd.,
1958. 19 pp. [Text is from A. W. Pollard's English Miracle
Plays, Moralities and Interludes].
BM.

3460 Noah's Flood. In, Cawley, A. C., ed. Everyman and Medieval
Miracle Plays. (New York, 1959), pp. 35-49.

3461 Noah's Flood. In, Browne, E. Martin, ed. Mystery and Morality
Plays. (New York, 1960), pp. 45-57.

3462 Noah's Deluge. In, Hussey, Maurice. The Chester Mystery
Plays ... Adapted into Modern English. (Melbourne, London,
Toronto, 1960), pp. 23-34.

3463 Noah's Flood. In, Malcolmson, Anne. Seven Medieval Plays for
Modern Players. (London, 1960).

3464 Noye's Fludde. The Chester Miracle Play Set to Music by Benjamin
Britten. Illustrated Libretto of the Recorded Performance in
Oxford Church at the XIVth Aldeburgh Festival. London: Argo
Record Company, Limited, 1961. 16 pp. [Based on Pollard's
text.]
BM.

3465 Noah's Flood. In, Hopper, Vincent F., and Gerald B. Lahey, eds.
Medieval Mystery Plays. (New York, 1962), pp. 90-107.

3466 Noah's Flood. In, Franklin, Alexander, ed. Seven Miracle Plays:
Cain and Abel, Noah's Flood, Abraham and Isaac, The Shep-
herds, The Three Kings, and Adam and Eve. (London and New
York, 1963).

3467 Noah's Flood. In, Franklin, Alexander, ed. Seven Miracle Plays:
Cain and Abel, Noah's Flood, Abraham and Isaac, The Shep-
herds, The Three Kings, and Adam and Eve. (London and New
York, 1965).

Abraham and Isaac

3468 Abraham and Isaak. In, Collier, J. P., ed. Five Miracle Plays, or Scriptural Dramas. (London, 1836).

3469 Abraham and Isaac. In, Marriott, William, ed. A Collection of English Miracle-Plays or Mysteries. (Basel, Paris, 1838).

3470 The Histories of Lot and Abraham. In, Wright, Thomas, ed. The Chester Plays. Vol. 1. (London, 1843), pp. 57-76.

3471 Sacrifice of Isaac. In, Pollard, Alfred W., ed. English Miracle Plays, Moralities and Interludes. (Oxford, 1890), pp. 21-30, 184-187.

3472 The Sacrifice of Isaac. In, Deimling, Hermann, ed. The Chester Plays. Vol. 1. (London, 1892), pp. 63-83.

3473 Abraham and Isaak; ein mittelenglisches Misterium aus einer Dubliner Handschrift. [Herausgegeben von Rudolf Brotanek]. Anglia, XXI (1899), 21-55.

3474 Abraham, Melchisedec, and Isaac. In, Everyman and Other Interludes. (London, [1909]), pp. 37-51.

3475 Abraham and Isaac. In, Waterhouse, Osborn, ed. The Non-Cycle Mystery Plays. (London, 1909).

3476 Abraham and Isaac, a Miracle Play Adapted from The Pageant of the Barbers and Wax-Chandlers, in the Chester Cycle of Miracles, and from the Book of Brome found at Brome Hall, Suffolk. Presented at the Municipal Theater, Northampton, Massachusetts, Christmas, 1918. In, Eliot, S. A., ed. Little Theatre Classics, 1918. Vol. 2, pp. [71]-112.

3477 Sacrifice of Isaac. In, Pollard, Alfred W., ed. English Miracle Plays, Moralities, and Interludes. (Oxford, 1927).

3478 Abraham and Isaac. In, Osgood, Phillips Endecott, ed. Old-time Church Drama Adapted: Mystery Plays and Moralities of Earlier Days for Sundry Churchly Uses To-day. (New York and London, 1928), pp. 99-123.

3479 Abraham, Melchisedec, and Isaac. In, Everyman And Other Interludes. London, New York, [1935].

3480 Abraham and Isaac. In, Hussey, Maurice. The Chester Mystery
Plays ... Adapted into Modern English. (Melbourne, London,
Toronto, 1960), pp. 34-41.

Balaam and Balak

3481 Balaam and His Ass. In, Wright, Thomas, ed. The Chester Plays.
Vol. 1. (London, 1843), pp. 77-93.

3482 Balaam and Balak. In, Deimling, Hermann, ed. The Chester
Plays. Vol. 1. (London, 1892), pp. 84-104.

3483 Balaam and His Ass. In, Manly, John Matthews, ed. Specimens
of the Pre-Shakesperean Drama. Vol. 1. (Boston, 1897), pp.
66-81.

3484 Balaam and His Ass. In, Adams, Joseph Quincy, ed. Chief Pre-
Shakespearean Dramas. (Boston, 1924), pp. 132-138.

Salutation and Nativity

3485 The Salutation and Nativity. In, Wright, Thomas, ed. The Chester
Plays. Vol. 1. (London, 1843), pp. 94-118.

3486 The Nativity. In, Deimling, Hermann, ed. The Chester Plays.
Vol. 1. (London, 1892), pp. 104-132.

3487 The Salutation and Nativity. In, Bridge, Joseph C., ed. Three
Chester Whitsun Plays. (Chester, 1906).

3488 The Salutation and Nativity. In, Hemingway, Samuel B., ed.
English Nativity Plays. (New York, 1909), pp. 5-35.

3489 The Nativity. In, Frost, Lesley, ed. Come Christmas. (New York,
1929), pp. 205-213.

3490 The Nativity. In, King, I. and O. Bolton, eds. The Chester Miracle
Plays. Done into Modern English and Arranged for Acting. (London, 1930), pp. 59-118. [In 16 scenes. Chester Plays 6-10
adapted.]

3491 The Nativity. In, Hussey, Maurice. The Chester Mystery Plays
... Adapted into Modern English. (Melbourne, London,
Toronto, 1960), pp. 42-48.

3492 Nativity. In, Hemingway, Samuel B., ed. English Nativity
      Plays. (New York, 1964).

Plays of the Shepherds

3493 The Play of the Shepherds. In, Wright, Thomas, ed. The Chester
      Plays. Vol. 1. (London, 1843), pp. 119-145.

3494 Adoration of the Shepherds. In, Deimling, Hermann, ed. The
      Chester Plays. Vol. 1. (London, 1892), pp. 132-160.

3495 The Shepherds' Offering. One of the Chester Miracle Plays.
      Edited by H. H. Barne. London: Arnold Fairbairns, 1906.
      53 pp.
            BM.

3496 The Play of the Shepherds. In, Bridge, Joseph C., ed. Three
      Chester Whitsun Plays. (Chester, 1906).

3497 The Play of the Shepherds. In, Hemingway, Samuel B., ed. Eng-
      lish Nativity Plays. (New York, 1909), pp. 36-67.

3498 The Sheaphardes' Play. In, Conroy, Frank M., and Roy Mitchell,
      eds. The Nativity and Adoration Cycle of the Chester Mys-
      teries, As Performed in New York on Christmas Eve at the
      Greenwich Village Theatre. (New York, 1917).

3499 The Shepherds' Play. In, Tickner, F. J., ed. Earlier English
      Drama, from Robin Hood to Everyman. (London and Edin-
      burgh, 1926).

3500 The Play of the Shepherds. In, Tickner, Frederick J., ed.
      Earlier English Drama from Robin Hood to Everyman. (New
      York, 1929), pp. 134-148.

3501 The Adoration of the Shepherds. In, Hussey, Maurice. The
      Chester Mystery Plays ... Adapted into Modern English.
      (Melbourne, London, Toronto, 1960), pp. 49-56.

3502 The Shepherds. In, Franklin, Alexander, ed. Seven Miracle
      Plays: Cain and Abel, Noah's Flood, Abraham and Isaac, The
      Shepherds, The Three Kings and Adam and Eve. (London and
      New York, 1963), pp. 72-93.

3503 Shepherds' Play. In, Hemingway, Samuel B., ed. English Nativity

Plays. (New York, 1964).

3504   The Shepherds. In, Franklin, Alexander, ed. Seven Miracle
       Plays: Cain and Abel, Noah's Flood, Abraham and Isaac,
       The Shepherds, The Three Kings, and Adam and Eve. (Lon-
       don and New York, 1965), pp. 72-93.

Adoration of the Magi

3505   Adoration of the Magi. In, Deimling, Hermann, ed. The Chester
       Plays. Vol. 1. (London, 1892), pp. 160-176.

3506   The Adoration of the Magi. In, Bridge, Joseph C., ed. Three
       Chester Whitsun Plays. (Chester, 1906).

3507   The Adoration of the Magi. In, Conroy, Frank M., and Roy
       Mitchell, eds. The Nativity and Adoration Cycle of the Chester
       Mysteries, As Performed in New York on Christmas Eve at
       the Greenwich Village Theatre. (New York, 1917).

3508   Adoration of the Magi. In, Hussey, Maurice. The Chester Mys-
       tery Plays ... Adapted into Modern English. (Melbourne,
       London, Toronto, 1960), pp. 56-63.

3509   King Herod. In, Franklin, Alexander, ed. Seven Miracle Plays:
       Cain and Abel, Noah's Flood, Abraham and Isaac, The Shep-
       herds, The Three Kings, and Adam and Eve. (London and
       New York, 1963), pp. 108-122.

3510   King Herod. In, Franklin, Alexander, ed. Seven Miracle Plays:
       Cain and Abel, Noah's Flood, Abraham and Isaac, The Shep-
       herds, The Three Kings, and Adam and Eve. (London and
       New York, 1965), pp. 108-122.

Magi's Oblation

3511   The Magi's Oblation. In, Deimling, Hermann, ed. The Chester
       Plays. Vol. 1. (London, 1892), pp. 177-186.

3512   The Magi's Oblation. In, Hussey, Maurice. The Chester Mys-
       tery Plays ... Adapted into Modern English. (Melbourne,
       London, Toronto, 1960), pp. 64-67.

Killing the Innocents

3513 De Occisione innocentium. In, Markland, James H., ed.
      Chester Mysteries. De Deluvio Noe. De Occisione Inno-
      centium. (London, 1818), pp. 39-70.

3514 De Occisione innocentium. In, Wright, Thomas, ed. The
      Chester Plays. Vol. 1. (London, 1843), pp. 172-188.

3515 Slaying of the Innocents. In, Deimling, Hermann, ed. The
      Chester Plays. Vol. 1. (London, 1892), pp. 186-205.

3516 Massacre of the Innocents. In, Tickner, Frederick J., ed.
      Earlier English Drama from Robin Hood to Everyman.
      (New York, 1929), pp. 171-181.

3517 The Slaying of the Innocents. In, Hussey, Maurice. The Chester
      Mystery Plays ... Adapted into Modern English. (Melbourne,
      London, Toronto, 1960), pp. 67-75.

Purification

3518 The Purification. In, Wright, Thomas, ed. The Chester Plays.
      Vol. 1. (London, 1843), pp. 189-200.

3519 Purification. In, Deimling, Hermann, ed. The Chester Plays.
      Vol. 1. (London, 1892), pp. 205-217.

Temptation

3520 The Temptation, and the Woman Taken in Adultery. In, Wright,
      Thomas, ed. The Chester Plays. Vol. 1. (London, 1843),
      pp. 201-211.

3521 The Temptation. In, Deimling, Hermann, ed. The Chester
      Plays. Vol. 1. (London, 1892), pp. 217-229.

Lazarus

3522 Lazarus. In, Wright, Thomas. The Chester Plays. Vol. 1.
      (London, 1843), pp. 212-231.

3523 Christ. The Adulteress. Chelidonius. In, Deimling, Hermann,
      ed. The Chester Plays. Vol. 1. (London, 1892), pp. 229-240;
      Vol. II. pp. 241-249.

3524 Christ's Ministry. In, Adams, Joseph Q., ed. Chief Pre-
Shakespearean Dramas. (Boston, 1924), pp. 167-174.

Simon the Leper

3525 Christ's Entry into Jerusalem. In, Wright, Thomas, ed. The
Chester Plays. Vol. 2. (London, 1847), pp. 1-17.

3526 Christ's Visit to Simon the Leper. In, Matthews, Dr. The
Chester Plays. Vol. 2. (London, 1916), pp. 249-265. [Part
of Deimling edition.]

3527 Simon the Leper. In, Hussey, Maurice. The Chester Mystery
Plays ... Adapted into Modern English. (Melbourne, London,
Toronto, 1960), pp. 76-84.

Christ's Betrayal

3528 Christ Betrayed. In, Wright, Thomas, ed. The Chester Plays.
Vol. 2. (London, 1847), pp. 18-32.

3529 Christ's Betrayal. In, Matthews, Dr. The Chester Plays. Vol.
2. (London, 1916), pp. 265-279. [Part of Deimling edition.]

3530 Christ Betrayed. In, Tickner, Frederick J., ed. Earlier English
Drama from Robin Hood to Everyman. (New York, 1929), pp.
191-200.

3531 The Betrayal of Christ. In, Hussey, Maurice. The Chester Mystery Plays.... Adapted into Modern English. (Melbourne, London, Toronto, 1960), pp. 85-94.

Christ's Passion

3532 The Passion. In, Wright, Thomas, ed. The Chester Plays. Vol.
2. (London, 1847), pp. 33-50.

3533 Christ's Passion, In, Matthews, Dr. The Chester Plays. Vol. 2.
(London, 1916), pp. 280-317. [Part of Deimling edition.]

3534 The Trial and Flagellation: A New Manuscript. By F. M. Salter.
In: The Trial & Flagellation With Other Studies in the Chester
Cycle. Malone Society Studies. London: Oxford University
Press, 1935. pp. 1-73.

3535 Salter, F. M. and W. W. Greg, eds. The Trial and Flagellation with

Other Studies in the Chester Cycle. The Malone Society Reprints. Oxford University Press, 1936. 172 pp.
  BM. DLC. ICU. MiU. MnU. OCU. PHC. PU-F.

3536 Christ's Passion. In, Hussey, Maurice. The Chester Mystery
      Plays ... Adapted into Modern English. (Melbourne, London,
      Toronto, 1960), pp. 95-107.

Harrowing of Hell

3537 The Harrowing of Hell. In, Wright, Thomas, ed. The Chester
      Plays. Vol. 2. (London, 1843), pp. 71-83.

3538 Christ's Descent into Hell. In, Matthews, Dr. The Chester
      Plays. Vol. 2. (London, 1916), pp. 318-331. [Part of Deim-
      ling edition.]

3539 The Harrowing of Hell. In, Adams, Joseph Q., ed. Chief Pre-
      Shakespearean Dramas. (Boston, 1924), 187-190.

3540 The Harrowing of Hell. In, Tickner, F. J., ed. Earlier English
      Drama from Robin Hood to Everyman. (New York, [1929]),
      pp. 223-232.

3541 The Harrowing of Hell. In, Cawley, A. C., ed. Everyman and
      Medieval Miracle Plays. (New York, 1959), pp. 157-169.

Resurrection

3542 The Resurrection. In, Wright, Thomas, ed. The Chester Plays.
      Vol. 2. (London, 1847), pp. 84-100.

3543 "The Resurrection." Manchester Guardian, May 19, 1883.
      [Fragment of the 19th Play, found in an old book cover, by
      C. W. Sutton.]

3544 Christ's Resurrection. In, Matthews, Dr. The Chester Plays.
      Vol. 2. (London, 1916), pp. 331-351. [Part of Deimling
      edition.]

3545 The Resurrection. In, Tickner, F. J., ed. Earlier English
      Drama from Robin Hood to Everyman. (New York, [1929]),
      pp. 232-244. [Lines 1-420.]

3546 Greg, W. W. "The Manchester Fragment of the 'Resurrection.'"

In, The Trial & Flagellation with Other Studies of the Cycle. Malone Society Studies. (London: Oxford University Press, 1935), pp. 85-100.

3547 Christ's Resurrection. In, Hussey, Maurice. The Chester Mystery Plays ... Adapted into Modern English. (Melbourne, London, Toronto, 1960), pp. 108-117.

Christ Appears to Two Disciples

3548 The Pilgrims of Emaus. In, Wright, Thomas, ed. The Chester Plays. Vol. 2. (London, 1847), pp. 101-112.

3549 Christ Appears to Two Disciples. In, Matthews, Dr. The Chester Plays. Vol. 2. (London, 1916), pp. 352-362. [Part of Deimling edition.]

3550 The Fourth Play, or Epilogue. [On the Road to Emmaus. Adapted.] In, Bolton King, I. and O. Chester Plays. (London, [1930]), pp. 157-162.

Christ's Ascension

3551 The Ascension. In, Wright, Thomas, ed. The Chester Plays. Vol. 2. (London, 1847), pp. 113-121.

3552 Christ's Ascension. In, Matthews, Dr. The Chester Plays. Vol. 2. (London, 1916), pp. 363-371. [Part of Deimling edition.]

3553 Christ's Ascension. In, Hussey, Maurice. The Chester Mystery Plays ... Adapted into Modern English. (Melbourne, London, Toronto, 1960), pp. 117-121.

Sending of the Holy Ghost

3554 The Emission of the Holy Ghost. In, Wright, Thomas, ed. The Chester Plays, Vol. 2. (London, 1847), pp. 122-138.

3555 The Sending of the Holy Ghost. In, Matthews, Dr. The Chester Plays. Vol. 2. (London, 1916), pp. 371-387. [Part of the Deimling edition.]

Antichrist

3556 The Advent of Antichrist. A Miracle Play. Now First Printed

from the Duke of Devonshire MS. [London: F. Shoberl, Jun.
1836?]. 39 pp. [Only 25 copies printed.]
O.

3557 The Advent of Antichrist. In, Collier, John Payne. Five Miracle
Plays. (London, 1836), pp. 1-39.

3558 Antichrist. In, Marriott, William. A Collection of English Miracle-
Plays or Mysteries. (Basel, 1838), pp. 16-38.

3559 Ezechiel. In, Wright, Thomas. The Chester Plays. Vol. 2. (London, 1847), pp. 139-149.

3560 Antichrist. In, Manly, John Matthews, ed. Specimens of Pre-
Shakespearean Drama. Vol. 1. (Boston, 1897), pp. 170-197.

3561 The Prophets and Antichrist. In, Matthews, Dr. The Chester
Plays. Vol. 2. (London, 1916), pp. 387-399. [Part of Deimling
edition.]

3562 The Coming of Antichrist. In, Matthews, Dr. The Chester Plays.
Vol. 2. (London, 1916), pp. 400-427. [Part of Deimling edition.]

3563 The Play of Antichrist from the Chester Cycle. Edited by W. W.
Greg. Oxford: At the Clarendon Press, 1935. xcix, [1], 90 pp.
BM. CtY. DLC. MH. MnU.

3564 Antichrist. In, Hussey, Maurice. The Chester Mystery Plays
... Adapted into Modern English. (Melbourne, London,
Toronto, 1960), pp. 122-141.

3565 Antichrist. In, Wright, Thomas, ed. The Chester Plays. Vol. 2.
(London, 1847), pp. 150-177.

Last Judgment (Doomsday)

3566 Doomsday. In, Wright, Thomas, ed. The Chester Plays. Vol. 2.
(London, 1847), pp. 178-201.

3567 The Last Judgment. In, Matthews, Dr. The Chester Plays. Vol.
2. (London, 1916), pp. 427-453. [Part of Deimling edition.]

3568 The Last Judgment. In, Hussey, Maurice. The Chester Mystery
Plays ... Adapted into Modern English. (Melbourne, London,
Toronto, 1960), pp. 142-152.

Studies

3569 A Concise History of the Country and City of Chester, from the
          Most Authentic and Respectable Authors; with Descriptive and
          Lively Observations on the Manners, Customs, &c. of the
          Inhabitants; also the Life of St. Werburgh, the Memorable
          Founder of the Cathedral of Chester, Containing Several
          Historical Facts, Worthy the Notice of the Traveller and
          the Man of Letters; Embellished with an Elegant Ground Plan
          of the City and Suburbs of Chester . . . Chester: Printed by
          J. Fletcher, for J. Poole. [Pref. 1791]. 116 pp.
             BM. MH.

3570 History of the City of Chester, from Its Foundation to the Present
          Time; Collected from Public Records, Private Manuscripts,
          and Other Authentic Sources. With an Account of Parochial
          and Other Charities, Never Before Published; and a Chronolo-
          gical Register of Important Events to the Year 1815. Illus-
          trated with five etchings, by G. Cuitt. Chester: Printed for
          T. Poole, 1815 [1816]. 334 pp.
             BM. DFo. ICN.

3571 Markland, James Heywood. A Dissertation on the Chester Mys-
          teries. Roxburghe Club, 1818. [Reprinted by Malone, Shake-
          speare, 1821].
             BM. ICN.

3572 Ormerod, George. The History of the County Palatine and City
          of Chester. 3 vol. London: Printed for Lackington, Hughes,
          Harding, Mavor, and Jones, 1819.
             BM. CSmH. DLC. ICN. MH. MiU. NN. PU.

3573 Collier, John Payne. "The Widkirk, Chester, and Coventry
          Miracle-Plays." The History of Dramatic Poetry. Vol. 2.
          (London, 1831), pp. 155-229.

*3574 Hemingway, Joseph. History of the City of Chester from Its
          Foundation to the Present Time; With an Account of Its Anti-
          quities, Curiosities, Local Customs, and Peculiar Immunities;
          and a Concise Political History. 2 vol. Chester, 1831.
             BM. CtY. ICN. MB. MH. OCl.

3575 Hume, A. [On the Chester Mystery Play, Presented before the
          Congress of the British Archaeological Association, 1849.]
          British Archaeological Association. Journal, V (1849), 317-320.

3576 Broadbent, R. J. Annals of the Chester Stage from the Earliest
      Times to the End of the Theatre Royal, by Letters Patent,
      1854.
            Typescript in Liverpool Public Library (Loewenberg, p.
            18).

3577 Christie, Richard Copley, ed. and tr. Annales Cestrienses; Or,
      Chronicle of the Abbey of S. Werburg, at Chester. [London]:
      Printed for the Record Society, 1887. 152 pp. (Latin and
      English on facing pages. Ends with year 1297.)
            BM. ICN. MiU.

3578 Weeks, S. B. "The Chester Mysteries." M.S. University of
      North Carolina, 1887.

3579 Hohlfeld, Alex. "Die altenglische Kollektivmisterien, unter
      besonderer Berücksichtigung des Verhältnisses der York-
      und-Towneley-Spiele." Anglia, XI (1888), 219-310.

3580 Deimling, Heinrich. Text-Gestalt und Text-Kritik der Chester
      Plays. Berlin: Mayer and Müller, 1890. [4], 32, [1] pp.
            BM. CtY. ICN. MH. NjP. NN. WaU.

3581 Hohlfeld, Alexander Rudolf. "Two Old English Mystery Plays
      on the Subject of Abraham's Sacrifice." Modern Language
      Notes, V (April, 1890), 222-237.

3582 Ungemach, Heinrich Gottfried. Die Quellen der fünf ersten
      Chester Plays. Erlangen und Leipzig: A. Deichert, 1890.
      [2], x, [2], 198 pp. Benützte Literatur, pp. [vii]-x.
            BM. CtY. ICN. MB. MH. MnU. NjP. NN. OCl. OCU.
            ViU. WU.

3583 Davidson, C. "Concerning English Mystery Plays." Modern
      Language Notes, VII (1892), 339-341.

3584 Morris, Rupert Hugh. Chester in the Plantagenet and Tudor
      Reigns. [Chester]: Printed for the Author, [1893]. x, 583 pp.
            BM. DLC. ICN. MH. NjP. OCl. OCU. PPL.

3585 -----. Chester. Published under the Direction of the Tract
      Committee. London: Society for Promoting Christian
      Knowledge. New York: E. and J. B. Young and Co., 1895.
      256 pp.
            BM. DLC. MB. NjP.

3586 Fenwick, George Lee. A History of the Ancient City of Chester
from the Earliest Times. (With Plans and Many Illustrations.)
Chester: Phillipson and Golder; London: Simpkin, Marshall,
Hamilton, Kent and Co., Ltd., 1896. 578 pp. Bibliography,
pp. 445-460.
BM. ICN. MH.

3587 Earwaker, J. P. The History of the Church and Parish of St.
Mary-on-the-Hill, Chester. Ed. Rupert H. Morris. London:
Love & Wyman, 1898.
BM.

3588 Bridge, Joseph C. "The Chester Miracle Plays; Some Facts Concerning Them, and the Supposed Authorship of Ralph Higden."
Journal of Chester and North Wales Architectural, Archaeological, and Historic Society, New Ser., IX (1903), 59-98.

3589 Chambers, E. K. "Chester, Cheshire." The Mediaeval Stage.
Vol. II (London, 1903), pp. 348-356.

3590 ----- "Chester Plays." The Mediaeval Stage. Vol. II. (London,
1903), pp. 407-409.

3591 Lawrence, William John. "Early Drama in Chester." Notes and
Queries, 10th Ser. II (1904), 29.

3592 Dale, Darley. "The Chester Plays. An Appreciation." Month,
CVII (1906), 266-278.

3593 Gollancz, Hermann. "The Chester Mystery Plays." Journal of
Chester and North Wales Architectural, Archaeological, and
Historic Society, New Ser., XIV (1908), 18-28.

3594 "Proposed Revival in Chester of the Chester Mystery Plays."
Journal of Chester and North Wales Architectural, Archaeological, and Historic Society, New Ser., XIV (1908), 269-272.

3595 Utesch, Hans. Die Quellen der Chester-Plays. Kiel: Kieler
Tagespost, G.m.b.H., 1909. [4], v, 94, [2] pp. Bibliography,
pp. [i]-iv.
CtY. MH. MiU. NN. OU.

3596 Harper, Carrie A. "A Comparison between the Brome and Chester
Plays of Abraham and Isaac. Studies in English and Compara-
ative Literature by Former and Present Students at Radcliffe

College Presented to Agnes Irwin. (Boston, 1910), pp. 51-73.

3597   Simpson, Frank. Chester City Gilds: The Barber-Surgeons'
         Company. Chester: G. R. Griffith, Ltd., 1911. 106 pp.
              BM. MH.

3598   ----- "The City Gilds of Chester." Journal of the Chester and
         North Wales Architectural, Archaeological, and Historic
         Society, New Ser., XVIII (1911), 98-203.

3599   Howells, W. D. "Chester 'Potted Pageant.'" North American Re-
         view, CXCV (1912), 607-617.

3600   Bridge, Joseph C. "Items of Expenditure from the 16th century
         accounts of the painters, glaziers, embroiderers, and station-
         ers' company, with special reference to the 'Shepherds Play.'"
         Chester and North Wales Architectural, Archaeological and
         Historic Society Journal. New Ser., XX (1914), [153]-191.
              NN.

3601   Farrall, L. M. Parish Register of the Holy & Undivided Trinity
         in the City of Chester, 1532-1837, Completely Indexed, In-
         dexes II-VI. Having an Epitome of Biographical and Genealo-
         gical Notes. Chester: Printed for the Editor by G. R. Griffith,
         Ltd., 1914. 870 pp.
              BM. ICN. MH.

*3602 Greg, Walter Wilson. Bibliographical and Textual Problems of
         the English Miracle Cycles. London: Alexander Moring, Ltd.,
         1914. 143 pp.
              BM.

3603   ----- "The Coming of Antichrist: Relation of the Manuscripts
         of the Chester Cycle." The Library, Series Three, V (1914),
         168-205. [Reprinted in, Bibliographical and Textual Problems
         of the English Miracle Plays. (London, 1914), pp. 32-69.]

3604   Bryant, Mary L. "Studies in the History and Structure of the
         Chester Cycle." M.A. University of Minnesota, 1915.

3605   Cook, Albert S. "The Chester Plays." Nation, May 27, 1915, p.
         599.

3606   Haller, Julius. "Der Dialog in den Chester-Spielen." Die Technik
         des Dialogs im mittelalterlichen Drama Englands. (Worms,

1916), pp. 1-29.

3607 Pierson, Merle. "Chester." In, "The Relation of the Corpus Christi Procession of the Corpus Christi Play in England." Transactions of the Wisconsin Academy of Sciences, Arts, and Letters, XVIII (1916), 125-126.

3608 Wells, John Edwin. "The Chester Plays." A Manual of the Writings in Middle English, 1050-1400. (New Haven, 1916-1951), pp. 546-551, 859, 1025, 1137, 1185, 1228, 1282-1283, 1318, 1368, 1416, 1523, 1586, 1636-1637, 1682, 1728.

3609 Frank, Grace. "Revisions in the English Mystery Plays." Modern Philology, XV (1918), 565-572.

3610 Rosé, Grace Norton. "A Miracle Play in a Country House. From the Old English Coventry or Chester Cycles Can Be Adapted a Play for Christmas Eve Or That Holiday House Party." House and Garden, XXXVI (December, 1919), 19-21, 62.

3611 Baugh, Albert C. "The Chester Plays and French Influence." In, Schelling Anniversary Papers. (New York, 1923), pp. 35-63.

3612 Cornelius, Brother Luke. The Role of the Virgin Mary in the Coventry, York, Chester, and Towneley Cycles. Washington, D.C.: Catholic University of America Press, 1923. 121 pp.

3613 "Play of the Shepherd's." Spectator, CXXXI (1923), 989-990.

3614 Dustoor, P. E. "The Origin of the Play of 'Moses and the Tables of the Law.'" Modern Language Review, XIX (1924), 459-463.

3615 Foster, Frances A., ed. A Stanzaic life of Christ, compiled from Higden's Polychronicon and the Legenda aurea, edited from MS Harley 3909. London: O.U.P., 1926. (Early English Text Society. Original series, no. 166, 1926 (for 1924). xliii, 456 pp.
          BM.

3616 Fort, Margaret Dancy. "The Metres of the Brome and Chester Abraham and Isaac Plays." Publications of the Modern Language Association, XLI (December, 1926), 832-839.

3617 Dustoor, P. E. "Textual Notes on the Chester Old Testament

Plays." Anglia, LII (June, 1928), 97-112.

3618 Dustoor, P. E. "Textual Notes on Three Non-Cycle Mystery Plays." Modern Language Review, XXIII (1928), 208-212.

3619 ----- "The Chester Fall of Lucifer." Allahabad University Studies, Arts Section, VI, Part I (1930), 19-57.

3620 ----- "The Chester MSS. and the Brome Plays." Allababad University Studies. Art Section. VI. 1930.

3621 Oakden, James Parker. Alliterative Poetry in Middle English. 2 vol. Manchester: University Press, 1930-1935. Biblio- graphy, Vol. 1, pp. 265-267.
    ICN.

3622 Wilson, Robert H. "The Stanzaic Life of Christ and the Chester Plays." Studies in Philology, XXVIII (July, 1931), 413-432.

3623 Carroll, Rev. Thomas J., O.M.C. "The Influence of the Festival of Corpus Christi upon the Cycle Plays; with Some Observa- tions about the View-Point of the Cambridge History of Eng- lish Literature." M.A. Catholic University of America, 1932.

3624 Greene, Richard L. "The Brome Manuscript." Times Literary Supplement, March 31, 1932, p. 229.

3625 Jones, Ellen Mattocks. "Stage Setting and Stage Business in the English Cycles." M.A. University of Minnesota, 1932.

3626 Kiho, Yosuke. "The Stanza-Divison of the Chester Play XVII." Studies in English Literature (Imperial University of Tokyo), XI (1932), 139-143.

3627 "Noah's Flood, Performed at Eynsham, Near Oxford." Lot, July 19, 1934, p. 9.

3628 Greg, W. W. "'Christ and the Doctors' and the York Play." The Trial and Flagellation With Other Studies in the Chester Cycle. (The Malone Society, 1935), pp. 101-120.

3629 ----- "The Lists and Banns of the Plays: Document I, from MS. Harley 2150; Document II, from MS. Harley 1944; Document III, from MS. Harley 1948; Document IV, from MS. Harley 2104." The Trial and Flagellation With Other Studies of the Chester Cycle. Malone Society. (London: Oxford University Press, 1935), pp. 121-171.

3630 Greg, W. W. "The Manchester Fragment of the Resurrection." The Trial and Flagellation with Other Studies in the Chester Cycle. Malone Society Reprints. (London, 1935), pp. 85-100. [From the MS. found in the Manchester Free Library.]

3631 ----- "Remarks on the Relation of the Manuscripts." The Trial and Flagellation with Other Studies of the Chester Cycle. Malone Society Studies. (London: Oxford University Press, 1935), pp. 74-83.

3632 Crocker, S. F. "The Production of the Chester Plays." West Virginia University Philological Studies, I (1936), 62-86.

*3633 Salter, Frederick Millet and Greg, Walter Wilson, eds. The Trial and Flagellation, with Other Studies in the Chester Cycle. [Oxford], Oxford University Press, 1936. 171 pp. (Malone Society Studies, 1935).
BM. CtY. DLC. ICN. ICU. MH. MiU. NN. OU. PU.

3634 Brady, Sister Mary Patrick. "A Study of the Characterizations of Abraham, Sarah, and Isaac in the English Abraham and Isaac Plays with Special Reference to Scripture and to Apocryphal Writings." M.A. Catholic University of America, 1938.

3635 Greg, W. W. "The Play of Anti-Christ from the Chester Cycle." Review of English Studies, XIV (1938), 79-80.

3636 Charles, B. G. "The Chester Play of Antichrist." National Library of Wales Journal, I (1939-40), 34.

3637 Salter, F. M. "The Banns of the Chester Plays." Review of English Studies, XV (1939), 432-457.

3638 Wells, Minnie E. "The Age of Isaac at the Time of the Sacrifice." Modern Language Notes, LIV (1939), 579-582.

3639 Harney, Sister Mary Camillus. "The Characterization of Cain and Abel in the English Mystery Plays; York, Chester, Ludus Coventriae and Towneley Cycles." M.A. Catholic University of America, 1940.

3640 Lucken, Brother Linus Urban. Antichrist and the Prophets of
    Antichrist in the Chester Cycle. Washington, D.C.: Catholic
    University Press, 1940. ix, 158 pp. Bibliography, 151-158.
        BM. CtY. DFo. DLC. ICN. MH. MiU. OC1. OU. WU.

*3641 Salter, F. M. "The Banns of the Chester Plays." Review of Eng-
    lish Studies, XVI (January, 1940), 1-17; (April, 1940), 137-
    148.

*3642 ----- The Banns of the Chester Plays. Oxford: Oxford University
    Press, 1940. 54 pp.
        BM.

3643 Clark, Sr. Mary Thaddeus. "Drama in the Cyclic Plays of Media-
    eval England." M.A. Fordham University, 1941.

3644 Lawlor, S. J., Richard Vincent. "The Music and Musical Ele-
    ments of the Craft Cycles." M.A. Boston College, 1941.

3645 Sullivan, S.S.J., Sr. John. "A Study of the Themes of the Passion
    in the Medieval Cyclic Drama." Ph.D. Catholic University of
    America, 1943.

3646 Clary, Dora Therese. "A Study of the Doctrinal Treatment of the
    Blessed Virgin Mary in the Chester Cycle." M.A. Catholic
    University of America, 1945.

3647 Severs, J. Burke. "The Relationship between the Brome and Chester
    Play of 'Abraham and Isaac.'" Modern Philology, XLII (February,
    1945), 137-151.

3648 Aquin, Sister M. "Vulgate and Eve-Concept in the English Cycles."
    Catholic Biblical Quarterly, IX (1947), 409-435.

3649 Homan, Delmar Charles. "A Study in the Medieval Miracle Plays:
    Judgment Day (With Two Plays Modernized)." M.A. University
    of Iowa, 1949.

3650 Beresford, J. R. "The Churchwardens' Accounts of Holy Trinity,
    Chester, 1532 to 1633." Journal of the Chester and North Wales
    Architectural, Archaeological and Historic Society, XXXVIII
    (1951), 95-172.

3651 Brown, Arthur. "A Tradition of the Chester Plays." London
    Mediaeval Studies, II, Part 1 (1951), 68-72.

3652 Seve, Nicholas Werner de. "The Marian Element in the Four
Great Cycles." M.A. Columbia University, 1951.

3653 Bryant, Joseph A., Jr. "Chester's Sermon for Catechumens."
Journal of English and Germanic Philology, LIII (July, 1954),
399-402. Bibliographical footnotes.

3654 Craig, Hardin. "The Chester Plays." English Religious Drama of
the Middle Ages. (Oxford, 1955), pp. 166-198.

3655 Salter, F. M. Medieval Drama in Chester. Toronto: University
Press, 1955; London: Cumberlege, 1956. xi, 138 pp.

3656 Coffee, Bernice French. "The Chester Plays: Interrelation of
Manuscripts." Ph.D. University of Missouri, 1956.

3657 French, Bernice. "The Chester Plays; Interrelation of Manuscripts." Ph.D. University of Missouri, 1956. [Delete].

3658 Pittock, M. J. W. "A Comparison of Noah and His Wife, and
of Octavian, in the Chester and Towneley Cycle of Miracle
Plays." Ph.D. University of Manchester, 1956.

3659 Savage, Donald James. "An Analysis of the Comic Element in
the Chester, York, Coventry, and Towneley Mystery Cycles."
Ph.D. University of Minnesota, 1956. [Delete 3809].

3660 Jones, Douglas Henry. The Church in Chester 1300-1540. Manchester: Cheltham Society, 1957. xii, 209, xvi pp. [Remains
Historical and Literary Connected with the Palatine Counties
of Lancaster and Chester, Ser. 3, Vol. 7.]
BM.

3661 Maltman, Sister Nicholas. "A Study of the Evil Characters in
the English Corpus Christi Cycles." Ph.D. University of
California, 1957.

3662 Devereaux, Sister Mary of the Holy Spirit. "Characterizations
in the Plays of the Chester Cycle." M.A. Fordham University,
1960.

3663 Lumiansky, R. M. "Comedy and Theme in the Chester Harrowing of Hell." Tulane Studies in English, X (1960), 5-12.

3664 Prosser, Eleanor. "Cain." Drama and Religion in the English

Mystery Plays. (Stanford, California, 1961), pp. 71-74.

3665 Prosser, Eleanor. "Joseph." Drama and Religion in the English
Mystery Plays. (Stanford, California, 1961), pp. 89-102.

3666 ----- "Magdalene." Drama and Religion in the English Mystery
Plays. (Stanford, California, 1961), pp. 114-119.

3667 ----- "Thomas." Drama and Religion in the English Mystery
Plays. (Stanford, California, 1961), pp. 160-163.

3668 ----- "The Woman Taken in Adultery." Dramas and Religion in
the English Mystery Plays. (Stanford, California, 1961),
pp. 103-109.

3669 The Chester Mystery Plays. Compiled from the City Archives.
[Chester]. Published by Chester Corporation [1962]. 36 pp.
[Introduction signed by Helen E. Boulton.]
BM.

3670 Bland, D. S. "The Chester Nativity: One Play or Two?" Notes
and Queries, X (April, 1963), 134-135.

3671 Kolve, V. A. "A Study of the Four English Medieval Play-Cycles
As Dramatic Literature." D. Phil. Oxford University (St.
Edmund Hall). 1963.

3672 Honeycombe, Gordon, ed. The Redemption: a play of the life of
Christ. Adapted from the medieval mystery cycles of York,
Towneley, Chester, and the Ludus Coventriae and the Corpus
Christi Plays. London: Methuen, 1964. 108 pp.
BM.

3673 Johnston, Alexandra Ferguson. "The Christ Figure in the Ministry Plays of the Four English Cycles." Ph.D. University of
Toronto, 1964. [Delete].

3674 Carpenter, Nan Cooke. "Music in the Chester Plays." Papers
on English Language and Literature, I (1965), 195-216.

3675 Macaulay, Peter S. "The Play of the Harrowing of Hell as a
Climax in The English Mystery Cycles." Studia Germanica
Gandensia, VIII (1966), 115-134.

3676 Coffee, Bernice F. "The Chester Play of Balaam and Balak."

Wisconsin Studies in Literature, No. 4 (1967), 103-118.

3677 Downing, Marjorie D. "The Influence of the Liturgy on the English Cycle Plays." Ph.D. Yale University, 1967.

3678 Johnston, Alexandra F. "The Christ Figure in the Ministry Plays of the Four English Cycles." Ph.D. University of Toronto, 1967.

3679 Strohm, Paul H., Jr. "The Dramatic and Rhetorical Technique of the Chester Mystery Plays." Ph.D. University of California (Berkeley), 1967.

3680 Stemmler, Theo. "Zur Datierung der Chester Plays." Germanische-Romanische Monatsschrift, Neue Ser. XVIII (July, 1968), 308-313.

3681 Brownstein, Oscar L. "Revision in the Deluge of the Chester Cycle." Speech Monographs, XXXVI (March, 1969), 54-65. [Based on Harley MS. 2124.]

3682 Walsh, O.S.B., Sister Mary Margaret. "The Judgment Plays of the English Cycles." The American Benedictine Review, XX (September, 1969), 378-394.

Clerkenwell

3683 Hassall, W. O. "Plays at Clerkenwell." Modern Language Review, XXXIII (1938), 564-567.

3684 ----- "Plays at Clerkenwell: a Correction." Modern Language Review, XXXIV (1939), 79.

Coggeshall

3685 Chambers, E. K. "Coggeshall, Essex." The Mediaeval Stage. Vol. 2. (London, 1903), p. 357.

Colchester

3686 ----- "Colchester, Essex." The Mediaeval Stage. Vol. 2. (London, 1903), p. 357.

Coleshill

3687 Chambers, E. K. "Coleshill, Warwickshire." The Mediaeval
        Stage. Vol. 2. (London, 1903), p. 357.

Cornwall

Manuscript

3688 Oxford. Bodleian MS. 791. Manuscript of 15th Century in Cornish.
        [Origo Mandi, Passio Domini, Resurrexio Domini.]

Collection

3689 Norris, Edwin, ed. and trans. The Ancient Cornish Drama. 2
        vol. Oxford: University, 1859.
                CtY. DLC. IaU. ICN. ICU. IU. MB. MH. MiU. NN.
                OCl. PU.

Individual Plays

GWRYANS AN BYS--Creation of the World

Manuscripts

3690 Oxford University, Bodleian MS. 219 (Written by William Jor-
        dan, 1611).

3691 Oxford University, Bodleian MS. 31,504 (A copy, with English
        translation by John Keigwyn, 1693).

3692 British Museum, Harleian MS. 1867 (Also a copy, with Keigwyn's
        translation).

Texts

3693 The Creation of the World, with Noah's Flood, Written in
        Cornish in the Year 1611 by William Jordan, with an English
        Translation by John Keigwin. Edited by Davies Gilbert.
        London: Printed by Nichols, 1827. viii, 186 pp. (Printed
        from Brit. Mus. Harl. MS. 1867).
                CtY.

3694 The Beginning of the World. Norris, Edwin, ed. Ancient Cornish
        Drama. Vol. 1. (Oxford, 1859), pp. 2-217.

3695 Gwrean An Bys--The Creation of the World, A Cornish Mystery,
        Edited and Translated by Whitley Stokes. Berlin: Published
        for the Philological Society by A. Asher & Co., 1863. [2], 208,
        [2] pp.

BM. CtY. DLC. ICU. MiU. MnU. O.

3696 Gwreans an bys. The Creation of the World, a Cornish Mystery, edited, with a Translation and Notes, by Whitley Stokes. Berlin: Published for the Philological Society by A. Asher & Co., 1863. [2], 208, [2] pp. (Philological Society. Transactions. 1864). [Cornish and English texts on facing pages. From MS. Bodley 219].
　　BM. CtY. DLC. ICU. MiU. MnU. NN. O.

3697 Gwreans an bys. The Creation of the World, a Cornish Mystery, edited, with a Translation and Notes, by Whitley Stokes. London and Edinburgh: Williams and Norgate, 1864. 208 pp.

3698 Noah's Flood. Tickner, Frederick James, ed. Earlier English Drama from Robin Hood to Everyman. (New York, [1929]), pp. 44-52. [Extract from the Cornish Origo Mundi.]

3699 I. David Takes the Shoots to Jerusalem. Browne, E. Martin, ed. Mystery and Morality Plays. (New York, 1960), pp. 70-76.

3700 II. David and Bathsheba. Browne, E. Martin, ed. Mystery and Morality Plays. (New York, 1960), pp. 76-85.

3701 Harris, Phyllis Pier. "Origo Mundi, First Play of the Cornish Mystery Cycle, The Ordinalia: A New Edition." Ph.D. University of Washington, 1964.

The Passion and Resurrection
Manuscripts

3702 British Museum. Harleian MS. 1782.

3703 Oxford. Bodleian MS. Cornwall 3.

3704 Oxford. Bodleian MS. Cornwall 4.

Texts

3705 Mount Calvary, or the History of the Passion, Death, and Resurrection of Our Lord and Saviour Jesus Christ. Written in Cornish (as may be conjectured) Some Centuries Past, Interpreted in the English Tongue in the Year 1682 by John Keigwin, Gent. Edited by Davies Gilbert. London, 1826. 98 pp. (Edited from MS. Harl. 1826.)

3706 The Passion of Our Lord Jesus Christ. Journey to Jerusalem. --
      Healing the Blind and Lame. -- Simon the Leper. -- Caiaphas
      Receives Judas. -- The Last Supper. -- The Betrayal. --
      Peter Denies Christ. -- Judas Hangs Himself. -- Jesus Be-
      fore Pilate. -- Beelzebub Goes to Pilate's Wife. -- The Con-
      demnation. -- The Smith. -- Crucifixion. -- Terror of
      Lucifer. -- Descent from the Cross. In, Norris, Edwin, ed.
      Ancient Cornish Drama. Vol. 1. (Oxford, 1859), pp. 222-477.

3707 The Resurrection of Our Lord Jesus Christ. Imprisonment of
      Nicodemus and Joseph. -- Harrowing of Hell. -- Soldiers
      Guard the Tomb. -- Resurrection. -- Soldiers Inform Pilate.
      -- The Three Maries at the Tomb. -- Mary Magdalene Informs
      the Apostles. -- Disciples Going to Emmaus. -- Thomas's
      Unbelief. -- Appearance of Jesus. -- Death of Pilate. --
      Ascension. In, Norris, Edwin, ed. Ancient Cornish Drama.
      Vol. 2. (Oxford, 1859), pp. 2-199. [2646 lines.]

3708 Stokes, Whitley, ed. and trans. "The Passion." Transactions of
      the Philological Society, (1860-1861), 1-100 (Appendix). [Sep-
      arately issued, Berlin, 1862.]

3709 Mystery Play of the Three Maries. In, Everyman and Other
      Interludes. (London, New York, 1909).

3710 Mystery Play of the Three Maries. In, Everyman and Other Inter-
      ludes. (London, New York [1935]).

3711 Halliday, F. E. The Legend of the Rood with The Three Maries
      and The Death of Pilate from the Cornish Miracle Plays.
      Done into English Verse with an Introduction. London: Gerald
      Duckworth & Co., Ltd., 1955. ix, [1], 11-142 pp. Bibliography,
      pp. 141-142.
          ICN. NN.

3712 The Death of Pilate. [Part of the Resurrection.] In, Cawley,
      A. C., ed. Everyman and Other Medieval Miracle Plays.
      (New York, 1959), pp. 235-263.

3713 The Three Maries. In, Browne, E. Martin, ed. Mystery and
      Morality Plays. (New York, 1960), pp. 237-245.

3714 The Cornish Mystery-Play of Mary Magdalene. In, Everyman, with
      Other Interludes, Including Eight Miracle Plays. (London, [1909]),
      pp. 128-136. [Lines 893-1188 of the Cornish Resurrection Play.

The text is the same as that in the Norris edition.]

3715   Mary Magdalene and the Apostles. In, Everyman and Other
       Interludes. (London, New York [1935]).

Life of St. Meriasek
                              Manuscript
3716   National Library of Wales. Ordinale de Vita Sancti Mereadoci
       Episcopi et Confessoris Peniarth MS. 105. (Late 15th cen-
       tury. "Finished by Ralph Ton, priest, in 1504.")

                               Texts
3717   Beunans Meriasek: The Life of St. Meriasek, A Cornish Drama.
       Edited by Whitley Stokes. London: Trübner and Co., 1872.
       xvi, 279 , 14 pp.
          CtY.

3718   Nance, R. M., and A. S. Smith, eds. St. Meriasek in Cornwall
       (Bewnans Meryasek, lines 587-1099). 2nd ed. [Rev. Enl.]
       Federation of Old Cornwall Societies, 1966.

                              Studies
3719   Gallagher, Dennis J. "A Critical Study of Buenans Meriasek, a
       Cornish Miracle Play." M.A. Catholic University of America,
       1967.

3720   Meyer, Robert T. "The Middle-Cornish Play Beunans Meriasek."
       Comparative Drama, III (Spring, 1969), 54-64.

General Studies of Cornish Drama

3721   Carew, Richard. Survey of Cornwall. London: Iaggard, 1602.
       159 ff.
          BM.

3722   Borlase, William. Antiquities, Historical and Monumental, of
       the County of Cornwall. London: W. Bowyer and J. Nichols,
       1769. xvi, 464 pp. [Includes ground plan of St. Just Amphi-
       theatre.]

3723   Gilbert, Davies. The Parochial History of Cornwall. Founded on
       the Manuscript Histories of Mr. Hals and Mr. Tonkin. 4 vol.
       London: J. B. Nichols and Son, 1838.
          BM. CtY.

3724 Chambers, E. K. "Cornwall." The Mediaeval Stage. Vol. 2.
      (London, 1903), pp. 433-436.

*3725 Jenner, H. "The Cornish Drama." Celtic Review, III (1906-1907),
      360-375.

3726 Peter, Thurston C. The Old Cornish Drama. London: Elliot Stock,
      1906. iv, 49 pp.
          BM. ICN. ICU. NN.

*3727 Jenner, H. "The Cornish Drama." Celtic Review, IV (1907-1908),
      41-68.

3728 Wells, John Edwin. "The Cornwall Plays." A Manual of the Writ-
      ings in Middle English, 1050-1400. (New Haven, 1916), pp.
      576, 863, 1229, 1417, 1524.

3729 Moore, John Robert. "Miracle Plays, Minstrels, and Jigs."
      Publications of the Modern Language Association, XLVIII
      (September, 1933), 942-945.

3730 Nance, R. Morton. "The 'plen an gwary' or Cornish playing-
      place." Journal of the Royal Institution of Cornwall, Truro,
      XXIV (1935), 190-211.
3731 Pollard, Peggy. Bewnana Alysaryn: gwary myr gans. (Arlodhes
      Ywerdhon). Porth la. Kernow: Pryntyes gans J. Lauham,
      1941. 37 pp.
          NN.

3732 Holman, Treve. "Cornish Plays and Playing Places." Theatre
      Notebook, IV (1949-1950), 52-54.

3733 Elliott-Binns, Leonard. Medieval Cornwall. London: Methuen
      & Co., Ltd., 1955. xii, 451 pp. Index.
          BM.

3734 Wellwarth, George E. "Methods of Production in the Medieval
      Cornish Drama." Speech Monographs, XXIV (August, 1957),
      212-218.

3735 Freeman, Arthur. "A 'Round' Outside Cornwall." Theatre Note-
      book, XVI (1961-1962), 10-11. [Recorded in Thomas Church-
      yard's Worthies of England, 1587.]

3736 Prosser, Eleanor. "Cain." Drama and Religion in the English

Mystery Plays. (Stanford, 1961), pp. 67-71.

3737 Prosser, Eleanor. "Magdalene." Drama and Religion in the
English Mystery Plays. (Stanford, 1961), pp. 113-114.

3738 ----- "Thomas." Drama and Religion in the English Mystery
Plays." (Stanford, 1961), pp. 167-178.

COVENTRY PLAYS

Collections

3739 Craig, Hardin, ed. Two Coventry Corpus Christi Plays: 1. The
Shearmen and Taylors' Pageant, Re-edited from the Edition
of Thomas Sharp, 1825; and 2. The Weavers' Pageant, Re-
edited from the Manuscript of Robert Croo, 1534; with a Plan
of Coventry, and Appendixes Containing the Chief Records
of the Coventry Plays. London: Published for the Early English
Text Society by Kegan Paul, Trench, Trübner & Co., Limited,
1902. xxxviii, 133 pp. (Early English Text Society. Extra
Series, LXXXVIII.) [Shermen and Tailors (Annunciation and
Nativity, Adoration of the Kings and Slaughter of the Innocents).
Pageant of the Weavers (Prophet Play, Purification, Disputa-
tion in the Temple.)]
BM. CtY. DLC. ICN. ICU. IU. MH. MiU. MnU. NjP.
NNC. O. PU.

3740 ----- Two Coventry Corpus Christi Plays: 1. The Shearmen and
Taylors' Pageant, Re-edited from the Edition of Thomas
Sharp, 1825; and 2. The Weavers' Pageant, Re-edited from
the Manuscript of Robert Croo, 1534: With a Plan of Coventry,
and Appendixes Containing the Chief Records of The Coventry
Plays. London: Published for the Early English Text Society,
by Humphrey Milford, Oxford University Press, 1931. xxxviii,
133 pp. [A reprint of the first edition of 1902.]

3741 ----- Two Coventry Corpus Christi Plays: 1. The Shearmen and
the Taylors' Pageant, Re-edited from the Edition of Thomas
Sharp, 1825; and 2. The Weavers' Pageant, Re-edited from
the Manuscript of Robert Croo, 1534; with a Plan of Coventry,
and Appendixes Containing the Chief Records of the Coventry
Plays. 2nd ed. London: Published for the Early English Text
Society by the Oxford University Press, 1957. xliii, 133 pp.
(Early English Text Society. Publications, Extra Series, No.
87).
BM.

Individual Plays

Pageant of the Company of Shearmen and Taylors

Texts

3742 The Pageant of the Company of Sheremen and Taylors, in Coven-
       try, As Performed by Them on the Festival of Corpus Christi;
       Together with Other Pageants, Exhibited on Occasion of
       Several Royal Visits to That City; and Two Specimens of
       Local Poetry. [Thomas Sharp.] Coventry: Printed by W.
       Reader, 1817. [4], 28, 14 pp. [Only 12 copies printed.]
          BM.

3743 The Pageant of the Company of Shearmen and Taylors, in Coven-
       try. In, Sharp, Thomas. A Dissertation on the Pageants or
       Dramatic Mysteries Anciently Performed at Coventry.
       (Coventry, 1825), pp. 83-112.

3744 The Pageant of the Company of Shearmen and Tailors, in Cov-
       entry: the Nativity. In, Marriott, William, ed. Collection
       of English Miracle-Plays or Mysteries. (Basel, 1838), pp.
       57-89.

3745 The Pageant of the Shearmen and Taylors [The Nativity and the
       Slaughter of the Innocents]. In, Manly, John Matthews, ed.
       Specimens of the Pre-Shakespearean Drama. Vol. 1. (Boston
       and New York, 1897-1898).

3746 The Pageant of the Shearmen and Taylors. In, Craig, Hardin,
       ed. Two Coventry Corpus Christi Plays. (London, 1902),
       pp. 1-32.

3747 The Presentation in the Temple. In, Craig, Hardin, ed. Two
       Coventry Corpus Christi Plays. (London, 1902), pp. 33-71.

3748 A Miracle Play of the Nativity. In, An English Garner. [Vol.
       12]. Fifteenth Century Prose and Verse, with an Intro-
       duction by A. W. Pollard. (Westminster, 1903), pp. 243-
       273. [The Pageant of the Shearmen and Tailors.]

3749 The Pageant of the Shearmen and Taylors. In, Manly, John
       Matthews, ed. Specimens of the Pre-Shakesperean Drama.
       (Boston and New York, 1903-1904).

3750 Coventry Nativity Play of the Company of Shearmen and Tailors.

In, Everyman, with Other Interludes Including Eight Miracle
Plays. (London, 1909), pp. 74-98.

3751 A Christmas Miracle Play, Adapted from The Pageant of the
Shearmen and Tailors in the Coventry Cycle of Miracles;
As Presented At the John Herron Art Institute in Indianapolis,
December, 1915. In, Eliot, Samuel Atkins, ed. Little
Theatre Classics. Vol. 1. (Boston, 1918), pp. [55]-104.

3752 The Magi, Herod, and the Slaughter of the Innocents. In, Adams,
Joseph Q., ed. Chief Pre-Shakespearean Dramas. (Boston,
1924), pp. 158-166. [Lines 475-900 of the Shearmen and Taylors'
pageant.]

3753 The Nativity. [Play of the Company of Shearmen and Tailors.] In,
Everyman, and Other Plays. (London, 1925), pp. 69-139.

3754 The Pageant of the Shearmen and Tailors. A Miracle Play Adapted
by John Mason Brown, In, Theatre Arts Monthly, IX (1925),
824-835.

3755 The Nativity. In, Tickner, F. J., ed. Earlier English Drama,
from Robin Hood to Everyman. (London and Edinburgh,
1926).

3756 "The Christmas Mystery of Shearmen's Guild of Coventry.
[Adapted.]" American Church Monthly, XXII (1927), 307-
320.

3757 The Pageant of the Shearmen and Tailors. In, Robinson, Donald
F., ed. The Harvard Dramatic Club Miracle Plays. (New
York, 1928), pp. 3-29. [A reprint of the John Mason Brown
adaptation which appeared in Theatre Arts Monthly, 1925.]

3758 Pageant of Shearmen and Taylors. In, Tickner, Frederick J., ed.
Earlier English Drama from Robin Hood to Everyman. (New
York, 1929), pp. 112-133.

3759 The Nativity Play. In, Everyman and Other Interludes. (London,
New York, [1935]).

3760 The Coventry Nativity Play. Adapted for Use in Schools. Edited
by I. L. Warner. London: S. French, Ltd., [1938]. 28 pp.
(French's Acting Edition.)
BM. DLC.

3761 Nativity Play. In, Feasey, Lynette. Old English at Play.
       (London, Toronto, 1944).

3762 Nativity Play. In, Allen, John, ed. Three Medieval Plays: The
       Coventry Nativity Play; Everyman; The Farce of Master
       Pierre Pathelin. (London, 1953).

3763 The Weavers' Pageant. In, Craig, Hardin, ed. Two Coventry
       Corpus Christi Plays. 2nd ed. (London, 1957).

3764 The Annunciation. In, Cawley, A. C., ed. Everyman and
       Medieval Miracle Plays. (New York, 1959), pp. 69-77.

3765 Herod and the Kings. In, Browne, E. Martin, ed. Mystery and
       Morality Plays. (New York, 1960), pp. 133-149.

3766 Herod and the Magi. Slaughter of the Innocents. In, Malcolm-
       son, Anne. Seven Medieval Plays for Modern Players. (Lon-
       don, 1960).

The Weaver's Pageant

Texts
3767 The Presentation in the Temple. A Pageant, As Originally Re-
       presented by the Corporation of Weavers in Coventry. Now
       First Printed from the Books of the Company. With a Pre-
       fatory Notice [by Thomas Sharp.] Edited by John B. Gracie.
       Edinburgh: Printed for the Abbotsford Club by the Edinburgh
       Printing Company, 1836. [6], 86 pp. [1st edition, prepared
       from MS.]
            BM. DLC. ICN. ICU. MH. MnU. O.

3768 Holthausen, Ferdinand, ed. "Das Spiel der Weber von Coventry.
       I." Anglia, XXV (1902), 209-250.

3769 Craig, Hardin, ed. "Fragments of Another Version of the
       Weavers' Pageant." Two Coventry Corpus Christi Plays.
       (London, 1931), pp. 119-122.

3770 The Shearmen and Taylors' Pageant. In, Craig, Hardin, ed.
       Two Coventry Corpus Christi Plays. 2nd ed. (London, 1957).

Studies
3771 Dugdale, William. The Antiquities of Warwickshire Illustrated;
       from Records, Ledger-Books, Manuscripts, Charters, Evi-

dences, Tombes, and Armes: Beautified with Maps, Prospects, and Portraictures. The Second Edition, in Two Volumes, Printed from a Copy Corrected by the Author Himself, and with the Original Copper Plates. The Whole Revised, Augmented, and Continued down to This Present Time; by William Thomas, D.D. With the Addition of Several Prospects of Gentlemens Seats, Churches, Tombs, and New and Correct Maps of the County, and of Several Hundreds, from an Actual Survey Made by Henry Beighton, F.R.S. Also Compleat Lists of the Members of Parliament and Sheriffs Taken from the Original Records; And an Alphabetical Index and Blazonry of the Arms upon the Several Plates. 2 vol. London: Printed for John Osborn and Thomas Longman, 1730. [See p. 183.]
BM.

3772 Dugdale, Sir William. The Antiquities of Coventre, Illustrated. From Records, Leidger-books, Manuscripts, Charters, Evidences, Tombes and Armes. Beautified with many curious copperplate cuts . . . Carefully Collected from His Edition of the Antiquities of Warwickshire, published in the year 1656. Coventry, 1765. 59 pp.
CtY. ICN.

*3773 Sharp, Thomas. A Dissertation on the Pageants or Dramatic Mysteries Anciently Performed at Coventry, by the Trading Companies of That City; Chiefly with Reference to the Vehicle, Characters, and Dresses of the Actors. Compiled in a Great Degree, from Sources Hitherto Unexplored. To Which Are Added, the Pageant of the Shearmen & Taylors' Company, and Other Municipal Entertainments of a Public Nature. Coventry: Published by Merridew and Son, 1825. [6], 226, [4] pp.
BM. CtY. DLC. ICN. ICU. MiU. NN. OU. TxU. WU.

3774 ----- "Processions on Corpus Christi Day, Midsummer and St. Peter's Eves." A Dissertation on the Pageants or Dramatic Mysteries Anciently Performed at Coventry. (Coventry, 1825), pp. 159-206.

3775 ----- The Pageant of the Company of Shearmen and Taylors, Anciently Performed in Coventry, With the Original Music and Songs, As Printed in the "Dissertation on the Coventry Mysteries." Coventry, Merridew, 1825. 118 pp.
BM. DLC. IaU. TxU.

3776 Dugdale, Sir William. Monasticon Anglicanum: A History of the
      Abbies and Other Monasteries, Hospitals, Frieries, and
      Cathedral and Collegiate Churches, with Their Dependencies,
      in England and Wales; Also of all Such Scottish, Irish, and
      French Monasteries As Were in Any Manner Connected with
      Religious Houses in England. Together with a Particular Ac-
      count of Their Respective Foundations, Grants, and Donations,
      and A Full Statement of Their Possessions, As Well Temporal
      As Spiritual. Originally Published in Latin by Sir William
      Dugdale. A New Edition ... by John Caley, Henry Ellis, and
      the Rev. Bulkeley Bandinel. Volume the Sixth -- Part I. Lon-
      don: Printed for Joseph Harding, Harding and Lepard, and
      Longman, Rees, Orme, Brown, and Green, 1830. xliii, xii,
      604 pp.
            BM.

3777 Poole, Benjamin. Coventry; Its History and Antiquities. London:
      J. R. Smith, 1870. xviii, 424 pp.
            CtY. ICN. MH.

*3778 Sharp, Thomas, Esq. Illustrative Papers on The History and
      Antiquities of the City of Coventry; Comprising the Churches
      of St. Michael, Holy Trinity, St. Nicholas, and St. John; The
      Grey Friars' Monastery; St. John's Hospital and Free Gram-
      mar School; Jesus Hall, Bablake Hall, and St. Mary's Hall.
      From Original, and Mostly Unpublished Documents. Care-
      fully Re-printed from an Original Copy. With Corrections,
      Additions, and a Brief Memoir of the Author, by William Geo-
      rge Fretton. Birmingham: Printed for the Subscriber, 1871.
      xv, [2], 239 pp.
            BM. ICN.

3779 Fretton, William George. Memorials of the Fullers' or Walkers'
      Guild, Coventry. Compiled from the Books of the Company,
      and from Other Sources. Coventry, 1878. x, 37 pp.
            BM.

3780 Fretton, William George. "Notes on the Guild of Corpus Christi
      or St. Nicholas Coventry." Reliquary, XXI (1880-1881), 68-
      71.

3781 Halliwell, James Orchard. Life of William Shakespeare, In-
      cluding Many Particulars Respecting the Poet and His Family
      Never before Printed. 4th ed. London: J. R. Smith, 1884.
      [See pp. 383-389.]

BM. MB. MH.

3782 Davidson, Charles. "The Play of the Weavers of Coventry."
Modern Language Notes, VII (1892), 184-185.

3783 Hohlfeld, Alexander B. "The Play of the Weavers of Coventry."
Modern Language Notes, VII (1892), 308-310.

3784 Harris, Mary Dormer. Life in An Old English Town; A History
of Coventry from the Earliest Times. Sonneschein & Co.,
Ltd.; New York: The Macmillan Co., Ltd., 1898. xxiii, 391
pp. "Authorities," pp. 377-380.
BM. CtY. ICN.

3785 "An Edition of the Weavers' Play of Coventry." The Princeton
University Bulletin, XIII (1901), 8-12.

3786 Chambers, E. K. "Coventry Plays." The Mediaeval Stage. Vol.
2. (London, 1903), pp. 422-424.

3787 ----- "Coventry, Warwickshire." The Mediaeval Stage. Vol.
2. (London, 1903), pp. 357-363.

3788 Hamelius, Paul. De dood van Kain in de engelsche mysteriespeln
van Coventry. Gent: Drukkerij C. Annoot-Broeckman, 1903.
11 pp.
ICN.

3789 "The Manuscripts of the Weavers' Pageant at Coventry." The
Princeton University Bulletin, XIV (1903), 199-207.

*3790 Harris, Mary Dormer. The Coventry Leet Book: or Mayor's
Register, Containing the Records of the City Court Leet
or View of Frankpledge, A. D. 1420-1555. With Divers Other
Matters. Transcribed and Edited. London: Published for the
Early English Text Society by Kegan Paul, Trench, Trübner
& Co., Ltd., and by Humphrey Milford, Oxford University
Press, 1907-1933. 4 parts, paged continuously. xi, 256; vi,
257-580; vii, 581-813; lii, 815-939 pp.
BM. CtY. CU. ICN. MH.

3791 Berkeley, Frances Campbell. "Were the Coventry Pageants Station-
ary or Processional." Publications of the Modern Language
Association, XXIV (1909), xxix.

3792 Munro, J. "Tyrly Tirlow' and The Coventry Play of the Nativity."
      Notes and Queries, 11th Ser. I (1910), 125.

*3793 Harris, Mary Dormer. The Story of Coventry. London: J. M.
      Dent and Sons, Ltd., 1911. xii, 355 pp.
         BM. ICN. MH.

3794 Craig, Hardin. "The Coventry Cycle of Plays." Athenaeum, CLXVI
      (August 16, 1913), 166.

3795 Greg, W. W. "The Coventry Cycle of Plays." Athenaeum, CLXVI,
      (1913), 262.

3796 Pierson, Merle. "Coventry." In, "The Relation of the Corpus
      Christi Procession to the Corpus Christi Play in England."
      Transactions of the Wisconsin Academy of Sciences, Arts, and
      Letters, XVIII (1916), 127-134.

3797 Wells, John Edwin. "The Coventry Plays." A Manual of the Writings
      in Middle English, 1050-1400. (New Haven, 1916-1951), pp.
      565-568, 861-862, 993, 1026, 1137, 1228, 1319, 1370, 1417,
      1524, 1637, 1729.

3798 Holthausen, F. "Zur Noah-Legende." Beiblatt zur Anglia, XXXI
      (1920), 90-92.

3799 Harris, Mary Dormer. "The 'World' In the Doomsday Mystery
      Play." Notes and Queries, CXLIV (1925), 243.

3800 Cady, F. W. "Towneley, York, and True-Coventry." Studies
      in Philology, XXVI (1929), 386-400.

3801 Craig, Hardin, ed. "Extracts from the Coventry Leet Book."
      Two Coventry Corpus Christi Plays. (London, 1931), pp. 72-
      81.

3802 ----- "Pageants on Special Occasions." Two Coventry Corpus
      Christi Plays. (London, 1931), pp. 109-118.

3803 ----- "Records and Accounts of the Trading Companies of
      Coventry Referring to the Corpus Christi Play." Two Coventry
      Corpus Christi Plays. (London, 1931), pp. 82-109.

3804 Steavens, T. W. "Shearmen and Tailors' Play; Note on the Set-
      ting." Theatre Arts Monthly, XVI (1932), 583-584.

3805 Luke, Brother Cornelius. The Role of the Virgin Mary in the
        Coventry, York, Chester, and Towneley Cycles. Washing-
        ton, D.C.: Catholic University of America, 1933. 121 pp.
        Bibliography, pp. 119-121.
            IaU. ICN. MnU. WU.

3806 Flower, R. "The Coventry Mysteries." British Museum Quarter-
        ly, VIII (1934), 98-100.

3807 Fox, L. "Administration of Gild Property in Coventry in the
        Fifteenth Century." English Historical Review, LV (1940),
        634-647.

3808 Craig, Hardin. "The Coventry Plays." English Religious Drama
        of the Middle Ages. (Oxford, 1955), pp. 281-298.

3809 Savage, Donald J. "An Analysis of the Comic Element in the
        Chester, York, Coventry and Towneley Mystery Cycles."
        Ph.D. University of Minnesota, 1955.   [Delete].

3810 Knowles, John A. "John Thorton of Coventry and the East Win-
        dow of Malvern Priory." Antiquaries Journal, XXXIX (July-
        October, 1959), 274-282.

3811 Harvey, Nancy Lenz. "Titus Andronicas and The Shearmen and
        Taylors' Play." Renaissance Quarterly, XXII (Spring, 1969),
        27-31.

Croxton Play of the Sacrament
                                Manuscript
3812   Trinity College, Dublin, F. 4. 20, Catalogue No. 652, ff.
            338^r-356^r. [Sixteenth century].

                                  Texts
3813 The Play of the Sacrament. Edited by Whitley Stokes. Trans-
        actions of the Philological Society. (Berlin, 1860-1861), pp.
        101-152 [Appendix].

3814 Play of the Sacrament. In, Manly, J. M. Specimens of the Pre-
        Shakespearean Drama. Vol. 1. (New York, 1897), pp. 239-
        276.

3815 The Play of the Sacrament. In, Waterhouse, Osborn, ed. The
        Non-Cycle Mystery Plays. (London, 1909).

3816 The Play of the Sacrament. In, Adams, Joseph Q., ed. Chief
Pre-Shakespearean Dramas. (Boston, New York, 1924), pp.
243-262.

Studies
3817 Holthausen, F. "The Play of the Sacrament." Englische Studien,
XVI (1892), 150-151. [Stokes' 1862 edition.]

3818 ----- "The Play of the Sacrament." Anglia, XV (1892), 198-200.

3819 Chambers, E. K. "Croxton Play: The Sacrament." The Mediaeval
Stage. Vol. 2. (London, 1903), p. 427.

3820 Wells, John Edwin. "The 'Croxton Sacrament.'" A Manual of the
Writings in Middle English, 1050-1400. (New Haven, 1916-
1951), pp. 572-573, 862, 1081, 1138, 1229, 1319, 1417,
1729.

3821 Coffman, George R. "The Miracle Play in England--Some Records of Presentation and Notes on Preserved Plays." Studies
in Philology, XVI (1919), 57-66.

3822 Patch, Howard Rollin. "The Ludus Coventriae and the Digby
Massacre." Publications of the Modern Language Association,
XXXV (1920), 324-343. [Croxton compared with Ludus Coven-
triae.]

3823 Barns, Florence Elberta. "The Background and Source of the
Croxton Play of the Sacrament." Ph.D. University of Chicago,
1926.

3824 Cutts, Cecilia. "The Background of the Play of the Sacrament."
Ph.D. Washington University, 1938.

3825 ----- "The Croxton Play: An Anti-Lollard Piece." Modern
Language Quarterly, V (1944), 45-60.

3826 Bevington, David. [Play of the Sacrament.] Tudor Drama and
Politics. (Cambridge, Massachusetts, 1968), 37-39.

Daventry

3827 Chambers, E. K. "Daventry, Northamptonshire." The Mediaeval
Stage. Vol. 2. (London, 1903), p. 363.

Digby Plays

Manuscript

3828 Oxford. Bodleian Digby MS. 133. [Killing of the Children; Conversion of St. Paul; Mary Magdalene].

Collections

3829 Sharp, Thomas, ed. Ancient Mysteries from the Digby Manuscripts. Preserved in the Bodleian Library, Oxford. Edinburgh: Printed for the Abbotsford Club, 1835. xlvii, [1], 200, viii pp.
BM. CSmH. ICN. MiD.

*3830 Furnivall, F. J., ed. The Digby Plays, with An Incomplete 'Morality' of Wisdom, Who Is Christ (Part of one of the Macro Moralities). Re-issued from the Plates of the Text Edited by F. J. Furnivall for the New Shakespeare Society in 1882. London: Published for the Early English Text Society by K. Paul, Trench, Trübner and Co., 1896. [4], v-xxxii, 239, [1] pp.
BM. ICN. MiU. NjP. NN. OC1. OO. PP. PU. ViU.

3831 The Digby Plays. With an Incomplete 'Morality' of 'Wisdom Who Is Christ.' (Part of One of the 'Macro Moralities.') Re-issued from the Plates of the Text Edited by F. J. Furnivall for the New Shakespeare Society in 1882. London: Published for the Early English Text Society by Humphrey Milford, Oxford University Press, 1930. xxxii, 239 pp.
BM.

3832 Devlin, V. M. "An Edition of the Digby Plays (Bodleian Digby 133), with Introduction, Notes and Glossary." Ph.D. University College, London, 1965-1966.

Individual Plays

Conversion of St. Paul

Texts

3833 The Conversion of St. Paul. In, Sharp, Thomas, ed. Ancient Mysteries from the Digby Manuscripts. (Edinburgh, 1835).

3834 The Conversion of St. Paul. In, Furnivall, Frederick J., ed. The Digby Mysteries. (London, 1882).

3835 The Conversion of St. Paul, In, Furnivall, F. J., ed. The Digby Plays. (London, 1896).

3836 The Conversion of St. Paul, In, Manly, J. M., ed. Specimens
     of the Pre-Shaksperean Drama. (Boston and New York, 1903-
     1904).

3837 The Conversion of St. Paul, In, Adams, Joseph Quincy, ed.
     Chief Pre-Shakespearean Dramas. (Boston and New York,
     1924).

3838 The Conversion of St. Paul, In, Tickner, F. J., ed. Earlier
     English Drama, from Robin Hood to Everyman. (New York,
     1929).

3839 The Conversion of St. Paul. In, The Digby Plays ... by F. J.
     Furnivall. (London, 1930), pp. 25-52.

3840 Ayliff, H. K. The Malvern Festival Plays, MCMXXXIII. Ar-
     ranged for Production by H. K. Ayliff, with an Introduction
     by Hugh Walpole, and preface by Sir Barry Jackson. London:
     Heath Crangon, Ltd., 1933. viii, 34 pp.
          NN.

Mary Magdalene
                              Texts
3841 Mary Magdalene. In, Sharp, Thomas, ed. Ancient Mysteries
     from the Digby Manuscripts. (Edinburgh, 1835).

3842 Mary Magdalene, in Two Parts. Part 1, in 20 Scenes ... Part
     2, in 31 Scenes ... In, Furnivall, F. J., ed. The Digby
     Plays. (London, 1882), pp. 53-136.

3843 Mary Magdalene. In, Furnivall, F. J., ed. The Digby Plays.
     (London, 1896).

3844 Mary Magdalene. In, Adams, J. G., ed. Chief Pre-Shakespearean
     Dramas. (Boston and New York, 1924), pp. 225-242.

3845 St. Mary Magdalene. In, Pollard, Alfred W., ed. English Miracle
     Plays, Moralities and Interludes. Oxford, 1927, p. 49. [Part
     only printed.]

3846 Sancta Maria Magdalene; Reproduced from MS Digby 133, fols.
     94-145 (recto) in the Bodleian Library, Oxford. 49 sheets and
     2 half sheets. The Modern Language Association of America.
     1929. (Collection of Photographic Facsimiles, No. 116.)

3847 Mary Magdalene. In, The Digby Plays ... by F. J. Furnivall.
      (London, 1930), pp. 53-136.

Killing of the Innocents
                              Texts
3848 Candlemas-Day, or The Killing of the Children of Israel. A
      Mystery. In, Hawkins, Thomas, ed. The Origin of the English
      Drama. Vol. 1. (Oxford, 1773), pp. 1-26.

3849 Candlemas Day. In, Sharp, Thomas, ed. Ancient Mysteries from
      the Digby Manuscripts. (Edinburgh, 1835).

3850 Candlemas-Day, or The Killing of the Children of Israel. In,
      Marriott, William. A Collection of English Miracle-Plays Or
      Mysteries. (Basel, 1838), pp. 197-219.

3851 "Candlemas Day: A Mystery." Kitto's Journal of Sacred Liter-
      ature, XXXVIII (1867), 413-429.

3852 Herod's Killing of the Children. In, Furnivall, Frederick J., ed.
      The Digby Mysteries. (London, 1882), pp. 1-24.

3853 Candlemas Day, or the Killing of the Children of Israel. In,
      Furnivall, F. J., ed. The Digby Plays. (London, 1896), pp.
      1-23.

3854 Herod's Killing of the Children (Candlemas Day). In, The Digby
      Plays ... by F. J. Furnivall. (London, 1930), pp. 1-25.

                              Studies
3855 Collier, John Payne. "The Digby Miracle Plays." The History of
      English Dramatic Poetry. Vol. 2. (London, 1831), pp. 230-235.

3856 "Towneley and Digby Mysteries." Gentleman's Magazine, New
      Ser., VI (1836), 563-572.

3857 Zupitza, Julius. "The Digby Mysteries." Academy, XXII (1882),
      281, 297.

*3858 Schmidt, Karl. Die Digby-Spiele. (Einleitung. Candlemas Day
      and the Kyllynge of the Children of Israeell. The Conuersyon
      of Seynt Paule.) Berlin: G. Bernstein, 1884. 30, [4] pp.
      NNC. O. WU.

3859 ----- "I. Maria Magdalena." In, "Die Digby-Spiele." Anglia,

VIII (1885), 371-390.

3860 Schmidt, K. "3. The Burial and Resurrection of Christ." In, "Die Digby-Spiele." Anglia, VIII (1885), 393-404.

3861 Chambers, E. K. "Digby Plays." The Mediaeval Stage. Vol. 2. (London, 1903), pp. 428-431.

*3862 Wells, John Edwin. "The 'Digby Plays.'" A Manual of the Writings in Middle English, 1050-1400. (New Haven, 1916-1951), pp. 573-575, 863, 1026, 1081, 1138, 1229, 1319, 1417, 1524, 1637.

3863 Campbell, Robert L. "The Digby Mary Magdalene." M.A. University of Chicago, 1920.

3864 Patch, Howard Rollin. "The Ludus Coventriae and the Digby Massacre." Publications of the Modern Language Association, XXXV (1920), 324-343.

3865 Vriend, Joannes, S.J. The Blessed Virgin Mary in the Medieval Drama of England. Purmerend: J. Musses, 1928. 160 pp. Select Bibliography, pp. [xiii]-xv.
      BM. DLC. IaU. ICN. ICU. IU. MH. MiU. MnU. NN. OCU.

3866 Anderson, Dice Robins, Jr. "The Digby Mary Magdalene. A Study of the Sources, Conventional Elements, and Originality." M.A. University of Chicago, 1929.

3867 Collins, Fletcher. "Music in the Craft Cycles." Publications of the Modern Language Association, XLVII (1932), 613-621.

3868 Mishrahi, Jean. "A 'Vita Sanctae Marie Magdalenae' (BHL 5456) in an Eleventh-Century Manuscript." Speculum, XVIII (1943), 335-339.

3869 Eaton, William. "'Paradise Lost' and the Digby 'Mary Magdalene.'" Modern Language Quarterly, IX (1948), 412-414.

3870 Abel, Patricia. "Grimaldi's Christus Redivivus and the Digby Resurrection Play." Modern Language Notes, LXX (May, 1955), 328-330.

3871 Craig, Hardin. "The Conversion of St. Paul." English Religious

Drama of the Middle Ages. (Oxford, 1955), pp. 311-313.

3872 Craig, Hardin. "The Digby Plays." English Religious Drama. (Oxford, 1955), pp. 310-317.

3873 ----- "The Slaughter of the Innocents and the Purification -- 'The Killing of the Children.'" English Religious Drama of the Middle Ages. (Oxford, 1955), pp. 313-315.

3874 ----- "St. Mary Magdalen." English Religious Drama of the Middle Ages. (Oxford, 1955), pp. 315-317.

3875 Hill, Betty. "The Digby Harrowing of Hell, Lines 232, 265." Notes and Queries, New Ser., XI (1964), 374.

3876 Bowers, Robert H. "The Tavern Scene in the Middle English Digby Play of Mary Magdalene." In, Bryan, Robert A., Alton C. Morris, A. A. Murphree, and Aubrey L. Williams, eds. All These to Teach: Essays in Honor of C. A. Robertson. (Gainesville, Florida, 1965), pp. 15-32.

3877 Baker, D. C., and J. L. Murphy. "The Late Medieval Plays of MS. Digby 133: Scribes, Dates, and Early History." Research Opportunities in Renaissance Drama, X (1967), 153-166.

3878 ----- "The Bodleian MS. E. Mus. 160 Burial and Resurrection and the Digby Plays." Review of English Studies, New Ser., XIX (1968), 290-293.

3879 Velz, John W. "Sovereignty in the Digby Mary Magdalene." Comparative Drama, II (1968), 32-43.

Doncaster

3880 [Hardy, William John, ed.]. A Calendar to the Records of the Borough of Doncaster. 4 vol. Doncaster, Corporation of Doncaster, 1899-1902. Indexes.
BM.

Dover

3881 Blair, Lawrence. "Dover." In, "A Note on the Relation of the Corpus Christi Procession to the Corpus Christi Play in England." Modern Language Notes, LV (February, 1940), 87-88.

3882 Dawson, Giles, ed. "Dover." Records of Plays and Players in
       Kent 1450-1642. The Malone Society. Collections. Vol. VII.
       (Oxford, 1965), pp. 22-53.

Dublin (Northampton)
Abraham and Isaac

Manuscript
3883 Trinity College, Dublin, D. 4, 18, No. 432, ff. 74^V-81^r.

Texts
3884 Sacrifice of Abraham. In, Collier, John Payne. Five Miracle
       Plays, Or Scriptural Dramas. (London, 1836).

3885 Abraham und Isaac. In, Brotanek, Rudolf. Abraham and Isaac.
       Ein mittelenglisches Misterium aus einer Dubliner Hand-
       schrift." Anglia, XXI (1898), 21-55. [Text, pp. 41-52.]

3886 "Abraham und Isaak: ein mittelenglisches Misterium aus einer
       Dubliner Handschrift." [Herausgegeben von Rudolf Brotanek.]
       Anglia, XXI (1899), 21-55.

3887 Abraham and Isaac. In, Waterhouse, Osborn, ed. The Non-Cycle
       Mystery Plays. (London, 1909), pp. 26-36.

3888 Abraham and Isaac. In, Eliot, Samuel A., ed. Little Theatre
       Classics. Vol. 2. (Boston, 1918-1922).

Studies
3889 Harris, Walter. "Of the Interludes and Plays Antiently Repre-
       sented on the Stage by the Several Corporations of the City of
       Dublin." The History and Antiquities of the City of Dublin.
       (London, 1766), pp. 142-150.

3890 Harris, Walter, Comp. The History and Antiquities of the City
       of Dublin, from the Earliest Accounts. With an Appendix,
       Containing an History of the Cathedrals of Christ-Church and
       St. Patrick, the University, the Hospitals and Other Public
       Buildings. Also Two Plans, One of the City As It Was in the
       Year 1610, Being the Earliest Extant; the Other As It Is At
       Present, from the Accurate Survey of Mr. Rocque. London:
       Printed for J. Knox, 1766. [8], 509, [1] pp.
            ICU.

3891 Walker, Joseph C. "An Historical Essay on the Irish Stage."

Transactions of the Royal Irish Academy, II (1788), 75-90.

3892 Gilbert, John T., ed. Calendar of Ancient Records of Dublin, in the Possession of the Municipal Corporation of That City. Published by the Authority of the Municipal Council. 7 vol. Dublin: J. Dollard, 1889.
BM. ICU.

3893 Chambers, E. K. "Abraham and Isaac (Dublin MS.)." The Mediaeval Stage. Vol. 2. (London, 1903), p. 426.

3894 ----- "Dublin, Ireland." The Mediaeval Stage. (London, 1903), pp. 363-366.

3895 Pierson, Merle. "Dublin." In, "The Relation of the Corpus Christi Procession to the Corpus Christi Play in England." Transactions of the Wisconsin Academy of Sciences, Arts, and Letters, XVIII (1916), p. 135.

*3896 Wells, John Edwin. "The Dublin Abraham." A Manual of the Writings in Middle English, 1050-1400. (New Haven, 1916-1951), pp. 571-572, 862, 1081, 1137, 1319, 1417.

3897 Patch, Howard Rollin. "The Ludus Coventriae and the Digby Massacre." Publications of the Modern Language Association, XXXV (1920), 324-343.

3898 Dustoor, P. E. "Textual Notes on Three Non-Cycle Mystery Plays." Modern Language Review, XXIII (April, 1928), 202-212.

3899 Craig, Hardin. "Abraham and Isaac -- Manuscripts from Brome Hall and from Dublin." English Religious Drama of the Middle Ages. (Oxford, 1955), pp. 305-310.

Dundee

3900 Maxwell, Alexander. The History of Old Dundee, Narrated Out of the Town Council Register, with Additions from Contemporary Annals. Edinburgh: D. Douglas, 1884. 610 pp.
ICN.

3901 Boyd, Frank. Records of the Dundee Stage from the Earliest Times to the Present Day. Dundee: W. and D. C. Thomson, 1886. [iii], ii, [1], 96, [2] pp.
MB. MH.

3902 Maxwell, Alexander. Old Dundee. Ecclesiastical, Burghal, and
        Social Prior to the Reformation. Edinburgh: David Douglas;
        Dundee: William Kidd, 1891. xvi, 424 pp. Index.
            BM.

Dunmow

3903 Mepham, W. A. "Village Plays at Dunmow, Essex, in the
        Sixteenth Century." Notes and Queries, (May 19, 1934), 345-
        348; (May 26, 1934), 362-366.

3904 Blair, Lawrence. "Dunmow." In, "A Note on the Relation of the
        Corpus Christi Procession to the Corpus Christi Play in Eng-
        land." Modern Language Notes, LV (February, 1940), 85.

3905 Mepham, William A. "Medieval Drama in Essex, Dunmow."
        Essex Review, LV (April, 1946), 58-65; (July, 1946), 129-
        136.

Dunstable

3906 Chambers, E. K. "Dunstable, Bedfordshire." The Mediaeval
        Stage. Vol. 2. (London, 1903), 366.

3907 Thomas, Catherine B. C. "The Miracle Play at Dunstable."
        Modern Language Notes, XXXII (June, 1917), 337-344. [See
        also, Coffman, G. R. A New Theory Concerning the Origin
        of the Miracle Play. (Menasha, 1914), pp. 72-78.]

Durham

3908 Lonstaffe, W. H. D. "The Banner and Cross of St. Cuthbert."
        Archaeologia Aeliana, New Ser., II (1848), 51-65.

3909 Chambers, E. K. "Durham Priory." The Mediaeval Stage. Vol.
        II. (Oxford, 1903), pp. 240-245.

3910 Dodds, Madeleine Hope. "The Northern Stage." Archaeologia
        Aeliana, Third Series, XI (1914), 31-64.

3911 Pierson, Merle. "Durham." In, "The Relation of the Corpus
        Christi Procession to the Corpus Christi Play in England."
        Transactions of the Wisconsin Academy of Sciences, Arts,
        and Letters, XVIII (1916), 156-157.

Dux Moraud

Manuscript

3912 Oxford. Bodleian MS. Eng. Poet. f. 2(R). [Play is 15th C.?]

Texts

3913 "Dux Moraud. Einzelrolle aus einem verlorenen Drama des 14.
        Jahrhunderts." [Edited by W. Heuser.] Anglia, XXX (1907),
        180-208.

3914 Dux Moraud. In, Adams, J. Q., ed. The Chief Pre-Shakespearean
        Drama. (Boston and New York, 1924).

Studies

3915 Heuser, W. "Dux Moraud, Einzelrolle aus einem verlorenen
        Drama des 14. Jahrhunderts." Anglia, XXX (1907), 180-208.

3916 "Dux Moraud." Wells, John Edwin. A Manual of the Writings of
        the Middle English, 1050-1400. (New Haven, 1916-1951), pp.
        545-546, 858, 1079, 1136, 1228, 1416.

Easterford

3917 Chambers, E. K. "Easterford, Essex." The Mediaeval Stage.
        Vol. 2. (London, 1903), p. 367.

Edinburg

3918 Chambers, E. K. "Edinburgh, Scotland." The Mediaeval Stage.
        Vol. 2. (London, 1903), pp. 366-367.

Essex

3919 Clark, The Rev. Andrew. "The 15th Century Drama in Essex."
        Essex Review, XIV (1905), 104-110.

3920 Mepham, William. "Village Plays at Dunmow, Essex, in the
        Sixteenth Century." Notes and Queries, CLXVI (May 19, 1934),
        345-348; (May 26, 1934), 362-366.

3921 ----- "A History of the Drama in Essex from the Fifteenth
        Century to the Present Time." Ph.D. University of London,
        1937.

3922 ----- "A General Survey of Mediaeval Companies in Essex,
        1537-1642." Essex Review, LIV (April-October, 1945),

52-58, 107-112, 139-142.

3923 Mepham, William A. "Visits of Professional Touring Companies
     to Essex, 1537-1642." Essex Review, LVII (October, 1948),
     205-216.

Exeter

3924 Robbins, Alfred F. "An Exeter Theatre in 1348." Notes and
     Queries, 9th Ser., VII (June 29, 1901), 506.

3925 Chope, R. Pearse. "The Early Exeter Theatre." Devon and
     Cornhill Notes and Queries, XI (October, 1920), 122-125.

3926 Radford, Cecily. "Early Drama in Exeter." Report and Trans-
     actions of the Devonshire Association for the Advancement of
     Science, Literature and Art, LVI (June, 1935), 361-370.

Faversham

3927 "Faversham." Dawson, Giles, ed. Records of Plays and Players
     in Kent 1450-1642. The Malone Society. Collections. Vol. VII.
     (Oxford, 1965), pp. 54-66.

Folkestone

3928 Chambers, E. K. "Folkstone, Kent." The Mediaeval Stage. Vol.
     2. (London, 1903), p. 367.

3929 Dawson, Giles, ed. "Folkestone." Records of Plays and Players
     in Kent 1450-1642. The Malone Society. Collections. Vol. VII.
     (Oxford, 1965), pp. 67-73.

Fordwich

3930 ----- "Fordwich." Records of Plays and Players in Kent 1450-
     1642. The Malone Society. Collections. Vol. VII. (Oxford,
     1965), pp. 74-79.

Foston

3931 Chambers, E. K. "Foston, Leicestershire." The Mediaeval Stage.
     Vol. 2. (London, 1903), p. 367.

Fyfield

3932 Chambers, E. K. "Fyfield, Oxfordshire." The Mediaeval Stage.
        Vol. 2. (London, 1903), p. 367.

Garboldisham

3933 ----- "Garboldisham, Norfolk." The Mediaeval Stage. Vol. 2.
        (London, 1903), p. 367.

Glastonbury

3934 Blair, Lawrence. "Glastonbury." In, "A Note on the Relation of
        the Corpus Christi Procession to the Corpus Christi Play in
        England." Modern Language Notes, LV (February, 1940), 92.

Gloucester

3935 Hart, William Henry, ed. Historia et cartularium monasterii
        Sancti Patri Gloucestriae. 3 vol. London: Longmans, 1863-
        1867. (Chronicles and memorials of Great Britain and Ireland
        during the Middle Ages. 'Rolls series'). ["Nota de festivitatae
        Corporis Christi" vol. 1, p. 44.]
            BM.

3936 Hannam-Clark, Theodore. Drama in Gloucestershire (the Cots-
        wold County). Some Accounts of Its Development from the
        Earliest Times Till To-day. Gloucester: Minchin and Gibbs;
        London: Simpkin, Marshall, Ltd., 1928. 240 pp. [Treats
        Tewskesbury, Gloucester, Cheltenham, Cirencester, Stroud,
        Berkeley.]
            BM. ICN.

Great Chart

3937 Chambers, E. K. "Great Chart, Kent." Vol. 2. The Mediaeval
        Stage. (London, 1903), p. 367.

Great Yarmouth

3938 Pierson, Merle. "Great Yarmouth." In, "The Relation of the
        Corpus Christi Procession to the Corpus Christi Play in Eng-
        land." Transactions of the Wisconsin Academy of Sciences,
        Arts, and Letters, XVIII (1916), 157.

Hadleigh

3939 Chambers, E. K. "Hadleigh, Essex." The Mediaeval Stage.
      Vol. 2. (London, 1903), p. 367.

Halstead

3940 ----- "Halstead, Essex." The Mediaeval Stage. Vol. 2. (Lon-
      don, 1903), p. 367.

Ham Street

3941 ----- "Ham Street, Kent." The Mediaeval Stage. Vol. 2.
      (London, 1903), p. 367.

Hanningfield

3942 ----- "Hanningfield, Essex." The Mediaeval Stage. Vol. 2.
      (London, 1903), p. 368.

Harling

3943 ----- "Harling, Norfolk." The Mediaeval Stage. Vol. 2.
      (London, 1903), p. 368.

Harrowing of Hell
                            Manuscripts
3944 British Museum. MS. Harl. 2253, ff. 55-56.

3945 Oxford. Bodleian MS. Digby 86, ff. 119-120.

3946 Advocates' Library. Auchinleck Manuscript, W. 4. I.

                              Texts
3947 The Harrowing of Hell. A Miracle Play. Printed from the Auchin-
      leck Manuscript. Edinburgh: Printed by Ballantine & Co. [1835].
      16 pp.
           BM.

3948 The Harrowing of Hell. In, Collier, J. Payne, ed. Five Miracle
      Plays, or Scriptural Dramas. (London, 1836). 16 pp.

3949 Owain Miles and Other Inedited Fragments of Ancient English
      Poetry. Edinburgh: [Privately Printed], 1837? 6 parts. [The
      Harrowing of Hell, 16 pp.]
           BM.

3950 The Harrowing of Hell, a Miracle Play Written in the Reign of
Edward the Second, Now First Published from the Original
Manuscript in the British Museum, with an Introduction,
Translation, and Notes. By James Orchard Halliwell. London:
J. R. Smith, 1840. 33 pp.
BM. ICN. NN.

3951 The Harrowing of Hell. In, Wright, Thomas, and James Orchard
Halliwell, eds. Reliquiae Antiquae. Vol. 1. (London, 1841), p.
253. [The prologue, which has variations from the one printed
in his edition. MS. Digby 86.]

3952 The Harrowing of Hell, In, Mall, Eduard. The Harrowing of Hell.
Das altenglische Spiel von Christi Höllenfahrt. Berlin: Druck
von Gebr. Unger (Th. Grim), 1871. 53 pp. [From MS Harl.
2253.]
BM. ICN. MdBP. MiU. NN. NNP.

3953 Christi Höllenfahrt [The Harrowing of Hell.] In, Altenglische
Dichtungen des MS. Harl. 2253. Mit Grammatik und Glossar.
Herausgegeben von Dr. K. Böddeker. Berlin: Weidmannsche
Buchhandlung, 1878. xvi, 463 pp. [The text is in Middle Eng-
lish.]
BM.

3954 The Harrowing of Hell. In, Pollard, A. W. English Miracle
Plays. (Oxford, 1890), pp. 166-172. [The Harleian text.]

3955 [Harrowing of Hell]. Editionis criticae vetustissimi quod sermone
anglico conscriptum est dramatis pars prior. Curavit Hermannus Varnahgen. Erlangae: Typis Friderici Innge Typographi
Aulae Reg. Bavar. et Univers. Erlangensis, 1898. [2], 34,
[12] pp. [Photographic reproduction of the pages of the MS.
on final 10 pages. Texts, pp. 7-21, with texts of MSS. Auchinleck and Digby.]
BM. ICU.

3956 The Middle-English Harrowing of Hell and Gospel of Nicodemus.
Now First Edited from All the Known Manuscripts, with Intro-
duction and Glossary, by William Henry Hulme. London: Pub-
lished for the Early English Text Society by Kegan, Paul,
Trench, Trübner & Co., Limited, 1907. lxx, 150 pp. (Early
English Text Society. Extra Series No. 100.) [In three parallel
columns the book contains the Bodleian Digby MS. 86; British
Museum MS. Harl. 2253; Auchinleck MS. W. 4, Advocates

Library, Edinburgh.]
BM. DLC. MiU. NjP. ODW. OU.

3957 Facsimile of British Museum MS. Harley 2253. With an Introduction by N. R. Ker. London, New York, Toronto: Published
for the Early English Text Society by the Oxford University
Press, 1965. xxiii, [1], ff. 49-142, [3].
BM.

Studies

3958 Harrowing of Hell. Codex manu scriptum. Digby 86 in Bibliotheca Bodleiana asservatum, descripsit, excerpsit, illustravit
dr. E[dmund] Stengel. Halis: Libraria Orphanotrophei, 1871.
xiv, 132 pp.
O.

3959 Wülker, Richard Paul. Das Evangelium Nicodemi in der Abend-
ländischen Literatur. Nebst drei Excursen über Joseph von
Arimathia als Apostel Englands, das Drama Harrowing of Hell
und Jehan Michels Passio Christi. Paderborn: F. Schoningh,
1872. 33 pp.
BM.

3960 Mall, Eduard. "Zu The Harrowing of Hell." Jahrbuch für
romanische und englische Sprache und Literatur, XIII (1874),
217-221.

3961 Altenglische Dichtungen des MS. Harl. 2253. Mit Grammatik
und Glossar. Herausgegeben von Dr. K. Böddeker. Berlin:
Weidmannsche Buchhandlung, 1878. xvi, 463 pp. [The text
is in Middle English].

3962 Kölbing, E. "Vier Romanzen-handschriften." Englische Studien,
VII (1884), 182.

3963 Kirkland, James Hampton. A Study of the Anglo-Saxon Poem
"The Harrowing of Hell." Inaugural Dissertation. Leipzig,
1885. 40 pp.
ICU.

3964 Crow, Charles Langley. Zur Geschichte des kurzen Reimpaars
im Mittelenglischen (Harrowing of Hell, Cursor Mundi,
Chaucer's House of Fame.) Göttingen: W. F. Kästner, 1892.
63, [1] pp. [MS. Harl. 2253].
BM.

3965 Cramer, Julius. Quelle, Verfasser und Text des altenglischen
      Gedichtes Christi Höllenfahrt. Halle a. S.: Bernhardt Karras,
      1896. [2], 38, [2] pp.

3966 Kretzmann, P. E. "A Few Notes on The Harrowing of Hell.
      Modern Philology, XIII (1915-1916), 49-51.

3967 Burstein, Sona Rosa. "The Harrowing of Hell." Folk-Lore,
      XXXIX (1928), 113-132.

3968 McCulloch, J. A. The Harrowing of Hell. A Comparative Study
      of an Early Christian Doctrine. Edinburgh, Clark, 1931.
      xiii, 352 pp.
          BM. CtY. DLC. ICU. MH. MnU. OC1. OCU. OO.

Hascombe

3969 Chambers, E. K. "Hascombe, Surrey." The Mediaeval Stage.
      Vol. 2. (London, 1903), p. 368.

Hereford

3970 Johnson, Richard. The Ancient Customs of the City of Hereford,
      with Translations of the Earlier City Charters and Grants;
      Also, Some Account of the Trades of the City, and Other In-
      formation Relative to Its Earlier History. London: J. B.
      Nichols and Sons; Hereford: E. K. Jakeman, 1868. viii, 176 pp.
          BM.

3971 ----- The Ancient Customs of the City of Hereford. With Trans-
      lations of the Earlier City Charters and Grants; Also, Some
      Account of the Trades of the City, and Other Information
      Relative to Its Early History. 2nd ed. London: T. Richards,
      1882. [12], 240 pp.
          BM. ICN.

3972 Bannister, A. T. "The Hereford Miracles." Woolhope Naturalists'
      Field Club. Hereford. Transactions (1902/04), 377-383.

3973 Chambers, E. K. "Hereford, Herefordshire." The Mediaeval
      Stage. Vol. 2. (London, 1903), pp. 368-369.

3974 Pierson, Merle. "Hereford." In, "The Relation of the Corpus
      Christi Procession to the Corpus Christi Play in England."
      Transactions of the Wisconsin Academy of Sciences, Arts,

and Letters, XVIII (1916), 136.

3975 Dew, Rev. E. N., translator. Extracts from the Cathedral
      Registers, A.D. 1275-1535. Hereford: Hereford Times for
      Diocese of Hereford, 1932. xv, 160 pp. Index.
          BM.

Herne

3976 Chambers, E. K. "Herne, Kent." The Mediaeval Stage. Vol. 2.
      (London, 1903), p. 370.

Heybridge

3977 ----- "Heybridge, Essex." The Mediaeval Stage. Vol. 2. (Lon-
      don, 1903), p. 370.

3978 Mepham, William A. "A XVIth Century Village Play at Heybridge,
      Essex." Notes and Queries, CLXVI (1933), 345-348; 362-366.

3979 ----- "A XVIth Century Village Play at Heybridge, Essex."
      Notes and Queries, CLXVII (August 4, 1934), 75-79.

3980 ----- "Mediaeval Plays in the 16th Century at Heybridge and
      Braintree." Essex Review, LV (January, 1946), 8-18.

High Easter

3981 Chambers, E. K. "High Easter, Essex." The Mediaeval Stage.
      Vol. 2. (London, 1903), p. 370.

High Halden

3982 ----- "High Halden, Kent." The Mediaeval Stage. Vol. 2. (Lon-
      don, 1903), p. 370.

Holbeach

3983 ----- "Holbeach, Lincolnshire." The Mediaeval Stage. Vol. 2.
      (London, 1903), p. 370.

Hull

3984 Hadley, George. A New and Complete History of the Town and
      Country Of the Town of Kingston-upon-Hull. Kingston-upon-

Hull: T. Briggs, 1788. iv, 887 pp.
BM.

3985 Chambers, E. K. "Hull, Yorkshire." The Mediaeval Stage. Vol.
2. (London, 1903), pp. 370-371.

3986 Sheppard, Thomas. Evolution of the Drama in Hull and District.
Hull: A. Brown and Sons, 1929. xii, 253 pp.
BM. ICN.

3987 Mill, Anna J. "The Hull Noah Play." Modern Language Review,
XXXIII (October, 1938), 489-505.

Hythe

3988 Chambers, E. K. "Hythe, Kent." The Mediaeval Stage. Vol.
2. (London, 1903), p. 371.

3989 Dawson, Giles, ed. "Hythe." Records of Plays and Players in
Kent 1450-1642. The Malone Society Collections. Vol. VII.
(Oxford, 1965), pp. 82-88.

Idbury

3990 Chambers, E. K. "Idbury, Oxfordshire." The Mediaeval Stage.
Vol. 2. (London, 1903), p. 371.

Interludium de Clerico et Puella

Manuscript
3991 British Museum Add. MS. 23986.

Texts
3992 Interludium de Clerico et Puella. In, Chambers, E. K. The
Mediaeval Stage. Vol. 2. (London, 1903), pp. 324-326.

3993 Interludium de Clerico et Puella. In, Brandl, A., and O. Zippel,
eds. Mittelenglische Sprach-und Literaturproben. (Berlin,
1917), p. 203.

3994 Interludium de Clerico et Puella. In, Brandl, A., und O. Zippel.
Mittelenglische Sprach-und Literaturproben. (Berlin, 1927),
p. 203.

3995 Interludium de Clerico et Puella. In, Brandl, A., and O. Zippel,

eds. 2nd ed. Mittelenglische Sprach-und Literatur-proben.
(Berlin, 1947), p. 203.

Studies

3996 Heuser, W. "Das Interludium de Clerico et Puella und das
      Fabliau von Dame Siriz." Anglia, XXX (1907), 306-319.

3997 "Interludium de Clerico et Puella." Wells, John Edwin. A
      Manual of the Writings in Middle English, 1050-1400. (New
      Haven, 1916-1951), pp. 546, 858, 1136, 1636.

3998 Craig, Hardin. [Interludium de Clerico et Puella]. English Reli-
      gious Drama of the Middle Ages. (Oxford, 1955), pp. 329-
      330.

3999 Richardson, Frances E. "Notes on the Text and Language of
      Interludium de Clerico et Puella." Notes and Queries, IX
      (1962), 133-134.

Ipswich

4000 Wodderspoon, John. Memorials of the Ancient Town of Ipswich.
      Ipswich: Pawsey; London: Longmans, Brown, Green & Long-
      mans; and J. R. Smith, 1850. xvi, 403 pp.
          BM.

4001 Chambers, E. K. "Ipswich, Suffolk." The Mediaeval Stage. Vol.
      2. (London, 1903), pp. 371-373.

4002 "Ipswich." Pierson, Merle. In, "The Relation of the Corpus
      Christi Procession to the Corpus Christi Play in England."
      Transactions of the Wisconsin Academy of Sciences, Arts,
      and Letters, XVIII (1916), 137-138.

4003 "Players at Ipswich." Malone Society Collections. II. Part III.
      (London, 1931), pp. 258-284.

Ixworth

4004 Chambers, E. K. "Ixworth, Suffolk." The Mediaeval Stage.
      Vol. 2. (London, 1903), p. 373.

Kendal

4005 ----- "Kendal, Westmoreland." The Mediaeval Stage.

Vol. 2. (London, 1903), pp. 373-374.

4006 Pierson, Merle. "Kendal." In, "The Relation of the Corpus
Christi Procession to the Corpus Christi Play in England."
Transactions of the Wisconsin Academy of Sciences, Arts,
and Letters, XVIII (1916), 158.

Kenninghall

4007 Chambers, E. K. "Kenninghall, Norfolk." The Mediaeval Stage.
Vol. 2. (London, 1903), p. 374.

Kilkenny

4008 ----- "Kilkenny, Ireland." The Mediaeval Stage. Vol. 2. (London, 1903), p. 374.

King's Lynn

4009 Harrod, Henry. Report on the Deeds & Records of the Borough
of King's Lynn. King's Lynn: Thew & Son, 1874. 153 pp.
BM.

4010 Chambers, E. K. "King's Lynn, Norfolk." The Mediaeval Stage.
Vol. 2. (London, 1903), p. 374.

4011 Pierson, Merle. "King's Lynn." In, "The Relation of the Corpus
Christi Procession to the Corpus Christi Play in England."
Transactions of the Wisconsin Academy of Sciences, Arts,
and Letters, XVIII (1916), 139.

Kingston-on-Thames

4012 Chambers, E. K. "Kingston-on-Thames, Surrey." The Mediaeval
Stage. Vol. 2. (London, 1903), pp. 374-375.

Lancashire

4013 ----- "Lancashire (?), Essex." The Mediaeval Stage. Vol. 2.
(London, 1903), p. 375.

Lancaster

4014 ----- "Lancaster." The Mediaeval Stage. Vol. 2. (London,
1903), p. 375.

Lavenham

4015 Chambers, E. K. "Lavenham, Suffolk." The Mediaeval Stage.
        Vol. 2. (London, 1903), p. 375.

Leconfield

4016 ----- "Leconfield, Yorkshire." The Mediaeval Stage. Vol. 2.
        (London, 1903), p. 375.

Leeds

4017 ----- "Leeds, Yorkshire." The Mediaeval Stage. Vol. 2.
        (London, 1903), pp. 375-376.

Leicester

4018 Bateson, Mary, ed. Records of the Borough of Leicester. Vols.
        1-6. Vols. 1-2. London: C. J. Clay & Sons; Vols. 3-4.
        Cambridge: University Press; Vols. 5-6. Leicester: Univer-
        sity Press, 1899-1967.
              BM.

4019 Liebermann, F. "Das Osterspiel zu Leicester." Archiv für
        das Studium der neuren Sprache und Literaturen, CVII
        (1900), 108.

4020 Chambers, E. K. "Leicester." The Mediaeval Stage. Vol. 2.
        (London, 1903), pp. 376-377.

4021 Pierson, Merle. "Leicester." In, "The Relation of the Corpus
        Christi Procession to the Corpus Christi Play in England."
        Transactions of the Wisconsin Academy of Sciences, Arts,
        and Letters, XVIII (1916), 157.

Lichfield

4022 Chambers, E. K. "Lichfield, Staffordshire." The Mediaeval
        Stage. Vol. 2. (London, 1903), p. 377.

Lincoln

4023 D., H. [Note on Stage Properties at Lincoln in 1564.] Gentleman's
        Magazine, LVII (July, 1787), 481-482. [See Notes and Queries,
        3rd Ser., X (October 6, 1866), 269.]

4024 Wordsworth, Christopher, ed. Statutes of Lincoln Cathedral,
Arranged by the Late Harry Bradshaw ... with Illustrative
Documents. 3 vol. Cambridge: University Press, 1892-1897.
BM. ICN.

4025 ----- Notes on Mediaeval Services in England, with an Index of
Lincoln Ceremonies. London: Thomas Baker, 1898. xiii, 313
pp. Index.
BM. ICU.

4026 Leach, Arthur F. "Some English Plays and Players (1220-1548)."
An English Miscellany Presented to Dr. Furnivall in Honor of
His Seventy-Fifth Birthday. (Oxford, 1901), pp. 205-234.

4027 Chambers, E. K. "Lincoln." The Mediaeval Stage. Vol. 2. (London, 1903), pp. 377-379.

4028 Craig, Hardin. "The Lincoln Cordwainer's Pageant." Modern
Philology, X (1913), 605-613.

4029 Foster, Frances A. "Lincoln Episcopal Records, 1571-1584."
Canterbury and York Society, L (1913), 138.

4030 Craig, Hardin. "An Elementary Account of Miracle Plays in
Lincoln." Lincoln Diocesan Magazine, XXX (1914), 135-139.

4031 Pierson, Merle. "Lincoln." In, "The Relation of the Corpus Christi
Procession to the Corpus Christi Play in England." Transactions
of the Wisconsin Academy of Sciences, Arts, and Letters,
XVIII (1916), 139-140.

4032 Craig, Hardin. "The Lincoln Cordwainers' Pageant." Publications
of the Modern Language Association, XXXII (December, 1917),
605-615.

4033 Shull, Virginia. "Clerical Drama in Lincoln Cathedral, 1318 to
1561." Publications of the Modern Language Association, LII
(December, 1937), 946-966.

4034 Loomis, Roger Sherman. "Lincoln as a Dramatic Centre [during
the Middle Ages]." In, Mélanges d'histoire du théâtre du
moyen-âge et de la renaissance offerts à Gustave Cohen.
(Paris, 1950), pp. 241-247.
BM.

4035 Anderson, M. D. The Choir Stalls of Lincoln Minster. London:
      Produced by Rainbird, Mchean Ltd., Published by The Friends
      of Lincoln Cathedral, 1951. 52 pp. 45 Illustrations.
          BM.

4036 Craig, Hardin. "Medieval Religious Drama at Lincoln." English
      Religious Drama of the Middle Ages. (Oxford, 1955), pp.
      265-280.

4037 ----- "Mystery Plays at Lincoln: Further Research Needed."
      Lincolnshire Historian, II (1964), 37-41.

4038 Cameron, Kenneth M. "The Lincoln Plays at Grantham." Re-
      search Opportunities in Renaissance Drama, X (1967), 141-
      151.

Little Baddow

4039 Chambers, E. K. "Little Baddow, Essex." The Mediaeval Stage.
      Vol. 2. (London, 1903), p. 379.

Little Walsingham

4040 Pierson, Merle. "Little Walsingham." In, "The Relation of the
      Corpus Christi Procession to the Corpus Christ Play in Eng-
      land." Transactions of the Wisconsin Academy of Sciences,
      Arts, and Letters, XVIII (1916), 158.

Liverpool

4041 Broadbent, R. J. Annals of the Liverpool Stage, from the Earliest
      Period to the Present Time. Together with Some Account of
      the Theatres and Music Halls in Bootle and Birkenhead. Liver-
      pool: E. Howell, 1908. [9], 393 pp.
          ICU.

London

4042 Baker, Henry Barton. The London Stage; Its History and Traditions
      from 1576 to 1888. 2 vol. London: W. H. Allen and Co., 1889.
      [2nd edition, 1904.]
          BM. ICN.

4043 Kitto, J. V., ed. St. Martin-in-the-Fields. The Accounts of the
      Churchwardens, 1525-1603. Transcribed and edited. London:

Simpkin, Marshall & Co., 1901. x, 638 pp.
BM.

4044 Chambers, E. K. "London." The Mediaeval Stage. Vol. 2. (London, 1903), pp. 379-383.

4045 Littlehales, Henry. The Medieval Records of a London City Church (St. Mary at Hill) A.D. 1420-1559. Transcribed and Edited. With Facsimiles and an Introduction. Part I. With Five Facsimiles and a Temporary Introductory Note. London: Published for the Early English Text Society by Kegan Paul, Trench, Trübner & Co., Limited, 1904. xxxiii pp. [Bound with the later part, published in 1905.]
BM.

4046 ----- The Medieval Records of a London City Church (St. Mary at Hill) A.D. 1420-1559. Transcribed and Edited. With Facsimiles and an Introduction. London: Published for the Early English Text Society by Kegan Paul, Trench, Trübner & Co., Limited, 1905. xcvi, [2], 449 pp. Indices. (Early English Text Society, Original Series, No. 128).
BM.

4047 London, Corporation. Dramatic Records of the City of London. The Remembrancia. Malone Society Collections. Vol. 1. Part 1. (Oxford, 1907), pp. 43-100.

4048 Pierson, Merle. "London." In, "The Relation of the Corpus Christi Procession to the Corpus Christi Play in England." Transactions of the Wisconsin Academy of Sciences, Arts, and Letters, XVIII (1916), 141-142.

4049 "Dramatic Records of the City of London: The Repertories, Journals, and Later Books." Malone Society. Collections. II, Part III (1931), pp. 285-320.

4050 Hassall, W. O. "Plays at Clerkenwell." Modern Language Review, XXXIII (October, 1938), 564-567.

4051 Blair, Lawrence. "London." In, "A Note on the Relation of the Corpus Christi Procession to the Corpus Christi Play in England." Modern Language Notes, LV (February, 1940), 88-91.

4052 Robertson, Jean, and D. J. Gordon, eds. A Calendar of Dramatic Records in the Books of the Livery Companies of London 1485-

1640. Malone Society. Collections. III. 1954. xlix, [1], 204 pp. Index.

Lopham

4053 Chambers, E. K. "Lopham, Norfolk." The Mediaeval Stage. Vol. 2. (London, 1903), p. 383.

Louth

4054 ----- "Louth, Lincolnshire." The Mediaeval Stage. Vol. 2. (London, 1903), p. 383.

4055 Pierson, Merle. "Louth." In, "The Relation of the Corpus Christi Procession to the Corpus Christi Play in England." Transactions of the Wisconsin Academy of Sciences, Arts, and Letters, XVIII (1916), 158.

4056 Kahrl, Stanley J. "Medieval Drama in Louth." Research Opportunities in Renaissance Drama, X (1967), 129-133.

Ludlow

4057 Blair, Lawrence. "Ludlow." In, "A Note on the Relation of the Corpus Christi Procession to the Corpus Christi Play in England." Modern Language Notes, LV (February, 1940), 92.

Ludus Coventriae -- Hegge
    N. Town Cycle
    [Lincoln?]
Manuscript
4058 British Museum MS. Cotton Vespasian D. VIII.

Collections
4059 Halliwell, James Orchard, ed. Ludus Coventriae. A Collection of Mysteries, Formerly Represented at Coventry on the Feast of Corpus Christi. London: Printed for the Shakespeare Society, 1841. xvi, 434 pp.
    BM. ICN. NN.

4060 First Five Plays: Creation; Fall of Man; Cain and Abel; Noah's Flood; Abraham's Sacrifice. In, Dugdale, Sir William. Monasticon Anglicanum. Vol. 6, Part 2. (London, 1846).

*4061 Block, K. S. Ludus Coventriae; or, The Plaie Called Corpus
        Christi, Cotton MS. Vespasian D. VIII. London: Published
        for the Early English Text Society by H. Milford, Oxford
        University Press, 1922. lx, 402, [2] pp. (Extra Series, No.
        CXX, 1922 (for 1917).) [Reprinted 1960.] [Text omits Nos.
        17 and 22. Repeats No. 10.]
            BM. CtY. DLC. ICN. MH. MiU. NjP. NN. OU. ViU.
            WU.

Individual Plays

Creation of Heaven and the Angels
        Fall of Lucifer

4062 Fall of Lucifer. In, Stevens, John. History of the Antient Abbeys,
        Monasteries, Hospitals, Cathedrals and Collegiate Churches.
        Vol. 1. (London, 1722), pp. 144-145.

4063 Fall of Lucifer. In, Dugdale, Sir William. Monasticon Anglicanum.
        Vol. 6, Part 3. (London, 1830), pp. 1537-1538.

4064 The Creation. In, Halliwell, James O., ed. Ludus Coventriae.
        (London, 1841), pp. 19-23.

4065 Creation. In, Dugdale, Sir William. Monasticon Anglicanum.
        Vol. 6. (London, 1846), Part 2.

4066 The Creation of Heaven and the Angels. Fall of Lucifer. In,
        Block, K. S., ed. Ludus Coventriae. (London, 1922), pp.
        16-19.

4067 The Fall of Lucifer. In, Adams, Joseph Quincy, ed. Chief Pre-
        Shakespearean Dramas. (Boston, New York, 1924), pp. 86-87.

4068 The Fall of Lucifer. In, Schweikert, Harry Christian, ed. Early
        Plays. (New York, 1928), pp. 71-73.

4069 The Creation. In, Tickner, Frederick James, ed. Earlier Eng-
        lish Drama from Robin Hood to Everyman. (New York, [1929]),
        pp. 99-103.

4070 The Creation and Fall of Man. In, Loomis, Roger Sherman, and
        Henry W. Wells. Representative Medieval and Tudor Plays.
        (New York, 1942), pp. 98-111. [Abridgment of the following
        plays: The Creation of Heaven and the Angels, Fall of Lucifer;

The Creation of the World and Man, Fall of Man. Plays 1
and 2.

Creation of the World and Man
    Fall of Man

4071 The Fall of Man. In, Stevens, John. History of the Antient Ab-
      beys, Monasteries, Hospitals, Cathedrals and Collegiate
      Churches. Vol. 1. (London, 1722), pp. 145-147.

4072 The Fall of Man. In, Dugdale, Sir William. Monasticon Angli-
      canum. New ed. Vol. 6, Part 3. (London, 1830), pp. 1538-
      1540.

4073 The Fall of Man. In, Halliwell, James, ed. Ludus Coventriae.
      (London, 1841), pp. 24-32.

4074 The Creation of the World and Man; Fall of Man. In, Block,
      K. S., ed. Ludus Coventriae. (London, 1922), pp. 19-29.

Cain and Abel

4075 Cain and Abel. In, Stevens, John. History of the Antient Abbeys,
      Monasteries, Hospitals, Cathedrals and Collegiate Churches.
      Vol. 1. (London, 1722), pp. 147-149.

4076 Cain and Abel. In, Dugdale, Sir William. Monasticon Anglicanum.
      Vol. 6, Part 3. (London, 1830), pp. 1540-1541.

4077 Cain and Abel. In, Halliwell, James O., ed. Ludus Coventriae.
      (London, 1841), pp. 33-39.

4078 Cain and Abel. In, Block, K. S., ed. Ludus Coventriae. (Lon-
      don, 1922), pp. 29-35.

4079 Cain and Abel. In, Cawley, A. C., ed. Everyman and Medieval
      Miracle Plays. (New York, 1959).

    Noah
Death of Lamech

4080 Noah's Flood. In, Stevens, John. History of the Antient Abbeys,
      Monasteries, Hospitals, Cathedrals and Collegiate Churches.
      Vol. 1. (London, 1722), pp. 149-151.

4081 Noah's Flood. In, Dugdale, Sir William. Monasticon Anglicanum. New ed. Vol. 6, Part 3. (London, 1830), pp. 1541-1542.

4082 Noah's Flood. In, Halliwell, James O., ed. Ludus Coventriae. (London, 1841), pp. 40-48.

4083 Noah's Flood. In, Manly, John Matthews, ed. Specimens of Pre-Shaksperean Dramas. Vol. 1. (Boston, 1897), pp. 31-40.

4084 Noah and Lamech. In, Manly, John Matthews, ed. Specimens of the Pre-Shaksperean Drama. Vol. 1. (Boston and New York, 1903-1904), pp. 31-40.

4085 Noah. In, Block, K. S., ed. Ludus Coventriae. (London, 1922), pp. 35-43.

Abraham and Isaac

4086 Abraham and Isaac.In, Stevens, John. History of the Antient Abbeys, Monasteries, Hospitals, Cathedrals and Collegiate Churches. Vol. 1. (London, 1722), pp. 151-153.

4087 Abraham and Isaac. In, Dugdale, Sir William. Monasticon Anglicanum. New ed. Vol. 6, Part 3. (London, 1830), pp. 1542-1544.

4088 Abraham and Isaac. In, Halliwell, James O., ed. Ludus Coventriae. (London, 1841), pp. 49-57.

4089 Abraham's Sacrifice. In, Dugdale, Sir William. Monasticon Anglicanum. Vol. 6. (London, 1846), Part 2.

4090 Abraham and Isaac. In, Block, K. S., ed. Ludus Coventriae. (London, 1922), pp. 43-51.

4091 Cain and Abel. In, Cawley, A. C., ed. Everyman and Medieval Miracle Plays. (New York, 1959), pp. 25-33.

Moses

4092 Moses and the Two Tables. In, Halliwell, James O., ed. Ludus Coventriae. (London, 1841), pp. 58-64.

4093 Moses. In, Block, K. S., ed. Ludus Coventriae. (London, 1922), pp. 51-57.

The Prophets

4094 The Prophets. In, Halliwell, James O., ed. Ludus Coventriae.
(London, 1841), pp. 65-69.

4095 The Prophets. In, Block, K. S., ed. Ludus Coventriae. (London,
1922), pp. 57-62.

4096 The Prophets. In, Tickner, F. J., ed. Earlier English Drama
from Robin Hood to Everyman. (New York, [1929]), pp. 110-
112. [A brief selection.]

4097 The Procession of the Prophets. In, Loomis, Roger Sherman,
and Henry W. Wells. Representative Medieval and Tudor
Plays. (New York, 1942), pp. 111-115. [Abridgment of Play
No. 7, The Prophets.]

The Conception of Mary

4098 Birth of Mary. In, Hone, William, ed. Ancient Mysteries
Described. (London, 1823), pp. 13-19. [Extracts, with interpolations by the editor.]

4099 The Barrenness of Anna. In, Halliwell, James O., ed. Ludus
Coventriae. (London, 1841), pp. 70-78.

4100 Prologue of Contemplacio. The Conception of Mary. In, Block, K.
S., ed. Ludus Coventriae. (London, 1922), pp. 62-71.

Mary in the Temple

4101 Mary's Education in the Temple, and Being Saved by Angels.
In, Hone, William, ed. Ancient Mysteries Described. (London,
1823), pp. 20-26. [Extracts, with interpolations by the editor.]

4102 Mary in the Temple. In, Halliwell, James O., ed. Ludus Coventriae. (London, 1841), pp. 79-80.

4103 Mary in the Temple. In, Block, K. S., ed. Ludus Coventriae.
(London, 1922), pp. 71-82.

The Betrothal of Mary

4104 The Miraculous Espousal of Mary and Joseph. In, Hone, William,
ed. Ancient Mysteries Described. (London, 1823), pp. 27-37.

[Extracts, with interpolations by the editor.]

4105 The Marriage of the Virgin. A Miracle Play. Now First Printed
from MS. Cotton Vespasian, D. VIII. [London: Privately
Printed for J. P. Collier, 1836]. 24 ppl
MWelC.

4106 The Marriage of the Virgin. A Miracle Play. Now First Printed
from MS. Cotton Vesp. D. VII. In, Collier, J. Payne. Five
Miracle Plays, or Scriptural Dramas. (London, 1836), pp. 1-24.

4107 Mary's Betrothment. In, Halliwell, James O., ed. Ludus Coventriae.
(London, 1841), pp. 90-104.

4108 The Betrothal of Mary. In, Block, K. S., ed. Ludus Coventriae.
(London, 1922), pp. 83-97.

4109 Browne, E. Martin. The Play of the Maid Mary, Adapted from
the Ludus Coventriae (XV Century). London: P. Allan [1932].
64 pp. (Religious Plays, Series No. 3.)
NN.

The Parliament of Heaven
The Salutation and Conception

4110 A Council of the Trinity and the Incarnation. In, Hone, William,
ed. Ancient Mysteries Described. (London, 1823), pp. 38-45.
[Extracts, with interpolations by the editor.]

4111 The Salutation and Conception. In, Halliwell, James O., ed.
Ludus Coventriae. (London, 1841), pp. 105-116.

4112 The Salutation and Conception. In, Pollard, Alfred W., ed. English Miracle Plays, Moralities and Interludes. (Oxford, 1890),
pp. 44-48, 191-193. [Printed in part.]

4113 The Salutation and Conception. In, Manly, John M., ed. Specimens
of the Pre-Shakesperean Drama. Vol. 1. (Boston, 1897), pp.
82-93.

4114 The Salutation and Conception. In, Manly, John Matthews, ed.
Specimens of the Pre-Shakesperean Drama. (Boston and New
York, 1903-1904), pp. 82-93.

4115 The Salutation and Conception, In, Hemingway, Samuel B., ed.

English Nativity Plays. (New York, 1909), pp. 71-83.

4116 The Parliament of Heaven. The Salutation and Conception. In,
       Block, K. S., ed. Ludus Coventriae. (London, 1922), pp.
       97-108.

4117 The Salutation and Conception. In, Adams, Joseph Q., ed.
       Chief Pre-Shakespearean Dramas. (Boston, 1924), pp. 139-
       141. [Lines 183-340].

4118 Annunciation. Play XI. In, Pollard, A. W., ed. English Miracle
       Plays, Moralities and Interludes. (Oxford, 1927).

4119 The Incarnation. In, Loomis, Roger Sherman, and Henry W.
       Wells. Representative Medieval and Tudor Plays. (New York,
       1942), pp. 115-124. [Abridgment of Play No. 11, The Parlia-
       ment of Heaven, and The Salutation and Conception.]

4120 The Parliament of Heaven: The Annunciation and Conception. In,
       Browne, E. Martin, ed. Mystery and Morality Plays. (New
       York, 1960), pp. 86-95.

Joseph's Return

4121 Joseph's Return. In, Hone, William. Ancient Mysteries Described.
       (London, 1823), pp. 46-52. [Extracts, with interpolations by
       the Editor.]

4122 Joseph's Jealousy. In, Marriott, William, ed. A Collection of
       English Miracle-Plays. (Basel, 1838), pp. 41-47.

4123 Joseph's Return. In, Halliwell, James O., ed. Ludus Coventriae.
       (London, 1841), pp. 117-123.

4124 Joseph's Return. In, Hemingway, Samuel B., ed. English Nativity
       Plays. (New York, 1909), pp. 84-91.

4125 Joseph's Return. In, Block, K. S., ed. Ludus Coventriae. (Lon-
       don, 1922), pp. 109-115.

The Visit to Elizabeth

4126 The Visit to Elizabeth. In, Hone, William, ed. Ancient
       Mysteries Described. (London, 1823), pp. 53-58. [Extracts,
       with interpolations by the editor.]

4127 The Visit to Elizabeth. In, Halliwell, James O., ed. Ludus
      Coventriae. (London, 1841), pp. 124-130.

4128 The Visit to Elizabeth. In, Hemingway, Samuel B., ed. English
      Nativity Plays. (New York, 1909), pp. 92-100.

4129 The Visit to Elizabeth. Prologue of Summoner. In, Block, K. S.,
      ed. Ludus Coventriae. (London, 1922), pp. 115-123.

The Trial of Joseph and Mary

4130 The Trial of Joseph and Mary. In, Hone, William, ed. Ancient
      Mysteries Described. (London, 1823), pp. 59-66. [Extracts,
      with interpolations by the editor.]

4131 The Trial of Joseph and Mary. In, Marriott, William, ed. A
      Collection of English Miracle-Plays. (Basel, 1838), pp. 48-56.

4132 The Trial of Joseph and Mary. In, Halliwell, James O., ed.
      Ludus Coventriae. (London, 1841), pp. 131-144.

4133 The Trial of Joseph and Mary. In, Block, K. S., ed. Ludus
      Coventriae. (London, 1922), pp. 124-135.

The Birth of Christ

4134 The Miraculous Birth and the Midwives. In, Hone, William, ed.
      Ancient Mysteries Described. (London, 1823), pp. 67-72.
      [Extracts, with interpolations by the editor.]

4135 The Birth of Christ. In, Halliwell, James O., ed. Ludus Coven-
      triae. (London, 1841), pp. 145-155.

4136 The Birth of Christ. In, Hemingway, Samuel B., ed. English
      Nativity Plays. (New York, 1909), pp. 101-112.

4137 The Birth of Christ. In, Block, K. S., ed. Ludus Coventriae.
      (London, 1922), pp. 135-145.

4138 The Cherry Tree. In, Loomis, Roger Sherman, and Henry
      W. Wells. Representative Medieval and Tudor Plays. (New
      York, 1942), pp. 124-126. [Abridgment of Play No. 15, The
      Birth of Christ.]

The Adoration of the Shepherds

4139 The Adoration of the Shepherds. In, Halliwell, James O., ed.
      Ludus Coventriae. (London, 1841), pp. 156-160.

4140 The Adoration of the Shepherds. In, Hemingway, Samuel B., ed.
      English Nativity Plays. (New York, 1909), 113-118.

4141 The Adoration of the Shepherds. In, Block, K. S., ed. Ludus
      Coventriae. (London, 1922), pp. 146-151.

4142 The Adoration of the Shepherds. In, Loomis, Roger Sherman,
      and Henry W. Wells. Representative Medieval and Tudor
      Plays. (New York, 1942), pp. 127-131.

The Adoration of the Magi

4143 The Adoration of the Magi. In, Halliwell, James O., ed. Ludus
      Coventriae. (London, 1841), pp. 161-171.

4144 The Adoration of the Magi. In, Block, K. S., ed. Ludus Coven-
      triae. (London, 1922), pp. 151-162.

4145 The Adoration of the Magi and the Death of Herod. In, Loomis,
      Roger Sherman, and Henry W. Wells. Representative Medieval
      and Tudor Plays. (New York, 1942), pp. 131-141. [Abridg-
      ment of Plays 15 and 17, The Adoration of the Shepherd; The
      Death of Herod.]

The Purification

4146 The Purification. In, Halliwell, James O., ed. Ludus Coventriae.
      (London, 1841), pp. 172-178.

4147 The Purification. In, Block, K. S., ed. Ludus Coventriae.
      (London, 1922), pp. 162-169.

The Massacre of the Innocents
   The Death of Herod

4148 The Slaughter of the Innocents. In, Halliwell, James O., ed.
      Ludus Coventriae. (London, 1841), pp. 179-188.

4149 The Massacre of the Innocents. The Death of Herod. In, Block,
      K. S., ed. Ludus Coventriae. (London, 1922), pp. 169-177.

Christ and the Doctors

4150 Christ Disputing in the Temple. In, Halliwell, James O., ed. Ludus Coventriae. (London, 1841), pp. 189-198.

4151 Christ and the Doctors. In, Block, K. S., ed. Ludus Coventriae. (London, 1922), pp. 178-187.

The Baptism

4152 The Baptism of Christ. In, Halliwell, James O., ed. Ludus Coventriae. (London, 1841), pp. 199-204.

4153 The Baptism. In, Block, K. S., ed. Ludus Coventriae. (London, 1922), pp. 188-193.

The Temptation

4154 The Temptation. In, Halliwell, James O., ed. Ludus Coventriae. (London, 1841), pp. 205-212.

4155 The Temptation. In, Block, K. S., ed. Ludus Coventriae. (London, 1922), pp. 193-200.

The Woman Taken in Adultery

4156 The Woman Taken in Adultery. In, Halliwell, James O., ed. Ludus Coventriae. (London, 1841), pp. 213-222.

4157 The Woman Taken in Adultery. In, Block, K. S., ed. Ludus Coventriae. (London, 1922), pp. 200-209.

4158 The Woman Taken in Adultery. In, Ault, Norman. The Poet's Life of Christ. (London, 1923), pp. 129-131. [A short extract, modernized, from Ludus Coventriae, No. 23.]

4159 The Woman Taken in Adultery. In, Cawley, A. C., ed. Everyman and Medieval Miracle Plays. (New York, 1959), pp. 131-142.

4160 The Woman Taken in Adultery. In, Browne, E. Martin, ed. Mystery and Morality Plays. (New York, 1960), pp. 157-167.

The Raising of Lazarus

4161 Lazarus. In, Halliwell, James O., ed. Ludus Coventriae. (London, 1841), pp. 223-238.

4162 The Raising of Lazarus. In, Block, K. S., ed. Ludus Coventriae. (London, 1922), pp. 210-225.

4163 The Raising of Lazarus. In, Loomis, Roger Sherman, and Henry W. Wells. Representative Medieval and Tudor Plays. (New York, 1942), pp. 141-148.

Prologues of Demon and of John the Baptist
    The Council of the Jews
    The Entry into Jerusalem

4164 The Council of the Jews. In, Halliwell, James O., ed. Ludus Coventriae. (London, 1841), pp. 239-251.

4165 The Entry into Jerusalem. In, Halliwell, James O., ed. Ludus Coventriae. (London, 1841), pp. 252-258.

4166 Passion Play. I. Prologue of Demon. The Council of the Jews. The Entry into Jerusalem. In, Block, K. S., ed. Ludus Coventriae. (London, 1922), pp. 225-242.

4167 The Passion Play. In, Loomis, Roger Sherman, and Henry W. Wells. Representative Medieval and Tudor Plays. (New York, 1942), pp. 152-197. [Abridgment of Plays 24-32, Conspiracy of the Jews and Judges; The Betrayal; Trial before Annas and Caiphas; Trial of Christ before Pilate; Death of Judas; Condemnation and Scourging; The Procession to Calvary; The Crucifixion; The Descent into Hell of Anima Christi; Descent from the Cross and Burial, Guarding of the Sepulchre, etc.]

The Last Supper and the Conspiracy of the Jews

4168 The Last Supper. In, Halliwell, James O., ed. Ludus Coventriae. (London, 1841), pp. 259-279.

4169 The Last Supper. Conspiracy of the Jews and Judas. In, Block, K. S., ed. Ludus Coventriae. (London, 1922), pp. 242-262.

The Betrayal

4170 The Betraying of Christ. In, Halliwell, James O., ed. Ludus
      Coventriae. (London, 1841), pp. 280-287.

4171 The Betrayal. Lament of the Virgin. In, Block, K. S., ed.
      Ludus Coventriae. (London, 1922), pp. 262-270.

4172 The Betraying of Christ. In, Adams, Joseph Q., ed. Chief Pre-
      Shakespearean Dramas. (Boston, 1924), pp. 175-178.

4173 Betrayal. In, Heilman, Robert B., ed. An Anthology of English
      Drama before Shakespeare. (New York, 1952), pp. 1-10.

            King Herod
The Trial of Christ before Annas and Caiaphas

4174 King Herod. In, Halliwell, James O., ed. Ludus Coventriae.
      (London, 1841), pp. 288-292.

4175 The Passion Play. II. King Herod. The Trial before Annas and
      Caiaphas. In, Block, K. S., ed. Ludus Coventriae. (London,
      1922), pp. 271-278.

      The Death of Judas
The Trial of Christ before Pilate
The Trial of Christ before Herod

4176 The Trial of Christ. In, Halliwell, James O., ed. Ludus Coven-
      triae. (London, 1841), pp. 293-307.

4177 The Death of Judas. The Trial before Pilate. The Trial before
      Herod. In, Block, K. S., ed. Ludus Coventriae. (London,
      1922), pp. 278-287.

4178 The Trial of Christ. In, Adams, Joseph Q., ed. Chief Pre-
      Shakespearean Dramas. (Boston, 1924), pp. 179-186.

4179 The Trial of Christ. In, Tickner, Frederick J., ed. Earlier
      English Drama from Robin Hood to Everyman. (New York,
      1929), pp. 200-212.

Pilate's Wife's Dream
The Trial of Christ and the Thieves before Pilate

4180 Pilate's Wife's Dream. In, Halliwell, James O., ed. Ludus
      Coventriae. (London, 1841), pp. 308-310.

4181 Pilate's Wife's Dream. The Trial of Christ and the Thieves be-
      fore Pilate. In, Block, K. S., ed. Ludus Coventriae. (London,
      1922), pp. 287-294.

The Procession to Calvary
  The Crucifixion

4182 The Condemnation and Crucifixion of Christ. In, Halliwell, James
      O., ed. Ludus Coventriae. (London, 1841), pp. 311-328.

4183 The Procession to Calvary. The Crucifixion. In, Block, K. S., ed.
      Ludus Coventriae. (London, 1922), pp. 294-305.

4184 The Crucifixion. In, Tickner, Frederick J., ed. Earlier English
      Drama from Robin Hood to Everyman. (New York, 1929), pp.
      212-224.

The Descent into Hell of Anima Christi

4185 The Descent into Hell. In, Halliwell, James O., ed. Ludus
      Coventriae. (London, 1841), pp. 329-330.

4186 The Descent into Hell of Anima Christi. In, Block, K. S., ed.
      Ludus Coventriae. (London, 1922), pp. 305-307. [Lines 971-
      1017.]

The Descent from the Cross and the Burial
  The Guarding of the Sepulchre

4187 The Burial of Christ. In, Halliwell, James O., ed. Ludus Coven-
      triae. (London, 1841), pp. 331-337.

4188 The Burial. The Guarding of the Sepulchre. In, Block, K. S., ed.
      Ludus Coventriae. (London, 1922), pp. 307-318.

The Harrowing of Hell
  The Resurrection

4189 The Resurrection. In, Halliwell, James O., ed. Ludus Coventriae.
      (London, 1841), pp. 338-353.

4190 The Harrowing of Hell. The Resurrection. In, Block, K. S., ed.
Ludus Coventriae. (London, 1922), pp. 312-327. [Lines 1176-
1343, The Guarding of the Sepulchre; lines 1344-1415, The
Harrowing of Hell; lines 1416-1479, The Resurrection and Ap-
pearance to the Virgin; lines 1480-1647, The Compacy of the
Soldiers and Pilate.]

The Announcement to the Three Maries

4191 The Three Maries. In, Halliwell, James O., ed. Ludus Coventriae.
(London, 1841), pp. 354-359.

4192 The Announcement to the Three Maries. In, Block, K. S., ed.
Ludus Coventriae. (London, 1922), pp. 327-333.

The Appearance to Mary Magdalen

4193 Christ Appearing to Mary. In, Halliwell, James O., ed. Ludus
Coventriae. (London, 1841), pp. 360-363.

4194 The Appearance to Mary Magdalen. In, Block, K. S., ed. Ludus
Coventriae. (London, 1922), pp. 333-337.

4195 The Appearance to Magdalene. In, Loomis, Roger Sherman,
and Henry W. Wells. Representative Medieval and Tudor
Plays. (New York, 1942), pp. 197-200. [Abridgment of Play
No. 35, The Appearance to Mary Magdalen.]

The Appearance on the Way to Emmaus
  The Appearance to Thomas

4196 The Pilgrim of Emaus. In, Halliwell, James O., ed. Ludus
Coventriae. (London, 1841), pp. 364-376.

4197 The Appearance to Cleophas and Luke. The Appearance to Thomas.
In, Block, K. S., ed. Ludus Coventriae. (London, 1922), pp.
337-349.

The Ascension

4198 The Ascension. In, Halliwell, James O., ed. Ludus Coventriae.
(London, 1841), pp. 377-380.

4199 The Ascension. In, Block, K. S., ed. Ludus Coventriae. (London,
1922), pp. 349-352.

The Day of Pentecost

4200 The Descent of the Holy Ghost. In, Halliwell, J. O., ed. Ludus
      Coventriae. (London, 1841), pp. 381-382.

4201 The Day of Pentecost. In, Block, K. S., ed. Ludus Coventriae.
      (London, 1922), pp. 352-354.

The Assumption of the Virgin

4202 The Assumption of the Virgin. In, Halliwell, James O., ed.
      Ludus Coventriae. (London, 1841), pp. 383-400.

4203 The Assumption of the Virgin. A Miracle Play from the N-town
      Cycle. Edited by W. W. Greg. Oxford: The Clarendon Press,
      1915. 75, [1] pp. (Studies in the Religious Drama. 1.)
              BM. CtY. ICN. MdBJ. MiU. MnU. NN. OC1W. PU.

4204 The Assumption of the Virgin. In, Block, K. S., ed. Ludus
      Coventriae. (London, 1922), pp. 354-373.

Doomsday

4205 Doomsday. In, Halliwell, J. O., ed. Ludus Coventriae. (London,
      1841), pp. 401-405.

4206 Doomsday. In, Block, K. S., ed. Ludus Coventriae. (London,
      1922), pp. 373-377.

4207 Doomsday. In, Tickner, F. J., ed. Earlier English Drama from
      Robin Hood to Everyman. (New York, [1929]), pp. 244-248.

4208 The Last Judgment. In, Loomis, Roger Sherman, and Henry W.
      Wells. Representative Medieval and Tudor Plays. (New York,
      1942), pp. 201-206. [Abridgment of Play No. 40, Doomsday.]

Studies

4209 Dugdale, Sir William, and Roger Dodsworth. Monasticon angli-
      canum; sive Pandectae coenobiorum benedictinorum, clunia-
      censium, cisterciensium, carthusianorum a primordiis ad
      eorum usque dissolutionem ex mss. Codd. ad monasteria
      olim pertinentibus; archivis Turrium londinensis, eboracensis;
      curarium scoccarii, augmantationum; Bibliothecis bodleiana;
      Coll. reg. ...aliisque digesti per Rogerum Dodsworth ...
      [et] Gulielmum Dugdale. 3 vol. Londini: typis R. Hodgkinsonne,

1665-1673. [Monasteries].
ICU.

4210 Dugdale, Sir William. Monasticon Anglicanum; a History of the
Abbies and Other Monasteries, Hospitals, Frieries, and
Cathedral and Collegiate Churches ... in England and Wales;
Also of Such Scotch, Irish, and French Monasteries As Were
in Any Manner Connected with Religious Houses in England...
A New Edition, Enriched with a Large Accession of Materials
Now First Printed ... the History of Each Religious Foundation
in English Being Prefixed to Its Respective Series of Latin
Charters. By John Caley ... Henry Ellis ..., and Rev. Bulkeley
Bandinel. 6 vol. in 8. London: Longman, 1817-1830.
ICU.

4211 Collier, John Payne. "The Widkirk, Chester, and Coventry Miracle-
Plays." The History of Dramatic Poetry. Vol. 2. (London, 1831),
pp. 155-229.

4212 Hohlfeld, Alex. "Die altenglische Killektivmisterien, unter besond-
erer Berücksichtigung des Verhältnisses der York-und Towneley-Spiele." Anglia. Zeitschrift für Englische Philologie, XI
(1888), 219-310.

4213 Kramer, Max. Sprache und Heimat des sogenannten Ludus
Coventriae. Eine Untersuchung zur mittelenglishcen Sprach-
geschichté. Halle, a.S., 1892. 69, [1] pp.
CtY. MH. MnU. NNC. O.

4214 Birt, Henry Norbert. "The Ancient Mystery Plays of Coventry."
Downside Review, XVI (1897), 1-20.

4215 Hackauf, Emil. Die älteste mittelenglische Version der Assumptio
Mariae. [Erfurt, Ohlenroth'sche buchdruckerei, 1902.]
CtY. ICN. MiU. MnU. NjP. PU.

4216 Chambers, E. K. "Ludus Coventriae." The Mediaeval Stage.
Vol. 2. (London, 1903), pp. 416-422.

4217 French, J. C. "A Note on the Miracle Plays." Modern Language
Notes, XIX (1904), 31-32.

4218 Thompson, Elbert N. S. "The Ludus Coventriae." Modern Language
Notes, XXI (January, 1906), 18-20.

4219 Falke, Ernest. Die Quellen des Sogen. Ludus coventriae. Leipzig:

Reudnitz, 1908. 100 pp. "Literatur," pp. 5-7.
BM. CtY. ICN. MH. MnU.

4220 Craig, Hardin. "The Coventry Cycle of Plays." The Athenaeum,
No. 4477 (August 16, 1913), p. 166. [Favors Lincoln as the
site of these plays.]

4221 ----- "So-Called Coventry Plays." Nation, XCVII (1913), 308-
309.

4222 Bonnell, John Kester. "The Source in Art of the So-Called Prophet's
Play in the Hegge Collection." Publications of the Modern Language Association, XXIX (1914), 327-340.

4223 Craig, Hardin. "Note on the Home of Ludus Coventriae." University of Minnesota Studies in Language and Literature, No.
1 (1914), 72-83.

4224 Dodds, Madeleine H. "The Problem of the Ludus Coventriae."
Modern Language Review, IX (1914), 78-91.

4225 Greg, W. W. "Ludus Coventriae." The Library, Third Series,
V (October, 1914), 365-399. [Part IV of his article, "Bibliographical and Textual Problems of the English Miracle Cycles."]

4226 Swenson, Esther Lydia. An Inquiry into the Composition and
Structure of Ludus Coventriae....with a Note on the Home of
Ludus Coventriae, by Hardin Craig. Minneapolis: The Uni-
versity, 1914. [4], 83 pp. (University of Minnesota. Studies
in Language and Literature 1.)
BM. ICN. NN.

4227 Wynne, Arnold. [On the Coventry Plays.] The Growth of English
Drama. (Oxford, 1914), pp. 25-38.

4228 Block, K. S. "Some Notes on the Problem of the Ludus Coventriae." Modern Language Review, X (1915), 45-57.

4229 Bonnell, John Kester. "The Easter Sepulchrum in Its Relation
to the Architecture of the High Altar. The Source in Art of
the So-called Prophet Play in the Hegge Collection." Ph.D.
University of Wisconsin, 1916.

4230 Haller, Julius. "Der Dialog im Ludus Coventriae." Die Technik
des Dialogs im mittelalterlichen Drama Englands. (Wormser,
1916), pp. 55-66.

4231 Wells, John Edwin. "The Ludus Coventriae or 'Hegge Plays.'"
A Manual of Writings in Middle English, 1050-1400. (New
Haven, 1916-1951), pp. 560-565, 861, 993, 1026, 1081,
1137, 1185, 1228, 1283, 1319, 1417, 1468, 1524, 1637, 1729.

4232 Craig, Hardin. "The Lincoln Cordwainer's Pageant." Publications
of the Modern Language Association, XXXII (1917), 605-615.

4233 Patch, Howard Rollin. "The Ludus Coventriae and the Digby
Massacre." Publications of the Modern Language Association,
XXXV (1920), 324-343.

4234 Bonnell, John Kester. "Cain's Jaw Bone." Publications of the
Modern Language Association, XXXIX (1924), 144-146.

4235 Erbacher, Sister Leo Gonzaga. "Glossary of Two Plays from
Ludus Coventriae." M.A. University of Kansas, 1926.

4236 Hartman, Herbert. "The Home of the 'Ludus Coventriae.'"
Modern Language Notes, XLI (December, 1926), 530-531.

4237 Taylor, George Coffin. "The Christus Redivivus of Nicholas
Grimald and the Hegge Resurrection Plays." Publications of
the Modern Language Association, XLI (December, 1926),
840-859.

4238 Frost, Inez. "Glossary of Five Plays from Ludus Coventriae."
M.A. University of Kansas, 1927.

4239 Skinner, Francis Marie. "Glossary of Five Plays from Ludus
Coventriae." M.A. University of Kansas, 1927.

4240 Wells, Henry W. "Ludus Coventriae." American Church Monthly,
XXII (1927), 273-286.

4241 Parker, Roscoe Edward, ed. The Middle English Stanzaic Versions of the Life of St. Anne. London: Published for the Early
English Text Society by H. Milford, Oxford University Press,
1928. liv, 139 pp. [As a source for the St. Anne Plays in the
cycle.]
    ICN.

4242 Vriend, S. J., Joannes. The Blessed Virgin Mary in the Mediaeval Drama of England. Purmerend: J. Musses, 1928. 160 pp.
"Select Bibliography," pp. [xiii]-xv.

BM. DLC. IaU. ICN. ICU. IU. MH. MiU. MnU. NN.
OCU.

4243 Harrison, Izola Curley. "The Staging of the Ludus Coventriae."
M.A. University of Chicago, 1929.

4244 Phillips, Elias H. "A Study of Some Epic Aspects of the Ludus
Coventriae." M.A. University of North Carolina, 1931.

4245 Carroll, O.M.C., Rev. Thomas J. "The Influence of the Festival of Corpus Christi upon the Cycle Plays; with Some Observations About the View-Point of the Cambridge History of
English Literature." M.A. Catholic University of America,
1932.

4246 Jones, Ellen Mattocks. "Stage Setting and Stage Business in the
English Cycles." M.A. University of Minnesota, 1932.

4247 Baugh, Albert C. "A Recent Theory of the Ludus Coventriae."
Philological Quarterly, XII (October, 1933), 403-406.

4248 Clark, Thomas Blake. "A New Theory Concerning the Identity
and History of the Ludus Coventriae Cycle of Mystery Plays."
Philological Quarterly, XII (April, 1933), 144-169.

4249 Salter, F. M. "The Old Testament Plays of Ludus Coventriae."
Philological Quarterly, XII (October, 1933), 406-409.

4250 Zisowitz, Milton L. "New Testament Apocryphal Elements in
Eight Plays of the Ludus Coventriae." M.A. Columbia
University, 1935.

4251 Harney, Sister Mary Camillus. "The Characterization of Cain
and Abel in the English Mystery Plays: York, Chester, Ludus
Coventriae and Towneley Cycles." M.A. Catholic University
of America, 1940.

4252 Clark, Sr. Mary Thaddeus. "Drama in the Cyclic Plays of Mediaeval England." M.A. Fordham University, 1941.

4253 Lawlor, S.J., Richard Vincent. "The Music and Musical Elements of the Craft Cycles." M.A. Boston College, 1941.

4254 Greg, Walter Wilson. Bibliographical and Textual Problems of
the English Miracle Cycles. London: Alexander Moring,

Limited, 1943. 143 pp.

4255 Sullivan, S.S.J., Sr. John. "A Study of the Themes of the Passion in the Medieval Cyclic Drama." Ph.D. Catholic University of America, 1943.

4256 Benkovitz, Miriam J. "Some Notes on the 'Prologue of Demon' of Ludus Coventriae." Modern Language Notes, LX (February, 1945), 78-85.

4257 Hammer, M. L. "The Saviour As Protagonist in the Ludus Coventriae." M.A. University of North Carolina, 1945.

4258 Aquin, Sister M. "Vulgate and Eve-concept in the English Cycles." Catholic Biblical Quarterly, IX (1947), 409-435.

4259 Branaham, Joel Scott. "The Hegge Cycle in Relation to the Medieval Church." M.A. Columbia University, 1947.

4260 Fry, Timothy Paul, O.S.B. "A Study of the Ludus Coventriae with Special Reference to the Doctrine of the Redemption." Ph.D. University of North Carolina, 1948.

4261 Homan, Delmar Charles. "A Study in the Medieval Miracle Plays: Judgment Day (With Two Plays Modernized)." M.A. University of Iowa, 1949.

4262 Kökeritz, H. "'Out Born' in Ludus Coventriae." Modern Language Notes, LXIV (February, 1949), 89-90.

4263 Fry, Timothy, O.S.B. "The Unity of the Ludus Coventriae." Studies in Philology, XLVIII (July, 1951), 527-570.

4264 Seve, Nicholas Werner de. "The Marian Element in the Four Great Cycles." M.A. Columbia University, 1951.

4265 Bryant, Joseph Allen, Jr. "The Function of Ludus Coventriae 14." Journal of English and Germanic Philology, LII (July, 1953), 340-345.

4266 Craig, Hardin. "The Hegge Plays." English Religious Drama of the Middle Ages. (Oxford, 1955), pp. 239-266.

4267 Savage, Donald J. "An Analysis of the Comic Element in the Chester, York, Coventry and Towneley Mystery Cycles."

Ph.D. University of Minnesota, 1955.

4268 Wassmer, Jessica Therese. "A Comparison of Two Cycles of English Mystery Plays Ludus Coventriae or the Plaie Called Corpus Christi and the Towneley Plays." M.A. Fordham University, 1955.

4269 Maltman, Sister Nicholas. "A Study of the Evil Characters in the English Corpus Christi Cycles." Ph.D. University of California, 1957.

4270 Gay, Anne C. "A Study of the Staging of the N. Towne Cycle." Ph.D. University of Missouri, 1961.

4271 Prosser, Eleanor. "Cain." Drama and Religion in the English Mystery Plays. (Stanford, California, 1961), pp. 87-88.

4272 ----- "Joseph." Drama and Religion in the English Mystery Plays. (Stanford, California, 1961), pp. 96-102.

4273 ----- "Magdalene." Drama and Religion in the English Mystery Plays. (Stanford, California, 1961), pp. 119-146.

4274 ----- "Thomas." Drama and Religion in the English Mystery Plays. (Stanford, California, 1961), pp. 163-167.

4275 ----- "The Woman Taken in Adultery." Drama and Religion in the English Mystery Plays. (Stanford, California, 1961), pp. 103-109.

4276 Johnston, Alexandra Ferguson. "The Christ Figure in the Ministry Plays of the Four English Cycles." Ph.D. University of Toronto, 1964. [Delete].

4277 Forrest, Sister Mary Patricia, O.S.F. "Sources and Style of the St. Anne Day Plays in the Hegge Cycle." Ph.D. Catholic University, 1965.

4278 ----- "Apocryphal Sources of St. Anne's Day Plays in the Hegge Cycle." Medievalia et Humanistica, XVII (1966), 38-50.

4279 ----- "The Role of the Expositor Contemplacio in the St. Anne's Day Plays of the Hegge Cycle." Medieval Studies, XXVIII (1966), 60-76.

4280 Macaulay, Peter S. "The Play of the Harrowing of Hell as a Climax in The English Mystery Cycles." Studia Germanica Gandensia, VIII (1966), 115-134.

4281 Cameron, Kenneth, and Stanley J. Kahrl. "Staging the N-Town Cycle." Theatre Notebook, XXI (Spring, 1967), 122-138, 152-165. [See, Theatre Notebook, XX (1965-1966), 61-69.]

4282 Downing, Marjorie D. "The Influence of the Liturgy on the English Cycle Plays." Ph.D. Yale University, 1967.

4283 Forrest, Sister M. Patricia, O.S.F. "The Role of the Expositor Contemplacio in the St. Anne's Day Plays of the Hegge Cycle." Mediaeval Studies, XXVIII (1967), 60-76.

4284 Gay, Anne C. "The 'Stage' and the Staging of the N-Town Plays." Research Opportunities in Renaissance Drama, X (1967), 135-140.

4285 Johnston, Alexandra F. "The Christ Figure in the Ministry Plays of the Four English Cycles." Ph.D. University of Toronto, 1967.

4286 Walsh, O.S.B., Sister Mary Margaret. "The Judgment Plays of the English Cycles." The American Benedictine Review, XX (September, 1969), 378-394.

Lydd

4287 Chambers, E. K. "Lydd, Kent." The Mediaeval Stage. Vol. 2. (London, 1903), p. 383.

4288 Dawson, Giles, ed. "Lydd." Records of Plays and Players in Kent 1450-1642. The Malone Society. Collections. Vol. VII. (Oxford, 1965), pp. 89-112.

Lyneham, Oxfordshire. See, Shipton.

Maidstone

4289 Dawson, Giles, ed. "Maidstone." Records of Plays and Players in Kent 1450-1642. The Malone Society. Collections. Vol. VII. (Oxford, 1965), pp. 113-117.

Maldon

4290 Chambers, E. K. "Malden, Essex." The Mediaeval Stage. Vol.
      2. (London, 1903), p. 384.

4291 Mepham, William A. "Municipal Drama at Maldon in the Sixteenth
      Century." Essex Review, LV (October, 1946), 169-175.

4292 ----- "Municipal Drama at Maldon in the Sixteenth Century."
      Essex Review, LVI (January, 1947), 34-41.

Manningtree

4293 Chambers, E. K. "Manningtree, Essex." The Mediaeval Stage.
      Vol. 2. (London, 1903), p. 384.

Maxstoke

4294 ----- "Maxstoke, Warwickshire." The Mediaeval Stage. Vol.
      2. (London, 1903), p. 384.

Middleton

4295 ----- "Middleton, Norfolk." The Mediaeval Stage. Vol. 2.
      (London, 1903), p. 384.

Mildenhall

4296 ----- "Mildenhall, Suffolk." The Mediaeval Stage. Vol. 2.
      (London, 1903), p. 384.

Mile End

4297 ----- "Mile End, Middlesex." The Mediaeval Stage. Vol. 2.
      (London, 1903), p. 384.

      "Milton, Oxfordshire." See, Shipton.

Morebath

4298 ----- "Morebath, Devonshire." The Mediaeval Stage. Vol.
      2. (London, 1903), p. 384.

Nayland

4299 Chambers, E. K. "Nayland, Essex." The Mediaeval Stage. Vol. 2. (London, 1903), p. 385.

New Romney

4300 Robertson, W. A. Scott. "The Passion Play and Interlude at New Romney." Archaeologia Cantiana, XIII (1880), 215-226.

4301 Chambers, E. K. "New Romney, Kent." The Mediaeval Stage. Vol. 2. (London, 1903), pp. 385-386.

4302 Dawson, Giles, ed. "New Romney." Records of Plays and Players in Kent 1450-1642. The Malone Society. Collections. Vol. VII. (Oxford, 1965), pp. 118-143.

Newcastle Upon Tyne

General Studies

4303 Bourne, Henry. The History of Newcastle upon Tyne; or, the Ancient and Present State of That Town. Newcastle-upon-Tyne: John White, 1736. viii, 245 pp.
        BM.

4304 Brand, John. History of Newcastle. 2 vol. London: B. White and Son, 1789. [Basically a reprint of the text.]

4305 Walker, James, and M. A. Richardson. The Armorial Bearings of the Several Incorporate Companies of Newcastle upon Tyne, With a Brief Historical Account of Each Company; Together with Notices of Corpus Christi, or Miracle Plays, Anciently Performed by the Trading Societies of Newcastle Upon Tyne. Also a Copious Glossary of the Technical Terms Used in the Work. Newcastle: E. Walker, 1824. 64 pp.
        BM. NN.

4306 Welford, Richard, ed. History of Newcastle and Gateshead. 3 vol. London: Walter Scott [1884?]-1887.
        BM. ICN.

4307 Chambers, E. K. "Newcastle-on-Tyne, Northumberland." The Mediaeval Stage. Vol. 2. (London, 1903), p. 385.

4308 ----- "Newcastle-upon-Tyne." The Mediaeval Stage. Vol. 2. (London, 1903), pp. 424-425.

4309 Welford, Richard. "Players and Minstrels at Newcastle-upon-
        Tyne (16th and 17th Century)." Notes and Queries, 10th ser.,
        XII (September 18, 1909), 222-223.

4310 Spencer, Matthew Lyle. "Corpus Christi Pageants in England."
        Ph.D. University of Chicago, 1910.

4311 Kretzman, P. E. "An Inquiry into the Origin and Theological
        Significance of the Corpus Christi Festival and Procession and
        Their Relation to the Corpus Christi Plays." M.A. University
        of Minnesota, 1913.

4312 Pierson, Merle. "Newcastle." In, "The Relation of the Corpus
        Christi Procession to the Corpus Christi Play in England."
        Transactions of the Wisconsin Academy of Sciences, Arts,
        and Letters, XVIII (1916), 143-144.

4313 Dendy, Frederick Walter. Three Lectures Delivered to the
        Literary and Philosophical Society, Newcastle-upon-Tyne, on Old
        Newcastle, Its Suburbs and Gilds, and an Essay on Northumber-
        land. Newcastle-upon-Tyne: Pub^d. by the Society, 1921. 85 pp.
        BM.

4314 Gleason, John MacArthur. "The Corpus Christi Pageants at New-
        castle in the Middle Ages." M.A. Yale University, 1928.

Noah's Ark
                                    Texts
4315 Bourne, Henry. "Shipwright's Dirge." In, History of Newcastle.
        (Newcastle upon Tyne, 1736).

4316 Brand, John. "Particulars Concerning the Corpus Christi Plays
        or Miracle Plays, with a Text of Noah's Ark." In, History of
        Newcastle. Vol. 2. (London, 1789), pp. 369-379. [The text is
        reprinted in Thomas Sharp. Brand's text is reprinted from
        Henry Bourne's edition.]

4317 Noah's Ark. In, Sharp, Thomas. A Dissertation on the Pageants
        or Dramatic Mysteries Anciently Performed at Coventry...
        (Coventry, 1825), pp. 223-225. [Text from Brand.]

4318 Holthausen, Ferd., ed. Das Noahspiel von Newcastle on Tyne.
        Göteburg: Wald. Zachrissons boktryckeri, 1897. 42, [2] pp.
        (Göteborgs högskolas årsskrift. Band 3 [no.] 3.) [Based on
        Bourne's text.] [See the note by Holthausen in Anglia, XXXI

(1920), 90-92.]
CSmH. MH. NN. O.

4319 Brotanek, Rudolf. "Noahs Arche. Ein Misterium aus Newcastle upon Tyne." Anglia, XXI (1899), 165-200. [Based on Sharp's edition.]

4320 Noah's Ship. In, Waterhouse, Osborn, ed. The Non-Cycle Mystery Plays. (London, 1909), pp. 19-25. [Based on Bourne.]

4321 Holthausen, F. "Zur Noah-Legende." Beiblatt zur Anglia, XXXI (1920), 90-92.

4322 Noah's Ark; the Only Surviving Mystery Play of the Newcastle Cycle. [Tynemouth: The Priory Press, 1922]. 45 pp. MnU.

4323 "Noah's Ark." The Newcastle Shipwright's Play. With a Modernized Version by M.S.D. Newcastle-upon-Tyne: Printed by M. S. Dodds [1925]. 20 pp. [Title comes from a short notice in Notes and Queries, CL (1926), 18.]

4324 Newcastle Shipwright's Play: Noah's Ark. In, Tickner, F. J., ed. Earlier English Drama, from Robin Hood to Everyman. (London and Edinburgh, 1926).

4325 Noah's Ark. In, Tickner, Frederick James, ed. Earlier English Drama from Robin Hood to Everyman. (New York, [1929]), pp. 53-59.

4326 Dustoor, P., ed. "The Newcastle's Noah's Ark." Allahabad University Studies, VIII, Part 1 (1931), 1-30.

Studies

4327 Wells, John Edwin. "The Newcastle-Upon-Tyne Noah's Ark." In, A Manual of the Writings in Middle English, 1050-1400. (New Haven, 1916-1951), pp. 570-571, 862, 1137, 1319, 1417, 1524, 1729.

4328 Dustoor, P. E. "Some Textual Notes on the English Mystery Plays." Modern Language Review, XXI (October, 1926), 427-431.

4329 ----- "Notes on the E. E. T. S. Edition of the Newcastle Noah's Ark." Modern Language Notes, XLIII (April, 1928), 252-255.

4330 Craig, Hardin. "Noah's Ark; Or, The Shipwrights' Ancient Play
      or Dirge Newcastle-upon-Tyne." English Religious Drama
      of the Middle Ages. (Oxford, 1955), pp. 303-305.

Norfolk

4331 Harrod, Henry. "A Few Particulars Concerning Early Norwich
      Pageants." Norfolk Archaeology, III (1852), 3-18.

4332 Fitch, R. "Norwich Pageants." Norfolk Archaeology, V (1859),
      8-31.

4333 Bolingbroke, L. C. "Pre-Elizabethan Plays and Players in Nor-
      folk." Norfolk Archaeology, XI (1892), 332-351.

Northampton

4334 Chambers, E. K. "Northampton, Northamptonshire." The Mediae-
      val Stage. Vol. 2. (London, 1903), p. 386.

Norwich
   Norwich Grocer's Play

                               Texts
4335 Norwich Pageants. The Grocer's Play. From a Manuscript in the
      Possession of Robert Fitch... Norwich: Charles Muskett,
      1856. [4], 24 pp. [The Story of the Creation of Eve, with the
      Expellyng of Adam and Eve out of Paradyce.]
          MH. O.

4336 [Norwich Grocers' Play]. "Norwich Pageants." Norfolk Archaeology,
      V (1859), 8-31. [The two texts are given, one dated June 16,
      1533, and the other, 1565. Same as above.]

4337 Norwich Whitsun Plays. The Story of the Creacion of Eve, with the
      Expellyng of Adam and Eve out of Paradyce. In, Manly, John
      Matthews, ed. Specimens of Pre-Shakesperean Drama. Vol. I.
      (Boston and New York, 1897), pp. 1-12. [Fitch version].

4338 Creation of Eve and the Fall. In, Waterhouse, Osborn, ed. The
      Non-Cycle Mystery Plays. (London, 1909), pp. 8-18.

4339 Norwich Grocers' Play. In, Adams, Joseph Quincy, ed. Chief
      Pre-Shakespearean Dramas. (Boston and New York, 1924),
      pp. 88-93.

Studies

4340 Harrod, Henry. "A Few Particulars Concerning Early Norwich Pageants." Norfolk Archaeology, III (1852), 3-18.

4341 Bolingbroke, L. C. "Pre-Elizabethan Plays and Players in Norfolk." Norfolk Archaeology, XI (1892), 332-351.

4342 Chambers, E. K. "Norwich, Norfolk." The Mediaeval Stage. Vol. 2. (London, 1903), pp. 386-389.

4343 ----- "Norwich." The Mediaeval Stage. Vol. 2. (London, 1903), pp. 425-426.

4344 Parsons, Edward S. "A Grocer's Play." Modern Language Notes, XXI (1906), 224.

4345 Pierson, Merle. "Norwich." In, "The Relation of the Corpus Christi Procession to the Corpus Christi Play in England." Transactions of the Wisconsin Academy of Sciences, Arts, and Letters, XVIII (1916), 145-146.

4346 Wells, John Edwin. "The Norwich Grocer's Play." A Manual of the Writings in Middle English, 1050-1400. (New Haven, 1916-1951), pp. 575-576, 863, 1229, 1319.

4347 Dustoor, P. E. "Textual Notes on Three Non-Cycle Mystery Plays." Modern Language Review, XXIII (April, 1928), 208-212.

4348 Woodforde, Christopher. The Norwich School of Glass-Painting in the Fifteenth Century. London: Oxford University Press, 1950. xiv, 233 pp. Index.

4349 Craig, Hardin. "Norwich Whitsun Plays." English Religious Drama of the Middle Ages. (Oxford, 1955), pp. 298-303.

Nottingham

4350 Godfrey, John Thomas. "Popular Amusements in Nottingham in the 15th and 16th Centuries." Reprinted from "The Newark Advertiser." Newark, 1896. 11 pp.

Nuneaton

4351 Chambers, E. K. "Nuneaton, Warwickshire." The Mediaeval Stage. Vol. 2. (London, 1903), p. 389.

Oxford

4352 Chambers, E. K. "Magdalen College, Oxford." The Mediaeval
     Stage, Vol. 2. (London, 1903), pp. 248-250.

4353 ----- "Oxford, Oxfordshire." The Mediaeval Stage. Vol. 2.
     (London, 1903), pp. 389-390.

4354 De Sausmorez, Fred B. "Early Theatricals at Oxford. With
     Prologue by Lewis Carroll." Nineteenth Century and After,
     III (February, 1932), 235-238.

4355 Blair, Lawrence. "Oxford." In, "A Note on the Relation of the
     Corpus Christi Procession to the Corpus Christi Play in Eng-
     land." Modern Language Notes, LV (February, 1940), 91.

4356 Alton, R. E., ed. "The Academic Drama in Oxford. Extracts
     from the Records of Four Colleges." Malone Society. Col-
     lections. V. 1959, (1960), pp. 28-95. [From 1480 to 1650].

4357 Driscoll, John P., S. J. "A Miracle Play at Oxford." Notes and
     Queries, VII (1960), 6. [In the 16th Century.]

Peniarth

4358 Jones, E. D. "The Date of the Peniarth Antichrist Manuscript."
     National Library of Wales. Journal, I (1939-1940), 145.

     "Penrhyn, Cornwall." See, Cornish. [No. 4359 omitted].

Perranzabulo

4360 Chambers, E. K. "Perranzabulo, Cornwall." The Mediaeval
     Stage. Vol. 2. (London, 1903), pp. 390-391.

Perth

4361 [Maidment, James, ed.] The Chronicle of Perth; A Register of
     Remarkable Occurrences, Chiefly Connected with That City,
     From the Year 1210 to 1668. Edinburgh [n.p.], 1831. [10],
     108 pp. [The Maitland Club.] [See p. 50, entry for July 1,
     1577, refers to playing Corpus Christi Play on June 6.]
          BM.

4362 Baxter, Peter. The Drama in Perth: Being a History of Perth's

Early Plays, Play Houses, Play Bills, Pageants, Concerts, etc. Perth: Thos. Hunter & Sons, 1907. [10], 335 pp. BM. ICU. MH.

Pilton

4363 Blair, Lawrence. "Pilton." In, "A Note on the Relation of the Corpus Christi Procession to the Corpus Christi Play in England." Modern Language Notes, LV (February, 1940), 93.

Preston

4364 Chambers, E. K. "Preston, Lancashire." The Mediaeval Stage. Vol. 2. (London, 1903), p. 392.

4365 Pierson, Merle. "Preston." In, "The Relation of the Corpus Christi Procession to the Corpus Christi Play in England." Transactions of the Wisconsin Academy of Sciences, Arts, and Letters, XVIII (1916), 159.

Processus Satanae

Manuscript
4366 The Duke of Portland, Welbeck Abbey. [Photographs of the Original are in the British Museum and the Bodleian Library.]

Text
4367 Processus Satanae. Malone Society Collections. Vol. II. Part III. (1931), pp. 239-250.

Reading

4368 Kerry, Rev. Charles. A History of the Municipal Church of St. Lawrence, Reading. Reading: The Author, 1883. viii, 256 pp. Index. [See pp. 234-238.] BM.

4369 Chambers, E. K. "Reading, Berkshire." The Mediaeval Stage. Vol. 2. (London, 1903), pp. 392-393.

4370 Pierson, Merle. "Reading." In, "The Relation of the Corpus Christi Procession to the Corpus Christi Play in England." Transactions of the Wisconsin Academy of Sciences, Arts, and Letters, XVIII (1916), 158.

4371 Blair, Lawrence. "Reading." In, "A Note on the Relation of the
      Corpus Christi Procession to the Corpus Christ Play in England."
      Modern Language Notes, LV (February, 1940), 85-96.

Ruckinge

4372 Chambers, E. K. "Ruckinge, Kent." The Mediaeval Stage. Vol.
      2. (London, 1903), p. 393.

Rye

4373 ----- "Rye, Sussex." The Mediaeval Stage. Vol. 2. (London,
      1903), p. 393.

Sabsford

4374 ----- "Sabsford (?), Essex." The Mediaeval Stage. Vol. 2.
      (London, 1903), p. 393.

Saffron Walden

4375 ----- "Saffron Walden, Essex." The Mediaeval Stage. Vol. 2.
      (London, 1903), p. 393.

Salisbury

4376 Swayne, Henry James Fowle. Churchwardens' Account of S.
      Edmund & S. Thomas, Sarum 1443-1702, with Other Docu-
      ments. With an Introduction by Amy M. Straton, and a Preface
      by The Lord Bishop of Salisbury. Salisbury: Printed by Bennett
      Brothers, 1896. xl, 403 pp. Index. (Wilts Record Society).
      BM.

4377 Chambers, E. K. "Salisbury, Wiltshire." The Mediaeval Stage.
      Vol. 2. (London, 1903), p. 393.

4378 Pierson, Merle. "Salisbury." In, "The Relation of the Corpus
      Christi Procession to the Corpus Christi Play in England."
      Transactions of the Wisconsin Academy of Sciences, Arts,
      and Letters, XVIII (1916), 147.

4379 Blair, Lawrence. "Salisbury." In, "A Note on the Relation of the
      Corpus Christi Procession to the Corpus Christi Play in Eng-
      land." Modern Language Notes, LV (February, 1940), 93.

Sandwich

4380 Blair, Lawrence. "Sandwich." In, "A Note on the Relation of
      the Corpus Christi Procession to the Corpus Christi Play in
      England." Modern Language Notes, LV (February, 1940), 88.

4381 Dawson, Giles, ed. "Sandwich." Records of Plays and Players in
      Kent 1450-1642. The Malone Society. Collections. Vol. VII.
      (Oxford, 1965), pp. 145-154.

Sheffield

4382 Addy, S. O. "Stage Plays in Sheffield in 1581." Transactions of The
      Hunter Archaeological Association, III (December, 1927), 243-
      246.

Shelfhanger

4383 Chambers, E. K. "Shelfhanger, Norfolk." The Mediaeval Stage.
      Vol. 2. (London, 1903), p. 393.

Shipton

4384 ----- "Shipton, Oxfordshire." The Mediaeval Stage. Vol. 2.
      (London, 1903), p. 394.

Shrewsbury
                        Manuscript
4385 Shrewsbury School VI, ff. 38^r-42^v. (15th Century).
      Latin Anthems with Music and Fragments of Three Mystery
      Plays. (Reproduction of, in the Modern Language Association
      of America, No. 33, Rotograph Series. 1925).

                     Individual Plays

[Officium Pastorum]
                         Texts
4386 The Angels and the Shepherds. In, Academy, XXXVII (1890), 27-
      28. [Shrewsbury Fragment No. 1. Published in the Academy
      by Dr. Skeat.]

4387 [Officium Pastorum.] In, Manly, John M., ed. Specimens of the
      Pre-Shaksperean Drama. Vol. 1. (Boston, 1897), pp. xxviii-
      xxx. [The MS. contains no heading. First printed in Academy,
      1890.]

4388 Officium Pastorum. In, Waterhouse, Osborn, ed. The Non-Cycle
         Mystery Plays. (London, 1909), pp. 1-2, Notes, pp. xix-xx.

4389 The Shepherds. In, Adams, Joseph Quincy, ed. Chief Pre-
         Shakespearean Dramas. (Boston, New York, 1924), pp. 77-78.

4390 [Officium Pastorum]. In, Young, Karl. The Drama of the Medieval
         Church. Vol. 2. (Oxford, 1933), pp. 514-516.

[Visitatio Sepulchri]
                                     Texts
4391 "The Three Maries At the Sepulchre." The Academy, XXXVII
         (1890), 28. [Shrewsbury fragment No. 2.]

4392 [Officium Resurrectionis]. In, Manly, John M., ed. Specimens of
         the Pre-Shaksperean Drama. Vol. 1. (Boston, 1897), pp. xxxi-
         xxxiii. [The MS. contains no heading. First printed in Academy,
         1890.]

4393 Officium Resurrectionis. In, Waterhouse, Osborn, ed. The Non-
         Cycle Mystery Plays. (London, 1909), pp. 1-2.

4394 The Sepulchre. In, Adams, Joseph Quincy, ed. Chief Pre-
         Shakespearean Dramas. (Boston, New York, 1924), pp. 73-
         74.

4395 [Visitatio Sepulchri]. In, Young, Karl. The Drama of the Medie-
         val Church. Vol. 2. (Oxford, 1933), pp. 516-518.

[Peregrinus]
                                     Texts
4396 The Two Disciples Going to Emmaus. In, Academy, XXXVII
         (1890), 28. [Shrewsbury Fragment No. 3.]

4397 [Officium Peregrinorum]. In, Manly, John M., ed. Specimens
         of the Pre-Shaksperean Drama. Vol. 1. (Boston, 1897), pp.
         xxxiii-xxxvii. [The MS. contains no heading. First printed
         in Academy, 1890.]

4398 Officium Peregrinorum. In, Waterhouse, Osborn, ed. The Non-
         Cycle Mystery Plays. (London, 1909), pp. 1-2.

4399 The Wayfarers. In, Adams, Joseph Quincy, ed. Chief Pre-
         Shakespearean Dramas. (Boston, New York, 1924), pp. 74-76.

4400 [Peregrinus]. In, Young, Karl, ed. The Drama of the Medieval
Church. Vol. 2. (Oxford, 1933), pp. 518-520.

General Studies

4401 Skeat, Walter W. "Fragments of Yorkshire Mysteries." Academy,
XXXVII (1890), 10-11; 27-28.

4402 Chambers, E. K. "Shrewsbury Corporation. The Mediaeval Stage.
Vol. 2. (London, 1903), pp. 250-255.

4403 ----- "Shrewsbury Fragments." The Mediaeval Stage. Vol. 2.
(London, 1903), p. 427.

4404 ----- "Shrewsbury, Shropshire." The Mediaeval Stage. Vol. 2.
(London, 1903), pp. 394-395.

4405 Pierson, Merle. "Shrewsbury." In, "The Relation of the Corpus
Christi Procession to the Corpus Christi Play in England."
Transactions of the Wisconsin Academy of Sciences, Arts,
and Letters, XVIII (1916), 147-148.

4406 Wells, John Edwin. "The Shrewsbury Fragments." A Manual of
the Writings in Middle English, 1050-1400. (New Haven, 1916-
1951), pp. 543-545, 858, 992, 1025, 1136, 1228, 1318.

4407 Miller, Frances H. "Metrical Affinities of the Shrewsbury 'Officium Pastorum' and Its York Correspondent." Modern
Language Notes, XXXIII (1918), 91-95.

*4408 Young, Karl. "The Shrewsbury Fragments." The Drama of the
Medieval Church. Vol. 2. (Oxford, 1933), pp. 514-523.
[Texts and study].

4409 Oldham, J. B. "Shrewsbury School Library: Its Earlier History
and Organization." Library, XVI (1935), 49-60.

Sleaford

4410 Oliver, George. History of the Holy Trinity Guild, at Sleaford,
with an Account of Its Miracle Plays, Religious Mysteries,
and Shows As Practised in the Fifteenth Century, and an Introduction Delineating the Changes That Have Taken Place in the
Localities of Heath and Fen, Castle and Mansion, Convent and
Hall, within the District about Sleaford Since That Period. To
Which Is Added an Appendix, Detailing the Traditions Which

Still Prevail, and a Description of the Lincoln Pageants, Ex-
hibited during the Visit of King James to That City. The
Whole Illustrated by Copious Notes, Critical, Historical and
Explanatory. Lincoln: Printed by Edward Bell Drury, 1837.
vii, [1], 3-135 pp.
   BM. DLC. ICN.

4411 Chambers, E. K. "Sleaford, Lincolnshire." The Mediaeval
      Stage. Vol. 2. (London, 1903), p. 395.

4412 Pierson, Merle. "Sleaford." In, "The Relation of the Corpus
      Christi Procession to the Corpus Christi Play in England."
      Transactions of the Wisconsin Academy of Sciences, Arts,
      and Letters, XVIII (1916), 159.

"St. Just, Cornwall." See Perranzabulo.

St. Thomas

4413 Blair, Lawrence. "St. Thomas." In, "A Note on the Relation of
      the Corpus Christi Procession to the Corpus Christi Play in
      England." Modern Language Notes, LV (February, 1940), 94.

Stoke-By-Nayland

4414 Chambers, E. K. "The Howards of Stoke-By-Nayland, Essex."
      The Mediaeval Stage. Vol. 2. (London, 1903), pp. 255-256.

4415 ----- "Stoke By Nayland, Essex." The Mediaeval Stage. Vol.
      2. (London, 1903), pp. 395-396.

Stone

4416 ----- "Stone, Kent." The Mediaeval Stage. Vol. 2. (London,
      1903), p. 396.

Southampton

4417 Burch, C. E. C. Minstrels and Players in Southampton, 1428-
      1635. [Southampton]: City of Southampton, 1969. 48 pp.
      (Southampton Papers, 7).

Stonyhurst Pageants
                        Manuscript
4418 Lancashire. Stonyhurst College Library, MS. A. VI. 33.

Collection

*4419 Brown, Carleton F., ed. The Stonyhurst Pageants. Baltimore: The Johns Hopkins Press, 1920. 302 pp.

Individual Plays

Texts

4420 [The 6 Pagean of Iacob]. In, Brown, Carleton, ed. The Stonyhurst Pageants. (Göttingen, Baltimore, 1920), pp. 1-4.

4421 The 7 pagean of Ioseph. In, Brown, Carleton, ed. The Stonyhurst Pageants. (Göttingen, Baltimore, 1920), pp. 5-40.

4422 The eight pagean of Moyses. In, Brown, Carleton, ed. The Stony- hurst Pageants. (Göttingen, Baltimore, 1920), pp. 41-95.

4423 The 9 pagean of Iosue. In, Brown, Carleton, ed. The Stonyhurst Pageants. (Göttingen, Baltimore, 1920), pp. 95-114.

4424 The 10 pagean of Gedeon. In, Brown, Carleton, ed. The Stony- hurst Pageants. (Göttingen, Baltimore, 1920), 114-124.

4425 The 11 pagean of Iephte. In, Brown, Carleton, ed. The Stony- hurst Pageants. (Göttingen, Baltimore, 1920), pp. 125-134.

4426 The 12 pagean of Samson. In, Brown, Carleton, ed. The Stony- hurst Pageants. (Göttingen, Baltimore, 1920), pp. 135-149.

4427 The 14 pagean of Saul. In, Brown, Carleton, ed. The Stony- hurst Pageants. (Göttingen, Baltimore, 1920), pp. 149-198.

4428 The 15 Pagean of Dauid. In, Brown, Carleton, ed. The Stony- hurst Pageants. (Göttingen, Baltimore, 1920), pp. 199-223.

4429 The 16 Pageant of Salomon. In, Brown, Carleton, ed. The Stony- hurst Pageants. (Göttingen, Baltimore, 1920), pp. 224-235.

4430 The 17 pageant [of Elias]. In, Brown, Carleton, ed. The Stony- hurst Pageants. (Göttingen, Baltimore, 1920), pp. 236-262.

4431 [The 18 Pageant of Naaman]. In, Brown, Carleton, ed. The Stony- hurst Pageants. (Göttingen, Baltimore, 1920), pp. 263-302.

Studies

4432 Wells, John Edwin. "The Stonyhurst Pageants." A Manual of the

Writings in Middle English, 1050-1400. (New Haven, 1916-
1951), pp. 1081-1082, 1138, 1229.

4433 Brown, Carleton. "The Stonyhurst Pageants." Modern Language
Review, XVI (April, 1921), 167-169.

4434 Cole, Helen Wieand. "The Influence of Plautus and Terence upon
the Stonyhurst Pageants." Modern Language Notes, XXXVIII
(November, 1923), 393-399.

4435 Craig, Hardin. "Terentius Christianus and the Stonyhurst
Pageants." Philological Quarterly, II (January, 1923), 56-62.

4436 ----- [Stonyhurst Pageants]. English Religious Drama of the
Middle Ages. (Oxford, 1955), 371-373.

Sussex

4437 Smith, L. B. "Sussex and Religious Drama." Sussex County
Magazine, V (January, 1931), 53-56.

4438 Browne, E. Martin. "Religious Drama in Sussex." Sussex
County Magazine, V (December, 1931), 817-820.

Tewkesbury

4439 Chambers, E. K. "Tewkesbury, Gloucestershire." The Mediaeval Stage. Vol. 2. (London, 1903), p. 396.

Thame

4440 Blair, Lawrence. "Thame." In, "A Note on the Relation of the
Corpus Christi Procession to the Corpus Christi Play in
England." Modern Language Notes, LV (February, 1940), 92.

Thetford

4441 Chambers, E. K. "Thetford Priory." The Mediaeval Stage. Vol.
2. (London, 1903), pp. 245-246.

Tintinhull

4442 ----- "Tintinhull, Somerset." The Mediaeval Stage. Vol. 2.
(London, 1903), p. 396.

TOWNELEY (WAKEFIELD) PLAYS

Manuscript
4443 California, San Marino. Huntington Library MS. HM. 1.

Collections
4444 Raine, James, and James Gordon, eds. The Towneley Mysteries.
London: J. B. Nichols and Son [1836]. xx, [2], 352 pp. (Publications of the Surtees Society...[3]). [Thirty-two Mysteries.
500 copies printed.]
BM. CtY. ICN. MnU. MH. NN. NNUT.

4445 England, George, ed. The Towneley Plays. Re-edited from the
Unique MS. by George England, with Side-notes and Intro-
duction by Alfred W. Pollard, M. A. London: Published for
the Early English Text Society by K. Paul, Trench, Trübner
& Co., 1897. xxiv, [2], 416, [2] pp. (Early English Text
Society. Extra Series, No. LXXI). [Reprinted 1907, 1925, 1952,
1966.]
BM. CtY. ICN. ICU. MH. MiU. NN. O. OU. PU.

4446 Cawley, A. C., ed. The Wakefield Pageants in the Towneley
Cycle. [Manchester]: Manchester University Press [c. 1958].
xxxix, 187 pp. (Old and Middle English Texts). [The text is
transcribed from photographs of MS. HM 1 in the Huntington
Library.]
BM. CtY. ICN. ICU.

4447 Rose, Martial, ed. The Wakefield Mystery Plays. London: Evans
Bros., 1962. 464 pp.

4448 Hamley, Dennis, ed. Three Towneley Plays. Adapted into Modern
English. London: Heinemann, 1962 [i.e., Jan. 1963]. xviii,
77 pp. (Kingswood Plays for Boys and Girls).
BM.

Individual Plays
Texts

Creation

4449 Creatio. In, The Towneley Mysteries. (London, 1836), pp. 1-7.

4450 The Creation. In, England, George, ed. The Towneley Plays.
(London, 1897), pp. 1-9.

4451 The Creation. In, Rose, Martial, ed. The Wakefield Mystery
        Plays. (London, 1961), pp. 49-62.

The Killing of Abel
                                    Texts
4452 Mactacio Abel. In, The Towneley Mysteries. (London, 1836),
        pp. 8-19.

4453 Killing of Abel. In, England, George, ed. The Towneley Plays.
        (London, 1897), pp. 9-22.

4454 The Killing of Abel. In, Adams, Joseph Quincy, ed. Chief Pre-
        Shakespearean Dramas. (Boston, New York, 1924), pp. 94-100.

4455 Mactacio Abel. In, Cawley, A. C., ed. The Wakefield Pageants
        in the Towneley Cycle. (Manchester, [1958]), pp. 1-13.

4456 The Killing of Abel. In, Rose, Martial, ed. The Wakefield Mys-
        tery Plays. (London, 1961), pp. 63-77.

4457 Cain and Abel. In, Franklin, Alexander, ed. Seven Miracle Plays:
        Cain and Abel, Noah's Flood, Abraham and Isaac, The Shep-
        herds, The Three Kings, and Adam and Eve. (London and New
        York, 1963).

4458 Cain and Abel. In, Franklin, Alexander, ed. Seven Miracle Plays:
        Cain and Abel, Noah's Flood, Abraham and Isaac, The Shep-
        herds, The Three Kings, and Adam and Eve. (London and New
        York, 1965).

Noah and the Ark
                                    Texts

4459 Processus Noe cum filiis. In, The Towneley Mysteries. (London,
        1836), pp. 20-34.

4460 Processus Noe cum Filiis. (Third Play). Edited by Edward Mätz-
        ner. Altenglische Sprachproben. (Berlin, 1867).

4461 Noah and the Ark. In, England, George, ed. The Towneley Plays.
        (London, 1897), pp. 23-40.

4462 Processus Noe cum filiis. In, Manly, John Matthews, ed. Speci-
        mens of the Pre-Shaksperean Drama. Vol. 1. (Boston, 1897),
        pp. 13-30.

4463 Processus Noe cum filiis. In, Tatlock, J. S. P., and R. G. Martin, eds. Representative English Plays. (New York, 1916), pp. 5-12.

4464 Processus Noe cum filiis. In, Adams, Joseph Quincy, ed. Chief Pre-Shakespearean Dramas. (Boston, 1924), pp. 101-110.

4465 Processus Noe cum filiis. In, Schweikert, Harry Christian, ed. Early English Plays. (New York, 1928), pp. 74-89.

4466 The Flood. In, Tickner, Frederick James, ed. Earlier English Drama from Robin Hood to Everyman. (New York, [1929]), pp. 59-73.

4467 Noah's Flood. In, Tatlock, J. S. P., and R. G. Martin, eds. Representative English Plays from the Miracle Plays to Pinero. 2nd ed. (New York, 1938), pp. 5-12.

4468 Noah and His Sons. Adapted from the Wakefield Cycle of Miracle Plays. In, Moore, Hortense, ed. Bread Loaf Book of Plays. (Middlebury, 1941).

4469 Noah. In, Heilman, Robert B. An Anthology of English Drama Before Shakespeare. (New York, 1952), pp. 23-43.

4470 Processus Noe Cum Filiis. In, Cawley, A. C., ed. The Wakefield Pageants in the Towneley Cycle. (Manchester, [1958]), pp. 14-28.

4471 Noah. In, Rose, Martial, ed. The Wakefield Mystery Plays. (London, 1961), pp. 77-92.

Abraham
Texts
4472 Abraham. In, The Towneley Mysteries. (London, 1836), pp. 35-42.

4473 Abraham. In, England, George, ed. The Towneley Plays. (London, 1897), pp. 40-49.

4474 Abraham, Melchisedec, and Isaac. In, Kreymborg, Alfred, ed. Poetic Drama. (New York, 1941), pp. 194-199.

4475 Abraham. In, Rose, Martial, ed. The Wakefield Mystery Plays. (London, 1961), pp. 92-101.

Isaac

Texts

4476   Isaac. In, The Towneley Mysteries. (London, 1836), pp. 43-44.

4477   Isaac. In, England, George, ed. The Towneley Plays. (London, 1897), pp. 49-51.

4478   Isaac. In, Manly, John Matthews, ed. Specimens of the Pre-Shaksperean Drama. Vol. 1. (Boston, 1897), pp. 58-60.

4479   Isaac. In, Rose, Martial, ed. The Wakefield Mystery Plays. (London, 1961), pp. 101-103.

Sequitur Iacob

Texts

4480   Sequitur Iacob. In, The Towneley Mysteries. (London, 1836), pp. 45-48.

4481   Sequitur Iacob. In, England, George, ed. The Towneley Plays. (London, 1897), pp. 52-56.

4482   Iacob. In, Manly, John Matthews, ed. Specimens of the Pre-Shaksperean Drama. Vol. 1. (Boston, 1897), pp. 60-65.

4483   Jacob. In, Rose, Martial, ed. The Wakefield Mystery Plays. (London, 1961), pp. 103-107.

The Prophets

Texts

4484   Processus Prophetarum. In, The Towneley Mysteries. (London, 1836), pp. 49-54.

4485   The Prophets. In, England, George, ed. The Towneley Plays. (London, 1897), pp. 56-64.

4486   The Procession of the Prophets. In, Rose, Martial, ed. The Wakefield Mystery Plays. (London, 1961), pp. 119-125.

Pharaoh

Texts

4487   Pharao. In, Marriott, William. A Collection of English Miracle-Plays. (Basel, 1838), pp. 93-108.

4488   Pharaoh. In, England, George, ed. The Towneley Plays. (London, 1897), pp. 64-78.

4489 Pharao. In, Adams, Joseph Quincy, ed. Chief Pre-Shake-
       spearean Dramas. (Boston, 1924), pp. 125-131.

4490 Pharaoh. In, Rose, Martial, ed. The Wakefield Mystery Plays.
       (London, 1961), pp. 107-118.

Caesar Augustus
                                    Texts
4491 Caesar Augustus. In, The Towneley Mysteries. (London, 1836),
       pp. 66-71.

4492 Caesar Augustus. In, England, George, ed. The Towneley Plays.
       (London, 1897), pp. 78-85.

4493 Caesar Augustus. In, Rose, Martial, ed. The Wakefield Mystery
       Plays. (London, 1961), pp. 126-132.

The Annunciation
                                    Texts
4494 Annunciacio. In, The Towneley Mysteries. (London, 1836), pp.
       72-80.

4495 The Annunciation. In, England, George, ed. The Towneley Plays.
       (London, 1897), pp. 86-97.

4496 Annunciacio. In, Hemingway, Samuel B., ed. English Nativity
       Plays. (New York, 1909), pp. 155-166.

4497 The Annunciation. In, Loomis, Roger Sherman, and Henry W.
       Wells. Representative Medieval and Tudor Plays. (New York,
       1942), pp. 61-66.

4498 The Annunciation. In, Rose, Martial, ed. The Wakefield Mystery
       Plays. (London, 1961), pp. 149-159.

4499 Annunciation. In, Hemingway, Samuel B., ed. English Nativity
       Plays. (New York, 1964).

The Salutation of Elizabeth
                                    Texts
4500 Salutacio Elizabeth. In, The Towneley Mysteries. (London, 1836),
       pp. 81-83.

4501 The Salutation of Elizabeth. In, England, George, ed. The
       Towneley Plays. (London, 1897), pp. 97-100.

4502   Salutacio Elizabeth. In, Hemingway, Samuel B., ed. English Nativity Plays. (New York, 1909), pp. 167-169.

4503   Salutacio Elizabeth. In, Tickner, Frederick J., ed. Earlier English Drama from Robin Hood to Everyman. (New York, 1929), pp. 181-184.

4504   The Salutation of Elizabeth. In, Rose, Martial, ed. The Wakefield Mystery Plays. (London, 1961), pp. 159-162.

4505   Salutation. In, Hemingway, Samuel B., ed. English Nativity Plays. (New York, 1964), pp. 167-169.

Shepherds' Play, I

Texts

4506   Prima pagina pastorum. In, The Towneley Mysteries. (London, 1836), pp. 84-97.

4507   Shepherds' Play, I. In, England, George, ed. The Towneley Plays. (London, 1897), pp. 100-116.

4508   First Shepherds' Play. In, Hemingway, Samuel B., ed. English Nativity Plays. (New York, 1909), pp. 170-187.

4509   Moorman, Frederic William. The Ewe Lamb, a Farce [in Two Acts], and in Yorkshire Dialect, (Based upon the Nativity Scene in the Wakefield Mystery Plays. (London, 1919), pp. 73-98.

4510   Prima Pastorum. In, Cawley, A. C., ed. The Wakefield Pageants in the Towneley Cycle. (Manchester, [1958]), pp. 29-42.

4511   The First Shepherds' Play. In, Rose, Martial, ed. The Wakefield Mystery Plays. (London, 1961), pp. 162-177.

4512   First Shepherds. In, Hemingway, Samuel B., ed. English Nativity Plays. (New York, 1964), pp. 170-187.

Second Shepherds' Play

Texts

4513   Secunda pagina pastorum. In, The Towneley Mysteries. (London, 1836), pp. 98-119.

4514   The Adoration of the Shepherds. A Miracle Play. Now First Printed from The Towneley MS. In, Collier, J. Payne. Five

Miracle Plays, or Scriptural Dramas. (London, 1836).

4515 Second Shepherds' Play. In, Marriott, William, ed. A Collection
      of English Miracle-Plays or Mysteries. (Basel, 1838), pp.
      109-136.

4516 Second Shepherds' Play. In, Morley, Henry, ed. English Plays.
      (London, Paris, and New York, [c. 1880]).

4517 Second Shepherds' Play. In, Pollard, Alfred W., ed. English
      Miracle Plays, Moralities and Interludes. (Oxford, 1890), pp.
      31-43, 188-191. [Abridged]

4518 Shepherds' Play, II. In, England, George, ed. The Towneley
      Plays. (London, 1897), pp. 116-140.

4519 Second Shepherds' Play. In, Manly, John M., ed. Specimens of
      the Pre-Shaksperean Drama. Vol. 1. (Boston, 1897), pp. 94-
      119.

4520 The Star of Bethlehem, a Miracle Play of the Nativity. Recon-
      structed from the Towneley and Other Old English Cycles
      (of the XIIIth, XIVth and XVth Centuries) and Supplemented
      and Adapted to Modern Conditions. Edited by Charles Mills
      Gayley. As Composed for Ben Greet, and Presented by His
      Company. New York: Fox, Duffield and Company [1904]. xix,
      [1], 70 pp.
          BM. MnU.

4521 Second Shepherds' Play. In, Everyman, with Other Interludes
      Including Eight Miracle Plays. (London, [1909]), pp. 52-73.

4522 Second Shepherds' Play. In, Hemingway, Samuel B., ed. English
      Nativity Plays. (New York, 1909), pp. 188-214.

4523 The Second Shepherds' Play. In, Child, Clarence Griffin. The
      Second Shepherds' Play, Everyman and Other Early Plays.
      (Boston, New York, and Chicago, 1910), pp. 27-64.

4524 Around the Manger -- the Shepherds' Address. In, Gosset,
      A.L.J. Lullabies of the Four Nations. (London, 1915), pp.
      210-211. [A short selection.]

4525 Second Shepherds' Play. In, Tatlock, J. S.P., and R. G. Martin,
      eds. Representative English Plays. (New York, 1916), pp.
      19-30.

4526 The Wakefield Second Nativity Play. Weybridge, 1917. 50 pp.
          BM. CtY.

4527 Secunda Pastorum. In, Brandl, A., and O. Zippel, eds. Mittel-
          englische Sprach-und Literaturproben. (Berlin, 1917).

4528 Second Shepherds Play (Episodes). In, Eliot, Samuel A., ed.
          Little Theatre Classics. Vol. 2. (Boston, 1918-1922).

4529 Second Shepherds' Play. In, Adams, Joseph Q., ed. Chief-Pre-
          Shakespearean Dramas. (Boston, 1924), pp. 145-157.

4530 Second Shepherds' Play. In, Matthews, Brander, and P. R.
          Lieder, eds. Chief British Dramatists. (Boston, 1924), pp.
          11-25.

4531 Acting Versions of Everyman and the Second Shepherds' Play.
          By William Duffey. Milwaukee, Wisconsin: Bruce Publishing
          Co., 1925. 88 pp.
          BM. DLC. MH. NN. OU.

4532 Second Shepherds' Play. In, Everyman and Other Plays. (London,
          1925), pp. 140-201.

4533 Second Shepherds. In, Brandl, A., und O. Zippel. Mittelenglische
          Sprach-und Literaturproben. (Berlin, 1927), pp. 208-222.

4534 Second Shepherds' Play. In, Hubbell, Jay B., and John O. Beaty.
          An Introduction to Drama. (New York, 1927), pp. 86-98.

4535 Secunda Pastorum. In, Pollard, Alfred W., ed. English Miracle
          Plays, Moralities and Interludes. (Oxford, 1927).

4536 A Wakefield Nativity. In, Rubinstein, H. F. Great English Plays.
          (London, 1928), pp. 9-26.

4537 The Second Shepherds' Play. In, Schweikert, Harry C., ed. Early
          English Plays. (New York, 1928), pp. 104-127.

4538 The Second Shepherds' Play. In, Lieder, P. R., ed. British
          Drama. (New York, 1929).

4539 The Shepherds. In, McCallum, James Dow., ed. English Liter-
          ature, the Beginnings to 1500. (New York, Chicago, Boston,
          1929).

4540 Second Shepherds' Play. In, Tickner, Frederick J., ed. Earlier English Drama from Robin Hood to Everyman. (New York, 1929), pp. 148-171. [Also 1926 edition.]

4541 Das Zweite Hirtenspiel der Wakefielder Spiele. Übersetzt von F. Holthausen. In, Englische Studien, LXIII (1929), 193-219. [A translation into modern German.]

4542 The Nativity. Adapted by Randall Cayford Burrell. In, Golden Book Magazine, XII (1930), 77-80. [In four scenes.]

4543 The Shepherds' Play. In, Parry, W. Dyfed, ed. Old Plays for Modern Players, Selected and Modernized. (London, [1930]), pp. 37-46.

4544 Second Shepherds' Play. In, Browne, E. Martin, ed. Religious Plays for Use in Churches. (London, 1932).

4545 The Second Shepherds' Play. In, Clark, Barrett H., ed. World Drama. (New York and London, 1933).

4546 A Shepherds' Play, the Fourteenth Century Miracle Play Known As 'Secunda Pastorum' from the Towneley Plays. Paraphrased by R. Nash. London: P. Allan [1933]. 32 pp. (Religious Plays, Series No. 9.)
    BM.

4547 Second Shepherds' Play. In, Everyman and Other Interludes. (London, New York [1935]).

4548 The Second Shepherds' Play. In, Parks, Edd Winfield, and Richmond Croom Beatty, eds. The English Drama. An Anthology 900-1642. (New York, 1935), pp. 23-43.

4549 Second Shepherds' Play. In, Clark, David Lee, William Brian Gates, and Ernest Edwin Leisy, eds. The Voices of England and America, Vol. 1 (New York, 1937).

4550 The Second Shepherds' Play. Edited by Harold Whitehall. New York, 1937. Works Progress Administration. New York. Federal Theatre Project. National Service Bureau Publication. Scripts. No. 34.
    NN.

4551 The Second Shepherds' Play. In, Tatlock, J. S. P., and R. G.

Martin, eds. Representative English Plays from the Miracle
Plays to Pinero. 2nd ed. (New York, 1938), pp. 19-30.

4552 The Second Shepherds' Play. In, Loomis, Roger Sherman, and
Henry W. Wells. Representative Medieval and Tudor Plays.
(New York, 1942), pp. 67-94.

4553 Secunda Pastorum. In, Brandl, A., and O. Zippel, eds. 2nd ed.
Mittelenglische Sprach-und Literaturproben. (Berlin, 1947).

4554 The Second Shepherds' Play. In, Schenkkan, Robert Frederick,
and Kai Jurgense, eds. Fourteen Plays for the Church. (New
Brunswick, New Jersey, 1948).

4555 The Second Shepherds' Play. In, Bentley, Gerald Eades, ed. The
Development of English Drama. An Anthology. (New York,
1950), pp. 21-34.

4556 A Modernized Version of the Wakefield 'Second Shepherd's Play.'
Edited by A. C. Cawley. Kendal, England: Printed for the
[Yorkshire Dialect] Society by Titus Wilson and Son, 1950.
(Transactions of the Yorkshire Dialect Society, VIII, Pt.
50), pp. 8-28.
    NN.

4557 The Second Shepherds' Play. In, Gassner, John, ed. A Treasury
of the Theatre. Rev. ed. (New York, 1951), pp. 194-203.

4558 Second Shepherds' Play. In, Heilman, Robert B. An Anthology of
English Drama Before Shakespeare. (New York, 1952), pp.
44-72.

4559 Secunda Pastorum. In, Cawley, A. C., ed. The Wakefield Pageants in the Towneley Cycle. (Manchester, [1958]), pp. 43-63.

4560 The Second Shepherds' Pageant. In, Cawley, A. C., ed. Everyman and Medieval Miracle Plays. (New York, 1959), pp. 79-108.

4561 The Play of the Shepherds. In, Browne, E. Martin, ed. Mystery
and Morality Plays. (New York, 1960), pp. 102-132.

4562 The Wakefield Shepherds' Play. Adapted and Abridged by H.
Coward. London: French [1960]. [4], 34 pp.
    BM.

4563 The Shepherds' Play. In, Malcolmson, Anne. Seven Medieval
    Plays for Modern Players. (London, 1960).

4564 The Second Shepherds' Play. In, Rose, Martial, ed. The Wake-
    field Mystery Plays. (London, 1961).

4565 The Second Shepherds' Play. In, Hopper, Vincent F., and Gerald
    B. Lahey, eds. Medieval Mystery Plays. (New York, 1962),
    pp. 108-146.

4566 Second Shepherds. In, Hemingway, Samuel B., ed. English Nati-
    vity Plays. (New York, 1964).

Offering of the Magi
                                Texts
4567 Offering of the Magi. In, England, George, ed. The Towneley
    Plays. (London, 1897), pp. 140-160.

4568 The Offering of the Magi. In, Rose, Martial, ed. The Wakefield
    Mystery Plays. (London, 1961), pp. 199-217.

The Flight into Egypt
                                Texts
4569 Fugacio Joseph et Mariae in Aegyptum. In, The Towneley Mys-
    teries. (London, 1836), pp. 135-139.

4570 The Flight into Egypt. In, England, George, ed. The Towneley
    Plays. (London, 1897), pp. 160-165.

4571 The Flight into Egypt. In, Rose, Martial, ed. The Wakefield
    Mystery Plays. (London, 1961), pp. 217-222.

Herod the Great
                                Texts
4572 Magnus Herodes. In, The Towneley Mysteries. (London, 1836),
    pp. 140-153.

4573 Herod the Great. In, England, George, ed. The Towneley Plays.
    (London, 1897), pp. 166-181.

4574 Magnus Herodes. In, Cawley, A. C., ed. The Wakefield Pageants
    in the Towneley Cycle. (Manchester, [1958]), pp. 64-77.

4575 Herod the Great. In, Cawley, A. C., ed. Everyman and Medieval
    Miracle Plays. (New York, 1959), pp. 109-129.

4576 Herod the Great. In, Rose, Martial, ed. The Wakefield Mystery
      Plays. (London, 1961), pp. 222-236.

The Purification of Mary
                              Texts
4577 Purificacio Mariae. In, The Towneley Mysteries. (London, 1836),
      pp. 154-157.

4578 The Purification of Mary. In, England, George, ed. The Towneley
      Plays. (London, 1897), pp. 181-185.

4579 The Purification of Mary. In, Rose, Martial, ed. The Wakefield
      Mystery Plays. (London, 1961), pp. 237-240.

The Play of the Doctors
                              Texts
4580 Pagina Doctorum. In, The Towneley Mysteries. (London, 1836),
      pp. 158-164.

4581 The Play of the Doctors. In, England, George, ed. The Towneley
      Plays. (London, 1897), pp. 186-194.

4582 The Play of the Doctors. In, Rose, Martial, ed. The Wakefield
      Mystery Plays. (London, 1961), pp. 241-248.

Iohn the Baptist
                              Texts
4583 Johannes Baptista. In, The Towneley Mysteries. (London, 1836),
      pp. 165-171.

4584 Iohn the Baptist. In, England, George, ed. The Towneley Plays.
      (London, 1897), pp. 195-203.

4585 John the Baptist. In, Rose, Martial, ed. The Wakefield Mystery
      Plays. (London, 1961), pp. 265-272.

The Conspiracy
                              Texts
4586 Conspiracio et Capcio. In, The Towneley Mysteries. (London,
      1836), pp. 172-189.

4587 The Conspiracy. In, England, George, ed. The Towneley Plays.
      (London, 1897), pp. 204-227.

4588 The Conspiracy. In, Rose, Martial, ed. The Wakefield Mystery
      Plays. (London, 1961), pp. 279-300.

The Buffeting

Texts

4589 Coliphizatio. In, The Towneley Mysteries. (London, 1836), pp. 190-202.

4590 The Buffeting. In, England, George, ed. The Towneley Plays. (London, 1897), pp. 228-242.

4591 Coliphizacio. In, Cawley, A. C., ed. The Wakefield Pageants in the Towneley Cycle. (Manchester, [1958]), pp. 78-90.

4592 The Buffeting. In, Rose, Martial, ed. The Wakefield Mystery Plays. (London, 1961), pp. 300-313.

The Scourging

Texts

4593 Flagellacio. In, The Towneley Mysteries. (London, 1836), pp. 203-215.

4594 The Scourging. In, England, George, ed. The Towneley Plays. (London, 1897), pp. 243-257.

4595 The Scourging. In, Rose, Martial, ed. The Wakefield Mystery Plays. (London, 1961), pp. 313-326.

The Crucifixion

Texts

4596 Crucifixio. In, The Towneley Mysteries. (London, 1836), pp. 216-223.

4597 Crucifixio. In, Marriott, William, ed. A Collection of English Miracle-Plays. (Basel, 1838), pp. 137-160.

4598 The Crucifixion. In, England, George, ed. The Towneley Plays. (London, 1897), pp. 258-278.

4599 Crucifixio. In, Everyman with Other Interludes Including Eight Miracle Plays. (London, 1909), pp. 99-119.

4600 Kirtlan, Ernest J. B. A Little Drama of the Crucifixion, Being a Modernization of the "Crucifixio" in the Towneley Mystery Plays circa 1400 A.D. London: Epworth Press [1920]. 45 pp. NN.

4601 The Crucifixion. In, Rose, Martial, ed. The Wakefield Mystery

Play. (London, 1961), pp. 329-348.

The Talents
Texts

4602 Processus Talentorum. In, The Towneley Mysteries. (London, 1836), pp. 233-243.

4603 The Talents. In, England, George, ed. The Towneley Plays. (London, 1897), pp. 279-292.

4604 The Talents. In, Rose, Martial, ed. The Wakefield Mystery Plays. (London, 1961), pp. 361-372.

The Harrowing of Hell
Texts

4605 Extractio animarum ab Inferno. In, The Towneley Mysteries. (London, 1836), pp. 244-253.

4606 Extractio Animarum ab Inferno. In, Marriott, William. A Collection of English Miracle-Plays Or Mysteries. (Basel, 1838), pp. 161-174.

4607 The Deliverance of Souls. In, England, George, ed. The Towneley Plays. (London, 1897), pp. 293-305.

4608 The Harrowing of Hell. In, Everyman and Other Interludes. (London, New York, 1909), pp. 137-152.

4609 The Harrowing of Hell. In, Everyman and Other Interludes. (London, New York [1935]).

4610 The Deliverance of Souls. In, Rose, Martial, ed. The Wakefield Mystery Plays. (London, 1961), pp. 372-384.

4611 Harrowing of Hell. In, Cozart, William R. "The Northern Middle English Harrowing of Hell Plays of the York and Towneley Cycles. An Edition and Commentary." Ph.D. Harvard University, 1963.

The Resurrection of the Lord
Texts

4612 Resurrectio Domini. In, The Towneley Mysteries. (London, 1836), pp. 254-269. [For the lines of this play which partly parallel the York Play No. 38, see Lucy Toulmin Smith, ed., York Plays (Oxford, 1885), pp. 396-420.]

4613 The Resurrection of the Lord. In, England, George, ed. The Towneley Plays. (London, 1897), pp. 306-325.

4614 Kirwan, Patrick Joseph. The Dawn of English Drama. [With a modernized version of "Resurreccio Domini" from the Towneley Plays.] London: Harding & More, 1920. 71 pp. BM. NN.

4615 The Resurrection of Christ. In, Adams, Joseph Quincy, ed. Chief Pre-Shakespearean Dramas. (Boston, New York, 1924), pp. 191-198.

4616 The Resurrection. In, Rose, Martial, ed. The Wakefield Mystery Plays. (London, 1961), pp. 384-402.

The Pilgrims
Texts
4617 Peregrini. In, The Towneley Mysteries. (London, 1836), pp. 270-279.

4618 The Pilgrims. In, England, George, ed. The Towneley Plays. (London, 1897), pp. 325-337.

4619 The Pilgrims. In, Rose, Martial, ed. The Wakefield Mystery Plays. (London, 1961), pp. 402-413.

Thomas of India
Texts
4620 Thomas Indiae. In, The Towneley Mysteries. (London, 1836), pp. 280-293.

4621 Thomas of India. In, England, George, ed. The Towneley Plays. (London, 1897), pp. 337-352.

4622 Thomas of India. In, Rose, Martial, ed. The Wakefield Mystery Plays. (London, 1961), pp. 413-427.

The Lord's Ascension
Texts
4623 Ascencio Domini. In, The Towneley Mysteries. (London, 1836), pp. 294-304.

4624 The Lord's Ascension. In, England, George, ed. The Towneley Plays. (London, 1897), pp. 353-366.

4625 The Ascension of the Lord. In, Rose, Martial, ed. The Wakefield
      Mystery Plays. (London, 1961), pp. 428-439.

The Judgment
                            Texts
4626 Juditium. Play XXX. In, Douce, Francis, ed. Roxburghe Club
      Publications. No. 16. (London, 1822). [50 copies].

4627 Juditium. In, The Towneley Mysteries. (London, 1836), pp. 305-
      321.

4628 Juditium. In, Marriott, William. A Collection of English Miracle-
      Plays. (Basel, 1838), pp. 175-195.

4629 The Judgment. In, England, George, ed. The Towneley Plays.
      (London, 1897), pp. 367-387.

4630 The Judgment. In, Rose, Martial, ed. The Wakefield Mystery
      Plays. (London, 1961), pp. 439-456.

Lazarus
                            Texts
4631 Lazarus. In, The Towneley Mysteries. (London, 1836), pp. 322-
      327.

4632 Lazarus. In, England, George, ed. The Towneley Plays. (Lon-
      don, 1897), pp. 387-393.

4633 Lazarus. In, Tickner, Frederick J., ed. Earlier English Drama
      from Robin Hood to Everyman. (New York, 1929), pp. 184-
      189.

4634 Lazarus. In, Rose, Martial, ed. The Wakefield Mystery Plays.
      (London, 1961), pp. 273-279.

The Hanging of Judas
                            Texts
4635 Suspentio Judae. In, The Towneley Mysteries. (London, 1836),
      pp. 328-330.

4636 The Hanging of Judas. In, England, George, ed. The Towneley
      Plays. (London, 1897), pp. 393-396.

4637 The Hanging of Judas. In, Rose, Martial, ed. The Wakefield Mys-
      tery Plays. (London, 1961), pp. 326-329.

Studies

4638 Dugdale, Sir William. Antiquities of Warwickshire. London:
Printed by Thomas Warren, 1656. [24], 826, [12] pp. Index.
BM.

4639 Collier, John Payne. "The Widkirk, Chester, and Coventry
Miracle-Plays." The History of Dramatic Poetry. Vol. 2.
(London, 1831), pp. 155-229.

4640 "Towneley and Digby Mysteries." Gentleman's Magazine, New
Ser., VI (1836), 563-572.

4641 Sharpe, Lancelot. "Remarks on the Towneley Mysteries." Archaeologia, XXVII (1837-1838), 251-256.

4642 Ebert, Adolf. "Die englischen Mysterien mit besonderer Berücksichtigung der Towneley-Sammlung." Jahrbuch für romanische
und Englische Sprache und Literatur, I (1859), 44-82; 131-170.

4643 Banks, W. A. A List of Provincial Words in Use at Wakefield in
Yorkshire. London: J. R. Smith; Wakefield: W. R. Hall, 1865.
viii, 82 pp.
BM.

4644 Ulrich, Jacob. "Le Sacrifice d'Abraham." Romania, VIII (1879),
374-391.

4645 Jusserand, Jean J. Le Théâtre en Angleterre depuis la Conquête
jusqu' aux prédécesseurs immédiats de Shakespeare. 2nd ed.
Paris: E. Leroux, 1881. 350 pp.

4646 Capes, F. M. "The Poetry of the Early Mysteries." Nineteenth
Century, XIV (1883), 654-673. [Extracts translated into
modern English.]

4647 Maskell, J. "Pilate a Saint." Notes and Queries, 6th Ser., XI
(1885), 384.

4648 Banzer, A. "Die Farce Pathelin und ihre Nachahmungen."
Zeitschrift für neufranzösischen Sprache und Litteratur, X
(1888), 93-112.

4649 Hohlfeld, Alex. "Die altenglische Kollektivmisterien, unter
besonderer Berücksichtigung des Verhältnisses der York-
und Towneley-Spiele." Anglia. Zeitschrift für Englische

Philologie, XI (1889), 219-310.

4650 Davidson, Charles. "Studies in the English Mystery Plays."
      Transactions of the Connecticut Academy of Arts and Sciences,
      IX (1892), 125-297. [Relations with the York Cycle.]

4651 Skeat, W. W. "The Locality of 'The Towneley Plays.'" Athenaeum,
      No. 3449 (December 2, 1893), 779.

4652 Bruce, J. Douglas. "The Anglo-Saxon Version of the Book of Psalms
      Commonly Known as the Paris Psalter." Publications of the
      Modern Language Association, IX (1894), 43-164.

4653 Kölbing, Eugen. "Kleine Beiträge zur Erklärung und Textkritik
      vor-Shakespeare'scher Dramen." Englische Studien, XXI
      (1895), 162-176.

4654 ----- "Die Secunda Pastorum der Towneley Plays und Archie
      Armstrang's Aith." Zeitschrift für Vergleichende Litteratur-
      Geschichte, N.S., XI (1897), 137-141.

4655 ----- "The Secunda Pastorum of the Towneley Plays and Archie
      Armstrang's Aith." In, England, George, ed. The Towneley
      Plays. (London, 1897), pp. xxxi-xxxiv.

4656 Peacock, Matthew H. "Towneley, Widkirk, or Wakefield Plays?"
      Yorkshire Archaeological Journal, XV (1898-1900), 94-103.

4657 Eaton, Horace A. "A Source for the Towneley Prima Pastorum."
      Modern Language Notes, XIV (1899), 265-268.

4658 Green, J. H. "Yorkshire Dialect As Spoken in the West Riding
      during the Fifteenth and Nineteenth Centuries." Transactions
      of the Yorkshire Dialect Society, I, Part 2 (1899), 54-68.

4659 Hugienin, Julian. "An Interpolation in the Towneley Abraham
      Play." Modern Language Notes, XIV (1899), 255-256.

4660 Peacock, Matthew H. "The Wakefield Mysteries. The Place of
      Representation." Anglia, XXIV (1901), 509-524.

4661 Bunzen, Asmus. Ein Beitrag zur Kritik der Wakefielder Mys-
      terien. Kiel: H. Fiencke, 1903. [6], 58, [2] pp. Litteratur,
      pp. 55-58.
            CtY. IaU. ICU. NjP. NN. OCl. OU. PU. WU.

*4662 Chambers, E. K. "Towneley Plays." The Medieval Stage. Vol.
2. (London, 1903), pp. 412-416.

4663 Hamelius, Paul. "The Character of Cain in the Towneley Plays."
Journal of Comparative Literature, I (September-December,
1903), 324-344.

4664 Gerould, Gordon Hall. "Moll of the Prima Pastorum." Modern
Language Notes, XIX (1904), 225-230.

4665 Gayley, Charles Mills. "The Later Miracle Plays of England.
1. The Wakefield Master of Comedy." International Quarterly,
XII (1905), 67-88.

4666 Traver, Hope. "The Relation of Musical Terms in the Woodkirk
Shepherds Plays to the Dates of Their Composition." Modern
Language Notes, XX (January, 1905), 1-5.

4667 Moorman, F. W. "The Wakefield Miracle Plays." Transactions
of the Yorkshire Dialect Society, I Part 7 (1906), 5-24.

4668 Lipsky, Abram. "An Old English Haggada. The Exodus in the form
of a Morality Play." Maccabaean, XII (1907), 125-131. [Towneley
Pharaoh Play adapted and modernized.]

4669 Taylor, George C. "The Relation of the English Corpus Christi
Play to the Middle English Lyric." Modern Philology, V (July,
1907), 1-38.

4670 Peacock, Matthew H. "Wildkirk: 'The Wakefield Mysteries.'"
Notes and Queries, 10th Ser., X (1908), 128-129.

4671 Skeat, W. W. "'Widkirk': 'The Wakefield Mysteries.'" Notes and
Queries, 10th Ser., X (1908), 177.

*4672 Cady, Frank W. "Liturgical Basis of the Towneley Mysteries."
Publications of the Modern Language Association, XXIV (1909),
419-469.

4673 Hanford, James Holly. "The Pastoral Elegy and Milton's Lycidas."
Publications of the Modern Language Association, XXV (1910), 403-
447.

4674 Cady, Frank W. "The Couplets and Quatrains in the Towneley Mystery Plays." Journal of English and Germanic Philology, X
(1911), 572-584.

4675 Foster, Frances A. "The Mystery Play and the Northern Pas-
        sion." Modern Language Notes, XXVI (June, 1911), 169-
        171.

4676 Cady, Frank W. "The Wakefield Group in Towneley." Journal
        of English and Germanic Philology, XI (1912), 244-262.

4677 Zupitza, Julius. Alt-und Mittelenglisches Übengsbuch. Wien
        & Leipzig: Wilhelm Braumüller, 1912. xiv, 347 pp. Wörter-
        buch, pp. 208-347. [10th edition].
                BM.

4678 Cady, Frank W. "The Passion Group in Towneley." Modern
        Philology, X (1913), 587-600.

4679 Greg, W. W. "Bibliographical and Textual Problems of the Eng-
        lish Miracle Cycles." The Library, Third Series, V (1914),
        280-319.

4680 Williams, E. F. "Comic Elements in the Wakefield Mysteries."
        Ph.D. University of California, 1914.

4681 Brown, Carleton. "The Towneley Play of the Doctors and the
        Speculum Christiani." Modern Language Notes, XXXI (1916),
        223-226.

4682 Cook, Albert S. "Another Parallel to the Mak Story." Studies in
        Philology, XIV (1916), 11-15.

4683 Haller, Julius. "Der Dialog in den Towneley-Spielen." Die Technik
        des Dialogs im mittelalterlichen Drama Englands. (Worms,
        1916), pp. 43-55.

*4684 Wells, John Edwin. "The Towneley Plays." A Manual of the
        Writings in Middle English, 1050-1400. (New Haven, 1916-
        1951), pp. 555-560, 860-861, 993, 1025-1026, 1081, 1137,
        1185, 1228, 1282, 1319, 1369, 1417, 1468, 1524, 1637,
        1682, 1728.

4685 Kinard, Charles C. "The Staging of the Towneley Plays." M.A.
        Columbia University, 1917.

4686 Baugh, Albert C. "Parallels to the Mak Story." Modern Philology,
        XV (1918), 729-734.

4687 Frank, Grace. "Revision in the English Mystery Plays."
Modern Philology, XV (1918), 565-572.

4688 Patch, Howard Rollin. "Some Elements in Medieval Descriptions
of the Otherworld." Publications of the Modern Language
Association, XXXIII (1918), 601-643.

4689 Wann, Louis. "The Influence of French Farce on the Towneley
Cycle of Mystery Plays." Transactions of the Wisconsin
Academy of Sciences, Arts, and Letters, XIX (1918), 356-368.

4690 Lyle, Marie Caroline. The Original Identity of the York and
Towneley Cycles. Minneapolis: University of Minnesota, 1919.
iv, [2], 113 pp. Bibliography, pp. 109-113.
BM. CtY. ICN. ICU. MnU. NjP. OC1. OU. PU. ViU.
WU.

4691 Miller, Frances H. "The Northern Passion and the Mysteries."
Modern Language Notes, XXXIV (1919), 88-92.

4692 Kirwan, Patrick. The Dawn of English Drama. London: Harding
& More, Ltd., The Ambrosden Press, 1920. 71, [1] pp.
BM.

4693 Coates, Sir E. F., bart. Catalogue of the Towneley Mysteries
and the York Missal, the Property of the Late Sir Edward
F. Coates. Which Will Be Sold by Auction by Messrs. Sotheby,
Wilkinson and Hodge . . . the 8th of February, 1922. [London]:
Dryden Press [1922]. 8 pp.
CtY. MnU. NN.

4694 "Play of the Shepherds; Criticism." Spectator, CXXXI (1923),
989-990.

4695 Schering, Karl. Die Quellen der Towneley Plays. Inaugural Dissertation. Kiel, 1923. 200 leaves.

4696 Holthausen, Ferdinand. "Studien zu den Towneley Plays."
Englische Studien, LVIII (1924), 161-178.

4697 Malone, Kemp. "A Note on the Towneley Secunda Pastorum."
Modern Language Notes, XL (January, 1925), 35-39.

4698 Peacock, M. H. "A Note on the Identity of the Towneley Plays
with the Wakefield Mysteries." Anglia Beiblatt, XXXVI (April,
1925), 111-114.

4699 Peacock, Matthew H. "The Wakefield Mysteries." Times Literary
        Supplement, March 5, 1925, p. 156.

4700 ----- "The Wakefield Mysteries." Times Literary Supplement,
        May 7, 1925, p. 316.

4701 Potter, Russell. "The Wakefield Mysteries." Times Literary
        Supplement, April 30, 1925, p. 300.

*4702 Cargill, Oscar. "The Authorship of the Secunda Pastorum."
        Publications of the Modern Language Association, XLI (Dec-
        ember, 1926), 810-831.

4703 Dustoor, P. E. "Some Textual Notes on the English Mystery
        Plays." Modern Language Review, XXI (October, 1926), 427-
        431.

4704 Peacock, Matthew H. "The Wakefield Mysteries." Yorkshire
        Archaeological Journal, XXVIII (January, 1926), 427-430.

4705 Vriend, J. "'That alle myghtys may' in the Towneley Secunda
        Pastorum." English Studies, VIII (December, 1926), 185-
        186.

4706 Cady, Frank W. "The Maker of Mak." University of California
        Chronicle, XXIX (1927), 261-272.

4707 Holthausen, F. "Das Wakefielder Spiel von Kain und Abel."
        Englische Studien, LXII (November, 1927), 132-151.

4708 Dustoor, P. E. "Textual Notes on the Towneley Old Testament
        Plays." Englische Studien, LXIII (1928-1929), 220-228.

4709 Foster, Frances A. "Was Gilbert Pilkington Author of Secunda
        Pastorum?" Publications of the Modern Language Association,
        XLIII (March, 1928), 124-136.

4710 Peacock, Matthew H. "Wakefield Mysteries." Times Literary
        Supplement, June 7, 1928, p. 431.

*4711 Wann, Louis. "A New Examination of the Manuscript of the
        Towneley Plays." Publications of the Modern Language Asso-
        ciation, XLIII (1928), 137-152.

4712 Cady, Frank W. "Towneley, York, and True-Coventry." Studies in Philology, XXVI (July, 1929), 386-400.

4713 Frank, Grace. "On the Relation Between the York and Towneley
      Plays." Publications of the Modern Language Association,
      XLIV (March, 1929), 313-319.

4714 Holthausen, Ferdinand. "Das zweite Hirtenspiel der Wakefielder
      Spiele." Englische Studien, LXIII (1929), 193-219.

4715 Lyle, Marie C. "The Original Identity of the York and Towneley
      Cycles--a Rejoinder." Publications of the Modern Language
      Association, XLIV (1929), 319-328.

4716 "Das zweite Hirtenspiel der Wakefielder Spiele." Englische
      Studien, LXIII (1929), 281-282.

4717 Carey, Millicent. The Wakefield Group of the Towneley Cycle;
      a Study to Determine the Conventional and Original Elements
      in the Four Plays Commonly Ascribed to the Wakefield Author
      ... Göttingen: Vandenhoeck & Ruprecht; Baltimore: The Johns
      Hopkins Press, 1930. [8], 251 pp. Bibliography, pp. 245-251.
      (Hesperia. Ergänzungsreihe: Schriften zur englischen Philologie.
      Heft 11.)
              BM. CtY. DLC. ICN. MB. MH. MiU. OCU. OU. PU.
              ViU. WU.

4718 Cargill, Oscar. "Studies in the Towneley Plays." Ph.D. Columbia
      University, 1930.

4719 Rogers, Genevieve. "Reductions of the Speakers' Parts in the
      Towneley Pharao." Philological Quarterly, IX (April, 1930), 216-218.

4720 Strunk, William. "Two Notes on the Towneley Second Shepherds'
      Play." Modern Language Notes, XLV (March, 1930), 151. [On
      lines 352 and 391.]

4721 Carroll, Rev. Thomas J., O.M.C. "The Influence of the Festival
      of Corpus Christi upon the Cycle Plays; with Some Observa-
      tions about the View Point of the Cambridge History of English
      Literature." M.A. Catholic University of America, 1932.

*4722 Frampton, Mendall G. "Gilbert Pilkington Once More." Publi-
      cations of the Modern Language Association, XLVII (September,
      1932), 622-635.

4723 Jones, Ellen Mattocks. "Stage Setting and Stage Business in the

English Cycles." M.A. University of Minnesota, 1932.

4724 Onions, C. T. "Middle English 'Alod, Olod.'" Medium Aevum,
     I (1932), 206-208; II (1933), 73.

4725 Scott, John Walter. "Notable Aspects of Satire in the Towneley
     Cycle." M.A. University of North Carolina, 1932.

4726 Whiting, B. J. "Analogues to the Mak Story: 'The Saturnalia'
     of Macrobius." Speculum, VII (October, 1932), 552.

4727 Cornelius, Brother Luke. The Role of the Virgin Mary in the
     Coventry, York, Chester and Towneley Cycles. Washington,
     D.C.: The Catholic University Press, 1933. vi, 121 pp.
         CU. DLC. ICU. MiU. MnU. OC1. PP. PU. ViU. WU.

4728 Curtiss, Chester G. "The York and Towneley Plays on The Har-
     rowing of Hell." Studies in Philology, XXX (January, 1933),
     24-33.

4729 Trusler, Margaret. "A Study of the Language of the Wakefield
     Group in Towneley on the Basis of the Significant Rime-Words
     with Comparison of Forms within the Line in Both the Towne-
     ley and the York Plays." Ph.D. University of Chicago, 1933.

4730 Waters, Samuel Horace. Wakefield in the 17th Century. A Social
     History of the Town and Neighborhood from 1550-1710.
     Wakefield: Sanderson & Clayton, Ltd., 1933. xv, 163 pp.
     Bibliography, pp. [153]-157.
         BM. ICN.

4731 Garvin, Katherine. "A Note on Noah's Wife." Modern Language
     Notes, XLIX (February, 1934), 88-90.

4732 Oxley, J. E. "Sam." Times Literary Supplement, July 5, 1934,
     p. 476.

4733 Smyser, H. M. and T. B. Stroup. "Analogues to the Mak Story."
     Journal of American Folklore, XLVII (October-December,
     1934), 378-381.

*4734 Frampton, Mendall G. "The Date of the Flourishing of the Wake-
     field Master." Publications of the Modern Language Association,
     L (September, 1935), 631-660.

4735 Gehman, Sara. "The Development of the Native English Domestic
      Braggart, with Particular Reference to Its Manifestation in
      the Towneley Plays." M.A. Columbia University, 1935.

4736 Trusler, Margaret. "Some Textual Notes Based on Examination
      of the Towneley Manuscript." Philological Quarterly, XIV
      (October, 1935), 301-306.

4737 Withington, Robert. "Water Fastand." Modern Language Notes,
      L (February, 1935), 95-96.

4738 Trusler, Margaret. "The Language of the Wakefield Playwright."
      Studies in Philology, XXXIII (January, 1936), 18-19.

*4739 Frampton, Mendal G. "The Early English Text Society Edition
      of the Towneley Plays." Anglia Beiblatt, XLVIII (1937), 330-
      333, 366-368; XLIX (1938), 3-7.

4740 Smith, John Harrington. "Another Allusion to Costume in the
      Work of the Wakefield Master." Publications of the Modern
      Language Association, LII (September, 1937), 901-902.

4741 Smith, Hart. Comparison of Towneley and Coventry Miracle
      Plays. M.A. University of Georgia, 1937.

*4742 Frampton, Mendall G. "The Date of the 'Wakefield Master':
      Bibliographical Evidence." Publications of the Modern Language
      Association, LIII (March, 1938), 87-117.

4743 Giddings, Joseph A. "The Language of the Towneley Plays."
      M.A. Cornell University, 1938.

4744 Smith, John Harrington. "The Date of Some Wakefield Borrowings
      from York." Publications of the Modern Language Association,
      LIII (June, 1938), 595-600.

4745 Kann, Sister Jean M. "Doctrinal Elements in the Towneley Plays."
      Ph.D. Yale University, 1939.

4746 Stroup, T. B. "Another Southern Analogue to the Mak Story."
      Southern Folklore Quarterly, III (1939), 5-6.

4747 Walker, J. W. "Gilds and Mystery Plays." Wakefield, Its History
      and People. 2nd ed. Vol. 1. (Wakefield, 1939), pp. 148-157.

4748 Walker, J. W. Wakefield: Its History and People. 2nd ed. 2 vols.
        Wakefield: Privately Printed, 1939. Indices.
        BM. ICU.

4749 Harney, Sister Mary Camillus. "The Characterization of Cain and
        Abel in the English Mystery Plays: York, Chester, Ludus
        Coventriae and Towneley Cycles." M.A. Catholic University of
        America, 1940.

4750 Watt, Homer A. "The Dramatic Unity of the 'Secunda Pastorum,'"
        In, Essays and Studies of Carleton Brown. (New York and Lon-
        don, 1940), pp. 158-166.

*4751 Clark, Edward Murray. "Liturgical Influences in the Towneley
        Plays." Orate Fratres, XVI (1941), 69-79.

4752 ----- "Liturgical Remains and Influences in the Towneley
        Plays." Ph.D. University of Oklahoma, 1941.

4753 ----- "A Restored Reading in the Towneley Purification Play."
        Modern Language Notes, LVI (May, 1941), 358-360.

4754 Clark, Sr. Mary Thaddeus. "Drama in the Cyclic Plays of Media-
        eval England." M.A. Fordham University, 1941.

4755 Frampton, Mendall G. "The Towneley Harrowing of Hell." Publi-
        cations of the Modern Language Association, LVI (March, 1941),
        105-119.

4756 Lawlor, S.J., Richard Vincent. "The Music and Musical Elements
        of the Craft Cycles." M.A. Boston College, 1941.

*4757 Marshall, Mary H. "The Dramatic Tradition Established by the
        Liturgical Plays." Publications of the Modern Language Asso-
        ciation, LVI (1941), 962-991.

4758 Mill, Anna Jean. "Noah's Wife Again." Publications of the Modern
        Language Association, LVI (September, 1941), 613-626.

4759 Utley, F. L. "The One Hundred and Three Names of Noah's Wife."
        Speculum, XVI (1941), 426.

4760 Benoit-Smullyan, Mary Louise. "Principles of Comedy in the
        Towneley 'Secunda Pastorum.'" M.A. Cornell University,
        1942.

*4761 Frampton, Mendall G. "Towneley XX: the 'Conspiracio (et
Capcio).'" Publications of the Modern Language Association, LVIII (December, 1943), 920-937.

4762 Spencer, Hazelton. "The Lost Lines of 'Secunda Pastorum.'"
Modern Language Notes, LVIII (January, 1943), 49-50.

4763 Sullivan, S.S.J., Sr. John. "A Study of the Themes of the Passion in the Medieval Cyclic Drama." Ph.D. Catholic University of America, 1943.

4764 Withington, Robert. "Three breefes to a long: Technical Musical Terms in the Secunda Pastorum." Modern Language Notes,
LVIII (February, 1943), 115-116.

4765 Frampton, Mendall G. "The Processus Talentorum (Towneley
XXIV)." Publications of the Modern Language Association,
LIX (1944), 646-654.

*4766 Parrott, T. M. "Mak and Archie Armstrang: What Professor
Kölbing Left Unsolved." Modern Language Notes, LIX
(May, 1944), 297-304.

*4767 Cosbey, Robert C. "The Mak Story and Its Folklore Analogues."
Speculum, XX (July, 1945), 310-317.

4768 Clark, Edward Murray. "The Towneley Peregrini, an Unnoticed
Step Toward the Vernacular." Modern Language Notes, LXI
(April, 1946), 236-241.

4769 Kökeritz, H. "Some Marginal Notes to the Towneley Resurrection
Included in Joseph Quincy Adam's Chief Pre-Shakespearean
Dramas." Modern Language Notes, LXI (December, 1946),
529-532.

4770 Aquin, Sister M. "Vulgate and Eve-concept in the English Cycles."
Catholic Biblical Quarterly, IX (1947), 409-435.

4771 Chidamian, Claude. "Mak and the Tossing in the Blanket."
Speculum, XXII (April, 1947), 186-190.

4772 Jean Marie, O.S.F., Sister. "The Cross in the Towneley Plays."
Traditio, V (1947), 331-334.

4773 Williams, Arnold. "Middle English 'Questmonger.'" Mediaeval

Studies, X (1948), 200-204.

4774 Homan, Delmar Charles. "A Study in the Medieval Miracle Plays:
     Judgment Day (With Two Plays Modernized)." M.A. University
     of Iowa, 1949.

4775 Slater, M. E. "Little Shepherds Going Toward Bethlehem."
     Catholic World, CLXX (1949), 179-185.

4776 Thompson, Francis J. "Unity in the Second Shepherds' Tale."
     Modern Language Notes, LXIV (1949), 302-306.

4777 Withington, Robert. "Mak, Op-Signorken and Mr. Hardwick."
     Notes and Queries, CXCIV (1949), 530-531.

*4778 Williams, Arnold. The Characterization of Pilate in the Towneley
     Cycle. Lansing: Michigan State College Press, 1950. xii, 112
     pp. Bibliography, pp. 103-108.
          CtY. CU. ICU. MH. MiU. WU.

*4779 Carpenter, Nan Cooke. "Music in the Secunda Pastorum."
     Speculum, XXVI (1951), 696-700.

4780 Seve, Nicholas Werner de. "The Marian Element in the Four
     Great Cycles." M.A. Columbia University, 1951.

4781 Speirs, J. "The Mystery Cycle, 1: Some Towneley Plays."
     Scrutiny, XVIII (1951), 86-117.

4782 ----- "Some Towneley Cycle Plays. Part III." Scrutiny, XVIII
     (1952), 246-265.

*4783 Cawley, A. C. "The Wakefield First Shepherds' Play." Pro-
     ceedings of the Leeds Philosophical and Literary Society,
     Literary and Historical Section, VII (October, 1953), 113-
     122.

4784 ----- "Iak Garcio of the Prima Pastorum in the Towneley
     Manuscript." Modern Language Notes, LXVIII (March, 1953),
     169-172.

4785 ----- An Edition of the Wakefield Group in the Towneley Cycle.
     Ph.D. University of London (External), 1954.

4786 Jones, Gertrude B. A Study of the Wakefield Group in the Towneley

Cycle. M.A. University of Leeds, 1954-1955.

4787 Cawley, A. C. "The 'Grotesque' Feast in the Prima Pastorum."
Speculum, XXX (April, 1955), 213-217.

4788 Craig, Hardin. "York-Wakefield Plays." English Religious
Drama of the Middle Ages. (Oxford, 1955), pp. 199-238.

4789 Savage, Donald J. "An Analysis of the Comic Element in the
Chester, York, Coventry and Towneley Mystery Cycles."
Ph.D. University of Minnesota, 1955.

4790 Scherer, Judith E. "The Passion Group in the York and Towneley
Cycles: a Study in Origins and Literary Techniques." M.A.
University of Rochester, 1955.

4791 Wassmer, Jessica Therese. "A Comparison of Two Cycles of
English Mystery Plays Ludus Coventriae or the Plaie Called
Corpus Christi and the Towneley Plays." M.A. Fordham
University, 1955.

4792 Savage, Donald James. "An Analysis of the Comic Element in
the Chester, York, Coventry, and Towneley Mystery Cycles."
Ph.D. University of Minnesota, 1956.

4793 Stevens, Martin. The Language of the Towneley Plays: A Comparative Analysis of the Identical York and Towneley Plays,
the Caesar Augustus, the Talents, and the Stanzas of the
Wakefield Master. Ph.D. Michigan State University, 1956.

4794 Berry, Francis. "Towneley Plays Syntonic Tense (First Shepherd's Play)." Blackfriars, XXXVIII (May, 1957), 221-226.

4795 Maltman, Sister Nicholas. "A Study of the Evil Characters in
the English Corpus Christi Cycles." Ph.D. University of
California, 1957.

*4796 Stevens, Martin. "The Accuracy of the Towneley Scribe."
Huntington Library Quarterly, XXII (November, 1958), 1-9.

4797 Zumwalt, Eugene E. "Irony in the Towneley Shepherds' Plays."
Research Studies of the State College of Washington, XXVI
(March, 1958), 37-53.

4798 Rynell, Alarik. "On the Meaning of 'Foyn' and 'Fo' in the

Towneley Plays." English Studies, XL (October, 1959), 379-381.

4799 Stevens, Martin. "Composition of the Towneley 'Talents' Play: A Linguistic Examination." Journal of English and Germanic Philology, LVIII (July, 1959), 422-433.

*4800 Dunn, Catherine E. "The Medieval Cycle As History Play: An Approach to the Wakefield Plays." Studies in the Renaissance, VII (1960), 76-89.

4801 Peel, Donald F. "The Allegory in 'Secunda Pastorum.'" Northwest Missouri State College Studies, XXIV (1960), 3-11.

4802 Dunn, Catherine E. "Lyrical Form and the Prophetic Principle in the Towneley Plays." Medieval Studies, XXIII (1961), 80-90.

4803 Maltman, Sister Nicholas, O.P. "Pilate--os Malleatoris in the Towneley Plays." Speculum, XXXVI (April, 1961), 308-311.

4804 Penninger, Frieda Elaine. "The Significance of the Corpus Christi Play As Drama with Particular Reference to the Towneley Cycle." Ph.D. Duke University, 1961.

4805 Prosser, Eleanor. "Cain." Drama and Religion in the English Mystery Plays. (Stanford, California, 1961), pp. 76-85.

4806 ----- "Joseph." Drama and Religion in the English Mystery Plays. (Stanford, California, 1961), pp. 92-96.

4807 ----- "Thomas." Drama and Religion in the English Mystery Plays. (Stanford, California, 1961), pp. 150-158.

4808 Samuels, Charles Thomas. "The Dramatic Rhythm of the Wakefield Crucifixion." College English, XXII (January, 1961), 343-344.

4809 Schless, Howard H. "The Comic Element in the Wakefield Noah." Studies in Medieval Literature, XVII (1961), 229-243.

4810 "Wakefield Mysteries." Time, April 14, 1961, p. 69. ["The Raising of Lazarus."]

4811 Kreutz, Irvin. "Three Collector's Items: 1961 Production of Wakefield Mysteries." Educational Theatre Journal, XIV (May, 1962), 141-147.

4812 Sisam, C. "Towneley Play of Noah: 'Bere'; 'Lufe.'" Review of
      English Studies, New Ser., XIII (November, 1962), 387-389.

4813 Bernbrock, John E. "Notes on the Towneley Cycle 'Slaying of
      Abel.'" Journal of English and Germanic Philology, LXII
      (April, 1963), 317-322.

4814 Cozart, William R. "The Northern Middle English Harrowing
      of Hell Plays of the York and Towneley Cycles. An Edition
      and Commentary." Ph.D. Harvard University, 1963.

*4815 Manly, William M. "Shepherds and Prophets: Religious Unity
      in the Towneley 'Secunda Pastorum.'" Publications of the
      Modern Language Association, LXXVIII (June, 1963), 151-
      155.

4816 Dunn, Catherine E. "The Prophetic Principle in the 'Prima
      Pastorum.'" Crisafulli, Allesandro S., ed. Linguistic and
      Literary Studies in Honor of Helmut A. Hatzfeld. (Washington,
      D.C., 1964), pp. 117-127.

4817 Johnston, Alexandra Ferguson. "The Christ Figure in the Minis-
      try Plays of the Four English Cycles." Ph.D. University of
      Toronto, 1964.   [Delete].

4818 Morgan, Margery M. "'High Fraud'" Paradox and Double Plot
      in the English Shepherds' Plays." Speculum, XXXIX (October,
      1964), 676-689.

4819 Nelson, Alan H. "'Sacred' and 'Secular' Currents in the Towneley
      Play of Noah." Drama Survey, III (February, 1964), 393-401.

4820 Gardner, John. "Theme and Irony in the Wakefield 'Mactatio
      Abel.'" Publications of the Modern Language Association,
      LXXX (1965), 515-521.

4821 McCabe, Bernard. "The 'Second Shepherds' Play.'" Explicator,
      XXIV (1965), Item 13.

4822 Munson, William Frederick. "Three Kinds of Dramatic Action
      in the Towneley Plays." Ph.D. Yale University, 1965.

4823 Cantelupe, Eugene B., and Richard Griffith. "The Gifts of the
      Shepherds in the Wakefield Secunda Pastorum: An Iconographical
      Interpretation." Mediaeval Studies, XXVIII (1966), 328-335.

*4824 Macaulay, Peter S. "The Play of the Harrowing of Hell as a
       Climax in the English Mystery Cycles." Studia Germanica
       Gandensia, VIII (1966), 115-134.

4825 Stevens, Martin. "The Dramatic Setting of the Wakefield 'An-
       nunciation.'" Publications of the Modern Language Association,
       LXXXI (June, 1966), 193-198.

4826 Davidson, Clifford. "The Unity of the Wakefield Mactacio Abel."
       Traditio, XXIII (1967), 495-500.

4827 Downing, Marjorie D. "The Influence of the Literary on the Eng-
       lish Cycle Plays." Ph.D. Yale University, 1967.

4828 Johnston, Alexandra F. "The Christ Figure in the Ministry Plays
       of the Four English Cycles." Ph.D. University of Toronto,
       1967.

*4829 Ross, Lawrence. "Symbol and Structure in the 'Secunda Pastorum.'"
       Comparative Drama, I (1967), 122-149.

4830 Weimann, Robert. "Realismus und Simultankonvention im Mister-
       iendrama: Mimesis, Parodie und Utopie in den Towneley-
       Hirtenszenen." Shakespeare-Jahrbuch (Weimar), CIII (1967),
       108-135.

4831 Gardner, John. "Imagery and Allusion in the Wakefield Noah
       Play." Papers on Language and Literature, IV (Winter, 1968),
       3-12.

4832 Meyers, Walter E. "A Study of the Middle English Wakefield
       Cycle Plays." Ph.D. University of Florida, 1968.

*4833 Munson, William F. "Typology and the Towneley Isaac." Re-
       search Opportunities in Renaissance Drama, XI (1968), 129-
       139.

4834 Roberts, Ian. "Another Parallel to the Mak Story?" Notes and
       Queries, CCXIII (1968), 204-205.

*4835 Stevens, Martin. "The Staging of the Wakefield Plays." Re-
       search Opportunities in Renaissance Drama, XI (1968), 115-
       128.

4836 Davidson, Clifford. "An Interpretation of the Wakefield Judicium."

Annuale Medievale, X (1969), 104-119.

4837 Walsh, O.S.B., Sister Mary Margaret. "The Judgment Plays of
the English Cycles." The American Benedictine Review, XX
(September, 1969), 378-394.

Walden

4838 Blair, Lawrence. "Walden." In, "A Note on the Relation of the
Corpus Christi Procession to the Corpus Christi Play in
England." Modern Language Notes, LV (February, 1940),
86.

Wimborne

4839 Chambers, E. K. "Wimborne, Minster." The Mediaeval Stage.
Vol. 2. (London, 1903), p. 396.

Winchester

4840 Chambers, E. K. "Winchester College." The Mediaeval Stage.
Vol. 2. (London, 1903), pp. 246-247.

4841 ----- "Winchester, Hampshire." The Mediaeval Stage. Vol. 2.
(London, 1903), p. 396.

4842 Handschin, J. "The Two Winchester Tropers." Journal of
Theological Studies, XXXVII, No. 145 (January, 1936), 34-
49; XXXVII, No. 146 (April, 1936), 156-172.

Windsor

4843 Chambers, E. K. "Windsor, Berks." The Mediaeval Stage.
Vol. 2. (London, 1903), pp. 396-397.

Witham

4844 ----- "Witham, Essex." The Mediaeval Stage. Vol. 2. (London,
1903), p. 397.

Wittersham

4845 ----- "Wittersham, Kent." The Mediaeval Stage. Vol. 2.
(London, 1903), p. 397.

Woodham Walter

4846 Chambers, E. K. "Woodham Walter, Essex." The Mediaeval
        Stage. Vol. 2. (London, 1903), p. 397.

Worcester

4847 ----- "Worcester, Worcestershire." The Mediaeval Stage. Vol.
        2. (London, 1903), p. 398.

4848 Pierson, Merle. "Worcester." In, "The Relation of the Corpus
        Christi Procession to the Corpus Christi Play in England."
        Transactions of the Wisconsin Academy of Sciences, Arts, and
        Letters, XVIII (1916), 159.

4849 Blair, Lawrence. "Worcester." In, "A Note on the Relation of
        the Corpus Christi Procession to the Corpus Christi Play in
        England." Modern Language Notes, LV (February, 1940), 94.

Wrexam

4850 Chambers, E. K. "Wrexham, Denbighshire." The Mediaeval
        Stage. Vol. 2. (London, 1903), p. 398.

Writtle

4851 ----- "Writtle, Essex." The Mediaeval Stage. Vol. 2. (London,
        1903), p. 398.

Wycombe

4852 ----- "Wycombe, Buckinghamshire." The Mediaeval Stage.
        Vol. 2. (London, 1903), p. 398.

Wye

4853 ----- "Wye, Kent." The Mediaeval Stage. Vol. 2. (London,
        1903), p. 398.

Wymondham

4854 ----- "Wymondham, Norfolk." The Mediaeval Stage. Vol.
        2. (London, 1903), p. 398.

Yarmouth

4855 Chambers, E. K. "Yarmouth, Norfolk." The Mediaeval Stage. Vol. 2. (London, 1903), p. 399.

Yeovil

4856 Blair, Lawrence. "Yeovil." In, "A Note on the Relation of the Corpus Christi Procession to the Corpus Christi Play in England." Modern Language Notes, LV (February, 1940), 93.

YORK PLAYS

Manuscripts

4857 British Museum. Additional MS. 35,290.

4858 Yorkshire, York Philosophical Society, Sykes MS. [Scrivener's play of "The Incredulity of Thomas."]

Collections

*4859 Smith, Lucy Toulmin, ed. York Plays: the Plays Performed by the Crafts or Mysteries of York on the Day of Corpus Christi in the 14th, 15th, and 16th Centuries; Now First Printed from the Unique Manuscript in the Library of Lord Ashburnham. With Introduction and Glossary. Oxford: Clarendon Press, 1885. lxxviii, 557 pp.
         BM. CtY. DFo. DLC. MH. MiU. NjP. NN. OC1W. ODW.

4860 Mooney, Margaret S. A Rosary of Mystery Plays. Fifteen Plays Selected from the York Cycle of Mysteries Performed by the Crafts on the Day of Corpus Christi in the 14th, 15th, and 16th Centuries. Translated from the Middle English of the Originals into Our Mother Tongue. Albany, New York: F. H. Evory and Co., 1915. 150 pp.
         CtY. DLC. ICN. ICU. MH. NN.

4861 Osgood, Phillips Endecott. Nativity Mysteries; from the Nativity Cycle of the York Mysteries. Translated and Adapted According to Ancient Precedent. Lebanon, Pennsylvania: The Christmas Tree Press, 1929. 45, [1] pp.
         NN.

4862 Purvis, J. S., ed. The York Cycle of Mystery Plays. A Shorter Version of the Ancient Cycle; with a Note on the Production Staged at the York Festival of 1951, by E. Martin Browne.

London: S.P.C.K., 1951. [4], 204 pp. (Gives 29 of the
original 48 plays.)
  BM. IaU. MH. NNC.

Individual Plays
Texts
The Creation, and the Fall of Lucifer

4863 The Creation, and the Fall of Lucifer. In, Smith, Lucy Toulmin,
      ed. York Plays. (Oxford, 1885), pp. 1-7.

4864 The Fall of Lucifer. In, Pollard, Alfred W., ed. English Miracle
      Plays, Moralities and Interludes. (Oxford, 1890), pp. 1-7,
      177-179.

4865 Dustoor, P. E., ed. "Creation of Adam and Eve." Allahabad
      University Studies, XIII (1937), 23-28.

4866 [The Creation, Fall of Lucifer.] The Barkers. In, Purvis, J. S.,
      ed. The York Cycle of Mystery Plays. A Shorter Version.
      (London, 1951).

4867 The Creation and the Fall of Lucifer. In, Cawley, A. C., ed.
      Everyman and Medieval Miracle Plays. (New York, 1959),
      pp. 1-9.

4868 The Fall of Lucifer. In, Browne, E. Martin, ed. Mystery and
      Morality Plays. (New York, 1960), pp. 23-28.

4869 [The Creation, and the Fall of Lucifer]. In, Purvis, J. S. The
      York Cycle of Mystery Plays. (London, 1962), pp. 15-19.

Creation, to the Fifth Day

4870 The Creation, to the fifth day. In, Smith, Lucy Toulmin, ed.
      York Plays. (Oxford, 1885), pp. 8-13.

4871 [The Creation, to the fifth day]. In, Purvis, J. S. The York
      Cycle of Mystery Plays. (London, 1962), pp. 20-24.

God Creates Adam and Eve

4872 God creates Adam and Eve. In, Smith, Lucy Toulmin, ed. York
      Plays. (Oxford, 1885), pp. 14-17.

4873 [God Creates Adam and Eve]. The Cardmakers' Play. In, Purvis, J. S., ed. The York Cycle of Mystery Plays. A Shorter Version. (London, 1951).

4874 The Creation of Adam and Eve. In, Cawley, A. C., ed. Everyman and Medieval Miracle Plays. (New York, 1959), pp. 11-16.

4875 The Creation of Man. In, Browne, E. Martin, ed. Mystery and Morality Plays. (New York, 1960), pp. 29-32. [Play No. 3].

4876 [God Creates Adam and Eve]. In, Purvis, J. S. The York Cycle of Mystery Plays. (London, 1962), pp. 25-27.

Adam and Eve in the Garden of Eden

4877 God puts Adam and Eve in the Garden of Eden. In, Smith, Lucy Toulmin, ed. York Plays. (Oxford, 1885), pp. 18-21.

4878 [Adam and Eve in the Garden of Eden]. The Fullers' Play. In, Purvis, J. S., ed. The York Cycle of Mystery Plays. A Shorter Version. (London, 1951).

4879 The Garden of Eden. In, Browne, E. Martin, ed. Mystery and Morality Plays. (New York, 1960), pp. 33-36.

4880 [God puts Adam and Eve in the Garden of Eden]. In, Purvis, J. S. The York Cycle of Mystery Plays. (London, 1962), pp. 28-30.

Man's Disobedience and Fall

4881 Man's disobedience and fall from Eden. In, Smith, Lucy Toulmin, ed. York Plays. (Oxford, 1885), pp. 22-28.

4882 [Man's Disobedience and Fall]. The Coopers' Play. In, Purvis, J. S., ed. The York Cycle of Mystery Plays. A Shorter Version. (London, 1951).

4883 The Fall of Man. In, Cawley, A. C., ed. Everyman and Medieval Miracle Plays. (New York, 1959), pp. 17-24.

4884 The Fall of Man. In, Browne, E. Martin, ed. Mystery and Morality Plays. (New York, 1960), pp. 37-44. [Play No. 5].

4885 [Man's disobedience and fall from Eden]. In, Purvis, J. S.
      The York Cycle of Mystery Plays. (London, 1962), pp. 31-35.

Adam and Eve Driven from Eden

4886 Adam and Eve driven from Eden. In, Smith, Lucy Toulmin, ed.
      York Plays. (Oxford, 1885), pp. 29-34.

4887 [Adam and Eve driven from Eden]. In, Purvis, J. S. The York
      Cycle of Mystery Plays. (London, 1962), pp. 36-40.

Sacrifice of Cain and Abel

4888 Sacrificium Cayme and Abell. In, Smith, Lucy Toulmin, ed.
      York Plays. (Oxford, 1885), pp. 35-39.

4889 [Sacrificium Cayme and Abell]. In, Purvis, J. S. The York Cycle
      of Mystery Plays. (London, 1962), pp. 41-44.

The Building of the Ark

4890 The Building of the Ark. In, Smith, Lucy Toulmin, ed. York
      Plays. (Oxford, 1885), pp. 40-44.

4891 [The Building of the Ark]. In, Purvis, J. S. The York Cycle of
      Mystery Plays. (London, 1962), pp. 45-48.

Noah and His Wife, the Flood

4892 Noah and His Wife, the Flood and its waning. In, Smith, Lucy
      Toulmin, ed. York Plays. (Oxford, 1885), pp. 45-55.

4893 The Fishers' and Mariners' Play The Flood. A Play from the
      York Cycle of Mystery Plays. A Version in Modern English
      by the Reverend J. S. Purvis. York: York Festival Society
      Limited, 1954. 15 pp. [Printed in England by Ben Johnson &
      Co., Ltd., York and London.]
            BM.

4894 [Noah and his wife, the Flood and its waning]. In, Purvis, J. S.
      The York Cycle of Mystery Plays. (London, 1962), pp. 49-57.

Abraham's Sacrifice of Isaac

4895 Abraham's Sacrifice of Isaac. In, Smith, Lucy Toulmin, ed.

York Plays. (Oxford, 1885), pp. 56-67.

4896 Abraham's Sacrifice of Isaac. In, Tickner, Frederick James,
ed. Earlier English Drama from Robin Hood to Everyman.
(New York, [1929]), pp. 73-82.

4897 [Abraham's sacrifice of Isaac]. In, Purvis, J. S. The York Cycle
of Mystery Plays. (London, 1962), pp. 58-67.

The Departure of the Israelites from Egypt

4898 The departure of the Israelites from Egypt, the ten plagues, and
the passage of the Red Sea. In, Smith, Lucy Toulmin, ed.
York Plays. (Oxford, 1885), pp. 68-92.

4899 [The departure of the Israelites from Egypt, the ten plagues,
and the passage of the Red Sea]. In, Purvis, J. S. The York
Cycle of Mystery Plays. (London, 1962), pp. 68-78.

The Annunciation, and Visit of Elizabeth to Mary

4900 The Annunciation, and Visit of Elizabeth to Mary. In, Smith,
Lucy Toulmin, ed. York Plays. (Oxford, 1885), pp. 93-101.

4901 The Annunciation [lines 1-196]. In, Mooney, Margaret S., Compiler. A Rosary of Mystery Plays. (Albany, New York, 1915),
pp. 21-27.

4902 The Visitation. In, Mooney, Margaret S. A Rosary of Mystery
Plays. (Albany, New York, 1915), pp. 28-30. [Lines 197-
240].

4903 The Annunciation. In, Osgood, Phillips E., ed. Old-Time Church
Drama Adapted. (New York, 1928), pp. 137-139. [Adaptation
of lines 145-192].

4904 [Annunciation, and Visit of Elizabeth to Mary]. The Spicer's Play.
In, Purvis, J. S., ed. The York Cycle of Mystery Plays. A
Shorter Version. (London, 1951).

4905 [The Annunciation, and visit of Elizabeth to Mary]. In, Purvis,
J. S. The York Cycle of Mystery Plays. (London, 1962), pp.
79-85.

Joseph's Trouble about Mary

4906 Joseph's Trouble about Mary. In, Smith, Lucy Toulmin, ed.
         York Plays. (Oxford, 1885), pp. 102-111.

4907 Joseph's Return. In, Hemingway, Samuel B., ed. English Nati-
         vity Plays. (New York, 1909), pp. 130-140.

4908 [Joseph's Trouble about Mary]. The Pewterers and Founders'
         Play. In, Purvis, J. S., ed. The York Cycle of Mystery Plays.
         A Shorter Version. (London, 1951).

4909 [Joseph's trouble about Mary]. In, Purvis, J. S. The York Cycle
         of Mystery Plays. (London, 1962), pp. 86-93.

4910 Joseph. In, Hemingway, Samuel B., ed. English Nativity Plays.
         (New York, 1964).

The Journey to Bethlehem; the Birth of Jesus

4911 The Journey to Bethlehem; the Birth of Jesus. In, Smith, Lucy
         Toulmin, ed. York Plays. (Oxford, 1885), pp. 112-117.

4912 The Journey to Bethlehem; the Birth of Jesus. In, Hemingway,
         Samuel B., ed. English Nativity Plays. (New York, 1909),
         pp. 141-146.

4913 The Journey to Bethlehem; the Birth of Jesus. In, Mooney,
         Margaret S. A Rosary of Mystery Plays. (Albany, New York,
         1915), pp. 31-35.

4914 The Birth of Jesus. In, Adams, Joseph Q., ed. Chief Pre-
         Shakespearean Dramas. (Boston, 1924), pp. 142-144.

4915 The Journey to Bethlehem. In, Brandl, A., and O. Zippel. Mit-
         telenglische Sprach-und Literaturproben. (Berlin, 1927), pp.
         204-205.

4916 Birth of Jesus. In, Osgood, Phillips E., ed. Old-Time Church
         Drama Adapted. (New York, 1928), pp. 139-146. [Adaptation].

4917 Birth of Jesus. In, Frost, Lesley, ed. Come Christmas. (New
         York, 1929), pp. 198-204.

4918 The York Nativity: a Miracle Play Based on the York Cycle and

Freely Arranged for Production. Edited by John F. Baird.
New York: S. French, 1932. 34 pp.
MnU.

4919 Nativity Play. In, Browne, E. Martin, ed. Religious Plays for
Use in Churches. (London, 1932).

4920 The York Nativity Play; Adapted from the York Mystery Cycle.
E. Martin Browne, Arranger. London: Allan, 1932. 47 pp.
(Religious Plays, Series No. 5.)
BM. (1952, Revised edition).

4921 The Journey to Bethlehem. In, Brandl, A., and O. Zippel, eds.
2nd ed. Mittelenglische Sprach-und Literaturproben. (Berlin,
1947), pp. 204-205.

4922 [Journey to Bethlehem: Birth of Jesus]. The Tile Thatchers'
Play. In, Purvis, J. S., ed. The York Cycle of Mystery Plays.
A Shorter Version. (London, 1951).

4923 The Birth of Christ. In, Browne, E. Martin, ed. Mystery and
Morality Plays. (New York, 1960), pp. 96-101.

4924 Nativity. In, Malcolmson, Anne. Seven Medieval Plays for
Modern Players. (London, 1960).

4925 [The Journey to Bethlehem; the Birth of Jesus]. In, Purvis, J. S.
The York Cycle of Mystery Plays. (London, 1962), pp. 94-98.

The Angels and the Shepherds

4926 The Angels and the Shepherds. In, Smith, Lucy Toulmin, ed.
York Plays. (Oxford, 1885), pp. 118-122.

4927 The Angels and the Shepherds. In, Hemingway, Samuel B., ed.
English Nativity Plays. (New York, 1909), pp. 147-151.

4928 The Angels and the Shepherds. In, Brandl, A., and O. Zippel,
eds. Mittelenglische Sprach-und Literaturproben. (Berlin,
1917), pp. 205-207.

4929 The Angels and the Shepherds. In, Osgood, Phillips E. Old-Time
Church Drama Adapted. (New York, 1928), pp. 146-152.
[Adaptation].

4930 Play of the Shepherds. In, Feasey, Lynette. Old English at Play.
      (London, 1944).

4931 The Angels and the Shepherds. In, Brandl, A., and O. Zippel,
      eds. Mittelenglische Sprach-und Literaturproben. 2nd ed.
      (Berlin, 1947).

4932 [The Angels and the Shepherds]. The Chandlers' Play. In, Purvis,
      J. S., ed. The York Cycle of Mystery Plays. A Shorter Ver-
      sion. (London, 1951).

4933 [The Angels and the Shepherds]. In, Purvis, J. S. The York
      Cycle of Mystery Plays. (London, 1962), pp. 99-102.

4934 Shepherds. In, Hemingway, Samuel B., ed. English Nativity
      Plays. (New York, 1964), pp. 147-151.

The Coming of the Three Kings to Herod

4935 The Coming of the Three Kings to Herod. In, Smith, Lucy Toulmin,
      ed. York Plays. (Oxford, 1885), pp. 123-125.

4936 The Coming of the Three Kings to Herod. In, Osgood, Phillips E.
      Old-Time Church Drama Adapted. (New York, 1928), pp.
      155-162. [Adaptation of York 16, and lines 73-216 of York 17.]

The Coming of the Three Kings to Herod; the Adoration

4937 The Coming of the Three Kings to Herod; the Adoration. In,
      Smith, Lucy Toulmin, ed. York Plays. (Oxford, 1885), pp.
      126-137.

4938 The Meeting of the Three Kings. In, Osgood, Phillip E. Old-Time
      Church Drama Adapted. (New York, 1928), pp. 152-155.
      [Adaptation of lines 217-304, and lines 26-36 of York No. 18
      is printed on pp. 163-167, as "The Adoration of the Three
      Kings."]

4939 [Coming of the Three Kings, the Adoration]. The Goldsmiths'
      Play. In, Purvis, J. S., ed. The York Cycle of Mystery
      Plays. A Shorter Version. (London, 1951).

4940 [The coming of the three Kings to Herod]. In, Purvis, J. S. The
      York Cycle of Mystery Plays. (London, 1962), pp. 103-113.
      [Includes the Adoration].

4941 The Three Kings. In, Franklin, Alexander, ed. Seven Miracle
        Plays: Cain and Abel, Noah's Flood, Abraham and Isaac, The
        Shepherds, The Three Kings, and Adam and Eve. (London and
        New York, 1963), pp. 94-107.

4942 The Three Kings. In, Franklin, Alexander, ed. Seven Miracle
        Plays: Cain and Abel, Noah's Flood, Abraham and Isaac,
        The Shepherds, The Three Kings, and Adam and Eve. (Lon-
        don and New York, 1965), pp. 94-107.

The Flight into Egypt

4943 The Flight into Egypt. In, Smith, Lucy Toulmin, ed. York Plays.
        (Oxford, 1885), pp. 138-145.

4944 [Flight into Egypt]. The Marshalls' Play. In, Purvis, J. S., ed.
        The York Cycle of Mystery Plays. A Shorter Version.
        (London, 1951).

4945 [The Flight into Egypt]. In, Purvis, J. S. The York Cycle of Mys-
        tery Plays. (London, 1962), pp. 114-120.

The Massacre of the Innocents

4946 The Massacre of the Innocents. In, Smith, Lucy Toulmin, ed.
        York Plays. (Oxford, 1885), pp. 146-155.

4947 [The Massacre of the Innocents]. In, Purvis, J. S. The York
        Cycle of Mystery Plays. (London, 1962), pp. 132-139.

Christ with the Doctors in the Temple

4948 Christ with the Doctors in the Temple. In, Smith, Lucy Toulmin,
        ed. York Plays. (Oxford, 1885), pp. 156-171.

4949 Christ with the Doctors in the Temple. In, Mooney, Margaret
        S. A Rosary of Mystery Plays. (Albany, New York, 1915),
        pp. 52-61.

4950 [Christ with the Doctors in the Temple]. In, Purvis, J. S. The
        York Cycle of Mystery Plays. (London, 1962), pp. 140-147.

The Baptism of Jesus

4951 The Baptism of Jesus. In, Smith, Lucy Toulmin, ed. York Plays.
        (Oxford, 1885), pp. 172-177.

4952 [Baptism of Jesus]. The Barbers' Play. In, Purvis, J. S., ed. The York Cycle of Mystery Plays. A Shorter Version. (London, 1951).

4953 [The Baptism of Jesus]. In, Purvis, J. S. The York Cycle of Mystery Plays. (London, 1962), pp. 148-152.

The Temptation of Jesus

4954 The Temptation of Jesus. In, Smith, Lucy Toulmin, ed. York Plays. (Oxford, 1885), pp. 178-184.

4955 [Temptation of Jesus]. The Locksmiths Play. In, Purvis, J. S., ed. The York Cycle of Mystery Plays. A Shorter Version. (London, 1951).

4956 The Temptation of Christ. In, Browne, E. Martin, ed. Mystery and Morality Plays. (New York, 1960), pp. 150-156.

4957 [The Temptation of Jesus]. In, Purvis, J. S. The York Cycle of Mystery Plays. (London, 1962), pp. 153-158.

The Transfiguration

4958 The Transfiguration. In, Smith, Lucy Toulmin, ed. York Plays. (Oxford, 1885), pp. 185-192.

4959 [The Transfiguration]. In, Purvis, J. S. The York Cycle of Mystery Plays. (London, 1962), pp. 159-165.

The Woman Taken in Adultery

4960 The Woman Taken in Adultery. The raising of Lazarus. In, Smith, Lucy Toulmin, ed. York Plays. (Oxford, 1885), pp. 193-200.

4961 [Woman Taken in Adultery, Raising of Lazarus]. The Capmakers' Play. In, Purvis, J. S., ed. The York Cycle of Mystery Plays. A Shorter Version. (London, 1951).

4962 [The Woman Taken in Adultery]. In, Purvis, J. S. The York Cycle of Mystery Plays. (London, 1962), pp. 166-171.

The Entry into Jerusalem upon the Ass

4963 The Entry into Jerusalem upon the Ass. In, Smith, Lucy Toulmin, ed. York Plays. (Oxford, 1885), pp. 201-218.

4964 [Entry into Jerusalem]. The Skinners' Play. In, Purvis, J. S., ed. The York Cycle of Mystery Plays. A Shorter Version. (London, 1951).

4965 Palm Sunday [Entry into Jerusalem]. In, Browne, E. Martin, ed. Mystery and Morality Plays. (New York, 1960), pp. 168-186.

4966 [The entry into Jerusalem upon the Ass]. In, Purvis, J. S. The York Cycle of Mystery Plays. (London, 1962), pp. 172-185.

The Conspiracy to Take Jesus

4967 The Conspiracy to Take Jesus. In, Smith, Lucy Toulmin, ed. York Plays. (Oxford, 1885), pp. 219-232.

4968 [Conspiracy to Take Jesus]. The Cutlers' Play. In, Purvis, J. S., ed. The York Cycle of Mystery Plays. A Shorter Version. (London, 1951).

4969 [The conspiracy to take Jesus]. In, Purvis, J. S. The York Cycle of Mystery Plays. (London, 1962), pp. 186-195.

The Last Supper

4970 The Last Supper. In, Smith, Lucy Toulmin, ed. York Plays. (Oxford, 1885), pp. 233-239.

4971 [The Last Supper]. In, Purvis, J. S. The York Cycle of Mystery Plays. (London, 1962), pp. 196-200.

The Agony and the Betrayal

4972 The Agony and the Betrayal. In, Smith, Lucy Toulmin, ed. York Plays. (Oxford, 1885), pp. 240-253.

4973 Christ's Agony in the Garden. In, Mooney, Margaret S. A Rosary of Mystery Plays. (Albany, New York, 1915), pp. 63-68.

4974 [The Agony and the Betrayal]. The Cordwainers Play. In, Purvis, J. S., ed. The York Cycle of Mystery Plays. A Shorter Version. (London, 1951).

4975 [The Agony and the Betrayal]. In, Purvis, J. S. The York Cycle
     of Mystery Plays. (London, 1962), pp. 201-209.

Peter Denies Jesus. Jesus Examined by Caiaphas

4976 Peter denies Jesus. Jesus Examined by Caiaphas. In, Smith,
     Lucy Toulmin. ed. York Plays. (Oxford, 1885), pp. 254-269.

4977 [Peter Denies Jesus: Jesus Examined by Caiaphas]. The Bowyers'
     and Fletchers' Play. In, Purvis, J. S., ed. The York Cycle
     of Mystery Plays. A Shorter Version. (London, 1951).

4978 [Peter denies Jesus; Jesus examined by Caiaphas]. In, Purvis,
     J. S. The York Ctcle of Mystery Plays. (London, 1962),
     pp. 210-220.

The Dream of Pilate's Wife; Jesus Before Pilate

4979 The Dream of Pilate's Wife; Jesus Before Pilate. In, Smith,
     Lucy Toulmin, ed. York Plays. (Oxford, 1885), pp. 270-
     291.

4980 [Dream of Pilate's Wife: Jesus before Pilate]. The Tapestry
     Makers' Play. In, Purvis, J. S., ed. The York Cycle of Mys-
     tery Plays. A Shorter Version. (London, 1951).

4981 [The Dream of Pilate's Wife: Jesus before Pilate]. In, Purvis,
     J. S. The York Cycle of Mystery Plays. (London, 1962), pp.
     221-235.

Trial Before Herod

4982 Trial Before Herod. In, Smith, Lucy Toulmin, ed. York Plays.
     (Oxford, 1885), 292-306.

4983 [Trial before Herod]. In, Purvis, J. S. The York Cycle Mystery
     Plays. (London, 1962), pp. 236-247.

Second Accusation before Pilate; Remorse of Judas,
   and Purchase of Field of Blood

4984 Second Accusation before Pilate; Remorse of Judas, and Purchase
     of Field of Blood. In, Smith, Lucy Toulmin, ed. York Plays.
     (Oxford, 1885), pp. 307-319.

4985 [Second Accusation before Pilate; Remorse of Judas; Purchase of
      Field of Blood]. The Cooks' and Waterleaders' Play. In, Purvis,
      J. S., ed. The York Cycle of Mystery Plays. A Shorter Version.
      (London, 1951).

4986 The Second Trial Before Pilate: The Scourging and Condemnation.
      In, Browne, E. Martin, ed. Mystery and Morality Plays.
      (New York, 1960), pp. 187-210.

4987 [Second accusation before Pilate; remorse of Judas, and Purchase
      of Field of Blood]. In, Purvis, J. S. The York Cycle of Mys-
      tery Plays. (London, 1962), pp. 248-258.

The Second Trial before Pilate Continued;
   the Judgment of Jesus

4988 The Second Trial before Pilate Continued; the Judgment of Jesus.
      In, Smith, Lucy Toulmin, ed. York Plays. (Oxford, 1885),
      pp. 320-336.

4989 The Scourging of Jesus by Pilate's Order (lines 1-386). The
      Crowning of Jesus with Thorns (lines 387-485). In, Mooney,
      Margaret S. A Rosary of Miracle Plays. (Albany, New York,
      1915), pp. 69-86.

4990 [Second Trial continued: Judgment of Jesus]. The Tilemakers'
      Play. In, Purvis, J. S., ed. The York Cycle of Mystery Plays.
      A Shorter Version. (London, 1951).

4991 [Second Trial before Pilate continued; the Judgment of Jesus].
      In, Purvis, J. S. The York Cycle of Mystery Plays. (London,
      1962), pp. 259-272.

Christ Led up to Calvary

4992 Christ Led up to Calvary. In, Smith, Lucy Toulmin, ed. York
      Plays. (Oxford, 1885), pp. 337-348.

4993 Christ Led Up to Calvary. Mooney, Margaret S. A Rosary of
      Mystery Plays. (Albany, New York, 1915), pp. 87-98.

4994 [Christ Led up to Calvary]. The Shearmens' Play. In, Purvis,
      J. S., ed. The York Cycle of Mystery Plays. A Shorter
      Version. (London, 1951).

4995 [Christ led up to Calvary]. In, Purvis, J. S. The York Cycle of
      Mystery Plays. (London, 1962), pp. 273-281.

Crucifixio Cristi

4996 Crucifixio Cristi. In, Smith, Lucy Toulmin, ed. York Plays.
      (Oxford, 1885), pp. 349-358.

4997 Crucifixio Cristi. In, Mooney, Margaret S. A Rosary of Mys-
      tery Plays. (Albany, New York, 1915), pp. 99-108.

4998 [Crucifixio Christi]. The Pinners' and Painters' Play. In, Purvis,
      J. S., ed. The York Cycle of Mystery Plays. A Shorter Ver-
      sion. (London, 1951).

4999 Crucifixion. In, Heilman, Robert B. An Anthology of English
      Drama before Shakespeare. (New York, 1952), pp. 11-22.

5000 The Crucifixion. In, Cawley, A. C., ed. Everyman and Medieval
      Miracle Plays. (New York, 1959), pp. 143-155.

5001 The Crucifixion. In, Browne, E. Martin, ed. Mystery and Moral-
      ity Plays. (New York, 1960), pp. 211-221.

5002 [Crucifixio Cristi]. In, Purvis, J. S. The York Cycle of Mystery
      Plays. (London, 1962), pp. 282-289.

Mortificacio Cristi

5003 Mortificacio Cristi [and burial of Jesus]. In, Smith, Lucy Toulmin,
      ed. York Plays. (Oxford, 1885), pp. 358-371.

5004 [Mortificacio Christi]. The Butchers' Play. In, Purvis, J. S., ed.
      The York Cycle of Mystery Plays. A Shorter Version. (Lon-
      don, 1951).

5005 [Mortificacio Cristi (and burial of Jesus)]. In, Purvis, J. S. The
      York Cycle of Mystery Plays. (London, 1962), pp. 290-300.

The Harrowing of Hell

5006 The Harrowing of Hell. In, Smith, Lucy Toulmin, ed. York
      Plays. (Oxford, 1885), pp. 372-395.

5007 [Harrowing of Hell]. The Sadlers' Play. In, Purvis, J. S., ed.

The York Cycle of Mystery Plays. A Shorter Version. (London, 1951).

5008 The Harrowing of Hell. In, Browne, E. Martin, ed. Mystery and Morality Plays. (New York, 1960), pp. 222-236.

5009 [The Harrowing of Hell]. In, Purvis, J. S. The York Cycle of Mystery Plays. (London, 1962), pp. 301-311.

The Resurrection; Fright of the Jews

5010 The Resurrection; Fright of the Jews. In, Smith, Lucy Toulmin, ed. York Plays. (Oxford, 1885), pp. 396-420.

5011 The Resurrection. In, Manly, J. M., ed. Specimens of the Pre-Shaksperean Drama. Vol. 1. (Boston, 1897), pp. 153-169.

5012 The Resurrection. In, Mooney, Margaret Sullivan, Comp. A Rosary of Mystery Plays. (Albany, 1915), pp. 109-127.

5013 [Resurrection, Fright of the Jews]. The Carpenters' Play. In, Purvis, J. S., ed. The York Cycle of Mystery Plays. A Shorter Version. (London, 1951).

5014 The Resurrection. In, Cawley, A. C., ed. Everyman and Medieval Miracle Plays. (New York, 1959), pp. 171-188.

5015 [The Resurrection; Fright of the Jews]. In, Purvis, J. S. The York Cycle of Mystery Plays. (London, 1962), pp. 312-323.

Jesus Appears to Mary Magdalene after the Resurrection

5016 Jesus Appears to Mary Magdalene after the Resurrection. In, Smith, Lucy Toulmin, ed. York Plays. (Oxford, 1885), pp. 421-425.

5017 [Jesus Appears to Mary Magdalen after the Resurrection]. The Winedrawers' Play. In, Purvis, J. S., ed. The York Cycle of Mystery Plays. A Shorter Version. (London, 1951).

5018 [Jesus appears to Mary Magdalene after the Resurrection]. In, Purvis, J. S. The York Cycle of Mystery Plays. (London, 1962), pp. 324-327.

The Travellers to Emmaus Meet Jesus

5019 The Travellers to Emmaus Meet Jesus. In, Smith, Lucy Toulmin,
        ed. York Plays. (Oxford, 1885), pp. 426-432.

5020 [The Travellers to Emmaus meet Jesus]. In, Purvis, J. S. The
        York Cycle of Mystery Plays. (London, 1962), pp. 328-333.

The Purification of Mary; Simeon and Anna Prophesy

5021 The Purification of Mary: Simeon and Anna Prophesy. In, Smith,
        Lucy Toulmin, ed. York Plays. (Oxford, 1885), pp. 433-447.

5022 The Presentation of the Child Jesus. In, Mooney, Margaret S. A
        Rosary of Mystery Plays. (Albany, New York, 1915), pp. 36-51.

5023 [The Purification of Mary; Simeon and Anna Prophesy]. In, Purvis,
        J. S. The York Cycle of Mystery Plays. (London, 1962), pp.
        120-131.

The Incredulity of Thomas

5024 "A Pageant Play, Copied from an Original MSS. amongst the
        Archives at Guildhall, York." In, [Croft, John]. Excerpta
        Antiqua; or, A Collection of Original Manuscripts. York:
        Printed by William Blanchard [1797]. [4], 112 pp. [See pages
        105-110].
              ICN.

5025 The Mystery of the Disbelief of Thomas. In, Halliwell-Phillipps,
        J. O. Yorkshire Anthology. (London, 1851), pp. 198-204.

5026 The Incredulity of St. Thomas. From a Manuscript in the Posses-
        sion of John Sykes, Esq. M.D. of Doncaster. Edited by J.
        Payne Collier. Printed for the Camden Society, 1859. 18 pp.
        (The Camden Miscellany, Vol. 4 [No. 3]).
              BM. ICN.

5027 The Incredulity of Thomas. In, Smith, Lucy Toulmin, ed. York
        Plays. (Oxford, 1885), pp. 448-455.

5028 [Incredulity of Thomas]. The Scriveners' Play. In, Purvis, J. S.,
        ed. The York Cycle of Mystery Plays. A Shorter Version.
        (London, 1951).

5029 [The Incredulity of Thomas]. In, Purvis, J. S. The York Cycle
of Mystery Plays. (London, 1962), pp. 334-339.

The Ascension

5030 The Ascension. In, Smith, Lucy Toulmin, ed. York Plays.
(Oxford, 1885), pp. 456-464.

5031 The Ascension. In, Mooney, Margaret Sullivan, Comp. A
Rosary of Mystery Plays. (Albany, 1915), pp. 128-136.

5032 [The Ascension]. The Tailors' Play. In, Purvis, J. S., ed. The
York Cycle of Mystery Plays. A Shorter Version. (London,
1951).

5033 The Ascension. In, Browne, E. Martin, ed. Mystery and Morality Plays. (New York, 1960), pp. 246-254.

5034 [The Ascension]. In, Purvis, J. S. The York Cycle of Mystery
Plays. (London, 1962), pp. 340-347.

The Descent of the Holy Spirit

5035 The Descent of the Holy Spirit. In, Smith, Lucy Toulmin, ed.
York Plays. (Oxford, 1885), pp. 465-472.

5036 The Descent of the Holy Spirit. In, Mooney, Margaret Sullivan,
Comp. A Rosary of Mystery Plays. (Albany, 1915), pp. 137-
144.

5037 [The Descent of the Holy Spirit]. In, Purvis, J. S. The York
Cycle of Mystery Plays. (London, 1962), pp. 348-353.

The Death of Mary

5038 The Death of Mary. In, Smith, Lucy Toulmin, ed. York Plays.
(Oxford, 1885), pp. 473-479.

5039 [The Death of Mary]. In, Purvis, J. S. The York Cycle of Mystery Plays. (London, 1962), pp. 354-359.

The Appearance of Our Lady to Thomas

5040 The Appearance of Our Lady to Thomas. In, Smith, Lucy Toulmin,
ed. York Plays. (Oxford, 1885), pp. 480-490.

5041 [The Appearance of our Lady to Thomas]. In, Purvis, J. S. The
       York Cycle of Mystery Plays. (London, 1962), pp. 360-367.

The Assumption and Coronation of the Virgin

5042 The Assumption and Coronation of the Virgin. In, Smith, Lucy
       Toulmin, ed. York Plays. (Oxford, 1885), pp. 491-496.

5043 The Assumption and Coronation of the Virgin. In, Mooney, Mar-
       garet S. A Rosary of Mystery Plays. (Albany, 1915), pp. 145-
       147.

5044 [The Assumption and Coronation of the Virgin]. In, Purvis, J. S.
       The York Cycle of Mystery Plays. (London, 1962), pp. 368-
       372.

The Judgment Day

5045 The Judgment Day. In, Smith, Lucy Toulmin, ed. York Plays.
       (Oxford, 1885), pp. 497-513.

5046 The Judgment Day. In, Manly, J. M., ed. Specimens of Pre-
       Shaksperean Drama. Vol. 1. (Boston, 1897), pp. 198-211.

5047 The Judgment Day. In, Adams, Joseph Quincy, ed. Chief Pre-
       Shakespearean Dramas. (Boston, New York, 1924), pp.
       199-204.

5048 The Judgment Day. In, Schweikert, H. C. Early English Plays.
       (New York [1928]), pp. 128-138.

5049 The Judgment. In, Cawley, A. C., ed. Everyman and Medieval
       Miracle Plays. (New York, 1959), pp. 189-203.

5050 The Last Judgment. In, Browne, E. Martin, ed. Mystery and
       Morality Plays. (New York, 1960), pp. 255-266.

5051 [The Judgment Day]. In, Purvis, J. S. The York Cycle of Mys-
       tery Plays. (London, 1962), pp. 373-382.

[The Coronation of Our Lady]

5052 [The Coronation of Our Lady]. In, Smith, Lucy Toulmin, ed.
       York Plays. (Oxford, 1885), pp. 514-515.

5053 [Coronation of Our Lady]. The Mercers' Play. In, Purvis, J.
S., ed. The York Cycle of Mystery Plays. A Shorter Version.
(London, 1951).

5054 [A fragment? of a Coronation]. In, Purvis, J. S. The York Cycle
of Mystery Plays. (London, 1962), pp. 383-384.

Composite Play

5055 Wright, Paul H., ed. The Word of God: a Miracle Play Adapted
from the Mediaeval York Cycle [Plays 1-18, 41]. With an
Introduction by the Rev. Paul Pinchard. York: The Church
Shop, 1926. 39, [1] pp.
BM. NN. NNC.

Studies
5056 Drake, Francis. Eboracum: or, The History and Antiquities
of the City of York, from its Original to the Present Times.
Together with the History of the Cathedral Church, and the
lives of the Archbishops of that See . . . Collected from Auth-
entick Manuscripts, Publick Records, Ancient Chronicles,
and Modern Historians. 2 vol. in 1. London: Printed by W.
Bowyer for the authors, 1736.
BM. CtY.

*5057 The History and Antiquities of the City of York, from Its Origin
to the Present Time. 3 vol. York: Printed by A. Ward, 1785.
BM. CtY.

5058 Hargrove, William. History and Description of the Ancient City
of York; Comprising All the Most Interesting Information,
Already Published in Drake's Eboracum; Enriched with
Much Entirely New Matter, from Other Authentic Sources.
2 vol. York: W. Alexander, 1816.
BM. CtY.

5059 Davies, Robert. Extracts from the Municipal Records of the City
of York, during the Reigns of Edward IV, Edward V, and
Richard III. With Notes Illustrative and Explanatory; and an
Appendix, Containing Some Account of the Celebration of the
Corpus Christi Festival at York, in the Fourteenth, Fifteenth,
and Sixteenth Centuries. London: J. B. Nichols and Son,
Printers, 1843. vii, 304 pp.
BM. MiU.

5060 Sheahan, James Joseph, comp. History and Topography of the
         City of York; and the North Riding of Yorkshire; Embracing
         a General Review of the Early History of Great Britain, and
         a General History and Description of the County of York. 2
         vol. Beverley: Printed for the Publishers, [T. Whellan and Co.]
         by J. Green, 1857-1859.
             BM. CtY.

*5061 [Skaife, Robert H.]. The Register of the Guild of Corpus Christi
         in the City of York; With an Appendix of Illustrative Documents,
         Containing Some Account of the Hospital of St. Thomas of Can-
         terbury, Without Micklegate-Bar in the Suburbs of the City.
         Durham: Andrews and Co.; London: Bernard Quaritch; Edin-
         burgh: Blackwood and Sons, 1872. xvi, 362, [1] pp.
             BM.

5062 Raine, James, ed. The Historians of the Church of York and Its
         Archbishops. 3 vol. London: Longman, 1879-1894. (Chronicles
         and memorials of Great Britain and Ireland during the Middle
         Ages. "Rolls series").
             BM.

5063 "The Ashburnham MS. of the York Mystery Plays." Academy,
         XXII (July 1, 1882), 9-10.

5064 Ornsby, George. York. Published under the Direction of the
         Tract Committee. London: Society for Promoting Christian
         Knowledge; New York: E. and J. B. Young and Co., [1882].
         440 pp. (Diocesan histories.)
             BM. CtY.

5065 Andrews, William. Historic Yorkshire. London: Reeves &
         Turner; Leeds: F. R. Spark [1884]. 204 pp. [See, "Mys-
         tery Plays in Yorkshire," pp. 36-44.]
             BM.

5066 Herttrich, Oswald. Studien zu den York Plays. Breslau: Buch-
         druckerei Lindner, 1886. [4], 31, [2] pp.
             CtY. MH. MnU. NN.

5067 Kamann, P. "Die Quellen der York-Spiele." Anglia, X (1887),
         189-226.

5068 Kamann, Paul Julius Gustav. Über Quellen und Sprache der
         York Plays. Halle, a.S.: Druck von E. Karras, 1887. [4],
         75, [1] pp.

BM. CtY. DLC. IaU. MB. MH. MiU. MnU. NjP. OCU.

5069 Herford, I. S. A. "Joseph and His Brethren: A Modern Yorkshire Mystery." New Englander, LI (1889), 284-299.

5070 Hohlfeld, Alex. "Altenglischen Kollektivmisterien, Unter besond-erer Berücksichtigung des Verhaltnisses der York-und Towneley-Spiele." Anglia, XI (1889), 219-310.

5071 Holthausen, F. "Beiträge zur Erklärung und Text Kritik der York Plays." Archiv für das Studium der neuren Sprachen und Liter-aturen, LXXXV (1890), 411-428.

5072 ----- "Nachtrag zu den Quellen der York Plays." Archiv für das Studium der neuren und Literaturen, LXXXVI (1891), 280-282. [Continuation].

*5073 Davidson, Charles. "Studies in the English Mystery Plays." Transactions of the Connecticut Academy of Arts and Sciences, IX (1892), 125-297.

5074 Rowe, Henry Kalloch. "The Corpus Christi Plays at York." Brown Magazine, III (1892), 110-114.

5075 Coblentz, H. E. "A Rime-Index to the Parent Cycle of the York Mystery Plays and a Portion of the Woodkirk Conspiracio et Capito." Publications of the Modern Language Association, X (1895), 487-557.

5076 ----- "Some Suggested Rime Emendations to the York Mystery Plays." Modern Language Notes, X (1895), 39-41; 77-81.

*5077 Kölbing, Eugen. "Beiträge zur Erklärung und Textkritik der York Plays." Englische Studien, XX (1895), 179-220.

5078 Holthausen, F. "Zur Textkritik der York Plays." Philologische Studien; Festgabe für Eduard Sievers zum 1. Oktober, 1896. (Halle, 1896), pp. 30-37.

5079 [Collins, Francis, ed.]. Register of the Freemen of the City of York, from the City Records 1272-1759. 2 vol. Durham: Andrews and Co., for the Society, 1897-1900. (Surtees Society Publications, Vols. 96, 102).
    BM. CtY. ICN.

5080 Holthausen, F. "Zu Alt- und Mittelenglischen Dichtungen."
      Anglia, XII (1899), 443-452.

5081 Hagen, Sivert N. "The Norse Loan-Words in the York Mystery
      Plays." Ph.D. Johns Hopkins University, 1900.

5082 Luick, Karl. "Zur Textkritik der Spiele von York." Anglia,
      XXII (1900), 384-391.

5083 Craigie, W. A. "The Gospels of Nicodemus and the York Mystery
      Plays." An English Miscellany: Presented to Dr. Furnivall.
      (Oxford, 1901), pp. 52-61.

5084 Chambers, E. K. "York Plays." The Mediaeval Stage. Vol. 2.
      (London, 1903), pp. 409-412.

5085 ----- "York, Yorkshire." The Mediaeval Stage. Vol. 2. (Lon-
      don, 1903), pp. 399-406.

5086 Gaaf, W. van der. "Miracles and Mysteries in South-East
      Yorkshire." Englische Studien, XXXVI (1906), 228-230.

5087 Sorg, Edward. "Miracles and Mysteries in Southeast Yorkshire."
      Englische Studien, XXXVII (1907), 172-173.

5088 Taylor, George C. "The Relation of the English Corpus Christi
      Play to the Middle English Lyric." Modern Philology, V
      (July, 1907), 1-38.

5089 Cooper, Thomas Parsons. "The Armorial Bearings of the Old
      Craft Guilds and Companies." The Book of the York Pageant
      1909. (York, 1909).

5090 O'Neill, F. "Blessed Virgin in the York Cycle of Miracle Plays."
      American Catholic Quarterly Review, XXXIV (1909), 439-
      455.

5091 Holthausen, F. "Zur Erklärung und Text Kritik der York Plays."
      Englische Studien, LXI (1910), 380-384.

5092 Livingston, A. A. "Some Early Italian Parallels to the Locution
      'the Sick Man of the East.'" Publications of the Modern
      Language Association, XXV (1910), 459-484.

5093 Bates, A. B. "York Pageant and Others." Chautauquan, LXII

(1911), 226-237.

5094 Foster, Frances A. "The Mystery Plays and the Northern Pas-
      sion." Modern Language Notes, XXVI (June, 1911), 169-171.

5095 Sellers, Maud, ed. York Memorandum Book. Lettered A/Y in
      the Guild-Hall Muniment Room. 2 vol. Durham: Published
      for the Society by Andrews and Co., etc., 1912-1915.
      (Publications of the Surtees Society, CXX, CXXV).
      BM. DLC.

*5096 Greg, Walter W. "Bibliographical and Textual Problems of the
      English Miracle Cycles." The Library, Third Series, V
      (1914), 280-319.

5097 Haller, Julius. "Der Dialog in den York-Spielen." Die Technik
      des Dialogs im mittelalterlichen Drama Englands. (Worms,
      1916), pp. 29-42.

5098 Pierson, Merle. "York." In, "The Relation of the Corpus Christi
      Procession to the Corpus Christi Play in England." Trans-
      actions of the Wisconsin Academy of Sciences, Arts, and
      Letters, XVIII (1916), 149-155.

*5099 Wells, John Edwin. "The York Plays." A Manual of the Writings
      in Middle English, 1050-1400. (New Haven, 1916-1951),
      pp. 551-555, 859-860, 1025, 1080, 1137, 1228, 1282, 1318-
      1319, 1369, 1416-1417, 1468, 1586, 1637, 1682, 1729.

5100 Craig, Hardin. "The Pater Noster Play." Nation, CIV (May 3,
      1917), 563-564.

5101 Wallis, J. P. R. "The Miracle Play of Crucifixio Christi in the
      York Cycle." Modern Language Review, XII (1917), 494-
      495.

5102 Miller, Frances H. "Metrical Affinities of the Shrewsbury
      'Officium Pastorum' and Its York Correspondent." Modern
      Language Notes, XXXIII (1918), 91-95.

*5103 Sellers, Maud, ed. The York Mercers and Merchant Adventurers,
      1356-1917. Durham: Published for the Society by Andrews and
      Co.; London: B. Quaritch, 1918. lxix, 356 pp. (Publications
      of the Surtees Society, CXXIX).
      BM. CtY. DLC.

*5104 Lyle, Marie Caroline. The Original Identity of the York
       and Towneley Cycles. Minneapolis, Minnesota: Uni-
       versity of Minnesota Press, 1919. iv, 113 pp. Biblio-
       graphy, pp. 109-113.
               BM. NN.

5105   Miller, Frances H. "The Northern Passion and the Mys-
       teries." Modern Language Notes, XXXIV (1919), 88-92.

5106   [Greg, W. W.] Emendations to the York Plays from Re-
       views by Joseph Hall and Julius Zupitza, 1885-1886;
       Also from Articles by Holthausen and Luick, [n.p.,
       191?]. 42 pp.
               DLC.

5107   Benson, Edwin. Life in a Mediaeval City, Illustrated by York
       in the XVth Century. London, Society for Promoting
       Christian Knowledge. New York: The Macmillan Co.,
       1920. v, 84 pp.
               BM. CtY.

5108   Miller, Frances H. "Stanzaic Division in York Play XXXIX."
       Modern Language Notes, XXXV (June, 1920), 379-380.

5109   Moore, J. R. "The Tradition of Angelic Singing in English
       Drama." Journal of English and Germanic Philology,
       XXII (1923), 89-99.

*5110 Allison, Tempe E. "The Pater Noster Play and the Origin of
       the Vices." Publications of the Modern Language Association,
       XXXIX (December, 1924), 789-804.

*5111 Dustoor, P. E. "Some Textual Notes on the English Mystery
       Plays." Modern Language Review, XXI (1926), 427-431.

5112   Lindkvist, Harald. "A Study of Early Medieval York." Anglia,
       L (1926), 345-394.

5113   Clark, Eleanor G. "The York Plays and the 'Gospel of Nicode-
       mus." Publications of the Modern Language Association,
       XLIII (March, 1928), 153-161.

5114   Dustoor, P. E. "Textual Notes on the York Old Testament
       Plays." Anglia, LII (March, 1928), 26-36.

5115 Cady, Frank W. "Towneley, York, and True-Coventry." Studies in Philology, XXVI (1929), 386-400.

*5116 Frank, Grace. "On the Relation Between the York and Towneley Plays." Publications of the Modern Language Association, XLIV (1929), 313-319.

5117 ----- "St. Martial of Limoges in the York Plays." Modern Language Notes, XLIV (April, 1929), 233-235.

5118 Lyle, Marie C. "The Original Identity of the York and Towneley Cycles--a Rejoinder." Publications of the Modern Language Association, XLIV (1929), 319-328.

5119 Freeman, Eva. "A Note on Play XXX of the York Cycle." Modern Language Notes, XLV (June, 1930), 392-394.

5120 MacKinnon, Effie. "Some Significant Aspects of the Dramatic Structure of the York Cycle." M.A. Wellsley College, 1930.

5121 Thomas, R. "A Note on Play XXX of the York Cycle." Modern Language Notes, XLV (1930), 392-394.

5122 MacKinnon, Effie. "Notes on the Dramatic Structure of the York Cycle." Studies in Philology, XXVIII (July, 1931), 433-449.

5123 Carroll, O.M.C., Rev. Thomas J. "The Influence of the Festival of Corpus Christi upon the Cycle Plays; with Some Observations About the View-Point of the Cambridge History of Literature." M.A. Catholic University of America, 1932.

5124 Jones, Ellen Mattocks. "Stage Setting and Stage Business in the English Cycles." M.A. University of Minnesota, 1932.

*5125 Young, Karl. "The Records of the York Play of the Pater Noster," (With Text). Speculum, VII (October, 1932), 540-546.

5126 Curtiss, Chester G. "The York and Towneley Plays on 'The Harrowing of Hell.'" Studies in Philology, XXX (1933), 24-33.

5127 Trusler, Margaret. "The York Sacrificium Cayme and Abell." Publications of the Modern Language Association, XLIX (1934), 956-959.

5128 Mill, Anna J. "The York Bakers' Play of the Last Supper."

Modern Language Review, XXX (April, 1935), 145-158.

5129 Frampton, Mendall G. "The Brewbarret Interpolation in the York
Play of the Sacrificium Cayme and Abell." Publications of
the Modern Language Association, LII (September, 1937),
895-900.

5130 Smith, John Harrington. "The Date of Some Wakefield Borrowings from York." Publications of the Modern Language Association, LIII (1938), 595-600.

5131 Raine, Angelo, ed. York Civic Records. I. York Civic Records
Vol. 1. Wakefield: Printed for the Society, 1939. viii, 192
pp. Index.
        BM.

5132 Harney, Sister Mary Camillus. "The Characterization of Cain
and Abel in the English Mystery Plays: York, Chester, Ludus
Coventriae and Towneley Cycles." M.A. Catholic University
of America, 1940.

5133 Sayles, G. "Dissolution of a Gild at York in 1306. With Text
of Assize Roll, No. 1107 (33-35 Edward I) m. 19." English
Historical Review, LV (1940), 83-98.

5134 Scherrinsky, Harald. Untersuchungen zum Sogenannten Anonymus
von York. Ph.D. Berlin University (Humboldt), 1940.

5135 Clark, Sr. Mary Thaddeus. "Drama in the Cyclic Plays of Mediaeval England." M.A. Fordham University, 1941.

5136 Frampton, Mendall G. "The York Play of Christ Led up to Calvary
(Play XXXIV)." Philological Quarterly, XX (July, 1941), 198-
204.

5137 ----- "The York Play of 'Christ Led Up to Calvary' (Play
XXXIV)." Renaissance Studies in Honor of Hardin Craig.
(California, 1941), pp. 6-12.

5138 Lawlor, S.J., Richard Vincent. "The Music and Musical Elements of the Craft Cycles." M.A. Boston College, 1941.

5139 Sullivan, S.S.J., Sr. John. "A Study of the Themes of the Passion in the Medieval Cyclic Drama." Ph.D. Catholic University
of America, 1943.

5140 Reese, Jesse Byers. "The York Plays and the Alliterative Tra-
        dition." Ph.D. University of North Carolina, 1946.

5141 Aquin, Sister M. "Vulgate and Eve-concept in the English Cycles."
        Catholic Biblical Quarterly, IX (1947), 409-435.

5142 Smith, A. H. "A York Pageant, 1486." London Mediaeval Studies,
        I, Part 3 (1948), 382-398. [For 1939].

5143 Homan, Delmar Charles. "A Study in the Medieval Miracle Plays:
        Judgment Day (With Two Plays Modernized)." M.A. University
        of Iowa, 1949.

5144 Hoffman, C. Fenno. "The Source of the Words to the Music in
        York XLVI." Modern Language Notes, LXV (April, 1950),
        236-239.

5145 Mill, Anna J. "The York Plays of the Dying, Assumption, and
        Coronation of Our Lady." Publications of the Modern Language
        Association, LXV (September, 1950), 866-876.

5146 Steinmetz, Charles. "The Preparation of an Acting and Production
        Edition of a Portion [Plays XII-XVII] in the York Cycle Mys-
        tery Play Adapted and Modernized from the Lucy Toulmin
        Smith Version of the Medieval Original." M.A. Catholic Uni-
        versity of America, 1950.

5147 Leeper, J. "York Cycle of Mystery Plays." Spectator, CLXXXVI
        (June 8, 1951), 748.

*5148 Mill, Anna J. "The Stations of the York Corpus Christi Play."
        Yorkshire Archaeological Journal, XXXVII (1951), 492-502.

5149 Read, H. "York Mystery Plays." New Statesman and Nation,
        XLI (June 9, 1951), 650.

5150 Reese, Jesse Byers. "Alliterative Verse in the York Cycle."
        Studies in Philology, XLVIII (July, 1951), 639-668.

5151 Seve, Nicholas Werner de. "The Marian Element in the Four
        Great Cycles." M.A. Columbia University, 1951.

5152 Cawley, A. C. "The Sykes Manuscript of the York Scriveners'
        Play." Leeds Studies in English and Kindred Languages, Nos.
        7/8 (1952), 45-80.

5153 Kirk, R. "York and Social Boredom." Sewanee Review, LXI
      (1953), 664-681.

5154 Flynn, Sister Dolorita. "A Study of the York Cycle Mary Plays."
      M.A. Catholic University of America, 1954.

5155 Purvis, J. S. The Flood; the Fishers' and Mariners' Play. A
      Play from the York Cycle of Mystery Plays. A Version in
      Modern English. [York]: York Festival Society [1954]. 15 pp.
      NN.

5156 "York Mystery Plays, Reviewed in 1951 and Performed Again
      This Year." Illustrated London News, CCIV (July 3, 1954).
      [Photograph]

*5157 Craig, Hardin. "York-Wakefield Plays." English Religious Drama
      of the Middle Ages." (Oxford, 1955), pp. 199-238.

5158 Savage, Donald J. "An Analysis of the Comic Element in the
      Chester, York, Coventry and Towneley Mystery Cycles."
      Ph.D. University of Minnesota, 1955.

5159 Scherer, Judith E. "The Passion Group in the York and Townley
      Cycles: a Study in Origins and Literary Techniques." M.A.
      University of Rochester, 1955.

5160 Stevens, Martin. "The Language of the Towneley Plays. A Com-
      parative Analysis of the Identical York and Towneley Plays,
      The Caesar Augustus, The Talents, and the Stanzas of the
      Wakefield Master." Ph.D. Michigan State University, 1956.

5161 Maltman, Sister Nicholas. "A Study of the Evil Characters in
      the English Corpus Christi Cycles." Ph.D. University of
      California, 1957.

5162 Speaight, Robert. "York Festival." New Statesman, LIII
      (June 29, 1957), 837-838.

5163 Vane, Henry. "Old Religion: The York Festival." Twentieth
      Century, CLXII (August, 1957), 174-177.

5164 Wood, G. Bernard. "Background of the York Mystery Plays."
      Country Life, June 20, 1957, pp. 1274-1275.

5165 Wyatt, Euphemia Van Rensselaer. "York Nativity Cycle: Produc-

1957），384.

5166 Wickham, Glynne. "Players at Selby Abbey, York, 1431-1532."
     Theatre Notebook, XII (Winter, 1958), 46-53.

5167 McDonald, Arthur Warren. "A Study of the York Mercers' Share
     in the Presentation of the Pageants of the Corpus Christi
     Festival." M.A. University of North Carolina, 1959.

5168 Scroggs, Joanna Hill. "A Phonological Study of the Riming Words
     of the York Plays." M.A. University of North Carolina, 1959.

5169 Driver, Tom F. "Misdirected Medievalism: York Mystery Plays."
     Christian Century, LXXVIII (August 10, 1960), 927-928.

5170 Laut, Stephen Joseph. "Drama Illustrating Dogma: A Study of the
     York Cycle." Ph.D. University of North Carolina, 1960.

5171 Prosser, Eleanor. "Cain." Drama and Religion in the English
     Mystery Plays. (Stanford, California, 1961), pp. 74-75.

5172 ----- "Joseph." Drama and Religion in the English Mystery
     Plays. (Stanford, California, 1961), pp. 90-92.

5173 ----- "Thomas." Drama and Religion in the English Mystery
     Plays. (Stanford, California, 1961), pp. 158-159.

5174 ----- "The Woman Taken in Adultery." Drama and Religion in
     the English Mystery Plays. (Stanford, California, 1961), pp.
     103-109.

5175 Young, Mark James. "The York Mystery Cycle As a Theatrical
     Experience, Illustrated by the Nativity Section." Ph.D. Uni-
     versity of Michigan, 1962.

*5176 Brown, Arthur. "Some Notes on Medieval Drama in York."
     Brown, Arthur, and Peter Foote, eds. Early English and
     Norse Studies: Presented to Hugh Smith in Honour of His
     Sixtieth Birthday. (London, 1963), pp. 1-5.

5177 Cozart, William R. "The Northern Middle English Harrowing of
     Hell Plays of the York and Towneley Cycles. An Edition and
     Commentary." Ph.D. Harvard University, 1963.

*5178 Robinson, J. W. "Art of the York Realist." Modern Philology,
         LX (May, 1963), 241-251.

5179 Claridge, Mary. "Blessed Margaret Clitherow and the York Plays."
         Month, XXXI (June, 1964), 347-354.

5180 Johnston, Alexandra Ferguson. "The Christ Figure in the Ministry
         Plays of the Four English Cycles." Ph.D. University of Toronto,
         1964. [Delete].

5181 Macaulay, Peter S. "The Play of the Harrowing of Hell as a Climax
         in the English Mystery Cycles." Studia Germanica Gandensia,
         VIII (1966), 115-134.

5182 Downing, Marjorie D. "The Influence of the Liturgy on the English
         Cycle Plays." Ph.D. Yale University, 1967.

5183 Young, M. James. "The York Pageant Wagon." Speech Monographs,
         XXXIII (1967), 1-20.

5184 Walsh, O.S.B., Sister Mary Margaret. "The Judgment Plays of
         the English Cycles." The American Benedictine Review, XX
         (September, 1969), 378-394.

E. Morality Plays and Interludes

1 General Studies

5185 "Mysteries, Moralities and Other Early Dramas." Retrospective
         Review, I (1820), 332-357.

5186 Lamb, Charles, ed. Specimens of English Dramatic Poets, Who
         Lived About the Time of Shakespeare. With Notes. New ed.
         2 vol. London: E. Moxon, 1835.
                  BM. CSmH. DLC. IaU. ICN. MB. MiU. NN. OC1. PU.

5187 Verney, Lady F. P. "Mysteries, Moralities and the Drama."
         Contemporary Review, XXV (1875), 595-609.

5188 "Morality Plays at Gloucester." Gloucestershire Notes and Queries,
         V (1894), 42-44.

5189 Galloo, E. "Eugénie Grandet." Modern Language Notes, XIV
         (1899), 128.

*5190 Cushman, Lysander W. The Devil and the Vice in the English
Dramatic Literature before Shakespeare. Halle a. S.: Max
Niemeyer, 1900. xiv, 148 pp.
BM. MB. MiU. NjP. NN. OCl. OCU. OU. PU. ViU.

5191 Holthausen, F. "Studien zum älteren englischen Drama."
Englische Studien, XXXI (1902), 77-103.

*5192 Chambers, E. K. "Moralities, Puppet-Plays and Pageants."
The Mediaeval Stage. Vol. 2. (London, 1903), pp. 149-176.

*5193 ----- "Players of Interludes." The Mediaeval Stage. Vol. 2.
(London, 1903), pp. 179-198.

5194 Dodgson, E. S. "Stage on Barrels." Notes and Queries, 9th Ser.,
XII (1903), 503.

5195 Harvey, Florence H. "The Morality Play in the Development of
English Drama." Dial, XXXIV (1903), 296-297.

*5196 Chambers, E. K. Notes on the History of the Revels Office
under the Tudors. London: A. H. Bullen, 1906. 80 pp.
BM. CtY. IaU. ICN. MB. MiU. MnU. NjP. NN. OC1W.
OCU. OU. PBm. PSC. PU.

5197 Moore, E. Hamilton. English Miracle Plays and Moralities.
London: Sherratt and Hughes, 1907. vi, 199 pp.
BM. MB. MiU. MnU. NjP. NN. OCl. OCU. PBm. WU.

*5198 Thompson, E. N. S. "The English Moral Plays." Connecticut
Academy of Arts and Sciences, No. 14 (1910), 291-414.
Bibliography of plays, pp. 404-408. Bibliography, pp. 409-
413.

5199 "The Ancient Morality Play and the Modern One." New English
Magazine, XLV (1911), 301-302.

5200 Fox, Harriet Ruth. "School Drama in England before 1580."
M.A. Columbia University, 1911.

5201 Barley, Joseph Wayne. The Morality Motive in Contemporary
English Drama. Mexico, Missouri: Missouri Printing and
Publishing Co., 1912. 118 pp.
PU.

*5202 Brooke, Charles F. T. Tudor Drama. A History of the English
        National Drama to the Retirement of Shakespeare. New York:
        Houghton, Mifflin and Co., 1912. xii, 461 pp.
               BM. MB. MH. NjP. OC1. OC1W. OU. PSC.

 5203 Dodds, Madeleine H. "Early Political Plays." The Library, Third
        Series, IV (1913), 393-408.

 5204 Hanford, J. H. "The Debate Element in Elizabethan Drama." In,
        Anniversary Papers by Colleagues and Pupils of G. L. Kittredge,
        Presented on the Completion of His Twenty-Fifth Year of Teach-
        ing in Harvard University, MCMXIII. Boston & London: Ginn &
        Co., 1913. vii, 462 pp.
               BM.

*5205 Mackenzie, William Roy. The English Moralities from the Point
        of View of Allegory. Boston and London: Ginn and Co., 1914.
        xv, 278 pp. (Harvard Studies in English, II).
               BM. ICN. MB. MiU. MnU. NN. OC1. OU. PU. ViU. WU.

*5206 ----- "The Origin of the English Morality." Washington University
        Studies, Series 4, Vol. 2, (1915), 141-164.

 5207 Calderhead, Iris G. "Morality Fragments from Norfolk." Modern
        Philology, XIV (1916), 1-9.

 5208 Compton, Mabel G. "Changing Religious Conceptions in the Eng-
        lish Morality Play." M.A. Columbia University, 1916.

 5209 Haller, Julius. "Buhne und Aufführungstechnik der Moralitäten."
        Die Technik des Dialogs im mittelalterlichen Drama Englands.
        (Worms, 1916), pp. 85-87.

 5210 Wieland, Günther. Lustspielelemente im mittelenglischen Drama
        (bis 1500). Ein Beitrag zur Kenntnis des mittelenglischen
        Dramas. Inaugural Dissertation. Kiel, 1916. 159 pp.

 5211 McGinnis, M. E. "The Morality Play: Medieval and Modern."
        M.A. University of Missouri, 1917.

 5212 Barnicle, Mary E. "The Exemplum of the Penitent Usurer."
        Publications of the Modern Language Association, XXXIII
        (1918), 409-428.

 5213 Johnston, Marie L. "The Tudor Morality." M.A. Columbia
        University, 1919.

5214 Scharpff, Paulua. Über ein englisches Auferstechungsspiel; ein
       Beitrag zur Geschichte des Dramas und der Lollarden. Winnen
       den (Würt): Lammle und Müllerschön, 1919. 63 pp.
           CtY.

5215 Wharey, J. B. "Bunyan's Holy War and the Conflict-type of Moral-
       ity Play." Modern Language Notes, XXXIV (1919), 65-73.

5216 Hundley, Frances Shelton. "The Reflection of Social Life in the
       Early Tudor Moralities." M.A. University of Chicago, 1920.

5217 Jelinek, Josephine. "The Music of the Morality Plays and Some
       Comparisons with the Mystery Plays." M.A. University of
       Chicago, 1921.

5218 Zandvoort, R. W. "The Messenger in the Early English Drama."
       English Studies, III (1921), 100-107.

5219 Moore, John Robert. "Ancestors of Autolycus in the English
       Moralities and Interludes." Washington University Studies,
       Humanistic Series, IX (April, 1922), 157-164.

5220 Cook, Jessie Lorene. "George Gascoigne's Glasse of Govern-
       ment As a Type of Prodigal Son Play." M.A. University of
       Chicago, 1923.

5221 Moore, John Robert. "The Tradition of Angelic Singing." The
       Journal of English and Germanic Philology, XXII (January,
       1923), 89-99.

5222 Roberts, Morris. "A Note on the Sources of the English Morality
       Play." Studies by Members of the Department of English, Uni-
       versity of Wisconsin, No. 18 (1923), 100-117.

5223 Hoffman, Helen Crissy. "The Elements of Comedy in the English
       Morality Play (1450-1550)." M.A. Columbia University, 1925.

5224 Reed, Arthur William. Early Tudor Drama. London: Methuen &
       Co., 1926. xv, 246 pp.
           BM. ICN.

*5225 Withington, R. "The Development of the 'Vice.'" Essays in
       Memory of Barrett Wendell, by His Assistants. (Cambridge,
       Mass., 1926), pp. 153-167.

5226 Albright, Evelyn May. Dramatic Publication in England, 1580-
      1640; A Study of Conditions Affecting Content and Form of
      Drama. New York: D. C. Heath and Co.; London: Oxford
      University Press, 1927. 442 pp. Bibliography, pp. 385-419.
            BM. DFo. IaU. ICN. ICU. MH. MiU. OU. PU. ViU.
            WU.

5227 Allison, Tempe Elizabeth. "The Moral Play, Its Fable and Its
      Folk. A Study in Mediaeval Dramatic Traditions and Techni-
      que." Ph.D. University of California, 1927.

5228 ----- "On the Body and Soul Legend." Modern Language Notes,
      XLII (1927), 102-106.

5229 Eckhardt, Eduard. "Die metrische Unterscheidung von Ernst und
      Komik in den englischen Moralitäten." Englische Studien,
      LXII (November, 1927), 152-169.

5230 Scholte, J. H. "Duitsche Moraliteiten uit de zestiende Eeuw."
      Neophilologus, XIII (1927-1928), 196-198.

5231 Albright, E. M. "Dramatic Publication in England, 1580-1640:
      A Reply." Review of English Studies, IV (1928), 193-202.

5232 Houck, Margaret. "The English Morality Play Studied in Reference
      to the Summa of St. Thomas Aquinas." Ph.D. University of
      California, 1928.

5233 Wright, L. B. "Variety-Show Clownery on the Pre-Restoration
      Stage." Anglia, LII (1928), 51-68.

5234 Fenton, Doris. "The Extra-Dramatic Moment in Elizabethan
      Plays before 1616." Ph.D. University of Pennsylvania, 1930.

*5235 Greg, W. W. "Notes on Some Early Plays." Library, New Ser.,
      XI (1930), 44-56; 162-172.

5236 Wright, Louis B. "Social Aspects of Some Belated Moralities."
      Anglia, LIV (July, 1930), 107-148.

5237 Banner, C. R. "Lessons to Youth in Tudor Drama to 1580."
      M.A. University of North Carolina, 1931.

5238 Bell, L. F. "Morality Theme in Book II of the Faerie Queene."
      Modern Language Notes, XLVI (1931), 371-379.

5239 Callaway, Margaret K. "Education in England During the Reign
of Henry VIII and the Part Played in It by Morality Plays."
M.A. University of Georgia, 1931.

5240 Collins, Fletcher. "The Relation of Tudor Halls to Elizabethan
Public Theatres." Philological Quarterly, X (1931), 313-316.

5241 Green, Adwin Wigfall. The Inns of Court and Early English Drama.
With a Preface by Roscoe Pound. New Haven: Yale University
Press; London: H. Milford, Oxford University Press, 1931.
xii, 199 pp. Bibliography, pp. 183-187.
BM. DFo. DLC. ICN. MB. MH. MnU. OCU. OU. PU-L.

5242 Lauf, Elisabeth. Die Bühnenanweisungen in den englischen Moralitäten und Interludien bis 1570. Emsdetten: H. & J. Lechte,
1932. xii, 109 pp. "Bibliographie," pp. vi-xi.
BM.

*5243 Withington, Robert. "The Ancestry of the 'Vice.'" Speculum,
VII (1932), 525-529.

*5244 Boas, Frederick Samuel. An Introduction to Tudor Drama. Ox-
ford: University Press, 1933. vi, 176 pp.
BM. CtY. DFo. DLC. ICU. ICN. MiU. NN. OC1. PU.

5245 Brindley, Bertha Elizabeth. "The Sixteenth Century Morality."
M.A. University of Pittsburgh, 1933.

5246 Brunner, Karl. "Der Streit der vier Himmelstöchter." Englische
Studien, LXVIII (September, 1933), 188-194. [Text].

5247 Raddatz, W. L. "Aspects of Characterization as Observed in Some
Selected Moralities (Including Moral 'Interludes') That Are
Broadly Theological, Secular, or Humanistic, and Controversial
in Tendency." M.A. University of North Carolina, 1934.

5248 Russell, Harry Kitsun. "Tudor and Stuart Dramatizations of the
Doctrines of Natural and Moral Philosophy." Studies in Philology,
XXXI (January, 1934), 1-27.

*5249 Withington, Robert. "Vice and Parasite; a Note on the Evolution
of the Elizabethan Villain." Publications of the Modern Language
Association, XLIX (September, 1934), 743-751.

5250 Collins, Sister Mary Emmanuel. "Allegory in the Early English
Moral Plays." Ph.D. Yale University, 1936.

5251 Jules, Eugene Bernard, Jr. "Song in the Tudor Interlude." M.A. Yale University, 1936.

5252 Withington, Robert. "Braggart, Devil, and 'Vice.' A Note on the Development of Comic Figures in the Early English Drama." Speculum, XI (1936), 124-129.

5253 Worthington, Mabel P., comp. English Miracle. Morality and Mystery Plays. A List. New York: Federal Theatre Project, 1936. 22 pp. [Mimeographed]. CSmH. OC1W.

5254 Bernard, Jules Eugene, Jr. "The Prosody of the Tudor Interlude." Ph.D. Yale University, 1937.

5255 Hulme, Hilda M. "Dialect in Tudor Drama." M.A. University of London, 1937.

*5256 Bernard, Jules Eugene. The Prosody of the Tudor Interlude. New Haven: Yale University Press; London: H. Milford, Oxford University Press, 1939. ix, 227 pp. (Yale Studies in English, Vol. 15.) BM. DFo. DLC. IaU. ICN. OC1. OO. OU. PU. ViU.

5257 Kincaid, Jr., Sterling. "The Dramaturgics of the English Morality Plays and Certain Moral Interludes." Ph.D. University of California, 1939.

5258 Brooks, N. C. "Latin Morality Dialogues of the Fifteenth Century." Journal of English and Germanic Philology, XLII (1943), 471-474.

5259 Miller, Edwin Shephard. "Medieval Biblical and Ritualistic Elements in English Drama, 1497-1562." Ph.D. University of North Carolina, 1943.

5260 Wilkinson, C. W. "A Thirteenth-Century Morality." Bulletin, Metropolitan Museum of Art, II (1943), 47-55.

5261 Coleman, Sr. Anne Gertrude. "The Seven Deadly Sins in the Pre-Reformation Morality Plays." M.A. Fordham University, 1944.

5262 Wright, N. "Morality Tradition in the Poetry of Edward Taylor." American Literature, XVIII (1946), 1-17.

5263 Holzknecht, K. J. Outlines of Tudor and Stuart Plays, 1497-
        1642. New York: Barnes and Noble, 1947. ix, 442 pp.
        BM.

5264 Smith, Sr. Mary Aquin. "The Milieu of the Early Tudor Inter-
        ludes." Ph.D. Fordham University, 1948.

5265 Heffernan, Sr. St. Regina Marie. "The Re-Emergence of the
        Morality Plays." M.A. Fordham University, 1949.

5266 Craig, Hardin. "Morality Plays and Elizabeth Drama." Shakespeare
        Quarterly, I (1950), 64-72.

5267 Feldman, Abraham. "Hans Ewouts, Artist of the Tudor Court
        Theatre." Notes and Queries, CXCV (1950), 257-258.

5268 Bland, D. S. "Interludes in Fifteenth-Century Revels at Furni-
        vall's Inn." Review of English Studies, III (July, 1952), 263-
        268.

5269 Craik, T. W. "Studies in the Tudor Interlude." Ph.D. University
        of Cambridge (Christs), 1952.

5270 Gilford, Charles Bernard. "A Critical Survey of the Morality
        Play." Ph.D. University of Denver, 1953.

5271 Allen, James S. "Changes in the Structure and Characterization
        of the English Moral Play after 1516." Ph.D. Vanderbilt
        University, 1954.

*5272 Boughner, Daniel C. "The Morality Vice and the English Brag-
        gart." The Braggart in Renaissance Comedy: A Study in Com-
        parative Drama from Aristophanes to Shakespeare. (Minne-
        apolis, 1954), pp. 145-178.

5273 ----- "The Vice, Braggart, and Falstaff." Anglia, LXXII (1954),
        35-61.

*5274 Ribner, Irving. "Morality Roots of the Tudor History Play."
        Tulane Studies in English, IV (1954), 21-43.

5275 Salter, K. W. "Lear and the Morality Tradition." Notes and
        Queries, CXCIX, New Ser., I (1954), 109-110.

*5276 Craig, Hardin. "The Morality Play." English Religious Drama of the Middle Ages. (Oxford, 1955), pp. 341-353.

*5277 Craig, Hardin. "Morality Plays." English Religious Drama
of the Middle Ages. (Oxford, 1955), pp. 377-389.

5278 Mares, Francis Hugh. "An Investigation of the Origin and Development of the Figure Called 'The Vice' in Tudor Drama." B. Litt.
Oxford University (Lincoln), 1955.

5279 Creeth, Edmund H. "From Moral to Tragic Recognition, A Study
of Plot Structure in the Morality Tradition." Ph.D. University
of California, 1956.

5280 Blackburn, Ruth Harriet. "Tudor Biblical Drama." Ph.D. Columbia
University, 1957.

5281 Bridges-Adams, W. "Moralities and Interludes." The Irresistible
Theatre. Vol. I. From the Conquest to the Commonwealth.
(London, 1957), pp. 61-75.

*5282 Craik, T. W. The Tudor Interlude. Stage, Costume and Acting.
Leicester: University Press, 1958. xiii, 158 pp.

*5283 Mares, Francis Hugh. "The Origin of the Figure Called 'The
Vice' in Tudor Drama." Huntington Library Quarterly, XXII
(November, 1958), 11-29.

5284 McCutchan, J. Wilson. "Justice and Equity in the English Morality
Play." Journal of the History of Ideas, XIX (June, 1958), 405-
410.

5285 Spivack, Bernard. "Bibliography of Morality Plays." Shakespeare
and the Allegory of Evil. The History of a Metaphor in Relation
to His Major Villains. (New York, 1958), pp. 483-493.

5286 ----- "The Morality Play." Shakespeare and the Allegory of Evil.
The History of a Metaphor in Relation to His Major Villains.
(New York, 1958), pp. 96-129.

5287 ----- Shakespeare and the Allegory of Evil. The History of a
Metaphor in Relation to His Major Villains. New York: Columbia
University Press; London: Oxford University Press, 1958. ix,
508 pp. [Revised edition of, Allegory of Evil.]
        BM. NN.

5288 Fehsenfeld, Erdmut. Der Dialog in den englischen Moralitaeten bis zur Mitte des 16. Jahrhunderts. Inaugural Dissertation. Goettingen, 1959.

*5289 Arnott, Peter D. "The Origins of Medieval Drama in the Round." Theatre Notebook, XV (Summer, 1961), 84-87.

5290 Borchardt, Donald A. "The Dramatic Nature of the English Morality Play." Ph.D. University of Utah, 1961.

*5291 Williams, Arnold. "The Drama of the Individual Christian: The Morality." The Drama of Medieval England. ([Lansing], 1961), pp. 142-162.

*5292 Bevington, David M. From Mankind to Marlowe: Growth of Structure in the Popular Drama of Tudor England. Cambridge, Massachusetts: Harvard University Press, 1962. 310 pp.
        CSmH. CtY. DLC. ICN. ICU. MH. NN. O. PU. WU.

5293 Matthews, Honor Mary V. Character and Symbol in Shakespeare's Plays. A Study of Certain Christian and Pre-Christian Elements in Their Structure and Imagery. Cambridge: University Press, 1962. viii, 211 pp.
        BM.

5294 Pineas, Rainer. "The English Morality Play As a Weapon of Religious Controversy." Studies in English Literature, II (Spring, 1962), 157-180.

5295 O'Neill, V. G. "The Dramatic Treatment of Religious and Political Themes in the Tudor Interlude." Ph.D. London University (University College), 1963-1964.

5296 Padhi, S. "Tudor Drama and Courtesy Literature." Ph.D. Aberdeen University, 1963.

*5297 Williams, Arnold. "The English Moral Play before 1500." Annuale Medievale, IV (1963), 5-22.

5298 Williamson, A. "More Sinned Against Than Sinning; Don Juan." The Opera News, XXVII (January 19, 1963), 2-5, 7.

5299 Dessen, Alec C. "Volpone and the Late Morality Tradition." Modern Language Quarterly, XXV (December, 1964), 383-399.

5300 Feldman, Sylvia Dollie. "The Morality Patterned Comedy of the Renaissance." Ph.D. Stanford University, 1965. [Delete].

5301 Happé, P. "Tragic Themes in Three Tudor Moralities." Studies in English Literature, V (Spring, 1965), 207-227.

5302 Potter, Robert Alonzo. "The Form and Concept of the English Morality Play." Ph.D. Claremont College, 1965.

*5303 Craik, T. W. "The Tudor Interlude and Later Elizabethan Drama." In, Brown, John Russell, and Bernard Harris, General Editors. Elizabethan Theatre. (London, 1966), pp. 37-57.

5304 Feldman, Sylvia Dollie. "The Morality-Patterned Comedy of the Renaissance." Ph.D. Stanford University, 1966.

5305 Fifield, Merle. The Castle in the Circle. Muncie, Indiana: Ball State University, 1967. vii, 48 pp. (Ball State Monograph Number Six).

5306 ----- "The Circular Theater and the Tradition." The Castle in the Circle. (Muncie, Indiana, 1967), pp. 1-17.

5307 Anglo, Sydney. "The Evolution of the Early Tudor Disguising, Pageant, and Mask." Renaissance Drama, New Ser., I (1968), 3-44.

5308 Kinghorn, A. M. "Morality Plays." Mediaeval Drama. (London, 1968), pp. 112-128.

5309 Nicholson, Jack L. "The Medieval Mystery, Miracle, and Morality Plays and Their Twentieth-Century Counterparts." M.A. University of Tulsa, 1968.

5310 Tompkins, Kenneth D. "The Wit Plays: Variations on a Tudor Dramatic Theme." Ph.D. University of Indiana, 1968.

5311 Williams, Marilyn E. "The Tudor Interlude 1495-1601: A Literary Historical Survey." Ph.D. New York University, 1968.

*5312 Wilson, F. P. "The Earlier Tudor Morality and Interlude." The English Drama 1485-1585. (Oxford, 1969), pp. 1-46.

*5313 ----- "The Late Tudor Morality Play." The English Drama, 1485-1585. (Oxford, 1969), pp. 47-77.

2 Authors and Texts of Plays

ABRAHAM'S SACRIFICE

5314 A Tragedie of Abrahams Sacrifice, Written in french by Theodore
Beza, and translated into Inglish, by A. G. Finished at Povvles
Belchamp in Essex, the xj. of August, 1575. Gen. 15. Rom. 4.
Abraham beleued God, and it was imputed to him for righteoujnes.
Imprinted at London by Thomas Vautroullier dwelling in the
Blacke Friers. 1577. 32 leaves, paged (B 1) 1-45. [See Greg, I,
pp. 151-152].
O.

ALBION KNIGHT
Texts
5315 [An interlude, in which Justice, Injury, Albion, and Division are
characters, known from six leaves only.] SR. 1565 c. Aug.
Ent. T. Colwell: a mery playe bothe pytthy and pleasaunt of
Albyon Knyghte. [See Greg, I, pp. 114-115, who dates the
work about Aug. 1565. STC. 275.]
CSmH.

5316 Albion, Knight: A Fragment of a Moral Play. From the Original
in the Library of His Grace the Duke of Devonshire. Edited by
J. Payne Collier. In, Shakespeare Society. Vol. 1. (London,
1844), pp. 55-68.

5317 Albion, Knight. A Moral Play of Albion Knight. In, Farmer, John
Stephen, ed. Six Anonymous Plays. (London, 1906).

5318 Albion, Knight. A Fragment of a Morality Printed by T. Colwell,
c. 1566. Edited by W. W. Greg. Malone Society Collections.
Part 3. (Oxford, 1909), pp. 229-242.

Studies
5319 Dodds, Madeleine Hope. "The Date of Albion, Knight." The
Library, Third Series, IV (1913), 157-170.

5320 Jones, Gwen Ann. "The Political Significance of the Play of Albion
Knight." Journal of English and Germanic Philology, XVII (1918),
267-280.

5321 Chambers, E. K. "Albion Knight." The Elizabethan Stage. Vol. 4.
(Oxford, 1923), p. 1.

5322 Wehrl, Heinz. A Merye Playe Bothe Pytthy and Pleasaunt of Albyon
       knyghte. Inaugural Dissertation. Erlangen, 1923. 41 pp.

Bale, John

1 Bibliography

5323 Davies, William T. "A Bibliography of John Bale." Oxford Biblio-
       graphical Society, Proceedings, V, Part 4 (1939), 201-279: New
       Series, I (1949), 44-45.

2 General Studies

5324 Cole, William. Warhafftige Zeitung vom Auffgang des Evangelis
        . . . aus einem Lateinischen Sendebrieff Guilielmi Colian den
       Herrn Joannem Baleum . . . werdeutscht. Geneva, 1539.

5325 Perry, George G. "John Bale, Bishop of Ossory." Contemporary
       Review, X (1869), 96-113.

5326 Barnwell, Charles H. "The Syntax of Bale's Plays." Ph.D. Harvard
       University, 1898.

5327 Preibler, Theodor. Christi Versuchung durch Satan bei John Bale,
       Giles Fletcher, und John Milton. Inaugural Dissertation. Wien,
       1898.

5328 Moser, Otto. Untersuchungen über die Sprache John Bale's.
       Berlin: Mayer and Müller, 1902. 31 pp.
            ICN. ICU.

5329 Chambers, E. K. "John Bale." The Mediaeval Stage. Vol. 2.
       (London, 1903), pp. 446-450.

5330 Wolf, Wilhelm. Das Thema der Versuchung Christi bei Bale,
       Fletcher und Milton. Inaugural Dissertation. Wien, 1910.

5331 Frame, Rita Chishold. "John Bale, a Study in Biography." M.A.
       Columbia University, 1923.

5332 Greg, W. W. "Notes on Some Early Plays." Library, XI, Fourth
       Series (1930), 44-56; 162-172.

5333 Hamilton, Mary G. "John Bale and His Anglorum Heliades."
       Ph.D. University of California, 1932.

5334 Andersen, Charles Darwin. "The Early Career of John Bale,
        1495-1552." M.A. University of Chicago, 1935.

5335 Harris, Jesse W. "The Life and Works of John Bale, 1495-1563."
        Ph.D. University of Illinois, 1935.

5336 McCusker, Honor. "John Bale; Controversialist, Antiquarian,
        Dramatist." Ph.D. Bryn Mawr, 1937.

5337 Harris, Jesse W. John Bale, A Study in the Minor Literature of
        the Reformation. Urbana: University of Illinois, 1940. 160 pp.
        Bibliography, pp. 137-150. (Illinois Studies in Language and
        Literature, XXV, No. 4.)
            BM. DFo. IaU. ICU. MnU. PU.

5338 McCusker, Honor Cecilia. John Bale, Dramatist and Antiquary.
        Bryn Mawr, Pennsylvania, 1942. xiii, 142 pp. Bibliography,
        pp. 129-138.
            BM. CtY. DLC. IaU. MiU. OC1W. OU. PU.

5339 Mozley, J. F. "John Bale." Notes and Queries, CLXXXIX (Dec-
        ember 29, 1945), 276-277.

5340 Miller, E. S. "The Antiphons in Bale's Cycle of Christ."
        Studies in Philology, XLVIII (July, 1951), 629-638.

5341 Miller, Edwin S. "Antitypes in Bale's Cycle of Christ." Annali
        Istituto Universitario Orientale, Napoli, Sezione Germanica.
        AION-SG, III (1960), 251-262.

5342 Duncan, Robert Lee. "Protestant Themes and Theses in the
        Drama of John Bale." Ph.D. University of Indiana, 1964.

5343 Blatt, Thora Balslev. The Plays of John Bale. A Study of Ideas,
        Technique and Style. Copenhagen: G.E.C. Gad, 1968. [Dis-
        sertation].

3 Collected Works

5344 Bale, John. Scriptorum Illustrium Maioris Brytanniae Catalogus.
        Basel, 1557-1559. [Contains: The Three Laws of Nature,
        Moses and Christ; God's Promises; John the Baptystes Preach-
        ynge in the Wyldernesse; The Temptatyon of Christ].
            BM. ICN.

5345 Christmas, Henry, ed. The Works of John Bale. Cambridge:
       for the Parker Society, 1849. xii, 647 pp.
              BM. ICN.

5346 Farmer, John S., ed. The Dramatic Writings of John Bale. Bishop
       of Ossory. London: Privately Printed for Subscribers by the
       Early English Drama Society, 1907. 347 pp.
              BM. ICN. MB. MH. MiU. MnU. NN. OC1. OU. PU. ViU.
              WU.

4 Individual Plays

GOD'S PROMISES

Texts

5347 A Tragedye or enterlude manyfestyng the chefe promyses of God
       vnto man by all ages in the olde lawe, from the fall of Adam to
       the incarnacyon of the lorde Iesus Christ. Compyled by Iohan
       Bale, Anno Domini M.D. XXXVIII. In the words (whych now is
       Christ the eternall sonne of God) was lyfe from the begynnynge,
       and that lyfe was the lyght of men. Thys lyght yet shyneth in
       the darkenesse, but the darkenesse comprehendeth it not.
       Ioannis primo. . . . Thus endeth thys Tragedy or enterlude
       manyfestynge the chefe promyses of God vnto Man by all ages
       in the olde lawe, from the fall of Adam, to the incarnacyon of
       the lorde Iesus Christ. Compyled by Iohan Bale. Anno domini,
       M.D. XXXVIII. 20 unnumbered leaves. [STC. 1305. See Greg,
       I, pp. 96-97, who dates the play about 1547-8.]
              BM. CtY.

5348 A Tragedie Or Enterlude, manifesting the chiefe promises of God
       vnto man, by all ages in the olde Lawe, from the fall of Adam
       to the Incarnation of the Lorde Iesus Christe. Compyled by
       Iohn Bale. An. Do. 1538. And now fyrst Imprinted. 1577. . . .
       Imprinted at London by Iohn Charlewoode, for Stephen Peele,
       and are to be solde at his shoppe in Roode Lane, 1577. 16
       unnumbered leaves. [STC. 1306. See Greg, I, pp. 97-98.]
              CSmH.

5349 God's Promises. A tragedye or enterlude, manyfestyng the chefe
       promyses of God unto man by all ages in the old lawe, from
       the fall of Adam to the incarnacyon of the Lorde Jesus Christ.
       In, Dodsley, R., ed. A Select Collection of Old Plays. Vol. 1.
       (London, 1744), pp. 1-37,

5350 God's Promises. In, Dodsley, R., ed. A Select Collection of Old

Plays. Vol. 1. (London, 1780), pp. 1-40.
BM.

5351 God's Promises. In, Dodsley, Robert, ed. A Select Collection of Old Plays. Vol. 1. (London, 1825), pp. 1-42.

5352 God's Promises. In, Marriott, William. A Collection of English Miracle-Plays Or Mysteries. (Basel, 1838), pp. 221-257.

5353 God's Promises. In, Dodsley, R., ed. A Select Collection of Old English Plays. Vol. 1. (London, 1874-1876), pp. 277-322.

5354 The Chief Promises of God unto Man. By John Bale Bishop of Ossory 1538. London and Edinburgh: Issued for Subscribers by T. C. & E. C. Jack, 1908. vii, [40] pp. (Tudor Facsimile Texts).
BM. IaU. MB. MH. MiU. NN. ViU.

5355 Jones, Emrys Edward, ed. John Bale's Drama God's Promises. Erlangen: Junge & Sohn, 1909. xx, 40 pp.
BM. CtY. NN. PU. WU.

5356 The Interlude of "God's Promises." In, Everyman, with Other Interludes Including Eight Miracle Plays. (London, [1909]), 153-182.

5357 God's Promises. Amersham, England: Issued for Subscribers by John S. Farmer, 1914. 38 pp. [Also 1908 edition.]
DFo. MnU.

5358 God's Promises. In, Everyman and Other Interludes. (London, New York [1935]).

Studies

5359 Chambers, E. K. "God's Promises." The Mediaeval Stage. Vol. 2. (London, 1903), p. 448.

5360 Steele, R. "A Tragedye or enterlude manyfesting the chefe promyses of God. . . . Compyled by Johan Bale. 1537." In, "Notes on English Books Printed Abroad, 1525-1548." Transactions of the Bibliographical Society, XI (October, 1909 - March, 1911), 235.

JOHN THE BAPTIST

Texts

5361 A brefe Comedy or Enterlude of Iohan Baptystes preachynge in
      the wyldernesse, openynge the craftye assaultes of the hypo-
      crytes, with the gloryouse Baptyme of the Lorde Jesus Christ.
      Compyled by Iohan Bale, Anno M.D. XXXVIII. The worde of
      God came unto Iohan the sonne of Zachary in the wyldernesse.
      And he resorted into all the coastes about Iordane, and
      preached the Baptysme of repentaunce for the remyssyon of
      synnes. Luce iii. Interlocutores. . . The text is found only in
      The Harleian Miscellany, Vol. 1. (London, 1744), pp. 97-
      110. [See Greg, II, p. 961. The work is not to be confused
      with the anonymous Johan the Evangelist. See Greg, I, p. 101.]
      BM.

Studies

5362 Chambers, E. K. "John Baptist." The Mediaeval Stage. Vol. 2.
      (London, 1903), p. 448.

5363 Greg, W. W. "Notes on Some Early Plays: Hycke Scorner, Re-
      construction of a Treveris Edition, Known Only from Two
      Leaves; Rastell's Nature of the Four Elements, Printer and
      Date; The Play of the Weather, an Alleged Edition by Robert
      Wyer; Bale's Play on the Baptism and Temptation." Library,
      XI (June, 1930), 44-56.

KING JOHN

Manuscript

5364 San Marino, California. Huntington Library MS. HM. 3.

Texts

5365 Kynge Johan. A Play in Two Parts. Edited by J. Payne Collier . . .
      from the MSS of the Author in the Library of His Grace
      the Duke of Devonshire. London: Printed for the Camden
      Society by J. B. Nichols & Son, 1838. xiv, 110 pp.
          BM. DFo. DLC. MH. MiU. NN. OU. PU. TxU. ViU.

5366 ----- In, Manly, J. M. Specimens of the Pre-Shakesperean
      Drama. Vol. 1. (Boston and New York, 1903-1904), pp.
      525-618.

5367 Bales Kynge Johan, nach der Handschrift in der Chatsworth Col-
      lection in Faksimile. Ed. by W. Bang. Louvain: A. Uystpruyst,
      1909. pl. lxiii, iv.

DFo. DLC. MH. MiU. NjP. NN. OU. PU. WU.

5368 King John. [Extracts.] In, Pollard, A. W., ed. English Miracle
      Plays, Moralities and Interludes. (Oxford, 1927), pp. 146-154.

5369 Pafford, J. H. P. "Kynge Johan, Re-edited with a Study of the
      Language of Bale." M.A. University of London (University Col-
      lege), 1929.

5370 King Johan, by John Bale . . . Prepared by John Henry Pyle Pafford
      and Checked by the General Editor, Who Has Also Collaborated
      in the Introduction, W. W. Greg. Printed for the Malone Society
      by J. Johnson at the Oxford University Press, 1931. xxxiv, [2],
      144 pp.

5371 Adams, Barry B. "John Bale's King Johan." Edited with an Intro-
      duction and Notes. Ph.D. University of North Carolina, 1963.

5372 King John. In, Armstrong, William A., ed. Elizabethan History
      Plays. (London, 1965).

5373 John Bale's King Johan. Edited with an Introduction and Notes by
      Barry B. Adams. San Marino, California: Huntington Library,
      1968. 220 pp.
      CSmH.

Studies

5374 Chambers, E. K. "King John." The Mediaeval Stage. Vol. 2.
      (London, 1903), 449-450.

5375 Wallerstein, Ruth C. "King John in Fact and Fiction." Ph.D.
      University of Pennsylvania, 1917.

5376 le Boutillier, Mrs. Martin. "Bale's Kynge Johan and The Troublesome
      Raigne." Modern Language Notes, XXXVI (January, 1921), 55-57.

5377 Greg, W. W. "Bale's Kynge Johan." Modern Language Notes, XXXVI
      (December, 1921), 505.

5378 Cason, Clarence E. "Additional Lines for Bale's Kynge Johan."
      Journal of English and Germanic Philology, XXVII (January,
      1928), 42-50.

5379 Pafford, J. H. P. "Bale's King John." Journal of English and Ger-
      manic Philology, XXX (April, 1931), 176-178.

5380 Barke, Herbert. Bales Kynge Johan und sein Verhältnis zur
      zeitgenössischen Geschichtsschreibung. Berlin, Würzburg:
      Verlag Konrad Triltsch, 1937. x, 145 pp.
          BM. MH.

5381 Stayton, Esther. "King John in Early English Drama." M.A. Uni-
      versity of Oregon, 1937.

5382 Shepherd, Louis P. "King John on the Elizabethan Stage." M.A.
      Columbia University, 1945.

5383 Elson, John. "Studies in the King John Plays." Joseph Quincy Adams,
      Memorial Studies. (Washington, D.C., 1948), pp. 183-197.

5384 Miller, Edwin Sheppard. "The Roman Rite in Bale's King John."
      Publications of the Modern Language Association, LXIV (Sept-
      ember, 1949), 802-822.

5385 Hankinson, Margie Mae. "Bale's Kynge Johan: a Work of Tudor
      Propaganda." M.A. Columbia University, 1951.

5386 Pafford, J. H. P. "Two Notes on Bale's King John." Modern
      Language Review, LVI (1961), 553-555.

5387 Bevington, David M. [King John]. From Mankind to Marlowe.
      (Cambridge, 1962), pp. 70, 76, 132, 170.

5388 Adams, Barry B. "Doubling in Bale's King Johan." Studies in
      Philology, LXII (1965), 111-120.

5389 Bevington, David. [King John]. Tudor Drama and Politics. (Cam-
      bridge, Massachusetts, 1968), pp. 97-105.

TEMPTATION OF OUR LORD

5390 A brefe Comedy or enterlude concernynge the temptacyon of our
      lorde and sauer Iesus Christ, by Sathan in the desart. Compyled
      by Iohan Bale, Anno M.D. XXXVIII. Iesus was led from thens
      of the sprete into the wyldernes, to be tempted of the deuyll. And
      whan he had fasted fourty dayes and fourty nyghtes, he was at
      last an hungered. Mathei iiii. . . . Thus endeth thys brefe
      Comedy concernynge the temptacyon of Iesus Christ in the wyl-
      dernes. Compyled by Iohan Bale, Anno M.D. XXXVIII. 9 un-
      numbered leaves. [STC. 1279. See Greg, I, p. 98, who dates
      the play "about 1547-8."]
          O.

5391 The Temptacyon of our Lorde: by John Bale Bishop of Ossory: Now
First Re-printed, and Edited by Rev. Alexander B. Grosart.
Printed for Private Circulation, 1870. 33 pp. [Or, pp. 123-155 in,
Miscellanies of The Fuller Worthies' Library, Vol. 1.]
BM. O.

5392 The Temptation of Our Lord. In, Grossart, A. B., ed. Miscellanies
of the Fuller Worthies Library. Vol. 1. (London, 1871-1876),
pp. 123-155.

5393 The Temptation of Our Lord. By John Bale, Bishop of Ossory, 1538.
London and Edinburgh: Issued for Subscribers by T. C. and E. C.
Jack, 1909. v, [18] pp. (Tudor Facsimile Texts).
BM. ICN. MB. MH. MiU. NjP. NN. ViU. WU.

5394 A brefe Comedy or enterlude concernynge the temptacyon of our
lorde and sauer Jesus Christ, by Sathan in the desart. Compyled
by Johan Bale, Anno M. D. XXXVIII. Amersham, England: Issued for Subscribers by John S. Farmer, 1914. 18 pp.
DFo. MnU. PU.

5395 Schwemmer, Paul, ed. John Bales Drama: A brefe Comedy or
Enterlude concernynge the temptacyon of our lorde and sauer
Jesus Christ by Sathan in the desart. Nürnberg: Friedr. Schwemmer,
1919. xvi, 26, [1] pp.
CtY. MH. MiU. MnU.

Studies
5396 Chambers, E. K. "Temptation." The Mediaeval Stage. Vol. 2.
(London, 1903), pp. 448-449.

5397 Greg, W. W. "Bale's Plays on the Baptism and Temptation." In,
"Notes on Some Early Plays." The Library, Fourth Series, XI
(June, 1930), 53-56.

THREE LAWS
Texts
5398 A Comedy concernynge thre lawes, of nature Moses, & Christ,
corrupted by the Sodomytes. Pharysees and Papystes. Compyled by Iohan Bale. Anno M.D. XXXVIII. [Colophon: Thus
endeth thys Comedy concernynge thre lawes, of Nature, Moses,
and Christ, corrupted by the Sodomytes, Pharisees & papystes
most wycked. Compyled by Iohan Bale. Anno M.D. XXXVIII,
and lately inprented by Nicolaum Baumburgensem [.] [STC. 1287.
See Greg, I, p. 99, who dates the edition "about 1547-8."]
BM. O. Marsh Library, Dublin.

5399 A Nevve Comedy or Enterlude concernyng thre lawes, of Nature, Moises, and Christe, corrupted by the Sodomytes, Pharysies, and Papistes: Compyled by Iohn Bale: and nowe newly Imprynted. The yere of our Lord, M, D, LXII, . . . [Colophon: Imprynted At London in S. brydes Churchyarde, ouer agaynste the North Doore of the Churche, by Thomas Colwell. Anno Domini. M.D. LXII. vi. Die Nouembris.] 44 unnumbered leaves. [STC. 1288. See Greg, I, pp. 99-100.]
           BM. CSmH.

*5400 Comedy concerynge thre lawes, mit Einleitung. Anmerkungen & einem Excurse ueber die Metrik herausgegeben. M. M. Arnold Schroeer, ed. Halle: Niemeyer, 1882. [6], 128 pp.
           CU. MH. PU. WU.

5401 Schroeer, Arnold, ed. "A Comedy Concernynge Three Lawes von John Bale." Anglia, V (1882), 137-264. [Text, pp. 160-225].

5402 A Comedy Concerning Three Laws of Nature, Moses and Christ. 1538. London and Edinburgh: Issued for Subscribers by T. C. and E. C. Jack, 1908. vi, [99] pp. (Tudor Facsimile Texts.)
           BM. DFo. ICN. MB. MiU. NjP. NN. PBm. PP. ViU. WU.

5403 A Comedy concernynge thre lawes, Compyled by Johan Bale. Anno M.D. XXXVIII. Amersham, England: Issued for Subscribers by John S. Farmer, 1914. 101 pp.
           BM. MnU. PU.

Studies

5404 Chambers, E. K. "Three Laws." The Mediaeval Stage. Vol. 2. (London, 1903), p. 449.

5405 Wheat, Cathleen Hayhurst. "A Poore Helpe, Ralph Roister Doister, and Three Laws." Philological Quarterly, XXVIII (April, 1949), 312-319.

5406 Bevington, David M. [Three Laws.] From Mankind to Marlowe. (Cambridge, 1962), pp. 51-52, 55, 70, 74, 87, 91, 93, 128-132, 133, 137, 139, 140, 141, 164, 210, 257.

Beauty and Good Properties of Women. See, Calisto and Melebea.

CALISTO AND MELEBEA

Texts

5407 A new comodye in englysh in maner Of an enterlude ryght elygant
& full of craft of rethoryk wherein is shewd & dyscrybyd as
well the betwe & good propertes of women as theyr vycys &
euyll codicios with a morall coclusion & exhortacyon to vertew
[.] [Colophon: Iohes rastell me imprimi fecit [.] Cum priuilegio
regali [.] 16 unnumbered leaves. STC. 20721, under John
Rastel. See Greg, I, p. 87, who dates the edition "?1530."]
O.

5408 The Spanish Bawd, Represented In Celestina: Or, The Tragicke-
Comedy of Calisto and Melibea. Wherein is contained, be-
sides the pleasantnesse and sweetenesse of the stile, many
Philosophicall Sentences, and profitable Instructions neces-
sary for the younger sort: Shewing the deceits and subtilties
housed in the bosomes of false seruants, and Cunny-catching
Bawds. London: Printed by I. B. And are to be sold by Ralph
Mabbe. 1631. 202 pp. [With errors in pagination. STC. 4911.
See Greg, II, pp. 589-590. A variant imprint: Printed by I.B.
And are to be sold by Robert Allot at the Signe of the Beare in
Pauls Church-yard. 1631.]
Dyce. Variant: BM. CSmH. CtY. DFo. DLC. MH. NN. O.

5409 Calisto and Melibaea. In, Dodsley, R., ed. A Select Collection
of Old English Plays. Vol. 1. (London, 1874-1876), pp. [51]-
92.

5410 Celestina; or, The Tragicke-comedy of Calisto and Melibea. Eng-
lished by James Mabbe, 1631. With Introduction by James
Fitzmaurice-Kelly. London: David Nutt, 1894. 287 pp. (Tudor
Translations, No. 6.)

5411 Calisto and Meliboea. In, Farmer, J. S., ed. Six Anonymous
Plays. Vol. 1, (London, 1905), pp. 47-87.

5412 The Interlude of Calisto and Melebea. Prepared by W. W. Greg.
[London: Printed for the Malone Society by C. Whittingham &
Co., at the Chiswick Press], 1908. viii, [28] pp.

5413 An Interlude of Calisto and Melebea. Edited by H. Warner Allen.
London and New York: E. P. Dutton, [1908], 345 pp.

5414 The Beauty and Good Properties of Women [Otherwise Calisto and
Melibaea c. 1530]. London and Edinburgh: Issued for Sub-

scribers by T. C. and E. C. Jack, 1909. v, [28] pp. (Tudor
Facsimile Texts.)
    ICN. MB. MH. MiU. NjP. OC1. ViU. WU.

5415 A new cömodye in englysh in maner Of an enterlude ryght elygant
    & full of craft of rethoryk wherein is shewd & descrybyd as well
    the bewte & good propertes of women as theyr vycys & euyll.
    Codicioš with a morall coclusion & exhortacyon to vertew.
    (Johēs rastell me imprimi fecit. Amersham, England: Issued for
    Subscribers by John S. Farmer, 1914?). 28 pp.
        OC1. PU.

5416 Celestina: or The Tragi-comedy of Calisto and Melibea, translated
    from the Spanish by James Mabbe, anno 1631; also an interlude
    of Calisto and Melebea (for the first time accurately reproduced
    from the original copy) printed by John Rastell, circa 1530.
    Edited, with introduction on the picaresque novel, and appendices
    by H. Warner Allen. London: G. Routledge & Sons, Ltd.; New
    York: E. P. Dutton & Co., [1923]. xci, 345 pp.
        DLC. ICU. MiU. NN. OC1. ViU. WU.

                            Studies
5417 House, Ralph E. "Present Status of the Problem of Authorship of
    the Celestina." Philological Quarterly, II (1923), 38-47.

5418 ----- "Notes on the Authorship of the Celestina." Philological
    Quarterly, III (1924), 81-91.

5419 Davis, Ruth. New Data on the Authorship of Act I of the Commedia
    de Calisto & Melibea. Iowa City: University of Iowa Press, 1928.
    58 pp. (University of Iowa Series, No. 152.)
        BM.

5420 Purcell, H. D. "The Celestina and the Interlude of Calisto and
    Melibea." Bulletin of Hispanic Studies, XLIV (1967), 1-15.

CASTLE OF PERSEVERANCE
                           Manuscript
5421 Washington, D.C. Folger Shakespeare Library. MS. of Macro
    Moralities.

                            Texts
5422 The Castle of Perseverance. In, Furnivall, F. J., and Alfred W.
    Pollard, eds. The Macro Plays. (London, 1904).

5423 The Castle of Perseverance. London and Edinburgh: Issued for

Subscribers by T.C. & E. C. Jack, 1908. [8], 154-191 numbered
leaves. (Tudor Facsimile Texts.)
CtY. DFo. ICN. MH. NN. WU.

5424 The Castle of Perseverance. Amersham, England: Issued for
Subscribers by John S. Farmer, 1914.
PU.

5425 The Castle of Perseverance. In, Adams, Joseph Quincy, ed. Chief
Pre-Shakespearean Dramas. (Boston and New York, 1924).

5426 The Castell of Perseverance (Extracts). In, Pollard, A. W., ed.
English Miracle Plays, Moralities and Interludes. (Oxford,
1927).

5427 The Castle of Perseverance: the Most Ancient Morality Extant,
1425 A.D. Translated, Adapted and Modified for Modern Church
Use in Approximately the Original Manner. Edited by Phillips
Endecott Osgood. Boston, Mass.; and Los Angeles, California:
[Walter H. Baker Co., c. 1940].
MH. MnU. NN.

5428 The Castle of Perseverance. A Free Adaptation from the Macro
Play Castell of Perseverance 1425. By Iwa Langentels, 1945.
London: Published for the Religious Drama Society by the
S.P.C.K., 1948. xiii, [1], 38 pp.
BM.

5429 The Castle of Perseverance (Abridged). In, Hopper, Vincent F.,
and Gerald B. Lahey, eds. Medieval Mystery Plays. (New York,
1962), pp. 147-195.

Studies
5430 Chambers, E. K. "The Castle of Perseverance." The Mediaeval
Stage. Vol. 2. (London, 1903), pp. 437-438.

5431 Haller, Julius. "Castle of Perseverance." Die Technik des Dialogs
im mittelalterlichen Drama Englands. (Wormser, 1916), pp.
87-96.

5432 Smart, Walter K. "The Castle of Perseverance: Place, Date, and
a Source." The Manly Anniversary Studies in Language and
Literature. (Chicago, 1923), pp. 42-53.

5433 Allison, Tempe E. "On the Body and Soul Legend." Modern Language
Notes, XLII (February, 1927), 102-106.

5434 Stoddard, Harriet Corwin. The Presentation of The Castle of
      Perseverance." M.A. University of Chicago, 1929.

5435 Withington, Robert. "The Castle of Perseverance, line 695."
      Philological Quarterly, XIV (July, 1935), 270.

5436 Hammerle, K. "The Castle of Perseverance und Pearl." Anglia,
      LX, Neue Folge, XLVIII (1936), 401-402.

5437 Z. "The Castell of Perseverance, 1. 26." English Studies, XXIV
      (1942), 178-179.

5438 Reddoch, Sister M. Callista. "Non-dramatic Sources and Analogues
      in a Typical English Morality The Castell of Perseverance."
      M.A. Catholic University of America, 1944.

5439 Chambers, E. K. ["The Castle of Perseverance."]. English Liter-
      ature at the Close of the Middle Ages. (Oxford, 1945), pp. 55-
      59.

5440 McCutchan, J. Wilson. "Covetousness in The Castle of Perseverance."
      University of Virginia Studies, IV (1951), 175-191.

5441 Towne, Rank. "Roister Doister's Assault on the Castle of Persever-
      ance." Research Studies of the State College of Washington,
      XVIII (1951), 175-180.

5442 Willis, James. "Stage Directions in the Castell of Perseverance."
      Modern Language Review, LI (July, 1956), 404-405.

5443 Southern, Richard. The Medieval Theatre in the Round: A study of
      the Staging of Castle of Perseverance and Related Matters.
      London: Faber and Faber, Ltd., 1957. xviii, 240 pp.
      BM. NN.

5444 Bennett, Jacob. "A Linguistic Study of the Castle of Perseverance."
      Ph.D. Boston University, 1960.

5445 ----- "The Castle of Perseverance: Redactions, Place, and Date."
      Mediaeval Studies, XXIV (1962), 141-152.

5446 Bevington, David M. [Castle of Perseverance]. From Mankind to
      Marlowe. (Cambridge, 1962), pp. 48-49, 65, 69, 70, 102,
      116, 117-123.

5447 Robinson, J. W. "Three Notes on the Medieval Theatre." Theatre

Notebook, XVI (1962), 60-62. [Reply to James Willis.]

5448 Henry, Avril K. "The Castle of Perseverance: The Stage Direction at Line 1767." Notes and Queries, XII (1965), 448.

5449 Schell, Edgar T. "On the Imitation of Life's Pilgrimage in The Castle of Perseverance." Journal of English and Germanic Philology, LXVII (1968), 235-248.

COMMON CONDITIONS

Texts

5450 An excellent and pleasant Comedie, termed after the name of the Vice, Common Condicions, drawne out of the most famous historie of galiarbus Duke of arabia, and of the good and eeuill successe of him and his two children, Sedmond his sun, and Clarisia his daughter: Set foorth with delectable mirth, and pleasant shewes. . . . Imprinted at London by William How, for Iohn Hunter, dwellynge on London Birdge, at the signe of the Blacke Lion. 28 leaves unnumbered. [STC. 5592. See Greg, I, pp. 149-150, who gives the date as 1576.]
CtY.

5451 [Common Conditions. Another edition, known from an imperfect copy.] 20 leaves unnumbered. [STC. 5592a. See Greg, I, pp. 150-151, who sees this as a later edition.]
CSmH.

5452 A pleasant Comedie called Common Conditions. In, Brandl, Alois. Quellen des weltlichen Dramas in England vor Shakespeare. (Strassburg, 1898), pp. 597-649.

5453 Common Conditions. In, Farmer, John Stephen, ed. Five Anonymous Plays. (London, 1908).
BM.

5454 Common Conditions. Edited by Tucker Brooke. From the Copy in the Library of the Elizabethan Club of Yale University Compared with the Chatsworth Copy now owned by Henry E. Huntington, esq. New Haven: Yale University Press, 1915. xv, 90 pp. (Elizabethan Club Reprints, I.)
BM. CtY. MH. WU.

Studies

5455 "Common Conditions." In, Brandl, Alois. Quellen des weltlichen Dramas in England vor Shakespeare. (Strassburg, 1898), pp. cxii-cxx.

5456 Brooke, C. F. Tucker. "On the Source of Common Conditions."
      Modern Language Notes, XXXI (1917), 471.

5457 Chambers, E. K. "Common Conditions." The Elizabethan Stage.
      Vol. 4. (Oxford, 1923), pp. 6-7.

5458 Bevington, David M. [Common Conditions]. From Mankind to Mar-
      lowe. (Cambridge, 1962), pp. 61-62, 66, 70, 72, 73, 88, 191-
      194.

THE CONTENTION BETWEEN LIBERALITY AND PRODIGALITY

Texts
5459 A Pleasant Comedie, Shewing the contention betweene Liberalitie
      and Prodigalitie. As it was playd before her Maiestie. London:
      Printed by Simon Stafford, for George Vincent: and are to be
      sold at the signe of the Hand in hand in Wood-street ouer against
      S. Michaels Church. 1602. 24 unnumbered leaves. [STC. 5593.
      See Greg, I, p. 302.]
          BM. CSmH. MH.

5460 The Contention between Liberality and Prodigality. In, Dodsley,
      Robert, ed. A Select Collection of Old English Plays. Vol. 4.
      (London, 1874-1876).

5461 The Contention between Liberality and Prodigality. 1602. London
      and Edinburgh: Issued for Subscribers by T. C. and E. C.
      Jack, 1912. 43 pp. (Tudor Facsimile Texts.)
          ICN. MH. WU.

5462 The Contention between Liberality and Prodigality 1602 . . . Pre-
      pared under the Direction of the General Editor, W. W. Greg.
      London: Printed for the Malone Society by H. Hart at the Ox-
      ford University Press, 1913. vii, [2], [43] pp.

5463 A Pleasant Comedie, Shewing the contention between Liberalitie
      and Prodigalitie. As it was played before her Maiestie. London,
      Printed by Simon Stafford, for George Vincent; and are to be sold
      at the signe of the Hand in hand in Wood-street ouer against S.
      Michaels Church, 1602. Amersham, England: Issued for Sub-
      scribers by John S. Farmer, 1913. 43 pp.
          BM. CSmH. DFo. MH. MnU. OCl. OU. PHC.

Studies
5464 Chambers, E. K. "Liberality and Prodigality." The Elizabethan
      Stage. Vol. 4. (Oxford, 1923), p. 26.

CRADLE OF SECURITY

5465 Halliwell-Philips, J. O. Outlines of the Life of Shakespeare.
      2 vol. London: Longmans, Green and Co., 1887. [Cradle of
      Security mentioned in Vol. 1, pp. 41-43.]
           BM.

5466 Bevington, David M. [The Cradle of Security]. From Mankind to
      Marlowe. (Cambridge, 1962), pp. 13-15, 19, 20.

5467 Wilson, F. P. [The Cradle of Security]. The English Drama,
      1485-1585. (Oxford, 1969), pp. 76-77.

CREED PLAY

5468 Chambers, E. K. "Creed Play." The Mediaeval Stage. Vol. 2.
      (London, 1903), pp. 404-406.

5469 Craig, Hardin. "The Creed Play of York and the Pater Noster
      Play." English Religious Drama of the Middle Ages. (Oxford,
      1955), pp. 334-337.

THE CRUEL DEBTOR
Texts
5470 [An interlude, in which Flattery, Rigour, Simulation, Ophiletis,
      Basilius, and Proniticus are characters, known from four
      leaves only.] [The running title is, "The Cruell Debtter."
      STC. 24934 (under W. Wager). See Greg, I, p. 122, who
      dates the fragment "about Mar. 1566." The entry in the
      Stationers' Register attributes the play to "Wager." There is
      no way to tell if it is Lewis or William. As a result I am list-
      ing the play as anonymous.]
           BM.

5471 The Cruel Debtor. A Fragment of a Morality Printed by Colwell,
      C. 1566. Malone Society. Collections. I. Parts IV and V
      (1911), pp. 315-323.

5472 The Cruel Debtor. Malone Society Reprints. 1923. II. Part 2, pp.
      142-144. [A further fragment.]

DARIUS
Texts
5473 A Pretie new Enterlude both pithie & pleasaunt of the Story of
      Kyng Daryus, Beinge taken out of the third and fourth Chapters
      of the thyrd booke of Esdras. . . . Imprynted At London In

Fletestreat beneath the Conduite, at the sygne of S. Iohn
Euangelyst by Thomas Colwell. Anno Domini. M.D. LXV.
[1565]. In October. 32 unnumbered leaves. [STC. 6277. See
Greg, I, pp. 117-118.]
> BM. CSmH. Pepys.

5474 A preaty new Enterlude, both pythie and pleasaunt, of the Story
of King Daryus. Being taken out of the thyrde and fourth
Chapter of the thyrde Booke of Esdras. . . . Imprinted at
London in Fleetestreate, beneath the Conduite, at the sygne
of S. Iohn Euangelist, by Hugh Iackson. Anno Domini. 1577.
32 unnumbered leaves. [STC. 6278. See Greg, I, pp. 118-
119.]
> BM.

5475 A preaty new Enterlude, both pythie and pleasaunt of the Story of
King Daryus . . . Now first Reprinted from the Original Edition
in 1565. Edited by James A. Halliwell. London: Thomas Richards,
1860. 60 pp. [One of an edition of twenty-six copies privately
printed. Reprinted from the edition of 1565.]
> BM.

5476 Kyng Daryus. In, Brandl, Alois. Quellen des weltlichen Dramas in
England vor Shakespeare. (Strassburg, 1898), pp. 359-418.

5477 Daryus. In, Farmer, J. S., ed. Anonymous Plays. (London, 1906).

5478 King Darius. An Hitherto (1906) Unknown Edition. London and
Edinburgh: Issued for Subscribers by T. C. & E. C. Jack, 1907.
[6], [64] pp. (Tudor Facsimile Texts). [Based on the 1577 text.]

5479 The Story of King Darius. 1565. Edited by John Farmer. London
and Edinburgh: Issued for Subscribers by T. C. & E. C. Jack,
1909. [6], [64] pp. (Tudor Facsimile Texts).

Studies
5480 "King Darius." In, Brandl, Alois. Quellen des weltlichen Dramas
in England vor Shakespeare. (Strassburg, 1898), pp. lxiii-lxx.

5481 Chambers, E. K. "King Darius." The Elizabethan Stage. Vol. 4.
(Oxford, 1923), pp. 8-9.

5482 Bevington, David M. [King Darius.] From Mankind to Marlowe.
(Cambridge, 1962), pp. 59-60, 61, 66, 175-178, 181, 189.

Edwards, Richard

Works

5483 Farmer, John Stephen, ed. The Dramatic Writings of Richard
      Edwards, Thomas Norton and Thomas Sackville. London:
      Privately printed for Subscribers by the Early English Drama
      Society, 1906. [4], 191 pp.
          DLC. ICN. MH. MnU. PU.

DAMON AND PITHIAS
                              Texts
5484 The excellent Comedie of two the moste faithfullest Freendes,
      Damon and Pithias. Newly Imprinted, as the same was shewed
      before the Queenes Maiestie, by the Children of her Graces
      Chappell, except the Prologue that is somewhat altered for the
      proper vse of them that hereafter shall haue occasion to plaie
      it, either in Priuate, or open Audience. Made by Maister
      Edvvards, then beynge Maister of the Children. 1571. Imprinted
      at London in Fleetelane by Richarde Iohnes, and are to be solde
      at his shop, ioyning to the Southwest doore of Paules Churche.
      30 unnumbered leaves. [STC. 7514. See Greg, I, pp. 137-138,
      who discusses a possible 1570 edition.]
          BM. CSmH.

5485 The excellent Comedie of two the most faithfullest friends, Damon
      and Pithias. Newly Imprinted, as the same was shewed before
      the Queenes Maiestie, by the Children of her Graces Chappell,
      excepting (only) the Prologue which is somewhat altered for
      the proper vse of them that hereafter shal haue occasion to
      play it, either in priuate, or open Audience. Made by Maister
      Edvvards, then being Maister of the Children. Imprinted at
      Londō, by Richarde Iones: dwelling neere vnto Holborne Bridge,
      ouer against the signe of the Faulcon. Anno 1582. 34 unnumbered
      leaves. [STC. 7515. See Greg, I, p. 138.]
          BM.

5486 Damon and Pithias. In, Dodsley, R., ed. A Select Collection of
      Old Plays. Vol. 1. (London, 1744), pp. 233-299.

5487 Damon and Pithias. In, Dodsley, Robert, ed. A Select Collection
      of Old Plays. Vol. 1. (London, 1780).

5488 Damon and Pithias. In, Ancient British Drama. Vol. 1. (London,
      1810), pp. 69-99.

5489 Damon and Pithias. In, Dodsley, R., ed. A Select Collection of
      Old Plays. Vol. 4. (London, 1874-1876), pp. [1]-104.

5490 Damon and Pithias. 1571. London and Edinburgh: Issued for Sub-
      scribers by T. C. and E. C. Jack, 1908. vi, [59] pp. (Tudor
      Facsimile Texts.)
      BM. ICN. ICU. MH.

5491 The Excellent Comedie of two the moste faithfullest Freendes,
      Damon and Pithias. 1571. Amersham, England: Issued for
      Subscribers by John S. Farmer, 1914. 57 pp.
      DFo. PU.

5492 Damon and Pithias. In, Adams, Joseph Quincy, ed. Chief Pre-
      Shakespearean Dramas. (Boston, New York, 1924), pp. 571-
      608.

5493 Jackson, James L. "An Edition of Richard Edwards' Damon and
      Pithias (1571 Printing)." Ph.D. University of Illinois, 1949.

5494 Damon and Pythias. Prepared by Arthur Brown, and F. P. Wilson.
      The Malone Society Reprints. 1957. xiv, [63] pp.

                              Studies
5495 Bradner, Leicester. "Richard Edwards and Early Court Drama."
      Ph.D. Yale University, 1926.

5496 Harvey, Walter Worth. "Damon and Pithias and Other Related
      Plays." Ph.D. University of Chicago, 1926.

5497 Mills, Laurens Joseph. "Some Aspects of Richard Edwards'
      Damon and Pithias." Indiana University Studies, XIV. Study No.
      75. Bloomington, Indiana, 1927. 11 pp.
      ICN.

5498 Jackson, James L. "Three Notes on Richard Edwards' Damon and
      Pithias." Philological Quarterly, XXIX (April, 1950), 209-213.

5499 Armstrong, William A. "Damon and Pithias and Renaissance
      Theories of Tragedy." English Studies, XXXIX (1958), 200-207.

5500 Cope, Jackson I. "'The Best for Comedy': Richard Edwards' Canon."
      Texas Studies in Literature and Language, II (1961), 501-519.

EVERYMAN

Texts

5501 [The Summoning of Every Man. An edition known from four mutilated leaves. Colophon: Imprynted at London in Fletestrete
at the Sygne of the George by Rycharde Pynson prynter vnto
the Kings noble grace. STC. 10604. See Greg, I, p. 83, who
dates the work "1510-?1519."]
O.

5502 [The Summoning of Every Man. Another edition, known from an
imperfect copy. Colophon: Imprynted at London in fletestrete
by me Rycharde Pynson prynter to the kynges moost noble
grace. [n.d.] 10 unnumbered leaves. STC. 10603. See Greg,
I, p. 83, who dates the work "1510-?1519.]
BM.

5503 Here begynneth a treatyse how e hye fader of heuen sendeth dethe
to somon euery creature to come and gyue a counte of theyr
lyues in this worlde and is in maner of a morall playe. [Colo-
phon: Thus endeth this morall playe of euery man. Imprynted
at London in Poules chyrche yarde by me Iohn Skot.] 16 unnumbered leaves. [STC. 10606. See Greg, I, pp. 83-84.]

5504 Here begynneth a treatyse how the hye fader of heuen sendeth
dethe to somon euery creature to come and gyue a counte of
theyr lyues in this worlde and is in maner of a morall playe.
[No colophon. John Skot's device is given where the colophon
would appear. STC. 10605. See Greg, I, p. 84. 16 leaves unnumbered.]
BM.

5505 Everyman. In, Hawkins, Thomas. The Origin of the English Drama
Vol. 1. (Oxford, 1773), pp. [27]-68.

5506 An Unknown Edition of the Interlude of Everyman Printed by
Pynson. The Shakespeare Society's Papers, III (1847),
147-155.

5507 An Unknown Edition of the Interlude of "Everyman," Printed by
Pynson. In, Shakespeare Society Publications. Vol. 3. (London,
1849), pp. 147-155.

5508 Everyman: A Moral Play. In, Dodsley, R., ed. A Select Collection
of Old English Plays. Vol. 1. (London, 1874-1876), Vol. 1,
pp. 93-142.

5509 Everyman, a Morality Play. With an Introduction and Notes.
        Edited by F. Sidgwick. 2d ed. London: A. H. Bullen, 1902.
        47 pp.
              BM. MiU. MnU.

5510 Everyman A Morality Play, with an Introduction and Notes. Edited
        by F. Sidgwick. 5th ed. London: A. H. Bullen, 1902. 47 pp.
              CSmH. ICN. PBa. PBm.

5511 Everyman: A Morality Play, with an Introduction and Notes. 6th
        ed. London: A. H. Bullen, 1902. 47 pp.
              ICU.

5512 Everyman. A Morality. New York: McLaughlin Brothers, 1902.
        31 pp.
              MH.

5513 Charles Frohman Presents the Fifteenth Century Morality Play
        Everyman: the Standard Edition. New York: [C. Frohman?,
        1902?]. 31 pp.
              MiU.

5514 Elckerlye-Everyman. De vraag naar de prioriteit opnieuw onder-
        zocht, door H. Logeman. Gand: Vuylsteke, 1902. 175 pp.
        (Université de Gand. Recueil de travaux publiés par la faculté
        de philosophie et lettres, 28. fasc.)
              IaU.

5515 Everyman, a Morality Play. Edited with an Introduction by Montrose
        J. Moses. New York: J. F. Taylor and Co., 1903. 69 pp. Biblio-
        graphy, pp. 63-69.
              DLC. MiU. MnU. NN. OCl. OClW. OO. PU. WU.

5516 Everyman, Old Morality Play, Arranged for Stage Performance
        by Percy Fitzgerald. London: Burns & Oates, Ltd., 1903. 54 pp.
              KAStB.

5517 Everyman: a Moral Play. New York: Fox, Duffield and Co., 1903.
        43 pp.
              IaU. MB. MiU. MnU. NjP. NNC. OCU. OO. PHC. PPD.

5518 Everyman: Being a Moralle Playe of the XV Centurie. Now done
        with a Forworde and mater of helpe. By Ben Greet. Boston: I.
        Sackse, 1903. 35 pp.
              CtY. ICN. MH. MiU. NBuG. NN. OCl. OClW. OO.

5519 Every-man: As Presented by the Elizabethan Stage Society of
London, Under the Personal Direction of Mr. Ben Greet.
[New York: McLaughlin, c. 1903]. 31 pp.
MWelC.

5520 Everyman. A Moral Play. London: George Routledge & Sons,
Limited; New York: E. P. Dutton & Co. [1903]. 63 pp. (The
Broadway Booklets).
BM.

5521 Every-man. A Morality. In, Bates, A. The Drama. Vol. 4.
(London, 1903), pp. 319-444.

5522 Everyman, a Play. Edited by E. Halderman-Julius. Girard,
Kansas: Haldeman-Julius Company. [c. 1903.] (Pocket Series,
No. 462.)
MnU. OCU.

5523 Everyman. In, An English Garner. Fifteenth Century Prose and
Verse. With an Introduction by Alfred W. Pollard. (Westminster, 1903), pp. [275]-304. [From John Skot's editions,
c. 1525.]

5524 Everyman. Reprinted by W. W. Greg from the Edition of John
Skot Preserved at Britwell Court. Louvain: Uystpruyst, 1904.
viii, 31 pp.
BM. MB. MiU. MnU. NjP. NN. OC1W. OCU. OU.

5525 Everyman: a Moral Play. New York: Fox, Duffield and Co., 1904.
43 pp.
MB.

5526 Everyman, Cantata Founded on the Old Morality Play. Edited by
Sir Henry Walford Davies. London: Novello, 1904. 123 pp.

5527 Comedia ofte spel van Homulus; herdrukt naar de ultgave van
Harmer van Borcule, met inleiding van J. W. van Bart.
Utrecht: P. den Boer, 1904. 96 pp.

5528 The Summoning of Everyman. In, Farmer, John S., ed. Six
Anonymous Plays. (London, 1904).

5529 Everyman: A Morality with Designs by Ambrose Dudley. London:
Arnold Fairbairns, 1906. 54 pp.
BM. MiU.

5530 Everyman. A Morality Play. Reprinted in Modern English from
        the First Edition. London and Glasgow: Gowans & Gray, Ltd.,
        1906. 52 pp.
            BM.

5531 The Summoning of Everyman [before 1500]. London: Published by
        Gibbins & Co., for the Early English Drama Society, 1906.
        36 pp.
            CtY. MH. NjP.

5532 Everyman: A Morality Play, with an Introduction and Notes. 23d
        ed. London: Bullen, 1906. 47 pp.
            OC1.

5533 Everyman. London: Routledge & Sons; New York: E. P. Dutton &
        Co. [1906]. 63 pp. (The Broadway Booklets).
            BM.

5534 Everyman, a Morality Play. Edited with an Introduction, Notes
        and Bibliography by Montrose J. Moses. New York: M. Kennerley
        [c. 1908]. 161 pp. Bibliography, pp. 148-161.
            DLC. IaU. OC1. PBa. PPGi.

5535 Everyman. A Morality Play. With an Introduction by A. T. Quiller-
        Couch. Oxford: Clarendon Press [1908]. 32 pp. (Select English
        Classics).
            BM.

5536 Everyman. Edited by Ernest Rhys. London: J. M. Dent & Co.:
        New York: E. P. Dutton & Co., 1909. 25 pp. (Everyman's
        Library).
            BM.

5537 Everyman, a Morality: with Designs by Ambrose Dudley. London:
        Chatto and Windus, 1909. 53 pp.
            BM. MiU. OU.

5538 Everyman. Reprinted by W. W. Greg from the Edition of John Skot
        in the Possession of Mr. A. H. Huth. Louvain: A. Uystpruyst,
        1909. viii, 31 pp.
            BM. IaU. MiU. MnU. NjP. NN. OC1W. OCU. PU. WU.

5539 Everyman, with Other Interludes, Including Eight Miracle Plays.
        London: J. M. Dent and Co.; New York: E. P. Dutton and Co.,
        1909. 208 pp. Bibliography, p. xx.
            MiU.

5540   Everyman. Reprinted by W. W. Greg from the Fragments of
       Two Editions by Pynson Preserved in the Bodleian Library
       and the British Museum, Together with Critical Apparatus.
       Louvain: A. Uystpruyst; Leipzig: O. Harrassowitz; London:
       David Nutt, 1910. vi, 69 pp.
         BM. MB. MiU. NjP. OCU. PU. WU.

5541   Everyman. In, Child, Clarence Griffin. The Second Shepherds'
       Play, Everyman and Other Early Plays. (Boston, New York,
       and Chicago, 1910), pp. 65-102.

5542   Everyman. Edited by J. Warschauer and G. Mott. Half-Hour
       Plays for Amateurs. London: Stead's Publishing House [1911].
       96 pp.
         BM.

5543   Everyman: a Morality Play. Edited by Frank Sidgwick. Illustrated
       after Drawings by John H. Amschewitz. London: P. L. Warner
       (Riccardi Press), 1911. xiii, 36 pp.
         BM. MH. MiU. OU. PSC.

5544   Everyman, with Other Interludes, Including Eight Miracle Plays.
       London: J. M. Dent and Co.; New York: E. P. Dutton and Co.,
       1912. 208 pp.
         OC1W.

5545   Everyman. London and Edinburgh: Issued for Subscribers by
       T. C. and E. C. Jack, 1912. 32 pp. (Tudor Facsimile Texts.)
         BM. IaU. MB. MiU. NjP. PPPD. PSC. ViU. WaU.

5546   Here Begynneth a treatyse how the hye fader of heuen sendeth
       dethe to somon euery creature to come and gyue a counte of
       theyr lyues in this Worlde and is in maner of a moral playe.
       Amersham, England: Issued for Subscribers by John S.
       Farmer, 1913. 32 pp.
         MnU. OC1.

5547   Everyman: Edited by Charles Saroleus. Special Belgian Relief
       Number. November, 1914. London, 1914. 120 pp.
         OC1. OC1W. WaU.

5548   Everyman, with Other Interludes, Including Eight Miracle
       Plays. London: J. M. Dent and Co.; New York: E. P. Dutton
       and Co., 1915. 208 pp.
         OC1W. PPTU.

5549 [Everyman]. <u>Envar</u>. Stockholm: Albert Bonnier, 1916. 112 pp.
     (The Version by Hugo von Hofmannsthal. Translated into Swedish
     by Emil Hillberg).

5550 The Play of Everyman, Based on the Old English Morality Play.
     New Version by Hugo von Hofmannsthal. Set to Blank Verse
     by George Sterling in Collaboration with Richard Ordynski.
     San Francisco: A. M. Robertson, 1917. 95 pp.
          BM. DLC. MiU.

5551 Sheard, A. E. W., ed. Living Parables. London: Skeffington &
     Son, Ltd. [1920]. 206 pp. [See pp. 198-206, "<u>Everyman</u>."
     A Simple Version for Children.]
          BM.

5552 Everyman. In, Adams, Joseph Quincy, ed. Chief Pre-Shake-
     spearean Dramas. (Boston and New York, 1924), pp. 288-303.

5553 Everyman & Other Plays. (The Nativity -- The Shepherds' Play).
     Decorated by John Austen. [London]: Chapman & Hall, 1925.
     201 pp.
          BM.

5554 Acting Versions of Everyman and the Second Shepherds' Play. By
     William Duffey. Milwaukee, Wisconsin: Bruce Publishing Co.,
     1925. 88 pp.
          BM. DLC. MH. NN. OU.

5555 Everyman, a Morality Play. New York: S. French; London: S.
     French, Ltd. [c. 1925]. 39 pp.
          IU.

5556 Everyman. In, Everyman and Other Plays. (London, 1925).

5557 Everyman, a Morality Play. New York: S. French; London:
     S. French, Ltd., 1927. 106 pp.
          NcD.

5558 The Moral Play of Everyman. In, Hubbell, J. B., and J. O. Beaty,
     comps. An Introduction to Drama. (New York, 1927), pp.
     107-121.

5559 Everyman. In, Pollard, A. W., ed. English Miracle Plays,
     Moralities and Interludes. (Oxford, 1927).

5560 Everyman. A Dutch Morality Play of the XVth Century Translated into English. Maastricht: Halcyon Press, 1929. 46 pp. [Text from Skot's 1537 edition.]
BM.

5561 Everyman. In, Baldwin, Thomas Whitfield. Early English Drama from Robin Hood to Everyman. (New York, 1929).

5562 Everyman. The text . . . arranged and pictured by Thomas Derrick. London and Toronto: J. M. Dent and Sons, Ltd.; New York: E. P. Dutton and Co., 1930. 100 pp.
BM. IU. MnU.

5563 Everyman and Other Interludes, Including Eight Miracle Plays. London and Toronto: J. M. Dent and Sons, Ltd.; New York: E. P. Dutton and Co., 1930. 198 pp.

5564 The Summoning of Everyman; With Helps for Reading and Acting. Edited by Francis Adam Hilbert. London: Society for Promoting Christian Knowledge, 1931. 64 pp. (Parish Plays, No. 39).

5565 Everyman -- The Interlude of Youth -- The World and the Child. Edited with Acting Notes by John Hampden. London & Edinburgh [1931]. 96 pp. (Nelson Playbooks, No. 120).
BM.

5566 The Summoning of Everyman; an Adapted Version from the Old Morality Play. Edited by John F. Baird. New York: Samuel French; London: Samuel French, Ltd., 1932. 45 pp.
PPB.

5567 The Summoning of Everyman: An Adapted Version from the Old Morality Play, by John F. Baird. In, Leverton, G. H., ed. Plays for the College Theater. (New York, 1932), pp. 13-27.

5568 Everyman, a Morality Play. The St. Bonaventure Version. Edited by Joseph Yanner. Allegany, New York: The Allegany Citizens Automatic Press, [c. 1932]. 54 pp.
OCl.

5569 [Everyman] Kazdy. Warsaw, 1933. 45 pp. (Bibljoteka Drama-tyczna Drogi. No. 4).
BM.

5570 Everyman . . . Written and Produced During the 16th Century.

In, Clark, Barrett H., ed. World Drama. Vol. 1. (New York, 1933), pp. 351-364.

5571 Everyman and Other Interludes, Including Eight Miracle Plays. London and Toronto: J. M. Dent and Sons, Ltd.; New York: E. P. Dutton and Co., Inc., 1935. 198 pp.

5572 Hentschel, Erhard, ed. Die Vorladung Jedermanns. Nach dem "Jedermann" des Mittelenglischen und des Hans Sachs für eine Feierstunde in der Kircher. Dresden: Ludwig Ungelenk [1935]. 40 pp. [Neue Volks- und Laienspiele, No. 38.] BM.

5573 Bennett, Henry Garland. Literature for the High School. New York, Cincinnati [etc.]: American Book Company, 1935. vii, 600 pp. [See pp. 402-421, Everyman.] BM.

5574 Everyman. In, Parks, Edd Winfield, and Richard Croom Beatty, eds. The English Drama. An Anthology, 900-1642. (New York, 1935), pp. 57-79.

5575 Everyman; a Morality Play in Three Acts . . . Freely Translated into Rhymed Couplets and Adapted for Stage Performance by Dr. William L. Lamers. Milwaukee, Wisconsin: The Catholic Dramatic Movement, 1936. 48 pp. (Library of Catholic Plays).

5576 The Morality Play of Everyman. Adaptation and Presentation by Clarus J. Graves. Collegeville, Minn., 1936. 38 pp. (Type-written).

5577 Everyman. In, Fluchère, Henri. "Tout-Homme, sur le thème de la moralité anglaise Everyman." Marseille, 1936. 63 pp. BM.

5578 The California Festival Edition of the Play of Everyman. Drama-tized by Hugo von Hofmannsthal, Translated into Blank Verse by George Sterling. Revised and Published on the Occasion of Its Presentation in the Hollywood Bowl, September, 1936. Direction, Johannes Poulsen. Los Angeles: The Primavera Press, 1936. 87 pp. DLC. MnU.

5579 Everyman. In, Clark, David Lee, William Brian Gates, and Ernest Edwin Leisy, eds. The Voices of England and America. (New York, 1937).

5580 Everyman. In, Tatlock, J. S. P., and R. G. Martin, eds. Representative English Plays from the Miracle Plays to Pinero. 2nd ed. (New York, 1938), pp. 31-44.

5581 Everyman: Radio Adaptation by Blevins Davis. Directed by Charles Warburton. New York, 1938. 42 pp. (Typewritten). (Great Plays. Series 1, No. 2.)

5582 Everyman, with Other Interludes, Including Eight Miracle Plays. London and Toronto: J. M. Dent and Sons, Ltd.; New York: E. P. Dutton and Co., Inc., 1939. 198 pp.

5583 The Summoning of Everyman. An Adapted Version from the Old Morality Play. Edited by John F. Baird. New York: S. French, 1940. 45 pp.

5584 Everyman, A Medieval Morality Play. Edited with Notes for Directions for Its Production by Esther Willard Bates. Boston, Mass., and Los Angeles, California: Baker's Plays. [c. 1940]. 48 pp.
         NN.

5585 Everyman. In, Cohen, Helen Louise (Mrs. William Stockwell), ed. Milestone of the Drama. (New York, Chicago, [c. 1940]).

5586 Everyman, a Morality, London: Chatto and Windus, 1941. 38 pp. BM. RPB.

5587 Everyman. In, Loomis, Roger Sherman, and Henry W. Wells, eds. Representative Medieval and Tudor Plays. (New York, 1942), pp. 209-244.

5588 Everyman, a New Version. The Classic Morality Play Expressed in the Language of the Bible. By Rev. P. Minwegan, O.M.I. White Bear Lake, Minn., 1943. 24 pp.

5589 Everyman, with Other Interludes, Including Eight Miracle Plays. London and Toronto: J. M. Dent and Sons, Ltd.; New York: E. P. Dutton and Co., Inc., 1943. 198 pp.

5590 Everyman: A Morality [Play]. Forest Hills, New York: Transatlantic Arts. 1943. 38 pp. [Zodiac Books.]

5591 Everyman: A Comparative Study of Texts and Sources. By Henry de Vocht. Louvain: C. Uystpruyst, for Libraire Universitaire,

1947. 228 pp. Bibliographie, pp. [215]-218. [Materials for the
Study of Old English Drama. New Series, V.)
        BM. IaU. NNC.

5592 The Summoning of Everyman, a Modern Version of the Medieval
      Morality Play. Edited by Herbert W. Payne. London: S. French,
      1947. 22 pp.

5593 The Summoning of Everyman. In, Bentley, Gerald Eades, ed. The
      Development of English Drama. An Anthology. (New York, 1950),
      pp. 35-49.

5594 Everyman. In, Gassner, John, ed. A Treasury of the Theatre.
      Rev. ed. (New York, 1951), pp. 204-212.

5595 Everyman. In, Heilman, Robert B., ed. An Anthology of English
      Drama Before Shakespeare. (New York, 1952), pp. 73-104.

5596 Everyman. In, Allen, John, ed. Three Medieval Plays: The Coventry
      Nativity Play; Everyman; The Farce of Master Pierre Pathelin.
      (London, 1953).

5597 Diest, Pieter van. Elckerlyc. Everyman. Moralité du XVme siècle.
      15th Century Morality. Adaptation moderne et francaise de
      Herman Teirlinck. English Adaptation by John Allen. Bruxelles,
      Paris: Olivier Perrin, 1955. 48 pp. [French and English].
        BM.

5598 Oram, Robert E. "A Production Text and Study of Everyman As
      Presented at Catholic University." M.F.A. Catholic University
      of America, 1958.

5599 Everyman. In, Cawley, A. C., ed. Everyman and Medieval
      Miracle Plays. (New York, 1959), pp. 205-234.

5600 Everyman. In, Browne, E. Martin, ed. Mystery and Morality
      Plays. (New York, 1960), pp. 267-304.

5601 Everyman. Edited by A. C. Cawley. Manchester: Manchester
      University Press [1961]. xxxviii, 47 pp. (Old and Middle
      English Texts. Edited by G. L. Brook).
        BM.

5602 Everyman. In, Hopper, Vincent F., and Gerald B. Lahey, eds.
      Medieval Mystery Plays. (New York, 1962), pp. 196-231.

5603 Juergens, Robert Oscar. "Production and Production Book of
      Everyman." M.F.A. Yale University, 1963.

5604 Everyman. In, Sanders, Thomas E. The Discovery of Drama.
      ([Glenview], 1968), pp. 459-489.

5605 Everyman: A Morality Play. With an Introduction by A. T. Quiller-
      Couch. Oxford: Clarendon Press [n.d.]. 32 pp. (Select English
      Classics.)
          WaU.

5606 Everyman: A Morality Play. Reprinted in Modern English from
      the First Edition. New York: F. A. Stockes Co. [n.d.]. 52
      pp. (International Library).
          MH.

5607 Everyman. London: G. Routledge & Sons; New York: E. P. Dutton
      & Co. [n.d.]. 63 pp. (The Broadway Booklets).

                              Studies
5608 Goedeke, Karl. Every-man, Homulus und Hekastus; ein Beitrag
      zur internationalen Literaturgeschichte. Hanover: C. Rümpler,
      1865. xii, 232 pp. Index.
          BM.

5609 Holthausen, Ferdinand. "Zu Everyman." Archiv für Das Studium
      Der neuren Sprachen und Literaturen, XCII (1894), 411-412.

5610 Holthausen, Ferdinand, and E. Kölbing. "Zu Everyman."
      Englische Studien, XXI (1895), 449-450.

5611 "Everyman and the Sacrifice of Abraham." Athenaeum, II (1901),
      103.

5612 Logeman, H. "Elckerlyc--Everyman." Athenaeum, II (1902),
      295-296.

5613 Cary, Elizabeth Luther. "Everyman, a Morality Play." Critic,
      XLII (January, 1903), 42-45.

5614 ----- "Summoning of Everyman." Independent, LV (April 16,
      1903), 906-911.

5615 "Link With the Past." Munsey's Magazine, XXVIII (1903), 946-
      947.

5616   Roersch, A. "Elckerlijk-Everyman-Homulus-Hekastus." Archiv für Das Studium Der neuren Sprachen Literaturen, CXVIII (1904), 13-16.

5617   Bang, W. "Zu Everyman." Englische Studien, XXXV (1905), 444-449.

5618   Manly, J. M. "Elckerlijk--Everyman: the Question of Priority." Modern Philology, VIII (1910), 269-302.

5619   Wood, Francis A. "Elckerlijc-Everyman: The Question of Priority." Modern Philology, VIII (1910), 279-302.

5620   Haller, Julius. "Everyman." Die Technik des Dialogs im mittelalterlichen Drama Englands. (Worms, 1916), pp. 112-115.

5621   Holthausen, Ferdinand. "Zu Everyman." Anglia Beiblatt, XXXII (September, 1921), 212-215.

5622   Young, S. "Production of Everyman." New Republic, LIII (1927), 164-165.

5623   James, S. B. "Everyman." Magnificat, XLVI (1930), 222-225.

5624   Everyman. Programme of the Performance Given by the Exeter College Dramatic Society on May 17, 18, 19, and 21, 1934. BM.

5625   Eliason, Norman E. "I Take My Cap in My Lappe." Philological Quarterly, XIV (July, 1935), 271-274.

5626   Grein, J. T. "Criticism of Everyman." Illustrated London News, CLXXXVI (1935), 592.

5627   Thaler, A. "Shakespeare and Everyman." Times Literary Supplement, July 18, 1936, p. 600.

5628   ----- "Shakespeare, Daniel, and Everyman." Philological Quarterly, XV (1936), 217-218.

5629   Taylor, Archer. Problems in German Literary History of the Fifteenth and Sixteenth Centuries. New York: M.L.A.; London: Oxford University Press, 1939. xviii, 211 pp. Bibliographies, pp. 151-172. Indices. BM.

5630 Tigg, E. R. "Is Elckerlijc Prior to Everyman?" Journal of English
      and Germanic Philology, XXXVIII (October, 1939), 568-596.

5631 Chambers, E. K. ["The Summoning of Everyman."] English
      Literature at the Close of the Middle Ages. (Oxford, 1945),
      pp. 62-64.

5632 Van Mierlo, Jozef. De prioriteit van Elckerlyck tegenover
      Everyman gebandhaafd. Antwerp: Standaard-Boekhandeln,
      1948. 105 pp.
          DLC.

5633 Lessmann, Ursula. Die Beziehungen von Hoffmannsthals Jeder-
      mann zu Everyman und Hecastus. Inaugural Dissertation.
      Marburg, 1949. 116 pp.

5634 Schulz, Ursula. Die Beziehungen von Hoffmannsthals Jedermann
      zu Everyman und Hecastus. Inaugural Dissertation. Marburg,
      1949.

5635 Takahashi, Genji. A Study of Everyman with Special Reference
      to Its Plot. [Tokyo]: Ai-tku-Sha [1953]. lxxx, 22 pp.
          CtY.

5636 Zandvoort, R. W. "Everyman-Elckerlijc." Etudes Anglaises, VI
      (February, 1953), 1-15.

5637 Steenbergen, Gerardus Johannes. Den Spiegel der Zaligheid van
      Elkerlijk. Zwolle: Tjeenk Willink, 1956. 66 pp. (Klassieken
      uit de Nederlandse Letterkunde, No. 9).
          MH.

5638 Adolf, Helen. "From Everyman and Elckerlijc to Hofmannsthal
      and Kafka." Comparative Literature, IX (Summer, 1957),
      204-214.

5639 Ryan, Lawrence V. "Doctrine and Dramatic Structure in Everyman."
      Speculum, XXXII (October, 1957), 722-735.

5640 Carlson, J. R. "A for Effort: Everyman Today." Christian Cen-
      tury, LXXV (February 5, 1958), 167.

5641 De Vocht, H. "Everyman." Professor W. Bang and His Work in
      English Philology. Materials for the Study of Old English
      Drama. New Series. Vol. 25. (Louvain, 1958), pp. 111-123.

5642 Stockum, Theodorus Cornelis van. Das Jedermann-Motiv und
      das Motiv des verlorenen Sohnes im niederländischen und
      im niederdeutschen Drama. Amsterdam, 1958. 22 pp.
      BM.

5643 Kaula, David. "Time and Timeless in Everyman and Dr. Faustus."
      College English, XXII (October, 1960), 9-14.

5644 Risser, Marjorie Alice Munns. "The Summoning of Everyman.
      A Creative Thesis in Dramatic Production." M.S. Illinois
      State Normal University, 1961.

5645 Thomas, Helen S. "The Meaning of the Character 'Knowledge' in
      Everyman." Mississippi Quarterly, XIV (1961), 3-13.

5646 ----- "Some Analogues of Everyman." Mississippi Quarterly, XVI
      (1963), 97-103.

5647 Van Laan, Thomas F. "Everyman: A Structural Analysis." Publi-
      cations of the Modern Language Association, LXXVIII (Dec-
      ember, 1963), 465-475.

5648 Kossman, H. "Felawship His Fer: A Note on Eueryman's False
      Friend." English Studies, XLV (1964), Supp. pp. 157-160.

5649 Lavery, E. "Everyman's Play." Today, XIX (February, 1964),
      19.

5650 Stratman, C.S.V., Carl J. "Everyman: The Way to Death."
      Drama Critique, VII (Winter, 1964), 61-64.

5651 Conley, John. "The Reference to Judas Maccabeus in Everyman."
      Notes and Queries, New Ser., XIV (1967), 50-51.

5652 Fifield, Merle. "Everyman." The Castle in the Circle. (Muncie,
      Indiana, 1967), 37-45.

5653 Bevington, David. [Everyman.] Tudor Drama and Politics.
      (Cambridge, Massachusetts, 1968), pp. 35-37.

5654 Johnson, Wallace H. "The Double Desertion of Everyman."
      American Notes and Queries, VI (1968), 85-87.

5655 Conley, John. "The Doctrine of Friendship in Everyman."
      Speculum, XLIV (July, 1969), 374-382.

THE FOUR CARDINAL VIRTUES

Texts and Criticism

5656 [An interlude in which Temperance, Wilful, Justice, Prudence,
and Fortitude are characters, known from the last quire, C.]
[12?] unnumbered leaves. [Colophon: Thus endeth the enterlude of the iiii. cardynal vertues, & y̆ᵉ vyces contrarye to them.
Imprynted at London in Fletestrete. at the signe of ꝑ George
by Wyllyam Myddylton.] [See Greg, IV, pp. 1643-1644.]
BM.

5657 The Four Cardinal Virtues. Edited by W. W. Greg. A Fragment
of a Morality Printed by W. Middleton between 1541 and 1547.
Malone Society. Collections. IV. (1956), pp. 41-54.

Fulwell, Ulpian

Works

5658 Farmer, John S., ed. The Dramatic Writings of Ulpian Fulwell.
Comprising Like Will to Like--Note-book and Word-List.
London: Privately Printed for Subscribers by the Early English
Drama Society, 1906. 67 pp.
ICN. ICU. MH. MiU. NN. OCl. OU. PU. ViU. WU.

LIKE WILL TO LIKE

Texts

5659 An Enterlude Intituled Like wil to like quod the Deuel to the Colier,
very godly and ful of plesant mirth. Wherin is declared not onely
what punishement followeth those that will rather followe licentious liuing, then to esteem & followe good councel: and what
great benefits and commodities they receiue that apply them vnto
vertuous liuing and good exercises. Made by Vlpian Fulwel.
. . . Imprinted at London at the long shop adioyning vnto S.
Mildreds Churche in the Pultrie by Iohn Allde. Anno Domini
1568. 22 leaves. [STC. 11473. See Greg, I, p. 128.]
O.

5660 An Enterlude intituled Like wil to like quod the Deuil to the Colier,
very godly & ful of pleasant mirth. Wherin is declared not onely
what punishment foloweth those that wil rather folowe licentious
liuing, then to esteem & folowe good councel: and what great
benefits and commodities they receiue that apply them vnto
vertuous liuing and good exercises. Made by Vlpian Fulwel.
. . . Imprinted at London at the long Shop adioyning vnto
Saint Mildreds Church in the Pultrie, by Iohn Allde. 22 unnumbered leaves.
DFo.

5661 A pleasant Enterlude, intituled, Like will to Like quoth the Deuill
     to the Collier. Wherin is declared what punishments followe
     those that will rather liue licentiously: then esteeme and fol-
     lowe good Councell. And what benefits they receiue that apply
     them selues to vertuous liuing and good exercises. Made by
     Vlpian Fulwel. . . . London [:] Printed by Edward Allde, and
     are to be Solde at the Long Shop adioyning vnto Sainte Mildreds
     Church in the Pultrie. 1587. 22 unnumbered leaves. [STC.
     11474. See Greg, I, p. 129.]
           BM. CSmH. CtY.

5662 Like Will to Like. In, Dodsley, Robert, ed. A Select Collection
     of Old English Plays. Vol. 3. (London, 1874-1876), pp. 303-
     359.

5663 Like Will to Like, by Ulpian Fulwell. 1587. London and Edinburgh,
     Issued for Subscribers by T. C. and E. C. Jack, 1909. vii,
     [43] pp. (Tudor Facsimile Texts.)
           ICN. ICU. MB. MH. MiU. NjP. NN. PP. ViU. WU.

5664 A pleasant Enterlude, intituled, Like will to Like quoth the Deuill
     to the Collier . . . 1587. Amersham, England, Issued for Sub-
     scribers by John S. Farmer, 1914. 40 pp.
           DFo. PU.

Studies

5665 Chambers, E. K. "Like Will to Like." The Elizabethan Stage.
     Vol. 3. (Oxford, 1923), p. 317.

5666 Ribner, Irving. "Ulpian Fulwell and His Family." Notes and
     Queries, CXCV (October 14, 1950), 444-448.

5667 ----- "Ulpian Fulwell and the Court of High Commission." Notes
     and Queries, CXCVI (June 23, 1951), 268-270.

5668 Sabol, Andrew J. "A Three-Man Song in Fulwell's Like Will to Like
     at the Folger." Renaissance News, X (1957), 139-142. [With
     music].

5669 Bevington, David M. [Like Will to Like.] From Mankind to Marlowe.
     (Cambridge, 1962), pp. 54-55, 155-158, 268-269.

Garter, Thomas

GODLY SUSANNA

Texts

5670 The Commody Of the most vertuous and Godlye Susanna, neuer
        before this type Printed. Compiled by Thomas Garter. . . .
        Imprinted At London, in Fleetestreate, beneath the Conduite,
        at the Signe of S. Iohn Euangelist, by Hugh Iackson, 1578.
        24 unnumbered leaves. [See Greg, I, pp. xxii-xxiii; IV, pp.
        1646-1647.]
             DFo.

5671 The Most Virtuous & Godly Susanna, by Thomas Garter . . .
        Prefared by B. Ifor Evans. London: Printed for the Malone
        Society by J. Johnson at the Oxford University Press, 1937.
        xiv, [2], [46] pp.

Studies

5672 Pilger, Robert. "Die dramatisierungen der Susanna im 16 Jahr-
        hundert." Zeitschrift für deutsche Philologie, XI (1889), 129-
        217.

5673 Evans, B. Ifor. "The Lost 'Commody' of Susanna." Times Liter-
        ary Supplement, May 2, 1936, p. 372.

5674 Bevington, David. [Godly Susanna.] Tudor Drama and Politics.
        (Cambridge, Massachusetts, 1968), pp. 160-163.

[The following is not by Garter. A new play.]

GENTLENESS AND NOBILITY

Texts

5675 Of Gentylnes & Nobylyte [.] A dyaloge betwen the marchaut the
        Knyght & the plowman dysputyng who is a verey gentylman &
        who is a noble man and how men shuld come to auctoryte
        compilid in maner of an enterlude with diuers toys & gestis
        addyd therto to make mery pastyme and disport. [Colophon:
        Iohes rastell me fieri fecti [.] Cum priuilegio regali. 14 un-
        numbered leaves. [STC. 20723. See Greg, I, p. 86, dates it
        "?1529." The Bodleian copy is imperfect.]
             C. O. Pepys.

5676 Gentleness and Nobility. In, Brydges, Robert, and Joseph Haslewood,
        eds. The British Bibliographer. Vol. 4. (London, 1814), pp. 270-
        275.

5677 Gentylnes and nobylyte: an Enterlude. [London, Privately Printed,
        1829. 51 pp. [25 copies printed.]
            BM. CSmH. DFo. DLC. MH. MiU.

5678 The Spider and the Fly, Together With an Attributed Interlude
        Entitled Gentleness and Nobility, by John Heywood; Edited by
        John S. Farmer. London: Privately Printed for Subscribers by
        the Early English Drama Society, 1908.
            BM. ICN. MH.

5679 Of Gentleness and Nobility. By John Heywood. London and Edinburgh:
        Issued for Subscribers by T. C. and E. C. Jack, 1908. [6],
        [28] pp. (Tudor Facsimile Texts.)
            BM. DFo. ICN. MB. MiU. NjP. NN. PP. ViU. WaU.

5680 Of Gentylnes and Nobylyte. Amersham, England: Issued for
        Subscribers by John S. Farmer, 1914. 28 pp.
            MiU. MnU. OC1. OU. PHC. PU.

5681 Gentleness and Nobility. In, E. Prestage, ed. Chivalry. (New
        York, 1928), pp. 217-219. [Selection].

5682 Gentleness and Nobility (1522-1523) by John Heywood (Originally
        Edited with a Philosopher's Epilogue by John Rastell) the Whole
        Now Re-edited from the Black-letter Original by Kenneth Walter
        Cameron. Raleigh, North Carolina: The Thistle Press, 1941.
        36 pp.
            BM. DLC. MH. OCU. OO. PU.

5683 Cameron, K. W. Authorship and Sources of "Gentleness and
        Nobility": A Study In Early Tudor Drama, Together With a
        Text of the Play Based on the Black-Letter Original. Raleigh,
        North Carolina: The Thistle Press, 1941. 132 pp. Bibliograph-
        ical footnotes.
            BM. DFo. DLC. MnU. NN. PU.

5684 Gentleness and Nobility. Prepared by A. C. Partridge and F. P.
        Wilson. London: Malone Society, 1950. xii, [32] pp.

5685 The Spider and the Fly, Together with an Attributed Interlude
        Entitled Gentleness and Nobility. Edited by John S. Farmer.
        New York: Barnes & Noble, 1966. vii, 472 pp. [First edition,
        1908].
            NN.

Studies

5686 Brooke, C. F. T. "Authorship and Sources of Gentleness and
  Nobility." Modern Language Review, VI (1911), 458-461.

5687 Dunn, Esther Cloudman. "John Rastell and Gentleness and Nobility."
  Modern Language Review, XII (1917), 266-278.

5688 Bevington, David M. [Gentleness and Nobility.] From Mankind to
  Marlowe. (Cambridge, 1962), pp. 42-43, 65.

5689 ----- [Of Gentleness and Nobility.] Tudor Drama and Politics.
  (Cambridge, Massachusetts, 1968), pp. 76-82, 83-84.

GISMOND OF SALERN

Manuscript

5690 Washington, D.C. Folger Shakespeare Library. MS 1232.3 Poems.

Texts

5691 Gismond of Salern in Loue. In, Brandl, Alois. Quellen des weltlichen Dramas in England vor Shakespeare. (Strassburg, 1898),
  pp. 539-595.

5692 Gismond of Salern. London and Edinburgh: Issued for Subscribers
  by T. C. and E. C. Jack, 1927. 27 pp. (Tudor Facsimile Texts.)

Studies

5693 "Gismond of Salern." In, Brandl, Alois. Quellen des weltlichen
  Dramas in England vor Shakespeare. (Strassburg, 1898),
  pp. xcvii-cxii.

5694 Griffin, Ernest G. "Gismond of Salerne: A Critical Appreciation."
  Review of English Literature, IV (1963), 94-107.

5695 Habicht, Werner. "Die Nutrix-Szenen in Gismond of Salern und
  Tancred and Gismund: zur akademischen Seneca-Nachahmung in
  England." Anglia, LXXX (1963), 394-411.

5696 Iriye, Kyoko. "A Stylistic Comparison of Gismond of Salerne and
  Tancred and Gismund." Shakespeare Studies, IV (1966), 1-35.

GODLY QUEEN HESTER

Texts

5697 A newe enterlude drawen oute of the holy scripture of godly queene
  Hester, verye necessary newly made and imprinted, this present

yere. M.D. LXI. [1561]. [Colophon: Imprynted at London by
Wyllyam Pickerynge and Thomas Hacket, and are to be solde
at theyre shoppes.] 24 unnumbered leaves. [STC. 13251. See
Greg, I, pp. 109-110.]
    CSmH.

5698 A Newe enterlude, drawen out of the Holy Scripture, of godley
Queen Hester, verye necessary; newly made and imprinted
MDLXI. In, Collier, J. P., ed. Illustrations of Early English
Popular Literature. (London, 1863-1864).

5699 Godly Queen Hester. In, Grosart, Alexander Balloch, ed. Miscellanies of the Fuller Worthies' Library. Vol. 2. (London,
1871-1874).

5700 Godly Queene Hester. In, Grosart, Rev. Alexander B., ed. Two
Enterludes: I. Jacke Jugeler: II. Godley Queen Hester. From
the Unique Originals in the Possession of His Grace the Duke
of Devonshire. Vol. 4. Fuller Worthies' Library Miscellany.
(London, 1873), pp. 544-610 [or, pp. 1-66].

5701 Godly Queene Hester. In, Bang, Willy, ed. Materialien zur Kunde
des älteren englischen Dramas. Vol. 5. (Louvain and London,
1902-1914).

5702 A New Enterlude of Godly Queene Hester. Edited from the Quarto
of 1561 by W. W. Greg. Louvain: A. Uystpruyst [etc., etc.],
1904. xvi, 62 pp. (Materialien zur kunde des älteren englischen
Dramas . . .). [Reprint of the quarto edition of 1561, in the
Devonshire Collection.]
    BM. DFo. DLC. ICN. MH. MiU. OU. PSC.

5703 Godly Queen Hester. In, Farmer, John Stephen, ed. Six Anonymous Plays. (2d Series). (London, 1905), pp. 245-287.

Studies
5704 De Vocht, H. "Queen Hester." Professor W. Bang and His Work
in English Philology. Materials for the Study of Old English
Drama. New Series. Vol. 25. (Louvain, 1958), pp. 48-49.

5705 Bevington, David M. [Godly Queen Hester]. From Mankind to
Marlowe. (Cambridge, 1962), pp. 30-31, 40, 59-60, 65.

GOOD ORDER
Texts

5706 [An interlude, in which Old Christmas, Good Order, Riot, Glut-
tony, and Prayer are characters, known from two mutilated
leaves.] [Colophon: Imprynted by w. Rastell the yere of our
lorde 1533. Cum priuilegio.] [See Greg, IV, p. 1643.] Owned
by R. Nash [According to Greg the fragment is on deposit at
Dartmouth College, Hanover, New Hampshire.]

5707 Frost, George L., and Ray Nash. "Good Order. A Morality
Fragment." Studies in Philology, XLI (October, 1944), 483-
491. [With Text.]

5708 Greg, W. W. "Old Christmas or Good Order. A Fragment of a
Morality Printed by William Rastell in 1533." Malone Society.
Collections. IV. (1956), pp. 33-39. [Includes photostats of
the fragment.]

Heywood, John

Bibliography

5709 Hillebrand, H. N. "The Canon of John Heywood's Play." Modern
Philology, XIII (1915), 91-104.

5710 Reed, A. W. "The Canon of J. H.'s Plays." Library, Third Series,
IX (1918), 25-57, 116-131.

5711 ----- The Canon of John Heywood's Plays. London: Alexander
Moring Limited, the De La More Press, 1918. 48 pp.
BM. ICN. ICU.

5712 Wood, P. M. "A Critical Bibliography of John Heywood." M.S.
University of Oklahoma, 1934.

5713 Phy, Wesley. "The Chronology of John Heywood's Plays."
Englische Studien, LXXIV (1940), 27-41.

5714 "John Heywood (1497? - 1580?)." The Cambridge Bibliography of
English Literature. Vol. 1. (New York, Cambridge, 1941), pp.
518-519; Vol. 5. (Cambridge, 1957), p. 248.

5715 Cameron, Kenneth Walter. "A Specialized Bibliography of John
Heywood." The Background of John Heywood's Witty and
Witless. (Raleigh, North Carolina, 1941), pp. [35]-41.

5716 Tannenbaum, Samuel A., and Dorothy R. Tannenbaum. John
      Heywood. (A Concise Bibliography). In, Elizabethan Biblio-
      graphies, No. 36. New York, Samuel A. Tannenbaum, 601
      West 113th Street, 1946. 31 leaves. Mimeographed. [Re-
      printed].
          BM. IaU. ICU. MH. MnU. PU.

Works

5717 Farmer, John S., ed. The Dramatic Writings of John Heywood,
      Comprising: The Pardoner and the Friar--The Four P.P.--
      John the Husband, Tyb his Wife, and Sir John the Priest--
      Play of the Weather--Play of Love--Dialogue Concerning Witty
      and Witless--Note-book and word-list. London: Privately
      Printed for Subscribers by the Early English Drama Society,
      1903 and 1905. 208 pp.
          BM. ICN. ICU. MH. MiU. NjP. OC1. OU. PU. ViU.

5718 de la Bere, R. John Heywood, Entertainer. London: George Allen
      and Unwin, Ltd., 1937. 272 pp. Bibliography, pp. 13-16. (Texts
      of four plays: A Play of Witty and Witles, The Pardoner and the
      Frere, The Foure PP, Johan Johan.)
          BM. ICU. MH. PU.

5719 John Heywood's Works and Miscellaneous Short Poems. Edited,
      with an Introduction and Notes, by Burton A. Milligan.
      Urbana: University of Illinois Press, 1956. xi, 297 pp. (Ill-
      inois Studies in Language and Literature. Vol. 41.)
          BM.

Individual Plays

THE FOUR PP
Texts

5720 The playe called the foure PP. A newe and a very mery enterlude
      of A palmer. A pardoner. A potycary. A pedler. Made by
      Iohn Heewood [.] [Colophon: Imprynted at London in Flete-
      strete at the sygne of the George by Wyllyam Myddylton.] 20
      unnumbered leaves. [STC. 13300. See Greg, I, p. 95, who
      dates the editon "? about 1544."]
          BM.

5721 The playe called the foure P [.] A new and very mery enterlude
      of A Palmer. A pardoner. A Poticary. A Pedler. Made by
      Iohn Heewode. [Colophon: Imprinted at London by Wyllyam
      Copland.] 20 unnumbered leaves. [STC. 13301, queries 1555

as the date of the edition. See Greg, I, p. 95.]   [CtY. O.]

5722   The Play called the foure P. A very mery Enterlude of A Palmer.
       A Pardoner. A Poticary. A Pedler. Imprinted at London at
       the long Shop adioyning vnto S. Mildreds Churche in the
       Pultrie, by Iohn Allde. Anno Domini. 1569. Septembris. 14.
       20 unnumbered leaves. [STC. 13302. See Greg, I, pp. 95-96.]
       BM. Pepys.

5723   The Play Called 'The 4 P's.' In, Dodsley, R., ed. A Select Col-
       lection of Old Plays. Vol. 1. (London, 1744), pp. 41-98.

5724   The Four P's by John Heywood. In, Dodsley, R., ed. A Select
       Collection of Old Plays. Vol. 1. (London, 1780), pp. [41]-98.
       BM.

5725   The Four P's by John Heywood. In, The Ancient British Drama.
       Vol. 1. (London, 1810), pp. 1-22.

5726   The Four P's. In, Dodsley, Robert, ed. A Select Collection of
       Old Plays. Vol. 1. (London, 1825), pp. [43]-103.

5727   The Four P's by John Heywood. In, Dodsley, R., ed. Vol. 1.
       (London, 1874-1876), pp. [323]-388.

5728   The Play Called 'The 4 P's.' Abridged. In, Morley, H., ed.
       English Plays. (London, [c. 1880]), pp. 18-21.

5729   The Four PP. In, Farmer, John S., ed. The Dramatic Writings
       of John Heywood. (London, 1903).

5730   The Play Called 'The 4 P's.' In, Manly, John Matthews, ed.
       Specimens of the Pre-Shakesperean Drama. Vol. 1. (Boston
       and New York, 1903-1904), pp. 483-522.

5731   The Play Called the Four PP, by John Heywood, 1545? London and
       Edinburgh: Issued for Subscribers by T. C. and E. C. Jack,
       1908. vi, [40] pp. (Tudor Facsimile Texts.)
       BM. IaU. MB. MH. MiU. NjP. NN. OU. ViU. WU.

5732   The playe called the four PP. A newe and a very mery enterlude
       of a palmer. A pardoner. A potcary. A pedler. Made by John
       Heywood. Imprynted at London in Fletestrete at the sygne of
       the George by Wyllyam Myddylton. Amersham, England:
       Issued for Subscribers by John S. Farmer, 1914. 40 pp.

DFo. MnU. OC1. PU.

5733 The Play called the Four P's. A new and a very mery interlude of
a palmer made by John Heywood. Modernized from the text in
John M. Manly. Specimens . . . by Allen Rogers Benham.
Seattle, Washington: Library of the University of Washington,
1921. 28 pp.

5734 The Foure PP. In, Adams, Joseph Quincy, ed. Chief Pre-Shakesperean Dramas. (Boston and New York, 1924), pp. 367-384.

5735 The Play Called 'The 4 P's.' In, Parry, W. D. Old Plays for
Modern Players. (London, 1930), pp. 47-63.

5736 The Play Called 'The 4 P's.' In, Boas, F. S. Five Pre-Shakespearean Comedies. (Oxford, 1934), pp. 73-112.
BM.

5737 The Play Called the Four PP. In, Hopper, Vincent F., and Gerald
B. Lahey. Medieval Mystery Plays. (New York, 1962), pp. 259-
297.

5738 Heywood, John. The Four P's. In, Hussey, Maurice, and Surendra
Agarwala, eds. The Play of the Weather by John Heywood and
Other·Tudor Comedies Adapted into Modern English. (New York,
1968).

5739 Four pp. copied by Mrs. Furnivall from the first edition. (Wyllyam
Myddyltòn. London, [n.d., but just before 1547].
MH.

Studies
5740 Chambers, E. K. "The Four Ps." The Mediaeval Stage. Vol. 2.
(London, 1903), p. 445.

5741 Ardagh, J. "The 4 P's: A Debt to Skelton." Notes and Queries,
CLXXIV (1938), 205.

5742 McCain, Jun., John Walker. "Heywood's The Four PP: A Debt to
Skelton." Notes and Queries, CLXXIV (March 19, 1938), 205.

5743 Miller, Edwin Shepard. "Guilt and Penalty in Heywood's Pardoner's
Lie." Modern Language Quarterly, X (March, 1949), 58-60.

5744 Bevington, David M. [Four PP.] From Mankind to Marlowe.

(Cambridge, 1962), pp. 9, 19, 38-39, 40, 41, 43, 47, 51, 66, 70, 72, 76.

5745 Bevington, David. [Four PP.] Tudor Drama and Politics. (Cambridge, Massachusetts, 1968), pp. 70-73.

JOHAN JOHAN

Texts

5746 A mery play betwene Iohan Iohan the husbande Tyb his wyfe & syr Ihan the preest. [Colophon: Impryntyd by Wyllyam Rastell the .xii day of February the yere of our lord. M.CCCCC. and .XXXIII. Cum priuilegio.] [1533]. 8 unnumbered leaves. [STC. 13298. See Greg, I, p. 88.]
O. Pepys.

5747 A mery play, between Johan Johan, the husband, Tyb, his wife, and Sir Jhan, the preest. Attributed to J. Heywood, 1533. London: Chiswick Press [1830?]. 34 pp.
BM. MH. NN.

5748 A mery play, between Johan, Johan, the husbande, Tyb, his wife, and Syr Jhan, the preest. In, Child, Four Old Plays. (Cambridge, 1848).

5749 A Mery Play betwene Johan Johan the husbande / Tyb his wyfe / and syr Johan the preest. In, Brandl, Alois. Quellen des weltlichen Dramas in England vor Shakespeare. (Strassburg, 1898), pp. 259-280.

5750 John John the husband, Tyb his wife, and Sir John the Priest. In, Gayley, Charles Mills, ed. Representative English Comedies. Vol. 1. (New York, 1903), pp. 61-86.

5751 Two Tudor "Shrew" plays: (1) John John the husband, Tib his wife, and Sir John the priest . . . (2) Tom Tiler and his wife . . . London: Gibbings, 1908. x, 72 pp. (The Museum Dramatists, No. 4.)
BM. DFo. IU. MH. NjP. OOxM.

5752 John John the husband, Tyb his wife, and Sir John the priest. By John Heywood, 1533. London and Edinburgh. Issued for Subscribers by T. C. and E. C. Jack, 1909. [6], 16 pp. (Tudor Facsimile Texts.)
BM. DLC. ICN. MH. MiU. NjP. NN. OU. ViU. WU.

5753 A mery play betwene Iohan Iohan the husbande Tyb his wife &
       sir Ihan the preest. Imprynted by Wyllyma Rastell the xii.
       day of February, the yere of our lord. M.CCCCC. and XXXIII.
       Amersham, England: Issued for Subscribers by John S. Far-
       mer, 1914. 16 pp.
            MnU. OCl. PU.

5754 Johan, Johan. In, Adams, Joseph Quincy, ed. Chief Pre-Shake-
       sperean Dramas. (Boston and New York, 1924), pp. 385-396.

5755 John John the husband, Tyb his wife, and Sir John the priest. In,
       Bere, R. de la. J. H. Entertainer. (London, 1927), pp. 83-
       87; 231-267.

5756 John, Tyb, and the curate. In, Rubinstein, H. F., ed. Great
       English Plays. (New York, 1928), pp. 26-58.

5757 A Merry Play Between John John, the Husband, Tyb, His Wife,
       and Sir John, the Priest. In, Parks, Edd Winfield, and Rich-
       mond Croom Beatty, eds. The English Drama. An Anthology,
       900-1642. (New York, 1935), pp. 80-97.

5758 John John the husband, Tyb his wife, and Sir John the Priest.
       Modernized. In, Loomis, R. S., and H. W. Wells, eds.
       Representative Medieval and Tudor Plays. (New York, 1942),
       pp. 245-274.

5759 A Merry Play Between Johan Johan, the Husband, Tyb, His Wife,
       and Sir Johan, the Priest. In, Hopper, Vincent F., and Ger-
       ald B. Lahey, eds. Medieval Mystery Plays. (New York, 1962),
       pp. 232-258.

5760 Heywood, John. John John, Tib and Father John. In, Hussey,
       Maurice, and Surendra Agarwala, eds. The Play of the
       Weather by John Heywood and Other Tudor Comedies Adapted
       into Modern English. (New York, 1968).

Studies

5761 Ash, M. "John Johan." British Bibliographer, IV (1814), 118-122.

5762 Chambers, E. K. "John, Tib and Sir John." The Mediaeval Stage.
       Vol. 2. (London, 1903), pp. 445-446.

5763 Craik, T. W. "The True Source of John Heywood's Johan Johan."
       Modern Language Review, XLV (July, 1950), 289-295.

5764 Elton, William. "John Heywood's 'Johan Johan.'" Times Literary
     Supplement, February 24, 1950, p. 128.

5765 Sultan, Stanley. "The Audience-Participation Episode in Johan
     Johan." Journal of English and Germanic Philology, LII (Oct-
     ober, 1953), 491-497.

5766 Elton, William. "Johan Johan and Its Debt to French Farce."
     Journal of English and Germanic Philology, LIII (April, 1954),
     271-272. [Reply to S. Sultan.]

5767 Sultan, Stanley. "Johan Johan and Its Debt to French Farce."
     Journal of English and Germanic Philology, LIII (January,
     1954), 23-37.

THE PARDONER AND THE FRIAR
                    Texts
5768 A mery play betwene the pardoner and the frere the curate and
     neybour Pratte. [Colophon: Imprynted by Wyllyam Rastell the
     .v. day of Apryll the yere of our lorde. M.CCCCC.XXXIII.
     Cum priuilegio.] [1533]. 8 unnumbered leaves. [STC. 13299.
     See Greg, I, p. 89.]
          CSmH. Pepys.

5769 A mery playe betweene the pardoner and the frere, the curate
     and neybour Pratte. [Imprynted by Wyllyam Rastell . . .
     M.CCCCC XXIII. London: Reprinted by G. Smeeton, 1830?]
     16 pp.
          BM. CSmH. DLC. MH. MiU.

5770 The pardoner and the frere. In, Child, Francis James, ed. Four
     Old Plays. (Cambridge, 1848), pp. 89-128.

5771 The Pardoner and the Friar. In, Dodsley, R., ed. A Select Col-
     lection of Old English Plays. Vol. 1. (London, 1874-1876), pp.
     197-238.

5772 The pardoner and the friar, the curate and neighbour Pratt (c.
     1533). The Four P.P. (c. 1540). By John Heywood. Edited with
     Introduction, Note-book, and Work-list by John S. Farmer.
     London, 1906. x, 78 pp.
          BM. ICU. MH. MnU. NjP. OOxM.

5773 The pardoner and the frere, the curate and naybour. Pratte. By
     John Heywood, 1532. London and Edinburgh: Issued for Sub-
     scribers by T. C. and E. C. Jack, 1909. vi, [16] pp. (Tudor

Facsimile Texts.)
BM. IaU. MH. MiU. NjP. NN. OU. ViU.

5774 A Mery Play Betwene the Pardoner and the Frere the Curate and
      Neybour Pratte. M. CCCCC. XXXIII. Amersham, England,
      Issued for Subscribers by John S. Farmer, 1914. 16 pp.
      DFo. MnU. PU.

5775 The Pardoner and the Frere. In, Pollard, A. W., ed. English
      Miracle Plays, Moralities and Interludes. (Oxford, 1927).

5776 The Pardoner and the Friar. With Introduction and Notes. In,
      de la Bere, R., ed. John Heywood, Entertainer. (London,
      1937), pp. 69-73; 145-182.

5777 A Merry Play between the Pardoner and the Frere, the Curate, &
      Neighbor Pratt. Modernized. In, Loomis, R. S. and H. W.
      Wells, eds. Representative Medieval and Tudor Plays. (New
      York, 1942), pp. 275-298.

5778 Heywood, John. The Pardoner and the Friar. In, Hussey, Maurice,
      and Surendra Agarwala, eds. The Play of the Weather by John
      Heywood and Other Tudor Comedies Adapted into Modern Eng-
      lish. (New York, 1968).

Studies
5779 Koelbing, C. "The Pardoner." Englische Studien, XX (1895), 174-
      176.

5780 Chambers, E. K. "The Pardoner and the Friar." The Mediaeval
      Stage. Vol. 2. (London, 1903), p. 444.

THE PLAY OF LOVE
Texts
5781 A play of loue, A newe and a mery enterlude concernyng pleasure
      and payne in loue, made by Ihon Heywood. . . . [Colophon:
      Prynted by. w. Rastell M.CCCCC.XXXIII. Cum priuilegio
      Regali.] [1533]. 20 unnumbered leaves. [STC. 13303. See
      Greg, I, p. 92.]
      Pepys.

5782 [The Play Of Love. Another edition, known from an imperfect
      copy.] [Colon: Printed at London in Farster Laen by Iohn
      Waley. Cum priuilegio ad imprimendum solum.] 28 un-
      numbered leaves. [STC. 13304. See Greg, I, pp. 92-93, who

suggests that this edition was printed "probably about 1560-5."]
O.

5783   The Play of Love. In, Brandl, Alois. Quellen des weltlichen
        Dramas in England vor Shakespeare. (Strassburg, 1898), pp.
        159-209.

5784   A Play of Love. Made by John Heywood. 1534. London and Edin-
        burgh: Issued for Subscribers by T. C. and E. C. Jack. 1909.
        viii, [39] pp.
                BM. DLC. IaU. MB. MH. MiU. NjP. NN. PP. ViU. WaU.
                WU.

5785   A play of loue, A newe and a mery enterlude concernyng pleasure
        and payne in loue, made by John Heywood. Printed by W. Rastell.
        M. CCCCC.XXXIII. Amersham, England: Issued for Subscribers
        by John S. Farmer, 1914. 37 pp.
                DFo. MnU. OC1. PU.

5786   The Play of Love, by John Heywood. Edited by Kenneth Walter
        Cameron. Raleigh, North Carolina: The Thistle Press, 1944.
        45 pp.
                BM. DLC. IaU. MH. NNU-W. PSC. WaU.

                                Studies
5787   Greg, W. W. "An Unknown Edition of Play of Love." Archiv für
        Das Studium Der Neuren Sprachen und Literaturen, CVI (1901),
        141-143.

5788   Chambers, E. K. "Love." The Mediaeval Stage. Vol. 2. (London,
        1903), pp. 444-445.

5789   Reed, A. W. "The Play of Love a Correction." Library, Fourth
        Series, IV (1923), 159.

5790   Schoeck, R. J. "Satire of Wolsey in Heywood's Play of Love."
        Notes and Queries, CXCVI (1951), 112-114.

5791   ----- "A Common Tudor Expletive and Legal Parody in Heywood's
        Play of Love." Notes and Queries, New Ser., III (1956), 375-
        376.

5792   ----- "A Legal Reading of John Heywood's The Play of Love."
        Studia Neophilologica, XXXIX (1967), 284-301.

THE PLAY OF THE WEATHER
Texts

5793 The play of the wether [.] A new and a very mery enterlude of
      all maner wethers made by Iohn Heywood, . . . [Colophon:
      Prynted by w. Rastell. 1533. Cum priuilegio.] 18 unnumbered
      leaves. [STC. 13305. See Greg, I, p. 89.]
          Pepys. St. John's College, Oxford.

5794 The play of the wether. A newe and very mery enterlude of all
      maner wethers made by Iohn Heywood. 24 unnumbered leaves.
      [STC. 13307a. See Greg, I, p. 90, thinks a date of 1544 is
      possible for the edition. The only copy is missing all after
      F 4.]
          C.

5795 The Play of the Wether. A New and a very mery enterlude of al
      maner wethers made by Iohn Heywood. . . . [Colophon: Im-
      printed at London in Paules Churche yearde, at the Sygne of
      the Sunne, by Anthonie Kytson.] 24 unnumbered leaves. [STC.
      13306 queries a 1560 date. See Greg, I, pp. 90-91, who sees
      the limits as about 1554 to 1560.]
          O.

5796 The playe of the weather. A newe and a very merye enterlude of
      all maner wethers made by Ihon Heywoode. . . . [Colophon:
      Imprinted at London by Ihon Awdeley dwelling in litle Britayne
      streete, beyonde Aldersgate.] 24 unnumbered leaves. [STC.
      13307, queries 1565 as the date of this edition. See Greg, I,
      p. 91.]
          BM.

5797 The Play of the Wether. In, Brandl, Alois. Quellen des welt-
      lichen Dramas in England vor Shakespeare. (Strassburg,
      1898), pp. 211-257.

5798 The Play of the Weather, and A mery play betweene Johan Johan,
      the husbande, Tyb, his wife, etc. Edited with Critical Essay
      and Notes by Alfred W. Pollard. In, Gayley, Charles Mills.
      Representative English Comedies. (New York, 1903), pp. 1-
      86.
          BM.

5799 The Play of the Weather. By John Heywood. An unrecorded Edition.
      London and Edinburgh: Issued for Subscribers by T. C. and
      E. C. Jack, 1908. vi, [47] pp. (Tudor Facsimile Texts).

BM. DLC. ICN. MB. MH. MiU. NjP. NN. ViU.

5800 The Play of the Weather. By John Heywood, 1533. London and
Edinburgh: Issued for Subscribers by T. C. and E. C. Jack,
1909. [6], [35] pp. (Tudor Facsimile Texts).
BM. ICN. MB. MH. MiU. NjP. ViU.

5801 The Playe of the Weather. Printed by W. Rastell. 1533. Amersham, England: Issued for Subscribers by John S. Farmer,
1914. 33 pp.
MnU. OCl. OU. PHC.

5802 The playe of the weather. Imprinted at London by John Awdeley.
Amersham, England: Issued for Subscribers by John S. Far-
mer, 1914. 45 pp.
DFo. MnU. OU. PHC. PU.

5803 The Play of the Weather. Edited by A. W. Pollard. In, Gayley,
Charles Mills. Representative English Comedies. Vol. 1.
(New York, 1921), pp. 19-59.

5804 The Play of the Weather. In, Adams, Joseph Quincy, ed. Chief
Pre-Shakesperean Dramas. (Boston and New York, 1924),
pp. 397-419.

5805 The Play of the Weather. In, Parry, W. D., comp. Old Plays
for Modern Players. (London, 1930), pp. 64-81.

5806 The Play of the Weather. In, A Book of Short Plays, XV-XX Centuries. (London, 1940), pp. 38-72.

5807 Cameron, K. W. Play of the Weather: A Study in Early Tudor
Drama. Raleigh, North Carolina: The Thistle Press, 1941.
65 pp.
BM. MnU. NN. PU.

5808 Hussey, Maurice, and Surendra Agarwala, eds. The Play of
the Weather by John Heywood and Other Tudor Comedies
Adapted into Modern English. With Introduction. New York:
Theatre Arts, 1968.

Studies

5809 Chambers, E. K. "Weather." The Mediaeval Stage. Vol. 2.
(London, 1903), p. 445.

5810 Adams, Joseph Quincy. "Lucian A Source for Heywood's Play of
        the Weather." Modern Language Notes, XXII (1907), 263.

5811 Greg, W. W. "The Play of the Weather: an Alleged Edition by
        Rober Wyer." In, "Notes on Some Early Plays." The Library,
        Fourth Series, XI (June, 1930), 50-53.

5812 Bevington, David M. [Play of the Weather.] From Mankind to
        Marlowe. (Cambridge, 1962), pp. 39-40, 65.

5813 ----- "Is John Heywood's Play of the Weather Really About the
        Weather?" Renaissance Drama, VII (1964), 11-19.

5814 ----- [The Play of the Weather]. Tudor Drama and Politics.
        (Cambridge, Massachusetts, 1968), pp. 65-70.

5815 Canzler, David G. "Quarto Editions of Play of the Wether."
        Papers of the Bibliographical Society of America, LXII
        (Third Quarter, 1968), 313-319.

WITTY AND WITLESS
                              Manuscript
5816 British Museum. Harleian MS. 367. 41.

                                Texts
5817 A Dialogue on Wit and Folly by John Heywood. Now First Printed
        from the Original Manuscript in the British Museum. To
        Which Is Prefixed, an Account of That Author, and His Dramatic
        Works, by Frederick W. Fairholt. London: Printed for the
        Percy Society by T. Richards, 1846. 32 pp.
             MB. MiU. MnU. NN. OC1. OU. PU. ViU.

5818 Dialogue on Wit and Folly, With an Account of the Author. Edited
        by F. W. Fairholt for the Percy Society. (London, 1852).
             NN.

5819 Witty and Witless. By John Heywood. London and Edinburgh: Is-
        sued for Subscribers by T. C. and E. C. Jack, 1909. 19 pp.
        (Tudor Facsimile Texts.)
             BM. DFo. InU. MB. MH. MiU. NjP. NN. OC1. PP.
             ViU. WaU.

5820 Witty and Witless. By John Heywood. Issued for Subscribers by
        John S. Farmer, 1914.
             MnU. PU.

5821 Witty and Witless. Bolwell, Robert W. The Life and Works of
John Heywood. (New York, 1922).

5822 Dialogue of Witty and Witless. With Introduction and Notes. In,
de la Bere, R., ed. John Heywood, Entertainer. (London,
1937), pp. 49-55; 117-143.

5823 Cameron, Kenneth Walter. The Background of John Heywood's
Witty and Witless. A Study in Early Tudor Drama. Together
With a Specialized Bibliography of Heywood Scholarship.
Raleigh, North Carolina: The Thistle Press, 1941. 46 pp.
Bibliography, pp. 35-41.
BM. ICN. MH. MnU. PU.

Studies
5824 Chambers, E. K. "Witty and Witless." The Mediaeval Stage.
Vol. 2. (London, 1903), p. 446.

5825 Bevington, David M. [Witty and Witless]. From Mankind to
Marlowe. (Cambridge, 1962), pp. 39, 41-42.

Biographical and Critical Studies

5826 J., F. "J. H's 'Pleasant Dialogues and Dramas." British Bibliographer, (1810), 450-452.

5827 Chalmers, Alexander. "John Heywood." Vol. 7. General Biographical Dictionary, 1814. Pp. 444-447.

5828 Fairholt, F. W. "An Account of [Heywood] and his Dramatic Works."
In, A Dialogue on Wit and Folly. (London, 1846).

5829 "John Heywood." Notes and Queries, XXVIII (1863), 247.

5830 Furnivall, F. J. "John Heywood and Geoffrey Chaucer." Notes
and Queries, XLV (1872), 177-178.

5831 Kittredge, George Lyman. "John Heywood and Chaucer." American Journal of Philology, IX (1888), 473-474.

5832 Swoboda, Wilhelm. John Heywood als Dramatiker. Wien: W.
Braumuller, 1888. 107 pp. (Ein Beitrag zur Entwickelungs-
geschichte des englischen Dramas.)
BM. ICN. IaU. MH. MnU.

5833 Hales, J. W. "The Date of the First English Comedy." Englische
        Studien, XVIII (1893), 408-421.

5834 "John Heywood." In, Brandl, Alois. Quellen des weltlichen Dramas
        in England vor Shakespeare. (Strassburg, 1898), pp. xlvii-
        lvii.

5835 Bayley, A. R. "Frankenstein: Rastell and Heywood: The First
        Prince of Wales." Notes and Queries, 9th ser., XII (1903),
        361-362.

5836 Chambers, E. K. "John Heywood." The Mediaeval Stage. Vol. 2.
        (London, 1903), pp. 443-446.

5837 Pollard, Alfred W. "John Heywood: Critical Essay." In, Gayley,
        C. M. Representative English Comedies. (New York, 1903),
        pp. 3-17.

5838 Young, Karl. "The Influence of French Farce upon the Plays of
        John Heywood." Modern Philology, II (1904), 97-124.

5839 Bang, W. "Acta Anglo-Lovaniensia: John Heywood und sein Kreis."
        Englische Studien, XXXVIII (1907), 243-250.

5840 Pemberton, H. "The Death of John Heywood." Notes and Queries,
        CXVI (1907), 367.

5841 Graves, Thornton S. "The Heywood Circle and the Reformation."
        Modern Philology, X (April, 1913), 553-572.

5842 Hanford, J. H. "The Debate Element in the Elizabethan Drama."
        Anniversary Papers by Colleagues and Pupils of George Lyman
        Kittredge. (Boston and London, 1913), pp. 445-456.

5843 Smith, G. C. Moore. "John Heywood the Dramatist a Freeman
        of London." Notes and Queries, 11th ser., X (1914), 128.

5844 Hillebrand, H. N. "On the Authorship of the Interludes Attributed
        to John Heywood." Modern Philology, XIII (1915-1916), 267-
        280.

5845 Colby, Elbridge. "John Heywood." American Catholic Quarterly
        Review, XLI (1916), 380-389.

5846 Reed, A. W. "Studies in the Life of John Heywood and the John
        Heywood Canon." M.S. University of London, 1916.

5847 Bolwell, R. "The Fabliau, the Farce, and the Works of John
       Heywood." M.S. Columbia University, 1917.

5848 Reed, Arthur William. John Heywood and His Friends. London:
       Alexander Moring, Ltd., 1917. 57 pp.
            BM. ICU. MnU.

5849 Zandvoort, R. W. "The Messenger in the Early English Drama."
       English Studies, III (1921), 100-107.

5850 Bolwell, Robert W. The Life and Works of John Heywood. New
       York: Columbia University Press, 1922. xiii, 188 pp.
       Bibliography, pp. 175-182.
            BM. IaU. ICN. ICU. MH. MnU. PU.

5851 "John Heywood, the Father of English Comedy." Times Literary
       Supplement, August 24, 1922, p. 543.

5852 Reed, Arthur William. The Beginning of English Secular and
       Romantic Drama. A Paper Read before the Shakespeare
       Association on Friday, February 29, 1920. London: Published
       for the Shakespeare Association by H. Milford, Oxford Uni-
       versity Press, 1922. 31 pp.
            BM. MB. MiU. NN. OC1. ODW. PBm. PU. PU-F. ViU.

5853 Graves, Thornton S. "On the Reputation of John Heywood."
       Modern Philology, XXI (1923), 209-214.

5854 Small, Miriam Rossiter. "The Literary Quality of John Heywood's
       Interludes." M.A. Yale University, 1923.

5855 Hughes, W. R. "They All Wrote Plays." More Books, CCXLII
       (1937), 70-84.

5856 "A Tudor Entertainer." Saturday Review of Literature, June 12,
       1937, p. 390.

5857 McCain, John W. "Certain Aspects of John Heywood's Vocabulary
       in Relation to His Cultural Interests." Ph.D. University of
       North Carolina, 1938.

5858 ----- "John Heywood and Classical Mythology." Notes and
       Queries, CLXXIV (May 21, 1938), 368.

5859 ----- "J. S. Farmer and J. H." Times Literary Supplement,
       August 13, 1938, p. 531.

5860 Cameron, Kenneth Walter. "John Heywood and Richard Stanley."
      Shakespeare Association Bulletin, XIV (January, 1939), 55-56.

5861 Withington, Robert. "Paronomasia in John Heywood's Plays."
      Smith College Studies in Modern Languages, XXI (1939), 221-
      239.

5862 Cameron, Kenneth W. "Three Plays of John Heywood." M.S. Yale
      University, 1940.

5863 McCain, John W. "Oratory, Rhetoric, and Logic in the Writings
      of John Heywood." Quarterly Journal of Speech, XXVI (Feb-
      ruary, 1940), 44-47.

5864 Neilson, W. A. "John Heywood's Plays." Modern Language
      Quarterly, III (1942), 129-131.

5865 Butler, Sr. M. Basil, C.S.J. "Religious Satire in the Works of
      Medwall, Rastell, Heywood, and More: A Spirit of Devotion
      to the Ideal of the Church Rather Than to That of the Re-
      formation." Ph.D. St. John's College, 1945. 162 pp.

5866 Holaday, Allan. "Robert Browne and the Date of Heywood's
      Lucrece." Journal of English and Germanic Philology, XLIV
      (1945), 171-180.

5867 Stroinska, Joanna. "John Heywood, 1494-1565. Earlier References
      from Heywood's Works." Notes and Queries, CLXXXIX (Oct-
      ober 20, 1945), 156-161.

5868 Maxwell, Ian Ramsay. French Farce and John Heywood. Mel-
      bourne and London: Melbourne University Press, and Oxford
      University Press, 1946. 175 pp. Bibliography, pp. 164-168.
      BM. CtY. DFo. ICN. ICU. MH. PU. TxU.

5869 Long, Richard A. "John Heywood, Chaucer, and Lydgate."
      Modern Language Notes, LXIV (January, 1949), 55-56.

5870 Schoeck, Richard J. "John Heywood and the Law." Ph.D. Princeton
      University, 1949.

5871 Ure, Peter. "Marriage and the Domestic Drama in Heywood and
      Ford." English Studies, XXXII (October, 1951), 200-216.

5872 Hogrefe, Pearl. The Sir Thomas More Circle. A Program of Ideas

and Their Impact on Secular Drama. Urbana: University of
Illinois Press, 1959. vi, 360 pp.
> BM. CtY. DLC. ICU. IU. MH. NNC.

5873 Canzler, David G. "A Concordance to the Dramatic Works of
John Heywood." Ph.D. University of Oregon, 1961.

5874 Craik, T. W. "Experiment and Variety in John Heywood's Plays."
Renaissance Drama, VII (1964), 6-11.

5875 Wilson, F. P. "Rastell and Heywood." The English Drama, 1485-
1585. (Oxford, 1969), pp. 27-32.

An Anonymous Play

HYCKESCORNER
Texts
5876 Hycke scorner. [Colophon: Enprynted by me Wynkyn de Worde.
18 leaves unnumbered. [STC. 14039. See Greg, I, p. 81, who
dates the edition "?1515-6."]
> BM.

5877 [Hycke Scorner. Another edition known from two leaves only.]
[See Greg, I, p. 82, who discusses the two leaves and the
typographical arrangement.]
> BM.

5878 Hycke scorner. [Colophon: Thus endeth the enterlude of Hycke
scorner. Imprinted at London in Foster laene by Iohn Waley.]
20 unnumbered leaves. [STC. 14040. See Greg, I, p. 82,
who gives a possible date "about 1550."]
> O.

5879 Hycke-scorner. In, Hawkins, Thomas, ed. The Origin of the
English Drama. Vol. 1. (London, 1773), pp. 69-111.

5880 Hyckescorner. In, Dodsley, R., ed. A Select Collection of Old
English Plays. Vol. 1. (London, 1874-1876), pp. 143-195.

5881 Hyckescorner. In, Manly, John Matthews, ed. Specimens of the
Pre-Shakespearean Drama. Vol. 1. (Boston and New York,
1903-1904), pp. 386-420.

5882 Hyckescorner. In, Farmer, John S., ed. Six Anonymous Plays.
(London, 1905), pp. 126-160.
> BM.

5883 Hickscorner [1497-1512]. London and Edinburgh. Issued for Sub-
        scribers by T. C. and E. C. Jack, 1908. vi, [36] pp. (Tudor
        Facsimile Texts.)
            BM. ICN. MB. MiU. NjP. NN. ViU. WU.

5884 Hyckescorner. Amersham, England. Issued for Subscribers by
        John S. Farmer, 1914. 34 pp.
            DFo. OC1. PU.

                              Studies
5885 Chambers, E. K. "Hickscorner." The Mediaeval Stage. Vol. 2.
        (London, 1903), p. 453.

5886 Greg, Walter W. "Notes on Some Early Plays: 'Hycke Scorner,
        Reconstruction of a Treveris Edition. Known only from Two
        Leaves; Rastell's 'Nature of the Four Elements,' Printer and
        Date; 'The Play of the Weather,' an alleged edition by Robert
        Wyer; Bale's Plays on the Baptism and Temptation." Library,
        XI (June, 1930), 44-56.

5887 Bevington, David M. [Hickescorner.] From Mankind to Marlowe.
        (Cambridge, 1962), pp. 50-51, 66, 69, 71, 72, 76, 90, 116,
        138-139, 141, 142.

                               Texts
IMPATIENT POVERTY

5888 A Newe Interlude of Impacyente pouerte newlye Imprynted.
        M.D.LX. [1560]. . . . [Colophon: Thus endeth the enterlute
        called Impacyente pouertye. Imprinted at London in Paules
        Churche yearde at the Sygne of the Swane by Iohn Kynge.] 18
        unnumbered leaves. [STC. 14114. See Greg, I, pp. 105-106.]
            BM.

5889 An new enterlude of Impacient pouerte newly Imprynted. . . .
        [No colophon]. 16 leaves [in extant copy]. [STC. 14113,
        queries 1561 for the date of this edition. See Greg, I, p. 106.
        The extant copy is missing all after D 4.]
            CSmH.

5890 Impatient Poverty. 1560. [London]: Privately Printed for Sub-
        scribers Only, 1907. [6], [36] pp. (Tudor Facsimile Texts).
            DFo. MH. MiU. NjP. NN. ViU. WU.

5891 An Interlude of Impatient Poverty. In, Farmer, John S., ed.

Recently Recovered "Lost" Tudor Plays. (London, 1907), pp. 311-348.

5892 Impatient Poverty, 1560. London, Privately Printed by Hazell, Watson and Viney, Ltd., 1909. 36 pp. (The Tudor Reprinted and Parallel Texts.)
MH. MoU. NjP. OC1. OC1W. OCU. OU. PU. TxU.

5893 A Newe Interlude of Impacyente Pouerte from the Quarto of 1560. Edited by Ronald Brunlees McKerrow. Louvain, A. Uystpruyst; Leipzig: O. Harrassowitz; London: David Nutt, 1911. 70 pp.
DFo. DLC. MH. MiU. NjP. OC1. OU. PBm. WU.

5894 A Newe Interlude of Impacyente pouerete newlye Imprynted. M.D.L.X. Imprinted at London, in Paules Churche yearde at the Sygne of the Swane by John Kynge. Amersham, England: Issued for Subscribers by John S. Farmer, 1914. 34 pp.
OC1. PU.

Studies
5895 Chambers, E. K. "Impatient Poverty." The Elizabethan Stage. Vol. 4. (Oxford, 1923), pp. 20-21.

5896 De Vocht, H. "Impacyente Pouerte." Professor W. Bang and His Work in English Philology. Materials for the Study of Old English Drama. New Series. Vol. 25. (Louvain, 1958), pp. 77-78.

5897 Bevington, David M. [Impatient Poverty.] From Mankind to Marlowe. (Cambridge, 1962), pp. 19, 20, 48, 53, 66, 69, 72, 91, 94, 141-143, 144, 145.

Ingelend, Thomas (fl. 1560)

Works
5898 Farmer, John S., ed. The Dramatic Writings of Richard Wever and Thomas Ingelend, Comprising Lusty Juventus--Disobedient Child--Nice Wanton--Note-book and word-list. London: Privately Printed for subscribers by the Early English Drama Society, 1905. 140 pp.
DLC. ICN. MH. MiU. NjP. NN. OC1. PU. ViU. WU.

THE DISOBEDIENT CHILD
Texts
5899 A pretie and Mery new Enterlude: called the Disobedient Child.
      Compiled by Thomas Ingelend late Student in Cambridge. Im-
      printed at London in Fletestrete, beneath the Conduit by
      Thomas Colwell. 30 unnumbered leaves. [STC. 14085. See
      Greg, I, pp. 132-133, says that it may "be as early as 1569-
      70." For its copy the British Museum queries a date of 1570.]
      BM. CSmH. CtY. IU. MH. O. Pforz.

5900 The Interlude of the Disobedient Child, by Thomas Ingelend.
      Edited by James Orchard Halliwell. London: Printed for the
      Percy Society by Richards, 1848. [6], 60 pp.
      BM. DFo. DLC. ICU. MH. MiU. OC1. OU. PU. ViU.

5901 The Disobedient Child. In, Dodsley, R., ed. A Select Collection
      of Old English Plays. Vol. 2. (London, 1874-1876), pp. 265-
      320.

5902 The Disobedient Child. In, The Dramatic Writings of Richard
      Wever and Thomas Ingelend, Comprising Lusty Juventus--
      Disobedient Child--Nice Wanton--Notes--Book and Word List.
      Edited by John S. Farmer. (London, 1905).

5903 The Disobedient Child. By Thomas Ingelend. [1570?]. London and
      Edinburgh: Issued for Subscribers by T. C. and E. C. Jack,
      1908. vi, [60] pp. (Tudor Facsimile Texts.)
      BM. DLC. ICU. MiU. OC1W. OCU. OO. PU.

5904 A pretie and Mery New Enterlude: called the Disobedient Child.
      Compiled by Thomas Ingelend late Student in Cambridge.
      Imprinted at London in Fletestrete, beneath the Conduit by
      Thomas Colwell. Amersham, England: Issued for Subscribers
      by John S. Farmer, 1914. 60 pp.
      DFo. OC1. PU.

Studies
5905 Holthausen, F. "Studien zum älteren englischen Drama." Eng-
      lische Studien, XXXI (1902), 77-103.

5906 Chambers, E. K. "Thomas Ingelend. The Disobedient Child."
      The Mediaeval Stage. Vol. 2. (London, 1903), p. 456.

5907 ----- "The Disobedient Child." The Elizabethan Stage. Vol. 3.
      (Oxford, 1923), p. 351.

5908 Bevington, David M. [The Disobedient Child.] From Mankind to
        Marlowe. (Cambridge, 1962), 29-30, 40, 65.

THE INTERLUDE OF MINDS

5909 A worke in Ryme contayning an Enterlude of Myndes witnessing
        the Mans Fall from God and Christ. Set forth by HN, and by
        Him newly perused and amended. Translated out of Base-
        almayne into English. . . . [No imprint or colophon.] 32 leaves.
        [STC. 18550 queries a date of 1574. See Greg, I, pp. 143-144,
        who accepts a date "? about 1574." Chambers, in The Eliz-
        abethan Stage (Oxford, 1923), says that the play is a translation
        of the Low German Comoedia: Ein Gedicht des Spels van Sinnen,
        anno 1575 of Henrick Niklaes. (Vol. 4, p. 31.) Greg spells the
        name "Niclas."]
            BM. CSmH. O.

JACK JUGGLER
Texts

5910 A new Enterlued for Chyldren to playe named Iacke Iugler, both
        wytte, very playsent and merye. Neuer before Imprented. . .
        [Colophon: Imprinted at London in Temes strete at the Vintre
        vnpon the thre Crayne wharge by me Wyllyam Copland.] 20
        unnumbered leaves. [STC. 14837, gives a date of 1563. See
        Greg, I, pp. 111-112, who dates it "about Nov. 1562." Greg
        lists a copy at A. S. W. Rosenbach.]

5911 A new Enterlued for Chyldren to playe, named Iacke Iugeler,
        both wytte, and very playsent. Newly Imprented. . . . [Colophon:
        Imprinted at London in Lothbury by me Wyllyam Copland.] 20
        unnumbered leaves. [STC. 14837a queries a date of 1565.]
            CSmH.

5912 An Enterlude for children to play named Iack Iugler both wittie
        and very plesant. Newly Imprinted. . . . Imprinted at London
        at the long Shop adioyning vnto Saint Mildreds Churche in the
        Pultrie, by Iohn Allde. 20 unnumbered leaves. [See Greg, IV,
        pp. 1644-1645, who says that most of Allde's dramatic publica-
        tions were between 1565-70, "the latter limit of which would
        seem most likely in the present case."]
            CSmH. DFo.

5913 Two Interludes: Jack Jugler and Thersytes. Kent: Printed at the
        Private Press of Lee Priory, by J. Warwick, 1820. 40 pp.

5914 Jack Juggler. In, Child, Francis James, ed. Four Old Plays.
         (Cambridge, 1848).

5915 Jack Jugeler. In, Grosart, Rev. Alexander B., ed. Two Enter-
         ludes: I. Jacke Jugeler: II. Godley Queene Hester. From the Unique
         Originals in the Possession of His Grace the Duke of Devonshire.
         Vol. 4. Fuller Worthies' Library Miscellany. (London, 1873),
         pp. 482-543 [or, pp. 27-88.]

5916 Jack Juggler. In, Dodsley, R., ed. A Select Collection of Old
         English Plays. Vol. 2. (London, 1874-1876), pp. [103]-157.

5917 Jacke Jugeler. (Reproduced from the Unique Original). Dramatic
         Fac-similes. Edited by Edmund W. Ashbee. London: for Pri-
         vate Circulation [1877?]. 40 pp. [100 copies].
         BM. DLC.

5918 Jack Juggler. In, Farmer, John Stephen, ed. Anonymous Plays.
         Vol. 3. (London, 1906), pp. 1-40.

5919 Jack Juggler [c. 1553-61]. [London]: Issued for Subscribers by
         the Editor of the Tudor Facsimile Texts, 1912. [6], [40] pp.
         (Tudor Facsimile Texts).
         BM. DLC. ICN. MH. MiU. NjP. ViU. WU.

5920 A New Enterlued for Chyldren to playe, named Jacke Jugeler, both
         wytte, and very playsent. Newly Imprented. Imprinted at Lon-
         don in Lothbury by me Wyllyam Copland. Amersham, England:
         Issued for Subscribers by John S. Farmer, 1913. 40 pp.

5921 Jack Jugeler. Edited by W. H. Williams. Cambridge, Cambridge
         University Press, 1914. xxii, 75 pp.
         BM. CtY. ICN. IU. MB. MH. NjP. OU. WU.

5922 Jack Juggler. Prepared by Eunice Lilian Smith, in Collaboration
         with W. W. Greg. The Malone Society Reprints. 1933. xx,
         [56] pp. [Has the first edition, and also another edition in
         fragmentary form.]

5923 Jack Juggler. Prepared by B. Ifor Evans and W. W. Greg. The
         Malone Society Reprints. 1936. (1937). xvi, [44] pp. [Third
         edition].

5924 Jack Juggler. In, Hussey, Maurice, and Surendra Agarwala, eds.
         The Play of the Weather by John Heywood and Other Tudor

Comedies Adapted into Modern English. (New York, 1968).

Studies

5925 Chambers, E. K. "Jack Juggler." The Mediaeval Stage. Vol. 2. (London, 1903), pp. 457-458.

5926 Williams, W. R. "The Date and Authorship of 'Jacke Jugeler.'" Modern Language Review, VII (1912), 289-295.

5927 Smith, G. C. Moore. "'Jacke Jugeler.' 11. 256-259." Modern Language Review, X (1915), 375.

5928 Marienstras, R. "Jack Juggler: Aspects de la conscience individuelle dans une farce du 16e siècle." Etudes Anglaises, XVI (1963), 321-332.

5929 Voisine, Jacques. "A propos de Jack Juggler." Etudes Anglaises, XVIII (1965), 166. [Reply by R. Marienstras, pp. 167-168.]

5930 Bevington, David. [Jack Juggler.] Tudor Drama and Politics. (Cambridge, Massachusetts, 1968), pp. 124-126.

JACOB AND ESAU

Texts

5931 A newe mery and wittie Comedie or Enterlude, newely imprinted, treating vpon the Historie of Iacob and Esau, taken out of the .xxvj. Chap. of the first booke of Moses entituled Genesis. The partes and names of the Players who are to be considered to be Hebrews and so should be apparailed with attire. . . . Imprinted at London by Henrie Bynneman, dvvelling in Knight-rider streate, at the signe of the Mermayde. Anno Domini. 1568. 28 unnumbered leaves. [STC. 14327. See Greg, I, p. 130.]
     BM. CSmH. CtY. DFo. O. Pforz.

5932 Jacob and Esau. In, Dodsley, R., ed. A Select Collection of Old English Plays. Vol. 2. (London, 1874-1876), pp. [185]-264.

5933 Jacob and Esau. In, Farmer, John Stephen, ed. Six Anonymous Plays. (London, 1906), pp. 1-90.

5934 Jacob and Esau. 1568. London and Edinburgh: Issued for Subscribers by T. C. and E. C. Jack, 1908. v, [56] pp. (Tudor Facsimile Texts.)
     DLC. ICN. MB. MH. MiU. NN. ViU. WU.

5935 Jacob and Esau. Amersham, England: Published for Subscribers
       by John S. Farmer, 1914. 56 pp.

5936 Jacob and Esau. Prepared by John Crow, and F. P. Wilson. The
       Malone Society Reprints. 1956. ix, [56] pp.

                                    Studies
5937 Herrlich, Joseph. Das englische Bibeldrama zur Zeit der Renais-
       sance und Reformation, mit besonderer Berücksichtigung
       von Udall's Komödie Jacob und Esau. Bad Aibling: Haack,
       [1907]. 70 pp. "Litteratur," pp. 3-5.
            NNC.

5938 Chambers, E. K. "Jacob and Esau." The Elizabethan Stage. Vol.
       4. (Oxford, 1923), p. 22. [See C. C. Stopes, Athenaeum,
       April 28, 1900, pp. 538-540.]

5939 Scheurweghs, George. "The Date of The History of Jacob and
       Esau." English Studies, XV (December, 1933), 218-219.

5940 Bevington, David. [Jacob and Esau.] Tudor Drama and Politics.
       (Cambridge, Massachusetts, 1968), pp. 109-113, 157-158.

5941 Thomas, Helen. "Jacob and Esau -- 'rigidly Calvinistic'?"
       Studies in English Literature, 1500-1900, IX (Spring, 1969),
       199-213.

JOHN THE EVANGELIST
                                     Texts
5942 Here begynneth the enterlude of Iohan the Euangelyst. [Colo-
       phon: Thus endeth the Enterlude of saynt Iohan the Euangelyste.
       Imprynted at London in Foster laene by Iohn Waley.] 12 un-
       numbered leaves. [STC. 14643. See, Greg I, p. 101, who
       suggests a date "? about 1550."]
            BM. Wise.

5943 John the Evangelist. In, Farmer, John Stephen, ed. Recently
       Recovered "Lost" Tudor Plays. (London, 1907), pp. 349-
       368.

5944 John the Evangelist. [London]: Privately Printed for Subscribers
       Only, 1907. [4], [23] pp. (Tudor Facsimile Texts).
            WU.

5945 The Interlude of John the Evangelist. Prepared by the General

Editor, W. W. Greg, and Checked by Arundell Esdaile.
London: Printed for the Malone Society by C. Whittingham &
Co., at the Chiswick Press, 1907. vii, [6], [20], [2] pp.

Studies

5946 Bradley, Henry. "Textual Notes on The Enterlude of Johan the
Evangelist." Modern Language Review, II (1906-1907), 350-
352.

5947 Williams, W. H. "'Irisdision,' in the Interlude of Johan the
Evangelyst." Modern Language Review, III (July, 1908), 369-
371.

5948 Dahlström, Carl E. W. L. "The Name Irisdision in the Interlude
of John the Evangelist." Modern Language Notes, LVIII (1943),
44-46.

5949 Bevington, David M. [John the Evangelist]. From Mankind to
Marlowe. (Cambridge, 1962), pp. 56-57, 67.

King Darius. See, Darius

A KNACK TO KNOW A KNAVE

Texts

5950 A most pleasant and merie nevv Comedie, Intituled, A Knacke
to knowe a Knaue. Newlie set foorth, as it hath sundrie tymes
bene played by Ed. Allen and his Companie. VVith Kemps
applauded Merrimentes of the men of Goteham, in receiuing
the King into Goteham. Imprinted at London by Richard Iones,
dwelling at the signe of the Rose and Crowne, nere Holborne
bridge. 1594. 28 unnumbered leaves. [STC. 15027. See Greg,
I, pp. 194-195.] [BM. CSmH. DYCE. O.]

5951 A Knacke to Knowe a Knave. 1594. In, Collier, J. P., ed. Five Old
Plays. (London, 1851), pp. 351-426.

5952 A Knack to Know a Knave. In, Dodsley, Robert, ed. A Select Collection of Old English Plays. Vol. 6. [London, 1874-1876], pp.
[503]-591.

5953 A Knack to Know a Knave. 1594. [London]: Issued for Subscribers
by the Editor of the Tudor Facsimile Texts, 1911. [6], [55] pp.
(Tudor Facsimile Texts).
CSmH. ICN. MB. MH. MiU. WU.

5954 A most pleasant and merie nevv Comedie, Intituled, a Knacke to
      knowe a Knaue. Newlie set foorth, as it hath sundrie tymes
      bene played by Ed. Allen and his Companie. With Kemps ap-
      plauded Merrimentes of the men of Goteham, in receiuing the
      King into Goteham. Imprinted at London by Richard Iones,
      dwelling at the signe of the Rose and Crowne, nere Holborne
      bridge. 1594. Amersham, England: Issued for Subscribers by
      John S. Farmer, 1913. 53 pp.
           MnU. OCl. PHC. PU. WaU.

5955 "A Knack to Know a Knave. A Critical Edition." By Paul Esmond
      Bennett. Ph.D. University of Pennsylvania, 1952.

5956 A Knack to Know a Knave. 1594. Prepared by G. R. Proudfoot.
      The Malone Society Reprints. 1963. (1964). xvii, [59] pp.

                              Studies
5957 Schütt, Hugo, ed. "Die Abfassungszeit von A Knack to Know a
      Knave." The Life and Death of Jack Straw. Ein Beitrag zur
      Geschichte des elisabethanischen Dramas. (Heidelberg, 1901),
      pp. 82-84.
           NN.

5958 Chambers, E. K. "A Knack to Know a Knave." The Elizabethan
      Stage. Vol. 4. (Oxford, 1923), pp. 24-25.

5959 Sykes, H. D. "The Authorship of A Knack to Know a Knave."
      Notes and Queries, CXLV (1924), 389-391, 410-412.

5960 Wainewright, John B. "A Knacke to Knowe a Knave: John Fisher."
      Notes and Queries, CXLIX (1925), 7-8.

5961 Adkins, Mary Grace Muse. "The Genesis of Dramatic Satire
      Against the Puritans, As Illustrated in A Knack to Know a
      Knave." Review of English Studies, XXII (April, 1946), 81-95.
      [Covers also, Respublica, Three Laws, New Custom, Conflict
      of Conscience.]

5962 Bennett, Paul E. "The Oswald Fragment and A Knack to Know a
      Knave." Notes and Queries, CXCVI (1951), 292-293.

5963 ----- "The Word 'Goths' in A Knack to Know a Knave." Notes and
      Queries, New Ser., II (November, 1955), 462-463.

5964 Freeman, Arthur. "Two Notes on A Knack to Know a Knave." Notes and Queries, IX (1962), 326-327.

5965 Bevington, David. [A Merry Knack to Know a Knave.] Tudor
Drama and Politics. (Cambridge, Massachusetts, 1968), pp.
227-229, 294-295.

Liberality and Prodigality. See, Contention between Liberality and
Prodigality

Lindsay, David

Bibliography

5966 Geddie, William. A Bibliography of Middle Scots Poets. Edinburgh: Printed for the [Scottish Text] Society by W. Blackwood,
1912. cix, 364 pp.

5967 Hamer, Douglas. "The Bibliography of Sir David Lindsay (1490-
1555)." Library, Fourth Series, X (1929), [1]-42.

5968 Hamer, Douglas, ed. "Bibliography." The Works of Sir David
Lindsay of the Mount. Vol. 4. (Edinburgh, 1936), pp. [1]-122.

Works
5969 Sir David Lyndesay's Works. London: Published for the Early
English Text Society, by N. Trubner and Co., 1865-1871.
5 parts in 1 vol. [See pt. 4.]
DFo.

5970 Lindsay, Sir David. Poetical Works. 2 vol. Edinburgh: William
Paterson, 1871.
BM.

5971 ----- Poetical Works. Edited by David Laing. 3 vol. Edinburgh:
William Paterson, 1879.
BM.

5972 The Works of Sir David Lindsay of the Mount, 1490-1555. Edited
by Douglas Hamer. 4 vol. Edinburgh and London: Printed for
the Society by W. Blackwood & Sons, Ltd., 1931-1936. (The
Scottish Text Society, 3d ser. Vols. 1-2, 6, 8.) [Bibliography,
Vol. 4, pp. 1-122.]
BM. DFo. ICU.

5973 The Works of Sir David Lindsay of the Mount, 1490-1555. Vol.
II: Ane Satyre of the Thrie Estaitis. Edinburgh and London:

Blackwood, for the Society, 1941. 405 pp. (Scottish Text
Society.)
     DLC. IaU. MiU. MnU. WU.

SATIRE OF THE THREE ESTATES
Texts

5974 Ane Satyre Of The Thrie Estaits, in commendation of vertew and
vituperation of vyce. Maid be Sir Dauid Lindesay of the Mont,
aliàs, Lyon King of Armes. At Einbvrgh Printed Be Robert
Charteris. 1602. [A variant imprint adds the following words
after the date: Cvm Privilegio Regis.] 77 leaves. [STC. 15681.
See Greg, I, p. 306.]
     CSmH. (Variant). O. (plus variant)

5975 The VVorkes Of the Famous and worthy Knight, Sir David Lindsaie
of the Mont, Alias Lyoun King of Armes. Newly corrected and
vindicate from the former errors, wherewith they were before
corrupted, and augmented with sundrie workes neuer before
imprinted. Viuet etiam post funera virtus. Militia est vita
hominis super terram. Imprinted at Edinburgh by Robert
Charteris, Printer to the Kinges most excellent Maiestie, and
are to be solde in London by Nathaniell Butter, at his shoppe
neare S. Austens Church in the old Change, 1604. [STC. 15682.
See Greg, I, pp. 306-307, who calls it another issue in which
a single-leaf cancel replaces the original title-leaf. He says
that it is known only from a single copy, Britwell sale, April,
1924; "seen Quaritch's, Mar. 1927."]

5976 Lindsay, Sir David. Ane Pleasant Satyre of the Thrie Estaitis.
Edited by James Sibbald. Edinburgh, 1802. xvi, 142, [1] pp.
[50 copies printed.]
     BM. DFo. MH.

5977 ----- Ane Plesant Satyre of the Three Estaitis. In, Poetical
Works. Edited by George Chalmers. Vol. 1. (London, 1806),
pp. 354-470.
     BM.

5978 Lyndesay, David. Ane Satyre of the Thrie Estaits, in Commendation of Vertew and Vitvperation of Vyce. Maid Be Sir David
Lindesay of the Mont, Alias, Lyon King of Armes. At Edin-
bvrg: Printed Be Robert Charteris, 1602. Cvm Privilegio Regis.
Edited by F. Hall, Esq. London: Published for the Early English Text Society, by N. Trübner &Co., 1869. pp. [375]-548.
[Part Four of Sir David Lyndesay's Works, Published by the

Early English Text Society. Original Series, No. 37.]
BM. MdBP. ODW.

5979 The Satire of the Three Estates of Sir David Lindsay of the Mount;
Edinburgh Festival Version. With an Introduction by Tyrone
Guthrie. Edited by Robert Kemp. London: W. Heinemann,
1951. xviii, 61 pp. (Drama Library Series.)
BM. IaU.

5980 Lindsay, Sir David. Ane Satyre of the Thrie Estaits . . . Edited
by James Kinsley with a Critical Introduction by Agnes Mure
Mackenzie, and a Foreword by Ivor Brown. London: Cassell &
Co., 1954. 236 pp.
BM. ICU.

5981 ----- A Satire of the Three Estates. A Play Adapted by Matthew
McDiarmid from the Acting Text Made by Robert Kemp for
Tyrone Guthrie's Production at the Edinburgh Festival 1948
with Music by Cedric Thorpe-Davie. Introduction and Notes by
Matthew McDiarmid. London: Heinemann Educational Books
Ltd., 1967. 170, [1] pp.

5982 McDiarmid, Matthew, ed. A Satire of the Three Estates. With
Introduction. New York: Theatre Arts, 1968. [Adaptation].

Studies
5983 Chambers, E. K. "Sir David Lyndsay (Ane Satyre of the Thrie
Estaitis)." The Mediaeval Stage. Vol. 2. (London, 1903), pp.
441-443.

5984 Mill, Anna J. "The Influence of the Continental Drama on Lyndsay's Satyre of the Thrie Estaitis." Modern Language Review,
XXV (October, 1930), 425-442.

5985 ----- "Representations of Lyndsay's Satyre of the Thrie
Estaitis." Publications of the Modern Language Association,
XLVII (September, 1932), 636-651.

5986 ----- "Representations of Lyndsay's Satyre of the Three Estaitis."
Publications of the Modern Language Association, XLVIII
(March, 1933), 315-316.

5987 Mohl, Ruth. The Three Estates in Medieval and Renaissance
Literature. New York: Columbia University Press, 1933. xi,
425 pp. (Columbia University Studies in English and Comparative Literature).
DLC.

5988 Houk, Raymond A. "Versions of Lindsay's Satire of the Three
      Estates." Publications of the Modern Language Association,
      LV (June, 1940), 396-405.

5989 Miller, Edwin Shepard. "The Christening in The Three Estates."
      Modern Language Notes, LX (January, 1945), 42-44.

5990 MacLaine, Allan H. "'Christis Kirk on the Grene' and Sir David
      Lindsay's Satyre of the Thrie Estaits." Journal of English and
      Germanic Philology, LVI (1957), 596-601.

5991 Dessen, Alan Charles. "Ben Jonson and the Estates Morality
      Tradition." Ph.D. Johns Hopkins University, 1963.

5992 ----- "The Estates Morality Play." Studies in Philology, LXII
      (April, 1965), 121-136.

                    General Biographical and Critical Studies

5993 Knauff, Gustav. Studien über Sir David Lyndsay. Berlin, [1885].
      91 pp.
            ICN. ICU.

5994 Kissel, Julius. Das Sprichwort bei dem Mittelschottischen Dichter
      Sir David Lyndesay. Inaugural Dissertation. Erlangen, 1892.

5995 Henderson, Thomas Finlayson. Scottish Vernacular Literature:
      A Succinct History. London: D. Nutt, 1898. viii, 462 pp.
            BM.

5996 Lindsay, John. The Lindsays of the Mount. Edinburgh: Lindsay
      & Co., 1938. 82 pp. (Clan Lindsay Society Publications V,
      No. 17).
            BM.

5997 Murison, William. Sir David Lyndsay, Poet and Satirist of the
      Old Church in Scotland. New York: Macmillan; Cambridge
      University Press, 1938. xiii, 227 pp. Bibliography pp. [205]-
      207.
            BM. DFo. DLC. IaU. ICN. ICU. MiU. OC1. OU. WU.

5998 Barclay, William R. "The Role of Sir David Lyndsay in the Scottish
      Reformation." Ph.D. University of Wisconsin, 1956.

5999 Wilson, F. P. "The Two 'Makers': Skelton and Lindsay." The

English Drama, 1485-1585. (Oxford, 1969), pp. 15-21.

Love. See, Heywood, John (Play of Love).

Love and Fortune. See, Rare Triumphs of Love and Fortune.

LOVE FEIGNED AND UNFEIGNED
Text
6000 Love Feigned and Unfeigned: A Fragmentary Morality. Malone
      Society Collections, I, Pt. I (1907), pp. 17-25.

Studies
6001 Daw, E. Beatrice. "Love Fayned and Unfayned and the English
      Anabaptists." Publications of the Modern Language Asso-
      ciation, XXXII (1917), 267-291.

6002 Chambers, E. K. "Love Feigned and Unfeigned." The Elizabethan
      Stage. Vol. 4. (Oxford, 1923), pp. 28-29.

LUCRECE
Texts
6003 The Enterlude of Youth. Nebst Fragmenten Des Playe of Lucres
      und von Nature. Herausgegen von W. Bang und R. B. McKerrow.
      Louvain: A. Ulystpruyst, 1905. 108 pp.
      ICN. MnU. MY. PU.

6004 The Play of Lucrece: A Fragment of an Interlude Printed c. 1530.
      Malone Society Collections, I, Part 2 (1908), 137-142.

Studies
6005 Chambers, E. K. "Lucrece." The Mediaeval Stage. Vol. 2.
      (London, 1903), p. 458.

Lupton, Thomas

ALL FOR MONEY
Texts
6006 A Moral and Pitiefvl Comedie, Intituled, All for Money. Plainly
      representing the maners of men, and fashion of the world
      noweadayes. Compiled by T. Lupton. The names of them that
      play this Comoedie. . . . At London: Printed by Roger Warde
      and Richard Mundee, dwelling at Temple Barre. Anno. 1578.
      20 unnumbered leaves. [STC. 16949. See Greg, I, pp. 152-
      153. Variants found in Bodleian copy.]
      BM. O.

6007 All for Money. In, Halliwell, James Orchard. The Literature of the Sixteenth and Seventeenth Century. Illustrated by Reprints of Very Rare Tracts. (London, 1851), pp. 103-173.

6008 Vogel, Ernst, ed. "All for Money. Ein Moralspiel aus der Zeit Shakespeares." Shakespeare Jahrbuch, XL (1904), 129-186. [Text, pp. 146-186].

6009 All for Money. By Thomas Lupton. 1578. London and Edinburgh: Issued for Subscribers by the Editor of the Tudor Facsimile Texts, 1910. [6], [37] pp.
        ICN. MB. MiU. NjP. PP. ViU. WU.

6010 A Moral And Pitiefvl Comedie, Intituled, All for Money. Plainly representing the maners of men, and fashion of the world noweadayes. Compiled by T. Lupton. At London. Printed by Roger Warde and Richard Mundee, and dwelling at Temple Barre. Anno. 1578. Amersham, England: Issued for Subscribers by John S. Farmer, 1913. 36 pp.
        DFo. MH. OCl. OU. PHC. PU.

Studies

6011 Chambers, E. K. "Thomas Lupton. All for Money." The Elizabethan Stage. Vol. 3. (Oxford, 1923), p. 411.

6012 Craik, T.W. "Some Notes on Thomas Lupton's All for Money." Notes and Queries, CXCIX (June, 1954), 233-235.

6013 Bevington, David M. [All for Money]. From Mankind to Marlowe. (Cambridge, 1962), pp. 55, 56, 70, 72, 73, 75, 76, 78, 93, 94, 165-169.

MACRO MORALITIES

Manuscripts

6014 MS of Macro plays in the Folger Shakespeare Library.

6015 Oxford. Bodleian, Digby MS 133.

Collections

*6016 Furnivall, F. J., and Alfred W. Pollard, eds. The Macro Plays: 1. Mankind (ca. 1475). 2. Wisdom (ca. 1460). 3. The Castle of Perseverance (ca. 1425). With Introduction and Glossarial Index. London: for the Early English Text Society by K. Paul, Trench, Trubner and Co., Ltd., 1904. xlii, 210 pp. (Early English Text Society. Extra Series, No. 91).
        BM. CtY. MH. NN. WU.

*6017 Eccles, Mark, ed. The Macro Plays: The Castle of Perseverance,
        Wisdom, Mankind. London, New York, Toronto: Oxford Uni-
        versity Press for the Early English Text Society, 1969. lii,
        280 pp. (E. E. T. S., 262).

6018 Chambers, E. K. "Macro Morals."The Mediaeval Stage. Vol. 2.
        (London, 1903), pp. 436-438.

        Individual Plays. See under individual titles.

CASTLE OF PERSERVERANCE
MANKIND
MIND, WILL, AND UNDERSTANDING

                            Studies
MANKIND
                             Texts
6019 Mankind. In, Brandl, Alois. Quellen des weltlichen Dramas in
        England vor Shakespeare. (Strassburg, 1898), pp. 37-72.

6020 Mankind. In, Manly, J. M., ed. Specimens of Pre-Shakespearean
        Drama. Vol. 1. (Boston and New York, 1903-1904), pp. 315-
        352.

6021 Mankind. In, Furnivall, F. J., and Alfred W. Pollard, eds.
        The Macro Plays. (London, 1904), pp. 1-34.

6022 Mankind. The Macro Plays. No. 1. London and Edinburgh: Is-
        sued for Subscribers by T. C. and E. C. Jack, 1907. [6],
        [26] pp. (Tudor Facsimile Texts.)
                DFo. DLC. ICN. MH. MiU. NjP. NN. O. ViU. WU.

6023 Mankind, c. 1475; a Morality Portraying the Life of Ne'er-do-
        wells in Late Plantagenet and Early Tudor Times. In, Farmer,
        John S., ed. Recently Recovered "Lost" Tudor Plays. (London,
        1907), pp. 1-40.

6024 Mankind, Amersham, England. Issued for Subscribers by John
        S. Farmer, 1914.
                MnU. OCl.

6025 Mankynd. A Morality Founded on and in Much Part Taken from
        The Castell of Perseverance, circa 1444 A.D. Edited by
        Francis Hartman Markoe. New York: The Premier Press
        [c. 1914]. 17 pp.

6026 Mankind. In, Adams, Joseph Quincy, ed. Pre-Shakespearean
       Plays. (Boston and New York, 1924), pp. 304-324.

6027 Mankind. A Copy Made by Mrs. Furnivall from Dr. Furnivall's
       Copy, the Latter Being Made by Dr. Furnivall Himself from
       the Macro Moralities.
          MH.

Studies

6028 "Mankind." In, Brandl, Alois. Quellen des weltlichen Dramas in
       England vor Shakespeare. (Strassburg, 1898), pp. xxi-xxxiii.

6029 Chambers, E. K. "Mankind." The Mediaeval Stage. Vol. 2.
       (London, 1903), p. 438.

6030 Keiller, M. M. "Influence of 'Piers Plowman' on the Macro Play
       of Mankind." Publications of the Modern Language Association,
       XXVI (1911), 339-355.

6031 MacKenzie, Roy W. "A New Source for Mankind." Publications
       of the Modern Language Association, XXVII (1912), 98-105.

6032 Haller, Julius. "Mankind." Die Technik des Dialogs im mittelalter-
       lichen Drama Englands. (Worms, 1916), pp. 99-101.

6033 Smart, W. K. "Some Notes on Mankind." Modern Philology, XIV
       (1916), 45-58, 293-313.

6034 ----- "Mankind and the Mumming Plays. Modern Language
       Notes, XXXII (1917), 21-25.

6035 Jones, Claude E. "Walsyngham Wystyll." Journal of English and
       Germanic Philology, XXXV (January, 1936), 139.

6036 Chambers, E. K. ["Mankind"]. English Literature at the Close
       of the Middle Ages. (Oxford, 1945), pp. 61-62.

6037 Coogan, Sr. Mary Philippa. An Interpretation of the Moral Play
       'Mankind.' Washington, D.C.: Catholic University of America
       Press, 1947. ix, 129 pp. Bibliography, pp. 121-125.
          BM. CU. DFo. DLC. PU.

6038 Bevington, David M. [Mankind]. From Mankind to Marlowe.
       (Cambridge, 1962), pp. 15-18, 137-138.

6039 Baker, Donald C. "The Date of <u>Mankind</u>." <u>Philological Quarterly,</u> XLII (January, 1963), 90-91.

6040 Fifield, Merle. "Mankind." The Castle in the Circle. (Muncie, Indiana, 1967), pp. 27-35.

Texts

MARRIAGE OF WIT AND SCIENCE

6041 A new and Pleasaunt enterlude intituled the mariage of Witte and Science. Imprinted at London in Fletestrete, neare vnto sainct Dunstones churche by Thomas Marshe. 22 unnumbered leaves. [STC. 17466. See Greg, I, p. 133, who dates the play "about Aug. 1569." "1570" is written on the title page of the Bodleian copy. This play is distinct from John Redford's play of <u>Wit and Science.</u>]
       O.

6042 The Marriage of Wit and Science. In, Dodsley, R., ed. A Select Collection of Old English Plays. Vol. 2. (London, 1874-1876), pp. 321-394.

6043 The Marriage of Wit and Science. In, Recently Recovered "Lost" Tudor Plays. Edited by John S. Farmer. (London, 1907), pp. 135-175.

6044 The Marriage of Wit and Science. In, Farmer, John S., ed. Five Anonymous Plays. (London, 1908), pp. 47-100.

6045 The Marriage of Wit and Science, 1569-1570. London and Edinburgh: Issued for Subscribers by T. C. and E. C. Jack, 1909. [6], [43] pp. (Tudor Facsimile Texts.)
       DLC. ICN. MB. MH. MiU. NjP. NN. PU. ViU. WU.

6046 A New and Pleasaunt Enterlude Intituled the Marriage of Witte and Science. Imprinted at London in Fletestret, neare vnto sainct Dunstones churche by Thomas Marshe, 1570. Amersham, England: Issued for Subscribers by John S. Farmer, 1914. 43 pp.
       DFo. MnU. OCl. PU.

6047 The Marriage of Wit and Science. In, Adams, Joseph Quincy, ed. Chief Pre-Shakesperean Dramas. (Boston and New York, 1924), pp. 325-342.

6048 The Marriage of Wit and Science. Prepared by Arthur Brown,
      with assistance from John Crow and F. P. Wilson. Oxford:
      Printed for the Malone Society by Vivian Ridler at the Uni-
      versity Press, 1961. xv, [43] pp.

Studies

6049 Seifert, J. Wit-und Science Moralitäten des 16 Jahrhunderts.
      Inaugural Dissertation. Prague, 1892.

6050 Haller, Julius. "Wyt and Science."Die Technik des Dialogs im
      mittelalterlichen Drama Englands. (Wormser, 1916), pp. 119-
      122.

6051 Chambers, E. K. "The Marriage of Wit and Science." The Eliz-
      abethan Stage. Vol. 4. (Oxford, 1923), pp. 29-30. [Indebed
      to Redford's Wit and Science.]

6052 Withington, Robert. "Experience the Mother of Science." Publi-
      cations of the Modern Language Association, LVII (1942), 592.

6053 Varma, R. S. "Act and Scene Divisions in The Marriage of Wit
      and Science." Notes and Queries, X (1963), 95-96.

6054 Habicht, Werner. "The Wit Interludes and the Form of Pre-
      Shakespearean 'Romantic Comedy.'" Renaissance Drama,
      VIII (1965), 73-88.

6055 Varma, R. S. "Philosophical and Moral Ideas in The Marriage
      of Wit and Science." Philological Quarterly, XLIV (1965),
      120-122.

6056 Tompkins, Kenneth D. "The Wit Plays: Variations on a Tudor
      Dramatic Theme." Ph.D. University of Indiana, 1968.

The Marriage of Wit and Wisdom. See Merbury, Francis.

Medwall, Henry

General Studies and Cricitism

6057 Chambers, E. K. "Henry Medwall." The Mediaeval Stage."
      (London, 1903), p. 443.

6058 Ross, Harold Truslow. "Henry Medwall: Life and Works." M.A.
      Columbia University, 1924.

6059 Reed, A. W. Early Tudor Drama: Medwall, the Rastells, Hey-
wood, and the More Circle. With Nine Illustrations. London:
Methuen and Co., Ltd., [1926]. 246 pp.
BM. ICN.

6060 Butler, Sr. M. Basil, C.S.J. "Religious Satire in the Works of
Medwall, Rastell, Heywood and More: A Spirit of Devotion
to the Ideal of the Church Rather Than to That of the Reformation." Ph.D. St. John's College, 1945.

6061 Waith, Eugene M. "'Controversia' in the English Drama: Medwall
and Massinger." Publications of the Modern Language Association, LXVIII (March, 1953), 286-303.

6062 Wilson, F. P. "Medwall and before Medwall." The English Drama
1485-1585. (Oxford, 1969), pp. 1-11.

FULGENS AND LUCRES
Texts
6063 Here is coteyned a godely interlude of Fulgens Cenatoure of Rome.
Lucres his doughter. Gayus flaminius. & Publi. Corneli. of the
disputacyon of noblenes. & is deuyded in two ptyes to be played
at ii. tymes. Copyled by mayster Henry medwall. late chapel-
ayne to $\bar{y}$ ryght reuerent fader in god Iohan Morton cardynall &
Archebysshop of Cauterbury. [Colophon: Emprynted at london
by Iohan rastell dwellynge on the south syde of paulys chyrche
by syde paulys cheyne.] 40 unnumbered leaves. [STC. 17778.
See Greg, I, p. 81, who dates the edition "1512-1516?"]
BM (Fragment of two leaves). CSmH.

6064 Here is coteyned a godely interlude of Fulgens Cenatoure of
Rome Lucres his daughter. In, Quellen und Forschungen zur
Sprachund Kulturgeschichte der germanischen Volker. (Strass-
burg, 1898), pp. 281-358.

6065 Fulgens and Lucres. A godely interlude of the disputacyon of
nobleness. Complyed by Mayster Henry Medwall. With an
Introductory Note by Seymour de Ricci. New York: G. D.
Smith, 1920. 76 pp.
DFo. DLC. MH. MiU. NN. OCU. PU. ViU. WU.

6066 Fulgens and Lucres. A Fifteenth-Century Secular Play. By
Henry Medwall. Edited by F. S. Boas and A. W. Reed. Ox-
ford: Clarendon Press, 1926. xxvii, 104 pp. (Tudor and
Stuart Library.)

BM. CSmH. DLC. ICU. MB. MH. MiU. OC1. OU. WU.

6067 Fulgens and Lucrece. In, Boas, F. S., ed. Five Pre-Shakespearean
      Comedies. (London, 1934), pp. 1-72.

Studies

6068 Greg, W. W. "Fulgens and Lucres." Times Literary Supplement,
      March 10, 1921, p. 160.

6069 Von Hecht, Prof. Dr. Hans. Medwalls Fulgens and Lucres. Eine
      Studie zu den Anfängen des weltlichen Dramas in England. In,
      Brandl, Alois. Untersuchungen zur englischen Philologie. Band
      II, Literaturgeschichte. Leipzig: Mayer & Müller, 1925.
      474 pp. (Palaestra, 148.)
         BM. ICN.

6070 Reed, A. W. "Sixt Birck and Henry Medwall, 'De Vera Nobilitate.'"
      Review of English Studies, II (1926), 411-415.

6071 Wright, Louis B. "Notes on Fulgens and Lucres: New Light on
      the Interlude." Modern Language Notes, XLI (February, 1926),
      97-100.

6072 Baskervill, Charles R. "Conventional Features of Medwall's
      Fulgens and Lucres." Modern Philology, XXIV (May, 1927),
      419-442.

6073 Purves, John. "A Note on Fulgens and Lucres." Times Literary
      Supplement, April 14, 1927, p. 265; July 7, 1927, p. 472.

6074 Jones, Claude E. "Notes on Fulgens and Lucres." Modern Lan-
      guage Notes, L (1935), 508-509.

6075 Lowers, James K. "High Comedy Elements in Medwall's Fulgens
      and Lucres." English Literary History, VIII (1941), 103-106.

6076 Bevington, David M. [Fulgens and Lucrece.] From Mankind to
      Marlowe. (Cambridge, 1962), pp. 43-44, 46, 47, 65, 70,
      128.

6077 ----- [Fulgens and Lucrece.] Tudor Drama and Politics. (Cam-
      bridge, Massachusetts, 1968), pp. 44-51.

NATURE
Texts
6078 Nature. A goodly interlude of Nature copylyd by mayster Henry
      Medwall chapleyn to the ryght reuerent father in god Iohan
      Morton somtyme Cardynall and archebyshop of Canterbury.
      [Colophon: None.] 36 leaves. [STC. 17779. See Greg, I, p.
      93, who suggests a date between 1530 and 1534.]
      BM. C. CSmH. O.

6079 Nature. In, Brandl, Alois. Quellen des weltlichen Dramas in
      England vor Shakespeare. (Strassburg, 1898), pp. 73-158.

6080 Nature: a goodly interlude of Nature. In, Farmer, John S., ed.
      Recently Recovered "Lost" Tudor Plays. (London, 1907), pp.
      41-133.

6081 Nature, by Henry Medwall. c. 1486-1500. London and Edinburgh,
      Issued for Subscribers by T. C. and E. C. Jack, 1908. viii,
      [71] pp. (Tudor Facsimile Texts.)
      BM. DLC. ICN. MB. MH. MiU. NjP. PP. ViU. WU.

6082 A goodly interlude of Nature copylyd by mayster Henry Medwall
      chapelyn to the ryght reuerent father in god Johan Morton
      somtyme Cardynall and arche byshop of Canterbury. Amer-
      sham, England: Issued for Subscribers by John S. Farmer,
      1914. 71 pp.
      DFo. OC1. PU.

Studies
6083 "Nature." In, Brandl, Alois. Quellen des weltlichen Dramas in
      in England vor Shakespeare. (Strassburg, 1898), pp. xxxiii-
      xlvi.

6084 Mackenzie, W. Roy. "Source for Medwall's Nature." Publications
      of the Modern Language Association, XXIX (1914), 189-199.

6085 Haller, Julius. "Nature." Die Technik des Dialogs im mittelalter-
      lichen Drama Englands. (Worms, 1916), pp. 105-112.

6086 McCutchan, J. Wilson. "Similarities between Falstaff and Glut-
      tony in Medwall's Nature." Shakespeare Association Bulletin,
      XXIV (July, 1949), 214-219.

6087 Bevington, David M. [Nature.] From Mankind to Marlowe. (Cam-
      bridge, 1962), pp. 44-45, 65, 70.

6088 Bevington, David. [Nature.] Tudor Drama and Politics. (Cambridge, Massachusetts, 1968), pp. 51-53.

Merbury, Francis

MARRIAGE OF WIT AND WISDOM
Manuscript
6089 A Marriage between Wit and Wisdom. British Museum Additional MS. 26782. [The date on the MS. is 1570 or 1579?. It has the name of Francis Merbury appended to the Epilogue. Because a number of scholars attribute the play to Merbury, I list it under his name.]

Texts
6090 The Marriage of Wit and Wisdom. Edited by James Orchard Halliwell. London: Shakespeare Society, 1846. xii, 147 pp. BM.

6091 The Marriage of Wit and Wisdom, an ancient interlude. To Which are Added Illustrations of Shakespeare and the Early English Drama. Edited by James O. Halliwell. London: Printed for the Shakespeare Society, 1846. 147 pp. In, Amyot, Thomas, ed. A Supplement to Dodsley's Old Plays. Vol. 2. (London, 1853).

6092 A Contract of Marriage between Wit and Wisdom [c. 1579]. London and Edinburgh: Issued for Subscribers by T. C. and E. C. Jack, 1909. v, [64] pp. (Tudor Facsimile Texts.) ICN. MH. MiU. NN. ViU.

6093 The Contract of Marriage betweene Wit and Wisdome very frutefull and mixed full of pleasant mirth as well for the beholders as the Readers or hearers neuer before imprinted. 1579. Amersham, England: Issued for Subscribers by John S. Farmer, 1914. OC1. PU.

Studies
6094 Haller, Julius. "Marriage of Wit and Wisdom." Die Technik des Dialogs im mittelalterlichen Drama Englands. (Worms, 1916), pp. 133-137.

6095 Chambers, E. K. "Francis Merbury. A Marriage between Wit and Wisdom c. 1579." The Elizabethan Stage. Vol. 3. (Oxford, 1923), pp. 436-437.

6096 Tannenbaum, Samuel A. "Comments on The Marriage of Wit and Wisdom." Philological Quarterly, IX (October, 1930), 321-340.

6097 Greg, Walter W. "The Date of Wit and Wisdom." Philological Quarterly, XI (October, 1932), 410.

6098 Tannenbaum, Samuel A. "Dr. Tannenbaum Replies." Philological Quarterly, XII (Janury, 1933), 88-89.

6099 Tilley, Morris P. "Notes on The Marriage of Wit and Wisdom." Shakespeare Association Bulletin, X (January, 1935), 45-57, 89-94.

6100 Race, Sidney. "The Marriage of Wit and Wisdom." Notes and Queries, CXCVIII (January, 1953), 18-20.

6101 Bevington, David M. [The Marriage of Wit and Wisdom.] From Mankind to Marlowe. (Cambridge, 1962), pp. 23-25.

6102 Lennam, Trevor Neville Shawe. "The 'Wit' Plays. A Study of the Dramatic Relations of Three Tudor Interludes. Wit and Science by John Redford, The Marriage of Wit and Science, Anon., and The Marriage between Wit and Wisdom by Francis Merbury." Ph.D. University of New Brunswick, 1964.

6103 Tompkins, Kenneth D. "The Wit Plays: Variations on a Tudor Dramatic Theme." Ph.D. University of Indiana, 1968.

Mind, Will, and Understanding. See, Wisdom Who Is Christ.

MISOGONUS

Manuscript

6104 California, San Marino. Huntington Library. HM. 452. [Dated 1577.]

Texts

6105 Misogonus. In, Brandl, Alois. Quellen des weltlichen Dramas in England vor Shakespeare. (Strassburg, 1898), pp. 419-489.

6106 Misogonus. In, Farmer, John Stephen, ed. Six Anonymous Plays. (London, 1906), pp. 133-243.

6107 Misogonus. In, Bond, Richard Warwick. Early Plays from the Italian. (Oxford, 1911), pp. 159-258; 303-323.

Studies

6108 "Misogonus." In, Brandl, Alois. Quellen des weltlichen Dramas
      in England vor Shakespeare. (Strassburg, 1898), pp. lxxv-
      lxxxvii.

6109 Kittredge, G. L. "The Misogonus and Laurence Johnson." Journal
      of English and Germanic Philology, III (1901), 335-341.

6110 Moore-Smith, G. C. "Misogonus." Times Literary Supplement,
      July 10, 1930, p. 576.

6111 Tannenbaum, Samuel A. "A Note on Misogonus." Modern Language
      Notes, XLV (1930), 308-310.

6112 ----- "The Author of Misogonus." Shaksperian Scraps and Other
      Elizabethan Fragments. (New York, 1933), pp. 129-141.

6113 Bevington, David M. "Misogonus and Laurentius Bari na." English
      Language Notes, II (1964), 9-10.

      Most Virtuous and Godly Susanna. See, Garter, Thomas.
      (Godly Susanna)

      Mundus et Infans. See, World and Child.

      Nature of the Four Elements. See, Rastell, John.
      (Nature of the Four Elements)

NEW CUSTOM
                                    Texts
6114 A new Enterlude No lesse wittie: then pleasant, entituled new
      Custome, deuised of late, and for diuerse causes nowe set
      forthe, neuer before this tyme Imprinted. 1573. . . . [Colophon:
      Imprinted at London in Fleetestreete by William How for
      Abraham Veale, dwelling in Paules churche yarde at the signe
      of the Lambe.] 16 unnumbered leaves. [STC. 6150. See Greg,
      I, pp. 138-139.]
            BM. CSmH. CtY. DFo. O.

6115 New Custome. In, Dodsley, R., ed. A Select Collection of Old
      Plays. Vol. 1. (London, 1744), pp. 39-81.

6116 New Custome. In, Dodsley, R., ed. A Select Collection of Old
      Plays. Vol. 1. (London, 1780), pp. [249]-292.

6117 New Custome. In, Dodsley, Robert, ed. A Select Collection of Old Plays. Vol. 1. (London, 1825), pp. [263]-308.

6118 New Custom. In, Dodsley, Robert, ed. A Select Collection of Old English Plays. 4th ed. Vol. 3. (London, 1874-1876), pp. [1]-52.

6119 New Custom. In, Farmer, John Stephen, ed. Anonymous Plays. (London, 1906), pp. 157-202.

6120 New Custom. 1573. London and Edinburgh. Issued for Subscribers by T. C. and E. C. Jack, 1908. [10], [32] pp. (Tudor Facsimile Texts.).
    DFo. DLC. ICN. MB. MH. NjP. NN. ViU. WU.

6121 A New Enterlude No Lesse wittie: then pleasant, entituled new Custome, deuised of late, and for diuers causes nowe set forthe, neuer before this tyme Imprinted. 1573. Amersham, England: Issued for Subscribers by John S. Farmer, 1914. 30 pp.
    DFo. OCl. OU. PU.

Studies

6122 Chambers, E. K. "New Custom." The Elizabethan Stage. Vol. 4. (Oxford, 1923), pp. 36-37.

6123 Oliver, Leslie Mahin. "John Foxe and the Drama New Custom." Huntington Library Quarterly, X (1947), 407-410.

6124 Bevington, David M. [New Custom]. From Mankind to Marlowe. (Cambridge, 1962), pp. 54-55, 66, 146-149.

6125 ----- [New Custom]. Tudor Drama and Politics. (Cambridge, Massachusetts, 1968), pp. 130-131.

NICE WANTON

Texts

6126 A Preaty Interlude called, Nice wanton,
    Wherein ye may see,
    Three braunces of an yll tree,
    The mother and her chyldren three,
    Twoo naught, and one godlye.
    Early sharpe, that wyll be thorne,
    Soone yll, that wyll be naught:
    To be naught, better unborne,
    Better vnsed, then naughtely taught.

Ut magnum magnos, pueros puerilia deocus . . . . Anno Domini.
M.D.L.X. [Colophon: Imprinted at London, in Paules Churche
yearde at the Sygne of the Swane by Iohn Kyng.]   10 unnumbered
leaves. [STC. 25016. Entered in SR on 10 June, 1560. See Greg,
I, pp. 106-107.]
    BM.

6127 A pretie Enterlude called Nice wanton.
    Wherin ye may see,
    Three braunches of an il tree:
    The mother and her Children three,
      Two naught and one godly.
    Early sharp that wilbe thorne,
    Soon il that wil be naught:
    To be naught better unborne,
      Better vnsed then naughtily taught.
    Et magnum magnos, pueros puerilia decus . . . . Imprinted
at London at the long Shop adioyning vnto Saint Mildreds
Church in the Pultrie, by Iohn Allde. 10 leaves unnumbered.
[STC. 25017 queries 1565 as the date. See Greg, I, pp. 107-
108.]
    BM. CSmH.

6128 Nice Wanton. In, Dodsley, Robert, ed. A Select Collection of
Old English Plays. 4th ed. Vol. 2. (London, 1874-1876).

6129 A preaty interlude called Nice Wanton. In, Manly, J. M., ed.
Specimens of the Pre-Shakesperean Drama. (Boston and New
York, 1903-1904), pp. 457-480.

6130 The Dramatic Writings of Richard Wever and Thomas Ingelend.
Comprising Lusty Juventus--Disobedient Child--Nice Wanton--
Note-book and word-list. Edited by John S. Farmer. (London,
1905).

6131 Nice Wanton, An Unrecorded Edition. London and Edinburgh:
Issued for Subscribers by T. C. and E. C. Jack, 1908. vi,
[20] pp. (Tudor Facsimile Texts.)
    DLC. ICN. MB. MH. MiU. NN. ViU. WU.

6132 Nice Wanton. 1560. London and Edinburgh: Issued for Subscribers
by T. C. and E. C. Jack, 1909. vii, [20] pp. (Tudor Facsimile
Texts.)
    DLC. MB. MH. MiU. NN. ViU. WU.

6133 A Preaty Interlude called, Nice Wanton. Anno Domini. M.D.L.X.
       Amersham, England: Issued for Subscribers by John S.
       Farmer, 1914. 20 pp.
          PU.

                              Studies
6134 Chambers, E. K. "T. R. Nice Wanton." The Mediaeval Drama.
       Vol. 2. (London, 1903), p. 460.

6135 Hollis, Gertrude Gray. "Nice Wanton." M.A. University of
       Chicago, 1921.

NOBODY AND SOMEBODY
                              Text
6136 Nobody and Somebody [c. 1592]. Issued for Subscribers by the
       Editor of the Tudor Facsimile Texts, 1911. [6], [68] pp.

OLD CUSTOM (Lost)

6137 Feuillerat, Albert. "Unknown Protestant Morality Play." Modern
       Language Review, IX (1914), 94-96.

6138 Baskervill, C. R. "On Two Old Plays." Modern Philology, XIV
       (1916-1917), 16.

PATER FILIUS ET VXOR, OR THE PRODIGAL SON
                              Texts
6139 [An interlude on the story of the Prodigal Son (related to Ravisius
       Textor's dialogue Iuuenis Pater et Vxor) in which Pater,
       Filius, Vxor, and Seruus are characters, known from a single
       leaf only.] [See Greg, I, p. 93, who gives the date as "?1530-
       1534."]
          C.

6140 The Prodigal Son. A Fragment of an Interlude Printed c. 1530.
       Malone Society Collections, I, Part I (1908), pp. 27-30.
       [A single leaf].

PATER NOSTER

6141 Chambers, E. K. "Pater-Noster Play." The Mediaeval Stage.
       Vol. 2. (London, 1903), pp. 403-404.

6142 Onions, C. Talbut. "A Thirteenth Century Paternoster by an
       Anglo-French Scribe." Modern Language Review, III (1907-
       1908), 69-71.

6143 Craig, Hardin. "Letter on the Pater Noster Play." Nation, May
       3, 1917, pp. 563-564.

6144 Allison, Tempe E. "The Paternoster Play and the Origin of the
       Vices." Publications of the Modern Language Association,
       XXXIX (December, 1924), 789-804.

6145 Chambers, E. K. ["Paternoster."] English Literature at the
       Close of the Middle Ages. Vol. 4. (Oxford, 1945), p. 51.

THE PEDLAR's PROPHECY
   (This play is often attributed to Robert Wilson.)

Texts
6146 The Pedlers Prophecie. London Printed by Tho. Creede, and are
       to be sold by William Barley, at his shop in Gratious streete.
       1595. 24 unnumbered leaves. [STC. 25782 lists the play under
       Robert Wilson. See Greg, I, p. 220.]
          BM. CSmH. DFo. MH. O. Pepys.

6147 The Pedler's Prophecy. 1595. [London]. Issued for Subscribers,
       1911. [6], [47] pp. (Tudor Facsimile Texts.)
          DLC. ICN. MH. MiU. NjP. PU. ViU. WU.

6148 The Pedlers Prophecie. London. Printed by Tho. Creede, and
       are to be sold by William Barley, at his shop in Gratious streete.
       1595. Amersham, England: Issued for Subscribers by John S.
       Farmer, 1913. 45 pp.
          DFo. MH. OCl. OU. PHC. PU.

6149 The Pedlar's Prophecy. 1595 . . . Prepared Under the Direction
       of the General Editor, W. W. Greg. Printed for the Malone
       Society by H. Hart at the Oxford University Press, 1914. vii,
       [47] pp.

Studies
6150 Chambers, E. K. "The Pedlar's Prophecy." The Elizabethan Stage.
       Vol. 4. (Oxford, 1923), p. 41.

6151 Kittredge, G. L. "The Date of the Pedlers Prophecie." Harvard
       Studies and Notes in Philology and Literature, XVI (1934),
       97-118.

6152 Pineas, Rainer. "Polemical Technique in The Pedlers Prophecie."
       English Language Notes, VI (December, 1968), 90-94.

Phillip, John

PATIENT GRISSIL
Texts

6153 The Commodye Of pacient and meeke Grissill, Whearin is
      declared, the good example, of her pacience towardes her Hus-
      band: and lykewise, the due obedience of Children, toward
      their Parentes. Newly. Compiled by Iohn Phillip. . . . Im-
      printed at London, in Fleetestreat beneath the Conduit, at the
      signe of Saint Iohn Euangelist by Thomas Colwell. 32 un-
      numbered leaves. [STC. 19865, queries a date of 1570. See
      Greg, I, p. 131, who dates the work "?about Feb. 1569."]
      CtY.

6154 The Play of Patient Grissell, by John Phillip. Prepared by the
      General Editor, W. W. Greg, and Ronald B. McKerrow.
      Printed for the Malone Society by C. Whittingham & Co.,
      1909. xvi, [62] pp.

6155 Roberts, Charles W. "An Edition of John Phillip's Commodye of
      Pacient and Meeke Grissil." Ph.D. University of Illinois, 1938.

Studies

6156 Huebsch, Gottlieb. "The Pleasant Comodie of Patient Grissill von
      John Phillip." Inaugural Dissertation. Erlangen, 1893.

6157 Bang, W. "Zur Patient Grissill." Archiv für das Studium der
      neuren Sprachen und Literaturen, CVII (1901), 110-112.

6158 Greg, W. W. John Phillip, Notes for a Bibliography. London:
      A. Moring, 1911. 54 pp. [Reprinted from Library, Third
      Series, I (July, 1910), 302-328; (October, 1910), 295-323.

6159 Paul, Heinrich. Uber the Comodye of Pacient and Meeke Grisill
      by John Phillip. Inaugural Dissertation. Erlangen, 1921.
      xviii, 260 pp.

6160 Chambers, E. K. "John Phillip. Patient Grissell. 1558-61."
      The Elizabethan Stage. Vol. 3. (Oxford, 1923), pp. 464-
      466.

6161 Wright, Louis B. "A Political Reflection in Phillip's Patient
      Grissell." Review of English Studies, IV (1928), 424-428.

6162 Swaen, A. E. H. "The Songs of John Phillip's Patient Grissell."
      Archiv, CLXVIII (1935), 77-79.

6163 Halstead, William L. "Collaboration on The Patient Grisill."
        Philological Quarterly, XVIII (1939), 381-394.

6164 Krzyzanowski, Julius. "Conjectural Remarks on Elizabethan
        Dramatists." Notes and Queries, CXCV (1950), 400-402.

6165 Bevington, David M. [Patient and Meek Grissell.] From Mankind
        to Marlowe. (Cambridge, 1962), pp. 62-63, 65, 272.

6166 ----- [Comedy of Patient and Meek Grissell]. Tudor Drama and
        Politics. (Cambridge, Massachusetts, 1968), pp. 147-150.

Pickeryng (Pykeryng), John

HORESTES
                                Texts
6167 A Newe Enterlude of Vice Conteyninge, the Historye of Horestes
        with the cruell reuengment of his Fathers death, vpon his one
        naturtll Mother. by Iohn Pikeryng. . . . Imprinted at London
        in Fletestrete, at the signe of the Falcon by William Gryffith,
        and are to be solde at his shope in S. Dunstons Churcheyearde.
        Anno. 1567. 20 unnumbered leaves. [STC. 19917. See Greg,
        I, pp. 126-127.]

6168 Horestes. In, Collier, John Payne, ed. Illustrations of Old English
        Literature. Vol. 2. (London, 1866).

6169 A Newe Enterlude of Vice, Conteyninge the Historye of Horestes,
        with the cruell revengement of his Fathers death, vpon his one
        naturtil Mother. In, Brandl, Alois. Quellen des weltlichen
        Dramas in England vor Shakespeare. (Strassburg, 1898),
        pp. 491-537.

6170 The History of Horestes. By John Pikering, 1567. [London]: Issued
        for Subscribers by the Editor of the Tudor Facsimile Texts,
        1910. [8], [40] pp. (Tudor Facsimile Texts).
            ICN. ICU. MH.

6171 A Newe Enterlude of Vice Conteyninge, the Historye of Horestes
        with the cruell reuengment of his Fathers death, vpon his
        own naturll Mother, by John Pikeryng . . . Imprinted at Lon-
        don in Fletestrete, at the signe of the Falcon by Wylliam
        Gryffith, and are to be solde at his shoppe in S. Dunstons
        Churche-yearde. Anno. 1567. Amersham, England: Issued
        for Subscribers by John S. Farmer, 1913. 40 pp.

6172 The Interlude of Vice (Horestes) 1567. Prepared by Daniel
Seltzer, with Assistance from Arthur Brown. Oxford: Printed
for the Malone Society by V. Ridler at the University Press,
1962. xii, [46] pp.

Studies

6173 "Horestes." In, Brandl, Alois. Quellen des weltlichen Dramas
in England vor Shakespeare. (Strassburg, 1898), pp. xc-xcvii.

6174 Brie, Friedrich. "Horestes von John Pikeryng." Englische Studien,
XLVI (1912/3), 66-72.

6175 Chambers, E. K. "John Pickering. Horestes. 1567-8." The
Elizabethan Stage. Vol. 3. (Oxford, 1923), p. 466.

6176 Phillips, James E. "A Revaluation of Horestes (1567)." Huntington
Library Quarterly, XVIII (May, 1955), 227-244.

6177 Chickera, E. B. de. "Horestes' Revenge -- Another Interpretation."
Notes and Queries, New Ser., VI (May, 1959), 190.

6178 Happé, P. "The Conception of Tragedy Embodied in Cambises,
The History of Horestes, and Apius and Virginia." M.A. University of London (Birkbeck College), 1960-1961.

6179 Bevington, David M. [Horestes.] From Mankind to Marlowe.
(Cambridge, 1962), pp. 60, 61, 66, 70, 72, 73, 77, 81-83,
85-90, 102-103, 178-183.

6180 ----- [Horestes.] Tudor Drama and Politics. (Cambridge,
Massachusetts, 1968), pp. 150-153, 154.

Play of Love. See, Heywood, John.

Play of the Weather. See, Heywood, John.

Preston, Thomas

CAMBISES

Texts

6181 A lamentable tragedy mixed ful of pleasant mirth, conteyning the
life of Cambises king of Percia, from the beginning of his kingdome vnto his death, his one good deed of execution, after that
many wicked deeds and tirannous murders, committed by and
through him, and last of all, his odious death by Gods Iustice

appointed. Doon in such order as foloweth. By Thomas Preston.
. . . [Colophon: Amen. Thomas Preston. Imprinted at London
by Iohn Allde.] 24 unnumbered leaves. [STC. 20287. See Greg,
I, pp. 133-134, who dates it "about Oct. 1569."]
BM. CSmH.

6182 A lamentable Tragedie, mixed full of plesant mirth, containing
the life of Cambises king of Percia, from the beginning of his
kingdome, vnto his death, his one good deede of execution,
after that many wicked deedes and tyrannous murders, committed by and through him, and last of all, his odious death
by Gods Iustice appointed. Done in such order as followeth.
By Thomas Preston. . . . [Colophon: Amen quod Thomas
Prestou. [Sic!] Imprinted at London by Edward Allde.] 24 unnumbered leaves. [STC. 20288, queries a date of 1585. See Greg,
I, pp. 135-136. There is a variant in the title.]
BM. CSmH. DFo. DLC. MH. O.

6183 [Cambises. Another edition known from two leaves.] [Colophon:
Finis. Thomas. Preston. Imprinted at London at the Long Shop
adioyning vnto Sainte Mildreds Churche in the Pultrie by Edward Allde.] [See Greg, I, p. 136, who says that Allde used the
address of the Long Shop in the Poultry from 1584 to 1588.]
O.

6184 Cambises. In, Hawkins, Thomas, ed. The Origin of the English
Drama. Vol. 1. (London, 1773), pp. [245]-319.

6185 Cambises. In, Dodsley, R., ed. A Select Collection of Old English Plays. Vol. 4. (1874-1876), pp. [157]-248.

6186 Cambises. In, Manly, John Matthews, ed. Specimens of Pre-
Shakesperean Drama. Vol. 2. (Boston and New York, 1903-
1904), pp. 159-210.

6187 Cambises King of Persia, by Thomas Preston. [C. 1584]. [London]:
Issued for Subscribers by the Editor of the Tudor Facsimile
Texts, 1910. [8], [48] pp. (Tudor Facsimile Texts).
DLC. ICN. ICU. MB. MH. MiU. NN. PP. ViU.

6188 A lamentable tragedy mixed ful of pleasant mirth, conteyning the
life of Cambises king of Percia, from the beginning of his
kingdome vnto his death, his one good deed of execution, after
that many wicked deeds and tirannous murders, committed by
and through him, and last of all, his odious death by God Iustice

appointed. Doon in such order as followeth. By Thomas Preston. Imprinted at London by Iohn Allde. [1570]. Amersham, England: Issued for Subscribers by John S. Farmer, 1913. 46 pp. OC1. PU.

6189 Cambises. In, Adams, Joseph Q., ed. Chief Pre-Shakespearean Dramas. (Boston, New York, 1924), pp. 638-666.

6190 Johnson, Robert Carl. "Thomas Preston's Cambises: A Critical Edition." Ph.D. University of Illinois, 1964.

Studies

6191 "The Early English Drama." Retrospective Review, II (1820), 70-91.

6192 Tilley, M. P. "Shakespeare and His Ridicule of Cambises." Modern Language Notes, XXIV (1909), 244-247.

6193 Chambers, E. K. "Thomas Preston. Cambyses 1570." The Elizabethan Stage. Vol. 3. (Oxford, 1923), pp. 469-470.

6194 Allen, Don Cameron. "A Source for Cambises." Modern Language Notes, XLIX (June, 1934), 384-387.

6195 Linthicum, M. Channing. "The Date of Cambyses." Publications of the Modern Language Association, XLIX (September, 1934), 959-962.

6196 St. John, Mary C. "A Discussion of the Life and Works of Thomas Preston, Author of Cambises." M.A. Columbia University, 1935.

6197 Armstrong, William A. "The Background and Sources of Preston's Cambises." English Studies, XXXI (1950), 129-135.

6198 Feldman, Abraham. "King Cambises' Vein." Notes and Queries, CXCVI (1951), 98-100.

6199 Armstrong, William A. "The Authorship and Political Meaning of Cambises." English Studies, XXXVI (1955), 289-299.

6200 Happé, P. "The Conception of Tragedy Embodied in Cambises, The History of Horestes, and Apius and Virginia." M.A. University of London (Birkbeck College), 1960-1961.

6201 Bevington, David M. [Cambises]. From Mankind to Marlowe.

(Cambridge, 1962), pp. 60-61, 70, 72, 73, 77, 78, 79, 81-
83, 85-89, 102, 105-107, 183-189, 211-216.

6202 Happé, P. "Tragic Themes in Three Tudor Moralities." Studies
in English Literature, 1500-1900, V (1965), 207-227.

6203 Bevington, David. [Cambises]. Tudor Drama and Politics. (Cambridge, Massachusetts, 1968), pp. 156-160, 161.

6204 Johnson, Robert Carl. "Antedatings from Cambises." Notes and
Queries, CCXIII (1968), 246.

6205 ----- "Press Variants in Cambises." Notes and Queries, CCXIII
(1968), 246-247.

6206 Johnson, Robert C. "The Third Quarto of Cambises." Notes and
Queries, CCXIII (1968), 247.

THE PRIDE OF LIFE

Texts

6207 Account Roll of the Priory of the Holy Trinity, Dublin, 1337-1346,
With the Middle English Moral Play "The Pride of Life" from
the Original in the Christ Church Collections in the Public
Record Office, Dublin. Edited with translation, Notes, and Introduction, by James Mills, Dublin: Royal Society of anti-
quaries of Ireland, 1891. 231 pp. "Authorities Referred to
in the Notes, pp. [215]-217.
DLC. MB. WU.

6208 The Pride of Life. In, Brandl, Alois. Quellen des weltlichen
Dramas in England vor Shakespeare. (Strassburg, 1898),
pp. 1-35.

6209 Holthausen, F., ed. "The Pride of Life." Archiv für das Studium
der Neuren Sprachen und Literaturen, CVIII (1902), 34-48.

6210 The Pride of Life. In, Waterhouse, Osborn, ed. The Non-Cycle
Mystery Plays, Together with the Croxton Play of the Sacrament and the Pride of Life. (London, 1909).

6211 Der Koenig des Lebens; metrische Uebersetzung von F. Holthausen.
In, Probleme der englishen Sprache und Kultur. (Heidelberg,
1925), pp. 152-168.
NN.

Studies

6212 "The Pride of Life." In, Brandl, Alois. Quellen des weltlichen
      Dramas in England vor Shakespeare. (Strassburg, 1898),
      pp. viii-xxi.

6213 Chambers, E. K. "The Pride of Life." The Mediaeval Stage.
      Vol. 2. (London, 1903), p. 436.

6214 Brown, Carleton. "The Pride of Life and the Twelve Abuses."
      Archiv für das Studium der Neuren Sprachen und Literaturen,
      CXXVIII (1912), 72-78.

6215 Haller, Julius. "The Pride of Life." Die Technik des Dialogs im
      mittelalterlichen Drama Englands. (Worms, 1916), pp. 102-105.

6216 Mackenzie, William Roy. "The Debate over the Soul in The Pride
      of Life." Washington University Studies. Humanistic Series,
      IX, No. 2 (1922), 263-274. ("Heller Memorial Volume.")

6217 Chambers, E. K. ["The Pride of Life."] English Literature at
      the Close of the Middle Ages. (Oxford, 1945), pp. 53-55.

6218 Fifield, Merle. "The Pride of Life." The Castle in the Circle.
      (Muncie, Indiana, 1967), pp. 19-22.

PROCESSUS SATANAE

6219 Processus Satanae. Malone Society Collections. II, Part 3 (1931).

      Prodigal Son. See, Pater, Filius et Vxor.

THE RARE TRIUMPHS OF LOVE AND FORTUNE

Texts

6220 The Rare Triumphes of Loue and Fortune. Plaide before the
      Queenes most excellent Maiestie: wherein are many fine Con-
      ceites with great delight. At London Printed by E.A. for
      Edward White, and are to be solde at the little North doore
      of S. Paules Church at the signe of the Gunne. 1589. 28 un-
      numbered leaves. [STC. 24286. See Greg, I, p. 170.]
      CSmH.

6221 The Rare Triumphs of Love and Fortune. In, Collier, John
      Payne, ed. Five Old Plays. (London, 1851), pp. [81]-155.

6222 Rare Triumphs of Love and Fortune. In, Dodsley, Robert, ed.

A Select Collection of Old English Plays. Vol. 6. (London, 1874-1876).

6223 The Rare Triumphs of Love and Fortune. Prepared under the Direction of the General Editor, W. W. Greg. Printed for the Malone Society by J. Johnson at the Oxford University Press, 1931. xi, [56] pp.

Studies

6224 Chambers, E. K. "The Rare Triumphs of Love and Fortune." The Elizabethan Stage. Vol. 4. (Oxford, 1923), p. 28.

Rastell, John

NATURE OF THE FOUR ELEMENTS

Texts

6225 A new iuterlude and a mery of the nature of the .iiii. elemente declarynge many proper poynte of phylosophy naturall and of dyuers straunge landys and of dyuers straunge effecte & causis whiche interlude yf $\overset{e}{y}$ hole matter be playd wyl conteyne the space of an hour and a halfe but yf ye list ye may leue out muche of the sad mater as the messengers pte and some of naturys parte and some of experyens pte & yet the matter wyl depend conuenyently and than it wyll not be paste thre quarters of an hour of length. [Imperfect copy.] 24 unnumbered leaves, plus. [STC. 20722. See Greg, I, p. 85, who says that the type undoubtedly belonged to John Rastell, and he suggests a probable date of "about 1526-7."]
BM (wants D and all after E).

6226 The Interlude of the Four Elements: An Early Moral Play. Edited by James Orchard Halliwell. London: Printed for the Percy Society by Richards, 1848. viii, 55 pp. (Percy Society. Early English Poetry, Vol. 22.)
BM. DFo. ICN. MB. MiU. NN. OC1. OCU. PU. ViU. WU.

6227 Interlude of the Four Elements. In, Dodsley, R., ed. A Select Collection of Old English Plays. Vol. 1. (London, 1874-1876), pp. [1]-50.

6228 Das Interlude of the Four Elements. Mit einer Einleitung neu herausgegeben . . . von Julius Fischer. Marburg: Universitäts-Buchdruckerei, 1902. 86 pp.
BM. NjP. WU.

6229 Das "Interlude of the Four Elements." Edited by Julius Fischer.
      Marburg: N. G. Elwert, 1903. 86 pp. (Reissue).
      BM. MiU. NN. OCU. OU. ViU. WU.

6230 Interlude of the Four Elements. In, Farmer, John S., ed. Six
      Anonymous Plays. (London, 1905), 45 pp.
      BM.

6231 The Nature of the Four Elements. London and Edinburgh: Issued
      for Subscribers by T. C. and E. C. Jack, 1908. [10], [64] pp.
      (Tudor Facsimile Texts.)
      DFo. ICN. ICU. MB. MiU. NN. ViU. WU.

6232 A new interlude! and a mery of the nature of the iiij. elements
      declarynge many propre poynts of phylosophy naturall and of
      dyuers strange landys. Amersham, England: Issued for Sub-
      scribers by John S. Farmer, 1914. 64 pp.

6233 Interlude of the Four Elements. In, Pollard, A. W. English
      Miracle Plays, Moralities and Interludes. (Oxford, 1927).

                              Studies
6234 Chambers, E. K. "John Rastell. The Nature of the Four Elements."
      The Mediaeval Stage. Vol. 2. (London, 1903), pp. 453-454.

6235 Baskervill, Charles Read. "John Rastell's Dramatic Activities."
      Modern Philology, XIII (1916), 557-560.

6236 Reed, Arthur W. "John Rastell's Plays." The Library, Third
      Series, X (January, 1919), 1-17.

6237 Stelle, Robert. "A Note on 'A New Interlude.'" Library, New
      Ser., IX (1928), 90-91.

6238 Greg, Walter W. "Notes on Some Early Plays: 'Hycke Scorner,'
      Reconstruction of a Treveris edition, Known Only From Two
      Leaves; Rastell's 'Nature of the Four Elements,' Printer and
      Date; 'The Play of the Weather,' an Alleged Edition by Robert
      Wyer; Bale's Plays on the Baptism and Temptation." Library,
      XI (1930), 44-56. [See pp. 46-50.]

6239 Borish, M. E. "Source and Intention of The Four Elements."
      Studies in Philology, XXXV (April, 1938), 149-163.

6240 Parks, George B. "The Geography of the Interlude of the Four

Elements." Philological Quarterly, XVII (July, 1938), 251-
262.

6241 Nugent, Elizabeth M. "Sources of John Rastell's The Nature of
the Four Elements." Publications of the Modern Language
Association, LVII (March, 1942), 74-88.

6242 Nash, Roy. "Rastell Fragments at Dartmouth." Library, XXIV
(June-September, 1943), 66-73.

6243 Parks, G. B. "Rastell and Waldseemüller's Map; Reply to E. M.
Nugent with Rejoinder." Publications of the Modern Language
Association, LVIII (June, 1943), 572-574.

6244 Butler, C.S.J., Sr. M. Basil. "Religious Satire in the Works of
Medwall, Rastell, Heywood, and More: A Spirit of Devotion to the
Ideal of the Church Rather Than to That of the Reformation."
Ph.D. St. John's College, 1945.

6245 Parr, Johnstone. "More Sources of Rastell's Interlude of the Four
Elements." Publications of the Modern Language Association,
LX (March, 1945), 48-58.

6246 ----- "John Rastell's Geographical Knowledge of America."
Philological Quarterly, XXVII (1948), 329-340.

6247 Bevington, David M. [Four Elements]. From Mankind to Marlowe.
(Cambridge, 1962), pp. 45-47, 65.

6248 Wilson, F. P. "Rastell and Heywood." The English Drama, 1485-
1585. (Oxford, 1969), pp. 21-27.

Redford, John

WIT AND SCIENCE
Manuscript
6249 British Museum. Additional MS. 15233.

Texts
6250 The Marriage of Wit and Science, an Interlude by John Redford.
[Extracts]. In, Shakespeare Society. Vol. 2. (London, 1845),
pp. 76-78.

6251 The Moral Play of Wit and Science, and Early Poetical Miscellanies. From an Unpublished Manuscript. Edited by James

Orchard Halliwell. London: Printed for the Shakespeare Society, 1848. 128 pp. (Shakespeare Society Publications, No. 37).

6252   Wit and Science. In, Amyot, Thomas, ed. A Supplement to Dodsley's Old Plays. Vol. 2. (London, 1853).

6253   Wit-und-Science, Moralitäten des 16. Jahrhunderts. Edited by Julius Seifert. Prag, 1892. 32 pp.

6254   Wyt and Science. In, Manly, John Matthews, ed. Specimens of the Pre-Shakesperean Drama. Vol. 1. (Boston and New York, 1903-1904), pp. 421-456.

6255   The Play of Wit and Science, Made by Master John Redford. [c. 1550]. London and Edinburgh: Issued for Subscribers by T. C. and E.C. Jack, 1908. vi, [34] pp. (Tudor Facsimile Texts.)

6256   Redford, John. Wit and Science. Prepared by Arthur Brown. London: The Malone Society, 1951. xii, 58 pp.

Studies

6257   Hauke, Hans. John Redfords Moral Play The Play of Wit and Science, und seine spätere Bearbeitung. Inaugural Dissertation. Wien, 1897.

6258   Chambers, E. K. "John Redford. Wit and Science." The Mediaeval Stage. Vol. 2. (London, 1903), p. 454.

6259   Haller, Julius. "Wyt and Science." Die Technik des Dialogs im mittelalterlichen Drama Englands. (Worms, 1916), pp. 119-122.

6260   Tannenbaum, Samuel A. "Editorial Notes on Wit and Science." Philological Quarterly, XIV (October, 1935), 307-326.

6261   Withington, Robert. "Experience the Mother of Science." Publications of the Modern Language Association, LVII (June, 1942), 592.

6262   Brown, Arthur. "Two Notes on John Redford." Modern Language Review, XLIII (October, 1948), 508-510.

6263   ----- "The Play of Wit and Science by John Redford." Philological Quarterly, XXVIII (October, 1949), 429-442.

6264 Race, Sidney. "The Moral Play of Wit and Science." Notes and
       Queries, CXCVIII (March, 1953), 96-99.

6265 Bevington, David M. [Wit and Science.] From Mankind to Marlowe.
       (Cambridge, 1962), pp. 22-23, 27, 65.

6266 Lennam, Trevor Neville Shawe. "The 'Wit' Plays. A Study of the
       Dramatic Relations of Three Tudor Interludes. Wit and Science
       by John Redford, The Marriage of Wit and Science, Anon., and
       The Marriage between Wit and Wisdom by Francis Merbury."
       Ph.D. University of New Brunswick, 1964.

6267 Tompkins, Kenneth D. "The Wit Plays: Variations on a Tudor
       Dramatic Theme." Ph.D. University of Indiana, 1968.

6268 Velz, John W., and Carl P. Dow, Jr. "Tradition and Originality
       in Wyt and Science." Studies in Philology, LXV (1968), 631-
       646.

6269 Wilson, F. P. "'Morals Teaching Education.'" The English
       Drama, 1485-1585. (Oxford, 1969), pp. 43-46.

RESPUBLICA

Manuscript
6270 New York City. Library of Carl H. Pforzheimer. MS. 40A.

Texts
6271 A mery enterlude entitled Respublica, made in the yeare of our
       Lorde 1553 and the first yeare of the moost prosperous reigne
       of our moste gracious soveraigne Quene Marye the first. In,
       Collier, John P., ed. Illustrations of Old English Literature.
       Green Series. Vol. 1. (London, 1866).

6272 Respublica. In, Brandl, Alois. Quellen des weltlichen Dramas in
       England vor Shakespeare. (Strassburg, 1898), pp. 281-358.

6273 Respublica, A. D. 1553. A Play on the Social Conditions of England
       at the Accession of Queen Mary. Edited by Leonard A. Magnus,
       LL.B. (from Mr. Gurney's Unique Macro MS. 115). With Intro-
       duction, Notes, and Glossaries. London: For the Early English
       Text Society by K. Paul, Trench, Trübner & Co., Ltd., 1905.
       84 pp.
       DLC. MH. MiU. NjP. NN. OCl. PU. WU.

6274 Respublica. A. D. 1553. A Drama of Real Life in the Early Days of

Queen Mary. In, Farmer, John S., ed. Recently Recovered "Lost" Tudor Plays. (London, 1907), pp. 177-272.

6275 Respublica. The Macro Plays No. 4. London and Edinburgh: Issued for Subscribers by T. C. and E. C. Jack, 1908. pp. 360-387. (Tudor Facsimile Texts.)
DFo. DLC. ICN. MB. MH. MiU. NjP. OCl. ViU. WU.

6276 A merye enterlude entitled Respublica, made in the yeare of owre Lorde. 1553, and the first year of the most prosperous raigne of our most gracious Soveraigne Quene Marye the first. Amersham, England: Issued for Subscribers by John S. Farmer, 1914.
DLC. PU.

6277 Udall, Nicholas [supposed author]. Respublica: an Interlude for Christmas, 1553, Attributed to Nicholas Udall. Re-edited by W. W. Greg. London: Published for the Early English Text Society by Oxford University Press, 1952. [i.e., January, 1953]. xxi, 83 pp. (Original Series, No. 226).
BM. NN.

Studies

6278 "Respublica." In, Brandl, Alois. Quellen des weltlichen Dramas in England vor Shakespeare. (Strassburg, 1898), pp. lvii-lxiii.

6279 Haller, Julius. "Respublica." Die Technik des Dialogs im mittelalterlichen Drama Englands. (Worms, 1916), pp. 138-143.

6280 Bradner, Leicester. "A Test for Udall's Authorship." Modern Language Notes, XLII (1927), 378-380.

6281 Bright, Lorrie Jacques. "Respublica: A Revaluation." M.A. University of Rochester, 1953.

6282 Craik, T. W. "The Text of Respublica: A Conjecture." Notes and Queries, CXCVIII (July, 1953), 279.

6283 Starr, G. A. "Notes on Respublica." Notes and Queries, New Ser., VIII (1961), 290-292.

6284 Bevington, David M. [Respublica.] From Mankind to Marlowe. (Cambridge, 1962), pp. 27-28, 40, 65.

6285 Bevington, David. [Respublica.] Tudor Drama and Politics.
      (Cambridge, Massachusetts, 1968), pp. 115-120, 121-124.

6286 Wilson, F. P. [Respublica.] The English Drama, 1485-1585. (Ox-
      ford, 1969), pp. 40-43.

Skelton, John

Bibliography

6287 Dale, Donald. "Editions of Skelton." Times Literary Supplement,
      February 18, 1939, p. 106.

6288 Whitmee, Dorothy E. "Bibliography of John Skelton, Poet Laureate,
      ?1460-1529." London University. Library Thesis, 1939.

Works

6289 Skelton, John. The Poetical Works of John Skelton: With Notes,
      and Some Account of the Author and His Writings, by the Rev.
      Alexander Dyce. 2 vol. London: Thomas Rodd, 1843. [See
      Vol. 1.]
             BM.

6290 ----- The Poetical Works of John Skelton: Principally According
      to the Edition of the Rev. Alexander Dyce. 3 vol. Boston: Little,
      Brown and Company. Shepard, Clark and Co.; Cincinnati: Moore,
      Wilstach Keys and Co., 1856. [See Vol. 2.]
             BM.

6291 ----- The Poetical Works of Skelton and Donne. With a Memoir
      of Each. Four Volumes in Two. Boston: Houghton, Mifflin and
      Company [1880]. [See Vol. 1 of 2 vols., or Vol. 2 of 4 vols.]
             BM.

6292 ----- The Complete Poems of John Skelton, Laureate. Edited by
      Philip Henderson. London and Toronto: J. M. Dent and Sons, Ltd.,
      1931. xl, [2], 470 pp. [Based on Dyce's edition of 1843.]
             BM.

6293 ----- The Complete Poems of John Skelton, Laureate. Edited by
      Philip Henderson. [2nd ed., revised.] London & Toronto: J.
      M. Dent and Sons, Ltd. [1948]. xxii, 446 pp.
             BM.

MAGNIFICENCE

Texts

6294 Magnyfycence, A goodly interlude and a mery deuysed and made
by mayster Skelton poet laureate late deceasyd. [No imprint.
Colophon: None. Only the words "Cum priuilegio."] 30 leaves.
[STC. 22607 says that the edition is printed by J. Rastell in
1533. There is no indication of printer or date. See Greg, I,
pp. 87-88, who suggests the date as "?1530."]
BM. C. O.

6295 Magnyfycence: An Interlude. By John Skelton, Poet Laureat to
Henry VIII. London: Reprinted by G. Woodfall, 1821. 34 pp.
(Roxburghe Club). [Fifty copies printed.]
BM. CSmH. DLC. ICU. MH.

6296 Magnyfycence, a Moral Play, by John Skelton. Edited by Robert
Lee Ramsay . . . from the Edition in the University Library.
Cambridge, with Introduction, Notes, and Glossary. London:
Published for the Early English Text Society by K. Paul, Trench,
Trübner and Co., Ltd., 1906. (Issued in 1908.) cxcvii, 100 pp.
BM. DLC. ICU. MiU. NjP. NN. OU. PU. ViU. WU.

6297 Magnificence, by John Skelton. c. 1515-1530. London and Edinburgh: Issued for Subscribers by T. C. and E. C. Jack, 1910.
58 pp. (Tudor Facsimile Texts.)
BM. DLC. ICN. ICU. MH. MiU. NjP. ViU. WaU. WU.

6298 Magnyfycence. A goodly interlude and a mery deuysed and made
by mayster Skelton poet laureate late deceasyd. Amersham,
England: Issued for Subscribers by John S. Farmer, 1914.
55 pp.
DFo. DLC. MnU. OC1. OCU. PU.

6299 Magnificence. In, Pollard, A. W., ed. English Miracle Plays,
Moralities and Interludes. (Oxford, 1927).

Studies

6300 Krumpholz, H. John Skelton und sein Morality Play Magnyfycence.
Inaugural Dissertation. Prossnitz, 1881.

6301 Hooper, E. S. "Skelton's Magnyfycence and Cardinal Wolsey."
Modern Language Notes, XVI (1901), 213-215.

6302 Chambers, E. K. "Magnificence." The Mediaeval Stage. Vol. 2.
(London, 1903), p. 441.

6303 Kölbing, Arthur. Zur Charakteristik John Skelton's. Stuttgart:
     Strecker & Schroder, 1904. x, 166 pp.
          BM. ICN. ICU.

6304 Thümmel, Bernhard Arno. Studien über John Skelton. Inaugural
     Dissertation. Leipzig, 1906. 98 pp.
          BM.

6305 Brie, Fredrich. "Skelton-studien." Englische Studien, XXXVII
     (1907), 84-86.

6306 Dodds, Madeleine Hope. "Early Political Plays." The Library,
     Third Series, IV (1913), 393-395.

6307 Berdan, J. M. "The Dating of Skelton's Satires." Publications of
     the Modern Language Association, XXIX (1914), 499-516.

6308 Bischoffsberger, Elise. Der Einfluss John Skeltons auf die eng-
     lische Literatur. Freiburg i. Br.: Hammerschlag. & Kahle,
     g.m.b.h., 1914. 80 pp.
          BM. ICU.

6309 Haller, Julius. "Magnyfycence." Die Technik des Dialogs im
     mittelalterlichen Drama Englands. (Worms, 1916), pp.
     122-128.

6310 Golding, Louis. "Merie Skelton." Saturday Review, CXXXIII
     (January 14, 1922), 30-31.

6311 Salter, F. M. "The Critical Ideas of John Skelton." M.A. Uni-
     versity of Chicago, 1922.

6312 Lloyd, Leslie John. "John Skelton, a Forgotten Poet." English
     Review, XL (1925), 659-665.

6313 Swain, Barbara. Fools and Folly During the Middle Ages and the
     Renaissance. New York: Columbia University Press, 1932.
     [8], 234 pp. (Columbia University Studies in English and
     Comparative Literature).
          BM.

6314 Salter, F. M. "Skelton's Speculum Principis." Speculum, IX
     (1934), 29-30.

6315 Nelson, William. "Skelton's Quarrel with Wolsey." Publications of the Modern Language Association, LI (1936), 59-82, 377-398.

6316 Lloyd, Leslie John. John Skelton; a Sketch of His Life and Writings. Oxford: Basil Blackwell, 1938. viii, 152 pp. Index.
BM. ICN. ICU. PU.

6317 Hibernicus. "Skelton's Reputation." Notes and Queries, CLXXVII (July 29, 1939), 84.

6318 Nelson, William. John Skelton. Laureate. New York: Columbia University Press; London: Oxford University Press, 1939. vi, 266 pp. Bibliography, pp. [249]-253. (Columbia University Studies in English and Comparative Literature, No. 139).
BM. IaU. ICN. ICU. MnU. PU.

6319 Gordon, Ian Alistair. John Skelton, Poet Laureate. Melbourne & London: Melbourne University Press, in Association with Oxford University Press, 1943. [8], 223 pp. Bibliography, pp. 211-216. Index.
BM. ICN. ICU.

6320 Whiting, B. J. "A Dramatic Clyster." Bulletin of the History of Medicine, XVI (1944), 511-513.

6321 Salter, F. M. "John Skelton's Contribution to the English Language." Transactions of the Royal Society of Canada, Section II, 3rd Ser., XXXIX (May, 1945), 119-217.

6322 Edwards, H. L. R. Skelton, the Life and Times of an Early Tudor Poet. London: Cape, [1949]. 325 pp. Bibliography, pp. 257-286.
BM. ICN. ICU. PU.

6323 Pollet, Maurice. "John Skelton. Poète lauréat (1460-1529)." Thèse. Lettres. Paris, 1955. 514 leaves.

6324 Holloway, John. Skelton. London: Oxford University Press, 1959. 20 pp. (Chatterton Lecture on an English Poet, 1958).
WU.

6325 Harris, William O. "Wolsey and Skelton's Magnyfycence: A Re-evaluation." Studies in Philology, LVII (1960), 99-122.

6326 Heiserman, A. R. Skelton and Satire. Chicago: The University of Chicago Press, 1961. [10], 326 pp. Bibliography, pp.

313-320. Index.
BM. ICU.

6327 Bevington, David M. [Magnificence.] From Mankind to Marlowe.
(Cambridge, 1962), pp. 52-53, 132-137, 144-145.

6328 Pollet, Maurice. John Skelton (c. 1460-1529). Contribution à l'
Histoire de la Prérenaissance Anglaise. Paris: Didier,
1962. 291, [2] pp. Bibliographie, pp. 259-277. Index.
BM.

6329 Harris, William O. "The Thematic Importance of Skelton's Allusion to Horace in Magnyfycence." Studies in English Literature, 1500-1900, III (1963), 9-18.

6330 ----- Skelton's Magnyfycence and the Cardinal Virtue Tradition.
Chapel Hill: The University of North Carolina Press, 1965.
x, [2], 177 pp. Index.
BM.

6331 Kinsman, Robert S. "Skelton's Magnyfycence: The Strategy of
the 'Olde Sayde Sawe.'" Studies in Philology, LXIII (1966),
99-125.

6332 Bevington, David. [Magnificence.] Tudor Drama and Politics.
(Cambridge, Massachusetts, 1968), pp. 54-63.

6333 Wilson, F. P. "The Two 'Makers': Skelton and Lindsay." The
English Drama, 1485-1585. (Oxford, 1969), pp. 11-15.

[SOMEBODY AND OTHERS, or THE SPOILING OF LADY VERITY]

Manuscript
6334 [An interlude, in which Somebody, Minister, Avarice, and Verity
are characters, known from two mutilated leaves.] [See Greg,
I, pp. 100-101, who suggests the date as "about 1547-1550."]
Lambeth Palace

Text
6335 Somebody and Others. In, Malone Society. Collections. Vol. II.
Part III. (London, 1931), pp. 251-257. [Fragment of a play.
Also a reproduction of the Lambeth Palace copy.]

TEMPERANCE AND HUMILITY
Texts
6336 [An interlude, in which Temperance, Disobedience, and Humility
      are characters, known from a single mutilated leaf.[[See
      Greg, I, p. 86, who dates it "?about 1528."]
      CSmH.

6337 Temperance and Humility. A Fragment of a Morality Printed, c.
      1530. Malone Society Reprints, I, Part 3 (1909), pp. 243-246.

Studies
6338 Craik, T. W. "The Political Interpretation of Two Tudor Inter-
      ludes: Temperance and Humility and Wealth and Health."
      Review of English Studies, New Ser., IV (April, 1953), 98-108.

THERSITES
Texts
6339 A new Enterlude called Thersytes Thys Enterlude Folowynge
      Dothe Declare howe that the greatest boesters are not the greatest
      doers. . . . [Colophon: Imprinted at London, by Iohn Tysdale
      and are to be solde at hys shop in the vpper ende of Lombard
      strete, in Alhallowes churche yarde neare vntoo grace church.]
      18 unnumbered leaves. [STC. 23949 queries a date of 1560,
      and the authorship by N. Udall. See Greg, I, p. 114, who sug-
      gests a date between 1561-1563.]
      CSmH. Pforz.

6340 Two Interludes: Jack Jugler and Thersytes. Kent: Printed at the
      Private Press of Lee Priory, by J. Warwick, 1820. 40 pp.
      MH.

6341 Thersytes. In, Child, Francis James, ed. Four Old Plays. Three
      Interludes: Thersytes, Jack Jugler and Heywoods Pardoner
      and Frere: and Jocasta, a Tragedy by Gascoigne and Kinwel-
      marsh. (Cambridge, 1848).

6342 A New Enterlude called Thersytes. In, Dodsley, R., ed. A
      Select Collection of Old Plays. Vol. 1. (London, 1874-1876),
      pp. 389-431.

6343 The Interlude of Thersytes. Printed by John Tisdale. From the
      Unique Original in the Collection of the Duke of Devonshire.
      Edited by Edmund W. Ashbee. London: For Private Circulation
      [187?]. 32 pp. [Dramatic Facsimiles].
      BM. PPL.

6344 Thersites. In, Farmer, John Stephen, ed. Six Anonymous Plays.
      (London, 1905), pp. [193]-226.

6345 Thersytes. c. 1550. London and Edinburgh: Issued for Subscribers
      by T. C. and E. C. Jack, 1912. 34 pp. (Tudor Facsimile Texts.)
      DLC. ICN. MH. MiU. NjP. ViU. WU.

6346 A New Enterlude called Thersytes. Thys Enterlude Folowynge
      Dothe Declare howe that the greatest boesters are not the
      greatest doers. Imprinted at London, by John Tysdale and are
      to be solde at hys shop in the upper ends of Lombard strete,
      in Alhallowes churche yarde neare untoo grace church.
      Amersham, England: Issued for Subscribers by John S. Far-
      mer, 1913. 34 pp.
          MnU. OCl. OU. PU.

6347 Thersites. In, Pollard, A. W., ed. English Miracle Plays.
      Moralities and Interludes. (Oxford, 1927), pp. 126-145.

                              Studies
6348 Holthausen, F. "Studien zum älteren englischen Drama."
      Englische Studien, XXXI (1902), 77-103.

6349 Chambers, E. K. "Thersites." The Mediaeval Stage. Vol. 2.
      (London, 1903), p. 456.

6350 Boas, F. S. "Thersites." Times Literary Supplement, July 25,
      1918, p. 349.

6351 Pollard, A. W. "Thersites." Times Literary Supplement, July 18,
      1918, p. 337.

6352 Swaen, A. E. H. "Thersytes." Neophilologus, V (1920), 160-162.

6353 Moon, A. R. "Was Nicholas Udall the Author of 'Thersites'?"
      Library, VII (September, 1926), 184-193.

TOM TYLER AND HIS WIFE
                              Texts
6354 Tom Tyler and His Wife. An Excellent Old Play, As It Was
      Printed and Acted About a Hundred Years Ago. The Second
      Impression. London, 1661.
          CtY. DFo. DLC.

6355 Tom Tyler and His Wife. In, Six Anonymous Plays. Edited by

John S. Farmer. (London, 1906), pp. 289-321.

6356   Tom Tyler and His Wife. In, Two Tudor "Shrew" Plays. (London, 1908), pp. 27-59.

6357   Tom Tyler and His Wife. c. 1551. London and Edinburgh: Issued for Subscribers by T. C. and E. C. Jack, 1910. 26 pp. (Tudor Facsimile Texts.)
BM. MiU. NjP. ViU.

6358   Tom Tyler and His Wife. Prepared by G. C. Moore Smith and W. W. Greg. The Malone Society Reprints, 1910. ix, [8], 26 pp. [Printed in 1661 as "The Second Impression." Chetwood, in his British Theatre of 1750, has a play of this name dated 1598.]

6359   Tom Tyler and His Wife. An Excellent Old Play, as It was Printed and Acted about a hundred years ago. Together, with an exact Catalogue of all the playes that were ever yet printed. The second Impression, London, Printed in the Year, 1661. Amersham, England: Issued for Subscribers by John S. Farmer, 1913. 26 pp.
OCl. OU.

THE TRIAL OF TREASURE

Texts

6360   A new and mery Enterlude, called the Triall of Treasure, newly set foorth, and neuer before this tyme imprinted. . . . Imprinted at Londo in Paules Churcheyarde, at the signe of the Lucrece by Thomas Purfoote. 1567. 22 unnumbered leaves. [STC. 24271. See Greg, I, pp. 127-128.]
BM. CSmH. O. Pforz.

6361   The Interlude of the Trial of Treasure. Reprinted from the Blackletter Edition of Thomas Purfoote, 1567. Edited by J. O. Halliwell. London: Printed for the Percy Society by Richard, 1850. viii, 48 pp. (Percy Society, Vol. 28.)
BM. DFo. DLC. MH. MiU. NN. OCl. PU-F. ViU. WU.

6362   The Trial of Treasure. In, Dodsley, R., ed. A Select Collection of Old English Plays. Vol. 3. (London, 1874-1876), pp. [257]-301.

6363   The Trial of Treasure. In, Farmer, John Stephen, ed. Anonymous Plays. (London, 1906), pp. 203-246.

6364 The Trial of Treasure. 1567. London and Edinburgh: Issued for
      Subscribers by T. C. and E. C. Jack, 1908. 38 pp. (Tudor
      Facsimile Texts.)
          DFo. DLC. ICN. MB. MH. MiU. NjP. NN. ViU. WU.

6365 A New and Mery Enterlude, Called the Trial of Treasure. Amer-
      sham, England: Issued for Subscribers by John S. Farmer,
      1914. 38 pp.
          OC1. PU.

Studies

6366 Greg, W. W. "The Trial of Treasure, 1567 - A Study in Ghosts."
      The Library, Third Series, I (1910), 28-35. [Bibliographical].

6367 Haller, Julius. "The Trial of Treasure." Die Technik des Dialogs
      im mittelalterlichen Drama Englands. (Worms, 1916), pp.
      129-133.

6368 Daw, E. Beatrice. "Two Notes on The Trial of Treasure." Modern
      Philology, XV (1918), 53-55.

6369 Chambers, E. K. "The Trial of Treasure." The Elizabethan Stage.
      Vol. 4. (Oxford, 1923), p. 51.

6370 Wright, L. B. "Social Aspects of Some Belated Moralities."
      Anglia, LIV (July, 1930), 107-148.

6371 Oliver, Leslie. "William Wager and The Trial of Treasure."
      Huntington Library Quarterly, IX (August, 1946), 419-429.

6372 Bevington, David M. [The Trial of Treasure.] From Mankind
      to Marlowe. (Cambridge, 1962), pp. 76-77, 95-96, 153-
      155.

      Triumphs of Love and Fortune. See, Rare Triumphs of Love
      and Fortune.

Wager, Lewis

Texts

MARY MAGDALENE

6373 A new Enterlude, neuer before this tyme imprinted, entreating
      of the Life and Repentaunce of Marie Magdalene: not only
      godlie, learned and fruitefull, but also well furnished with

pleasaunt myrth and pastime, very delectable for those which
shall heare or reade the same. Made by the learned clarke
Lewis Wager. . . . Imprinted at London, by Iohn Carlevvood,
dwelling in Barbican, at the signe of the halfe Eagle and the
key. Anno. 1566. 36 unnumbered leaves. [STC. 24932. See
Greg, I, pp. 125-126. There is a variant imprint with the date
of 1567. This imprint of 1567 is noted in STC. 24932a as
another issue.]
> BM (1566). CSmH (1567).

6374 Life and Repentaunce of Marie Magdalene. A Morality Play Reprinted from the Original Edition of 1566. Edited by F. I.
Carpenter with Introduction, Notes, Glossarial Index. Chicago:
University of Chicago Press, 1902. xxxv, 91 pp. (University
of Chicago, Decennial Publications. 2nd Ser., Vol. 1).
> BM. IaU. ICU. MB. MiU. MnU. NN. OC1. OU. ViU.

6375 The Life and Repentaunce of Mary Magdalene. 1567. London and
Edinburgh: Issued for Subscribers by T. C. and E. C. Jack,
1908. 68 pp. (Tudor Facsimile Texts.)
> BM. DLC. ICN. MB. MH.MiU. NjP. NN. ViU.

6376 A New Enterlude, neuer before this tyme imprinted, entreating
of the Life of Repentaunce of Marie Magdalene: not only godlie,
learned and fruitefull, but also well furnished with pleasaunt
myrth and pastime. Made by the learned clarke Lewis Wager.
Imprinted at London, by Iohn Charlewood, dwelling in Barbican,
at the signe of the halfe EAgle and the Key. Anno 1567. Amersham, England: Issued for Subscribers by John S. Farmer,
1914. 68 pp.
> DFo. MnU. OC1. PU.

6377 Mary Magdalene. In, Pollard, Alfred W., ed. English Miracle
Plays, Moralities and Interludes. (Oxford, 1927).

Studies

6378 Chambers, E. K. "Lewis Wager. The Life and Repentance of
Mary Magdalene 1566." The Elizabethan Stage. Vol. 3. (Oxford, 1923), pp. 503-504.

6379 Kiner, Grace Isabel. "A Theory for the Staging of Mary Magdalene."
M.A. University of Chicago, 1927.

6380 Knoll, Friedrich Otto. Die Rolle der Maria Magdalena im geistlichen Spiel des Mittelalters. Ein Beitrag zur Kultur- und

Theatergeschichte Deutschlands. Berlin und Leipzig: Walter
de Gruyter and Co., 1934. 122 pp.
    BM. IaU. ICN. MnU. OU.

6381 Bevington, David M. [Mary Magdalene.] From Mankind to Marlowe.
(Cambridge, 1962), pp. 58-59, 66, 80-81, 94-95, 98-99, 171-
175.

Wager, W.

ENOUGH IS AS GOOD AS A FEAST
                          Texts
6382 A Comedy or Enterlude intituled, Inough is as good as a feast, very
fruteful godly and ful of pleasant mirth. Compiled by W.
Wager. . . . Imprinted At London at the long shop adioyning
vnto S. Mildreds Church in the Pultrie, by Iohn Allde. 26
unnumbered leaves. [STC. 24933. See Greg, I, pp. 136-137,
who dates the edition "about 1565-1570." Ascribed to W. Wager.]
    BM (Def.). CSmH. CtY. IU. MH. O.

6383 Wager, E. Enough Is As Good As a Feast. From the Unique Copy
in the Henry E. Huntington Library. With an Introductory Note
by Seymour De Ricci. New York: George D. Smith, 1920.
8, [52] pp. (The Henry E. Huntington Facsimile Reprints II.)
    BM. DFo. DLC. MH. MiU. NN. OU. ViU.

                          Studies
6384 Chambers, E. K. Enough Is As Good As a Feast. c. 1560."
The Elizabethan Stage. Vol. 3. (Oxford, 1923), pp. 504-505.

6385 Bevington, David M. [Enough Is As Good As a Feast.] From Mankind to Marlowe. (Cambridge, 1962), pp. 54, 66, 70, 72, 74,
81-83, 85, 107, 158-161.

6386 ----- [Enough Is As Good As a Feast.] Tudor Drama and Politics.
(Cambridge, Massachusetts, 1968), 131-133.

THE LONGER THOU LIVEST
                          Texts
6387 A very mery and Pythie Commedie, called The longer thou liuest,
the more foole thou art. A Myrrour very necessarie for youth,
and specially for such as are like to come to dignitie and
promotion: As it maye well appeare in the Matter folowynge.
Newly compiled by VV. VVager. Imprinted at London, by
Wyllyam How for Richarde Iohnes: and are to be solde

at his shop vnder the Lotterie house. 28 unnumbered leaves.
[STC. 24935. See Greg, I, p. 132, who suggests a date
"about Apr. 1569."]
BM.

6388 "The Longer Thou Livest the More Fool Thou Art. Ein Drama
aus den ersten Regierungsjahren der Konigin Elisabeth. Zum
ersten Male neu gedruckt." Edited by Alois Brandl. Shakespeare
Jahrbuch, XXXVI (1900), 1-64.

6389 Wager, W. The Longer Thou Livest the More Fool Thou Art.
[c. 1568]. [London]: Issued for Subscribers by the Editor of
The Tudor Facsimile Texts, 1910. [8], [56] pp.
BM. ICN. MB. MH. MiU. NjP. ViU. WU.

6390 A very mery and Pythie Commedie, called The Longer thou liuest,
the more foole thou art. Amersham, England: Issued for Subscribers by John S. Farmer, 1913. 56 pp.
DFo. MnU. OC1.

Studies

6391 Chambers, E. K. "The Longer Thou Livest, the More Fool Thou
Art. c. 1559." The Elizabethan Stage. Vol. 3. (Oxford, 1923),
p. 504.

6392 Bevington, David M. [The Longer Thou Livest.] From Mankind to
Marlowe. (Cambridge, 1962), pp. 70, 72, 77-78, 81-82, 91-92,
95-99, 163-165.

6393 ----- [The Longer Thou Livest the More Fool Thou Art.] Tudor
Drama and Politics. (Cambridge, Massachusetts, 1968), pp.
131-133.

Wapull, George

THE TIDE TARRIETH NO MAN

Texts

6394 The Tyde taryeth no Man. A Moste Pleasant and merry commody,
right pythie and full of delight. Compiled by George Wapull.
. . . Imprinted at London, in Fleetestreate, beneath the Conduite, at the Signe of Saynt Iohn Euaungelist, by Hugh Iackson.
1576. 28 unnumbered leaves. [STC. 25018. See Greg, I, p.
151.]
BM. C. CSmH. CtY. DFo. Pforz.

6395   The Tyde Taryeth No Man. A moste pleasant and merry commody, right pythie and full of delight. London: Hugh Jackson, 1576. In, Collier, J. P., ed. Illustrations of Early English Popular Literature. Vol. 2. (London, 1863-1864).

6396   Wapull, George. The Tide Taryeth No Man. Ein Moralspiel aus Shakespeares Jugendzeit. Herausgegeben von E. Rühl. Deutsche Shakespeare-Gesellschaft. Jahrbuch, XLIII (1907), 1-52.

6397   Wapull, George. The Tide Tarrieth No Man. 1576. [London]: Issued for Subscribers by the Editor of The Tudor Facsimile Texts, 1910. [6], [55] pp.
         BM. MH. MiU. WU.

6398   The Tyde Taryeth no Man. A Moste Pleasant and mery commody right pythie and full of delight. Compiled by George Wapul. Imprinted at London, in Fleetestreate, beneath the Conduite, at the Signe of Saynt Iohn Euaungelist, by Hugh Jackson, 1576. Amersham, England: Issued for Subscribers by John S. Farmer, 1913. 54 pp.
         BM. DFo. OC1. PU.

Studies

6399   Bevington, David M. [Tide Tarrieth No Man.] From Mankind to Marlowe. (Cambridge, 1962), pp. 54, 66, 70, 72, 75-76, 149-151, 272-273.

WEALTH AND HEALTH

Texts

6400   An enterlude of Welth, and Helth, very mery and full of Pastyme, newly at this tyme Imprinted. . . . [No imprint or colophon.] 16 unnumbered leaves. [STC. 14110. See Greg, I, p. 102, who dates the edition "?about Sept. 1557."]
         BM.

6401   Wealth and Health. c. 1557-1558. London and Edinburgh: Issued for Subscribers by T. C. and E. C. Jack, 1907. 28 pp. (Tudor Facsimile Texts.)
         DFo. MiU. NjP. OU. ViU. WaU. WU.

6402   An Interlude of Wealth and Health, Very Merry and Full of Pastime, Newly at This Time Imprinted. In, Farmer, John S., ed. Recently Recovered "Lost" Tudor Plays. (London, 1907), pp. 273-309.

6403 The Interlude of Wealth and Health . . . Prepared by the General
       Editor, W. W. Greg, and Checked by Percy Simpson. London:
       Printed for the Malone Society by C. Whittingham & Co., at
       the Chiswick Press, 1907. xii, [32] pp.

6404 An Enterlude of Welth und Helth. Eine englische Moralität des
       xvi. Jahrhunderts. Edited by F. Holthausen. Kiel: Lipsius
       & Tischer, 1908. 65 pp.
          BM. NjP. OC1W. WU.

6405 An Enterlude of Welth, and Helth. Very Mery and Full of Past-
       yme, Newly At this Tyme Imprinted. Amersham, England:
       Issued for Subscribers by John S. Farmer. 1914. 30 pp.
          PU.

6406 An Enterlude of Welth und Helth. Eine englische Moralitat des
       xvi. Jahrhunderts. Edited by F. Holthausen. 2d ed.;
       Heidelberg: C. Winter, 1922. xvii, 50 pp. (Englische Text-
       bibliothek, XVII.)
          BM. DLC. MH. MiU. NJP. NNU-W. OCU. PU. WU.

                              Studies
6407 Hunter, Mark. "Notes on the Interlude of Wealth and Health."
       Modern Language Review, III (1907-1908), 366-369.

6408 "Notes on the Society's Publications, with Contributions by W.
       Bang and L. Brandin." The Malone Society. Collections. I.
       Part I. (1907), pp. 3-15.

6409 Craik, T. W. "The Political Interpretation of Two Tudor Inter-
       ludes: Temperance and Humility and Wealth and Health."
       Review of English Studies, New Ser., IV (April, 1953), 98-
       108.

6410 Bevington, David M. [Wealth and Health.] From Mankind to
       Marlowe. (Cambridge, 1962), pp. 53-54, 66.

6411 Pineas, Rainer. "The Revision of Wealth and Health."
       Philological Quarterly, XLIV (1965), 560-562.

6412 Bevington, David. [Wealth and Health.] Tudor Drama and Politics.
       (Cambridge, Massachusetts, 1968), pp. 133-134.

       Weather. See, Heywood, John (Play of the Weather).

Wever, Richard

Works

6413   The Dramatic Writings of Richard Wever and Thomas Ingelend.
Comprising Lusty Juventus--Disobedient Child--Nice Wanton--
Note-book and word-list. London: Privately Printed for Sub-
scribers by the Early English Drama Society, 1905. 140 pp.
DLC. ICN. MH. MiU. NN. OC1. PU. WU.

LUSTY JUVENTUS

Texts

6414   An Enterlude called lusty Iuuentus, Lyuely discribing the frailtye
of youth: of nature, prone to vice: by grace and good counsayll,
trayneable to vertue. . . . [Imprinted at London by Iohn Awdely
dwelling in litle Britayne strete without Aldersgate.] 22 unnumbered leaves. [STC. 25149 queries a date about 1570. See Greg,
I, pp. 119-120, who favors 1565 for the date of the edition.]
BM. CSmH.

6415   An Enterlude called lusty Iuuentus. Lyuely describing the frailtie
of youth: of natur, prone to vyce: by grace and good counsayll,
traynable to vertue. . . . [Colophon: Finis Quod R. Weuer.
Imprynted at London, in Lothbury, ouer agaynst Sainct
Margarits Church, by Wyllyam Copland.] 20 unnumbered leaves.
[STC. 25147 queries a date "c. 1565." See Greg, I, p. 120.]
BM. CSmH. Pforz.

6416   An Enterlude called Lusty Iuuentus. Liuely descibyng the frailtie
of youth: of nature, prone to vyce: by grace and good councell
traynable to vertue. . . . [Colophon: Finis, quod R. Weuer.
Imprinted at London in Paules churche yeard, by Abraham
Vele, at the sygne of the Lambe.] 18 unnumbered leaves.
[STC. 25148 queries "c. 1565" as the date of the edition. See
Greg, I, pp. 120-121.]
O.

6417   Lusty Juventus. A Morality. In, Hawkins, Thomas, ed. The
Origin of theEnglish Drama. Vol. 1. (Oxford, 1773), pp.
[113]-163.

6418   Lusty Juventus. A Morality. In, Dodsley, R., ed. A Select Collection of Old English Plays. Vol. 2. (London, 1874-1876),
pp. 41-102.

6419   Lusty Juventus, by Richard Wever. A Hitherto (1906) Unrecorded

Edition. London and Edinburgh: Issued for Subscribers by
T. C. and E. C. Jack, 1907. 43 pp. (Tudor Facsimile Texts.)
DLC. ICN. MiU. ViU.

6420 An Enterlude called Lusty Juventus. Lyuely discribing the frailtye
of youth: of nature, prone to vice: by grace and good counsayll,
trayneable to vertue. Imprinted at London by John Awdeley
dwelling in little Britayne strete without Aldersgate. Amersham,
England: Issued for Subscribers by John S. Farmer, 1914. 43
pp.
DFo. MnU. OC1. PU.

Studies
6421 Chambers, E. K. "R. Wever. Lusty Juventus." The Mediaeval
Stage. Vol. 2. (London, 1903), p. 460.

6422 Kelly, Virginia Stuart. "Lusty Juventus: A Study in Lutheran
Drama." M.A. Fordham University, 1944.

6423 Bevington, David M. [Lusty Juventus.] From Mankind to Marlowe.
(Cambridge, 1962), pp. 143-146.

6424 ----- [Lusty Juventus.] Tudor Drama and Politics. (Cambridge,
Massachusetts, 1968), pp. 107-108.

Wilson, Robert

General Studies

6425 Martin, Mildred Lillian. "Robert Wilson, Actor and Playwright."
M.A. Columbia University, 1924.

6426 Baldwin, T. W. "Nathaniel Field and Robert Wilson." Modern
Language Notes, XLI (January, 1926), 32-34.

6427 Gourvith, I. "Robert Wilson; 'the Elder and the Younger.'"
Notes and Queries, CL (1926), 4-6.

6428 Gatch, Katherine H. "Robert Wilson, Actor and Dramatist." Ph.D.
Yale University, 1928.

6429 Mann, Irene Rose. "The Text of the Plays of Robert Wilson."
Ph.D. University of Virginia, 1942.

6430 ----- "More Wilson Parallels." Notes and Queries, CLXXXVI

(June 17, 1944), 287-288.

6431 Mithal, H. S. D. "The Two-Wilsons Controversy." Notes and
      Queries, New Ser., VI (1959), 106-109.

Individual Plays

COBLER'S PROPHECY
                              Texts
6432 The Coblers Prophesie. Written by Robert Wilson, Gent.
      Printed at London by Iohn Danter for Cuthbert Burbie: and are
      to be sold at his shop nere the Royall-Exchange. 1594. 28 un-
      numbered leaves. [STC. 25781. See Greg, I, p. 209.]
         BM. CSmH. DFo (Impf.). MH. O. Pforz.

6433 Wilson, Robert. The Coblers Prophecy. Herausgegeben von
      Wilhelm Dibelius. Jahrbuch der Deutschen Shakespeare-
      Gesellschaft, XXXIII (1897), 3-48.

6434 The Cobler's Prophecy. London and Edinburgh: Issued for Sub-
      scribers by T. C. and E. C. Jack, 1911. 50 pp. (Tudor Fac-
      simile Texts.)
         ICN. MB. MH. MiU. NjP. NN. ViU. WU.

6435 The Coblers Prophesie. Written by Robert Wilson. Gent. Printed
      at London by Iohn Danter for Cuthbert Burbie: and are to be
      sold at his shop nere the Royall-Exchange. 1594. Amersham,
      England: Issued for Subscribers by John S. Farmer, 1913.
      50 pp.
         PU.

6436 Wilson, Robert. The Cobler's Prophecy. 1594 . . . Prepared by
      A. C. Wood, with the Assistance of the General Editor, W.
      W. Greg. London: Printed for the Malone Society by H. Hart
      at the Oxford University Press, 1914. ix, [58] pp.

6437 Sisson, Sarah Trumbull. "The Coblers Prophesie, a Morality:
      Edited with Introduction and Notes." Ph.D. Urbana, Illinois.
      University of Illinois, 1942.

                             Studies
6438 Chambers, E. K. "The Cobler's Prophecy 1594." The Elizabethan
      Stage. Vol. 3. (Oxford, 1923), p. 516.

6439 Mann, Irene. "A Political Cancel in The Cobblers Prophesie."

Library, New Ser., XXIII (September-December, 1942), 94-100.

6440 Mann, Irene. "The Dibelius Edition of The Coblers Prophesie." Notes and Queries, CLXXXIX (August 11, 1945), 48-50.

6441 ----- "Notes on the Malone Society Reprint of The Cobler's Prophecy." The Library, New Ser., XXVI (September-December, 1945), 181-189.

6442 Lavin, J. A. "Two Notes on The Cobler's Prophecy." Notes and Queries, New Ser., IX (1962), 137-139.

6443 Bevington, David. [The Cobler's Prophecy.] Tudor Drama and Politics. (Cambridge, Massachusetts, 1968), pp. 191-194, 195.

THE THREE LADIES OF LONDON

Texts

6444 A right excellent and famous Comoedy called the three Ladies of London. Wherein Is Notablie Declared And Set foorth, how by the meanes of Lucar, Loue and Conscience is so corrupted, that the one is married to Dissimulation, the other fraught with all abhomination. A Perfect Patterne For All Estates to looke into, and a worke right worthie to be marked. Written by R. W. as it hath been publiquely played. At London, Printed by Roger Warde, dwelling neere Holburne Conduit, at the signe of the Talbot. 1584. 24 unnumbered leaves. [STC. 25784. See Greg, I, pp. 164-165.]
BM. CSmH. O. Pepys.

6445 A Right excellent and famous Comedy, called The Three Ladies of London. VVherein Is Notablie declared and set forth, how by the meanes of Lucar, Loue and Conscience is so corrupted, that the one is married to Dissimulation, the other fraught with all abhomination. A perfect patterne for all Estates to looke into, and a worke right worthie to be marked. Written by R. W. as it hath been publiquely plaied. At London, Printed by Iohn Danter, dwelling in Ducke Lane, neere Smithfield. 1592. 24 unnumbered leaves. [STC. 25785. See Greg, I, p. 165.]
BM. CSmH. DFo. MH. Pforz.

6446 A right excellent and famous comoedy called the Three Ladies of London. Written by R. W. as it hath been publiquely played.

In, Collier, J. P., ed. Five Old Plays. (London, 1851), pp. [157]-244.

6447 The Three Ladies of London. In, Dodsley, R., ed. A Select Collection of Old English Plays. Vol. 6. (London, 1874-1876), pp. [245]-370.

6448 The Three Ladies of London, by R. W. 1584. London and Edinburgh: Issued for Subscribers by T. C. and E. C. Jack, 1911. 46 pp. (Tudor Facsimile Texts.)
       DLC. ICN. MH. MiU. NjP. ViU. WU.

6449 A Right Excellent and Famous Comoedy Called the Three Ladies of London. 1584. Amersham, England: Issued for Subscribers by John S. Farmer, 1913. 44 pp.
       PU.

Studies

6450 Chambers, E. K. "The Three Ladies of London, c. 1581." The Elizabethan Stage. Vol. 3. (Oxford, 1923), p. 515.

6451 Mann, Irene. "The Copy of the 1592 Quarto of The Three Ladies of London." Philological Quarterly, XXIII (January, 1944), 86-89.

6452 ----- "A Lost Version of The Three Ladies of London" Publications of the Modern Language Association, LIX (June, 1944), 586-589.

6453 Nathanson, Leonard. "A Quip for an Upstart Courtier and The Three Ladies of London." Notes and Queries, New Ser., III (September, 1956), 376-377.

6454 Bevington, David M. [The Three Ladies of London.] From Mankind to Marlowe. (Cambridge, 1962), pp. 88, 90, 92, 94-95.

6455 ----- [The Three Ladies of London.] Tudor Drama and Politics. (Cambridge, Massachusetts, 1968), pp. 138-140.

THE THREE LORDS AND THREE LADIES OF LONDON
Texts

6456 The pleasant and Stately Morall, of the three Lordes and three Ladies of London. With the great Ioy and Pompe, Solempnized at their Mariages: Commically interlaced with much honest Mirth, for pleasure and recreation, among many Morall ob-

seruations and other important matters of due Regard. by R.
W. London. Printed by R. Ihones, at the Rose and Crowne
neere Holburne Bridge. 1590. 34 unnumbered leaves. [STC.
25783. See Greg, I, pp. 170-171.]
   BM. CSmH. DFo. Dyce. O. Pforz.

6457 The Pleasant and Stately Morall of the Three Lordes and Three
      Ladies of London. 1590. In, Collier, J. P., ed. Five Old
      Plays. (London, 1851), pp. [245]-349.

6458 The Three Lords and Three Ladies of London. In, Dodsley, R.,
      ed. A Select Collection of Old English Plays. Vol. 6. (London,
      1874-1876), pp. [371]-502.

6459 The Three Lords and Three Ladies of London. 1590. London and
      Edinburgh: Issued for Subscribers by T. C. and E. C. Jack,
      1912. 65 pp. (Tudor Facsimile Texts.)
      DLC. ICN. MH. MiU. NjP. ViU. WU.

6460 The Three Lords and Three Ladies of London. 1590. Amersham,
      England: Issued for Subscribers by John S. Farmer, 1913.
      65 pp.
         OCl. PU.

6461 Mithal, H. S. D. "An Edition of Robert Wilson's The Three Ladies
      of London, and The Three Lords and Three Ladies of London."
      Ph.D. University of Birmingham, 1959.

                                  Studies
6462 Fernow, Hans. The Three Lords and Three Ladies of London.
      Ein Beitrag zur Geschichte des englischen Dramas. [Hamburg,
      1885]. [3], 29 pp. [Programm - Realgymnasium des Johanneums
      zu Hamburg.]
         BM. ICU.

6463 Chambers, E. K. "The Three Lords and Three Ladies of London."
      The Elizabethan Stage. Vol. 3. (Oxford, 1923), p. 515.

6464 Nathanson, Leonard. "Variants in Robert Wilson's The Three
      Lords." The Library, Fifth Series, XIII (March, 1958), 57-
      59. [Bibliographical].

6465 Mithal, H. S. D. "'Chipping Norton a Mile from Chapel of the
      Heath.'" Notes and Queries, New Ser., VI (1959), 193.

6466 Mithal, H. S. D. "The Variants in Robert Wilson's The Three
      Lords of London." Library, XVIII (1963), 142-144.

6467 Bevington, David. [The Three Lords and Three Ladies of London.]
      Tudor Drama and Politics. (Cambridge, Massachusetts, 1968),
      pp. 189-192.

WISDOM WHO IS CHRIST
                            Manuscripts
6468 Macro MS. of Plays in the Folger Shakespeare Library.

6469 Oxford. Bodleian MS. Digby 133, ff. 158-169 (Fragment).

                              Texts
6470 A Morality [Wisdom]. In, Sharp, Thomas, ed. Ancient Mysteries
      from the Digby Manuscripts. (Edinburgh, 1835).

6471 Mind, Will, and Understanding: A Morality. From the Macro MS.
      in the Possession of Hudson Gurney. Edinburgh, 1837. 25 pp.
      (Abbotsford Club, Publication No. 10). [By W. B. D. Turn-
      bull. Supplements the 1835 edition of the fragment from the
      Digby MS.]
          CSmH. CtY. MB. MH. O.

6472 A Morality of Wisdom Who Is Christ. In, Furnivall, Frederick
      J., ed. The Digby Mysteries. (London, 1882).

6473 A Morality of Wisdom, Who Is Christ. In, Furnivall, F. J., ed.
      The Digby Plays, with an Incomplete Morality of Wisdom,
      Who Is Christ. (London, 1896).

6474 Wisdom, Who Is Christ. In, Furnivall, F. J., and Alfred W.
      Pollard, eds. The Macro Plays. (London, 1904).

6475 Wisdom; or, Mind, Will, and Understanding. The Macro Plays.
      No. 2. London and Edinburgh: Issued for Subscribers by T. C.
      and E. C. Jack, 1907. (Tudor Facsimile Texts.)
          DFo. DLC. ICN. MB. MH. MiU. NjP. OCl. ViU.

6476 A Morality of Wisdom, Who Is Christ. In, The Digby Plays.
      (London, 1930), pp. 137-168.

                            Studies
6477 Schmidt, K. "Morälitat Wisdom." In, "Die Digby-Spiele."
      Anglia, VIII (1885), 390-393.

6478 Chambers, E. K. "Mind, Will, and Understanding." The Mediaeval
     Stage. Vol. 2. (London, 1903), p. 438.

6479 Smart, Walter Kay. Some English and Latin Sources and Parallels
     for the Morality of Wisdom. Menasha, Wisconsin: G. Banta
     Publishing Company, 1912. [4], 93 pp.
     BM. DLC.

6480 Haller, Julius. "Wisdom Who Is Christ." Die Technik des Dialogs
     im mittelalterlichen Drama Englands. (Worms, 1916), pp. 96-99.

6481 Green, Joseph Coleman. "The Medieval Morality of Wisdom Who is
     Christ: a Study of Origins." Ph.D. Vanderbilt University, 1938.

6482 Chambers, E. K. ["Wisdom."] English Literature at the Close of
     the Middle Ages. (Oxford, 1945), pp. 59-61.

6483 Molloy, John Joseph. A Theological Interpretation of the Moral
     Play, Wisdom, Who Is Christ. Washington, D.C.: Catholic
     University of America Press, 1952. xviii, 225 pp. Bibliography,
     pp. 217-221.
     BM.

6484 Bevington, David M. [Wisdom Who Is Christ.] From Mankind to
     Marlowe. (Cambridge, 1962), pp. 124-127.

6485 Fifield, Merle. "The Use of Doubling and Extras in Wisdom."
     Ball State University Forum, VI (Autumn, 1965), 65-68.

6486 ----- "Wisdom Who Is Christ." The Castle in the Circle.
     (Muncie, Indiana, 1967), pp. 23-26.

6487 Bevington, David. [Wisdom Who Is Christ.] Tudor Drama and
     Politics. (Cambridge, Massachusetts, 1968), pp. 28-34.

Woodes, Nathaniel

CONFLICT OF CONSCIENCE

Texts

6488 An excellent new Commedie, Intituled: The Conflict of Conscience.
     Contayninge, The most lamentable Hystorie, of the desperation
     of Frauncis Spera, who forsooke the trueth of Gods Gospell,
     for feare of the losse of life and worldly goodes. Compiled, by
     Nathaniell Woodes. Minister, in Norwich . . . . At London
     Printed, by Richarde Bradocke dwellinge in Aldermanburie,

a little aboue the Conduict. Anno 1581. 36 leaves unnumbered.
[STC. 25966. See Greg, I, pp. 157-158.]
NPf. O.

6489 An excellent new Commedie, Intituled: The Conflict of Conscience.
Contayninge, A most lamentable example, of the dolefull
desperation of a miserable worldlinge, termed, by the name of
Philologvs, who forsooke the trueth of Gods Gospel, for feare of
the losse of lyfe, & worldly goods. Compiled, by Nathaniell
Woodes. Minister, in Norwich. At London Printed, by Richard
Bradocke dwellinge in Aldermanburie, a little aboue the Conduict.
Anno 1581. 36 unnumbered leaves. [Another issue. See Greg, I,
p. 158, who notes the differences.]
BM. CSmH. CtY. DFo. MH. O (Imperfect).

6490 Conflict of Conscience. In, Collier, John Payne, ed. Five Old
Plays. (London, 1851). [Of the second issue.]
BM.

6491 Conflict of Conscience. In, Dodsley, R., ed. A Select Collection
of Old English Plays. Vol. 6. (London, 1874-1876), pp. [29]-
142.
BM.

6492 The Conflict of Conscience, by Nathaniel Woodes. 1581. London
and Edinburgh: Issued for Subscribers by T. C. and E. C.
Jack, 1911. 71 pp. (Tudor Facsimile Texts.)
BM. MH. WU.

6493 An excellent new Commedie, Intituled: The Conflict of Conscience.
Contayninge, The Most Iamentable Hystoire, of the desper-
ation of Frauncis Spera, who forsooke the trueth of Gods
Gospell, for feare of the losse of life and worldly goodes.
Compiled, by Nathaniell Woodes, Minister, in Norwich at
London. Printed, by Richare Bradocke dwellinge in Alder-
manburie, a little aboue the Conduict. Anno. 1581. Amersham,
England: Issued for Subscribers by John S. Farmer, 1913. 71
pp.
MH. PU.

6494 Woodes, Nathaniel. The Conflict of Conscience, 1581. Prepared
by Herbert Davis and F. P. Wilson. Malone Society, 1952.
xii, [85] pp.

Studies

6495 Chambers, E. K. "The Conflict of Conscience, 1581." The
Elizabethan Stage. Vol. 3. (Oxford, 1923), p. 517.

6496 Jackson, William A. "Woodes's Conflict of Conscience." Times
Literary Supplement, September 7, 1933, p. 592.

6497 Wine, Celesta. "Woode's Conflict of Conscience." Times Literary Supplement, November 23, 1933, p. 840.

6498 ----- "Nathaniel Wood's Conflict of Conscience." Ph.D. University of Chicago, 1934.

6499 ----- "Nathaniel Wood's Conflict of Conscience." Publications
of the Modern Language Association, L (September, 1935),
661-678.

6500 ----- "Nathaniel Woodes, Author of the Morality Play The Conflict of Conscience." Review of English Studies, XV (1939),
458-463.

6501 Oliver, Leslie Mahin. "John Foxe and The Conflict of Conscience."
Review of English Studies, XXV (January, 1949), 1-9.

6502 Bevington, David M. [The Conflict of Conscience.] From Mankind to Marlowe. (Cambridge, 1962), pp. 57-58, 64, 67,
245-251.

6503 ----- [The Conflict of Conscience.] Tudor Drama and Politics.
(Cambridge, Massachusetts, 1968), pp. 129-130.

THE WORLD AND THE CHILD

Texts

6504 Here begynneth a propre newe Interlude of the worlde and the
chylde otherwyse called Mundus & Infans & it sheweth of the
estate of Chyldehode and Manhode. Mundus. [Colophon:
Here endeth the Interlude of Mundus & Infans. Imprynted at
London in Fletestrete at the signe of ỹ Sone by me Wynkyn
de worde. The yere of our Lorde M.CCCCC. and .XXII. The
xvii. daye of July.] 18 unnumbered leaves. [1522]. [STC.
25982. See Greg, I, pp. 84-85.]
Trinity College, Dublin.

6505 The Worlde and the Chylde. In, Dodsley, Robert, ed. A Select
Collection of Old Plays. Vol. 2. (London, 1780).

6506 A Propre Newe Interlude of the Worlde and the Chylde, Other-
      wyse Called Mundus et Infans. London: Shakespeare Press,
      1817. 36 pp. (For the Roxburghe Club). [From the edition
      of Wynkyn de Worde, 1522.]
          BM. DLC. OCl.

6507 The World and the Chylde. In, Dodsley, R., ed. A Select Col-
      lection of Old Plays. Vol. 12. (London, 1825-1827), pp. [305]-
      336.

6508 The World and the Child. In, Dodsley, R., ed. A Select Collec-
      tion of Old Plays. Vol. 1. (London, 1874-1876), pp. [239]-
      275.

6509 Mundus et Infans. In, Manly, John Matthews, ed. Specimens of
      the Pre-Shakesperean Drama. (Boston and New York, 1903-
      1904).

6510 The World and the Child. In, Farmer, John S., ed. Six Anonymous
      Plays. (London, 1905), pp. 162-192.

6511 The World and the Child Otherwise Mundus & Infans, 1522. Lon-
      don and Edinburgh: Issued for Subscribers by T. C. and E. C.
      Jack, 1909. 36 pp. (Tudor Facsimile Texts.)
          BM. DLC. ICN. MB. MiU. NjP. NN. WaU.

6512 Here begynneth a propre newe Interlude of the Worlde and the
      chulde. 1522. Amersham, England: Issued for Subscribers by
      John S. Farmer, 1914. 36 pp.
          OCl. PU.

6513 The World and the Child. With Introduction and Notes. In, Pollard,
      A. W., ed. English Miracle Plays, Moralities and Interludes.
      (Oxford, 1927), pp. lv-lviii, 114-125, 210-213.

6514 Everyman -- The Interlude of Youth -- The World and the Child.
      Edited with Acting Notes by John Hampden. London & Edin-
      burgh [1931]. 96 pp. (Nelson Playbooks, No. 120).
          BM.

6515 The World and the Child; a Mediaeval Morality Play. Edited by
      John Hampden. In, Vallance, R., ed. Little Plays from Eng-
      lish Drama. (London, 1935), pp. 217-247.

Studies

6516 Chambers, E. K. "The World and the Child." The Mediaeval
Stage. Vol. 2. (London, 1903), pp. 439-441.

6517 MacCracken, H. N. "A Source of Mundus et Infans." Publications
of the Modern Language Association, XXIII (1908), 486-496.

6518 Bevington, David M. [Mundus et Infans.] From Mankind to
Marlowe. (Cambridge, 1962), pp. 50-51, 66, 116-124.

YOUTH

Texts

6519 Thenterlude of youth, [An edition known from a mutilated copy
of the first sheet only. Greg, I, p. 94 dates it "1530-1535."
STC. 14111.]
Lambeth Palace.

6520 Theterlude of youth. [Colophon: Imprinted at London, by Iohn
waley dwellyng in Foster lane.] 12 unnumbered leaves.
[STC. 14111a dates it 1557?. See Greg, I, p. 94, thinks that
the SR entry of 1557 probably refers to this edition.]
BM. CSmH. CtY. O. Pforz.

6521 The Enterlude of Youth. [Colophon: Imprented at London in
Lothbury ouer against Sainct Margarytes church by me Wyllyam
Copland.] 12 unnumbered leaves. [STC. 14112 dates it "1560?"
See Greg, I, pp. 94-95, who says that Copland settled in
Lothbury between the winter of 1562-3 and 1565, and remained
there until his death in 1568-9.]
BM. CSmH.

6522 The interlude of Youth; from the rare black-letter edition printed
by Waley about the year 1554. Edited by James Orchard Halliwell.
Brixton Hill: For Private Circulation Only. 1849. 44 pp.
BM. ICN. MH. MiU. NjP. NN. PU-F.

6523 The Interlude of Youth. In, Dodsley, R., ed. A Select Collection
of Old English Plays. Vol. 2. (London, 1874-1876), pp. 1-40.

6524 Enterlude of Youth. In, Bang, Willy, ed. Materialien zur Kunde
des älteren englischen Dramas. Vol. 12. (Louvain and London, 1902-1914).

6525 The Enterlude of Youth nebst Fragmenten des Playe of Lucres
und von Nature. In, McKerrow, R. B., and W. Bang, ed.
Louvain: A. Uystruyst; Leipzig: O. Harrassowitz; London:

David Nutt, 1905. xxiv, 108 pp. (Materialien zur Kunde des
älteren englischen Dramas.)
BM. MB. MH. MiU. NjP. NN. OC1. OU. PU. WU.

6526 The enterlude of Youth. In, Farmer, John S., ed. Six Anonymous
Plays. (London, 1906), pp. 91-116.

6527 The Interlude of Youth: a Morality, As Edited and Given in the
Month of October, 1907, in Birmingham. Birmingham Printers,
Ltd., 1907. 24 pp.
BM. NNC.

6528 Youth. C. 1560-1562. London and Edinburgh: Issued for Subscribers
by T. C. and E. C. Jack, 1908. 24 pp. (Tudor Facsimile Texts.)
ICN. MH.

6529 Youth. (1) Fragment of eight pages now preserved in Lambeth
Palace Library. (2) Waley's edition. c. 1557. London and Edinburgh: Issued for Subscribers by T. C. and E. C. Jack, 1909. 24
pp. (Tudor Facsimile Texts.)
BM. CtY. MB. MH. MiU. NjP. ViU.

6530 The Enterlude of Youth. Printed by William Copland. Amersham,
England: Issued for Subscribers by John S. Farmer, 1914.
DFo.

6531 The Interlude of Youth, Reprinted in Modern English; with Introduction by John Drinkwater. London and Glasgow: Gowans
and Gray, Ltd.; Boston: L. Phillips, 1923. 39 pp.
BM.

6532 Everyman -- The Interlude of Youth -- The World and the Child.
Edited with Acting Notes by John Hampden. London & Edin-
burgh [1931]. 96 pp. (Nelson Playbooks, No. 120).
BM.

Studies
6533 Chambers, E. K. "Youth." The Mediaeval Stage. Vol. 2. (London, 1903), p. 453.

6534 "Another Old Morality Play Produced in England." The Theatre,
VI (February, 1906), 50. [Production of Youth by The English
Drama Society at Bloomsbury Hall, London, December 12,
13, and 14, 1906.]

6535 Haller, Julius. "Youth." Die Technik des Dialogs im mittelalterlichen Drama Englands. (Worms, 1916), pp. 116-119.

6536 De Vocht, H. "Enterlude of Youth." Professor W. Bang and His
Work in English Philology. Materials for the Study of Old
English Drama. New Series. Vol. 25. (Louvain, 1958), pp.
41-46.

6537 Bevington, David M. [Youth.] From Mankind to Marlowe. (Cambridge, 1962), pp. 50-51, 66, 139-140.

6538 ----- [The Interlude of Youth.] Tudor Drama and Politics.
(Cambridge, Massachusetts, 1968), pp. 40-41.

F Folk Drama

Texts

LINCOLNSHIRE PLOUGH PLAY

6539 Rudkin, Mrs. E. H. "Lincolnshire Plough Play." Folk-lore, L
(1939), 88-97. (Text. Two versions.)

ROBIN HOOD PLAYS

6540 A mery geste of Robyn Hoode and of hys lyfe, wyth a newe playe
for to be played in Maye games very ple-saunte and full of
pastyme. [Colophon: Imprinted at London vpon the thre Crane
Wharfe by wyllyam Copland. 1560?] 34 unnumbered leaves.
[There are two pieces: 1) "Robin Hood and the Friar"; 2)
"Robin Hood and the Potter."]
BM.

6541 A merry Iest of Robin Hood, and of his life, VVith a newe play
for to be plaied in May-games. Very pleasant and full of
pastime. London: Printed for Edward White [after 1577?].
Chapin. O.

6542 Robin Hood and the Knight. In, Manly, John Matthews, ed. Specimens of the Pre-Shakspearean Drama. Vol. 1. (Boston and
New York, 1897), pp. 279-281.

6543 Robin Hood and the Friar. In, Manly, John Matthews, ed. Specimens of the Pre-Shakspearean Drama. Vol. 1. (Boston and
New York, 1897), pp. 281-285.

6544 Robin Hood and the Potter. In, Manly, John Matthews, ed.

Specimens of the Pre-Shakspearean Drama. Vol. 1. (Boston and New York, 1897), pp. 285-288.

6545 Robin Hood and the Sheriff of Nottingham. A Dramatic Fragment, c. 1475. Malone Society. Collections. I. Part II. (1908), pp. 117-124.

6546 A Play of Robin Hood for May-Games. From the Edition by William Copland, c. 1560. Malone Society. Collections. I. Part 2. (1908), pp. 125-136.

6547 Robin Hood and the Knight. In, Child, Clarence Griffin. The Second Shepherds' Play, Everyman and Other Early Plays. (Boston, New York, and Chicago, 1910), pp. 103-106.

6548 Robin Hood and the Potter. In, Child, Clarence Griffin. The Second Shepherds' Play, Everyman and Other Early Plays. (Boston, New York, and Chicago, 1910), pp. 106-114.

6549 Robin Hood. C. 1561-9. Issued for Subscribers by the Editor of the Tudor Facsimile Texts, 1914. [6], [68] pp.

6550 Robin Hood and the Sheriff of Nottingham. In, Adams, Joseph Quincy, ed. Chief Pre-Shakespearean Dramas. (Boston, New York, 1924), pp. 345-346.

6551 Robin Hood and the Friar. In, Adams, Joseph Quincy, ed. Chief Pre-Shakespearean Dramas. (Boston, New York, 1924), pp. 347-349.

6552 Robinhood and the Friar. In, Schweikert, Harry Christian, ed. Early Plays. (New York, 1928).

6553 Robin Hood and the Friar. In, Parks, Edd Winfield, and Richmond Croom Beatty, eds. The English Drama. An Anthology, 900-1642. (New York, 1935), pp. 44-47.

SWORD PLAYS

6554 Revesby Sword Play. In, Manly, John Matthews, ed. Specimens of the Pre-Shakspearean Drama. Vol. 1. (Boston and New York, 1897), pp. 296-311.

6555 The Revesby Sword Play. In, Adams, Joseph Quincy, ed. Chief Pre-Shakespearean Dramas. (Boston and New York, 1924), pp. 357-364.

6556 Shetland Sword Dance. In, Adams, Joseph Quincy, ed. Chief
        Pre-Shakespearean Dramas. (Boston, New York, 1924),
        pp. 350-352.

6557 Shetland Sword Dance. In, Parks, Edd Winfield, and Richmond
        Croom Beatty, eds. The English Drama. An Anthology, 900-
        1642. (New York, 1935), pp. 48-52.

ST. GEORGE PLAYS

6558 Lutterworth Christmas Play. In, Manly, John Matthews, ed.
        Specimens of the Pre-Shakspearean Drama. Vol. 1. (Boston
        and New York, 1897), pp. 292-295.

6559 The Lutterworth St. George Play. Vol. 2. In, Chambers, E. K.
        The Mediaeval Stage. (London, 1903), pp. 276-279.

6560 Leicestershire St. George Play. In, Adams, Joseph Quincy, ed.
        Chief Pre-Shakespearean Dramas. (Boston, New York, 1924),
        pp. 355-356.

6561 An Anglo-Saxon Passion of Saint George. Edited by C. Hardwick.
        London: Percy Society, 1850. viii, 29 pp.
            BM.

6562 Oxfordshire St. George Play. In, Manly, John Matthews, ed.
        Specimens of the Pre-Shakspearean Drama. Vol. 1. (Boston
        and New York, 1897), pp. 289-292.

6563 The Oxfordshire Saint George Play. In, Child, Clarence Griffin.
        The Second Shepherds' Play, Everyman and Other Early Plays.
        (Boston, New York, and Chicago, 1910), pp. 115-121.

6564 Oxfordshire St. George Play. In, Adams, Joseph Quincy, ed.
        Chief Pre-Shakespearean Dramas. (Boston, New York, 1924),
        pp. 353-354.

6565 Oxfordshire St. George Play. In, Parks, Edd Winfield, and
        Richmond Croom Beatty, eds. The English Drama. An Anth-
        ology, 900-1642. (New York, 1935), pp. 53-56.

Studies
6566 Sharp, Thomas. "Hox Tuesday Play." A Dissertation on the
        Pageants or Dramatic Mysteries Anciently Performed at
        Coventry. (Coventry, 1825), pp. 125-132.

6567 Douce, Francis. "Dissertation on the Ancient English Morris
     Dance." Gutch, John Mathew, ed. A lytell geste of Robin
     Hode . . . Vol. 1. (Longman, 1847), pp. 329-365.

6568 Gutch, John Mathew. A lytell geste of Robin Hode, with other
     ancient & modern ballads and songs relating to this celebrated
     yeoman to which is prefixed his history and character, grounded
     upon other documents than those made use of by his former
     biographer, "Mister Ritson." Edited by John Mathew Gutch,
     F.S.A., and Adorned with cuts by F. W. Fairholt, F.S.A. 2
     vol. London: Longman, Brown, Green, & Longmans, 1847.
     ICN.

6569 [Hone, W.] "Dissertation upon the Morris Dance and Maid Marian."
     Gutch, John Mathew, ed. A lytell geste of Robin Hode . . . Vol. 1.
     (Longman, 1847), pp. [301]-328.

6570 Smith, Horatio. Festivals, Games and Amusements; Ancient and
     Modern. With Additions, by Samuel Woodworth. New York:
     Harper, 1862. 355 pp.

6571 Kelly, William. "The Christmas Mummers' Play." Notices Il-
     lustrative of the Drama. (London, 1865), pp. 53-56.

6572 Sawyer, Frederick Ernest. Sussex "Tipteerer's" Play: A Christmas
     Mystery. London: [n.p.], 1884. 8 pp. [Reprinted from Folk-
     Lore Society's Journal for January, 1884.]
     BM.

6573 Child, F. J. English and Scottish Popular Ballads. 5 vol. Boston
     and New York: Houghton, Mifflin and Company, 1886-1898.
     [See Vol. 3, pp. 114, 127.]
     ICN. ICU.

6574 Ordish, Thomas Fairman. "Folk Drama." Folk-lore, II (1891),
     314-335.

6575 Matthews, James Brander. "The Folk Theatre." Cosmopolitan,
     XXX (March, 1901), 535-543.

6576 Chambers, E. K. "The Coventry Hock-Tuesday Show." The
     Mediaeval Stage. Vol. 2. (London, 1903), pp. 264-266.

6577 Beatty, A. "The St. George, or Mummer's Play: A Study in the
     Protology of the Drama." Transactions of the Wisconsin

Academy of Science and Letters, XV (1906), 273-324.

6578 Long, Doris. "The Relation of Robin Hood to the Early English
       Stage." M.A. Columbia University, 1911.

6579 Sharp, Cecil James. The Sword Dances of Northern England,
       Together with the Horn Dance of Abbets Bromley. 3 vol. Lon-
       don: Novella and Company, Ltd. [1911-1913].

6580 De M., J. E. G. "The Christmas Mummers." Contemporary
       Review, CIII (1913), 129-134.

6581 Montmorency, J. E. G., ed. "Christmas Mummers." Contem-
       porary Review, CIII (1913), 129-134.

6582 Pietschmann, Tony. Robin Hood im englischen Drama mit besond-
       erer Berücksichtigung von Tennysons Foresters. Inaugural
       Dissertation. Wien, 1913.

6583 Gordon, Margery. "Robin Hood in the Drama." M.A. Columbia
       University, 1914.

6584 Smart, W. K. "Mankind and the Mumming Plays." Modern
       Language Notes, XXXII (1917), 21-25.

6585 Olson, Mabel Beatrice. "Robin Hood Elements in Elizabethan
       Drama." M.A. University of Chicago, 1918.

6586 Baskervill, Charles Read. "Dramatic Aspects of Medieval Folk
       Festivals in England." Studies in Philology, XVII (1920), 19-87.

6587 Olson, Beatrice. "The Morris Dance in Drama before 1640."
       Quarterly Journal of the University of North Dakota, X (1920),
       422-435.

6588 John, Col. Gwen. "The Derbyshire Mumming Play of St. George
       and the Dragon." Folk-Lore, XXXII (September, 1921), 181-
       193.

6589 Sharp, Cecil. "Oldest Play: Discovery of an Old Folk Play."
       Nation, XXVIII (1921), 503-505.

6590 Chambers, E. K. "Robin Hood." The Elizabethan Stage. Vol. 4.
       (Oxford, 1923), p. 44.

6591 Fairfax-Blakeborough, J. "Plough Monday Plays." Notes and Queries, XII (January 13, 1923), 37.

6592 Smith, K. "Christmas Mummers in England." Theatre Arts Monthly, VII (1923), 58-68.

6593 Tiddy, Reginald J. E. The Mummer's Play. Oxford: Clarendon Press, 1923. 257 pp.
     BM. ICN. ICU. MiU. NjP. NN. OC1. OO. OU. ViU.

6594 A., G. E. P. "The Mummers' Play." Notes and Queries, CXLVI (1924), 135, 199, 435-437, 453-455.

6595 Baskervill, Charles Read. "Mummers' Wooing Plays in England." Modern Philology, XXI (February, 1924), 225-272. (Text of plays with discussion.)

6596 A., G. E. P. "The Mummers' Play." Notes and Queries, CXLVI (1924), 435-437, 453-455. [Delete].

6597 Dodds, M. H. "Northern Minstrels and Folk Drama." Archaeologia Aeliana, 4th ser., I (1925), 121-146.

6598 Harris, Mary Dormer. "Christmas Mummers of Stoneleigh." Notes and Queries, CXLVIII (1925), 42-43.

6599 Askew, H. "Three Folk Plays." Transactions of the Yorkshire Dialect Society, XXVII (April, 1926), 29-35.

6600 Dowson, Frank W. "Notes on the Goathland Folk Plays." Transactions of the Yorkshire Dialect Society, XXVII (April, 1926), 36-38.

6601 Noyes, Gertrude Elizabeth. "A Study of the St. George Play." M.A. Yale University, 1926.

6602 Beckett, Arthur. "The Sussex Mummers' Play." Sussex County Magazine, I (December, 1927), 545-552.

6603 Ferguson, Lucille. "Some Early Masks and Morris Dances." Modern Philology, XXIV (1927), 409-417.

6604 Piggott, Stuart. "Berkshire Mummers' Plays." Folk-lore, XXXIX (September, 1928), 271-279.

6605 Gomme, Alice B. "The Character of Beelzebub in the Mummers' Play." Folk-lore, XL (September, 1929), 292-293.

6606 Kronenberg, M. G. "Het mirakelspel van Mariken van Nieumeghen en het Engelsche volksboek." De Nieuwe Taalgids, XXIII (1929), 23-43.

6607 Piggott, Stuart. "The Character of Beelzebub in the Mummers' Play." Folk-lore, XL (June, 1929), 193-195.

6608 ----- "Mummers' Plays from Berkshire, Derbyshire, Cumberland, and Isle of Man." Folk-lore, XL (September, 1929), 262-277.

6609 Boyd, A. W. "The Tichborne Mummers' Christmas Play." Notes and Queries, CLX (1930), 93-97.

6610 Gomme, Alice B. "Some Incidents in Mummers' Plays." Folk-lore, XLI (June, 1930), 195-198.

6611 Jenkinson, A. J. "Ploughboy Plays." Cornhill Magazine, LXVII (1930), 96-105.

6612 Newman, L. F. "Mummers' Play from Middlesex." Folk-lore, XLI (March, 1930), 95-98.

6613 Lake, H. Coote. "Versions of Mummers' Play of England and Thrace." Folk-lore, XLII (1931), 141-149.

6614 A., G. E. P. "The Mummers' Play." Notes and Queries, CLXII (January 23, 1932), 65-66.

6615 Lake, H. Coote. "Mummers' Plays and the 'Sacer Ludus.'" Folk-lore, XLII (June, 1932), 141-149.

6616 Massingham, H. J. "Mummers' Play." Saturday Review of Literature, CLII (1932), 809.

6617 Myres, M. W. "English Mumming Play. The Frodsham Version and Text of the Soul-caking Play." Folk-lore, XLIII (1932), 97-104.

6618 Chambers, Sir Edmund K. The English Folk Play. Oxford: Clarendon Press, 1933. 248 pp. "Lists of Texts," pp. 236-244. [Reprinted in 1969.]
      CtY. MB. MiU. OC1. OC1W. OCU. OO. OU. PU. ViU.

6619 L., P. "The Mummers' Play." Times Literary Supplement, Jan-
     uary 4, 1934, p. 12.

6620 Rhodes, R. Crompton. "The Mummers' Play." Times Literary
     Supplement, January 25, 1934, p. 60.

6621 Tod, D. A. N. "Christmas Mummers' Play from Gloucester-
     shire, England." Folk-lore, XLVI (December, 1935), 361-374.

6622 Finny, W. E. St. Lawrence. "Medieval Games and Gaderings
     at Kingston-upon-Thames." Surrey Archaeological Collections,
     XLIV (1936), 108-110.

6623 Flower, R. "The Revesby Play." British Museum Quarterly, XI
     (October, 1936), 23-24.

6624 Magriel, Paul David, comp. Bibliography of Dancing. A List of
     Books and Articles on the Dance and Related Subjects. New
     York: H. W. Wilson, 1936. 229 pp.

6625 Withington, Robert. "Braggart, Devil, and 'Vice.' A Note on
     the Development of Comic Figures in the Early English Drama."
     Speculum, XI (1936), 124-129.

6626 Campbell, Marie. "Survivals of Old Folk Drama in the Kentucky
     Mountains." Journal of American Folklore, LI (1938), 10-24.

6627 J., W. H. "Mummers' Play at Christmas." Notes and Queries,
     CLXXI (December 24, 1938), 34-46. (Text, with music.)

6628 Wilson, E. M. "The Pace-eggers' Play in England." Folk-lore,
     XLIX (1938), 34-46. (Text, with music.)

6629 Bidgood, Mary E. "The Metamorphosis of the Robin Hood Legend
     As Exemplified in Sixteenth Century Literature." M.A. Col-
     umbia University, 1939.

6630 Bowers, F. T. "A Sixteenth-Century Plough Monday Play Cast."
     Review of English Studies, XV (1939), 192-194.

6631 Boyd, A. W. "Mummers' Play at Christmas." Notes and Queries,
     CLXXVI (January 14, 1939), 30-31.

6632 ----- "Mummers' Play." Notes and Queries, CLXXVI (January
     21, 1939), 44.

6633 Bradbrooke, William. "Mummers' Play." Notes and Queries,
      CLXXVI (January 14, 1939), 31.

6634 Cope, J. Hauteville. "Mummers' Play." Notes and Queries,
      CLXXVI (February 4, 1939), 87.

6635 Gable, J. Harris. Bibliography of Robin Hood. Lincoln, Nebraska:
      University of Nebraska Press, 1939. 163 pp. (University of
      Nebraska Studies in Language, Literature, and Criticism, No.
      17).
           BM. ICU.

6636 Greg, W. W. "Robin Hood." A Bibliography of the English Printed
      Drama to the Restoration. Vol. 1. (London, 1939), pp. 108-109.

6637 Rudkin, Mrs. E. H. "Plough-Jack's Play from Willoughton, Lin-
      colnshire." Folk-lore, L (1939), 291-294.

6638 Lindsay, Jack. The English Folk-Play." Times Literary Supple-
      ment, April 20, 1940, p. 195.

6639 Cosbey, Robert C. "The Mak Story and Its Folklore Analogues."
      Speculum, XX (1945), 310-317.

6640 Hewitt, Douglas. "Very pompes of the Divell--Popular and Folk
      Elements in Elizabethan and Jacobean Drama." Review of
      English Studies, XXV (January, 1949), 10-23.

6641 Dodds, M. H. "A Few Notes on Yorkshire Folk-Drama." Notes
      and Queries, CXCV (1950), 472-473.

6642 Bessinger, Jr., Jess B. "The Beginnings of the Robin Hood Tra-
      dition; with an Annotated Bibliographical Supplement to 1951."
      Ph.D. Harvard University, 1952.

6643 Brown, Arthur. "Folklore Elements in the Medieval Drama."
      Folk-lore, LXIII (1952), 65-78.

6644 Wilson, Richard Middlewood. The Lost Literature of Medieval
      England. London: Methuen and Co., 1952. xiv, 272 pp.
           BM.

6645 Dean-Smith, Margaret. "Cast of a Plough Monday Play at Donington."
      Review of English Studies, New Ser., V (1954), 394-396.

6646 Dean-Smith, Margaret. "Folk-Play Origins of the English Mas-
      que." Folk-Lore, LXV (1954), 74-86.

6647 Morse, J. Mitchell. "The Unity of the Revesby Sword Play."
      Philological Quarterly, XXXIII (January, 1954), 81-86.

6648 Flett, J. F., and T. M. "Dramatic Jigs in Scotland." Folklore,
      LXVII (1956), 84-96.

6649 Smith, S. A. "The Folk Element in Tudor Drama." M.A. Uni-
      versity of London (King's College), 1956.

6650 Dean-Smith, Margaret. "The Life-Cycle Play or Folk Play."
      Folklore, LXIX (December, 1958), 237-253.

6651 Walter, Marie. "Grateful Dead: An Old Tale Newly Told."
      Southern Folklore Quarterly, XXIII (September, 1959), 190-
      195.

6652 Nelson, Malcolm A. "Look About You and the Robin Hood Tra-
      dition." Notes and Queries, IX (1962), 141-143.

6653 Miller, B. D. H. "The Early History of Bodleian MSS. Digby 86."
      Annuale Medievale, IV (1963), 23-56. [Unique texts of The Fox
      and the Wolf, and Dame Sirith.]

6654 Happé, P. "The Vice and the Folk-Drama." Folklore, LXXV
      (1964), 161-193.

6655 Newman, T. G. "The St. George Legend in England up to the
      Seventeenth Century." M.A. University of Durham (St. Cuth-
      bert's), 1965-1966.

6656 Thorne, William Barry. "The Influence of Folk Drama upon
      Shakespearian Comedy." Ph.D. University of Wisconsin, 1965.

6657 Green, Robert J. "Some Notes on the St. George Play." Theatre
      Survey, IX (1968), 21-35.

6658 Helm, Alex, comp. Cheshire Folk Drama. Ibstock, Leicestershire:
      Guizer Press [1968]. 58 pp.
            ICU.

6659 Hilton, R. H. "The Origins of Robin Hood." Past and Present, No.
      14 (November, 1968), 30-45.

6660 Malin, Stephen Durboraw. "Character Origins in the English
      Folk Play." Ph.D. University of Florida, 1968.

6661 Chambers, Edmund. The English Folk-Play. Oxford, England;
      New York: Oxford University Press, 1969. vi, 248 pp. [First
      published in 1933.]